Women
and
Irish Society

A Sociological Reader

305
42

Edited by
Anne Byrne
Madeleine Leonard

First published in 1997
by
Beyond the Pale Publications
PO Box 337
Belfast BT9 7BT
Tel: +44 (0)1232 431170
Fax: +44 (0)1232 301299
E-mail: btpale@unite.co.uk
Internet site: http://www.unite.net/customers/btp/

British Library Cataloguing-in-Publication Data.
A catalogue record for this book is available from the British Library.

ISBN 1-900960-03-6

Cover design based on a photograph by Derek Speirs

Printed by
Colour Books Ltd, Dublin

Contents

Notes on the Contributors

Anne Byrne is a member of the Department of Political Science and Sociology, University College Galway where she teaches Irish Sociology, research methods and Women's Studies. Her current interests include the lives and identities of never-married women, feminist methodologies and pedagogies. She has published work on women in rural development, poverty and feminist pedagogy.

Derek Birrell is a professor of Social Administration and Policy in the University of Ulster. He has published widely on government and social policy. He is currently writing a book on direct rule in Northern Ireland.

Sara Cantillon is an Economic and Social Policy Analyst in the Department of the Taoiseach. Previously in the Economic and Social Research Institute she worked in the gender and poverty area. She holds an MA in Economics (TCD) and an MA in Equality Studies (UCD) where she teaches a course in Economics of Social Policy.

Margaret Carey was awarded her PhD from Queen's University, Belfast in 1995. She is currently employed as Training Officer with the Women Into Trades Project, based at Craigavon, County Armagh. Prior to this, she worked as a research officer with the Centre for Research on Women at the University of Ulster.

Tanya M Cassidy is soon to complete her doctoral studies from the University of Chicago in the Department of Sociology. Her research examines the historical and cultural influences surrounding the ambiguity associated with drinking in Ireland. Currently, she is living and working as a sociologist in Maynooth, Co Kildare, Ireland.

Anne Cleary has worked as a researcher in the health services and in the Health Research Board. Her main areas of research interest are women's health and mental health and she has produced a number of reports on health including one on women and depression. She is a lecturer in the Department of Sociology, University College Dublin.

Anne Coakley, BSoc.Sc. MA is completing a PhD on the social construction of mothers on social welfare in the Department of Sociology, Trinity College Dublin. She has worked for a number of years in the field of health and social welfare and has lectured in sociology and social policy.

Bríd Connolly teaches in the Centre for Adult and Community Education, Maynooth College and is completing her PhD in Adult Education. She has researched and published on democracy and community development, gender and community education. Her current interests include group-work and facilitation skills in participative democracy.

Linda Connolly has just completed a PhD in Sociology at Maynooth College. She is a member of the Centre for Adult and Community Education at Maynooth, and has researched and published on feminist politics and the women's movement, contemporary social movements, adult and community education and political sociology. She is currently writing a book on the contemporary Irish women's movement as a social movement.

Geoffrey Cook is a lecturer in Social Policy in the Department of Sociology and Social Policy, University College Dublin. He is a graduate of Bristol University and undertook post-graduate study in social policy at Manchester University and the London School of Economics. He was awarded his PhD from LSE in 1991 for his thesis on the Irish system of social security.

Ethel Crowley is a lecturer in the Department of Sociology, University College, Cork. She is currently working on her doctorate on the impact of EU policy on Irish farming. She is a feminist and hispanophile.

Breda Grey is currently completing a PhD on Irish national identity, gender and emigration at the Department of Sociology and the Centre for Women's studies, Lancaster University. A graduate in Social Science from University College, Dublin, she worked for the Probation and Welfare Service in Dublin before undertaking a Masters Degree at the University of British Columbia, Canada. She has lived and worked (in statutory and voluntary sectors and in Higher Education) in England since 1986.

Damian F Hannan (PhD Michigan State University 1967) worked in the Economic and Social Research Institute (ESRI) as a Research Officer from 1967-1971, as a Professor of Social Theory and Institutions in University College Cork from 1971-1976 and is currently Research Professor with the ESRI. His main areas of research include the sociology of education, school to work transitions, coeducation, poverty and inequality. His most recent publication is *Coeducation and Gender Equality* 1996 Oaktree Press.

Deirdre Heenan PhD is a lecturer in Social Administration and Policy at the University of Ulster. Her doctoral thesis examined the role and contribution of farm wives in Northern Ireland. She is currently jointly responsible for a major research project examining the use of quangos.

Abbey Hyde is a lecturer in Nursing Studies at University College Dublin. Her research interests are in power, in nursing work and the politics of reproduction. A graduate of University College Cork, she completed her doctoral research on non-marital pregnancy at Trinity College Dublin in 1996.

Patricia Kennedy, B.Soc.Sc. M.Soc.Sc is a lecturer in Social Policy in the Department of Social Policy and Social Work in University College Dublin. She also teaches Feminist Social Policy in the Women's Education Research Resource Centre (WERRC), UCD. She is currently completing a PhD thesis on *A Feminist Critique of Irish Social Policy: Women's Experience of Pregnancy and Maternity*. For the past ten years Patricia has worked as a community worker in Cork, Inner City Dublin and North West London and as a Probation and Welfare Officer with the Department of Justice. She is the mother of two young children.

Elizabeth Kiely is a lecturer in Social Policy in the Department of Applied Social Studies, University College Cork. She has also worked as a facilitator with a number of lone parent groups and women's groups. Her research interests include gender, education and youth work. She has published in the area of youth work.

Maire Leane is a lecturer in Social Policy in the Department of Applied Social Studies, University College Cork. Her research interests include women's issues, learning disability, gender and social policy. She has published work in the area of learning difficulty, mental health and elder care.

Madeleine Leonard is a lecturer in Sociology at Queen's University, Belfast. Her current research interests include the informal economy, women and work, the economic activity of children and m,ature students in higher education. She has published work on each of these areas.

E Maria Lohan is researching her PhD in the Department of Sociology, Trinity College Dublin. Her research interests focus on the sociology of technologies and the constructions of masculinities and femininities. She is involved in European research teams on technology and society and corporate research on Gender and Telephony for British Telecom.

Anthony McCashin is a lecturer in Social Policy in the Department of Social Studies, Trinity College, Dublin. He is a graduate of University College, Dublin, and pursued post-graduate study at Essex University. Prior to joining Trinity College he was a Social Policy analyst with the National Economic and Social Council and was earlier a member of the Commission on Social Welfare's secretariat.

Joan McKiernan is currently working on research and investigations at the Equal Opportunities Commission for Northern Ireland. Previously, she was Research Officer in the Centre for Research on Women in the University of Ulster where she worked on projects on women's employment and child-care and co-authored a study on domestic violence with Monica McWilliams. She has also lectured in Sociology and Women's Studies.

Monica McWilliams is a senior lecturer in Social Policy and a member of the Centre for Research on Women at the University of Ulster where she has been responsible for the postgraduate and outreach Women's Studies programmes. She has published work on the changing role of women and on domestic violence. Most recently she has co-authored, with Linda Spence, *A Criminal Justice Response to Domestic Violence in Northern Ireland* (1996).

Rosie R Meade has been a member of the Cork Women's Support Group since May 1994. She is a lecturer in the Department of Applied Social Studies, University College, Cork. Her other research interests include community development, social movements, money lending and informal credit.

Geraldine Moane teaches in psychology, women's studies and equality studies in University College, Dublin. She has been active in the women's movement since 1976 in the areas of violence, reproductive rights and lesbian issues. She has published on women's psychological development, health care, lesbian issues, and gender and colonialism.

Barbara Murray studied at University College, Dublin where she took her Bachelor's and Master's degrees, and at the University of Zurich where she obtained a doctorate in Sociology. She has worked with the National Rehabilitation Board in Dublin since 1985 and is currently on leave of absence, based in Bangkok.

Audrey O'Carroll graduated from Trinity College, Dublin, with a BA in Social Studies and a BA (mod) in Sociology. She qualified as a nurse/midwife before going to college and has had an interest in women's health since then. Her research interests include women and the law and women with disabilities.

Patricia O'Hara has a PhD in Sociology from Trinity College, Dublin. Formerly a senior research officer in Teagasc, where she works as a consultant sociologist combining teaching (mainly at University College, Cork), research (rural development, gender and social exclusion) and consultancy (to government departments, universities, agencies, NGOs and the European Union). Her book *Partners in Production? Women, Farm and Family in Ireland* will be published in Autumn 1997.

Pauline Prior has a DPhil in Social Policy from the University of York and an MSc (Econ) in social work studies from the London School of Economics. She is a lecturer in Social Policy at Queen's University, Belfast with a special research interest in mental health policy. Among her forthcoming publications is a text on *Gender and Mental Illness* for Macmillan Press.

Wendy Richards, PhD, is a graduate of Trinity College Dublin and is lecturer in Idustrial Relations in the Department of Human Resource Management and Industrial Relations, Keele University, Staffs. She retains an interest in Irish industrial relations and is co-author of the Irish Volume in the *European Employment and Industrial Relations Glossary* series and of the forthcoming edition of von Ptondzynski and McCarthy's *Employment Law in Ireland*.

Jocelyne Rigal is a professional nomad of French descent. She has been living and researching in France and the United States before settling in Ireland where she completed research on Irish Travellers at Trinity College Dublin. She has written on Traveller ethnicity, fertility control among Irish Travellers and Irish Traveller women. She now works in the voluntary sector.

Eilish Rooney is currently working on an ESRC funded project on democracy and the politics of women's inclusion in various organisations (community, church and trade union bodies) in the North of Ireland. Most of her women-centred research has been carried out with the Centre for Research on Women, University of Ulster. This has included work on nationalisms and feminisms in conflict; political inclusion and exclusion and citizenship.

Anne Bridget Ryan is currently writing a doctoral thesis on feminist pedagogy at the Centre for Adult and Community Education, Maynooth College. She has worked in second level and in adult education.

Louise Ryan graduated from University College Cork with a PhD in 1992. Since then she has been lecturing in Sociology and Women's Studies at the University of Central Lancashire, Preston. Her book *Irish Feminism and the Vote* (Folens Publisher) was published in 1996.

Sandra Ryan is a Registered General Nurse and works as a lecturer in the School of Nursing and Midwifery, Queen's University, Belfast. Her research interests are women's health – specifically childbirth and chronic illness, and gender in professional relationships.

Wendy Saunderson, BSSc., D.Phil., is a lecturer in the School of Social and Community Sciences at the University of Ulster, Coleraine, and is currently Course Director of the BSc in Social Administration and Policy. Her specialist research area is gender, urban planning and the policy process. She is currently the Ireland Representative for the International Women and Environments Network.

Sally Shortall, PhD is at Department of Sociology and Social Policy, Queen's University, Belfast and she is a member of the Centre for Rural Studies at Queen's. Her research interests are farm women, rural development and gender studies.

Emer Smyth is a Research Officer at the Economic and Social Research Institute. She holds a doctorate from University College, Dublin. Her research interests include gender equality issues in education, second-level schooling process, youth labour market transitions and women's employment.

Nicola Yeates, PhD, lectures in Social Policy at the Department of Social Policy and Social Policy, Queen's University, Belfast. Her research interests lie in gender and social welfare and in the implications of European social policy and European integration for national welfare regimes.

Acknowledgements

We would like to thank the referees who greatly assisted the editors and authors in preparing material for publication; we are also indebted to our colleagues in the Department of Political Science and Sociology, University College Galway and the Department of Sociology and Social Policy, the Queen's University Belfast for supporting us in this endeavour. The following people deserve special mention for the myriad ways (from child-minding to proof-reading) in which they helped to realise the work; Caitriona Byrne, Jenny Clavin, Ricca Edmondson, Róisin Forde, Val Gibson, Paul Gosling, Ruth Lynch, Ann Lyons, Claire Shryne. Madeleine Leonard would like to acknowledge the friendship of Mary Kintner, Kate McAnulty, Patricia McBride, Pam McIntyre and Margaret Woods. The editors would also like to express their appreciation and gratitude to Ruth Burke-Kennedy who assisted us with this project.

Introduction
Anne Byrne and Madeleine Leonard

The growing importance of gender in sociology and the growth of Women's Studies courses and scholarship in community, third-level and continuing education in Ireland prompted us to bring together gender-based social science research in a single text. Examining gender relations enhances our knowledge of the social. Using this knowledge, we are aware that inequality is not a natural state, but a social product. Feminists have described and theorised about social relations and practices which dominate, shape and constrain women's lives. Gender relations are based on the understanding that men have greater economic, social and productive power than women. The male gender is considered dominant, the female gender subordinate and oppressive gender relations are both recreated and maintained when we continue to observe these forms. Feminist theorising and the facts of gender inequality continue to be documented in the social sciences and this text is part of that endeavour. Gender is a key concept for feminist social scientists; and in this text we examine the gendered character of social relations, institutions, structures, practices and discourses. Moreover, gender is considered to be problematic; particularly as inequality can be one of the consequences of gender relations. However, as gender is considered to be a social product by many theorists, it is believed that oppressive gender relations can be altered.

Women and Irish Society

The contributors in this text use gender as an organising category in their analyses; theorise on the basis of women's experiences of oppressive social relations; seek to examine the relationship between the researcher, the research participants and the research process; make visible hidden aspects of women's lives and identify alternative strategies which empower women to act as agents of social reform. These practices are considered to be part of the process of doing feminist research. A standard criticism of social science research is that

1

in the main it has been concerned with those areas of life which men have found problematic. Research topics and questions have tended to be based on only those aspects of social life which are apparent or important to men. It has also been assumed that women's concerns about and interests in social relations are similar to men's. Feminist social scientists reject this assumption and stress the importance of identifying those questions which emerge from women's often problematic and difficult experiences of the world. Trying to explain and understand the human condition only from the viewpoint of a male experience leads to an incomplete and even 'perverse understanding of social life' (Harding, 1987). Feminist research methodologies have now moved on from simply 'adding in' women to the research topic. It can be argued that a new sociological paradigm has been created and feminist methodologies have contributed to changing the practice and process of doing research. Feminist sociologists have criticised existing sociological theories and methodologies, discovered new research areas, emphasised interdisciplinary approaches in research and writing, and politicised the research process (see Harding, 1987, Wallace, 1989). Feminist social science research is research for the emancipation of women rather than merely research on women.

The text reflects a combination of research methodologies, both qualitative and quantitative. The range of methods include ethnography, in-depth interviews, participant observation, large scale surveys and longitudinal studies. Census and statistical data, archival material, case study material, published and unpublished documents, recorded interviews, and existing research publications are all used in innovative and creative ways to explore aspects of women's lives heretofore little known and unacknowledged. Women's support and activist groups contributed to the research, both as participants and researchers, as well as many individual women committed to making visible the paucity of scholarship on women's lives in Northern Ireland and in the Republic of Ireland. Contributors draw on feminist theorising to make sense of their data; for example authors make use of feminist poststructuralist critiques to understand the regulation of sexuality among young women or feminist structural arguments to examine the impact of modernisation on equality issues. Feminist critiques of Irish society, North and South, of the prevalence of patriarchal practices in the welfare state, in the Catholic Church and in the family are recurrent elements of many of the analyses. However, the enduring and persistent character of inequality permeates all of the research findings. Differences between women are revealed, showing up the heterogeneity of the category 'woman'. The research in this text also exposes, not only inequality and differences connected to gender, but those also associated with sexual orientation, intellectual and physical abilities, ethnic group membership and economic class. Bringing together the evidence of inequality in Irish society and making visible the hidden aspects of women's lives are significant elements of this text.

The development and expansion of Women's Studies programmes in Ireland also prompted us to bring together social science research on women's lives. As teachers of Women's Studies, we realised the need for a text based on Irish society which would add a comparative dimension to courses which use UK, European or US source material. We are also aware of the exponential growth of feminist scholarship in Ireland, particularly within social science and we felt a text drawing this scholarship together was required. In addition, bringing together research from both parts of Ireland, North and South, allowed us to view the effects of gender in two very different societies. The text is based on a call for papers, to which we received an immense response — much more than we first anticipated. The sections represent current areas of Irish social science scholarship in Women's Studies; education, work, citizenship and the welfare state, mental health, reproduction, motherhood, violence, rurality, power and politics. Disability, sexuality and the negotiation of power within households are also treated in the section on 'hidden lives'. But while these contributions continue to advance our explorations of inequality and place feminist research firmly on the Irish sociological agenda, there are of course absences — absences which we hope will be filled in the future by another volume.

Irish sociology began to pay attention to 'the social differences between men and women' with the publication of *Gender in Irish Society* (Curtin, C, Jackson, P, O'Connor, B. (eds.), 1987). This was preceded by two Women's Studies publications in 1986 — *Women in Ireland: Voices of Change*, (Beale, J.) and *Personally Speaking: Women's Thoughts on Women's Issues* (Steiner-Scott, L. (ed.)) — both of which explore changes in Irish society through the eyes and voices of women. These and other publications have helped to mark and push out the boundaries of gender-based research so that additional dimensions of inequality can be unravelled and vital connections made between scholarship and activism (see for example Smyth, A. (ed.), 1993 *Irish Women's Studies Reader*; contributions to Clancy, P, Drudy, S, Lynch, K, O'Dowd, L. (eds.) 1995 *Irish Society: Sociological Perspectives*, UCG *Women's Studies Centre Review*, Vol. 1-4, 1992-1996, Lentin, R. (ed.) 1995-1996 *In from the Shadows: UL Women's Studies Collection* Vol. 1-2, *Irish Journal of Feminist Studies*, 1996). In a survey of feminist research in Ireland, Lentin (1993) however, laments the lack of a feminist perspective in most gender-based sociological research as well as the dearth of 'empirical data to make visible the material realities of Irish women's lives'. It is the editors' aspiration that this challenge has been at least partially met with the publication of this text. Aspects of Irish social, political and cultural systems are revealed in the volume and we hope that *Women and Irish Society: A Sociological Reader* will be useful to students in higher and adult education as well as the those interested in understanding women's lives in Irish society at the end of the twentieth century. The research contained within this volume is inspired by the women's movement and constructed from feminist perspectives. In exposing social, economic and political inequalities, it promotes the liberation and emancipation of women.

References

Beale, J. 1986 *Women in Ireland: Voices of Change* UK: Macmillan.

Clancy, P, Drudy, S, Lynch, K, O'Dowd, L. (eds.) 1996 *Irish Society: Sociological Perspectives* Dublin: IPA/SAI.

Curtin, C, Jackson, P, O'Connor, B. (eds.) 1987 *Gender in Irish Society* Galway: Galway University Press.

Harding, S. (ed.) 1987 *Feminism and Methodology* UK: OUP.

Irish Journal of Feminist Studies, 1996 Cork: Cork University Press.

Lentin, R. 'Feminist Methodologies' in *Irish Journal of Sociology*, Vol.3, 1993 pp.119-138.

Lentin, R. (ed.) 1995-1996 *In from the Shadows: UL Women's Studies Collection Vol. 1-2* Limerick: University of Limerick.

Smyth, A. (ed.) 1993 *Irish Women's Studies Reader* Dublin: Attic Press.

Steiner-Scott, L. (ed.) 1986 *Personally Speaking: Women's Thoughts on Women's Issues* Dublin: Attic Press.

UCG Women's Studies Centre Review. Vols. 1-4, 1992-1996, Galway: UCG WSC.

Wallace, R A. (ed.) 1989 *Feminism and Sociological Theory* UK: Sage.

Section 1:
Women and Education

The educational system is one of the most important institutions of society and remains a central focus for feminists concerned to eradicate inequalities between men and women. Early feminists considered education as having the potential to radically transform women's position in both the private and the public sphere. However, feminist research, particularly from the 1970s onwards, suggested that not only were girls and young women disadvantaged in the educational system but it was there they learned to accept dominant ideologies concerning femininity and masculinity. Rather than neutrally educating pupils, schools were accused of reflecting patriarchal assumptions about the world. For example, in economics, the contribution of women's unpaid work to the economy was often ignored or defined as non-economic.

The attention drawn to gender inequalities in education by the women's movement and feminist researchers raised awareness of sexism in education and lead to the implementation of several initiatives to improve educational opportunities for girls and young women. Changes in curriculum content, school organisational structures and legislative acts have largely realised the liberal agenda and formal equality in terms of access, disadvantage, under-representation and under-achievement is increasingly apparent, at least in first and second level educational institutions. However, what goes on in the classroom remains a more complex arena of reform. Sexual inequalities continue to cast their shadow on schooling and education more generally.

Research into education has often been contradictory rather than complementary and different analyses have generated different solutions and strategies for change. The three chapters in this section reflect these controversies and add interesting and important dimensions to our awareness of the relationship between education and masculinity and femininity in Irish society.

Emer Smyth and Damian Hannan report on a large-scale survey carried out by the Economic and Social Research Institute into the impact of coeducational and single-sex schools on girls' educational achievement. Drawing on a sample

size of over ten thousand pupils in over one hundred schools, the research
indicated that the type of school attended had a minimal impact on girls' and
boys' examination performance. Rather, the important factors influencing both
girls' and boys' examination performance were family background and prior
ability. Smyth and Hannan found that girls tended to outperform boys regardless
of the type of school attended. This was particularly evident at Junior Certificate
level. However, there was some evidence to indicate that girls tended to under-
perform in mathematics in coeducational schools.

While this issue was not directly explored by the authors, other research
(Archer and McDonald, 1991) suggests that females receive and perceive
different messages about their aptitudes and abilities from those of males. In
particular, assumptions concerning masculinity and femininity remain embedded
in certain subjects and act as subtle barriers to the promotion of true equality.
This is why feminist research which challenges girls' perceptions of 'masculine'
curriculum subjects is so important. While Smyth and Hannan's study was
limited to performance in mathematics, they suggest that future research should
examine whether the discovered effects are prevalent in other 'male' subjects
such as physics.

Weiner (1994) suggests that some of the most illuminating aspects of current
research into male-female schooling are analyses that place the often neglected
realm of sexuality and the social control of girls in education to the forefront of
educational research. This is the theme of Anne Bridget Ryan's chapter. She
regards coeducational schools as sites where boys practice and establish their
domination over girls. Ryan demonstrates how boys control girls' behaviour in
the classroom through their use of the sexual double standard. Boys were
expected to 'sow wild oats' but similar behaviour was censured in girls and was
likely to lead to derogatory labels such as 'slag' or 'slut'. This sexual labelling
had little to do with actual sexual practices but was linked to the extent to which
girls' behaviour deviated from popular ideas of femininity. To remain a 'nice
girl', girls had to suppress any real sexual desire and conform to expectations of
romantic love and monogamy. Hence, only girls in steady relationships with
one male escaped the labelling. Other girls found themselves in a no-win
situation. Those who interacted freely with boys were labelled as 'sluts' while
those who tried to avoid male company were labelled as 'frigid' or 'lesbians'.

Female teachers were also victims of such labels and often the institutional
response was to suggest that teachers were 'nice' and couldn't possibly be
'sluts' leaving intact the implication that other women might be labelled this
way. While the effect of this on girls' educational potential was not examined
by Ryan, other research indicates that girls' educational opportunities are
restricted by the exercise of male sexuality. Lees (1986) for example, suggests

that abusive behaviour and language from boys in school which often has a sexual connotation can alienate girls from education and learning.

Bríd Connolly reminds us that education is a life-long process by examining the participation of women in community education. She suggests that education can be potentially liberating but not in its present form. Only by adopting a feminist pedagogy can education be truly transformative. Connolly describes her own feminist pedagogical techniques which she believes will contribute to a more meaningful educational agenda. She places group-work activities which encourage students to develop a critical awareness of their own positioning within educational discourses as central to her approach. Drawing on feminist poststructuralism, Connolly emphasises a pedagogy that enables educational practitioners and students to explore how oppression works, is experienced and where resistances may be possible. If reducing gender inequality continues to be a major goal for teachers, feminists and policy-makers, then the often contradictory research into girls and women's day to day experiences of education remain central to feminist enquiry.

References and Further Reading

Archer, J and McDonald, M. 1991 Gender Roles and School Subjects in *Adolescent Girls Educational Research* No.33 pp.55-64.
Lees, S. 1986 *Losing Out: Sexuality and Adolescent Girls* London: Hutchinson.
Weiner, G. 1994 *Feminism in Education* Buckingham: Open University Press.

1.

Girls and Coeducation in the Republic of Ireland[1]

Emer Smyth, Damian F Hannan

Introduction

The impact of coeducation on girls' and boys' experiences of schooling has been the subject of much international debate. Since the 1970s, a large number of studies have been carried out in Britain, the United States and elsewhere which examine the influence of coeducation on a range of pupil outcomes, including examination performance, and personal and social development. Due to the long tradition of single-sex schooling, these issues have been given much less attention in Ireland. However, the recent growth in the proportion of pupils educated within coed schools has prompted some debate on the role of coeducation, and highlighted the necessity to assess policy in this area. In order to provide such an assessment, a large-scale national study of second-level schools, *Coeducation and Gender Equality* (Hannan, Smyth, McCullagh, O'Leary, McMahon, 1996), was carried out by the Economic and Social Research Institute.[2]

The study's main objective was to determine whether coeducational schools, relative to single-sex schools, have negative effects on girls' educational achievement and personal and social development. To address these questions, a nation-wide survey was carried out of more than 10,000 pupils in Junior and Leaving Certificate classes within a national sample of 116 second level schools. While the study was concerned with both educational and developmental outcomes of coeducation, this chapter focuses on differences between single-sex and coed schools in educational performance. This is measured using pupils' examination performance in the Junior and Leaving Certificate examinations. Research has indicated the crucial role of exam results in obtaining access to further education and to employment (Breen, Hannan and O'Leary, 1995). Given the rapid growth in coeducation in Ireland, it is vital to assess whether such a development adversely affects girls' educational and occupational achievements.

9

The remainder of this chapter is divided into five sections. The first section briefly outlines some of the main findings from international research on coeducation. The second describes the nature of coeducational schooling in the Republic of Ireland. The third section describes the study methods and outlines the main factors found to influence exam performance among girls and boys. The fourth section assesses the impact of coeducation on overall educational performance at the Junior and Leaving Certificate levels, while the final section describes differences between coed and single-sex pupils in Mathematics performance.

International Research on Coeducation

Research on coeducation has been concerned both with describing differences between coed and single-sex schools, and with assessing the impact of these differences on aspects of girls' and boys' experiences, including their educational performance, and their personal and social development. Coed and single-sex schools have been found to differ in three main respects: school policy and practice, pupil-teacher interaction, and pupil-pupil interaction.

School policy and practice may impact differently on single-sex and coed pupils, and on girls and boys within coed schools; for example, the nature of the curriculum provided and the associated rules regarding subject allocation may vary by school type. However, much more attention has been paid to the 'hidden curriculum' within schools, 'the social norms and values that are implicitly communicated to pupils in schools by the way in which school and classroom life is organised' (Drudy and Lynch, 1993, p.182). Single-sex and coed schools have been found to differ in their overall ethos (see Trickett et al., 1982) and in their 'engenderment', or the way in which they socialise girls and boys to gender roles. However, gendered patterns of behaviour are not only found in coed schools. One American study found that 'sexist incidents' (including active and embedded discrimination, gender reinforcement, sex-role stereotyping, and gender domination) were found in all types of school, although the particular form of such behaviour varied by school type (Lee, Marks and Byrd, 1994).

Qualitative studies of classroom interaction indicate that boys receive more attention from teachers than girls. Teachers initiate more interactions with boys than girls. In addition, boys demand more attention from teachers by calling out unprompted answers and by being more disruptive in class (Spender, 1982, Askew and Ross, 1988, Wilson, 1991). Consequently, girls' involvement in pupil-teacher interaction tends to be higher in single-sex than in coed classrooms (Cocklin, 1982, Trickett et al., 1982). While these tendencies appear to apply across all subject areas, other research indicates that differences in pupil-teacher interaction between boys and girls may be even more pronounced in non-traditional subject areas (Crossman, 1987).

The nature of pupil-pupil interaction has been found to differ between coed and single-sex schools. Being educated with boys appears to result in greater pressure on girls to conform to traditional gender role stereotypes (see Lees, 1993). In addition, a number of studies have reported overt harassment of girls by boys in coed schools, behaviour which reinforces girls' greater reluctance to speak out in class (Stanworth, 1981, Jones, 1985, Mahony, 1985, Hanafin, 1995).

While there has been a remarkable consistency between studies which highlight the differences in schooling experiences of coed and single-sex pupils, there has been much greater controversy about the impact of these differences on the educational performance of girls and boys in coed schools. The first major study of coeducation in Britain (Dale, 1969, 1971, 1974) found that being in a coeducational school had no negative impact on girls' overall educational performance. Later research on the British context contradicted Dale's findings, indicating that girls tend to achieve more highly in single-sex schools, or at least in single-sex classes within coed schools. In contrast, boys were found to do better academically in coed than in single-sex schools (Shaw, 1976, Deem, 1978, Spender and Sarah, 1980, Arnot, 1983). However, most of these studies did not adequately take account of social class and ability differences in pupil intakes between school types, or were based on unrepresentative case-studies of single-sex and coed classes. Later large-scale studies indicated few consistent advantages to single-sex schooling, once other factors (such as social background and prior performance) were taken into account (see review by Bone, 1983, Steedman, 1983). Recent studies have used improved statistical techniques (multi-level modelling) in order to separate the effects of school type from that of school composition. The results of these studies have been somewhat inconclusive, with one study of London schools indicating no significant differences between school types when other factors are taken into account (Goldstein et al., 1993) but another study indicating higher performance among boys and girls in single-sex schools (Nuttall et al., 1989). These results should be interpreted with caution since neither study controlled fully for pupil background characteristics in assessing school type differences.

Research on coeducation in Australia has been consistent with more recent British studies, indicating little overall effect of coeducation per se on girls' academic achievement (see, for example, Carpenter, 1985). In contrast, recent American research has indicated clear positive effects for girls' overall academic achievement in single-sex schools; the effects for boys have been found to be positive but somewhat less consistent (Bryk, Lee and Holland, 1993).

While research on the effect of coeducation on girls' overall educational performance has been somewhat inconclusive, clearer effects have been indicated in relation to particular subject areas. A number of studies have shown that a polarisation in attitudes to subjects is more common in coed schools, with subject take-up being used to assert gender role identity (see Dale, 1974, Stables, 1990, Riddell, 1992). Consequently, girls appear more likely to take, and perform well in, 'male' subjects, such as science and technical subjects, in single-sex classes or schools (Ormerod, 1975, Shaw, 1976, Deem, 1978, Spender and Sarah, 1980, Arnot, 1983 on the British context). Australian research has also shown advantages for single-sex girls in relation to science (Young and Fraser, 1990) and mathematics (Yates and Firkin, 1986, Gill, 1992).

Comparatively little research has been carried out on coeducation in Ireland. The main Irish study on coeducation (Hanafin, 1992, Hanafin and Ní Chárthaigh, 1993) was based on seventeen second level schools in the Limerick area. The study found that single-sex schools significantly advantaged girls in terms of academic achievement at Leaving Certificate level but had a neutral effect on boys' performance. Hanafin found that this difference was due to higher educational expectations among girls in single-sex schools. The findings of this study must be interpreted with caution, however. Firstly, although the study took account of social background and school-level differences in assessing the impact of coeducation on Leaving Certificate performance, it failed to take account of initial ability differences between pupils in coed and single-sex schools. Secondly, the sample included only one vocational school, even though these make up over half of all coed schools in Ireland. An unpublished study (Brennan, 1986, reported in Drudy and Lynch, 1993), used data collected for the nationally representative *Schooling and Sex Roles* study (Hannan, Breen et al., 1983) to compare Leaving Certificate performance in coed and single-sex secondary schools. In contrast to Hanafin, Brennan found that, controlling for social background, coeducation had a slightly positive effect on girls' Leaving Certificate performance in Irish, English and Mathematics. However, this study did not control fully for prior ability/performance and differential pupil drop-out rates.

In summary, existing research suggests a slightly negative or, at best, neutral effect of coeducation on girls' overall educational performance, with a somewhat stronger negative effect on girls' take-up and performance in non-traditional subject areas (such as mathematics, physical sciences and technical subjects). However, it should be noted that findings have varied by country, over time and according to the other factors considered. The degree to which international findings apply to the Irish situation will be discussed in a later section.

Coeducation in Ireland

The prevalence of coeducational schooling in the Republic of Ireland has increased dramatically in recent years: from just under half of second-level schools in 1978/79 to over sixty per cent in 1994 (see Figure 1). The majority of girls and boys are now educated in coeducational schools, although the proportion is lower for girls than for boys. Growth in the level of coeducation is likely to continue in the future as second-level enrolments begin to decline and school amalgamations increase (National Education Convention, 1994).

Figure 1: *Growth in Second Level Coeducation, 1979-1994*

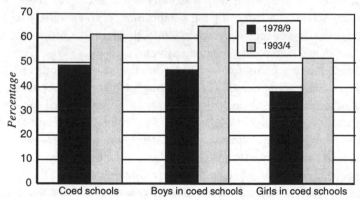

Source: Department of Education, Tuarascáil Staitistiúil, 1978/79 and 1993/94.

In the Irish context, the meaning of 'coeducation' is quite complex. Firstly, there are different types of coed school — secondary, vocational and community/comprehensive — with resulting variation in ethos, subject specialisation, management structure, and so on. Secondary schools have traditionally been more academic in orientation, in contrast to a greater practical and technical focus in vocational schools. Community and comprehensive schools were established in an attempt to bridge the gap between the secondary and vocational sectors, by providing a broad curriculum catering for pupils of different backgrounds and ability levels (see Hannan, Breen et al., 1983). In contrast, single-sex schools are overwhelmingly located in the secondary sector; in 1994, secondary schools made up over ninety-eight per cent of all single-sex schools. Secondly, coed schools differ in their gender composition; schools can be classified as 'coed' even when girls make up as little as one per cent of the pupil body. Thirdly, a small number of coed schools allocate boys and girls to separate classes so, while the school is nominally coed, pupils' classroom experiences may be closer to those of single-sex pupils. Because of the diversity of coed schools, pupils' experiences of coeducation may differ significantly by type of school. These factors have to be taken into account in assessing the impact of coeducation.

Coeducational and single-sex schools in Ireland differ in a number of respects that are not related to coeducation as such (see *Coeducation and Gender Equality*). Firstly, single-sex schools tend to be more selective in their intake than coed schools. This selectivity results in a very different social and ability profile of pupils in the two school types, with working-class and lower ability pupils disproportionately concentrated in coed schools (particularly vocational schools). For example, lower ability pupils make up thirty-one per cent of those in vocational schools compared with only ten per cent of those in boys' secondary schools. In terms of pupil composition, coed secondary schools are more like single-sex secondary schools than they are like other coed schools (vocational, and community/comprehensive).

Secondly, coed schools are more likely to allocate their pupils to classes on the basis of their academic ability ('streaming' or 'banding'). As a result, many pupils in lower streamed/banded classes have a more restricted subject choice and limited access to higher level courses. Thirdly, coed and single-sex schools differ in the type of curriculum taught and the way in which subjects and levels are made available to classes and pupils. However, these differences are related not to coeducation as such but rather to the institutional origins and development of the secondary, vocational and community/comprehensive sectors. In a number of respects, coed secondary schools more closely resemble single-sex secondary schools than they do other coed schools. It is necessary to take these differences into account in assessing the impact of coeducation on exam performance.

Influences on Exam Performance

The findings in this and the following sections are drawn from a large-scale national study of *Coeducation and Gender Equality*. This study involved administering questionnaires to 5,961 Junior Certificate pupils and 4,813 Leaving Certificate pupils in a random sample of 116 schools around the country. Information was collected on pupils' social background, their perceptions of their schooling, and their educational and occupational aspirations. This information was supplemented by scores on numerical and verbal reasoning ability tests administered to Junior Certificate pupils approximately three months before their exam, and information on pupils' subsequent examination performance in the summer of 1994. In addition, in-depth interviews covering aspects of the school organisation were conducted with school principals and guidance counsellors.

Figure 2: *Model of Relationships Between Factors Influencing Examination Performance*

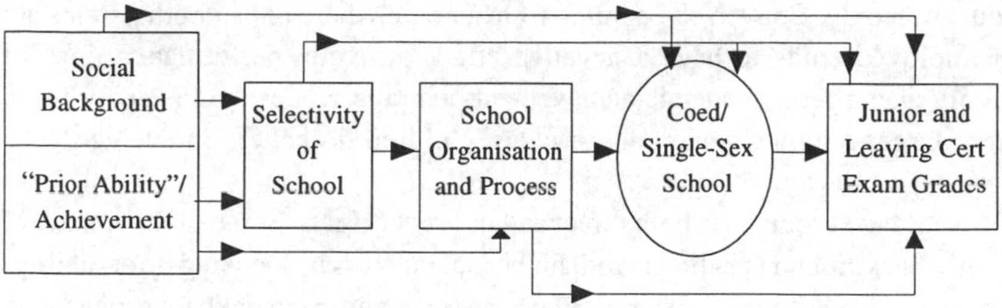

Source: Coeducation and Gender Equality study.

This section outlines some of the main factors which influence exam performance, before assessing the impact of coeducation net of these factors. The relationships between these factors are mapped out in Figure 2. Examination performance is seen to be influenced by both background and schooling factors. Pupils' social background and prior ability influence the type of second-level school they attend but also have a direct effect on how they get on in later examinations. School organisation and process mediate the effects of social background and prior ability; that is, the way in which schools 'manage' initial differences between pupils affects their subsequent educational performance. In order to assess the impact of coeducation on exam performance, it is necessary to control for these other factors so that we are comparing 'like with like'.

The outcome of concern here is overall performance in the Junior and Leaving Certificate examinations. The measure used to assess academic performance is the grade point average (GPA). This is calculated by allocating points to pupils according to the exam grades obtained, and then dividing by the total number of subjects taken.[3] Only those students who sat at least four subjects in the Junior or Leaving Certificate are included in the analysis.

(i) Family Background

Research in Ireland and elsewhere has indicated the significant impact of social background on educational participation and performance (see Drudy and Lynch, 1993 Chapter 7, Clancy, 1995). This pattern is also evident from the *Coeducation and Gender Equality* study. Among both the Junior and Leaving Certificate groups, pupils from higher social classes tend to achieve higher exam grades than those from lower social classes; this effect is apparent even when prior ability or performance is controlled for.[4] Mother's employment in a professional occupation has a positive effect on exam performance, over and above the effects of social class. Similarly, pupils whose mothers have had third level education tend to do better than those whose mothers had a primary education only. Conversely, coming from a home where one or both parents are unemployed tends to have a negative effect on exam performance. Size of family also affects academic achievement; average grades are lower for those from larger families while only or eldest children do better, on average, than younger siblings.

Social background has both direct and indirect effects. Some of the impact of family background is indirect, with higher social class influencing prior 'ability' which in turn influences exam performance. However, social background also has a direct effect on educational performance; for example, pupils with similar Junior Certificate grades but from different social classes tend to obtain different Leaving Certificate grades.

The study indicates that schools in Ireland vary significantly in the average exam performance of their pupils, but that a substantial proportion (fifty-seven per cent at Junior Cert level, forty-three per cent at Leaving Cert level) of the inter-school variance in performance is due to the differing social backgrounds of their pupils (see Appendix, Tables 1 and 2).

(ii) 'Ability'/Prior Performance[5]

Schools may differ from each other because of differences in the prior ability levels of their pupils. The study collected two measures of ability/performance: the verbal reasoning and numerical ability test for Junior Certificate pupils, and Junior Certificate performance for Leaving Certificate pupils. Ability tests were carried out during the pupils' third year of the junior cycle. While it would have been preferable to have tested pupils on entry to second-level schooling, this was not possible within the time and resource constraints of the study. Entry test scores were, however, obtained from a small number of schools in the sample. Using this information, it was found that, while they should be interpreted with caution, estimates of the net impact of coeducation are not affected substantively by using third year test results. (This issue is discussed in greater detail in *Coeducation and Gender Equality*.) As might be expected, verbal and numerical reasoning ability has a positive and significant association with Junior Certificate exam performance, explaining a substantial proportion of the variance between schools and among pupils (Appendix Table 1).

At the Leaving Cert level, achievement in the Junior Cert exam is used as a measure of prior performance. As might be expected, those who do well in the Junior Certificate tend to do well in the Leaving Cert. In fact, most of the difference between schools in average Leaving Cert performance is due to differences in the social background and prior performance characteristics of their pupils (Appendix Table 2).

(iii) Pupil and School Selectivity

School selectivity plays an important role in shaping the social composition of its pupil body. Some schools may be over-subscribed and 'get the better pupils' while other schools may suffer from 'cream off', where other schools in the area 'get the better pupils' and the school ends up with lower ability pupils. Pupils in schools which are suffering from cream-off are found to have lower exam grades than those in other schools.

Since most schools in Ireland are in multi-school catchment areas, parental choice of school is likely to be an important predictor of educational achievement. The findings confirm that pupils whose parents actively chose their present school do significantly better than those whose parents wanted them to go to another school, although this effect holds for Junior Certificate pupils only.

(iv) School Process and Organisation

The way in which schools organise and manage the educational process impacts significantly on pupils' exam performance. One of the most influential aspects of school organisation is the approach taken to the allocation of pupils to classes. Approaches vary from 'streaming', where schools rank pupils according to academic ability and allocate pupils to classes on this basis, to 'mixed ability', where base classes contain a broad mix of ability levels. At the Junior Certificate level, streaming is found to have a negative impact on the average performance of pupils within the school. Controlling for other factors, Junior Certificate pupils in schools where classes are mixed ability score just under half a grade higher than pupils in rigidly streamed schools. Being in a 'top' class boosts performance while being placed in a 'bottom' or 'remedial' class tends to lower performance. Among Leaving Certificate pupils, streaming has little impact on average performance but being placed in a 'bottom'/'remedial' class within a streamed/banded school has a strongly negative impact on performance. This effect holds even when Junior Certificate performance is controlled for.

Another aspect of the school context is relevant to performance. The average social class of pupils within the school has a significant and negative effect on exam performance, over and above individual social class differences; that is, pupils tend to do worse in schools with a high concentration of working-class pupils, regardless of their own social background. Thus, schools with a high proportion of disadvantaged pupils tend to experience disproportionate educational disadvantage.

Coeducation and Examination Performance

The *Coeducation and Gender Equality* study used multi-level modelling techniques to examine the effects of coeducation on exam performance. This approach allows us to distinguish between the factors influencing the average exam performance of schools and those influencing the performance of pupils within schools (see Goldstein, 1995). It also allows us to 'control' for the effects of differences in pupil intakes between coed and single-sex schools, and so provide an accurate estimate of the impact of attendance at a coeducational school on academic performance.

Controlling for background, ability and schooling factors, girls achieve higher grades in the Junior Certificate than boys. On average, girls score the equivalent of an 'A' grade on an ordinary level paper (or a 'D' grade on a higher level paper), while boys score the equivalent of a 'B' grade on an ordinary level paper. This pattern applies across both coed and single-sex schools and across school types — secondary, vocational and community/comprehensive.

Figure 3: *Predicted Junior Certificate Grade Point Average by Gender and School Type*

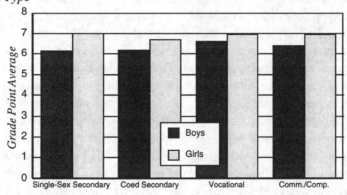

Source: Coeducation and Gender Equality study.

Coeducation has very little impact on Junior Certificate performance, when differences in social background, ability and school organisation are taken into account. Most of the differences in average exam performance between coed and single-sex schools are, in fact, due to differences in the social background and ability of their pupil intakes. In contrast, coeducation explains less than one per cent of the variance between schools in overall exam results (Appendix Table 1).

The impact of coed on academic achievement can best be understood by examining the predicted exam scores for the 'average' pupil within each school type.[6] Figure 3 indicates that performance is highest for girls in single-sex schools and lowest for boys in single-sex schools. Girls in single-sex schools do slightly better than those in coed schools. However, the effect is substantively small and girls in coed schools still do better than their male counterparts. Average exam results vary by type of school (secondary, vocational, community/comprehensive). In the case of boys, those in non-secondary (particularly vocational) schools do better than those in secondary schools (whether coed or single-sex). This is likely to be associated with curricular differences between secondary and non-secondary schools. Greater access to, and take-up of, technical/practical subjects among boys, particularly lower ability boys, in vocational and community/comprehensive schools is likely to contribute to an improvement in boys' overall examination performance.

The impact of coeducation is strongest among lower ability pupils, where boys in coed schools do somewhat better, and girls in coed schools slightly worse, than their single-sex counterparts. In contrast, coeducation has little impact on middle and higher ability pupils.

Figure 4: *Predicted Leaving Certificate Grade Point Average by Gender and School Type*

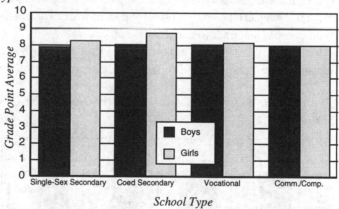

Source: Coeducation and Gender Equality study.

At the Leaving Certificate level, girls outperform boys on average, although the 'gender gap' is narrower than at the Junior Cert level. Coeducation appears to have little independent impact on overall performance in the Leaving Certificate, when allowance is made for social background, prior performance and school organisation. The highest predicted exam scores are found among girls (regardless of the coed/single-sex distinction) while boys in single-sex schools score marginally lower (0.2 grades) than their coed counterparts. The pattern varies by school type; girls in coed secondary schools do slightly better, and girls in vocational or community/comprehensive schools slightly worse, than girls in single-sex schools (see Figure 4). However, none of these differences are statistically significant.

Coeducation and Mathematics Performance

A number of international studies have suggested that coeducation may have negative effects on girls' take-up of, and performance in, traditionally 'male' subjects, such as Mathematics and Science. Research in Ireland has indicated very striking gender differences in patterns of subject take-up at both Junior and Leaving Certificate levels (see Hannan, Breen et al., 1983). However, no systematic study has yet been undertaken on the impact of coeducation on patterns of subject take-up in Ireland. Drudy and Lynch (1993) suggest that, while patterns of provision and take-up do vary by school type, 'the patterns appear to reflect attitudes among schools and pupils concerning sex-appropriate subjects, the traditions of the three school sectors, and the social class composition of the different types of schools' (p.195), rather than coeducation per se. While a consideration of differences in patterns of subject take-up and performance by school type is outside the scope of this chapter, examining patterns of performance in Mathematics, a subject taken by almost all pupils, provides a useful illustration of school differences in a traditionally 'male' subject.

At the Junior Certificate level, girls do better than boys in Mathematics, controlling for background and ability factors. Being in a coed school has a

Figure 5: *Predicted Junior Certificate Mathematics Grade by Gender and School Type*

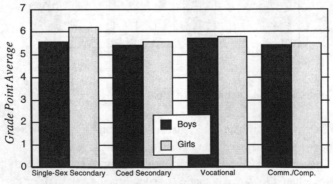

School Type

Source: Coeducation and Gender Equality study.

significant and negative effect on Mathematics performance among girls, a difference of over half a grade from their single-sex counterparts (see Figure 5). This effect does not appear to be related to sectoral differences since it applies across all types of coed school. Some of the differences between coed and single-sex girls' grades is due to more positive attitudes to Maths and Science among single-sex girls. However, a more in-depth analysis of teacher-pupil and pupil-pupil interaction in Maths classes is needed in order to fully explore the reasons for these differences.

On average, there is no significant difference between girls and boys in Leaving Certificate Mathematics grades. Controlling for background factors and Junior Certificate Mathematics grade, pupils (both girls and boys) in coed schools perform slightly worse than their counterparts in single-sex schools. In the case of boys, lower Maths performance appears to be the result of lower take-up of higher level Maths in coed schools.[7] However, in the case of girls, there is little difference between coed and single-sex schools in the take-up of higher level Maths, when other factors are taken into account. Consequently, Leaving Cert girls in coed schools appear to show a tendency towards under-performance in Maths similar to that of their Junior Cert counterparts.

Figure 6: *Predicted Leaving Certificate Mathematics Grade by Gender and School Type*

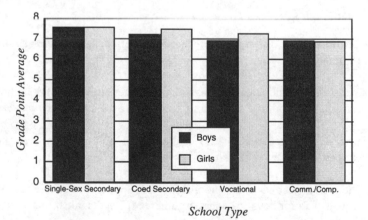

School Type

Source: Coeducation and Gender Equality study.

Conclusion

In summary, school type is less important as a predictor of exam success than family background, prior ability and certain aspects of the schooling process (such as streaming). Coeducation has a slight negative effect on girls' overall exam performance at Junior Cert level. However, the effect is substantively small and is limited to those of below average academic ability. Being in a coed school has no significant impact on Leaving Cert performance, when we control for social background, prior performance and other schooling factors. There are, however, clear indications that coed girls under-perform in Mathematics, relative to girls in single-sex schools, at both Junior and Leaving Cert levels. This pattern is of particular concern, since it indicates a cumulative process of under-performance in Maths among girls in coed schools over the whole period of second level schooling. Further research is needed to examine whether coeducation disadvantages girls in their take-up of, and performance in, other 'male' subjects, such as Physics.

Much of the early research on gender and education focused on girls' educational disadvantage in relation to boys. In contrast, this study indicates that girls tend to outperform boys at both Junior and Leaving Certificate exam levels. However, gender differences are still apparent in the type of exam subjects taken in second-level schools. These gender differences are also apparent in the level and nature of participation in third level education (Clancy, 1995) and in young people's occupational position after leaving school (Murphy and Whelan, 1995). As a result, educational policy needs to address the type of education girls receive, rather than focusing on the level of performance alone.

Discussion Topics

1.   Outline the main differences between coeducational and single-sex schools in Ireland.

2.   Apart from educational performance, what other outcomes of the schooling performance should be considered in assessing the impact of coeducation?

3.   Suggest some reasons for the difference in Mathematics performance between girls in coed and single-sex schools.

4.   'The current second-level schooling system appears to be more favourable for girls than for boys'. Discuss arguments for and against this view.

Notes

1.   We wish to acknowledge the contribution of our colleagues John McCullagh, Richard O'Leary and Dorren McMahon to the study on which this chapter is based.
2.   This study was funded by the Department of Education.
3.   For Junior Certificate pupils, points range from 1 for a 'D' grade on a Foundation level paper to 10 for an 'A' grade on a Higher level paper. For Leaving Certificate

pupils, points range from 1 for a 'D3' on an Ordinary level paper to 20 for an 'A1' on a Higher level paper.

4. Pupils are allocated to social classes on the basis of the Census of Population classification; there are six social class groups, ranging from 'Higher Professional' to 'Unskilled Manual'. Previous studies of educational attainment have often used father's occupation as the only basis for class allocation. However, in this study pupils are assigned on the basis of either mother's or father's occupation, depending on which yields the higher class position.

5. It is not intended to imply that 'ability' is unidimensional or reducible to verbal reasoning and numerical ability scores (see Gardner, 1983, on the multidimensional nature of intelligence). These measures do, however, capture the kind of aptitudes which are highly predictive of performance in formal examinations.

6. Multilevel modelling provides an estimate of the effect of coeducation on exam scores, 'all other things being equal'. These estimates are termed 'predicted scores', whereas 'actual grades' refer to scores which fail to control for differences in social background, ability and other schooling factors.

7. On the scale used, the maximum score for pupils taking ordinary level Maths is 12 ('A1'), compared with 20 for those taking higher level Maths. Therefore, low take-up of higher Maths in coed schools is likely to lower the average points received.

Appendix Table 1: *Variance in Junior Cert Grade Point Average*

	% Variance	Explained
Factors	School level	Pupil level
Social Background	57.3	13.1
+ Selectivity	67.3	13.5
+ Coeducation	68.2	13.5
+ School Organisation	68.9	35.6
+ Ability	84.7	63.0

Source: Coeducation and Gender Equality study.

Appendix Table 2: *Variance in Leaving Cert Grade Point Average*

	% Variance	Explained
Factors	School level	Pupil level
Social Background	42.8	6.7
+ Prior Preformance	74.2	58.5
+ Coeducation	74.4	58.5
+ Selectivity	76.6	58.5
+ School Orgaisation	81.8	59.0

Source: Coeducation and Gender Equality study.

References and Further Reading

Arnot, M. 1983 'A Cloud over Coeducation: An Analysis of the Forms and Transmission of Class and Gender Relations' in Walker, S and Barton, L. (eds.) *Gender, Class and Education* Sussex: Falmer Press.

Askew, S and Ross, C. 1988 *Boys Don't Cry* Milton Keynes: Open University Press.

Bone, A. 1983 *Girls and Girl-Only Schools* Manchester: Equal Opportunities Commission.

Breen, R, Hannan, D F and O'Leary, R. 1995 'Returns to Education: Taking Account of Employers' Perceptions and Use of Educational Credentials' *European Sociological Review* Vol.11, No.1 pp.59-73.

Brennan, M. 1986 *Factors Affecting Attainment in the Irish Leaving Certificate Examination* M.Ed. Thesis, University College Dublin.

Bryk, A, Lee, V and Holland, P. 1993 *Catholic Schools and the Common Good* Cambridge: Harvard University Press.

Carpenter, P. 1985 'Single-Sex Schooling and Girls' Academic Achievements' *The Australian and New Zealand Journal of Sociology* Vol.21, No.3 pp.456-472.

Clancy, P. 1995 'Education in the Republic of Ireland: The Project of Modernity?' in Clancy, P, Drudy, S, Lynch, K and O'Dowd, L. (eds.) *Irish Society: Sociological Perspectives* Dublin: Institute of Public Administration.

Cocklin, B. 1982 'The Coeducational versus Single Sex Schools Debate' *Delta* Vol.31, pp.19-31.

Crossman, M. 1987 'Teachers' Interactions with Girls and Boys in Science Lessons' in Kelly, A. (ed.) *Girls and Science* Stockholm: Almquist and Wiksell.

Dale, R. 1969 *Mixed or Single-Sex School? Vol.1, A Research Study in Pupil-Teacher Relationships* London: Routledge and Kegan Paul.

Dale, R. 1971 *Mixed or Single Sex School? Vol.2, Some Social Aspects* London: Routledge and Kegan Paul.

Dale, R. 1974 *Mixed or Single Sex School? Vol.3, Attainment, Attitudes and Overview* London: Routledge and Kegan Paul.

Deem, R. 1978 *Women and Schooling* London: Routledge and Kegan Paul.

Department of Education. 1980 *Tuarascáil Staitistiúil 1978/79* Dublin: Stationery Office.

Department of Education. 1995 *Tuarascáil Staitistiúil 1993/94* Dublin: Stationery Office.

Drudy, S and Lynch, K. 1993 *Schools and Society in Ireland* Dublin: Gill and Macmillan.

Gardner, H. 1983 *Frames of Mind: the Theory of Multiple Intelligences* London: Paladin.

Gill, J. 1992 'Re-Phrasing the Question about Single Sex Schooling' in Reid, A and Johnson, B. (eds.) *Critical Issues in Australian Education in the 1990s* Adelaide: Painters Prints.

Goldstein, H. 1995 *Multilevel Statistical Models* London: Edward Arnold.

Goldstein, H, Rasbash, J, Yang, M, Woodhouse, G, Pan, H, Nuttall, D and Thomas, S. 1993 'A Multilevel Analysis of Examination Results' *Oxford Review of Education* Vol.19, No.4 pp.425-432.

Hanafin, J. 1992 *Coeducation and Attainment: A Study of the Gender Effects of Mixed and Single-Sex Schooling on Examination Performance* Ph.D. Thesis, University of Limerick.

Hanafin, J. 1995 'Moving Beyond the Figures: Quantitative Methods in Education Research' *Irish Educational Studies* Vol.14 pp.184-210.

Hanafin, J and Ní Chárthaigh, D. 1993 *Coeducation and Attainment: A Research Summary Centre for Studies in Gender and Education*, University of Limerick.

Hannan, D F, Breen, R, Murray, B, Hardiman, N, Watson, D and O'Higgins, K. 1983 *Schooling and Sex Roles: Sex Differences in Subject Provision and Student Choice in Irish Post-Primary Schools* Dublin: The Economic and Social Research Institute.

Hannan, D F, Smyth, E, McCullagh, J, O'Leary, R and McMahon, D. 1996 *The Impact of Coeducation: Exam Performance, Stress and Personal Development* Dublin: Oak Tree Press/ESRI.

Jones, C. 1985 'Sexual Tyranny: Male Violence in a Mixed Secondary School' in Weiner, G. (ed.) *Just a Bunch of Girls* Milton Keynes: Open University Press.

Lee, V E, Marks, H and Byrd, T. 1994 'Sexism in Single-Sex and Coeducational Independent Secondary School Classrooms' *Sociology of Education* Vol. 67 pp.92-120.

Lees, S. 1993 *Sugar and Spice: Sexuality and Adolescent Girls* Harmondsworth: Penguin.

Mahony, P. 1985 *Schools for the Boys? Coeducation Reassessed* London: Hutchinson.

Murphy, M, Whelan, B J. 1995 *The Economic Status of School Leavers 1992-1994* Dublin: The Economic and Social Research Institute.

National Education Convention. 1994 *Report on the National Education Convention* Dublin: The Convention Secretariat.

Nuttall, D L, Goldstein, H, Prosser, R and Rasbash, J. 1989 'Differential School Effectiveness' *International Journal of Educational Research* Vol.13, No.7 pp.769-776.

Ormerod, M B. 1975 'Subject Preference and Choice in Coeducational and Single-Sex Secondary Schools' *British Journal of Educational Psychology* Vol.45 pp.257-267.

Riddell, S. 1992 *Gender and the Politics of the Curriculum* London: Routledge and Kegan Paul.

Shaw, J. 1976 'Finishing School: Some Implications of Sex-Segregated Education' in Barker, D L and Allen, S. (eds.) *Sexual Divisions and Society: Process and Change* London: Tavistock.

Spender, D. 1982 *Invisible Women: The Schooling Scandal* London: Writers and Readers Publishing Co-operative Society Ltd.

Spender, D and Sarah, E. 1980 *Learning to Lose: Sexism and Education* London: Women's Press.

Stables, A. 1990. 'Differences Between Pupils from Mixed and Single Sex Schools in Their Enjoyment of School Subjects and in Their Attitudes to Sciences and to School' *Education Review* Vol.42, No.93 pp.221-230.

Stanworth, M. 1981 *Gender and Schooling* London: Hutchinson.

Steedman, J. 1983. *Examination Results in Mixed and Single-Sex Schools* Manchester: Equal Opportunities Commission.

Trickett, E, Trickett, P K, Custro, J J and Schuffner, P. 1982 'The Independent School Experience: Aspects of the Normative Environments of Single-Sex and Coeducation Secondary Schools' *Journal of Educational Psychology* Vol.74, No.3 pp.374-381.

Wilson, M. (ed.) 1991 *Girls and Young Women in Education: A European Perspective* Oxford: Pergamon Press.

Yates, J and Firkin, J. 1986 *Student Participation in Mathematics: Gender Differences in the Last Decade* Victorian Curriculum Assessment Board.

Young, D J and Fraser, B J. 1990 'Science Achievement of Girls in Single-Sex and Coeducational Schools' *Research in Science and Technology Education* Vol.8, No.1, pp.5-20.

2.

Gender Discourses in School Social Relations
Anne Bridget Ryan

Introduction

Education is a central institution in Irish social life (Drudy and Lynch, 1993, p.ix), reflecting wider social attitudes, including attitudes to gender equality (Lynch and Morgan, 1995, p 556). It plays important and complex roles in shaping identity and social relations. This chapter uses the concept of discourse to examine how the subjective experience of being a girl or woman is shaped in everyday school social relations. Discourse, as I use the term here, refers to historically constructed regimes of knowledge which function as filters for interpreting experience (Holland and Eisenhart, 1990, p.95). Within discourses and their related practices, subjectivity, including gender identity, is formed. Subjectivity is understood as the complex subjective sense of oneself, including 'ideas, beliefs and emotions' (Frosh, 1987, p.11). Social relations, including gender relations, also operate in this discursive framework. Dominant discourses are implicated in the operation of power and agency. These in turn are implicated in the regulation of girls. The regulatory discourses which I discuss here centre on sexuality, naturalness and normality. These understandings of discourse, subjectivity and power arise from a feminist poststructuralist perspective.

Feminist poststructuralism is a diverse body of work which offers a view of gender as constructed in social relations in complex ways and which disputes the idea that there exists essential, that is, pregiven or asocial, female or male identities. It draws attention to the inadequacy of sex-role socialisation and internalisation theories as explanations for gender differentiated behaviour, attainment, and choices. It points to the need to problematise the content of gender difference and to deal with the operation of power.

Dominant discourses concerning essential female nature are often not recognised as oppressive or as sexist, because they are seen to represent reality and naturalness, or natural differences, and are placed in exclusive opposition

26

to equality (Scott, 1988). Such discourses are rarely spelled out explicitly. They are comprised of self-evident 'givens' that structure common-sense explanations for the way things are. They are contained in institutions, organisations and practices as well as in words (ibid). Awareness of dominant discourses and the articulation of challenges can begin when people feel contradictions and unfairness and when they reflect and act on them (Weedon, 1987).

Internationally, studies using discourse analysis have shown that discourses which depend on essentialist ideas about gender difference operate as barriers to equality. These include Connell (1989) and Davies (1989, 1990a, 1990b) in Australia; Holland and Eisenhart (1990) in the USA; Lees (1986, 1993) in Britain and Lewis (1993) in Canada. Studies which take the content and operation of discourse and the discursive formation of subjectivities into account are useful contributions to the study of gender in Irish schooling. Gendered choices and provision of subjects and choices of careers have been examined by Breen (1986), Clancy and Brannick (1990), Hannan and Breen (1987) and McQuillan (1995). Attainment has been examined by Hanafin and Ní Chartaigh (1993). An overview is provided by Drudy (1991) and Drudy and Lynch (1993). Drudy (1991, p.118) points to the room for ethnographic techniques of investigation in Irish sociological research on education. Discourse analysis, such as this chapter provides, attends to such issues, in examining the actual content of gender and the way that differential powers and values are attached to different gender positions.

Methodology

The implications for research of a feminist poststructuralist framework are that a feminist woman researcher draws considerably on her own experiences of being a woman and a girl and moves between theory, experience and interpretation (see Hollway, 1989, pp.40-42). Having used discourse as a heuristic device to examine the construction of my own subjectivity and my positioning in sexist regimes of knowledge (Ryan, 1992), I recognised its usefulness as both a research tool and a consciousness-raising method (cf Weedon, 1987, p.85). Between 1990 and 1992, I began to explore the issues which are discussed in the main part of this chapter with a group of twelve girls with whom I ran a school extra-curricular outdoor activities programme. Through contacts with feminist women teachers in five other schools, over the next three years, I met other girls for similar discussions.

In all, thirty-two pupils between the ages of fourteen and seventeen are represented in this study. They attended six schools, all co-educational and located in the greater Dublin area. Twelve women teachers from the same schools are represented. There were two vocational schools, one community college, two community schools and one comprehensive. Since a feminist poststructuralist perspective regards gender as constructed in social relations between the sexes, it was important to research in a co-educational context. The data represented here are based on taped discussions with the pupils (in pairs, or in groups no bigger than five), as well as letters from and conversations with the teachers. In each discussion, I told the participants about my research concerns. I wanted to explore with them whether there were conflicts and contradictions as a result of their positioning in sexist discourses. In analysing discourses thus, it is the systems of meaning-making which are important. I make no claims as to the representative nature of the data, but assert that I am analysing examples of how social and cultural categories are implicated in the production of subjective experience (cf McCracken, 1988, p.17).

The Discourse of Essential Female Sexuality

The discourse of 'essential' female sexuality has facilitated the regulation of girls through the concept of 'reputation'. It has also operated through the ways in which a girl's, or a woman's, sexuality are given relevance in a wide variety of situations — even when these situations have no overt sexual content. It is a discourse recognised in radical feminist theorising, as well as in feminist poststructuralist work. In this study of adolescents, in the girls' talk, to speak of a girl's 'reputation' was to refer primarily to her sexual behaviour, but to speak of a boy's 'reputation' was to refer not just to his sexual behaviour, but also to his standing with other boys, his sporting or musical ability or his ability to entertain people. A boy's 'reputation' was enhanced if it was known that he had slept with a lot of girls. On the other hand, the opposite applied for a girl if she slept with people other than a steady boyfriend, or even if she was seen to be friendly with a lot of different boys. For a girl 'having a reputation' invariably meant having a bad reputation for sexual 'looseness'. Defending their reputations with both boys and girls was a crucial concern for individual girls.

> *Susan:* If a girl gets a reputation, most people just think that's the way she is and it stays with her.
>
> *Q:* What kind of a reputation can a boy get?
>
> *Susan:* For being cheeky, or talking back to teachers or making fun of them.
>
> *Q:* And in relation to sex, what sort of a reputation can he get?
>
> *Lorraine:* Oh, he's a hero, if he goes with loads of girls, but a girl immediately gets called a slut.
>
> *Q:* If she goes with loads of boys?
>
> *Lorraine:* Yeah, or well, sometimes even if she just goes round with lots of different young fellas.

Reputation, for a girl, centred around her relations or perceived relations with boys and was encapsulated in the terms 'slut', 'slag', 'tart', 'slapper' and 'tramp'. Terms such as 'frigid', 'tight' or 'lesbian' were also used, to refer to girls who were not seen to show interest in boys. In the interviews and discussions, the concept of 'slut' always arose in the context of discussions about boy/girl relations. Whenever the term came up, I would ask the girls to say what people meant when they used the word. Definitions varied:

- a young one that'll go with anyone
- a girl that has one fella after another
- a young one that's always going of with loads of different fellas
- someone that takes another girl's fella

In the discussions that followed the introduction of the term, it became clear that the actual ways it was applied were far from straightforward. It was necessary to look for underlying rules of interpretation and recognition, which decided how the term and related ones were used. The emphasis in the analysis was on language as material process, not as a mere reflection of some underlying structures, but as part of the process of structures, reproducing and producing practices (cf Lees, 1986).

The ways 'slut' was used showed a variety of situations and behaviours where it and similar terms could be applied and find recognised social currency. Its usage regulated the way the girls 'tread the thin line between sexuality and decency' (ibid). They had to be seen to be attractive and interested in sex, but not so interested that they could appear 'easy'. On the other hand, they could not afford to appear too uninterested in sex and boys, for fear of being labelled 'frigid', 'stuck up' or 'lesbian'.

> *Sharon:* You might be just walking by a crowd and someone would call you something
>
> *Q:* What would you do if that happens?
>
> *Sharon:* Well, the worst thing is if you don't know who said it, because then — well, you can't try to get even.
>
> *Q:* What can you do to get even, if you know who said it?
>
> *Elaine:* If a fella said that to me, I'd go over and slap him, just to even the score. I know it wouldn't be the same, but I just couldn't let any fella get away with it, calling me that. I just wouldn't put up with it.
>
> *Elaine:* But they don't usually say it when they're on their own, because they either ignore you, or else it's somebody you're friends with, that cares

how you feel. But when there's a gang of them, they can get a laugh out of it in front of their mates and they can all jeer you.

The concept of sexual reputation made Elaine and Sharon uneasy. They felt there was something not right in the way boys could abuse them while they had no effective means of retaliation. As Holland and Eisenhart (1990) found in their study of young women, in handling such attacks, all the energy was channelled into self-defence, not to challenging the legitimacy of the concept. The girls recognised the disparity in power involved: they saw that 'reputation' for them was invariably a bad thing; they also knew that the abuse of girls in this way could raise a laugh with a group of boys and that their protests could be negated by the laughter and further jeering of the group. They had no claim to agency within this discourse of sexuality. Its practices made it unthinkable or undo-able for them to assert their right to be sexual or not and to be free from uninvited comment (cf Davies, 1990a).

The Other Side of the Coin

Audrey and her friend told me they did not socialise much with the people from their school. They received the abuse reserved for girls who were perceived not to be interested in boys.

Audrey: Everyone in this school thinks we're really stuck up ...

Q: How do you know they think you're stuck up?

Audrey: Well, they make comments about us when we pass by, or if we say anything in class, like, yesterday in our tutor class, Mr O'Connell was asking if we had any ideas about what we would like to do after school and when I said I would like to study physics, some boys went 'ooh' and one of them said something really insulting.

Q: What did he say?

Audrey: Well, he didn't say it straight to my face, he said it to his friend. He said, 'that frigid bitch, what does she want to study physics for? She'd be better off getting fucked on a Friday night'. But they were sitting right behind me and they knew I could hear.

Q: What did you do?

Audrey: I just pretended not to hear. I mean, what could I do? I couldn't put up my hand and tell Sir, could I?

Q: Why did you feel you couldn't do that?

Audrey: Well, you're supposed to be able to take that sort of thing, aren't you? You couldn't repeat that sort of a thing to a teacher, in class, everybody would laugh.

Q: Could you tell a teacher about it privately?

Audrey: Well, I'm telling you now, but that's okay, because I know you and I know you're not going to make a show of me. But what could a teacher do, they can't do anything about what people say to you and if you complain, it only makes people worse.

Audrey's study aspirations were being connected to her sexual/social identity, through the discourse that places sexuality at the core of female identity. Her aspirations were a bit out of the ordinary, in wanting to study physics, so the power of the sexual discourse was called into play, to 'put her in her place'. She had no recognisable means of contesting this positioning and saw her only option as pretending not to hear the comments made by the boy. She had never seen a teacher tackle that kind of abuse in a way that dealt with it effectively. She recognised her tutor's lack of power in challenging her positioning in a discourse of essential female sexuality . Moreover, this kind of treatment did not surprise her.

Self-Regulation through Sexuality

Girls could be policed by boys as Audrey was. They also policed themselves, through the categories produced in gender relations.

Nicola: Some young ones just go round looking for attention, you know, with the way they dress an' all. I know you shouldn't really say it, but it's the only way to take them down a peg or two.

Q: Say what?

Nicola: Call her a tramp

Lorraine: But it's not just the young fellas that call girls that. Young ones (girls) do it too sometimes.

Such positioning was also mediated by relations with adults (teachers) in the schools.

Girls who don't conform can be called a 'madam', or a 'hussy', or once I heard someone refer to a girl as 'a right trollop'. (Correspondence from a teacher)

These terms were not said directly to girls by teachers, but could be used to talk about girls who resisted or did not conform, illustrating acceptance that sexuality is at the heart of a girl's identity.

Teachers reported that school staff often spoke admiringly about girls who 'deal with' this kind of thing, or were 'well able to handle it' (cf Lees, 1986, p.113). But this admiration was usually for the ways girls could 'give as good as they get', ignoring that the girls were accepting the terms of the abuse and using energy to deny their applicability to them as individuals. No framework was provided for them in their schools to challenge the acceptability of the abuse itself, except where individual teachers made efforts.

The achievement of respectability through self-regulation produced a certain satisfaction (cf Walkerdine, 1987, 1988, Gavey, 1993). But the other side of this was the pain caused by not being thought respectable, if one followed some other desire, produced in a muted discourse.

> *Elizabeth:* It's all very well talking about standing out against the crowd, if that's the way you feel, but it doesn't stop you feeling miserable and hurt when people jeer and mock you and say things to put you in your place.

Male Sexual Drive Discourse and the Missing Discourse of Female Desire

Boys also had access to positions of power through a socially recognised discourse of aggressive male sexuality (Hollway 1984, 1989). Belief in a naturally occurring aggressive male sexuality could be drawn on to justify and make sense of the kinds of abuse girls received. This discourse was expressed in gestures and language and it recognised as 'natural' that boys are obsessed with sex, especially in the adolescent years. Teachers reported that it was generally accepted that boys were obsessed with sex and that this was generally sympathetically dealt with.

> They really need the sex-ed programme. Once they get into second year, they never stop drawing penises on the desks and talking about sex. The sooner it starts the better. (Conversation with teacher).

Girls who did not comply with the positions boys expected them to take up and who showed little interest in boys, could be told that their lack of interest was unnatural and that the reason they thought sex-obsessed boys were 'perverts' was because they were afraid of sex, or 'frigid', or because they were 'lemos' (lesbians). On the other hand, if a girl did act as the positioning seemed to expect, and complied in meeting a boy's 'legitimate' sexual needs, she ran the risk of being abused as a slut.

Crucial through its absence was any discourse that supplied positive ways of thinking and talking about active adolescent female sexual desire and activity (cf Fine, 1988). The girls were interested in sex and had sexual feelings and desires, but I picked this up more from observation than from any direct references they made. Sexual feelings were not acknowledged in any discourses to which they, nor their teachers or peers, had easy access. Age seemed to make a difference here: some girls felt that, as they got older, acknowledging sexual feelings would be more acceptable, although only in the heterosexual context of 'going steady' with one partner and not free from the discourses around reputation.

> *Sharon:* People wouldn't talk about you if you were going with your fella ages and you were a bit older. Then it would be just between the two people and maybe their close friends.

Connell (1989) and Hunter (1993) point out how aggressive masculinity is produced in relation to female passivity and to other forms of less aggressive masculinity. While female activity and non-aggressive masculinity are recognised by many people, their existence and validity are suppressed in dominant discourses. This makes it difficult for teachers of lifeskills, where sexuality may be a topic, to discuss it in ways which do not allow the discussion to fall back on the dominant discursive interpretive devices.

> You would think that by getting them to talk about sexuality, they would revise their attitudes. But it just seems to give an opportunity to the loud ones to say all the old sexist things. I tried to discuss with a transition year group what we should do about offensive graffiti, such as the stuff we get here all the time, 'X is a slut', 'Y is tight', etc. I didn't go into it cold. I had done all the stuff about brainstorming slang words for sex, about feelings, about assertiveness and being able to decide what it was you wanted. This was the fourth week of the programme. The responses depressed me terribly. They ranged from 'do nothing'. to 'say it's not true', to 'have a good laugh', to 'have a vote on it' (to decide if it was true).
>
> I had been trying to promote the idea that women are entitled to have sexual desires if they want, or to be sexually inactive if they want. Boys too. But I had completely failed. They could see from my reactions that I was disappointed, I couldn't hide it. That makes some of them act up even more. (Letter from woman lifeskills teacher).

Assertiveness training and building of self-esteem are common official institutional strategies for combating sexism in language and practice. Such strategies are useful, but they need to be initiated in ways which recognise power relations (Kenway and Willis, 1990). The responses by girls were, as described, to ignore or deny their labelling. Rather than disrupt the power of the discourses, such responses highlight it. Liberal approaches, including liberal feminism, tend to assume that talking about sexuality will shatter 'old-fashioned' attitudes and behaviour. However, such talk can reproduce sexuality according to dominant discourses and continue to structure it in ways that reinforce women's essential sexuality and passivity.

As Potter and Wetherell point out, it is valid in discourse analysis to 'analyse, too, in a fine-grained way, one-off representatives of what are unmistakably commonplace phenomena' (1987, p.161). It is common-place for women teachers to experience being positioned in a discourse of sexuality. Liberal feminist discourses have led to people being able to discuss such issues openly, even if their strategies for challenge have been largely ineffective. One teacher told me how a card had been left on her desk, in which she was described as 'a fat slut' and 'a bloody tramp'. She had a good idea who had put it there and told her house-head, who found out for certain who the culprits (three boys) were. She described a session in the house-head's office, at which she and the boys were present:

> He (the house-head) was great, really supportive. He really let them have it ... told them it was disgusting and cheap to think such things about a teacher. He asked what their parents would say when they found out and how they thought I felt, being described like that. (Conversation)

While it was encouraging that she could approach her house-head and know that the matter would be treated seriously, the concept of 'slut' and 'tramp' was not challenged here. It was 'disgusting' to think of a teacher in this way, but remaining was the implication that it might be all right to think of some women like that. The house-head tackled a subject which others in his situation frequently avoid (especially when abuse is directed at girls, rather than teachers). But lack of critical analysis of the underlying assumptions meant that the discourse went unexamined.

Access to powerful positions was available to whoever activated the dominant discourse around female sexuality, as Noel and the other boys did in the following incident:

> During class, Noel kept shouting that Denise was pregnant. She can normally stand up for herself and give as good as she gets, but this time she was becoming upset by his accusations. I warned Noel to stay quiet, but he persisted, eventually saying, 'Look, Denise's tits are getting bigger'. This, of course, caused the other boys to get a laugh at Denise's expense. Denise and the other girls were shouting at the boys to shut up, that it was not true. I could not get any work done. The boys then started a string of abuse at Denise, one kept repeating that she was a bitch, and one kept saying that she had no character to lose, as she already had a reputation. The class became chaotic for a while. I eventually got them quiet and doing some work, but muttered comments of the same kind were still going round the room. I reported the whole thing to their tutor. I am only a few months in my school and I felt that I just did not have the authority to deal with it. The tutor said he would talk to them, but his attitude seemed to be that these things happen. I also felt he was implying that if I had better control, there would not have been as much disruption, as I could get them to stop it more quickly. I talked about this to a few friends in the staffroom (all women). They have all had similar experiences. (Teacher, writing about a second-year class)

A class became chaotic and the girls became angry and upset, through the positioning of one of them as essentially sexual. The woman teacher was affected too, as her class management was shown to be vulnerable in the face of this discourse. In the tutor's reaction, there was an implication that this was reality ('these things happen') and that the problem is one for individual teachers in the classroom, rather than a problem that could be tackled collectively through the institution of the school.

Feminist Poststructuralist Practice

Workers for gender justice in schools often find themselves in difficulty when they try to challenge the dominant discourses surrounding sexuality. Work with young children of both sexes has shown that they draw on discourses of sexuality to position themselves powerfully from at least primary school age, if not earlier (Davies, 1990b, Walkerdine, 1984). Sexist discourses are mediated by the peer group and in family and local community settings, as well as in the school. In this respect, they are different from racist and classist discourses, where it is clear who is privileged through the operation of the discourse and who is disadvantaged (Holland and Eisenhart, 1990). Where a family member or friend is the one positioning a girl, in discourses of essential female sexuality, normality and heterosexuality, it can be difficult to identify such positioning as oppressive or regulatory. And a teacher who identifies it as such may be rejected, because of the pain associated with going against entrenched and emotionally resonant values of family and peer group.

Girls are not just positioned in sexist discourses. They are also positioned in discourses of ethnicity, class, ability, race, age and personality. Shaping all of these discourses are the metadiscourses of normality/naturalness (including heterosexuality) and reality, set in opposition to equality. Feminist teachers working for change cannot ignore any of these discourses and the ways that they shape subjectivity and pedagogical practices. Poststructuralist feminist discourse can attend to these simultaneous positionings, as well as to power, pleasure, pain and emotion, in the formation of current gender identities. It can contribute to the development of feminist pedagogies which provide a nurturing and challenging atmosphere for the creation of new discourses or the emergence of muted ones. Of course, emancipation does not occur at the level of discourse alone. The importance of political and economic factors must be recognised also (Soper, 1991).

Young people are often aware of the unfairness of sexist discourse. Supportive groupwork led by well trained teacher facilitators can provide the 'nurturing dimension' (Kenway et al., 1994, p.203) which can help make the leap from awareness to challenge. Groups can include girls and boys, women and men teachers. The key element here is the teacher training, which must include poststructuralist insights, in order for teachers to move beyond the limitations of essentialist perspectives. Poststructuralism offers us a view of ourselves and of pupils that is able to accommodate complexity. It does not insist that we are all the time either active or passive, rational or emotional. It recognises that there will be no overall strategy for gender reform. Each instance of positioning in sexist discourses will need to be dealt with specifically and support given to pupils and teachers in working out possibilities for strategies which will challenge the discourse, rather than deny it or see it as representing reality. It also implies taking a view of communication which acknowledges pupils as active interpreters of feminist pedagogies and which trusts them to rewrite what they receive from a teacher, to suit their own particular circumstances (ibid). It implies that feminist teachers must not show disappointment when pupils do not reach 'correct' conclusions. Feminist poststructuralism avoids feminist dogma and challenges stereotyping of feminism (ibid).

Attending to feminist poststructuralism in the education of teachers (both pre- and in-service) does not mean that other feminist discourses need be forgotten. Liberal feminist initiatives about access, school policies and equal representation of sexes in schooling are necessary and effective in particular circumstances. Cultural/radical feminist discourse which emphasises the value of femaleness and female collectivity can provide a welcome sense of solidarity and support for girls and women in same-sex groups. Nevertheless, without work at the level of discourse, equality measures will be confined to 'add women and stir' (Fisher and Todd, 1988). Teachers need to be helped to see different feminisms as strategies for making changes at local sites of power. 'Change does not occur ... by transforming the whole at once but only by resisting injustices at the particular points where they manifest themselves.' (Hoy, 1986, p.143)

This chapter has concentrated on how girls are positioned within discourses of sexuality. It is clear that boys too can be positioned in ways that are constraining and contradictory (see Reay, 1990, Hunter, 1993). Feminist poststructuralist initiatives support wide ranges of ways to be female and male and encourage people to experiment with gender identity. The experience of contradiction can be used to explore ways of not allowing taken-for-granted meanings to define who we are. There are few spaces in schools for exploring contradictions. They need to be created. Before engaging in such work with girls or boys, teachers need to be able to engage in critical and ongoing reflection on their own gender identities. However, there is little professional development available for teachers in the area of gender reform, which recognises poststructuralist work. Add to this the general institutional tendency to avoid confronting the complexity of issues (Reay, 1990, p.270), and the difficulty of the task is clear. Individual feminists are most often left to do their own development in this area, along with some initiatives from the teacher unions.

Conclusion

If we want to account for the reproduction of inequality and male privilege in gender relations, we must ask why girls 'choose' certain paths which could rationally be shown to be 'bad' for them. In this study, many individual teachers were attempting to contest inequality, yet failing to see changes. Gender relations were structured through discourses which were mediated by the peer group, the family and wider social relations. These relations were commonly taken to be an expression of normal and natural differences, which acted against critical examination of language and practices. Power was invested in the subject position which could define a girl according to her sexuality and reputation. Both girls and boys took up these subject positions, recognising the power invested in them, although some felt uncomfortable with them and recognised them as unfair. Teachers too recognised the power of the categories. The unfortunate 'reality' of girls' and women's essentially sexual nature was seen to be inescapable and the equal opportunities ideal unattainable. The idea 'only natural' functioned to eliminate the perception of oppression and to create self-regulating subjectivities. Nevertheless, awareness of contradictions existed, revealing that the discourses did not have entirely unitary effects.

Feminist poststructuralist insights need to be combined with radical and liberal feminist approaches to gender justice, in order to push beyond limiting essentialist beliefs about women and men. As yet, such practice remains undeveloped, except in isolated cases. It needs to be worked out in dynamic and collective ways which include girls and boys, women and men teachers, as well as feminist poststructuralist theorist-practitioners.

Discussion Topics

1. Discourses of essential female sexuality constitute a form of social control of women. Discuss and illustrate.

2. To what extent is gender identity constructed, rather than pregiven?

3. In what ways does talking about sexuality reproduce dominant discourses?

4. How can regulatory discourses of sexuality and normality be effectively challenged?

References and Further Reading

Breen, R. 1986 *Subject Availability and Student Performance in the Senior Cycle of Irish Post Primary schools* Dublin: ESRI.

Clancy, P and Brannick, T. 1990 'Subject Specialisation at Second Level and Third Level Field of Study: Some Gender Differences' *Irish Educational Studies* 9, pp.158-173

Connell, R W. 1989 'Cool Guys, Swots and Wimps: The Interplay of Masculinity and Education' *Oxford Review of Education* 15(3), pp.291-304.

Davies, B. 1989 'The Discursive Production of the Male/Female Dualism in School Settings' *Oxford Review of Education* 15(3), pp.229-242.

Davies, B. 1990a 'Agency as a Form of Classroom Practice: A Classroom Scene Observed' *British Journal of the Sociology of Education* 11(3), pp.341-361.

Davies, B. 1990b *Frogs and Snails and Feminist Tales: Pre-school Children and Gender* Sydney: Allen and Unwin.

Drudy, S. 1991 'Developments in the Sociology of Education in Ireland' *Irish Journal of Sociology* 1, pp.107-127.

Drudy S, and Lynch K. 1993 *Schools and Society in Ireland* Dublin: Gill and Macmillan

Fine M. 1988 'Sexuality, Schooling and Adolescent Females: The Missing Discourse of Desire' *Harvard Educational Review* 58(1), pp.29-53.

Fisher, S, and Todd, A D. 1988 (eds.) *Gender and Discourse* New Jersey: Ablex.

Frosh, S. 1987 *The Politics of Psychoanalysis* London: Macmillan.

Gavey, N. 1993 'Technologies and Effects of Heterosexual Coercion' in Wilkinson, S and Kitzinger C. (eds.) *Heterosexuality: A Feminism and Psychology Reader* London: Sage.

Hanafin, J, and Ní Chartaigh, D. 1993 *Co-Education and Attainment* Limerick: Centre for Studies in Gender and Education, University of Limerick.

Hannan, D, and Breen, R. 1987 'Schools and Gender Roles' in Cullen, M. (ed.) *Girls Don't Do Honours: Irish Women in Education in the 19th and 20th Centuries* Dublin: WEB.

Holland, D, and Eisenhart, M. 1990 *Educated in Romance: Women, Achievement and College Culture* Chicago: University of Chicago Press.

Hollway, W. 1984 'Gender Difference and the Production of Subjectivity' in Henriques J, Hollway, W, Urwin, C, Venn, C and Walkerdine, V. *Changing the Subject: Psychology, Social Regulation and Subjectivity* London: Methuen.

Hollway, W. 1989 *Subjectivity and Method in Psychology: Gender, Meaning and Science* London: Sage.

Hoy, D C. 1986 'Power, Repression, Progression: Foucault, Lukes and the Frankfurt School' in Hoy, D C. (ed.) *Foucault: A Critical Reader* Oxford: Blackwell.

Hunter, A. 1993 Same Door, Different Closet: A Heterosexual Sissy's Coming-out Party in Wilkinson, S and Kitzinger, C. (eds.) *Heterosexuality: A Feminism and Psychology Reader* London: Sage.

Kenway, J, and Willis, S. 1990 (eds.) *Hearts and Minds: Self-esteem and the Schooling of Girls* Barcombe: The Falmer Press.

Kenway, J, Willis, S, Blackmore, J and Rennie, L. 1994 Making Hope Practical Rather than Despair Convincing: Feminist Post-Structuralism, Gender Reform and Educational Change in *British Journal of the Sociology of Education* 15(2), pp.187-210.

Lees, S. 1986 *Losing Out: Sexuality and Adolescent Girls* London: Hutchinson.

Lees, S. 1993 *Sugar and Spice: Sexuality and Adolescent Girls* Harmondsworth: Penguin.

Lewis, M. 1993 *Without a Word: Teaching Beyond Women's Silence* London and New York: Routledge.

Lynch, K, and Morgan, V. 1995 Gender and Education, North and South in Clancy, P, Drudy, S, Lynch, K and O'Dowd, L. (eds.) *Irish Society: Sociological Perspectives* Dublin: IPA.

McCracken, G. 1988 *The Long Interview Sage University Paper Series on Qualitative Research Methods*, Vol.13 Beverly Hills, CA: Sage.

McQuillan, H. 1995 Options and Opportunities: An Exploration of Gender Differences in Subject and Career Choice in Lentin R. (ed.) *In from the Shadows: The UL Women's Studies Collection* Limerick: Department of Government and Society, University of Limerick.

Potter J, and Wetherell M. 1987 *Discourse and Social Psychology: Beyond Attitudes and Beliefs* London: Sage.

Reay, D. 1990 Working with Boys in *Gender and Education* 2(3), pp.269-282.

Ryan, A. 1992 *Gender Difference and Discourse in School Relations* Unpublished M.A. thesis Maynooth: Centre for Adult and Community Education, St.Patrick's College.

Scott, J W. 1988 Deconstructing Equality Versus Difference: or, The Uses of Poststructuralist Theory for Feminism in *Feminist Studies* 14, pp.33-50.

Soper, K. 1991 Postmodernism and its Discontents in *Feminist Review* 39, pp.97-108.

Walkerdine, V. 1984 Developmental Psychology and the Child-Centered Pedagogy: The Insertion of Piaget into Early Education in Henriques, J, Hollway, W, Urwin, C, Venn, C and Walkerdine, V. *Changing the Subject: Psychology, Social Regulation and Subjectivity* London: Methuen.

Walkerdine, V. 1987 No Laughing Matter: Girls' Comics and the Preparation for Adult Sexuality in Broughton, J M. (ed.) *Critical Theories of Psychological Development* New York: Plenum Press.

Walkerdine, V. 1988 *The Mastery of Reason: Cognitive Development and the Production of Rationality* London: Routledge.

Weedon, C. 1987 *Feminist Practice and Poststructuralist Theory* Oxford: Blackwell.

3.

Women in Community Education and Development – Liberation or Domestication?

Bríd Connolly

Introduction

This chapter examines theories which underpin current practice in both the women's movement and community education and development. The current practice of community education and development, while endeavouring to address issues of social disadvantage, is incompatible with the emancipation of women, underscored, as it is, by a philosophy which is influenced by Freirean principles but mediated through liberal discourse. The agencies involved in community education and development who wish to address gender inequality need to recognise and learn from feminist theory, the processes and practices which have emerged from feminist groupwork, research and women's studies, especially where they have incorporated poststructural insights.

Current Limitations

Community education and development is perceived by the state and by many statutory and voluntary agencies, operating within a liberal discourse, as the route to empowerment for many marginalised groups in modern Irish society. It is advocated as a positive response to disadvantage, for example, gender inequality, poverty, unemployment, drug misuse, lack of community services, educational disadvantage and so on. Resources are channelled into community groups through ADM,[1] LEADER[2] programmes, Social Welfare and Combat Poverty Agency[3] grants. Community education and development is asked to address major fundamental social problems.

Women have a very high profile in community education and development. Women are involved at all levels from basic women's support groups to membership of the partnership boards. While this is impossible to quantify, Coulter (1993) uses the example that, in 1992 1,000 women turned up to meet President Robinson in the west of Ireland representing forty-two separate groups. The Department of Social Welfare have funded projects in 873 women's groups with small grants in 1995 (Department of Social Welfare, 1996). Women comprise the vast majority of voluntary participants in community education and development, yet they are not present in powerful positions. The Centre for Adult and Community Education, for example, estimate that more than eighty per cent of the participants on extra-mural courses are women out of about 2,000 in total. Almost 100 per cent of the local unpaid co-ordinators are women. These figures would be endorsed by Aontas,[4] the adult education umbrella group. This point is addressed by President Robinson when she appealed in her Allan Lane lecture in February 1992, for a marshalling:

> of new energies and real creative forces which still remain outside the power structures of the established order (Coulter, 1993, p.52).

The discourses underpinning community education and development stem from a spectrum which include the liberal equality of opportunity and Freire's (1972) emancipatory agendas. The thinking underpinning the women's movement in contemporary Irish society similarly draws from a parallel spectrum. The question must be posed, therefore: why are women, generally, not achieving an equal share in the benefits and power from this social movement? Are the discourses insufficient to address gender inequality? Or is the practice of community education and development inconsistent with the emancipation of women?

It appears that, despite the huge numbers of women involved in this movement, the power structures which serve to exclude women are not even affected, much less challenged. Further, the responses of existing institutions of power may be interpreted as being covertly opposed to them, maintaining their powerlessness by not changing. This is consistent with the experience of most movements involving women over the past two hundred years, so much so that women have had to find ways of organising outside those institutions (Coulter, 1993, p.59). This gives rise to two points: that the process of community education and development is not addressing exclusion and powerlessness, much less inequality, in a meaningful way; that women, as a group, are the most significant losers.

Community Development: Origins

Community development, which aimed to bring about social change, was identified and described by the United Nations in 1948 as a process by which the population collaborates with governmental authorities to improve economic, social and cultural conditions of communities, to integrate these communities into the life of the nation and to help them to contribute to the progress of the state. This process comprises two essential elements:

the participation of the people themselves in efforts to improve their level of living with as much reliance as possible on their own initiative; and the provision of technical and other services in ways which encourage initiative, self-help and mutual help and make these more effective. [It is] essentially both an educational and organisational process.' (Quoted in Mezirow, 1963, p.10).

The process was seen as a way of bringing about social, economic and cultural change to rural peoples based in villages, who were removed from the rapid industrialisation and modernisation processes which were occurring globally after the 2nd World War. The essence of community development was that these people could act collectively, through the medium of community education, to identify their needs and problems as isolated and marginalised and to formulate responses by self-reliance and with the help of governmental and non governmental agencies, thereby moving towards a different, 'more mature' (Mezirow, 1963, p.15) political awareness, strongly influenced by western style democracy and underpinned by industrialisation.

On the basis of its success in rural areas in Asia and Africa, community development was transposed to marginalised urban settings in the USA, and subsequently to Britain and Ireland.

Essentially, the community development process was seen as a social movement which aimed to bring about the assimilation of marginalised groups into the mainstream society. The underlying discourse of industrialisation and modernisation as the model of progress, and the prevailing political will which supported it, was not questioned in the process as people were enlisted as the agents of their own modernisation.

Freire (1972) saw this type of community development as domesticating. He maintained that modernisation benefited 'metropolitan' society and left others marginal. Moreover, it created passive, self-regulating citizens who did not criticize the institutions of power (Freire, 1972, p.130).

Community development, as postulated, was an oppressive force perpetuated by a political discourse grounded in western, capitalist economics.

Strategies in Ireland

O'Cinnéide and Walsh (1990, pp.327-330) described four main strategies in community development in Ireland since the 1960s. The connecting elements incorporate the notion of self-determination and self-expression by people belonging to one community, whether geographical or issue based, who do not necessarily have access to political or social power.

1. Community Social Services Councils, which endeavoured to provide basic, community-based social services, such as meals on wheels and community playgroups.

2. Community Development Co-operatives, which attempted to redress the disadvantage which prevailed, particularly in the West of Ireland, in spite of the economic boom of the 1960s. These community development co-operatives had two main aims: (i) to develop local natural resources such as handicrafts and tourism; (ii) to provide community facilities such as water and electricity.

3. Community Employment and Training Centres, which saw unemployment as a symptom of social disadvantage and which aimed to address it through interventions such as unemployed action groups, job creation schemes, training and personal development projects.

4. Community Anti-Poverty Projects. This strategy stemmed from the belief that poverty and powerlessness are closely connected. If poverty is to be combated, then the issue of power is central to this process.

In 1992, Kelleher and Whelan incorporated this dimension of power into their description, which includes the notions of self-determination and expression, but goes further:

> The process or way the work is carried out is as important as the programme of development being undertaken… This logically leads communities to seek changes at policy and institutional levels, often highlighting the need for the redistribution of society's resources (Kelleher and Whelan, 1992, p.1).

While this description goes far beyond the original concept of community development, it does not recognise the issue of power in gender relations, patriarchal power, and its influence in maintaining the status quo, even in the midst of other political changes.

Community Education

As can be seen from the first description of community development, education has been integral to the process. Lynch (1989), argued, convincingly, that education within a liberal discourse does not change the power relations in society. An emerging radical trend in community development is endeavouring to bring social and political change, but is not overt about how participants will be agents of that change. Kelleher and Whelan (1992) imply it when they say that community awareness and collective action logically leads to political change, but steps in that logical progression are not clear.

Community education is adult education which is located physically in the community, whether the community is geographic or issue based. Community education adopts a person centred approach, or in Knowles' (1970) parlance, an andragogical approach. This is contrasted with an approach which situates all the knowledge, power and status in the teacher.

Community education responds to the needs of the community. It imparts the knowledge and skills the community needs in order to become agents of change.

Adult education, endeavours to facilitate three ways of learning, identified by Bassett, Brady, Fleming and Inglis (1989) as firstly, technical learning, which involves the learner acquiring the skills to enable her/him to control and manipulate the environment; secondly, practical learning, enabling the learner to understand communication and social interaction; thirdly, critical reflection which centres on learning to reason and reflect about life and the nature of society and culture. Critical reflection aims to empower people to take control of their lives, by examining how attitudes and values are formed (Bassett et al., 1989, pp.27-31).

Inglis (1992) distinguishes between empowerment and emancipation. Empowerment is the enabling of people to work within existing power structures; emancipation refers to the struggle against the structures.

The skills needed to utilise this learning, such as communication skills, scientific enquiry and reflexivity flow from these types of knowledge. Thus, in adult education, the process underpins the practical with the intellectual and psychological human functions.

However, it is flawed. The problem with a word such as andragogy is, of course, that is translates literally, and in reality, to 'male-centred' learning. A person centred approach in a patriarchal discourse, as the word andragogy clearly shows may not be sufficiently conscious of itself to become explicit to allow critical reflection.

In addition, a person centred approach may remain in the personal: personal awareness and change contains a message that the participant may change only her or himself. This ideology informs personal development, self awareness, assertiveness, counselling and parenting courses, as well as skills acquisition courses. Community education, underscored by this thinking, rests the responsibility for change in the personal arena, and cannot make the link with collective action. That is not to say that social change does not occur: participants report a change in their families and communities as a result of community education. Social change, in this person centred perspective, is the cumulative effect of individual, personal change rather than a coherent movement.

This person centred perspective of social change is consistent with the view of society which sees it made up of a collection of small groups and individuals which interact with society (Broughton, 1987).

This perspective does not see that the social is something present in the person, with its own structural processes. Furthermore, it implies a view of the person as having an asocial core, separate from the social and pre-existing it, which can be revealed ('the real person') underneath the veneer of socialisation. The implication is that, once the real person is revealed, and 'bad' or 'unequal' socialisation cast aside, equality will emerge as a matter of course. This is implicitly a modernist (and liberal-humanist) view of both society and individual.

A post-structuralist approach tries to overcome this dualism. This translates into an attempt to deconstruct all dualities, eg. oppression/liberation (Ryan, 1995).

The Women's Movement

The women's movement is the term used to describe the political movement which endeavours to bring about emancipatory change for women. It is useful to explore briefly some of the discussions on the terms, such as women's liberation, women's rights, women's emancipation, feminism and so on, that are used almost interchangeably in normal communication.

Lerner (1986) sees the women's movement in general as concerned with the unjust inequality of women in society. Feminism is a blanket term, concealing strong, distinct trends. Thus, a women's rights group see the solution to inequality as a rights issue: if rights are extended to women, then equality will follow. Women's emancipation means freedom from oppression, self-determination and autonomy. The implications of emancipation, — as the roots of the word imply, — 'to come out from under the hand of' — are radical transformation of existing institutions, values and theories. The term women's liberation, according to Lerner, necessarily implies victimisation, which she assesses does not always describe accurately the subordination of women (1986, pp.232-237).

Jane Mills (1991) quotes Rebecca West, who said in 1913:

> I myself have never been able to find out precisely what feminism is: I only know that people call me a feminist whenever I express sentiments that differentiate me from a doormat or a prostitute.

Mills finds that the definitions of feminisms are perplexing, but concludes that the complexity of the term ensures its plurality, encompassing the ideology of difference: radical, marxist, socialist, Black, lesbian (pp.86-88).

Zappone (1991, pp.8-10) muses that the word 'woman' is less threatening and therefore much more palatable than the word 'feminism'. She identifies the following elements of feminism as crucial: consciousness of the patriarchal culture which inhibits human development, including that of people who are poor and people of colour as well as women; a vision of what society would be like freed of the dominant culture; a set of activities which challenge the present social structures and the evolution of a culture which is person-centred and ecological.

Further, feminism is a term that can encompass a social and political spectrum from the liberal discourse of equality of opportunity to the post-structuralist examination of the relation between language, subjectivity, social organisation and power (Weedon, 1991, p.12).

Women and feminism are not identical (Zappone, 1991, p.8). Women's groups may or may not be feminist, and some feminist groups contain men. However, it is true to say that women as a group, comprising feminists, non-partisan and anti-feminists as well as all the shades of belief in between, have benefited from the political and social changes brought about by feminism. It is now a matter of 'common sense' that women be admitted to educational institutions and employment, that women can vote (Bryson, 1992, p.261), and that women have special rights such as maternity leave and children's allowance.

Evans (1982), Eisenstein (1984), Tong (1992) and Humm (1992), together with many other writers, provide us with extensive introductions to feminist theories and feminisms. Humm asserts that, although the word 'feminism' did not come into English use until 1890, the term can stand for a belief in sexual equality combined with a commitment to eliminate gender domination and to change society, dating back at least 400 years. Feminisms range from political activism to academic theorising. Feminism is shaped by the culture in which it is activated, as well as the thinking that underpins it (pp.1-2).

A broad sweep of feminist thinking includes the history of feminisms. Humm describes the first wave of feminism, in the US, as emerging from the anti-slavery movement. When women were excluded from the World Anti-Slavery Convention in London in 1840, Elizabeth Cady Stanton and Susan Anthony organised the famous Seneca Falls Convention in 1848 which sought to apply the principles of the American Declaration of Independence to women. In Britain, Mary Wollstonecraft's 'A Vindication of the Rights of Women' in 1792 formed the basis of thinking around women's rights eventually culminating in the liberal argument for equal rights, as postulated by Harriet Taylor and John Stuart Mill in Britain in 1869.

In Ireland, nationalism was the underlying cause where women struggled alongside men to usher in a new, nationalist state. Coulter (1993) estimated the first women's political association was founded in 1865 by the relatives of Fenians, the Ladies Committee. Although some of the (male) Fenians were influenced by Victorian values with regards to what was and was not appropriate behaviour for women, the women themselves contested those views, and they engaged in 'unwomanly' activities such as the smuggling and manufacture of arms. By the same token, the Ladies Land League advocated such a radical agenda, that the Land League split with them, causing deep bitterness. However, while these women were active in the social and political movements, a distinct women's agenda did not emerge until 1880 (Coulter, 1993, p.15).

Coulter shows that a number of emancipatory movements were intertwined in the nationalist movement such as the labour movement and the cultural movement. They were not distinct or separate, rather they were integral to a generalised resistance to the status quo. Countess Markievicz, Maud Gonne,

Kathleen Clarke and Lady Gregory as well as some men, notably James Connolly were fully behind the principle of the equality of women and were influential enough to have 'Irishwomen' inserted into the 1916 proclamation, despite some opposition (pp.16-21).

The second waves of feminisms again differed in the US and Britain and Ireland was influenced by both. Post-structuralist theory provides exciting thinking, for women and for lessons which may be transposed to other situations. If feminism is about changing the social structures which are the root cause of oppression and inequality, then feminism can provide the thinking and social action that will underpin the praxis.

Post-structuralism, according to Weedon (1991) is plural: it does not have one fixed meaning but is applied to a range of work. Post-structuralism enables us to understand some of the questions which constantly undermine the principles of feminism, eg, why do women tolerate social relations which subordinate their interests to those of men? Why can a privileged, middle class white woman be termed oppressed, especially in contrast with an unemployed, resourceless man?

Feminism has always appropriated existing theories and has attempted to develop radical alternatives.

> Both in the appropriation of existing theory and the development of new theories, feminists require criteria of adequacy which might usefully focus on the basic assumption, the degree of explanatory power and the political implications which a particular type of analysis yields (Weedon, 1991, p.19).

Thus can feminism look at the underlying discourses of society, look at what is working and what is not, and attempt to develop innovatory ways of seeing in order to bring about the nub of feminism: the transformation of society to true equality? This necessarily means that other emancipatory movements must include the emancipation of women, and that all other measures must be critiqued in order to illuminate the ideologies which prevent emancipation.

As has been seen from history, women struggling alongside men in so many social movements, the anti-slavery in the US, socialism in Europe, and nationalism in Ireland and other colonised countries have been excluded as soon as a new status quo has been attained. Therefore, it is not enough for women to participate, to be 'included', to come in from the margins. A self conscious feminist input must be included in any strategy which attempts to deal with the problems that community education and development are addressing.

Feminism, Community Development and the role of Community Education

Feminism and community development are both political movements. They aim to bring about social change, to endeavour to empower people to take control over their own lives, to develop their human potential and to act collectively to change the power relations which created the inequality. However, it is useful to look at the differences in the philosophies underpinning these movements.

Community education and development, even underpinned by radical aspirations which seek to redress disadvantage remains stuck in a relatively helpless position arising out of three problematic issues, areas which are not adequately scrutinised in current thinking:

(i)   the pedagogical approach
(ii) the inadequacy of thinking on the process of collective action
(iii) the types of outcomes desired.

The Pedagogical Approach

Firstly, Weiler (1991) points out that feminist pedagogy as it is usually defined and Freirean pedagogy see their function in terms of social transformation. Both are underpinned by common assumptions concerning oppression, consciousness and historical change. Both see consciousness as more than a sum of dominating discourses. They see:

> human beings as subjects and actors in history and [both] hold a strong commitment to justice and a vision of a better world and of the potential for liberation (Weiler, 1991, p.450).

However, Freirean pedagogy does not recognise the overlapping forms of oppressions (Weiler, 1991, p.453): oppressions where the oppressed are oppressors as in a patriarchal power structure. More than conscientization and critical reflection is needed. Integral to feminism is a consciousness raising process which is a way for women to analyse their condition, develop new theory and plan action' (Ryan, 1992, p.167). Further, it is focused on oppression. Hart (1990) asserts that social membership is reclaimed and the theoretical perception of power as it operates as a social structure is adopted. Finally, emancipatory action is initiated (pp. 70-71).

What is required is consciousness raising which enables women to see their condition as political or social rather than individuated. Activity aimed at bringing about change which is not underpinned by this process of consciousness raising is not likely to challenge the status quo. Consciousness raising politicises action. Conscientization (Friere, 1972) encompasses critical awareness and the impetus to act but does not goes so far as challenging the dominant discourses especially in relation to patriarchy. Consciousness raising, with the capacity to reflect on experience, to developing thinking on the nature of power structures, and to make sense of it by challenging the discourses is what is required. That is, consciousness raising recognises that the prevailing discourses may themselves mask the reality that critical reflection seeks to address. Further, they may reproduce them unchanged. This is crucial in regard to patriarchy, which supersedes all other forms of human oppression, but which is not overtly dealt within the liberal discourse. The feminist pedagogical approach is clearly in the strongest position to make this explicit and is essential if this problem is to be overcome.

Secondly, while the pedagogical approach is crucial, it does not adequately respond to the problem of moving from the personal to the political. The need for participants to behave in an equalitarian manner, to develop group cohesiveness and to act collectively has to be addressed. And, thirdly, it does not necessarily address the nature of the type of change that is required. But social change can be domesticating rather than liberating, turning participants into self-regulating citizens.

Discussions on the issue of feminist pedagogy centre on what is it, how does it differ from other pedagogies and what does it do? Maher (1987) says that feminist pedagogy emerged as a response to the traditional content and theory of knowledge which prevails in mainstream educational institutions. That is, education which locates elite white heterosexual males as the norm of experience and knowledge. Further, she points out that Freirean analysis of oppression ignores gender oppression, that Freire subsumes gender oppression into class subordination, without recognising the implications of patriarchy and of difference. She asserts that Freire overlooks the private sphere, where gender oppression is especially acute, focusing on the public, where oppression is more visible (Maher, 1987, pp.91,97-98) And, it may be inferred, more male.

Maher's exploration of the roots of feminist pedagogy sheds light on the usefulness of Freirean liberation models, in spite of the drawbacks already mentioned with regards to gender, and the evolution of what she terms the 'gender model'. This model is characterised by a celebration of women's attributes such as care, love, empathy, compassion, sensitivity whether these are natural or socially proscribed. This model analyses the partiality of knowledge, stemming from the gendered, classed and cultured division of experience and thought. Primarily, it identifies the subjectivity of 'truth' (p.96). That is, that truth is not objective or impartial, rather, it resides in the subject. Crucially, she finds that gender models 'do not see the importance of collective, political and politically conscious resistance experiences' (p.98). This may be because gender models lack a consciousness of the liberal discourse. In spite of the appearance of tackling the issue, the underlying ideology subverts the outcomes. Maher finds that the liberation and gender models, when combined, comprise the basis of feminist pedagogy.

Honor Fagan (1991), in her work with the Centre for Adult and Community Education, Maynooth, describes her own feminist pedagogical approach which she believes will contribute to a new politics that aims to achieve radical democracy (p.65). Her practice includes a statement of her own political stance: critical socialist feminism. Her pedagogical methodology includes dialogue, discussion, input by herself as tutor and a supportive, non-competitive learning ambience. Content centres on how society operates, firstly, as a system, and secondly, how society impinges on the participants lives (p.70).

> A feminist critical pedagogy makes gendered subjectivities of the teacher and students part of the text or subject matter. A critical inquiry is grounded in gender subjectivity as an example that allows the addressing of and inquiry into, other axes of oppression such as class, race and global positioning (Fagan, 1991, p.74).

Feminist pedagogy is more than a way of looking at women's oppression. It provides a lens through which all other forms of oppression can be viewed clearly and changes planned.

Weiler (1991) adds the dimension of difference to feminist pedagogy. She explicitly invokes post structuralist feminism as a way of encompassing difference. Feminist post-structuralism attempts to analyse historical and social data to explain the way in which power operates in the interest of the dominant discourse, and to identify specific opportunities for resistance (Weedon, 1991, p.41).

The dominant influence in a pedagogical approach which sees universalities in women and inequalities, is the discourse of white middle-class heterosexual women, who do not see beyond their own subjectivity. While post-structuralism is intimately concerned with subjectivity, it recognises subjectivity as unique to the subject rather than attempting to draw generalisations. Further, it is concerned with knowledge, social institutions, power and ways of bringing about change.

> Feminist post structuralism, then, is a mode of knowledge production which uses poststructuralist theories of language, subjectivity, social processes and institutions to understand existing power relations and to identify areas and strategies for change (Weedon, 1991, pp.40-41).

Weiler concludes:

> [The feminist pedagogical position of difference] challenges the use of such universal terms as oppression and liberation without locating these terms in a concrete historical or social context (Weiler, 1991, p.469).

Essentially, feminist pedagogy, developed through liberatory and feminist models of teaching, does far more than focus on the oppression of women. It provides us with a medium through which to view discourse, knowledge, difference, subjectivity, language, social institutions and processes in order to enable us to understand power structures, the way in which those power structures work and to learn the routes to bring about change in those structures towards equality in the distribution of power.

The methodologies of feminist pedagogy, as was stated in reference to Fagan's self-assessment, comprise dialogue, discussion and a supportive learning environment, in addition to input on the social institutions and power relations. This process requires that participants recognise the value of their own and the others' subjectivity and whence their values and attitudes emerged. These skills are not normally imparted in mainstream education, where the prevailing discourse encourages competitiveness, silence, objectivity, and an hierarchical power relation between teacher and student.

Byrne, (1995) speaks of the difficulties she experiences in her own work when a feminist methodology is implemented. She lists at length some of the factors which may have contributed to the difficulties.

> At the beginning ... most of the students did not have the skills to do the tasks I set, could not listen to each other, did not appreciate feedback from other students, wanted more structure and affirmation from me (p.33).

My own experience amounts to ten years of adult and community education. I implement a feminist pedagogical approach, which I evolved over time, based on assumptions of the equality of all the participants of a group, including myself as facilitator. For many groups, the feminist pedagogical approach is comfortable and enriching, enabling the participants to develop their potentialities in such areas as speaking in public, speaking from their own experience, becoming motivated by consciousness raising towards action and continuing their growth and education through voluntary community activity or paid employment.

However, feminist pedagogy is so counter to the prevailing pedagogical approach that it takes some while for the participants to accept it and enjoy it. Women only groups are usually the quickest to adapt but groups comprising men and women tend towards dominant participation by some men, even when this tendency is known, and the participants have undergone skills education in participating equally. There may be hostility to explicit radical agendas, such as feminism or socialism, even in courses like women's studies or social analysis. Subjectivity is sometimes perceived as invalid and participants do not have skills such as listening and making the links between the subjective and the theoretical.

When problems arising out of these areas occur, my experience concurs with Anne Byrne's: the participants strongly express a need for a more directive, authoritarian style of facilitation and less cathartic and disclosing. My response remains in the optimistic framework of feminist pedagogy, and seeks to address the problems rather than repress them.

It is in precisely this area that group work is needed: the skills and education for acting collectively.

Group Work and Collective Action

The underscoring principle of group work in this context is that collective action challenges the liberal discourse of aiming to enable more people to take part in the process, but not challenging the structures which are causing exclusion: structures which are fundamentally incompatible with emancipation. Collective action is only meaningful when it brings about social change towards equality, not if it brings about self-regulation or domestication.

The humanistic approach to adult and community education comprise the following concepts or principles:

1.   Holistic emphasis, which focuses attention on the whole person, rather than how specific psychological processes work.
2.   Phenomenological approach, in which the focus is on subjective awareness, on how a participant experiences her/his world and self.
3.   Existential perspective, the awareness of being intrinsically involved in the process of existence.
4.   Personal agency, participants experience themselves as agents of their own lives, capable of initiating thoughts and actions, especially in relation to bringing about personal change (Open University, 1984).

That is, participants in an adult and community education process have the opportunity to develop to their full potential, in a group setting. However, as was stated earlier, this implies that the person has an asocial core, with no connection with the others members of the group or community. Unless this perspective is underpinned by a discourse which challenges it, participants will experience tremendous personal development, — and this has been documented many times — but it will not translate into social change.

Butler and Wintram (1991) describe this in their work, Feminist Groupwork. Their practice is underpinned by a feminist philosophy, so that the impact of group work is increased esteem and sense of self, as a prelude to collective action.

> Collective action which involves sublimation of the Self becomes training in conformity in the name of a sense of belonging. The last thing a women's group wants to do is to provide yet another source of social pressure for women, in which the words may be different, but the song remains the same (p.152).

They develop this theme when they say that women generalise from their membership of the group to an appraisal of their role in other social groups. This appraisal is measured in terms of oppression, discrimination and violence. This type of appraisal helps women to understand that they, as group members, are part of a continual state of socio-political education. This is the essence of politicisation harnessed by solidarity (p.156).

That is, feminist group work adds a political dimension to humanistic group work. However, as we have seen, a liberal feminist perspective colludes in the notion of personal power: that when all the legal and civil rights blocks are removed, then each woman can take her place alongside men. A liberal-humanistic approach to group work is precisely the crux of the problem: it empowers participants to take control of their own lives, but it does not emancipate them. It does not provide the wherewithal to 'come out from under the hand' of patriarchal, classed, raced and heterosexual society. It may make a difference to each participant and her family and perhaps her community. But it does not challenge the status quo.

A post-structuralist feminist analysis of power relations, of the dominant discourses, of the colonisation of knowledge is integral to feminist group work.

This, then, is the link that is needed to see that, against the odds, it is possible to move from the personal to the political. The insights that feminism has given to people is that the political is not a separate world: it is intrinsically intertwined with everyday experience and existence. These insights can be transposed to all of social life: they can contribute to creating a more democratic, more equal society.

The precise skills that are required to act collectively are those of group work. But the pedagogical approach, the underscoring principles and a vision of what is possible are crucial. No where is this clearer than in feminism.

> By defining a vision of how things can be different, women's groups have a dramatic impact across historical and cultural division ... Every time this happens, the world does not remain the same (Butler and Wintram, 1991, pp.188-9).

The Type of Outcomes

> The whole discussion about adult education and social change, ...as Tawney indicated, rests on a particular view of the nature and capabilities of men and women and the sort of society which would assist their development (Lovett, 1988, p.300).

The type of social change envisaged by the newer strategies in community education and development is to a society where marginalised groups: women, people who are unemployed, people who are poor, people with disabilities, drug misusers, gays and lesbians, travellers, have an equal share in the benefits of society. This is termed by the liberal discourse as inclusion, meaning that the status quo is fine, so long as everyone has the opportunity to share in it. That is, inclusion means tinkering at the protective boundaries of mainstream society so that everyone can get in.

A feminist critique of patriarchy shows that this patently is not sufficient. In a liberal discourse, the liberation of women amounts to inclusion into a patriarchal power structure. Patriarchy, in and of itself, is responsible for the subordination of women: that is what it means. Therefore, the liberal solution is incompatible with emancipation. Patriarchy has implications not just for women.

> Patriarchy is a form of social organisation in which a man heads and controls the family unit. This definition has been broadened by feminists to describe the dominant position of men and male values throughout society (Norton, 1994, p.399).

Patriarchy ultimately benefits all men. The sons of the father may be in competition with him, but eventually they will head up their own families and control them just as their fathers did. As a conduit for resisting the redistribution of power, it is practically flawless.

Gerda Lerner (1986) says that the appropriation by men of women's sexual and reproductive capacity occurred prior to the formation of private property and class society: that archaic states were organised in the form of patriarchy. Women's sexual subordination was institutionalised in the earliest laws, securing women's co-operation by various means such as force and economic dependence. Men learned to dominate other people by their earlier practice of dominance over women in their own group (Lerner, 1986, pp.8-9).

If class stratification is taken as the starting point of an analysis of oppression, the position that underpins the Freirean analysis, then the root of that stratification is overlooked. As Lerner says, the implications of patriarchy are far beyond the effects on women. Inclusion into a patriarchal, socially divided society is impossible. Without patriarchy, society would not have the subordination of women, the competition between people for seemingly scarce resources such as power and property, the dominance of the discourse which underpins these occurrences and a defensive attitude to any discussion which challenges it.

The political system reflects and implements the values and attitudes of the dominant discourse and is the bulwark against the challenges. David Held (1989) says the new movements, such as the women's movement, the anti-Vietnam war, the student movement, the rise of the New-Left, sexual freedom

> seemed to define themselves against almost everything that the traditional political system defended ... Widespread dissent was met by, among other things, the 'heavy hand' of state power (p.116).

Because the traditional, parliamentary political system enforces the status quo, it is in here that new models of democracy need to be implemented. Representational democracy has its roots in access to the means of production.

For example, the vote for women did not bring about the social change it was hoped it would. This points to the fact that the redistribution of power does not lie in current models of representational democracy. Legislative changes have brought about some attitudinal changes in society's perception of women but most change for women has come from outside the established structures of power. Thus, representational democracy, perceived as the fail-safe device in the distribution of power, has not the capacity to address the powerlessness of women in society.

Thompson (1983) says:

> It is only when women cross the line drawn by patriarchy and choose to do things on our own, and when our collusion with racism, homophobia and class oppression can no longer be guaranteed, that real resistance and real possibilities begin to emerge (p.200).

In historical accounts of community development, education and feminism, it is clear that while women have a high participation ratio, this does not translate into an equal share of the benefits of the movements and the social change which they may bring about. Therefore, while community education and development can appropriate the learning and insights of feminism, it has to retain a distinct gender consciousness. Otherwise, women will again be the losers.

Conclusion

In this chapter, the origins of community education, community development and feminism are examined. I explored the liberal discourse in each of the areas and concluded that it was not compatible with the emancipation of women or of the groups that community education and development serve. I focused on three areas where current practice is underpinned by inadequate thinking: pedagogical approaches, collective action and a vision of what is possible. I have endeavoured to show that feminist post-structuralist thinking can broaden the ambit of social change for all marginalised groups and especially for women. Finally, I conclude that emancipatory movements which do not have a specific gender dimension are doomed to reproduce the status quo.

Discussion Topics

1. To what extent can community education and development be considered as part of a social movement?

2. What discourse underpins education in general?

3. Critically evaluate the feminist pedagogical approach to education and learning.

4. Has feminist theory and practice anything to say to non-academic people?

Notes

1. Area Development Management (ADM) is the intermediary company established by the Irish Government in agreement with the European Commission to support local social and economic development. It has direct responsibility for the management of Integrated Development of Designated Disadvantaged and Other Areas (ADM, 1995).
2. LEADER (Liaisons entre actions de development de l'economie rurale) is an initiative launched in 1992, encouraging local rural groups to prepare and submit business plans for the economic development of their areas (Kearney, 1994).
3. The Combat Poverty Agency is a statutory body established in 1986 to provide support for overcoming poverty and to act as a resource for community development.
4. AONTAS is a natioanl umbrella organisation which promotes, develops and supports adult learning and issues relevant to adult education.

References and Further Reading

ADM. 1995 *Integrated Local Development Handbook* Dublin: ADM

Bassett, M, Brady, B, Fleming, T and Inglis, T. 1989 *For Adults Only: A Case for Adult Education in Ireland* Dublin: Aontas.

Broughton, J. 1987 *Critical Theories of Psychological Development* New York: Plenum Press.

Bryson, V. 1992 *Feminist Political Theory: An Introduction* London: Macmillan.

Butler, S and Wintram, C. 1991 *Feminist Groupwork* London: Sage.

Byrne, A. 1995 'Issues for Irish Feminist Pedagogy: What it is and how to do it?' in Lentin, R. *In from the Shadows: The UL Women's Studies Collection* Limerick: UL.

Coulter, C. 1993 *The Hidden Tradition: Feminism and Nationalism in Ireland* Cork: Cork University Press.

Eisenstein, H. 1984. *Contemporary Feminist Thought* London :Unwin Paperbacks.

Evans, M. (ed.) 1982 *The Woman Question: Readings on the Subordination of Women* Oxford: Fontana.

Fagan, H. 1991 'Local Struggles: Women in the Home and Critical Feminist Pedagogy in Ireland' in *Journal of Education* Vol.173 No.1.

Freire, P. 1972 *Pedagogy of the Oppressed* London: Penguin.

Hart, M. 1990 'Liberation through Consciousness Raising' in Mezirow, J. *Fostering Critical Reflection in Adulthood* Oxford: Jossy-Bass.

Held, D. 1989 *Political Theory and the Modern State* Oxford: Polity Press.

Humm, M. (ed.) 1992 *Feminisms: A Reader* New York: Harvester, Wheatsheaf.

Inglis, T. 'Learning about Power, Empowerment and Emancipation' paper presented to Sociology Department, University College, Dublin.

Kearney, B, Boyle, G E and Walsh, J A. 1994 *EU LEADER 1 Initiative in Ireland, Evaluation and Recommendations* Dublin: Dept. of Agriculture, Food and Forestry and Commission of EC.

Kelleher, P and Whelan, M. 1992 *Dublin Communities in Action* Dublin: CAN and CPA.

Knowles, M. 1970 *The Modern Practice of Adult Education: Andragogy versus Pedagogy* New York: Association Press.

Lerner, G. 1986 *The Creation of Patriarchy* Oxford: Oxford University Press.

Lovett, T. 1988 'Radical Adult Education' in Lovett, T. (ed.) *Radical Approaches to Adult Education* London: Routledge.

Lynch, K. 1989 *The Hidden Curriculum: Reproduction in Education: A Reappraisal* London: Falmer.

Maher, F. 1987 'Towards a Richer Theory of Feminist Pedagogy: A Comparison of 'Liberation' and 'Gender' Models for Teaching and Learning' in *Journal of Education* Vol.169 No.3

Mezirow, J. 1963 *Dynamics of Community Development* Washington: Scarecrow Press.

Mills, J. 1991 *Womanwords* London: Virago.

Norton, A. 1994 *The Hutchinson Dictionary of Ideas* Oxford: Helicon.

O'Cinnéide, S and Walsh, J. 1990 'Multiplication and Division: Trends in Community Development since 1960s' in *Community Development Journal* Vol.25 No.4

Open University 1984 *Education for Adults* Milton Keynes: Open University Press.

Ryan, A. 1995 Personal correspondance with the writer.

Ryan, B. 1992 *Feminism and the Women's Movement: Dynamics of Change in Social Movement, Ideology and Activism* London: Routledge.

Tong, R. 1992 *Feminist Thought: A Comprehensive Introduction* London: Routledge.

Thompson, J. 1983 *Learning Liberation: Women's Response to Men's Education* Croom Helm.

Weedon, C. 1991 *Feminist Practice and Poststructuralist Theory* Oxford: Basil Blackwell.

Weiler, K. 1991 'Freire and a Feminist Pedagogy of Difference' in *Harvard Education Review* Vol.61 No.4 November.

Zappone, K. 1991 *The Hope the Wholeness* Twenty-Third Publication, Connecticut: Mystic.

Section 2:
Women and Work

In Ireland, as in many other societies, women's waged employment is women's work'. Women and men are not spread evenly or equally in the different sectors of the economy. Women are often concentrated in low-paid, low-status employment. Their work remains differentiated from that of men's in terms of pay, power and skill (Adkins, 1994, Hanson and Pratt, 1995). These patterns are a complex interconnected process of employers' strategies, trade union practices, traditional cultural stereotypes and of the choices that individual men and women make. Moreover, women's participation in waged employment remains intimately connected to their unpaid domestic roles as mothers and housewives. The strength of the chapters in this section is that they focus on recent empirical data to address a range of explanations for women's disadvantaged position in the labour market and to uncover hitherto neglected aspects of women's working lives. They draw on a range of methodologies including large-scale surveys, in-depth interviews and ethnography. The collective aim of the chapters is to examine the reasons for the persistence of gender inequalities in women's waged and unwaged work and to suggest ways in which this cycle of disadvantage might be eliminated.

Emer Smyth's chapter analyses the most prominent trends in the level and pattern of female employment in the Republic of Ireland. She suggests that theories of women's employment fall into two main types 'supply side' theories and 'demand side' theories. Each of these approaches provide a partial explanation for women's employment patterns and Smyth advocates a more integrated approach drawing on the interplay of demand and supply factors in explaining women's labour market positions. Within supply side theories, households are viewed as consensual units, women's responsibility for childcare and housework is taken for granted and the labour market is seen as gender neutral. In the process, the demand factors operating within the labour market itself are rendered unimportant and the differences in the employment situation of men and women with similar characteristics are not acknowledged.

Demand side theories provide a more holistic view of women's employment patterns by locating women's labour market position within the context of overall changes in employment and unemployment. However, often demand side theories present a simplistic dualistic model of the labour market divided into core and peripheral sectors with men dominating the core while women are relegated to the periphery. Smyth argues that closer examination of women's employment patterns reveal a much more complex picture. For example, one quarter of women in employment in the Republic of Ireland are in professional/ technical occupations. This contrasts with only thirteen per cent of male workers. By focusing on women's actual employment patterns, Smyth provides a readable and accessible account of trends of gender segregation in Ireland and a critique of the main theoretical approaches which seek to explain them.

Ethel Crowley examines the demand side factor of women's employment by describing the extent to which multinational corporations (MNCs) actively recruit women workers. She suggests that MNCs contribute to the already existing patriarchal order within Irish industry. Since most of the jobs that women undertake in these industries are unskilled or semi-skilled then MNCs do little to elevate women's economic status in Irish society. Crowley argues that the only type of industrial employment which is increasing in Ireland is in manufacturing. However, if one examines the types of work women undertake in manufacturing one finds that women occupy jobs which depend on the supposedly feminine traits of nimbleness and frugality. Such jobs do little to challenge the segregated nature of the labour market along gender lines.

Crowley is sceptical of the potential of trade unions to improve women's working conditions. She suggests that women tend to view trade unions as male dominated organisations concerned with advancing the concerns of men while marginalising the concerns of women. In her view, MNCs favour workers who are least likely to take trade union membership seriously. Again, this makes women ideal recruits for MNCs. Crowley argues that women need to diversify into all areas of industry in order to strengthen their labour market potential and suggests that education and training schemes need to tackle first-hand the segregated nature of the labour market by preparing women for jobs in areas currently dominated by males.

Margaret Carey reminds us that while the labour market remains segmented along gender lines, nonetheless some women do end up in areas of employment traditionally seen as men's work. However, she suggests that because most women find employment in stereotypical gender specific types of work such as teaching, nursing and service work, women who step outside these boundaries are often rendered invisible. Her chapter attempts to rectify this neglect by focusing on women in non-traditional employment in Northern Ireland.

While the numbers of women employed in male dominated areas of employment remain small, nonetheless their experiences challenge the view that women are unwilling or unable to undertake physically demanding and often dirty work. Contrary to popular expectations, Carey did not find sexual harassment to be a major problem for the women in her study. However, Carey warns that since so few women participate in areas of non-traditional employment and since those that do are generally employed in relatively powerless positions, women do not as yet constitute a threat to male models of employment and under such circumstances, tolerance may flourish. This situation could however reverse if more women moved away from stereotypical expectations surrounding employment destinations.

In the opening chapter in this section, Smyth suggests that official statistics on labour market participation tend to view work in male terms, that is, as full-time formal employment and as a result tend to underestimate or ignore certain types of women's work. The chapters by Madeleine Leonard and Wendy Richards highlight these often invisible aspects of women's work. Leonard applies the concept of the 'caring community' to one working class area of high, long-term unemployment in Belfast. Her research shows that caring for others both within and outside the household is primarily a female task. Drawing on the concept of 'love labour', Leonard suggests that while many women find caring for others fulfilling, nonetheless the gendered nature of caring activities results in the economic value of such work at a community and household level remaining hidden or undervalued. Rather caring work was constructed as part of traditional, stereotypical views regarding activities to which women are 'naturally' suited. In the process, the sheer effort attached to such work went unrecognised. Moreover, since women did not receive adequate help from other family members, particularly males, then caring for others outside the household had to be combined with primary responsibility for caring for others within the household. As a result, traditional attitudes concerning male and female work roles remained unchallenged and a division of labour along gender lines remained firmly entrenched.

Richards' chapter moves the focus to work within the household for money. Her research on homeworkers in the Republic of Ireland backs up research elsewhere into the exploitative nature of homework. Drawing on a sample of nineteen homeworkers located through newspaper advertisements, Richards documents the lived reality of homeworking in Ireland. The homeworkers in Richards' study worked long hours for very low rates of pay. Under the guise of flexibility, the homeworkers had to combine their paid activities with primary responsibility for housework and childcare. Richards warns that the trend towards flexibility is likely to increase the opportunities for homeworking. Locating work in the home provides employers with a host of advantages. They avoid responsibility for health and safety regulations and often have no legal commitment towards their workers. Workers are paid by piece rate and such a mechanism enables the employer to control and intensify the work process. Many homeworkers are not recorded in labour market participation statistics, hence their economic output remains hidden. Indeed, Richards suggests that many employers and homeworkers regard their work as a hobby. Clearly, such attitudes do little to enhance women's bargaining power outside the household or to challenge women's roles within the household.

Collectively these chapters suggest that without a change in the domestic division of labour and with women concentrated in low-paid, low-status, often part-time work, waged employment may have little liberating effect for women. Yet, the future is not all bleak. Smyth's chapter does indicate that women are making inroads into higher-paid, high-status employment while Carey demonstrates that the gender specific nature of the labour force is no longer as firmly entrenched as more and more women gain entrance to jobs once seen solely as men's work. Within this framework, there is ample room for women to mobilise and improve their situation both within and outside the household.

References and Further Reading

Adkins, L. (ed.) 1994 *Gendered Work* Buckingham: Open University Press.
Hanson, S and Pratt, G. 1995 *Gender, Work and Space* London: Routledge.

4.

Labour Market Structures and Women's Employment in the Republic of Ireland[1]

Emer Smyth

Introduction

The period since the 1960s has seen significant changes in the nature of women's position in the Irish labour market. In spite of these changes, however, women and men in Ireland continue to differ in the extent of their involvement in paid employment, the type of jobs they hold and the wages they earn (Durkan, 1995).

This chapter is concerned with analysing the factors shaping trends in the level and pattern of female employment in the Republic of Ireland.[2] Previous analyses of women's employment in Ireland have tended to operate within a 'supply-side' perspective, emphasising the central role of individual and family characteristics in shaping women's position in the labour market. However, recent theoretical developments have emphasised the demand for labour, focusing on the role of labour market structures in shaping the level and pattern of female employment. This chapter discusses both 'supply-side' and 'demand-side' frameworks and assesses their contribution to the understanding of women's position in the Irish labour market.

Trends in Female Labour Force Participation in Ireland

Figure 1 reveals contrasting trends in labour force participation for men and women for the period 1961 to 1994. The labour force participation rate refers to the number of those in paid employment or unemployed as a proportion of all those over fifteen years of age. Male participation rates have decreased from eighty-five per cent in 1961 to seventy per cent in 1994, mainly because of increased educational participation among the fifteen to nineteen age-group. In contrast, the proportion of women in the labour force has increased from thirty per cent in 1961 to thirty-six per cent in 1994.

Figure 1: *Labour Force Participation Rates by Gender, 1961-1994*

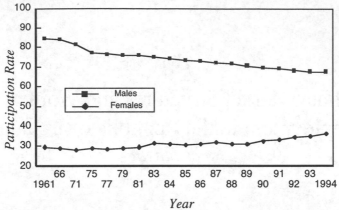

Year

Source: *Census of Population of Ireland* and *Labour Force Survey,* various years.

Overall figures on female participation rates conceal significant differences by marital status (see Figure 2). Participation rates are highest for single women, although there has been a decline among this group due to increasing levels of educational participation within the youngest age-group and earlier retirement among the older age-group. A similar decline in levels of participation is apparent among widowed females; much of this decline can be attributed to the decreasing numbers engaged in agriculture (where retirement is later) along with increased access to social welfare benefits. In contrast, the proportion of married women in the labour force has increased dramatically, from five per cent in 1961 to thirty-three per cent in 1994.[3] By 1994, just under half (forty-nine per cent) of the female labour force was made up of married women.

Figure 2: *Female Labour Force Participation by Marital Status, 1961-1994*

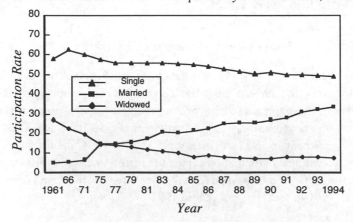

Year

Source: *Census of Population of Ireland* and *Labour Force Survey,* various years.

These figures are based on data collected on the 'usual employment situation' (Principal Economic Status) of respondents to the Census of Population and the Labour Force Survey. An alternative approach to the measurement of labour force participation is provided by the International Labour Organisation (ILO) Economic Status measure. This measure includes those who had worked for payment or profit for at least one hour in the previous week, along with those who were actively seeking work, among those in the labour force. The ILO approach provides a higher estimate of married women's participation than the Principal Economic Status approach, yielding rates of thirty-eight per cent (ILO) compared with thirty-three per cent (PES) in 1994.

Measurement of the numbers of women in employment and unemployment cannot be regarded as unproblematic, however. It has been argued that official statistics present labour market participation in 'male' terms (i.e., as a permanent, full-time relationship), thus leading to a distorted or inadequate coverage of the female labour force. In particular, using figures based on women's 'usual employment situation' underestimates less regular forms of employment, such as seasonal or casual work, some types of part-time work, as well as unpaid labour carried out in the home, farm or business (Blackwell, 1986, 1987, Fahey, 1990, Lynch and McLaughlin, 1995).

While official statistics on women's employment should be interpreted with some caution, there does appear to have been a marked increase in the proportion of married women engaged in paid employment since the 1960s, at least in the more 'regular' forms of employment captured in official statistics. There are two sets of theories which can be used to explain these trends. The first set of theories focuses on labour supply, examining the factors which facilitate or constrain the entry of women into the labour force; these include neo-classical theory and status attainment theory. The second set of theories focuses on the demand for labour, examining the processes operating within the labour market itself and their influence on the level and pattern of female employment; these include reserve army of labour theory and labour market segmentation theory. These theories will be discussed, and their application to the Irish situation assessed, in the following sections of the chapter.

Neo-Classical Theory

Neo-classical theorists view labour force participation decisions as the outcome of rational choices on the part of individuals. They tend to view the situation of women in the labour market in relation to their 'supply' characteristics, specifically focusing on the position of women within the family. They argue that the household, rather than the individual, is the unit which allocates time between market (paid) work, household labour and leisure. Decisions about labour force participation are thus made by weighing up the comparative advantage (or potential value) of time spent in paid employment against that spent in household labour or leisure. It is argued that men and women have different comparative advantages in relation to market and household labour, partly derived from biological differences and subsequently reinforced by differences in investment in education, training and time spent in employment (Becker, 1981). An increase in wages within the market is expected to raise the opportunity cost of spending time in domestic labour or childcare and thus result in increased female participation. In addition, women's labour force participation will increase with education (because more educated women can expect higher wages) and decrease with increasing family size (due to the increased time that must be allocated to childcare).

The labour market is seen as fully competitive; workers differ from each other only in terms of their 'human capital', that is, their investment in education, training and work experience. It is assumed that workers, both male and female, can obtain equal returns to their education and training; thus, those with similar levels of human capital have equal access to employment and can secure similar wage levels.

There are a number of problems with this approach to women's position in the labour market. Firstly, the theory assumes that differences in work behaviour between men and women are somehow innate. Thus, women's responsibility for child-care is seen as unproblematic, 'a heavy biological commitment' (Becker, 1981, p.21), rather than a social and cultural arrangement. Secondly, it obscures power and labour inequalities within the household by assuming that the household is a harmonious unit in which welfare can be maximised for all. In contrast, feminist theorists have argued that the household division of labour reflects gender inequality in power and cultural constraints on female employment (Delphy and Leonard, 1992). International studies have shown that women carry out the bulk of child-care and household labour, even when they are in paid employment and their husbands are unemployed (Anderson et al., 1994). Thirdly, the theory fails to explain why men and women occupy very different types of jobs and earn different levels of wages, even when they have similar levels of 'human capital'.

Status Attainment Theory

Like neo-classical theory, status attainment theory focuses on the characteristics of individual workers. Status attainment theory maps out the relationship between family background, education and the type of occupations people hold, with a particular emphasis on the extent of occupational or social mobility between and within generations (see Blau and Duncan, 1967).[4] Status attainment theorists tend to adopt a similar view of the labour market to neo-classical theorists: the emphasis is on the characteristics people bring to the labour market (particularly their education), rather than on the factors operating within the labour market itself. In contrast, later studies of social mobility have emphasised the role of social structural factors in occupational allocation (see, for example, Erikson and Goldthorpe, 1992); however, these theorists are not concerned with analysing the factors shaping changes in the occupational structure itself.

Much of the research carried out on occupational or social mobility has excluded women from the analysis. This exclusion was initially justified as a 'legitimate preliminary simplification' (Blau and Duncan, 1967, p.113) but later researchers have explicitly argued for the exclusion of women, particularly married women, from research on social mobility (Goldthorpe, 1983). Briefly, Goldthorpe (1983) argues that a (married) woman's class position is derived from that of the (male) household head since women's paid work has little impact on the household's life-chances. Goldthorpe's approach has been the subject of much criticism on both theoretical and empirical grounds (see Crompton and Mann, 1986).

Earlier studies of social mobility in Ireland (e.g. Whelan and Whelan, 1984) followed Goldthorpe in excluding women from the analysis. Later research (e.g. Breen and Whelan, 1995) has taken into account women's own occupational position in examining mobility patterns.[5] As is the case for men, the class background of women impacts on their own subsequent class position. However, the destination of women is very different to that of men from similar social backgrounds, a pattern Breen and Whelan attribute to gender segregation rather than class processes. Hayes and Miller (1989) expand the analysis of women's family background to examine the impact of mother's occupational status on the occupational status of their daughters. They have found that whether a woman works and the type of job she holds have a direct effect on the occupational status of her daughter(s); this effect is both equal to, and independent of, that of the father's occupational position (see also Hayes, 1987).

While the inclusion of women in studies of occupational and/or social mobility is to be welcomed, many researchers have argued that existing 'male' mobility models are inadequate for the analysis of female occupational mobility. Firstly, it is argued that existing occupational classifications can be too broad and often obscure the degree of gender segregation within the labour market. For example, the category of clerical workers (in which women predominate) contains workers with very different occupational characteristics, while categories for manufacturing work (in which men predominate) are quite detailed and specific. Secondly, traditional mobility models fail to take account of the discontinuous nature of many women's employment histories and are thus unsuitable for analysing women's intragenerational mobility (see Dex, 1987).

Status attainment theory does, however, have potentially useful applications to the study of women's employment. In particular, it allows us to assess the impact of social and educational background on the subsequent employment position of women. However, it provides only a partial explanation since it fails to account for differences in the employment situation of men and women from similar backgrounds.

Supply-Side Theories and Women in the Irish Labour Market

Much of the research carried out on female labour force participation in Ireland has drawn on supply-side theories, in particular neo-classical theory. This research indicates that women are more likely to be in the labour market if they have higher levels of education ('human capital') and less likely to be in the labour market if they have larger families, pre-school children and/or husbands with relatively high earnings (Walsh and Whelan, 1973, Callan and Farrell, 1991, Walsh, 1993). In addition, it is argued that the most significant influence on the level of married women's participation in the labour market since the 1960s has been rising real wages, an effect which has been reinforced by changes in fertility patterns.

It is clear that significant changes in 'supply' characteristics have taken place since the 1960s; in particular, an increase in post-compulsory educational participation among women, an increase in the proportion of married women in the population, a decrease in marital fertility rates and earlier completion of families. In some respects, the increasing proportion of married women in the labour force must be seen in relation to the 'freeing' of their labour (through declining fertility rates and earlier completion of families) at a time when the proportion of single women available for employment was in decline (through increased educational participation and a reduction in the proportion of the single population).

This is only a partial explanation, however, since it can only address relative rather than absolute differences in participation rates. Although fertility rates have been higher in Ireland than in other EU countries, participation rates are still lower in Ireland than elsewhere for women with children (Callan and Farrell, 1991). Thus, it is not supply factors *per se* that influence female participation rates but their impact in the context of labour market, legislative and other socio-cultural constraints on female employment. Furthermore, by reducing participation decisions to economic incentives, this approach fails to take into account power and labour inequalities within the household, and the way in which these inequalities are reinforced by lack of State provision for child-care (see Pyle, 1990). In addition, this approach fails to account for occupational and industrial segregation on the basis of gender; it does not explain why women and men occupy different types of jobs, even when they have equal levels of 'human capital', and why men tend to earn more than similarly qualified women (Nolan, 1992), even within the same occupational groups (Callan and Wren, 1994).

Focusing only on changes in the nature of the labour supply ignores the impact of a number of factors operating since the 1960s. Firstly, the increasing proportion of married women in the labour force must be seen, at least in part, as a response to legislative change in the 1970s, including the removal of the 'marriage bar' in the civil service and financial sectors, along with the introduction of equal opportunity and equal pay legislation.[6] Secondly, the growth in the number of women in work must be seen in relation to trends in the type of jobs available; the 1970s, in particular, saw a dramatic increase in jobs that had been traditionally female, such as clerical and service work.[7] Thus, it is necessary to consider the impact of changes within the labour market on female labour force participation; the following sections consider theories which focus on the impact of the demand for labour on women's employment.

Reserve Army of Labour Theory

The concept of a reserve army of labour is central to Marxist economic theory. The reserve army of labour is made up of workers expelled from capitalist industries, those in pre-capitalist forms of employment (e.g. agriculture), and the casually employed. Marx argued that the reserve army of labour acted both as a source of labour for industrial expansion and as a means of producing competition between workers.

Twentieth century Marxist and Marxist-feminist theorists have argued that women, particularly married women, can be seen as a latent labour reserve, with female labour force participation falling in response to early industrial development, as production moves from the home to the factory, and later increasing as industrialisation progresses. In the shorter term, women's employment is seen to be responsive to cyclical fluctuations, with women being drawn into the workforce in times of economic expansion and being laid off in times of recession (Humphries, 1983). It is argued that married women constitute a particular form of reserve labour: firstly, their labour is cheap because of their economic dependence on their husbands, and secondly, they are considered dispensable, since they can be reabsorbed into the family during economic recessions (Beechey, 1987).

This approach provides some insight into women's position in the labour market, firstly, by placing it in the context of overall trends in employment and unemployment, rather than focusing on women's family position alone; and secondly, because it adopts an historical perspective, placing more recent trends in female employment in the context of changes over a much longer period.

At first glance, longer term trends in female labour force participation in Ireland appear consistent with the predictions of reserve army of labour theory: a decline in female labour force participation followed early industrialisation, with a subsequent increase in participation, particularly among married women. Thus, taking a more historical perspective reveals a very different pattern from that apparent over the most recent period; trends in women's labour force participation since the nineteenth century have followed a U-shaped pattern rather than showing a simple increase over time (see Figure 3).

Figure 3: *Women's Labour Force Participation, 1841-1991*[8]

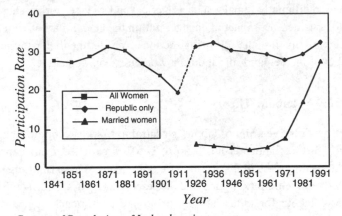

Source: *Census of Population of Ireland*, various years.

However, this perspective glosses over some of the complexities of Irish industrial development. The decline in female labour force participation was related not only to a shift away from home production but also to the decline in traditional Irish industries resulting from the spread of the factory system in Britain, changes in the nature of agricultural production in the post-Famine period, along with a decline in the number of domestic servants. Thus, the traditional areas of female labour — domestic, agricultural and textiles — all declined over the same period (Daly, 1981).

A further problem with this approach is its tendency towards determinism; it appears to assume that all women at any point in time are equally responsive to changes in the demand for labour and fails to account for differences in participation between groups of women.

In relation to shorter term trends in female employment, reserve army of labour theory maintains that women will be drawn into the labour market in times of expansion and 'dispensed with' in periods of recession. However, this is not consistent with overall trends in employment in Ireland; during recessionary conditions in the 1980s, for example, female employment continued to increase while male employment was decreasing.

Reserve army of labour theory has been criticised for failing to account for the factors shaping industrial and occupational segregation within the labour market. Given that trends in female employment cannot be explained in terms of changes in the aggregate demand for labour, it is necessary to examine how the demand for workers may be differentiated, and indeed gendered.

Labour Market Segmentation Theory

Labour market segmentation theory is concerned with how industries, firms and occupations are differentiated and how these structures interact with workforce characteristics. Initial formulations of segmentation theory conceptualised the workforce in dualistic terms, with occupations divided into primary and secondary sector jobs and industries divided into core and periphery. Primary sector workers (or those in 'core' industries) enjoy higher pay, more stable employment and have access to promotional ladders. The result is the operation of an internal labour market (ILM) whereby only lower grade jobs are filled from outside the firm and higher grade workers are protected from external competition. In contrast, workers in the secondary sector (or peripheral industries) experience low pay, unstable employment chances and have no access to promotion within their occupation or firm (Doeringer and Piore, 1971). Increasingly, this dualistic division has been seen merely as an ideal type with more recent theorists emphasising the variety and complexity of segmentation within the labour market (Rubery and Wilkinson, 1994).

A number of explanations have been advanced for the emergence of labour market segmentation. Early theorists emphasised the role of technological factors, with high technology, capital-intensive production processes requiring greater workforce stability and employer investment in on-the-job training for workers. Consequently, employers encourage worker stability through the provision of higher pay, better working conditions and access to promotion within the firm (Doeringer and Piore, 1971). Later writers, such as the radical labour market theorists (Gordon et al., 1982), have emphasised the employers' need to 'divide and rule' the workforce as the reason for the development of segmentation. According to this view, employers exploit social divisions (such as ethnicity and gender) to promote competition between groups of workers. However, this explanation tends to assume worker passivity in the face of managerial strategies. As Rubery (1978) has argued, workforce divisions can also be utilised by groups of workers to improve their bargaining position, for example, by excluding women and other minority groups.

Increasingly, segmentation theorists have moved away from these more deterministic approaches to view labour market structuration as the outcome of competing strategies on the part of both employers and workers (Rubery and Wilkinson, 1994). The structure of jobs is not automatically determined (Garnsey et al., 1985); employers act to maximise their interests but are not always 'successful' since they are constrained by general labour market conditions, State regulations and worker organisations.

Labour market segmentation theorists argue that existing social divisions serve to segment the labour force:

> there are systematic processes at work which segment labour markets, creating inequalities within the labour force which interact with and reinforce social divisions among the population at large (Garnsey et al., 1985, p.40).

They maintain that those in more vulnerable labour market positions are those who have sources of income other than personal wages (for example, married women and young people living with their parents), and those who are unable to exert organised control over the labour they supply. Consequently, the social and gender differentiation of the labour supply reinforces and develops labour market structuring (Burchell and Rubery, 1994).

No systematic study of segmentation in Ireland has yet been undertaken, primarily because of the lack of available information on pay, conditions and workforce characteristics among those working in different industries, firms and occupations. What little information does exist tends to relate to the manufacturing sector, where only a minority of women are employed. It is possible, however, to examine the extent to which segmentation theory yields general insights into the position of women in the Irish labour market. The next section examines the extent to which women and men work in different types of industries. This is followed by a discussion of gender differences in occupational allocation in Ireland; these differences are placed in the context of the segmentation of the labour market into primary ('good') and secondary ('bad') jobs.

Industrial Segmentation in Ireland

Segmentation theory maintains that industries are segmented into core and periphery sectors. Core industries tend to be larger, more capital intensive, more productive, with better pay, conditions and promotional opportunities for their workers. In contrast, peripheral industries tend to be smaller, more unstable with lower pay and poorer conditions for their workers. While no systematic information on the existence and nature of industrial segmentation in the Irish labour market is available, information on the manufacturing sector over the 1960s and 1970s shows the way in which industrial characteristics interact with workforce characteristics. Women are more likely to work in industries that could be termed 'peripheral', that is, industries which tend to be family-run, more unstable and lower paid (e.g. the textiles and clothing sector). In contrast, women are under-represented in 'core' industries, those that are capital intensive, highly productive and higher paying, such as brewing and printing (see Smyth, 1993).

This pattern of women's over-representation in peripheral industries and under-representation in core industries appears broadly consistent with the pattern predicted by segmentation theorists. However, industrial segmentation does not provide a wholly adequate explanation of the pattern of female employment in Ireland. Firstly, not all industries fall neatly into the core/periphery divide; for example, female workers in electronics firms are paid higher wages than their female counterparts in other manufacturing industries, but, compared with their male co-workers, they tend to work in lower grade jobs with little access to promotion (Wickham and Murray, 1987, Jackson and Barry, 1989). Secondly, industrial segmentation does not explain why some periphery industries are female-intensive (e.g. textiles/clothing) while others are male-intensive (e.g. the timber/furniture industry), nor why men and women occupy very different jobs within the same industry (Smyth, 1993). Thus, it is necessary to look at how women and men are allocated to different jobs in order to complete the picture.

Occupational Segregation in Ireland

Figure 4 indicates the degree of occupational segregation in the Irish labour market.[9] Women are over-represented in clerical, professional/ technical and service occupations; over half of the female workforce are concentrated in just two occupational groups (clerical workers, and professional/ technical workers), while only eighteen per cent of men are employed in these groups.

The degree of segregation across all occupations can be assessed using a segregation index (see Blackwell, 1986); the segregation index for 1994 is 51.4, indicating that over half (51.4 per cent) of employed women would have to move to male-dominated jobs in order to eliminate gender segregation.[10] The degree of segregation has declined somewhat since 1961, although the process is a complex one with the proportion of women declining in some occupations and increasing in others (see Canny et al., 1995).

Figure 4: *Distribution of Male and Female Workers Across Occupational Groups, 1994*

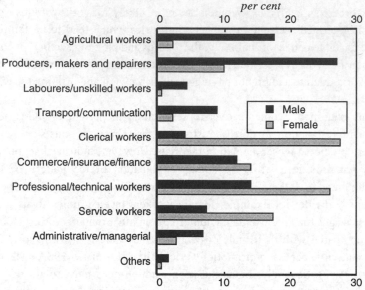

Source: *Labour Force Survey,* 1994.

Occupational Segmentation in Ireland

According to labour market segmentation theory, there are different types of jobs in the labour market, with distinct criteria for hiring, conditions and pay, generally filled by different groups of workers. Early theorists distinguished between three separate occupational segments: the independent primary market, the subordinate primary market, and the secondary market. Secondary jobs require no previous training, and are characterised by low pay, lack of job security, high turnover and little prospect for advancement. Jobs in the subordinate primary market are better-paying and more stable, with some prospects for advancement. The skills required by these workers are usually acquired on the job, and job ladders tend to be firm-specific. Independent primary jobs offer stable employment with considerable job security, established patterns of career progression and relatively high pay. These workers usually have general educational qualifications or skills that are transferable from one employer to another (Edwards, 1979).

Initially, researchers focused on allocating particular occupations to these segments and investigating the distribution of workers across segments; estimates of the over-representation of women in the secondary segment varied significantly according to the particular typology used. Increasingly, this approach has become subject to criticism. Firstly, grouping occupations into very broad categories often conceals important differences between them; for example, both consultants and nurses tend to be allocated to the independent primary sector which serves to obscure important differences in pay, working conditions and control over the labour process between the two groups. As a result, such typologies fail to take account of gender segregation.[11]

Secondly, the concept of 'skill' has been seen as unproblematic by these theorists. This view has increasingly been challenged by feminist theorists who argue that the classification of women's jobs as unskilled and men's jobs as skilled may bear little relation to the amount of ability required for the job (Gaskell, 1986). In response to these issues, more recent analyses of occupational segmentation have focused on detailed case-studies of particular occupations and industries in order to trace the factors shaping labour market structuration.

The lack of detailed information on pay and working conditions in particular occupations in Ireland means that we cannot assess how many women workers are in each occupational segment. However, viewing the Irish labour market in terms of sets of occupational segments provides us with a useful framework for interpreting differences within and between labour market positions. Cleaning work provides a prime example of a highly feminised area of employment which displays classic secondary characteristics, such as low pay, lack of promotional opportunities, and insecurity of tenure. Daly's (1985) study reveals that contract cleaners tend to be female, married with children, with relatively low levels of education and a limited range of work experience. These women's limited bargaining power in the labour market interacts with employment structures in the cleaning industry to produce a pool of cheap reserve labour for cleaning work.

Within particular industries, women may disproportionately occupy lower grade ('secondary') jobs with little access to promotional ladders. Studies of the electronics industry have indicated that women are more or less excluded from professional and technical grades. Instead, they form a preferred labour supply for the assembly grades, where pay rates are lower and they are unlikely to achieve internal promotion (Wickham and Murray, 1987, Jackson and Barry, 1989).

It is far too simplistic to regard all women workers in Ireland as occupying 'secondary' jobs, however. Professional employment is usually regarded as 'primary' in nature, with higher levels of pay, better working conditions, and access to career ladders. A relatively high proportion of women workers in Ireland are employed in such jobs; in 1994, one quarter of women in employment worked in professional/ technical occupations, compared with only thirteen per cent of male workers. Thus, in Ireland women in paid employment are over-represented in professional employment compared with Irish men and in comparison with women in other EU countries (see Rubery and Fagan, 1995).

Furthermore, the overall pattern of employment appears more complex than a primary/secondary dichotomy allows for. The position of clerical workers, for example, cannot be easily allocated to one segment or the other. In addition, there appears to be segmentation within the clerical sector itself. Research on the civil service (Mahon, 1991a, 1991b) indicates that the grade structure can usefully be seen as a segmented one with little mobility between lower grade clerical work and higher grade administrative work.

Segmentation alone does not provide a wholly adequate explanation for the existence of gender segregation in the Irish labour market. Gender segregation is found to occur within broad occupational segments; even among professional workers, for example, women tend to occupy very different jobs to men, with female professional workers disproportionately concentrated in traditionally 'female' areas such as teaching and nursing. Within specific occupations, women and men tend to occupy different grades in the career structure and specialise in different types of work (or particular tasks). Among academics, for example, women tend to work in different faculties and tend to be over-represented among the lower grades of the academic hierarchy (HEA, 1987). In addition, the degree to which men and women achieve access to promotional ladders tends to differ, even when they are in the same occupations (see Geoghegan, 1985, Mahon, 1991b).

The importance of gender in shaping differentiation within, as well as between, segments highlights the need to take account of the contributions of feminist theorists to the analysis of gender segregation. A number of feminist theorists argue that the labour market is 'not a sexually-neutral entity' (Beechey, 1988, p.50) and the labour market itself is gendered. They argue that the labour market does not consist of 'empty places' but that assumptions about the gender of workers are built into the labour process from the outset. Employers view particular jobs or tasks as more 'suitable' or 'appropriate' for women or men, which results in gender segregation within the labour market (Game and Pringle, 1983, Bradley, 1989). While much of the research on 'gendered jobs' has emphasised the centrality of employers' preferences for male or female labour, more recent studies have emphasised the role of trade unions and professional associations (Witz, 1992), (male) informal work cultures (Cockburn, 1991), and management strategy (Collinson et al., 1990) in maintaining the distinction between 'men's jobs' and 'women's jobs'.

Conclusion

Each of the theories discussed is seen to have particular strengths and weaknesses in providing an explanation for recent trends in the level and pattern of female employment in Ireland. Supply-side theories provide a way of looking at the differences between groups of women in their labour market behaviour. However, these theories tend to ignore processes within the labour market itself and tend to see gender inequalities in the household and the labour market as unproblematic. Theories that emphasise the demand for labour have the advantage of placing women's employment position in the context of overall changes in employment and unemployment. However, these theories have often ignored differences between women workers as well as paying inadequate attention to the way in which the labour market is gendered. An integrated approach, which develops the concept of labour market segmentation to incorporate supply factors, would appear to provide the most satisfactory way of understanding the position of women in the Irish labour market.

Discussion Topics

1.   How do official statistics on employment and unemployment affect perceptions of women's work?

2.   Discuss the ways in which State policy can directly and indirectly impact on the level and nature of women's employment.

3.   Identify three jobs that are typically seen as 'women's jobs'. What characteristics do these jobs have in common? In what ways do they differ from each other?

4.   Within manufacturing industry, women continue to earn lower hourly wages than men. Indicate some of the factors which might account for this difference.

Notes

1. I would like to thank Maureen Lyons, Seosamh MacCárthaigh and colleagues at the ESRI for their comments on an earlier version of this paper.
2. Hereafter, 'Ireland' refers to the Republic of Ireland unless otherwise stated.
3. Here 'married' includes women who are separated or divorced.
4. Social mobility refers to shifts in class position while occupational mobility refers to shifts in occupational position, which may or may not reflect changes in class position.
5. However, Breen and Whelan (1995) argue that the family, rather than the individual, is the appropriate unit for class analysis.
6. The 'marriage bar' required women to resign from employment on marriage; married women could not be appointed to jobs in particular sectors.
7. Shift-share analysis indicates that the increase in female employment over the period 1961 to 1990 is primarily related to an increase in the size of 'female' occupations (see Smyth, 1993).

8. Participation rates for the pre-1926 and post-1926 periods are not directly comparable. The pattern of change is roughly similar when the rates are standardised, but the increase between 1911 and 1926 becomes much less dramatic.

9. This discussion refers to horizontal segregation, where men and women hold different types of jobs. The Irish labour market is also vertically segregated, with women over-represented in lower-grade jobs within particular sectors (see Durkan, 1995).

10. The index is calculated on the basis of segregation across twenty-two occupational categories.

11. It also obscures the difference between part-time and full-time workers. Part-time employees often have lower pay, poorer conditions and less access to promotion than full-time employees (see Drew, 1990).

References and Further Reading

Anderson, M, Bechhofer, F and Gershuny, J. (eds.) 1994 *The Social and Political Economy of the Household* Oxford: Oxford University Press.

Becker, G S. 1981 *A Treatise on the Family* Cambridge: Harvard University Press.

Beechey, V. 1987 *Unequal Work* London: Verso.

Beechey, V. 1988 'Rethinking the Definition of Work: Gender and Work' in Jenson, J, Hagen, E and Reddy, C. (eds.) *Feminization of the Labour Force* Cambridge: Polity Press.

Blackwell, J. 1986 *Women in the Labour Force* Dublin: EEA.

Blackwell, J. 1987 'Gender and Statistics' in Curtin, C, Jackson, P and O'Connor, B. (eds.) *Gender in Irish Society* Galway: Galway University Press.

Blau, P M and Duncan, O D. 1967 *The American Occupational Structure* New York: Wiley.

Bradley, H. 1989 *Men's Work, Women's Work* Cambridge: Polity Press.

Breen, R and Whelan, C T. 1995 'Gender and Class Mobility: Evidence from the Republic of Ireland' *Sociology* Vol.29, No.1 pp.1-22.

Burchell, B and Rubery, J. 1994 'Divided Women: Labour Market Segmentation and Gender Segregation' in Scott MacEwen, A. (ed.) *Gender Segregation and Social Change* Oxford: Oxford University Press.

Callan, T and Farrell, B. 1991 *Women's Participation in the Irish Labour Market* Dublin: NESC.

Callan, T and Wren, A. 1994 *Male-Female Wage Differentials* Dublin: ESRI.

Canny, A, Hughes, G and Sexton, J J. 1995 *Occupational Employment Forecasts* 1998 Dublin: ESRI.

Cockburn, C. 1991 *In the Way of Women* London: Macmillan.

Collinson, D L, Knights, D and Collinson, M. 1990 *Managing to Discriminate*. London: Routledge.

Crompton, R and Mann, M. (eds.) 1986 *Gender and Stratification* Cambridge: Polity Press.

Daly, M. 1985 *The Hidden Workers* Dublin: EEA.

Daly, M E. 1981 'Women in the Irish Workforce from Pre-Industrial to Modern Times' *Saothar* Vol.7 pp.74-82.

Delphy, C and Leonard, D. 1992 *Familiar Exploitation* Cambridge: Polity Press.

Dex, S. 1987 *Women's Occupational Mobility* London: Macmillan.

Doeringer, P B and Piore, M J. 1971 *Internal Labor Markets and Manpower Analysis* Lexington: D C Heath.

Drew, E. 1990 *Who Needs Flexibility?* Dublin: EEA.

Durkan, J. 1995 *Women in the Labour* Force Dublin: EEA.

Edwards, R C. 1979 *Contested Terrain* London: Heinemann.

Erikson, R and Goldthorpe, J H. 1992 *The Constant Flux* Oxford: Clarendon Press.

Fahey, T. 1990 'Measuring the Female Labour Supply: Conceptual and Procedural Problems in Irish Official Statistics' *Economic and Social Review* Vol.21, No.2 pp.163-191.

Game, A and Pringle, R. 1983 *Gender at Work* Sydney: Allen and Unwin.

Garnsey, E, Rubery, J and Wilkinson, F. 1985 'Labour Market Structures and Work-Force Divisions' in Deem, R and Salaman, G. (eds.) *Work, Culture and Society* Milton Keynes: Open University Press.

Gaskell, J. 1986 'Conceptions of Skill and the Work of Women: Some Historical and Political Issues' in Hamilton, R and Barrett, M. (eds.) *The Politics of Diversity* London: Verso.

Geoghegan, C. 1985 *Barriers to Women's Progression: A Study in Banking* MBS Thesis no.594, University College Dublin.

Goldthorpe, J H. 1983 'Women and Class Analysis: In Defence of the Conventional View' *Sociology* Vol.17, No.4 pp.465-488.

Gordon, D M, Edwards, R C and Reich, M. 1982 *Segmented Work, Divided Workers.* Cambridge: Cambridge University Press.

Hayes, B. 1987 'Female Intergenerational Mobility within Northern Ireland and the Republic of Ireland' *British Journal of Sociology* Vol.38, No.1 pp.66-76.

Hayes, Bernadette and Miller, Robert L. 1989 'Intergenerational Occupational Mobility within the Republic of Ireland' *Women's Studies International Forum* Vol.12, No.4, pp.439-445.

Higher Education Authority. 1987 *Women Academics in Ireland* Dublin: HEA.

Humphries, J. 1983 'The 'Emancipation' of Women in the 1970s and 1980s: From the Latent to the Floating' *Capital and Class* Vol.20 pp.6-28.

Jackson, P and Barry, U. 1989 'Women's Employment and Multinationals in the Republic of Ireland' in Elson, D and Pearson, R. (eds.) *Women's Employment and Multinationals in Europe* London: Macmillan.

Lynch, K and McLaughlin, E. 1995. 'Caring Labour and Love Labour' in Clancy, P, Drudy, S, Lynch, K and O'Dowd, L. (eds.) *Irish Society: Sociological Perspectives* Dublin: IPA.

Mahon, E. 1991a *Motherhood, Work and Equal Opportunity: A Case Study of Irish Civil Servants* Dublin: Stationery Office.

Mahon, E. 1991b. 'Women and Equality in the Irish Civil Service' in Meehan, E and Sevenhaijsen, S. (eds.) *Equality Politics and Gender* London: Sage.

Nolan, B. 1992 *Low Pay in Ireland* Dublin: ESRI.

Pyle, J L. 1990 *The State and Women in the Economy* New York: SUNY Press.

Rubery, J. 1978 'Structured Labour Markets, Worker Organisation and Low Pay' *Cambridge Journal of Economics* Vol.2, No.1 pp.17-36.

Rubery, J and Fagan, C. 1995 'Gender Segregation in Societal Context' *Work, Employment and Society* Vol.9, No. 2 pp.213-240.

Rubery, J and Wilkinson, F. (eds.) 1994 *Employer Strategy and the Labour Market* Oxford: Oxford University Press.

Smyth, E. 1993 *Labour Market Structures and Women's Employment in Ireland* Ph.D. Thesis, University College Dublin.

Walsh, B M. 1993 'Labour Force Participation and the Growth of Women's Employment, Ireland 1971-1991' *Economic and Social Review* Vol.24, No.4 pp.369-400.

Walsh, B M and Whelan, B J. 1973 'The Determinants of Female Labour Force Participation' paper to the Statistical and Social Inquiry Society of Ireland.

Whelan, C T and Whelan, B J. 1984 *Social Mobility in the Republic of Ireland* Dublin: ESRI.

Wickham, J and Murray, P. 1987 *Women in the Irish Electronics Industry* Dublin: EEA.

Witz, A. 1992 *Professions and Patriarchy* London: Routledge.

5.

Making a Difference? Female Employment and Multinationals in the Republic of Ireland
Ethel Crowley

Introduction

Much debate has ensued in recent years about the real contribution of multinational corporations (MNCs) to the economy of the Republic of Ireland. What differences have they made to Irish society? This chapter argues that the way that MNCs interact with the Irish state maintains both Ireland's dependent status in the international economy and the increasing feminisation of that dependency. Most of the work done by women in these industries is unskilled or semi-skilled, and contributes little to the elevation of their status in society at large. Analysis of the industrial workplace must be understood with reference to other elements of society that serve to discourage women from expressing their full potential.

The Emergence of Export-Led Development in Ireland

Beginning in the late nineteen fifties, the Irish government adopted a specific strategy of attracting MNCs to locate part of their production process in Ireland. This was meant to counteract the decades of economic protectionism which preceded it (Jackson and Barry, 1989, p.38) and has involved giving MNCs huge incentives for locating in Ireland in the form of grants, tax relief, advance factories and Free Trade Zones. This type of industrial policy led Murray and Wickham to the conclusion that the Industrial Development Authority (IDA), reflecting state policy, perceived technology as 'rationalised ideology', that is, everything to do with modern technology must necessarily be positive, and capitalism uses science and technology to legitimate the specific type of inegalitarian society it breeds (Murray and Wickham, 1982, p.179). The type of inequality and indeed displacement of humans caused by technology in the workplace is seen as inevitable and outside of human control. Technology is thus deemed an autonomous force which is devoid of human power relations and is unaccountable to society for the consequences of its actions.

In 1974, seventy-four per cent of IDA funding was allocated to the attraction of foreign firms (Wickham, 1982). Other factors such as proximity to European markets, lax environmental legislation and a low level of unionisation among workers were also important (Harris, 1983, p.101). This policy of export-led development, with the IDA as watchdog, led to the complete restructuring of the Irish industrial landscape, both in terms of location and content. A deliberate policy of attracting MNCs and dispersing them to peripheral rural areas was adopted (O'Malley, 1994). Between 1961 and 1971, when manufacturing employment in Ireland increased by 19.6 per cent overall, it increased in rural areas by 44.5 per cent and in urban areas by 15.8 per cent (Breathnach, 1985, p.179). Whole new sectors of MNC-dominated industry such as electronics, chemicals and pharmaceuticals have also been created (Jackson and Barry, 1989, p.41).

Table 1: *Industries which Increased Overall Employment in Ireland (1979-1987) and Extent of Foreign Dependence.*

SECTOR	OVERALL JOB INCREASE (%)	% OF FEMALE IND. WORKFORCE	FOREIGN CONTROLLED (%)
Chemicals	+4.9	5.8	79.3
Pharmaceuticals	+51.6	3	80.8
Office & Data-Processing Machinery	+53.7	4.9	97.3
Electrical Engineering	+24.4	16.7	83.5
Instrument Engineering	+8.5	6.2	97.4
Plastics	+8.3	2.7	60.2

Source: CSO, 1990, CSO, 1991.

Table 1 shows that Irish industry was almost entirely reliant on foreign investment for employment in the 1980s, a period which witnessed very slow growth in indigenous investment. These sectors which grew in terms of overall employment are also substantial employers of women, for example, electrical engineering and instrument engineering. Exactly in what capacity they were employed will be revealed in the subsequent section on women's work in MNCs in Ireland.

These sectors now constitute a huge proportion of our export industry. By 1982, MNCs accounted for over seventy per cent of manufacturing exports and over one third of manufacturing employment (O'Malley, 1988). The National Economic and Social Council (NESC) deemed the Irish industrial promotion effort 'one of the most highly intensive and organised of its type among competing countries' (quoted in Pyle, 1990, p.139). Intensive and organised this promotion effort may have been, but successful it was not. This was illustrated by the fact that throughout the 1980s, there was an overall decline in manufacturing employment (Blackwell, 1989, p.31). The only sectors which grew at all were those shown in Table 1. In recent years, of course, the IDA has sub-divided into Forbairt, which is in charge of the development of indigenous industry, and IDA Ireland, which focuses on the attraction of MNCs. There is far more emphasis since the late 1980s on helping smaller Irish industries to start up. The macro-economic context, however, has not changed.

In order to illustrate the dynamics of the modern Irish industrial landscape, the concept of the New International Division of Labour (NIDL) is useful (Frobel et al., 1980). This is defined by economic restructuring according to the needs and dictates of multinational corporations. These companies obtain maximum benefit from differential supplies of resources throughout the world, be they in the form of mineral wealth, good infrastructures or cheap labour. The power of MNCs stems in part from their ability to fragment the production process, locating and relocating at will in order to maximise their profits (Massey, 1984, p.36). Headquarters are almost always retained in the mother country and those functions which require more labour are dispersed throughout developing countries, particularly in the NICs of South East Asia and Latin America. This process has been made easy by technological innovations in transport, communications and production technology (Mitter, 1986, p.8). The effect of an 'external' factor like MNCs depends of course on the specifics of the host country, the economic, social and political conditions that exist prior to location there.

In the Irish context, O'Malley outlines two characteristics of foreign industries which are similar for Ireland and the NICs. Firstly, they are 'foot-loose' labour-intensive industries and secondly, among the newer, more sophisticated industries, only those stages of the production process which require little skill are located both in Ireland and the NICs (O'Malley, 1988, p.254). Those countries which set up Free Trade Zones (FTZs), the first ever of which was Shannon in the South West of Ireland, presumably do so in order to improve their position in the international economy, to earn revenue and to provide employment. However, according to Frobel and others:

> ...the employment effects of world market oriented production are extremely disruptive. Their multiplier effects are minimal and often unbalancing in their consequences on the respective domestic economies (Frobel et al., 1980, p.369).

They also comment that countries virtually abandon national sovereignty over the territory that FTZs occupy, both politically and legally (p.385).

A comprehensive report examining the effects of foreign investment in Ireland was drawn up by the Telesis Consultancy Group in 1982. In this report, the damning criticisms of MNCs put forward by Frobel and others were echoed in the Irish context:

> Foreign-owned industrial operation in Ireland with few exceptions do not embody the key competitive activities of the businesses in which they participate; do not employ significant numbers of skilled workers; and are not significantly integrated into traded and skilled sub-supply industries in Ireland (Telesis, 1982 quoted in O'Malley, 1988).

It becomes clear, then, that multinational investment in Ireland has created the preconditions for dependency in the economic sphere and have indeed been very disruptive influences in the Irish economy.[1] Ireland mostly gets the unskilled phases of the production process, while the core countries are characterised by HQ functions and high-grade tertiary activities, like research and development. O'Hearn defines dependency as 'a structural attribute of a country or region that is dependent on external sources for its primary engine of economic growth' (O'Hearn, 1990, p.325). The industrial sector has become increasingly dependent on exports by foreign investors in increasingly few sectors. The manner in which the Irish state has adopted a free trade policy model is obviously essential to this analysis.

Those sectors which have expanded most rapidly, electronics and pharmaceuticals, are those which are most renowned for repatriation of profits from the country (O'Malley, 1988). The extent of the perfectly legal activity of capital flight from Ireland in 1986, for example, was equivalent to 8.4 per cent of total GNP (Breathnach, 1988); in 1989 this had increased to ten per cent (Breathnach, 1993). With this level of repatriation of profits, the losses involved in foreign investment for the Irish economy quite obviously outweigh the gains. Murphy (1994) estimates that profit repatriation rose from £1,358m in 1986 to £3,350m in 1993; and he suggests that it would be more realistic to count this outflow as imports in order to calculate a more accurate balance of payments (Murphy, 1994, pp.17-20).

Women's Work in Multinationals in Ireland

Women's industrial work must be analysed in the context of the fact that women are rather severely under-represented in all aspects of the public sphere in Ireland. One does not find many women in any 'corridor of power' (see Gardiner, 1993). The overall female work participation rate in Ireland, for example, is the lowest in Europe (see Pyle, 1990). Table 2 shows that the work participation rates of women have hardly changed in thirty years, increasing only by three per cent, while for men it has dropped by fourteen percentage points. When this is broken down by age, it appears that only sixty-nine per cent of all women aged between twenty and twenty-four and sixty-two per cent of those between twenty-five and thirty-four are in employment (EEA, 1995, p.10).

Table 2: *Female Participation Rates in the Irish Labour Force, 1961-91.*

MARITAL STATUS	1961	1971	1981	1991
Married	5	8	17	27
Single	59	60	56	50
Widowed	26	19	11	7
All women	30	28	30	33
Men	85	82	76	71

Source: Adapted from Table 3, Mahon, 1994, p.1286.

This does not point to a healthy economy, and certainly not one which is 'woman-friendly'. Mahon (1994) goes on to explain in detail how the tax system and lack of state child-care discriminates against women in the workplace. One can thus understand how in such an economic climate, MNCs would be welcomed with open arms.

Research on women's employment in MNCs in Ireland has shown that the majority of work done by women is classified as unskilled or semi-skilled (Harris, 1983). Phillips and Taylor argue that 'far from being an objective economic fact, skill is often an ideological category imposed on certain types of work by virtue of the sex and power of the workers who perform it' (Phillips and Taylor, 1980, p.79). Thus it is specifically because some types of work in the public sphere of the paid economy are largely done by women that they are undervalued, as is the work done by women in the private sphere of the home. Dual labour market theorists claim that sexual divisions are very convenient ones on which employers can capitalise (Barron and Norris, 1976). They assert that it is one's gender which often determines one's status in the labour market, not one's inherent skill or ability.

There are two types of relations into which women enter, those which are gender ascriptive and those which are bearers of gender. Marriage is the prime example of the former, that is, where one must necessarily be of a certain gender to become involved; the sexual division of labour is the main example of the latter, because it creates and is created by societal gender roles (Elson and Pearson, 1981, p.95). Thus examining the concept of skill in relation to gender is an important step in challenging the idea that a woman's bargaining power in society is increased by working outside the home. This is often not the case.

Table 3 shows the sectors of industry which employ the most women in Ireland and the proportion of these which are dependent on MNCs.

Table 3: *Female Manufacturing Employment by Broad Industrial Sector and the Extent of Foreign Dependence, Irish Republic, 1988.*

INDUSTRIAL SECTOR	SHARE OF FEMALE EMPLOYMENT (%)	FOREIGN (%)
Chemicals/Pharmaceuticals	9	80
Metals & Engineering	34	82.5
Food	15	25.4
Textiles	8	66
Clothing, Footwear & Leather	18	36.4
Paper & Printing	7	13
Miscellaneous	6	69.2
Plastics	3	60.2
TOTAL	100	56.7

Source: CSO, 1991.

This table shows that women's industrial employment is indeed very dependent on foreign investors since they provide almost two-thirds of all women's factory jobs. It is significant that metals and engineering is the sector that is most foreign-dominated at 82.5 per cent and also that it accounts for over one third of all female industrial employment. This chapter will later argue, by providing a breakdown of types of work done by women in industry, that MNCs capitalised upon the already existing patriarchal order within Irish industry, exemplified by the mainly Irish-owned sectors of foodstuffs, clothing and apparel, and footwear and leather.

The employment of women by MNCs in Ireland is comparable, but not identical to that in the NICs. In the case of the latter, substantial pools of cheap female labour are the main attraction for MNCs, whereas in Ireland government incentives for location take priority. This is reflected in the fact that the proportion of women employed in these firms is much higher in the NICs than in Ireland (Pyle, 1990). For example, in Sri Lanka's Free Trade Zones, eighty-five per cent of its 42,000 (app.) industrial workers are young, mostly single women (Rosa, 1991, p.196). Therefore, several economic factors intersect to produce varying levels and types of female exploitation throughout the world. The manner in which MNCs interact with different states produce differing conditions both inside and outside the workplace. Patriarchy itself, with its characteristic flexibility, is the only universal.

Table 4 shows how significant foreign investors are to Irish industry. It shows that in 1988, they were responsible for the employment of 44.2 per cent of the industrial workforce. It also shows that they employ a relatively high proportion of women (German firms, 48.5 per cent female; American firms, 40.1 per cent female) compared to Irish firms, where less than a quarter are female, or the overall manufacturing employment figure of 31.4 per cent female.

Table 4: *Male-Female Breakdown of Manufacturing Employment, by Nationality of Ownership, Irish Republic, 1988.*

NATIONALITY OF OWNERS	TOTAL No.	EMPLOYMENT %	FEMALE %	MALE %
Irish	103,215	55.8	24.4	75.6
Other EC	31,411	17	40.1	59.9
UK	15,324	8.3	35.6	64.4
German	10,093	5.4	48.5	51.5
Other	5,994	3.3		
Non-EC	50,414	27.2	40.3	59.7
US	40,493	21.9	40.1	59.9
Other	9,921	5.3	-	
Total Foreign	81,825	44.2	40.2	59.8
TOTAL	185,040	100	31.4	68.6

Source: CSO, 1991.

Breathnach (1993) shows that in the 1981-86 period, metals and engineering showed a marked increase in female employment, with a rise of twenty-one percentage points (the equivalent figure for men in that sector being 1.5 per cent) (Breathnach, 1993, p.22). This surpassed every other sector by a long stretch.

Even if these statistics were not available, the MNCs' preference for female labour was illustrated by events in Ireland in the early 1970s. In 1969, when the IDA noticed that foreign firms were creating rather too many unskilled, female (these characteristics being synonymous) jobs, they introduced the new stipulation that in order to receive grant assistance, foreign firms should employ seventy-five per cent males. This would presumably raise the level of skill of the new jobs. However, because there was such a sharp fallback in the take-up of these grants, the IDA dropped this criterion in 1975 (Mahon, 1994, p.1285). This clearly shows that the availability of a female workforce was rather important to MNCs.

As is shown in Table 5, those industries which grew at all in the 1980s in terms of employment are those which are almost completely dominated by foreign investors and also have a disproportionate share of female manual workers. It is shown that this is especially true for electrical and instrument engineering, with eighty-five per cent and eighty-four per cent female manual workers respectively and under five per cent of women in managerial and technical work in both cases. These new industries thus follow the patriarchal status quo which existed and contribute little or nothing to the elevation of women's status in Irish society. Blackwell, in his study of women in the Irish labour force, points out that 'one crucial issue ... is the extent to which women are 'crowded' into a relatively small number of industrial sectors' (Blackwell, 1989, p.22). The increasing concentration of women industrial workers into these sectors has profound implications for their future in terms of the effects of new technology, training policies and trade union activity.

Table 5: *Occupational Breakdown of Women's Work in Growing Industries, Ireland, 1988.* *

INDUSTRIAL SECTOR	MANAGERIAL/ TECHNICAL(%)	CLERICAL(%)	MANUAL(%)
Chemicals	17.3	31.4	49.3
Pharmaceuticals	24	26	47
Office & Data-Processing Machinery	7	20.5	70
Electrical Engineering	3.2	10.2	85
Instrument Engineering	4.7	10.4	84
Plastics	2.6	24.6	70

*These percentages do not always add up to 100 per cent because I have omitted apprentices and outside piece workers.

Source: CSO, 1991.

In the industrial arena, technology is and always has been used to simultaneously raise productivity and to reduce the need for skilled labour. It has been well documented that it is those sectors of industry and those stages of the production process in which women are ghettoised that are most vulnerable to displacement by new technology. Mitter describes how in Malaysia alone, 10,000 electronics workers were replaced by machines in 1986 (Mitter, 1986, p.70). This observation is as valid now as it was in the early 1900s, when weaving and spinning, which had been predominantly done by women, became mechanised, centralised into factories, and then a male preserve (Hartmann, 1976, p.149). I will argue that MNCs have been primary facilitators of the maintenance of women in unskilled positions, or the secondary labour market. This should become a major factor in the determination of future industrial and training policy in Ireland as elsewhere. I intend to show how women, traditionally the 'reserve army of labour' (Braverman, 1974), are particularly affected by technological innovations in services and manufacturing industry, relating both in their turn to the Irish context.

In quantitative terms, the service sector is also worrying with regard to the employment effects of new technology. Even though a detailed discussion is outside the scope of this chapter, we can briefly observe that every business now processes data with the aid of sophisticated computer technology, eliminating the need for the traditional type of clerical worker (Mallier and Rosser, 1987, p.163). Office work has become increasingly routinised and deskilled because of new technology and is now also more under the control of management than previously (Jackson and Barry, 1989). Of all women workers, seventy-seven per cent are employed in services, the corresponding figure for men being forty-eight per cent (Blackwell, 1989, p.21). The implications of this are quite grave, as it implies that more workers in those areas become proletarianised.

It is in qualitative terms that we need to study the impact of new technology on women in manufacturing industry. By this is meant that while the absolute numbers of women involved in manufacturing are quite small, the increasing level of both female unemployment and proletarianisation in the growing sectors is quite alarming.

The NIDL has been facilitated by technological change. Within the NIDL, it is those sectors of industry which are the most 'foot-loose' in which technology is mostly used to fragment the production process. Within these sectors (mainly electronics, textiles and chemicals) it is women who perform most of the repetitive tasks, precisely those which are most liable both to monotonous routinisation and/or complete displacement. The processes of displacement and routinisation are very visible within these sectors in Ireland, shown by the fact, for example, that while the growth of assembly work in the electronics industry was very slow in the 1980s, its output reached unprecedented levels (Breathnach, 1990, p.14); that is, while production increases, employment decreases. The only sector which showed an increase in terms of female employment in the 1980s was metals and engineering, and that was only by 2,200 (Blackwell, 1989, p.31). This surely is a strong indictment of IDA industrial policy in these years. While unemployment of course affects men too and indeed society at large, its ideological ramifications are very serious for women. It means that the only kind of jobs now available for women in manufacturing industry are those in which 'the criteria for women are the same as of an efficient housewife: tidyness, nimbleness, frugality with time and movement and, perhaps most importantly, a personal method of getting through work' (Harris, 1983, p.111). It is very difficult for women to develop a group identity when the type of skill requirements and power relations evident in the workplace are almost identical to those in the home. It is quite alarming that this is the only type of industrial employment which is increasing at all in Ireland as we approach the year 2000.

This restructuring of employment within modern capitalism points to the fact that worker requirements will change profoundly in the future. With increased use of computer technology, skilled workers will necessarily be computer literate in order to monitor and maintain production. At present, it is mostly men who do these kinds of jobs so if women are to challenge this particular manifestation of male dominance, they need to diversify into all areas of industry. This must be taken into account by education and training schemes now and in the future, so that women can diversify their skills and become valued in all areas of work. This has been facilitated by the EU-sponsored New Opportunities for Women (NOW) programme in recent years in Ireland (NOW, 1994). Women will not achieve their rightful status solely by becoming equal in the workplace, however. This must be part of a much larger project of challenging the conservative elements in society that keep women, and especially working class women, in a subordinate, powerless position in Irish society. The forthcoming section on workplace politics must be viewed in this context, as part of a larger project of ending sex discrimination.

Women and Trade Unions

Much of the literature on discrimination against women in the workplace point to trade unions as a vehicle for the advancement of women's status in this sphere. However, women find male-dominated unions very off-putting and difficult to penetrate, both on ideological and practical levels. In the following section, it will be explained why they alienate women and how MNCs contribute to this also.

The traditional role of trade unions has been to represent the interests of the working class in their struggles with the bourgeoisie under capitalism. C W Mills described them as 'managers of discontent' in the antagonistic relationship between labour and capital (Mills, 1948, p.8). Hill outlines two modern Marxist arguments against the revolutionary potential of trade unions. The first argues that unions are not revolutionary, but accommodationist, that their very survival depends on labour conflict under capitalism. The second holds that because unions follow divisions laid down by industry, they militate against unity and promote divisions among the working class. This idea is based upon the Leninist perception of unions as being based on individualistic principles instead of universalistic ones (Hill, 1981, p.124).

Trade unions often reproduce the oppressive sexual divisions in the world of work. Women within the trade union movement are often doubly marginalised, both as workers and as women:

weakly organised women workers... have to battle against the bureaucratisation and collaboration of their union (and) also, at every level, they have to struggle as women against being ground down by a male-dominated union hierarchy (Pollert, 1981, p.180).

To illustrate this in the Irish context, we must examine female participation in unions at two levels, that of ordinary member and that of elected official. Women constituted one third of total union membership in 1986, with particularly high representation in the service worker's and teacher's unions (Blackwell, 1989, p.67). However, that said, they represented only thirteen per cent of the membership of union executives. In the twelve unions which represented eighty-eight per cent of female union members, only 3.3 per cent of their elected officials were women (Tansey, 1984, p.116).

By 1993/4, the situation had not improved appreciably, with total female membership of all unions staying at thirty-seven per cent (EEA, 1995, p.43). While unions with a majority of female members certainly do sometimes engage in public action, the voices that are heard in the media are invariably male, as with MANDATE and the INO in 1995 (see *Irish Reporter*, No 20, 1995).

On the positive side, nine unions have national women's committees, two have equality officers and three have women's committees at branch level (Clancy and MacKeogh, 1987, p.152). While these initiatives are somewhat progressive, integration of women into workplace politics is still very slow. The ramifications of this lack of involvement of women in unions are very serious because their interests are thus not properly represented in national wage agreements. Consequently, there follows a shift of power away from female workers and a maintenance of the patriarchal status quo once again.

What are the reasons for the lack of female involvement in unions and how do MNCs help to perpetuate this situation? All of the factors involved are intimately linked and ultimately inseparable. Firstly, many foreign firms in Ireland now use modern management techniques and adopt a specific non-union policy, that is, their workers are not affiliated to any trade union. Jones (1995), in her case study of an American electronics company, provides us with a Gramscian analysis of the importance of the ideology of the 'company ethos' in gaining employee's loyalty. She points out that there are very clear ideas about what is acceptable behaviour or 'the way we do things around here' (Jones, 1995, p.71), within an atmosphere which is perceived to be flexible and informal. However, Jones asserts that:

Consensus is achieved in the workplace by means of corporate cultures which equate the interest of the individual with that of the company, and which actively discourage dissent. The mechanisms through which acquiescence and consent are achieved include the fostering of a corporate ethos which interprets disagreement as disloyalty, and the careful granting of concessions and compromises. These compromises, while effective in gaining the goodwill and commitment of women workers, make no attempt to restructure... patriarchal relations (Jones, 1995, p.70).

So while women employees are encouraged to believe that 'we are all on an adventure together' (Jones, 1995, p.46), capitalist relations of production nevertheless underlie the ideology of community propounded by the company. Consent is thus subtly maintained.

Secondly, many foreign firms, especially in the electronics sector, make 'sweetheart deals' with unions prior to setting up in Ireland (Breathnach, 1990, p.11). This means that the firms and the unions collaborate in a mutually beneficial arrangement and 'trade union membership is a fait accompli for incoming assembly workers' (Breathnach, 1993, p.25). The unions get paid their dues and the companies get more leverage with the unions. This naturally has the effect of alienating the (mostly female) workforce and creating suspicion among them as to the union's real allegiances. This is exacerbated by the fact that the vast majority of union officials are men who are not interested in the daily issues which pertain primarily to women (King, 1984, p.82). Therefore, instead of challenging gender divisions, the unions instead perpetuate them (Harris, 1983, p.105). Unions thus become the 'men's affair' and this becomes a self-fulfilling prophesy for women (Beynon and Blackburn, 1984, p.77).

The main reason given by women union members themselves for their lack of active involvement in their union is commitment to domestic duties. For this reason, they do not have the time to actively pursue workplace politics and are often discouraged from doing so by men (Pollert, 1981, p.186). This is a symptom of a much larger social problem, that is, that of the primacy of the nuclear family and the maintenance of strict sex roles therein. The young working class woman's vision of her future role as wife and mother often serves to discourage her from taking her work experience as seriously as her male counterparts (Hunt, 1980). Therefore, as long as women still perceive their primary role as that of homemaker, workplace politics will inevitably take a back seat.

Like in the NICs, MNCs usually show a preference for hiring young women, inexperienced in the workplace, or married women; these are the two groups who are least likely to take their unions seriously (Clancy and MacKeogh, 1987, p.158). Considering the male bias of most unions, this is understandable. The effect of this is augmented if these workers are located in a small plant in a rural area where there is no tradition of unionism (Moore, 1986). One of the respondents in Harris' study expresses this well:

In a factory like Naguishi there's an awful lot of people who have an agricultural background and who do part-time farming and that. There's a different tradition... We haven't had fathers and grandfathers who've been fitters in Guinness's (in Dublin) for twenty-five years (Harris, 1983, p.103).

While the aforementioned dispersalist policy did a lot to stem rural depopulation and unemployment, the lack of a history of unions was also convenient for foreign companies. It is previous experience of work and unions that determines both male and female attitudes towards unions, that is, the more experience one has, the more positive the attitude (Beynon and Blackburn, 1984, p.80). Therefore, as long as women's work is perceived as transitory, and as long as this ideology is fostered by MNCs, women's equality in the workplace will never be taken seriously and given the attention it deserves.

Conclusion

Ireland's peripheral location in the new international division of labour has been created and fostered by multinational corporations. This situation emerged with the encouragement of the state and its representative body, the IDA, and continues under the auspices of its 1990s successor, IDA Ireland. MNCs usually locate those phases of the production process which require lower quality of labour in Ireland. This process has been intensified by innovations in new technology. During the 1980s, foreign investors dominated the only growing sectors in Ireland: chemicals, pharmaceuticals, plastics, and metals and engineering.

Ireland's subservient position in the international economy is mirrored by women's subordinate status in the industrial sector in Ireland. Those expanding sectors of manufacturing industry have capitalised on women's weak bargaining power in the Irish workplace and in Irish public life in general. Women are usually required to do manual or clerical work and rarely reach the upper echelons of the managerial or technical spheres of work.

Capitalism, whose interests are defended in Ireland by the state at almost any cost, very effectively utilises existing male domination in the private sphere to legitimise its action in the public sphere. The male/female power dynamic evident in the home and in public life is reproduced in the factory. Both the public and private spheres must thus be tackled in unison in order to begin to effect any real change in the daily lives of working class women.

The trade union movement, whose job it is to represent working class interests, is generally very male-dominated. Women rarely get involved in union politics because they perceive the union as the 'men's affair'. A 'Catch 22' situation has emerged within workplace politics; women are not interested in becoming elected officials until unions are seen to defend women's interests.

MNCs further contribute to the subordination of women by entering into 'sweetheart deals' with the unions when they arrive.

So, to proffer an answer to the question in the title — do MNCs make a real difference to the improvement of women's status in society — the answer must unfortunately be no, apart from the minimal requirement of providing some jobs. They instead maintain sexual and class inequality. More fundamental questions need to be asked about the impact of MNCs in Ireland, both at the macro-economic level concerning their 'souffle effect' (Murphy, 1994, p.2) on the economy, and at the micro-social level of affecting women's everyday lives.

Discussion Topics

1.   To what extent does the employment of women in multinational corporations promote the feminisation of women's labour?

2.   In what ways is women's secondary status in industry maintained?

3.   Women's work is underestimated and undervalued throughout the world. Discuss and illustrate with case study material.

4.   How could trade unions be improved to become more responsive to the needs of women workers?

Notes

1.   For a rather damning exposition of the environmental effects of the operations of some MNCs in Ireland, see Allen and Jones, 1990.

References and Further Reading:

Allen, R and Jones, T. 1990 *Guests of the Nation: People of Ireland versus the Multinationals* London: Earthscan.

Barron, R D Norris, G M. 1976 'Sexual Divisions and the Dual Labour Market' in Barker, D L and Allen S. (eds.) *Dependence and Exploitation in Work and Marriage* London: Longman.

Beynon, H and Blackburn, R. 1984 'Unions: The Men's Affair?' in Siltanen, J and Stanworth M. (eds.) *Women and the Public Sphere — A Critique of Sociology and Politics* London: Hutchinson.

Blackwell, J. 1989 *Women in the Labour Force* Dublin: Employment Equality Agency.

Braverman, H. 1974 *Labor and Monopoly Capital* London: Monthly Review Press.

Breathnach, P. 1985 'Rural Industrialisation in the West of Ireland' in Healey, M J and Ilbury B W. (eds.) *The Industrialisation of the Countryside* Norwich: Short Run Press.

Breathnach, P. 1988 'Uneven Development and Capitalist Peripheralisation: The Case of Ireland' *Antipode* Vol.20, No.2 pp.122-141.

Breathnach, P, 1990 'Women's Employment and the European Spatial Division of Labour: the Case of Ireland' Paper presented at Conference on Ireland after 1992, Institute of Irish Studies, University of Liverpool, May, 1990.

Breathnach, P, 1993 'Women's Employment and Peripheralisation: the Case of Ireland's Branch Plant Economy' *Geoforum* Vol.24, No.1, pp.19-29.

Central Statistics Office (CSO). 1990 *Census of Industrial Production 1987*. Dublin: CSO.

Central Statistics Office (CSO). 1991 *Census of Industrial Production 1988*. Dublin: CSO.

Clancy, P and MacKeogh, K. 1987 'Gender and Trade Union Participation' in Curtin, C, Jackson, P and O'Connor B. (eds.) *Gender in Irish Society* Galway: Galway University Press.

Elson, D and Pearson, R. 1981 'Nimble Fingers Make Cheap Workers: An Analysis of Women's Employment in Third World Export Manufacturing' *Feminist Review* No 7 Spring.

Employment Equality Agency (EEA). 1995 *Women in the Labour Force* Dublin: EEA.

Frobel, F, Heinrichs, J and Kreye, O. 1980 *The New International Division of Labour* Cambridge: Cambridge University Press.

Gardiner, F. 1993 'Political Interest and Participation of Irish Women 1922-1992: The Unfinished Revolution' in Smyth, A. (ed.) *Irish Women's Studies Reader* Dublin: Attic Press.

Harris, L. 1983 'Industrialisation, Women and Working Class Politics in the West of Ireland' *Capital and Class* Spring pp.100-117.

Hartmann, H. 1976 'Capitalism, Patriarchy and Job Segregation by Sex' in Blaxall, M and Reagan, B. (eds.) *Women and the Workplace* Chicago: University of Chicago Press.

Hill, S. 1981 *Competition and Control at Work* London: Heinemann.

Hunt, P. 1980 *Gender and Class Consciousness* London: Macmillan.

Irish Reporter. 1995 Full issue, No. 2.

Jackson, P and Barry, U. 1989 'Women's Employment and Multinationals in the Republic of Ireland: the Creation of a New Female Labour Force' in Elson, D and Pearson R. (eds.) *Women's Employment and Multinationals in Europe* London: Macmillan.

Jones, C. 1995 *Patriarchal Hegemony, Women and the Workplace: A Case Study of Women in an Irish Electronics Company* Unpublished Women's Studies MA thesis, University College Cork.

King, D S. 1984 'Ireland' in Cook, A H and Lorwin, U R. (eds.) *Women and Trade Unions in Eleven Industrialized Countries* Philadelphia: Temple University Press.

Mahon, E. 1994 'Ireland: A Private Patriarchy' *Environment and Planning* A Vol.26 pp.1277-1296.

Mallier, A T and Rosser, M J. 1987 *Women and the Economy* London: Macmillan.

Massey, D, 1984 *Spatial Divisions of Labour* London: Macmillan.

Mills, C W. 1948 *The New Men of Power: America's New Labour Leaders* New York: Augustus M Kelly.

Mitter, S. 1986 *Common Fate, Common Bond* London: Pluto.

Moore, T S. 1986 'Are Women Workers Hard to Organise?' *Work and Occupations* Vol.13 February pp.97-111.

Murphy, A E. 1994 *The Irish Economy: Celtic Tiger or Tortoise?* Dublin: Money Markets International.

Murray, P and Wickham, J. 1982 'Technocratic Ideology and the Reproduction of Inequality: the Case of the Electronics Industry in the Republic of Ireland' in Day, G. (ed.) *Diversity and Decomposition in the Labour Market* London: Gower.

NOW. *1994 List of Approved Projects and their Transnational Partners* Dublin: Council for the Status of Women (CSW).

O'Hearn, D, 1990 'Tales and Realities' *American Sociological Review* August pp.603-608.

O'Malley, E. 1988 'The Problem of Late Industrialisation and the Experience of the Republic of Ireland' in Farmar, A. (ed.) *The Developing World* Maynooth: DESC.

O'Malley, E. 1994 'The Impact of Transnational Corporations in the Republic of Ireland' in Dicken P and Quevit M. (eds.) *Transnational Corporations and European Restructuring Netherlands* Geographical Studies No.181, Utrecht.

Phillips, A and Taylor, B. 1980 'Sex and Skill: Notes Towards a Feminist Economics' *Feminist Review* Vol.6 pp.79-88.

Pollert, A. 1981 *Girls, Wives, Factory Lives* London: Macmillan.

Pyle, J L. 1990 'Female Employment and Export-Led Development in Ireland: Labour Market Impact of State-Reinforced Gender Inequality in the Household' in Stichter, S and Parpart J L. (eds.) *Women's Employment and the Family in the International Division of Labour* London: Macmillan.

Rosa, K. 1991 'Export-Oriented Industries and Women Workers in Sri Lanka' in Afshar, H and Agarwal B. (eds.) *Women, Poverty and Ideology in Asia* London: Macmillan.

Tansey, J. 1984 *Women in Ireland* Dublin: Council for the Status of Women.

Wickham, A. 1982 'Women, Industrial Transition and Training Policy in the Republic of Ireland' in Kelly, M, O'Dowd, L and Wickham J. (eds.) *Power, Conflict and Inequality* Dublin: Turoe Press.

6.

Women in Non-Traditional Employment in Northern Ireland: A Marginalised Form of Femininity
Margaret Carey

Introduction

The gendered division of labour in the family, and in society more generally, is now a recognised and well-documented phenomenon. A wide sociological literature has sought to demonstrate and explain how gender roles are learned primarily in the family, and then reinforced by the education and training systems, the media, religion, peer group pressure, and so on.[1] But, that is not the end of the story. The cultivation of gendered roles during childhood and adolescence culminates in a gendered division of labour within the workforce, with women clustered in a narrow range of 'female' occupations. Consequently, fewer women than men will be classified as 'manual' workers, and within the manual category of employment, men are much more likely to be categorised as skilled (craft and similar) workers (Abbott and Wallace, 1991, p.133).

Commentators such as Brewer (1991), Game and Pringle (1984), and Walshok (1987), have noted a tendency in the past for sociologists to overlook women in studies of work. Where they have been studied, the focus has often been on stereotypical 'female' areas of employment such as teaching, nursing and clerical work. However, despite a consistent failure to recognise their existence, there have always been women who have 'stepped outside the stereotype'. According to Connell (1993, p.188), what is hidden from conventional historiography are the experiences of such 'unconventional' women, including manual workers. In an effort to redress this situation, or, to recover one such 'marginalised form of femininity', the reader will be introduced to a number of such women in the following pages.

Two particular areas of employment where women can be said to have 'stepped outside the stereotype' can be identified: male-dominated professions, and, to a lesser extent, male-dominated blue-collar or manual employment. In compensation for the earlier dearth of literature on the subject, a considerable corpus of work has now been developed which examines the position of women in male-dominated professions.[2] Conversely, as Walshok notes (1987, p.xvi), 'most studies of blue-collar workers have emphasised the concerns and attitudes of males.' There have been a limited number of researchers who have examined women's involvement in blue-collar, non-traditional employment, particularly, it would appear, in Northern Ireland. Where such studies have been conducted, they have very often been American in origin.[3]

This chapter attempts to rectify this omission in two ways. First, it will assess the participation of women in non-traditional employment in Northern Ireland, and demonstrate that numbers here have been increasing (albeit slowly) over the past two decades. Second, by reference to a series of semi-structured, in-depth interviews, the chapter qualitatively examines the lived-experiences of some of Northern Ireland's non-traditionally employed women. However, before turning to this assessment, some definition of the term 'non-traditional' is necessary.

For the purposes of this chapter, non-traditional employment can be taken to denote any occupation of a manual nature, which is, or has been, traditionally undertaken by a man. While areas such as transport, construction, and other trade jobs are of particular interest, there are a plethora of occupations which may still be considered as non-traditional for women. Recent research by the author uncovered the fact that women in Northern Ireland are employed in occupations as diverse as foreperson with a road gang, motor cycle courier, saddler, stone carver, and stained-glass window installer (many women interviewed are 'tokens', the sole representatives of their kind in Northern Ireland). A few professional occupations, such as outdoor pursuits instructor and acoustic engineer, were also included. Such occupations can be considered as either 'physical' or 'manual', and are normally associated with males.

Women's Participation Rates in Non-Traditional Employment in Northern Ireland

As in Ireland generally, the late twentieth century has seen numerous changes in the Northern Irish labour market as the nature of work has changed. Due to the decline in traditional heavy industries, and a subsequent increase in service sector employment, many new jobs have been created, a high percentage of these going to women. Subsequently, men's and women's employment patterns have altered dramatically. The number of women in paid employment has risen consistently over the past two decades, so much so that they now represent over forty-five per cent of the Northern Irish labour force (McCorry, 1988, p.7). Data from the Northern Ireland Economic Activity Report, 1991, indicate a total of 275,294 economically active women (aged sixteen and over), of whom 168,573 are married. However, despite these increases there has been little improvement in the breadth of women's employment opportunities. In Northern Ireland, as elsewhere, they predominate in low-pay, low status occupations and part-time employment, and remain congregated in a relatively small number of industries and occupations. For example, data from the 1991 Northern Ireland Census Economic Activity Report shows that the majority of economically active women over the age of sixteen are employed in clerical and secretarial occupations (23.7 per cent). According to Kremer and Montgomery (1993), thirty three per cent of Northern Irish women employed in this category are working on a part-time basis.

According to Beechey (1989, p.86), while statistics show that women are not formally precluded from many occupations in contemporary society, there remains a pronounced form of occupational segregation, defined as the division of the labour market into predominantly female and predominantly male occupations.[4] As Bradley (1989, p.1) comments:

> There are few tasks, even those seen as typically 'masculine' to us in twentieth century Britain such as mining and forestry, which have not in some time or place been performed by women. Despite this fact, today, in virtually every society of which we have knowledge men and women perform different types of work.

Purcell (1989, p.160) notes how the overall pattern of gender segregation has remained surprisingly stable despite increasing female activity rates, the introduction of equal opportunities legislation in the 1970s, occupational diversification and industrial restructuring. Indeed, the separation of the sexes into different occupations, has become so entrenched as to have, in many people's minds, the force of a natural law, i.e. 'women can't be bricklayers'. This assumption is reflected in official statistics which reveal the paucity of Northern Irish women employed in non-traditional occupations:

Table 1: *Women in Selected Non-Traditional Occupations in Northern Ireland, 1991.*

SOC Unit Groups	Males	Female	Per cent of Total
500. Bricklayers, Masons,	3,210	5	0.1
502. Plasterers	1,660	2	0.1
507. Painters & Decorators	3,851	56	1.4
521. Electricians, electrical maintenance fitters	7,021	82	1.1
532. Plumbers, heating & ventilating engineers/related	3,144	26	0.8
540. Motor Mechanics, auto engineers	5,179	59	1.1
570. Carpenters & Joiners	9,860	38	0.3
594. Gardeners, Groundsmen/women	2,636	51	1.8
872. Drivers of road goods vehicles	13,143	121	0.9
873. Bus & Coach Drivers	2,448	62	2.5
887. Fork lift truck & mechanical truck drivers	1,673	11	0.6

Source: Unpublished Census Data, 1991.

At first glance, Table 1 presents a rather pessimistic scenario. However, when data are compared to those from previous Northern Irish Economic Activity Reports, some improvement in women's participation rates can be identified. For example, in 1971, just before the introduction of sex equality legislation, the Census listed only one woman engineer, eighteen female motor mechanics, forty-three female drivers of road goods vehicles, and no female bus or coach drivers. Following the introduction of sex equality legislation, by the next Census, a minimal upward trend could be detected. By 1981, Northern Ireland boasted twelve female engineers, twenty-seven female motor mechanics, and 128 women employed as bus, coach or lorry drivers.[5] Table 1, which presents statistical data from the 1991 Census, indicates a continuation of this upward trend, although, as the data also establish, the percentage of women in such occupations, in comparison to men, remains small.

The table replicates data based mainly on private sector employment. However, occupational segregation of the sexes is also a feature of public sector employment in Northern Ireland. According to the Northern Ireland Annual Abstract of Statistics, in 1991, 115,811 women were working in the public sector in comparison to 86,676 men. From these figures, an examination of three areas of public sector employment illustrate the continued existence of occupational segregation — the DHSS, associated with traditional 'female' occupations (such as clerical work), and the prison and fire services, usually associated with traditional 'male' occupations (further examples of occupational segregation can be found in areas such as Local Government and the Royal Ulster Constabulary).

In 1975, no vast chasm existed between the numbers of men and women employed by the DHSS, 2,857 women in comparison to 2,307 men. Between 1975 and 1991, the number of women employees rose from fifty-five per cent to 61.5 per cent of the total, a rise of just over six per cent. By 1991, therefore, 4,390 women were employed, in comparison to 2,746 men. This pattern is not reflected in the other areas of public sector employment examined here, the prison and fire services (both can still be considered as relatively non-traditional for women). The number of female employees in the prison service rose by only one per cent between 1975 — 1991; in the fire service there has been no rise in the number of women employed as a percentage of the total (although more women were employed). Female employees here accounted for approximately seven per cent of the total in 1975 and this figure remained the same in 1991.

While an expansion in the numbers of female prisoners in Northern Ireland (due in part to The Troubles) accounts to some extent for the rise in female employees in the prison service, women's position within the fire service looks particularly bleak. Although there has been some increase in the employment of women here, they continue to be employed in traditional female roles; in Northern Ireland only one woman is employed as a fire fighter.[6]

In summing up this brief examination of women's employment in Northern Ireland we can note how patterns of occupational segregation here approximate those in Britain, and indeed, Europe.[7] As with their counterparts in other countries, Northern Irish women continue to find employment in traditionally 'female' areas of employment, where they are often employed on a low-paid, insecure and part-time basis. Thus, while the female workforce in Northern Ireland has expanded, particularly since the introduction of sex equality legislation in the 1970s, upward trends in women's employment have tended to mirror the amount of part-time work available. While there have been marginal increases in the numbers of women employed in non-traditional work, both in the private and public sector, this rise has not been significant. Indeed, if the numbers of women and girls currently engaged in training in non-traditional skills are indicative of future developments in this area, then change in the future will continue to be slow.[8]

Nevertheless, while there may not have been a substantial increase in the numbers of non-traditionally employed women in Northern Ireland, data do signify that there are women out there, working at non-traditional occupations on a day-to-day basis. Therefore, in order to render visible this 'marginalised form of femininity', the chapter now turns to an account of the lived experience of such women. As far as possible, and in keeping with much current feminist methodological thinking (for example, Fonow & Cook, 1991, Opie, 1992, Rheinharz, 1992, Roberts, 1981), the women described here are given 'a voice'. The following pages centre around what they have to say, utilising quotes from a series of in-depth, semi-structured interviews.[9] Data from the author's recent survey of almost 1,000 fifth-form schoolgirls (N=980), which assessed their attitudes to non-traditional training and employment, are also utilised.[10]

The Lived Experience of Women in Non-Traditional Employment

When asked why they had chosen to pursue a non-traditional career, it was often the case that women had been influenced by families, and, by fathers in particular. For instance, when asked what had inspired her to choose mechanical engineering as a career, one young woman said:

> My dad and his brothers were all navy and they were all mechanical engineers. From I was wee he was getting me books on it — on engineering.

And a thirty year-old lorry driver:

> I used to, when I was younger, go out with daddy in the lorry, and it used to fascinate me, driving the lorry. It was just something I had to do.

Careers education at school was generally described in scathing terms. The following quote, from a twenty two year old electrical engineer, was typical of most:

> Careers teaching? Yes, a girl came in for careers — teaching was non-existent. I went in to her and said I want to be an electrical engineer and she said, oh, have you ever thought of doing anything about office skills. And I just got this wonderful reaction that I should learn to type!

Evidence from the author's recent survey of fifth form schoolgirls (see Footnote 10) suggests that substantial numbers of girls would be interested in taking non-traditional subjects, such as Technology or CDT, at school, and the majority expressed an interest in non-traditional careers. However, little appears to be happening in schools to foster such ambition (such as visits to industry, careers talks by non-traditional representatives, and so on). Of almost 1,000 girls questioned, a mere nine per cent were studying non-traditional subjects such as Technology and CDT. And, of 630 girls who had decided on a future career, only twenty-five had decided on a non-traditional option, mainly engineering-related. The majority of career choices remained gender stereotypical in nature, with the highest single number of girls expressing an interest in a career as a secretary or personal assistant.

As previous research indicates (see for example Spencer and Podmore, 1987), some male-dominated professions, such as academia, medicine and law, have become more accessible to women, if only in terms of numbers. However, as Table 1 shows, this has not been the case to any large extent in non-traditional areas of employment. Because of the nature of the work, which can be physically demanding and often dirty, it stubbornly continues to be regarded as a male domain. Women who seek admittance are often regarded with suspicion. As a woman carpenter says of the construction industry: 'women must be clearly superior to survive or there will be a hundred reasons to lay them off.' Fear of such behaviour often leads women to strive to perform better than male colleagues. 'Outperformance', or 'overcompensation', appears to be commonplace for non-traditionally employed women. As a forty nine year-old HGV driver put it:

> You can't afford to make mistakes cos you're noticed more than a man. Let's face it, if it takes me two shunts to get on a boat and it takes a man ten, they're going to criticise me more. A man could come after me and take twice as long and they wouldn't even notice.

The fact that women are usually physically weaker than men, and no interviewee denied this, is often used as a reason to exclude them from non-traditional employment. A second HGV driver, a woman of comparatively slight build, explained how she was having difficulty in finding a job because of this attitude. According to her, the firm which had employed her for fourteen years had refused to train her to work on the factory lorry, despite the fact that her occupation at the time was, she claimed, more demanding than lorry work. When the lorry work was passed to a newly appointed male employee, the woman quit factory work, and has since driven large Scania and Volvo lorries for a number of companies, finally finding permanent employment as a Post Office driver.

Evidence from interviews indicates that excessive physical strength is not necessarily a prerequisite of non-traditional employment. Numerous women, over the course of the interviews, explained how heavy tasks, such as a car mechanic lifting a gear box, are usually undertaken by two or more people, even where no women are employed. Besides, special machinery, such as hoists, are available for such tasks. Moreover, some women find alternative ways to cope with heavy work, such as dragging something instead of lifting it. A thirty year-old saddler says of her work, which is often very physically demanding:

> I've never found myself stuck with anything yet. I've always managed to find some way round it. Sometimes I find I do a job better because I don't use brute force and ignorance to get a thing done. I'll sit there and think about it and if there's a quicker and easier way to do it, I'll do it. Quite often the men just bull on through.

Apart from this physical aspect of non-traditional employment, the 'dirty' aspect of such work is often used as a further excuse to exclude women. According to some training instructors, interviewed over the course of the research, 'women don't like getting dirty'. But, as a twenty-nine year-old zoo keeper remarks about cleaning out drains:

> You're up to your arms in shit there basically — but that doesn't bother me. The only time it bothered me was when I was pregnant — but that only happened in the first couple of months. Don't get me wrong — I'd happily do something else other than lift a drain, but it has to be done, so I do it, and I don't make a fuss.

Such comments were fairly typical. One young acoustic engineer commented that she did not consider she had done a proper day's work unless she came home filthy at the end of it.

The above are problems which women may encounter when attempting to gain access to non-traditional employment, or have been cited as reasons for excluding them. Interviews with non-traditionally employed women suggest that the grounds for such exclusion are often unfounded. Undue physical strength is not always a necessary prerequisite of non-traditional employment, nor are all women averse to getting dirty. However, gaining access to non-traditional employment is only the first hurdle to be overcome; the second is gaining acceptance.

Unlike male-dominated professions, where women may have the opportunity to befriend other women, in non-traditional situations the female employee is invariably the 'one-of-a-kind', or the 'token' (see Kanter, 1977). This was the case for one young electrical engineer, a solitary woman working alongside four hundred men. Nevertheless, few of the women interviewed complained of feeling isolated, although often, they were required to 'make the first move'. Of her first visit to the canteen, during a Construction Industry Training Board (CITB) course on which she was the only woman, a forty year-old partner in a construction company says:

> I can remember my tea-cup was shaking like this — and I was trying to keep my stiff upper lip and my back up. And I'd just go and plonk myself down in the middle, and say 'Hullo, how are you?' (she laughs). I don't think men would realise the effort that takes!

Like this woman, most interviewees explained that they had attempted to understand how their male workmates felt, realising that men were unsure of how to respond to the presence of a woman in a traditionally male environment. Accommodating men's feelings in this way, or putting them at their ease, was a common reaction from many women interviewed.

According to both Kanter (1977), and Yount (1991), a 'thick skin', a sense of humour, and acting as 'one of the boys', are all prerequisites for gaining respect in a male-dominated environment. Becoming 'one of the boys' is often made easier for women in non-traditional employment because the work they perform may demand that they dress in a particular way, often considered to be 'mannish'. In particular, those women who worked outdoors, such as gardeners and construction workers, dressed in trousers, big jackets, safety hats and wellington boots. Those who worked indoors often appeared for interview in boiler suits and steel-capped boots. Besides the practical purposes which such clothing affords, as Kanter (1977) has discovered, women in male-dominated employment often dress in this way to minimize their visibility. Consequently, such women are often mistaken, by the public, for men. A gardener explained:

> You'll get granny and granda out with the wee toddler, and you'll hear them, there's a man there, you see? And then I'll look round and the wee lad'll go, that's a woman (she laughs)! Oh, and granny and granda are all embarrassed you see. The number of times they've apologised for calling me a man!

Such mistakes can lead to less amusing results, as a twenty-five year-old former motor cycle courier discovered. She had been continually mistaken for a man at security force road checks; on one such occasion a police officer began to frisk her before he realised that he had made a significant mistake.

Despite their sometimes 'masculine' appearance, as a number of interviewees admitted, they would sometimes resort to 'feminine wiles' to escape more arduous tasks. In the words of one: 'I feel at an advantage being a girl — I can get away with more.' However, generally speaking there is little room for the trappings of 'femininity', jewellery, painted fingernails, high-heeled shoes and so on, in such occupations. The majority of women were at ease, or even revelled in their so-called 'masculine' appearance (see Carey, 1994). Besides, some women, such as the gardener quoted above, believe that it is wrong from the outset to describe individuals in either 'masculine' or 'feminine' terms. In her opinion:

> It's misleading to use terminology like that. I'm not afraid of the masculine side of the person. I'm not afraid to adopt comfortable masculine poses. Rather than wearing something that's damaging to your health. It doesn't bother me to stand with my hands in my pockets and wear men's shirts. If that means I'm more masculine, then yes. I think it's a particular type of person you're talking about, rather than the male/female thing.

It may also be that it is this necessity to become 'one of the boys' that leads to what Walshok (1987) has described as an essentially peer-like relationship between men and women in non-traditional employment. Evidence from the author's own research also suggests that having overcome the obstacles of gaining access to employment and initial acceptance, it would be feasible to describe the relationship between Northern Ireland's non-traditionally employed women and their male fellow-workers as 'peer-like'. Certainly, hierarchical relationships, described in much of the literature on women in male-dominated professions, appear to be absent. Comments such as the following, from a woman lorry driver, were common:

> The ones coming from here (male lorry drivers) were always very helpful from the start, my own crowd out of Ireland. I travel on all the boats and I've been going so often that I've met them all at various stages and they're all very supportive.

According to interviewees (perhaps surprisingly) active harassment of women in non-traditional settings does not appear to be the norm. However, more subtle forms of discrimination can sometimes be detected. For instance, a thirty-nine year-old outdoor pursuits instructor related how a misplaced form of protectiveness led her male colleagues to 'look after her'. Consequently she was steered away from her preferred line of work to tasks which were considered to be less arduous. In relation to taking charge of schoolchildren she told me:

> Quite often if we're deciding where we're going he'll (the boss) say, right, we'll have a really tough walk among three peaks, and then we'll have a medium walk and do one peak — and Susan, you can go to the forest (laughs). And maybe you didn't want to go to the forest, but I think he thinks he's doing me a favour!

'Looking after' women in this way was a factor experienced by a number of interviewees. As one young woman put it:

> A lot of them (male co-workers) are like surrogate fathers, you know? Very protective of me. I'm the wee girl, our kid.

Men's behaviour in non-traditional settings, may not, however, always be so agreeable. Sexually related jokes, girl watching, pornographic displays, and profanity were regarded by Reimer (1979) as being commonplace in his study of the American construction industry. While some research indicates that men may modify their behaviour in the presence of women, the author's interviews with non-traditionally employed women suggested that such modification may be short-lived. Men soon resumed, what for some of them, was normal behaviour. A young postwoman commented:

> Language is bad. Somebody would say, there's ladies sitting there, and they'd turn round and go, where? But they don't really mean any harm in it. I suppose they're just used to working with me. It doesn't bother me, and I don't expect them to change cos they wouldn't.

Moreover, one woman, the partner in the construction company, admitted that bad language was 'like water off a duck's back' to her, while several admitted to swearing as often as (and sometimes more than) male co-workers. Although pornographic displays (as described by Reimer) were not found to be commonplace at non-traditional workplaces in Northern Ireland, where they did exist, or had existed, there was a mixed reaction to these by women. Some interviewees were highly offended by such displays, but admitted that they were usually removed on request; others appeared relatively unconcerned by pornography in whatever shape or form:

> Going across on a freight boat I'll be the only female passenger. Occasionally a good blue movie will come out ... It's blaring away and I don't even see it. It doesn't embarrass them and it doesn't embarrass me because I'm sitting doing my own thing.

Other women, such as one electrician, go so far as to add their own male pin-ups to the selection of Page Three Girls on display.

Overt harassment, therefore, did not appear in general to be a problem for women interviewed by the author.[11] Indeed, as the zoo-keeper told me:

> They'd probably say that I harass them more than they do me (laughs). I think maybe some women have taken this harassment thing too far. Jesus, we all have to have a sense of humour, you know?

Some areas, however, can be problematic: first, it appears that where a non-traditionally employed women is in a position of authority (although few are), some harassment may occur. For example, following an argument with a young male employee in her charge, during which he objected to taking orders from a woman, a female foreperson with a road gang found that he had left a used condom on the seat of her lorry. However, this was an isolated incident, and other women interviewed, such as the gardener, an engineering manager, and the partner in the construction firm, maintained friendly relations with their subordinates. Second, where a woman is totally isolated, as with women taxi drivers, serious harassment, such as rape, may occur. According to one such interviewee, this did indeed happen to a friend, a woman employed in similar work. But, since making a living was the interviewee's first priority, she remained philosophical about the incident:

The way I look at it is, if I started to worry about what would happen I wouldn't do anything. If something's going to happen to you, the chances are it's going to happen to you once and you can't live in expectation of it really.

Conclusion

How then can the position of women in non-traditional employment in Northern Ireland be assessed? First, we can point to the fact that while the female working population has dramatically increased in the past twenty years, few women are employed in a non-traditional capacity. In part, this can be attributed to the image that non-traditional employment presents to many women. In addition to the often physical, and sometimes dirty nature of this work, difficult hours, and the usual lack of childcare facilities, may combine to discourage women. Nevertheless, despite the obstacles in their way, when one speaks to women who are employed in a non-traditional capacity, it is clear that they are very much capable of doing their respective jobs, both in physical terms and despite the dirty element involved. Indeed, it is now accepted in some circles that women have 'special' qualities which they can bring to such employment. For example, Gale (1992) argues that the construction industry's male culture must 'feminise' if conflict within it is to be reduced. Women interviewed during the author's research listed a variety of so-called 'female' qualities which they believed would enhance their respective areas of employment. These included tidiness, attention to detail, being more approachable and better communicators, and being less stubborn than men. According to a female construction worker:

> More women would benefit the construction industry because when men and women go to buy a house it's actually the wife's input which says whether the house is bought or not — I think if they had a woman to deal with, and a woman involved in the planning and maintenance and so on, the industry would be much better.

However, there is a danger here: by steering women into such areas, a division of labour could develop. Greed (1990, 1994), for example, notes how the 'caring' qualities traditionally associated with women have led to just such a phenomenon in the area of quantity surveying. Other writers, such as Brewer (1991) and Spencer and Podmore (1987) have noted similar effects in other male-dominated professions such as the police force and law. However, those same 'caring qualities' which these writers discuss, are not a prerequisite for non-traditional employment, for mucking out animal's cages, servicing an engine, or driving a lorry. Only in one instance did this become a factor: a young coastguard explained how, as the only woman in her station, the onus of breaking bad news to families of accident victims often fell upon her shoulders.

Thus, it can be concluded that having surmounted the barriers of finding non-traditional employment, and becoming accepted there, non-traditionally employed women (certainly those interviewed) appear to find their work immensely enjoyable and, generally, do not report high levels of harassment. Of course, that is not to say that this state of affairs may not change in the future. As more attention is focused on training for women, and as more girls and women are encouraged to see non-traditional employment as a viable option, the possibility remains that their numbers in these areas may continue to increase.[12] To date, as demonstrated above, numbers remain small, with few women having had the opportunity to advance to positions of power in any area of non-traditional employment. When, or if this happens, will the peer-like relationship which appears to exist between women and men here be transformed into the hierarchical male/female model which, according to the relevant literature, is commonplace across male-dominated professions? Time alone will provide us with an answer to this question.

Discussion Topics

1. Why are so few women working in non-traditional areas of employment?

2. Discuss the view that while women may gain access to non-traditional employment, it may be more difficult to gain acceptance.

3. Women in non-traditional occupations are sometimes described as being 'masculine'. Should we describe women and men as being either 'masculine' or 'feminine'?

4. If a division of labour were to develop within non-traditional employment what would the likely consequences of this be for the women employed there?

Notes

1. See for example: Chodorow, 1978, Deem, 1978, Spender, 1982, Stanworth, 1983.
2. See Agnew et al., 1987, Brewer, 1991, Greed, 1990, 1994, Spencer and Podmore, 1987.
3. For American studies see: Lunneborg, 1990, Padavic and Reskin, 1990, Reskin and Padavic, 1988, Schroedel, 1985, Walshok, 1987. There have been some British studies. See for example Gale (1992), Rees (1992) and Greed (1990, 1994).
4. In terms of existing legislation: In Northern Ireland, the Equal Pay Act (1970), and the Sex Discrimination (NI) Order, 1976. The Equal Opportunities Commission for NI was set up under the provisions of the latter.
5. There are numerous difficulties in drawing comparisons between occupational data from Northern Ireland's Economic Activity Reports (see Carey, 1995). Nevertheless,

utilisation of the data permits the detection of some broad trends in the pattern of occupational segregation in Northern Ireland over that period of time.

6. This is interesting in light of data from the author's schools' survey. When asked which, if any, non-traditional employment they would prefer to work at, most girls (forty-seven per cent) opted for fire-fighter.

7. See Women of Europe Supplement, No.36, (1992) for an overview of women's position in the labour market across all member states.

8. The Training and Employment Agency (T&EA) is Northern Ireland's largest and most important centralised training organisation. A 1994 T&EA report indicates that of 1,614 non-programme trainees across Northern Ireland's eleven Training Centres, only fourteen, or a mere one per cent, were female. Of this small number, the majority were engaged on a computer course.

9. The thirty five interviewees were selected by snowball sampling, a method chosen because of the 'hard-to-locate' nature of the target population. The youngest interviewee was twenty-one, and the eldest was fifty-six. The latter had been a bus driver for sixteen years (the first woman driver with Citybus) which was the longest spell of non-traditional employment among the interviewees. The majority of women — 68.5 per cent — were single, and only eight of those interviewed had children.

10. Girls surveyed came from a proportionate stratified sample of single-sex (all-girl) and mixed-sex schools across Northern Ireland (549 from Secondary Intermediate schools; 354 from Secondary Grammar schools; 77 attended FE College).

11. But bearing in mind the relatively small sample of women interviewed.

12. See the author's (Carey, 1995) discussion of the innovative Women Into Trades Project, based in Craigavon, Co. Armagh.

References and Further Reading

Abbott, P and Wallace C. 1991 *An Introduction to Sociology: Feminist Perspectives* London: Routledge.

Agnew, U, Fulton J, Malcolm S, McEwen A. 1987 *Women in the Professions* Belfast: Equal Opportunities Commission (NI).

Beechey, V. 1989 'Women's Employment in Contemporary Britain' Beechey V and Whitelegg E (eds.) *Women in Britain Today* Milton Keynes: Open University Press.

Bradley, A. 1989 *Men's Work, Women's Work* Cambridge: Polity Press.

Brewer, J D. 1991 'Hercules, Hippolyte and the Amazons — or Policewomen in the RUC' *The British Journal of Sociology* Vol.42, No.2, June, pp.231-247.

Carey, M. 1995 *Women in Non-Traditional Employment in Northern Ireland* Unpublished PhD Thesis.

Carey, M. 1994 'Gender and Power: Boys Will be Boys and So Will Girls', *Irish Journal of Sociology*, Vol.4, pp.105-127.

Chodorow, N. 1978 *The Reproduction of Mothering*, Berkeley: University of California Press.

Connell, R W. 1993 *Gender and Power*, Cambridge: Polity Press.

Deem, R. 1978 *Women and Schooling*, London: Routledge Paul.

Equality of Opportunity Monitoring Results: 1994 Disability, Gender and Community Background Belfast: T&EA.

Fonow, M M & Cook, J A. (eds.) 1991 *Beyond Methodology* Indiana University Press.

Gale, A W. 1992 'The Construction Industry's Male Culture must Feminise if Conflict is to be Reduced' *Construction Conflict: Management and Resolution* Fenn P and Gameson R. (eds.) E and F N. Spon, pp.416-427.

Game, A and Pringle, R. 1984 *Gender at Work* London: Pluto Press.

Greed, C. 1990 'The Professional and the Personal: a Study of Women Quantity Surveyors' Stanley L. (ed.) *Feminist Praxis* London: Routledge.

Greed, C. 1994 'Women Surveyors: Constructing Careers' Evetts J. (ed.) *Women and Careers: Themes and Issues in Advanced Industrial Societies* London: Longman.

Kanter, R M. 1977 'Some Effects of Proportions on Group Life: Skewed Sex Ratios and Responses to Token Women' *American Journal of Sociology* Vol.82, No.5, pp.965-990.

Kremer, J and Montgomery, P. (eds.) 1993 *Women's Working Lives* Belfast: Equal Opportunities Commission (NI).

Lunneborg, P W. 1990 *Women Changing Work* USA: Greenwood Press.

McCorry, M. 1988 *Women and the Need for Training* Belfast: Women's Education Project.

Northern Ireland Abstract of Statistics, No.10, 1991, Belfast: PPRU.

Northern Ireland Census 1991: Economic Activity Report Belfast: HMSO.

Northern Ireland Census 1981: Economic Activity Report Belfast: HMSO.

Northern Ireland Census 1971: Economic Activity Report Belfast: HMSO.

Opie, A. 1992 'Quantitative Research Appropriation of the 'Other' and Empowerment' *Feminist Review* No.40, Spring, pp.52-69.

Padavic, I, and Reskin, B. 1990 'Men's Behaviour and Women's Interest in Blue Collar Jobs' *Social Problems* Vol.37, No.4, November, pp. 613-628.

Purcell, K. 1989 'Gender and the Experience of Employment' Gallie D. (ed.) *Employment in Britain* Oxford, New York: Basil Blackwell Ltd.

Rees, T. 1992 *Women in the Labour Market* London, New York: Routledge.

Reimer, J W. 1979 *Hard Hats* London: Sage.

Reskin, B F, Padavic, I. 1988 'Supervisors as Gatekeepers: Male Supervisor's Response to Women's Integration in Plant Jobs' *Social Problems* Vol.35, No.5, pp.536-550.

Rheinharz, S. 1992 *Feminist Methods in Social Research* Oxford: Oxford University Press.

Roberts, H. (ed.) 1981 *Doing Feminist Research* London: Routledge & Kegan Paul.

Rowbotham, S. 1974 *Hidden from History* London: Pluto Press.

Schroedel, J R. 1985 *Alone in a Crowd: Women in the Trades Tell Their Stories* Temple University Press.

Spencer, A, Podmore, D. (eds.) 1987 *In a Man's World* London, NewYork: Tavistock Publications.

Spender, D. 1982 *Invisible Women: The Schooling Scandal* London: Writers' and Readers' Publishing Co-Operative.

Stanworth, M. 1983 *Gender and Schooling: a Study of Sexual Divisions in the Classroom* London: Hutchinson.

Walshok, L M. 1987 *Blue Collar Women: Pioneers on the Male Frontier* Garden City, New York: Anchor Press.

Women of Europe Supplement. 1992 No.36, 'The Position of Women in the Labour Market: Trends and Developments in the Twelve Member States of the EC, 1983-1990', Brussels: Commission of the European Communities.

Yount, K R. 1991 'Ladies, Flirts and Tomboys' *Journal of Contemporary Ethnography* Vol.19., No.4, pp.396-422.

7.

Women Caring and Sharing in Belfast
Madeleine Leonard

Introduction

The purpose of this chapter is to examine the potential of one stable, working class community in West Belfast to provide care and support for its weaker members. Such a focus is timely given the renewed political interest in the concept of 'community care' which has dominated policy decision-making regarding welfare provision for the most vulnerable in society. Right wing governments anxious to dismantle the welfare state and cut back on spending money on welfare services, particularly to the poor and needy have invoked the concept of the 'caring community' as a moral justification for their increasing stringent policies. By examining kinship and neighbourhood ties in an area characterised by poverty, deprivation, high long-term unemployment and geographical immobility, the chapter will examine the potential of these ties to form the basis for community care. The chapter will demonstrate that these ties are most prominent among female members of the community. Hence, any movement towards community care will tend to place the burden of that care on female shoulders rather than the community in general.

Problems with Terminology

Defining the term community is no easy task. Often the word is imbued with highly positive connotations conveying an image of warm, helpful, friendly interactions between individuals based upon personal knowledge and face to face contact. Hence, the geographical dimension of the concept is highlighted at the expense of the impact of wider macro influences in shaping social relationships. In this context, then, a 'loss of community' is defined as the decreasing relevance of locally based social relationships in determining the lives of local inhabitants. Pahl (1966) however, warns that there is no exact relationship between place and way of life. Community relationships can transcend geographical boundaries. While recognising that community relationships can exist in a myriad of different spatial and institutional settings, nonetheless, the thrust of this chapter is to utilise the concept to refer to the intimacy of association among people living in close proximity to one another. Such a usage is motivated by a recognition that ties between people are, at least in part, shaped and constrained by the geographical and material conditions which characterise an individual's life. Hence, in areas of high unemployment and widespread poverty, people, through lack of choice as much as anything else, are thrown back on their neighbours, friends and relatives as sources of support.

While the term 'community care' is similarly open to wide interpretation, nonetheless, the geographical definition of community is often highlighted in notions of community care. Finch (1993) in charting the different meanings attached to the term 'community care' outlines the significant transformation in emphasis from care *in* the community to care *by* the community. She points out that initially community care focused on the community as the location for care and referred to attempts to transfer large impersonal, isolated residential units to small-scale units located within specific communities. This policy was accompanied by measures to normalise inhabitants' experiences by attempting to integrate their life-styles into those of the surrounding community. However, gradually this policy subtly shifted to care by the community rather than care in the community and was based on the assumption that families, friends and neighbours 'are uniquely well placed to identify and respond to the needs of their relatives and friends' (Griffiths, 1988). Griffiths went on to point out that not only was this how things were in most communities but emphasised that 'this is how it should be'. Hence, living in the midst of friendly, supportive social networks was one of the most positive and desirable features of community life and policy makers were morally responsible to ensure that they 'sustain and where necessary develop but never displace such support and care' (DHSS, 1981, para. 1.9).

The notion of the locality as the locus for community caring and the capacity of friends, neighbours and relatives to provide the basis of that care was promoted as a panacea for society's current ills ranging from juvenile crime to the loneliness of the elderly. This viewpoint emerged in a number of policy documents on community care. For example, DH *et al.* (1989, p.4) stated 'the great bulk of community care is provided by friends, families and neighbours... many people make that choice and it is right that they should be able to play their part in looking after those close to them'. However, Wenger (1984) questions the capacity of communities to uniformly provide support to families, friends and relatives in need. She suggests that different communities promote different types of relationships and argues that supportive networks are more likely to emerge in stable, working-class neighbourhoods.

Background to the Data

In many ways, the locality (pseudonym Newbury), where the research took place provided a number of conducive conditions for the emergence of strong personal ties between neighbours, friends and relatives. High long-term unemployment was a common feature of life on the estate. A survey of one in four households in the area, generating a sample size of 150 households, revealed that the majority of males and females from the estate had no access to formal employment. Hence opportunities for social mobility were low and the estate was characterised by poverty and a high reliance on various sources of welfare benefits. These high levels of unemployment combined with the shared precarious economic situation of the majority of inhabitants compelled residents to create and maintain supportive relationships within the locality.

Kinship connections often formed the backbone of these relationships. Seventy-eight per cent of the overall sample were related to other households within the estate and women tended to have more relations on the estate than males. Moreover, intermarriage among community members was also a strong feature of life on the estate. Fifty per cent of males between the ages of twenty-six to forty in the households sampled had been born within Newbury while seventy-two per cent of the females in the same age range were born in the estate. Hence, a substantial number of respondents were brought up and had lived all their lives in Newbury. This helped to strengthen social ties and often made the distinction between friends and neighbours indistinguishable. Eighty six per cent of males and ninety per cent of females stated that most of their friends came from within the estate. Hence, in many instances, friends and neighbours were one and the same and were discussed together by most informants. Indeed, Allan (1979) suggests that working-class friendships are likely to be situational rather than based on shared tastes or interests. Thus, in the ensuing discussion on support between households, I intend to discuss friends and neighbours together.

St Leger and Gillespie (1991) point out that in Northern Ireland, the family and therefore household size is considerably larger than other industrialised countries with the exception of the Republic of Ireland. This in turn means that social networks are larger leading to more potential sources of support being available. Among inhabitants of the estate over fifty years of age, family sizes in excess of eight children were not uncommon. These large family sizes combined with limited opportunities for social mobility meant that a considerable number of households within the estate were related to other households. This supports McLaughlin's (1992) observation that social networks in Northern Ireland are based to a greater extent on kinship than in most urban areas in Great Britain.

My survey was primarily concerned with making visible the myriad of informal work practices that existed within the estate and providing support and practical help to others was seen in this light (Leonard, 1994). Since much of this work was undertaken by females as an extension of the mother-housewife role then often the work was invisible and undervalued or even where recognised dismissed as not proper or real work. This has implications for encouraging care in the community since as Finch and Groves (1980) point out, care in the community means care by women in the community. Hence, promoting community care may in practice heighten women's burden within and outside the household while simultaneously contributing to the marginality of women as economic agents.

The chapter will look at support among households during periods of crises, practical support among households in relation to shopping and childcare and community support for the sick and elderly. Parker (1992) suggests that there are two different types of caring activity outlined in government reports. The first refers to people who are extensively involved in providing physical care for others in their household and for substantially long hours. The second type of carer, she refers to as informal helpers. These people 'provide practical help to friends, neighbours and... relatives who do not live in the same household and for relatively few hours' (1992, p.14). This chapter is concerned with the activities of informal helpers in the locality under investigation and will examine the extent to which gender influences the level of support available. While this may seem a very limited conception of community care, nonetheless, the supposed existence of close networks of friends, neighbours and relatives provides the moral rationale for policies aimed at transforming care in the community to care by the community. Examining the day to day practicalities and motivations for looking after the needs of friends, neighbours and relatives can provide a useful indication of the ability of such networks to provide the foundation for more extensive care arrangements.

Support between Neighbours

Respondents were asked if they could rely on their neighbours for help and support. Of course, I am aware, as Cecil et al. (1987) point out that anyone who comments about neighbours is also a neighbour. Hence, to suggest that neighbours would help out if needed enables everybody to consider themselves to be good neighbours whether or not they have ever been involved in neighbourly activities. Furthermore, those who have never asked for support may nevertheless feel that such support would be forthcoming, if requested. I attempted to partly deal with this problem by distinguishing between perceived availability and actual exchange. Hence, neighbours were asked if they could be relied on to provide assistance and support to others and were further requested to list the various sources of help they had given to or received from their neighbours, particularly during crisis periods. More women than men reported giving and receiving help during a crisis. Hence, most help tended to flow from women to other women. Crises were defined by the informants rather than the researcher. Hence, crises may have occurred which informants declined to mention. Surprisingly, in an area characterised by widespread long-term unemployment, the potential stress, social isolation and the coping strategies in place to deal with these possibilities were not mentioned by the majority of respondents. This was mainly because unemployment was viewed as a way of life for most of the inhabitants of the estate.

Since unemployment was also a shared experience, this diluted the feelings of anxiety and increased social isolation highlighted in other studies of the unemployed. The research supported the observations of Meegan (1989) who found that in areas of high, long-term unemployment, the stigma, social isolation and possible negative health effects stemming from unemployment were considerably weak. On the other hand, in some instances the need to borrow money from neighbours was specified and this may have been linked to unemployment.

The two most common crises mentioned by respondents were acute illness and bereavement. In these instances, neighbours and relatives could be relied upon to provide short-term emotional and practical support. In the case of bereavement, street collections were often made if the inhabitant of a particular street died. The money was given to the family to 'tide them over' the crisis period. Neighbours played an active role in organising the wake arrangements supplying food for visitors and providing limited emotional support for the bereaved. The street collections and subsequent practical and emotional support were largely undertaken by female members of the estate.

Female neighbours could also be relied upon to provide limited help and support during periods of sickness, although the help tended to be short-term responses to acute illnesses rather than the long-term support associated with caring for the chronically ill. Moreover, since male and female domestic responsibilities were strongly demarcated, the extent of help given to men and women differed substantially. Wives, with husbands in hospital were given minor help mainly with shopping and childcare tasks whereas men with wives in hospital were given much more extensive assistance with a range of household chores including cleaning and washing. Two of the women interviewed justified their help as follows:

> You know what men are like, leave them on their own for ten minutes and the house is in chaos.

> God help him, he doesn't know what hit him. He does his best but he just can't manage you know.

On the whole, then the data indicated that while neighbours acted as a helping resource, nonetheless, the help given tended to be piecemeal and immediate. Long-term assistance was less common and was connected to kinship obligations rather than neighbouring ties.

The most frequently mentioned non-crisis form of practical help mentioned was childcare. Northern Ireland's position as the worst provider of childcare in Europe has been widely documented (Hinds, 1991, Kremer and Montgomery, 1993). These studies illustrate how the absence of formal childcare facilities militates against women taking up formal employment or has a causal effect on women's decision to engage in part-time rather than full-time formal employment. In Newbury, the unemployed status of husbands had an equally restraining impact on women's opportunities to engage in paid employment outside the home as such employment would have an adverse effect on the family's welfare benefit entitlements. Often, the women from the estate in part-time employment worked unsocial hours and were thus able to combine their childcare duties with employment outside the home with minimal assistance from their husbands (Leonard, 1993). Hence, while neighbours, friends and relatives provided informal sources of childcare provision largely on a reciprocal basis, this was largely for women with no access to formal or informal paid employment. The availability of these informal sources of help with childminding, nonetheless increased the flexibility of many women in the estate although in some cases, the 'free time' was utilised to perform caring duties for adult relatives.

Support between Kin

St Leger and Gillespie (1991) from a study of informal welfare in three communities in Northern Ireland suggest that relatives provide a major source of emotional support, advice and guidance particularly between generations. This finding is supported by this current study. The most significant support relationships existed between parents and children. Middle aged mothers tended to initiate most aid obligations and these were directed towards married daughters or daughters who were unmarried mothers.

In some cases, married daughters remained in the family home with their new husbands. This was often at extreme inconvenience to other family members as space was usually limited. Sometimes these were temporary arrangements until the newly wed couple had saved up the deposit for a mortgage. At other times, particularly if the new husband was unemployed, these arrangements could last several years until the young couples had commenced families of their own and qualified for council housing.

Married daughters who moved out of the parental home, often continued to live in the estate, sometimes in the same street or a few streets away from their mothers. Again, almost daily interaction occurred between married daughters and mothers. Mothers and daughters shopped for each other and mothers often minded grandchildren. Emotional and financial support were frequently exchanged and the flow tended to be from mothers to daughters. Financial assistance was particularly prevalent when the son-in-law was unemployed. In one household, while the interview was taking place, the respondent's daughter called in to borrow money. When she left, the mother stated:

> Look at that wee girl. She has four kids and she just can't feed them. He [the husband] just can't get a job, no matter how hard he tries. I've to help her out nearly every day. Sometimes she has nothing at all for the dinner and she doesn't like to say to me. But you've only to look at her. She's like an old woman with all the worry. You know, she's only twenty eight. I bet you thought she was older. Everybody does.

While this level of support typifies studies of interaction between daughters and mothers in working-class communities in general (Willmott, 1987), McCafferty (1985) from her study of informal support in nine villages in Northern Ireland, suggests that such support is likely to be more prevalent in working-class Catholic areas (like Newbury) because of inherent conservative attitudes to the family derived from religious teaching.

Support for the Elderly

Parker (1990) argues that one of the most persistent misconceptions about modern society is that the family no longer cares for the elderly. This misjudgement is particularly likely to be made where the elderly live alone. However, a number of studies have indicated that even where the elderly do live alone, support was often available from relatives, particularly from children who live close at hand (O'Connor and Ruddle, 1988, McLaughlin, 1993). The Newbury study focused on help and support given to the elderly living outside the household. To some extent, such a focus may under-estimate the amount of care provided by males as research by Parker (1990) indicates that where males were involved in providing care for the elderly, it was mainly in connection with elderly men caring for their elderly wives. However, when studies have concentrated on elderly people who are cared for by relatives of a younger generation, the research indicates that daughters are the most heavily involved and the Newbury study supports this general trend.

As has been reflected in research elsewhere (Willmott, 1987), the women in the sample were the main sustainers of the kinship structure. The data revealed a bias towards contact with the woman's side of the family and this is reflected in the tendency mentioned earlier for females to be related to more households in the estate compared to males. Most contact tended to occur between elderly women living alone and their married daughters. Daughters often shopped and undertook laundering duties for elderly mothers. Apart from frequent visits, daughters tried to reduce the isolation of elderly mothers by buying consumer durables such as colour televisions and radios. Visits were also supplemented by telephone calls and in a number of cases, married daughters paid for the installation of a telephone for their mothers so that they could keep in daily touch and function as a safeguard if anything were to happen:

> I feel happier now that my mother has the phone. Like if she falls or anything she can telephone me for help.

> Well I worry about her at nights and a quick phone call before she goes to bed puts my mind at rest.

Arber et al. (1988) point out that while the provision of statutory services to elderly people has increased substantially over recent years, nonetheless, this has been largely aimed at supporting elderly people without families close by rather than replace or supplement female care.

Motivations for Providing Support

Throughout this chapter, I have focused on practical help and support outside the household and suggested that such aid was mainly performed by women. Women's roles outside the household are inextricably related to their roles within the household. Elsewhere, I have outlined how women were mainly responsible within the household for caring for the needs of other household members (Leonard, 1993). Even in the midst of high long-term unemployment, gender roles remained specific and unequal. Women in part-time formal or informal paid employment were rarely relieved of the burdens of domesticity even where the male had no access to formal or informal paid employment. Indeed, in the absence of opportunities to sustain macho identity through paid employment, men sought to enhance their male identity through their relationships with other males from the estate whom they met frequently in pubs and clubs. Whereas women's friendships tended to be home-based and comprised more of relatives and neighbours, men's friendships extended throughout the estate. While inter-generational friendships were common among women, men tended to befriend males in the same age range as themselves and this was most pronounced among men of working age. In these circumstances, significantly helping out in the household was seen as further diluting the male identity and resisted by many men and indeed their wives. Several women I spoke to stated that they felt it would be 'degrading' to expect men to substantially undertake domestic tasks.

Where men helped and supported others outside the household, this tended to be related to practical gender-specific tasks rather than concerned with relationships per se and was mainly influenced by the principle of reciprocity (Leonard, 1995). Reciprocity concerns the obligation to give and to receive and is based on the premise that both parties will eventually mutually benefit from such exchanges. Hence, when males were interviewed concerning the extent and type of help they gave to others, the majority were able to immediately specific favours given and expectation of returns. Women, on the other hand, seemed more unaware of the level of support they gave to others and indeed, in contrast to the males, the extent of this support emerged in general conversation during the in-depth interviews rather than in response to specific questions. Rather caring and supporting others inside and outside the household was seen by many women as fitting naturally with their perceptions of their roles in society. From a feminist standpoint, Finch (1993) argues that this is the most potentially damaging aspect of any movement towards community care. Finch demonstrates that the concept of 'community care' is inherently sexist as it is based on the premise that any dividing line between the services women specifically provide for members of their households and caring for others outside the household is artificial and unnatural. The remainder of this chapter will examine Finch's distinction between caring for and caring about; labour and love; and duty and affection as ways of understanding informal support networks in Newbury.

Caring For and Caring About

Finch suggests that 'caring for' someone is often seen as a logical extension of 'caring about' someone. Hence, since we care about our relatives, friends and possibly our neighbours, then it seems reasonable to assume that caring for these people will present us with little difficulties. However, the two do not necessarily coincide in practice. For example, one can think of a host of occupations where caring for people is an inherent part of the job without the expectation that caring about such people is a necessary appendage. The main problem here is that such occupations tend to be gender specific and based on idealised extensions of the mother-role. Hence, caring for and about people becomes part of the make-up of the natural female.

Land (1991) discusses men's collective choice to leave caring to women and outlines how men often have the power and resources to choose not to become involved in caring work whereas women are often denied such choices. There is no reason to suppose that men in Newbury do not care about their children or their relatives yet the persistence of sexist attitudes concerning who does what inside and outside the household enabled most men to blamelessly opt out of making the transition from caring about to caring for others due to the presence of women in the estate seemingly content to take on board caring responsibilities. This was particularly the case for married men who could discharge their responsibilities for elderly parents on to their wives shoulders.

Labour and Love

Because of modern industrial society's preoccupation with formal paid labour as the purest form of economic activity, the economic value of forms of labour which exist outside this limited definition tend to be under-rated. The main intention of the Newbury survey was to make visible the numerous types of work undertaken by both men and women outside the realm of formal paid employment. The invisibility of such economic practices was at its height among the activities typically undertaken by women both within and outside the household. Caring for people crosses the boundary between the formal and informal economy. For example, caring for the elderly in an institutional setting involves a range of occupations including nurse, cleaner and caterer. While these occupations tend to be low-paid and dominated by women, nonetheless, they are recognised as valid work and there is an acknowledgement that each demands a certain level of skills. However, when these activities are performed within the household or community, particularly by a family member, they are dismissed as non-work and ideologies concerning the supposed natural traits of femininity are invoked to undermine the skills and sheer physical labour involved in accomplishing such tasks. Indeed, performing these tasks 'for free' within the household has a negative effect on the pay and gender composition of these occupations when they are transferred to the formal economy. Nonetheless, the existence of such occupations in the formal economy has gradually promoted changes in the way such tasks are viewed when performed informally. Hence, in many European countries, caring for people in an informal setting is termed 'care-giving work' to underline the conceptualisation of such activities as proper work (Leira, 1993).

Of course, men are also involved in performing a wide range of economic tasks in the informal sector. However, much of men's labour has tangible results. During the survey, the tasks most frequently undertaken by men concerned painting and decorating, fixing electrical household products, car maintenance and a host of major or minor household repairs and renovations. These activities have a lasting visibility and confusion over whether the task can be considered as work or not is less pronounced. Apart from knitting and dressmaking, most of the tasks women were involved in had limited or extremely short-term visibility. Hence, looking after a neighbour's children or cooking a meal for an elderly neighbour or relative did not match the permanency of men's informal economic activities. Moreover, because these tasks were performed on a daily basis anyway as part of the mother-housewife role, then extensions of these activities to cover the needs of other people often remained hidden.

The data further revealed a stronger tendency for women to be concerned with maintaining close relationships with friends, neighbours and relatives rather than to simply perform practical tasks for others on a reciprocal basis. Hence, women were often involved in intangible activities such as providing emotional support to others or calling in to visit a friend, neighbour or relative. Such activities fall into what Lynch and McLaughlin (1995) term love labour. They argue that love labour is a fundamental aspect of caring about or for others, although they emphasise that not all caring is love labour. Lynch and McLaughlin are careful not to romanticise love labour, hence their analysis outlines the shifting boundaries between love and labour and formal and informal care. They also suggest that in most cases, like the practical tasks outlined earlier, love labour involves some element of reciprocity. This issue will be returned to in the next section.

Duty and Obligation

In examining the variety of practical help tasks performed by males in Newbury for other households in the estate, the notion of mutual self-interest was clearly evident. While an element of reciprocity characterised female motivations for doing favours for others, nonetheless, female participation in informal support networks was closely associated with strong norms and overtones of obligation concerning women's roles in society. This influenced the type of favour men and women were likely to perform for others and the likely recipient of such favours. Men tended to perform tangible favours for those seemingly able to reciprocate including people with whom they had little prior relationship. Women, on the other hand, tended to engage in intangible as well as tangible favours for others and the stronger the prior relationship with the recipient of the favour, the weaker the expectation of reciprocity influenced the exchange. This was particularly the case when favours were performed for extended kinship network members.

This is not to say that reciprocity was entirely absent from these exchanges. Most favours were performed by middle-aged women for young married daughters or for elderly relatives. These favours seemed to be one-way as young married daughters and elderly relatives seemed unable to reciprocate these favours. However, if one considers these exchanges between generations, then the notion of delayed reciprocity seems useful for exploring motivations for engaging in such support mechanisms. Middle-aged women by helping younger family members set in motion expectations of deferred gain for their assistance. It seems likely that when young married daughters reach middle age they will reciprocate the favours previously given to them by their now elderly mothers. What is notable here is that the equivalence is not calculated precisely on the basis of what each party consumes. Rather each side feels a commitment to the other and a moral obligation to provide one another with support when needed. The nature of the support and its direction will vary over the life course. This is similar to Antonucci and Jackson's (1989) notion of a social support bank in which individuals amass credits for later use. This camouflages the centrality of exchange to the relationship and questions the apparent altruism involved.

Hence, I do not want to present an idealised, romantic image of self-interested males and caring, altruistic females. Women's motivations for engaging in informal helping networks were closely bound to culturally defined rules regarding gender specific obligations both within and outside the household. Kinship and gender interacted to place the onus for caring for others on to female shoulders as part of traditional gender-role expectations surrounding women's obligation and duty within the family. Once females took on board this role, other family members opted out of taking responsibility for care. Land and Rose (1985) refer to this as compulsory altruism. Women have little choice regarding their willingness to care for others inside or outside the household since participation is so closely bound up with normative expectations of kinship obligations. Moreover, in the absence of viable alternative roles, women's identity and self-esteem was often linked to looking after the needs of others both within and outside the household. Hence, many women remained unconscious of the altruism involved whether compulsory or voluntary.

Conclusion

While the study confirms the general trend of helping networks found in working-class, close-kin communities, nonetheless, there was little evidence to suggest that such networks could be utilised to play any great part in the care of heavily dependent people. As this study indicates, these networks were beneficial sources of help during the periods of need associated with the average life-cycle such as helping with childcare, helping out during temporary illnesses or providing short-term support for the bereaved. However, on closer examination what looks like lots of support being extended between households is instead one category of people providing support both up and down the generational ladder during a specific period of their lives. In other words, most care in this study was provided by women providing support to daughters in the early stages of family formation and daughters providing support for elderly mothers. Neighbours tended to provide banal, mundane favours that enabled others to cope with the haphazard contingencies they face rather than provide a consistent source of long-term effective support. Hence, as a foundation for community care policies, the potential of such networks to meet the needs of the most vulnerable in society seems limited.

As the study indicated, it is those who do not have an adult daughter, daughter-in-law and possibly bachelor son or competent spouse who are at risk. Thus never married people (who have always formed a significant group in institutional care for exactly this reason), people (married or not) who have never had children, those whose spouses and/or offspring have died prematurely, and/or those whose offspring have been geographically mobile may be unable to hold their own in a reciprocal relationship and thus remain outside the realm of community support networks. This is an important point because as I have argued earlier, it is the supposed existence of these supportive networks that provides the *sine qua non* for transferring responsibility for the needy and vulnerable on to the shoulders of community members.

In focusing on self-help, working class networks, there is a danger of romanticising 'the world we have lost' and thus ignoring the downside of working class community life. Hence the poverty, deprivation and entrenched patriarchy which characterise such communities are often ignored. Thus, Abrams (Bulmer, 1986) warns against encouraging a return to the conditions which seem to generate 'neighbourliness'. These conditions tend to go against the interests of women and limit their opportunities. This is because women are more likely to be accorded the role of family 'kin-keeper' and initiate and maintain ties with kin. The research indicated that the informal helping networks prevalent in the estate extended and perpetuated gender divisions within the family and community.

On the other hand, caring and loving others is for many women much more life enhancing than the mundane badly paid formal work carried out under the exploitative conditions which most women have to endure. Indeed, for many women, caring and loving others is the raison d'etre of their lives. The main problem is the conditions under which caring is carried out and the low regard for women's caring role held by many men and the state. With proper informal support from men and formal support from the state through social services and the social security system, caring could be a liberating emotional and economically valued experience for many women.

Discussion Topics

1. Outline the distinction between 'caring for' someone and 'caring about' someone.

2. Do women care for others out of duty or out of love?

3. Is caring for others a form of love labour?

4. Discuss the view that women have little choice regarding their willingness to care for others inside or outside the household as participation is related to normative expectations surrounding kinship obligations.

References and Further Reading:

Allan, G. 1979 *A Sociology of Friendship and Kinship*, London: Harvester Wheatsheaf.

Antonucci, T, and Jackson, J. 1989 'Successful Ageing and Life Course Reciprocity', in Warnes, A. *Human Ageing and Later Life*, London: Age Concern and Institute of Gerontology.

Arber, S, Gilbert G and Evandrow, M. 1988 'Gender, Household Compostion and Receipt of Domiciliary Services by the Elderly Disabled', *Journal of Social Policy*, Vol 17 (2), pp153-176.

Bulmer, M. 1986 *Neighbours. The Work of Philip Abrams*, Cambridge: Cambridge University Press.

Cecil, R, Offer, J and St Leger, F. 1987 *Informal Welfare: A Sociological Study of Care in Northern Ireland*, Aldershot: Gower.

Cecil, R 1989 'Care and Community in a Northern Irish Town', in Donnan, H. and McFarlane, G. *Social Anthropology and Public Policy in Northern Ireland*, Aldershot: Avebury.

Department of Health and Social Security 1981 *Growing Older*, Cmnd 8173, London: HMSO.

DH/ DSS/ Welsh Office/Scottish HHD. 1989 *Caring for People: Community Care in the Next Decade and Beyond*, Cm. 849. London: HMSO.

Finch, J. 1993 'The Concept of Caring: Feminist and Other Perspectives', in Twigg, J (ed.) *Informal Care in Europe*, University of York: Social Policy Research Unit.

Finch, J, and Groves, D. 1980 'Community Care and the Family: a case for equal opportunities?', *Journal of Social Policy*, 9, 4: 487-511.

Griffiths, Sir R. 1988 *Community Care: Agenda for Action, A Report to the Secretary of State for Social Services*, London: HMSO.

Hinds, B. 1991 'Childcare Provision and Policy', in Davies, C and McLaughlin, E. *Women, Employment and Social Policy in Northern Ireland: a problem postponed?* Belfast: Policy Research Institute.

Kremer, J, and Montgomery, P. 1993 *Women's Working Lives*, Belfast: HMSO.

Land, H, and Rose, H. 1985 'Compulsory Altruism for some or an altruistic society for all?' in Bean, P, Ferris, J and Whynes, D. (eds.) *In Defence of Welfare*, London: Tavistock.

Land, H. 1991 'Time to Care' in Maclean, M and Groves, D. *Women's Issues in Social Policy*, London: Routledge.

Leira, A. 1993 'Concepts of Care: Loving, Thinking and Doing', in Twigg, J. (ed.) *Informal Care in Europe*, University of York: Social Policy Research Unit.

Leonard, M. 1995 'Women and Informal Economic Activity in Belfast', in Clancy, P. Drudy, S, Lynch, K. and O'Dowd, L. (eds.) *Irish Society: Sociological Perspectives*, Dublin: Institute of Public Administration.

Leonard, M. 1994 *Informal Economic Activity in Belfast*, Aldershot: Avebury.

Leonard, M. 1993. 'The Modern Cinderellas: Women and the Contract Cleaning Industry in Belfast', in Arber, S. and Gilbert, N. (eds.) *Women and working lives: Divisions and Change*, London: Macmillan.

Lynch, K, and McLaughlin, E. 1995 'Caring Labour and Love Labour', in Clancy, P et al. (ibid).

McCafferty, M. 1985 *Family and Kin in North Antrim and South Derry — a Geographical Perspective*, unpublished M.Phil Thesis, Coleraine: University of Ulster.

McLaughlin, E. 1993 'Women and the Family in Northern Ireland: a review', *Women's Studies Internation Forum*, 16, 6, 553-568.

McLaughlin, E. 1992 'Informal Care' in Kremer, J. and Montgomery, P. (eds.) *Women's Working Lives*, Belfast: HMSO.

Meegan, R. 1989 'Paradise Postponed: The Growth and Decline of Merseyside', in Cooke, P. (ed.) *Localities: The Changing Face of Urban Britain*, London: Unwin Hyman.

O'Connor, J, and Ruddle, H. 1988 *Caring for the Elderly*, Dublin: National Council for the aged.

Pahl, R E. 1966 'The Rural-urban continuum' *Sociological Ruralis*, Vol 6. No.3/4 pp. 299-329.

Parker, G. 1992 'Counting Care: Numbers and Types of informal carers', in Twigg, J. *Carers: Research and Practice*, London: HHSO.

Parker, G. 1990 *With Due Care and Attention: A Review of Research on Informal Care*, London: Family Policy Studies Centre.

St Leger, F, and Gillespie, N. 1991 *Informal Welfare in Belfast: Caring Communities,* Aldershot: Avebury.

Wenger, C. 1984 *The Supportive Network: Coping with old age*, London: Allen and Unwin.

Willmott, P. 1987 *Friendship Networks and Social Support*, London: Policy Studies Institute.

8.

Behind Closed Doors: Homeworkers in Ireland
Wendy Richards

Introduction

Homeworking, working at home for a wage or salary, is attracting increasing interest from employers seeing the possibilities of new technology. However, homeworking is no new phenomenon and research evidence highlights the myth that such work provides flexibility and advantages for workers as well as employers. This form of work has tended to be overlooked by mainstream labour market and gender analyses. This chapter attempts to remedy this omission by considering some of the important analytical and empirical issues involved in homeworking, arguing that debates surrounding the gendered nature of the labour market are incomplete without consideration of this marginalised, low paid and invisible workforce.

Homeworking: Marginalised and Invisible

According to official records, Ireland has a relatively low rate of female labour force participation. Only thirty-eight per cent of Irish women are engaged in paid employment, compared to sixty-four per cent in the UK and seventy-six per cent in Denmark (Hansard, 1.5.95, col. 29).

These statistics can give a false impression of women's waged labour: many Irish women work part-time, and as there is no accepted definition of part-time employment, may not be recorded. Many married women, in response to population census and the Labour Force Survey, classify themselves as being occupied on home duties despite working part-time, and others who work on family farms are not recorded as engaging in paid employment (Blackwell, 1986). Homeworking is rarely identified in official statistics, and so there are no reliable estimates of the numbers doing this work; however, a number of studies have highlighted its existence in Ireland. Similar studies have examined homeworking in Britain and in Northern Ireland (ICTU, 1994), and estimates suggest that there were 656,000 homeworkers in Britain in 1992; the 1982 estimate was half that figure (Department of Employment, 1994a and 1994b).

Homeworking in the context of this chapter refers to people who are employed to carry out work in their own home, and are paid a wage; this definition encompasses office workers using new technology at home as well as the more traditional forms of homeworking: toy-making, knitters and clothing workers.[1]

Homeworking is an extreme form of the marginalised and atypical forms of work into which many women are segregated. Like other 'atypical' workers, homeworkers are treated as casual labour, a temporary workforce, even though many engage in this work for several years. In addition, homeworkers are rarely considered to be employees: they are generally designated by those providing and paying for the work as self-employed, 'housewives supported by a husband's wage, seeking a bit of "pin-money" for work in their spare time' (Allen and Wolkowitz, 1987, p.3). The lack of employee status means that homeworkers are deprived of normal entitlements including statutory employment protection, sick pay, pension schemes and holidays; the question of the employment status of homeworkers is covered in detail in Richards (1989). Homeworkers' reputation as casuals, a 'hidden workforce' (Pennington and Westover, 1989) means that to onlookers, including in some cases the media, such workers are part of the 'black economy'.[2]

However, homeworking has received less attention than other low-paid and marginal female employment, and Allen and Wolkovitz suggest that one reason may be the influence of assumptions that waged work takes place outside the home, freeing women from domestic constraints (1987, p.2). In contrast to such assumptions, homeworking is an inevitable consequence of a patriarchal system in which domestic labour and caring responsibilities are assumed to be women's role. As a form of waged labour it tends to be ignored or excluded in literature on discrimination, with relatively few exceptions, such as Allen and Wolkowitz supra, and Richards (1988) who locates homeworking within the context of gender and labour market segmentation.

New technology homeworking is perceived as different from traditional forms of homeworking which are associated with low pay, marginalisation and feminisation. With advances in computer technology and the Internet, many white-collar jobs need not be located in an office. It is claimed that technology can be liberating, offering flexibility and autonomy, eliminating the need to travel and to work to employer-dictated hours; however, research evidence on new technology homeworking shows that in comparison to on-site workers, these 'new' homeworkers fare little better than their traditional counterparts. Their pay may be higher than traditional homeworkers but is lower than on-site employees, they incur work-related expenses which are not always reimbursed and they also experience job insecurity and lack of employment protection, making them vulnerable to exploitation (Huws, 1984). Allen and Wolkowitz (1987) point out that despite suggestions that this type of homeworking is suitable for higher-level employees, the majority of 'new' homeworkers are female, engaged in various types of clerical work. Data processing, they comment, is little different from traditional homeworking: 'these girls [sic] are behind computers, but they could just as easily be behind a sewing machine' (p.55). There is no evidence that 'new' homeworking has yet become prevalent among middle-class workers (Allen and Wolkovitz, 1987, p.67); like traditional homeworking, it is a working-class phenomenon. In her study of new technology homeworking in British Telecom, Bannister (1992) found that BT did not view homeworkers as employees. Potential problems with health and safety existed which were not given adequate consideration by BT; and interestingly, given the reasons why many women work at home, BT made clear its view that homeworking was not an answer to childcare problems. She comments: 'BT took the intrusion of the family into work very seriously... the manager pointed out that the teleworkers' families had been warned not to interrupt them at work if possible' (1992, p.52).

The Origins of Homeworking

Homeworking was the normal pattern of work organisation in the sixteenth and seventeenth centuries. All family members helped to produce the typical pre-industrial society goods: cotton and woollen cloth, lace, hosiery, footwear, rope and so on, with local organisations in each area, similar to co-operatives; a 'master' took charge of selling the finished goods (Gregg, 1976). With industrialisation from the 1850s onwards the major part of the economic process moved outside the home, concentrating capital, workers (mainly women and children, in industries such as cotton and textiles: Davis, 1993, pp.12, 18-19) and machinery in factories. Homework continued, but in isolation, and homeworkers were dependent on factory employers having a surplus of work when demand was high and were thus a domestic reserve army of labour. Hope et al. (1976) comment that homeworkers at this time worked longer hours than their counterparts in factories, for 'starvation wages', and outside the scope of existing factory legislation (p.88).

The growth of homeworking in the nineteenth century is discussed in more detail by Pennington and Westover (1989). Around 1885 homeworking became the subject of public interest. A number of reports drew attention to its low pay and poor working conditions: the 1890 Report of the House of Lords Select Committee on Sweating, which considered the 'sweated trades' and included homeworking in its deliberations, and the Royal Commission on Labour in 1893 which remarked, inter alia, on the prevalence of homeworking in the lace industry in Limerick and in the weaving industry in Skibbereen (Morris, 1984). Other reports drew attention to the unhealthy working conditions and inadequate pay of homeworkers during this period, which, among other factors, contributed to the establishment by the Westminster government of the first four Trade Boards in 1909 (predecessors of the Joint Labour Committee system). In addition, in 1911 a statutory requirement was introduced obliging all firms employing homeworkers to submit lists of these workers to the local authorities.

Homeworking also caught the attention of writers of fiction: this extract from The Rat Pit, first published in 1915, illustrates not only the poor wages compared with the employer's profit on goods produced, but also workers' acceptance of this treatment without question:

> 'Knitting!' exclaimed Fergus, rising to his feet and striding up and down the cabin. 'God look sideways on the knitting! How much are you paid for your work? One shilling and threepence for a dozen pairs of stockings that take the two of you more than a whole week to make. You might as well be slaves, slaves to the very middle of your bones! How much does Fawley McKeown get for stockings in the big towns away from here? Four shillings a pair, I am after hearing. You get a penny farthing a pair, a penny farthing...' (Macgill, 1982, p.43.)

By the 1920s concern was fading: a report by the Chief Inspectorate of Factories and Workshops in 1925 commented that 'there is a consensus of opinion that homework is on the decline...[there] is not much room for casual work in modern industry' (Morris, 1984). It is often assumed that from the First World War onwards homework virtually died out, but Pennington and Westover (1989) argue that the Factory Inspector's report drew too sweeping a conclusion and that during the inter-war years homework 'declined but not disappeared' (p.147). The lack of attention from government or pressure groups aided the impression that homework had diminished, and it was not until 1974 when the London-based Low Pay Unit published its first pamphlet, a study of homeworking (Brown, 1974), that attention was again drawn to the existence of this work.

Sweated Labour: British Studies of Homework

During the 1970s and 1980s in Britain homeworking was the focus of considerable research, by the Department of Employment, independent researchers and pressure groups. Estimates were produced of numbers engaged in homeworking: 29,000 in Wages Council industries alone, according to the House of Commons Employment Committee in 1980, and an estimate of between 200,000 and 400,000 by the Select Committee on Employment in

1981. There are problems with these and other estimates (eg Hakim, 1984a): this is discussed in more detail in Richards (1988, pp.236-9).

The studies examine the reasons why women undertake homework: they confirm that women perform homework due to financial need, rather than for so-called 'pin-money'. Brown (1974, p.17) remarks that eight homeworkers in her small study had husbands who earned only a little above the State poverty line, while a further two families needed the extra income to meet housing costs. A study of homeworkers in North London (Hope et al., 1976, p.97) showed earnings spent on food or children's clothes; in no instance did homeworkers indicate that money was spent on themselves.

Domestic and caring responsibilities are significant factors tying women to the home, but in addition, many women experience difficulty in finding employment outside the home due to lack of available work in the local area, or at convenient hours. Occasionally disabilities prevent women obtaining alternative employment: Huws' (1984) study of new technology homeworkers found two out of seventy-eight whose disability ruled out work-based employment, and Hakim (1980) quotes one woman who, although medically capable of work, faced discrimination:

> I've got a green card [registered disabled]... and as soon as employers see
> that, they don't want to know. I even got the sack from one firm when I got
> it out (p.1106).

The casual, hidden nature of homeworking is illustrated by the various methods in which work was obtained: word-of-mouth and other informal networks are common, as are advertisements in shop windows or community centres (Hakim, 1980, Bisset and Huws, 1984). In some cases, 'new' homeworkers particularly, women had altered their location of work at their employers' suggestion, and others who had left employment for domestic reasons were subsequently recruited by their employers to work at home (see eg Hakim, 1980, Huws, 1984).

Homeworkers are generally paid by piece-rate, which Allen and Wolkowitz (1987) argue is a mechanism through which the supplier controls output and maintains or increases work intensity. In in-work situations, piecework can become an issue for collective bargaining as workers and their representatives attempt to influence the measurement of a 'piece', the rate of payment and production line speeds (see inter alia Roy, 1952, Lupton, 1962). However, the isolation inherent in homeworking makes it easier for suppliers to push down piece-rates, and as Allen and Wolkowitz argue (p.115) and research has shown, homeworkers' families frequently help to meet targets or deadlines. Allen and Wolkowitz also point out that to increase earnings significantly on piecework, workers need to build up speed and accuracy with a particular process or product; yet tasks or products may be changed frequently, making the speed which comes with familiarisation difficult (p.116). This inevitably leads to work intensification in order to earn anything approaching a reasonable amount; as one homeworker comments, 'To earn anything worthwhile... you'd have to chain yourself to the envelopes', and according to another 'the less I did the less I got paid, so the incentive was there to do more' (p.116). However, the 'flexibility' which it is claimed that homework offers can lead to workers blaming themselves rather than the suppliers for their long working hours: again, from Allen and Wolkowitz's study, a homeworker earning between £15 and £20 for forty-two hours' work argued that 'this is my own fault, I needn't take all the work I do' (p.116).

In terms of pay, Brown's (1974) study showed that homeworkers earned significantly less than women working outside the home. Hourly pay for full-timers (defined by Brown as more than 30 hours per week) was twenty-four per cent of national average hourly earnings for women in manufacturing. A later study (Crine, 1979) showed homeworkers earning between twenty-six per cent and forty per cent of the Low Pay Unit's low pay threshold, which is set at two-thirds median male earnings. Hakim's (1980) more comprehensive study produced an average hourly rate of pay for homeworkers engaged in manufacturing which was half of the then Low Pay Unit threshold. A further study by Hakim, carried out in the winter of 1978-79 and described as a 'homework blitz', concentrated on Wages Inspectorate records of homeworkers in the clothing industry in London (Hakim, 1982). This study covered about 500 homeworkers, and while it used a much lower definition of low pay than that of the Low Pay Unit (ninety pence per hour rather than £1.50), fifty-seven per cent of those surveyed were low-paid. Homeworkers were also far more likely to be low paid than on-site workers. However, this study may underestimate the incidence of low pay as it only covered homeworkers registered by employers with the Wages Inspectorate. This registration is rare.

Other studies confirm these findings in relation to pay (Cragg and Dawson, 1981, TUC, 1985, Bisset and Huws, 1984). Allen and Wolkowitz (1987) studied homeworkers in West Yorkshire: while twenty-two worked in industries covered by Wages Councils, sixteen were earning below the set rate.[3] These quotes from respondents illustrate the scale of low pay (p.117):

> Earned £5 a week on average – occasionally I had thicker wool and earned about £6 per week. (Hand-knitter; average hours 30 per week).

> Earned £9.25 last week, usually £7–£8 per week. If I get all the higher paid overalls I can earn £10 per week. (Machinist; average hours 16´ per week).

There is, of course, a striking difference between the rates of pay offered to homeworkers and the price for which the goods are eventually sold in retail stores or through catalogues, and Allen and Wolkowitz found that the homeworkers were well aware of this disparity, but powerless, in their unequal supplier-worker relationship, to do anything about it.

The low rates of pay are further eroded by the fact that carrying out work at home inevitably involves the workers in expenses – heat, light, telephone and so on – which would normally be part of an employer's overheads. In addition, homeworkers may often have to incur the costs of collecting or delivering their work, and of course receive no payment for time spent doing this. Equipment used for the work, such as sewing or knitting machines, pliers or other tools, is frequently not provided (Brown, 1974, Crine, 1979, Allen and Wolkowitz, 1987).

Given the low pay, additional costs and health and safety hazards arising from homeworking (see, for instance, ACAS, 1978a, ACAS, 1978b, Allen and Wolkowitz, 1987, Richards, 1988) it might be asked why women continue to do homework. These quotes from Hakim's study (1980, p.1108) are illustrative:

> I rely on it. I don't get regular maintenance from my ex-husband, so whatever job I'm given I won't refuse. He [the supplier] knows I need the money.

> We must have the money... we've got a bigger mortgage than we can afford, a bank overdraft, a pile of debts... I've just got to help out.

Homeworking in Ireland

There is much less research evidence on the incidence and extent of homeworking in Ireland. The ICTU Women's Committee published a report on atypical work in Northern Ireland (ICTU, 1994) which included some evidence on homeworking in the Province; to the author's knowledge, the only research in the Republic of Ireland apart from the author's own (Richards, 1988, 1989, 1994), is a study carried out in Tallaght, south county Dublin, in 1982 (Jones, 1982).

The ICTU study targeted firms which might potentially employ homeworkers and sent letters to about 300 such organisations; only 25 replied and few of these were making use of homeworkers. The researchers then carried out a survey of advertisements in the press and in shop windows, and concluded that much homeworking had shifted from the clothing and manufacturing sectors to clerical, retail and service sectors (ICTU, 1994, pp.26-27). Much of the work does not conform to the usual understanding of homeworking, or to the definition used in this paper; the study cites women advertising their services for ironing, typing or doing alterations. As usual with studies of homeworking, it proved difficult to obtain participants, and in fact only twelve women took part; the report comments on 'the obvious fear of those women who were engaged in homework – largely due to the fact that their money making occupations were likely to affect the rates of social security benefits coming into the house' (1994, p.27).

These women were engaging in homework for the same reasons as homeworkers elsewhere: 'for many women, and particularly those with dependent children – homeworking is possibly the only alternative to unemployment' (ICTU, p.28). As a further example of how such work is not seen as 'convenient' by those who perform it, the 'freedom' or 'flexibility' of homework was rarely mentioned; instead respondents complained about the intrusion of work into their domestic lives. This study again showed how 'flexibility' can lead to longer hours: a number of respondents worked in the evenings and at weekends in addition to daytime (p.30). This confirms Allen and Wolkowitz's (1987) argument that the piecework system and low pay act as pressure on workers to extend their working day to meet deadlines or earn sufficient money.

Jones' study of homeworkers in Dublin, funded by FAS (at the time AnCO) was carried out by a house-to-house investigation in three working-class estates in Tallaght. She reasonably expected to find evidence of homeworking in this area, as well as reluctance to admit to its existence: Tallaght is an area with unemployment levels well above the national average (Jones, 1982). Jones found significant evidence of homeworking, including hand-sewing moccasins, knitting, assembling rosary beads, making mass cards and sewing. Pay rates varied considerably, though in relation to the moccasin sewing (a difficult and often painful task) average pay was between 25p and 30p per hour. The fourteen moccasin stitchers interviewed by Jones were working directly for a factory and were aware of the difference between their pay and that of in-workers. For machinists, a communion dress, from cut-out to completion, earned the homeworker £10, and a fully-lined skirt with accessories earned 50p. Footwear sewers in this study were part of a division of labour: the material was cut out in the factory and sewn up by the homeworker. A similar process took place in relation to some handknitters, who would knit the pieces of garments which were then sewn up and finished elsewhere, thus depriving the knitter of the satisfaction of seeing the finished garment.

The British studies comment on expenses incurred by homeworkers; Jones gives as an example a rosary bead assembler who had to provide her own pliers. At a cost of £4, this represented eight hours of her labour. She also had to collect and deliver her own work, which involved a four-bus return journey (1982, p.45).

The author's own study of homeworking in Ireland was carried out between 1986 and 1987, by means of a postal questionnaire of women engaged in homework and a study of suppliers of homework by means of questionnaires and interviews. The significant difficulties in identifying homeworkers willing to participate meant that the sample had to be self-selecting; it was impossible to carry out the research in such a way that a representative sample could be obtained. An article was published in the Evening Press newspaper (Richards, 1986) which explained the research, and this was followed by an interview on the Gay Byrne Show on RTÉ Radio One in which the author appealed for homeworkers to contact her. Forty-six letters were received in response, and these resulted in nineteen usable questionnaires. This is a small sample, but compares favourably with many UK studies and the ICTU study which had twelve respondents.

The geographical spread covered most of the twenty-six counties, and all respondents were women. Fifteen were hand-knitters, three were machine-knitters and one was a moccasin-stitcher. This woman worked directly for a factory where her husband was an in-worker and knew many other homeworkers engaged in the same work. Since all but one of the homeworkers were knitters, the study investigated the views of suppliers of this type of work. Many knitters work directly for wool shops which offer a knitting service to their customers. Twenty-four wool shops in the Dublin area were visited, and twelve of these were found to be supplying work to homeworkers. Between them, these shops were employing fifty-two homeworkers, who were generally recruited through word-of-mouth.

Of the respondents to the questionnaire study of homeworkers, fifteen of the nineteen were married, and nine of these had dependent children; the other four were widowed. Two respondents were disabled, and the respondents' ages ranged from mid-twenties to late seventies. Six respondents had never worked outside the home, including one 26-year-old with two young children. Others had worked until they married, some leaving under a marriage bar and others due to traditional views; as one argued, 'as a parent it [home] is the right place to be to look after one's family.' She added, repeating a view which has often been voiced in Ireland, 'there are too many young people unemployed: should we go and join the workforce to make competition greater...?' One woman left her job because her employer refused to give her sick pay or holiday pay, and another was made redundant.

All respondents had good reasons for working at home. Three were not trained for anything else and believed that they would not be able to get a job. Four helped on family farms, and others expressly mentioned their isolation at home: one said that she was 'housebound with no transport', while another lived eight miles from the nearest town with no adequate public transport. Thus it seems that many women still face difficulties in competing in the labour market. Unsuitable working hours and a shortage of affordable childcare facilities, particularly in rural areas, do not allow mothers to combine childcare with employment; an apparent lack of training opportunities means that those who have been out of the labour market are disadvantaged in their attempts at re-entry. In addition, societal attitudes, strongly felt in rural communities, which insist that a married woman should be supported by her husband or must stay at home with her children, are often so pervasive that women themselves accept their legitimacy.

The study attempted to ascertain the women's dependency on their earnings from homework. Some did rely on their earnings: one wrote 'I am forced to knit to help my daughter who is attending UCG [University College Galway]. I would love to give it up as it is extremely hard staying up at night.' Another, a widow on a pension, said that the extra £10 per week was vital as she had two daughters in full-time education. Only one respondent described her earnings as 'pocket money', yet she worked 25 hours per week in order to earn £10, and she also pointed out that as she could not drive, lived some distance from a town and was 'not trained with any other skill' this was the only work she could do.

Some of the respondents in this study did describe the work as 'convenient' in that they were able to remain at home and work when they wanted; an illustration of this is the handknitter who remarked that she 'liked to do a bit of knitting at my own leisure', but revealed that she knits for twenty hours per week and had to work on the farm as well as manage her housework. On the other hand, several respondents pointed out that their work encroached into time which they felt was their own or into other activities. One mentioned the continual pressure to complete orders, while others gave the impression that their work was occupying more time than they would have liked:

> You spend all your time in the home and I try to do one garment a week and cope with all the other household chores as well.

> I have to spend a lot of time working in order to feel any monetary benefit.

> I do not enjoy the work because of the number of hours I spend at it and the small amount of money I get for it.

These responses provide further evidence of Allen and Wolkowitz's (1987) argument about piecework and work intensification. Further evidence came from the interviews with employers: several insisted on garments being completed within strict time-limits. During the course of one such interview, a young girl came into the shop, delivering a garment on behalf of her mother and apologising because it was a few days late. The proprietor later explained that the garment had been promised to a customer who had by this time left on holiday, and so a sale had been lost. It appeared unlikely that this knitter would be offered further work.

As with other studies, pay rates were very poor, ranging from 25p to 75p per hour. Some hand-knitters worked for an agency which then sold the garments overseas. In relation to Aran knitwear, prices can start from around £100, while the knitter earns between £10 and £20 for a garment which takes two weeks to knit. Others worked directly for a wool shop, and also earned between £10 and £20 for a completed garment. This was confirmed by the wool shop interviews, most of which took a mark-up of ten to fifteen pounds on the work. Some of the hand-knitters were well aware of the prices their work sold for, and also felt that they were underpaid for what they did:

> I think it needs some organisation and proper rates of pay for the time and skill that is put into the work.

> Terribly long hours for the lowest paid job.

> I would love it if we were paid a right wage for what we do. Hand knitting can be very hard work and very slow…

> I earn about £10 per week for 25 hours' hard work. I think it's scandalous but I really need the money.

Most appeared pessimistic about their chances of improving their pay. One, a former trade union member, commented that 'there is strength in numbers', and others argued that unions should negotiate a basic hourly wage and that there was a need for standardisation of pay rates But most felt that trade unions or collective organisation had little to offer. There had been an attempt to organise the shoe stitchers by the factory's union, but this had not worked, according to the respondent, because the women were anxious about tax and PRSI, and their husbands who were employed at the factory were afraid that they might be victimised if their wives became unionised.

These negative attitudes about trade unions are consistent with most other studies, including Allen and Wolkowitz's (1987) research in West Yorkshire, and recruitment attempts by the National Union of Hosiery and Knitwear Employees, which concluded that homeworkers did not want to be connected with a trade union for fear of losing their jobs (TUC, 1985, pp.33-34). On the other hand, the Rossendale Union of Boot and Shoe Operators managed successfully to recruit homeworkers and to organise on their behalf (1985, pp.27-28). Historical hostility to homeworkers on the part of trade unions has made matters difficult, although Allen and Wolkowitz (1987, p.149) comment that examples from India suggest that it is possible for homeworkers to be organised.

Conclusion: Flexibility or Exploitation?

Flexibility in employment tends to be presented as a desirable ideal, both for employer and employee; particularly in the UK where it is claimed to lead to greater labour productivity (eg Metcalf, 1989). However, in practice flexibility for the employer tends to lead to low pay and labour casualisation for the worker (Huws et al., 1989, Richards, 1994). Allen and Wolkowitz (1987) argue that although attempts to deregulate the labour market are seen as progressive and represent 'modernisation', ironically they frequently involve a return to 'methods of production previously discussed as archaic' (p.164). They argue that '"working in one's own home" conjures up a myth of autonomy which is quite misleading' (1987, p.133).

Homeworking, the research shows, is not something done casually, in odd moments of free time, despite the claims of employers. The flexibility which homeworkers are presumed to have rarely exists: piecework and production quotas ensure that any 'flexibility' is in the employer's favour, generally in relation to the avoidance of employer's on-costs, benefits and statutory entitlements. Homeworking, as Allen and Wolkowitz argue (1987, p.125) must be seen in the context of a full, very long working week. This was particularly the case in relation to the shoe-stitcher in this study, for whom production quotas meant that she had to work eight hours per day seven days a week. As most homeworkers also tended to be housewives, a break from one kind of work is usually used just to continue with another.

The present author's study illustrates extreme forms of labour force casualisation affecting women workers in Ireland. The crucial issue with regard to homeworkers is their invisibility in the labour force, which arises partly as a consequence of such workers not being perceived, even by themselves, as being engaged in paid employment. Suppliers of homework do not consider the women as workers but merely as housewives with a hobby. This, incidentally, is in stark contrast to a small-scale study of a weaving firm employing male homeworkers, which found that homeworkers enjoyed the same pay, terms and conditions as inworkers, including employment status (Richards, 1988, pp.310-313).

All evidence points to the continuation and expansion of homeworking as a method of production. It is a form of employment which is almost exclusively female, it is very badly paid, completely unregulated, and fraught with health and safety dangers. Yet with advances in technology there is increasing interest in homework as a means of cutting costs for employers. As a result, there is a clear case for regulation of this work, for it to be recognised as a form of employment rather than a 'hobby' or 'side-line', and for its exploitative, discriminatory nature to be highlighted by further research.

Discussion Topics

1. Why do you think much research on women's employment has ignored the existence of homeworking?

2. Patriarchy and capitalism combine to create systems where women are oppressed and disadvantaged at home and in employment; homeworking is an extreme example of this. What needs to change in order to improve the position of women?

3. Improvements to homeworkers' pay and working conditions will not come about through organisation in existing trade unions as the interests of unions and homeworkers are incompatible. Discuss.

4. Homeworking is part of the 'black economy', and the arrangement seems to suit homeworkers. Why should public policy have any interest in regulating homework, other than collecting taxes due?

Notes

1. See Richards, 1988 for a discussion of definitional problems in relation to homeworking.
2. For example, the author's radio interview with Gay Byrne on 11 December 1986, in which Byrne argued that 'isn't it the sort of work that suits women very well... I would say ninety-five per cent of the people you're talking about are not registered for tax and they're getting cash into their pocket.'
3. The UK equivalent of Joint Labour Committees, abolished under the Trade Union Reform and Employment Relations Act 1993.

References and Further Reading

ACAS 1978a *The Button Manufacturing Wages Council Report No. 11*, London: Advisory, Conciliation and Arbitration Service.
ACAS 1978b *The Toy Manufacturing Wages Council Report No. 13*, London: Advisory, Conciliation and Arbitration Service.
Allen, S and Wolkowitz, C. 1987 *Homeworking: Myths and Realities* London: Macmillan.
Bannister, P. 1992 *Telework: Perceptions and Realities — a Case Study of the BT Telework Project* unpublished dissertation, Department of Human Resource Management and Industrial Relations, Keele University.
Bisset, L and Huws, U. 1984 *Sweated Labour: Homeworking in Britain Today* London: Low Pay Unit Pamphlet No. 33.
Blackwell, J. 1986 *Women in the Labour Force* Dublin: Employment Equality Agency.
Brown, M. 1974 *Sweated Labour: a Study of Homework* London: Low Pay Unit Pamphlet No. 1.
Cragg, A and Dawson, T. 1981 *Qualitative Research among Homeworkers* Department of Employment Research Paper No. 21, London.
Crine, S. 1979 *The Hidden Army* Pamphlet No. 11, London: Low Pay Unit.

Davis, M. 1993 *Comrade or Brother? The history of the British labour movement 1789–1951* London: Pluto Press.

Department of Employment 1994a *Research News Bulletin* January, London: Department of Employment.

Department of Employment 1994b *Employment Gazette* January, London: Department of Employment.

Gregg, P. 1976 *Black Death to Industrial Revolution: a Social and Economic History of England* London: Harrap.

Hakim, C. 1980 'Homeworking: some new evidence' in *Department of Employment Gazette* October, p.1105.

Hakim, C. 1982 'Homeworking in the London clothing industry' in *Department of Employment Gazette* September, p.369.

Hakim, C. 1984a 'Homework and Outwork: national estimates from two surveys' in *Department of Employment Gazette* January, p.7.

Hakim, C. 1984b 'Employers' use of Homework, Outwork and Freelances' in *Department of Employment* Gazette April, p.144.

Hansard, House of Commons Reports, 1 May 1995, Col.29.

Hope, E, Kennedy, M, and DeWinter, A. 1976 'Homeworkers in North London' in Barker, D L and Allen, S. (eds.) *Dependence and Exploitation in Work and Marriage* London: Longmans.

Huws, U. 1984 *The New Homeworkers: New Technology and the Changing Location of White-Collar Work* London: Low Pay Unit Pamphlet No. 28.

Huws, U, Hurstfield, J. and Holtmat, R. 1989 *What Price Flexibility? The Casualisation of Women's Employment* London: Low Pay Unit Pamphlet No. 54.

ICTU 1994 *On the Edge* Belfast: Women's Committee of ICTU.

Jones, M. 1982 *Homeworkers Research Project* unpublished dissertation, Department of Social Studies, Trinity College Dublin.

Lupton, T. 1962 *On the Shop Floor — Two Studies of Workshop Organisation and Output* Oxford: Pergamon Press.

Macgill, P. 1982 *The Rat Pit* (1st ed. 1915) Sussex: Caliban Books.

Metcalf, D. 1989 'Water Notes Dry Up: The Impact of the Donovan Reform Proposals and Thatcherism at Work on Labour Productivity in British Manufacturing Industry' *British Journal of Industrial Relations* Vol. XXVII (I), pp.1-31.

Morris, J. 1984 *Women Workers and the Sweated Trades: The Origins of Minimum Wage Legislation* unpublished PhD thesis, London: London School of Economics.

Pennington, S and Westover, B. 1989 *A Hidden Workforce* London: Macmillan.

Richards, W M 1986 'The Homeworker: Exploited and Underpaid' *Evening Press*, 19 November.

Richards, W M 1988 *Women in the Labour Market: Gender and Disadvantage* unpublished PhD thesis, Department of Business and Administrative Studies, Trinity College Dublin.

Richards, W M 1989 'Working in the Comfort of Your Own Home: A New Way of Working for the Future' *Journal of the Irish Society for Labour Law*, Vol. 7, pp.9-22.

Richards, W M 1994 'The Flexible Labour Market: The Case of Homeworking' *Irish Business and Administrative Research* Vol. 15, pp.165-177.

Roy, D. 1952 'Quota Restrictions and Gold-Bricking in a Machine Shop' *American Journal of Sociology* Vol. 57, pp.427-442.

TUC 1985 *Homeworking: A TUC Statement* London: Trades Union Congress.

Section 3:
Women and the Welfare System

State welfare systems are usually understood to be mechanisms of social reform and expressions of citizenship rights; hence many democratic states in the modern world provide a modicum of health care, educational facilities and financial support to vulnerable members of the population such as the unemployed, the elderly, the young, the sick and disabled. The welfare system in the Republic of Ireland has had a complex history of development (see O'Connell and Rottman, 1992, Cousins, 1995); nevertheless it can be assessed in terms of its effectiveness as an agent of social reform and as a provider of citizenship rights. Welfare provision guarantees the citizen a minimum standard of economic security. While civil and political rights are provided in most states in modern Europe, social rights, which include welfare provision, can be less well developed. The provision of social rights often depends on lobbying, campaigning and strong voices on behalf of the most marginalised or deprived in society. Equal treatment of all citizens has to be worked for and planned. It is not a given, even in the most advanced models of democratic societies.

The chapters in this section of the text are mainly concerned with social welfare policies in the Republic of Ireland and their particular impact on women. The gendered character of the social welfare system is emphasised in all of the contributions, as are the inequalities that are reproduced by the policy-making process.

Women are not given full citizenship rights within the confines of the Irish social welfare system. What emerges from the research is that women, in the main, are not treated as individuals within the welfare system, but are regarded as wives, mothers, daughters — dependants of a male breadwinner. The direct material effect of a gendered social welfare policy is to impoverish women. Furthermore, the haphazard development of Irish social policy is made apparent, as is the inadequacy of the policy-making process. The lack of long-term planning and the poor strategic capacity to effect change are serious defects which have impacted heavily on the social rights of women in the welfare system.

In an historical review of the development of social welfare in the Republic, Nicola Yeates offers a gender-based critique of social welfare and points to the inherent inequalities present within the system, since its inception. She argues that the state regards women as members of familiy units only (wives, mothers, daughters) and economically dependent on the male breadwinner. Women's dependency is assumed by policy-makers, so that the inequalities upon which the system is based have yet to be addressed. The Irish welfare system is based on the British model in which women's dependency on the male breadwinner was a fundamental element. In the effort to legitimise the newly independent State in 1937, women's social rights were provided for in the context of a dependence within the family. Drawing on previous Irish-based research, Yeates shows that the Irish Poor Law made distinctions in providing relief from hunger and destitution on the basis of gender. Later, the National Insurance Act (1911) established different contribution and benefit rates for women and men, girls and boys. The 1930s were crucial in the marginalisation of women, according to Yeates. Irish identity was closely aligned to the importance of the family as a fundamental unit in society. The role of married women as home-makers economically dependent on their spouses was essential to the maintenance of this unit. It was assumed that women would be provided for and protected by the family. Even in the face of more progressive welfare policies introduced in the 1970s, and attempts to introduce equality, women's experiences as consumers of social welfare have not substantially altered since the mid-1840s.

What are the possibilities for reform? While Yeates stresses the urgent need to introduce an individual model of welfare entitlements to guarantee gender equality, Geoffrey Cook and Anthony McCashin point out that the concept of equality in social security has not received much attention or analysis in the Irish context. Drawing on the work of Abel Smith, five dimensions of equality within social security are presented and the authors ask what type of equality Irish women themselves want. Some forms of equality, such as actuarial and insurance status equality in social security schemes, disadvantage women. Insurance benefits are based on contribution records and women are often unable to build up a sequential record similar to men's because of pregnancy and movement in and out of the labour market. Sex role equality seeks to equalise roles between the sexes, allowing both women and men to work outside the home and care for the family. However, as Cook and McCashin demonstrate, the Irish debate on sex equality within social security has not dwelt on the variety of dimensions that exist, nor has there been any considered review of the long-term strategies that are required for reform. This is more than apparent in Ireland's response to the European Community Directive on Sex Equality which was partially implemented on the basis of a least-cost, minimalist strategy. While some degree of gender equality was achieved, ironically the cost to the State was far more expensive than intended. In addition, Cook and

McCashin show that the implementation of the Equality Directive benefited middle-class female taxpayers but impoverished women married to unemployed men. The case presented by these authors clearly shows the worst effects of a hastily-implemented policy.

Anne Coakley examines the impact of the Equality Directive on mothers. She argues that a series of policy measures have been put in place that have produced a dual concept of social citizenship for mothers. Earning and caring confer different sets of social rights on mothers. Mothers who are full-time caring in the home are treated as dependants within a familist conception of welfare, while both mothers who are full-time in the labour market and lone parents dependant on welfare are treated as individuals in their own right. Married couples continue to be assessed for welfare assistance on the basis of aggregate means of the household, which assumes the equal distribution of resources within households. Coakley shows that not all married women are treated equally in social welfare as a result of the Equality Directive.

The final chapter in this section focuses on the distribution of resources within the Irish household and attempts to assess differences in living standards between husband and wife in the same household. Sara Cantillon shows that there are inequalities in relation to access and consumption of resources within the home, the overall balance favouring the husband. As the social welfare system distributes benefits on the basis of the household, internal inequalities and conflicts between women and men are masked. Women's lack of control over resources is a contributing factor to women's poverty. While the household may be relatively well-off, individuals within the household may not. Using the household as a unit of analysis compromises the capacity of the welfare system to care for and protect the most vulnerable of its citizens. The piecemeal reform of the welfare system has occurred without a thorough examination of the bases on which this system rests. While some inequalities are being removed, they are replaced by others. It is difficult to disagree with the conclusion reached by O'Connel and Rottman (1992) that the expansion of social rights as they affect life chances in the Republic of Ireland is 'more nominal than real', particularly in the case of women. It is apparent that a debate on the nature of equality, not only within the welfare system, but within all of the institutions of the state, is urgently required.

References

Cousins, M. 1995 The Irish Social Welfare System: Law and Social Policy Dublin: The Round Hall Press.

O'Connell, P J and Rottman, D B. 1992 'The Irish Welfare State in Comparative Perspective' in Goldthorpe, JH and Whelan, CT. (eds.) The Development of Industrial Society in Ireland Oxford: Oxford University Press.

9.

Gender and the Development of the Irish Social Welfare System

Nicola Yeates

Introduction

T his chapter examines the role of the State in the institutionalisation of gender inequality in Ireland. This is undertaken in the context of the historical development of women's social welfare entitlements. It is argued that although these entitlements are key to understanding the forces which create and sustain women's unequal social, economic and political status within a number of countries, they have particular resonance within Ireland. As Daly (1989) has argued, the social welfare system has been 'planned mainly by men and with the life patterns of men in mind' (p.52). It thus questions the assumption that social welfare systems are designed solely to meet need. Instead, gender inequality has been an organising concept of the system from the foundation of the social welfare system in the nineteenth-century to the present day. It affirms that the aims and consequences have been to leave women 'financially dependent upon the resources of husbands, lovers or friends' (Daly, 1989, p.52). In other words, women have been incorporated not as individuals equal to men, but as their dependants (Donnelly, 1993, Evason, 1993).

The principles and rules governing social welfare entitlements have not fundamentally changed since the mid-nineteenth century. The reason for this lies in the conceptualisation of women as a separate and unequal category to men. While the source of this assumption is found in the model of statehood founded on the 1937 Constitution, the origins of women's dependency can be traced right back to the foundations of the English social welfare system which was transposed onto Ireland. Notwithstanding the emergence of a Welfare State, the introduction of equality legislation and the individualisation of rights, the structural position of women within the social welfare system has not fundamentally changed. Further, the very categories of reform are gendered as it is women's family status that continues to determine their access to social rights. Thus, at most, the manifestation of women's inequality has merely been modified.

Thus, it is proposed that the structure and content of social welfare rights explain women's historical and contemporary marginalisation within a social protection system ostensibly covering all citizens. I shall show that the development of social citizenship is not only compatible with profound gender inequalities, but that social welfare has been exclusionary and premised on the devaluation of women. It is concluded that an alternative framework for social policy development based on individual rights is a prerequisite for substantive gender equality.

Conceptualising Gender Equality in Social Policy

Feminist social policy analysis has steadily gained ground since the late 1970s (Wilson, 1977). Feminist analyses of the Welfare State stress the relationship between paid, unpaid work and welfare regarding gender as a central organising principle of the Welfare State (Wilson, 1977, Pascall, 1986, Bryson, 1992). During the 1990s comparative social policy has turned its attention to the gender structure of welfare and there is now a substantial literature mapping the extent of gender inequality in social policies in a wide range of countries (see Langan and Ostner, 1991, Lewis, 1992, Lewis and Ostner, 1994, Sainsbury 1994a, Duncan, 1995).

The current trend by mainstream schools to 'gender welfare' may however amount to the appropriation of feminist analyses by mainstream theoreticians who attempt to assmiliate them into non-gendered theoretical frameworks based on class. While welcoming the growing influence of feminist analysis in social policy, the result of this has often been the grafting of women onto originally non-gendered frameworks. As a result, feminist theoretical models of equality are narrowed and 'gender' becomes equated merely with the status of women (Young, Fort and Danner, 1994). Women are still treated as a deviant of the male norm whose situation can be noted and then forgotten about (e.g. Cook, 1983, McCashin, 1985, Cook and McCashin, 1992, Cousins, 1995). Thiele (1990) calls this pseudo-inclusion: women appear to be accounted for but ultimately remain a problematic category and sex differences in outcomes are regarded as a side-effect of otherwise sound policies. This phenomenon can be seen in Ireland at the political level: the State's attempt to rectify profound gender inequalities in social welfare entitlements has consisted of women's 'insertion' into systems based on male lifestyles and needs. The practical difficulties and resultant inefficiencies of such an essentially gender-blind approach form a key theme of this discussion.

The Foundations of the Male Breadwinner Regime

The concept of the male breadwinner regime is an attractive one for interpreting Irish social policy. The pioneering work of Jane Lewis and Illona Ostner has highlighted how western Welfare States are organised on the basis of the male breadwinner family model. They argue that although the male breadwinner principle is a characteristic of all social welfare regimes, national variations exist. Accordingly Lewis and Ostner distinguish between three forms or 'strengths': strong (U.K., Ireland, Germany), modified (France) and weak (Sweden, Denmark) (see Lewis, 1992, Lewis and Ostner, 1994). (See Figure 1 in this volume in Cook and McCashin, 1997 for a schematic representation of the Lewis typology of welfare regimes). It is therefore important to note that although this discussion focuses on the Irish system, Ireland is by no means unique in the manner that it treats women in social welfare.[1]

As a strong male breadwinner regime, women's status as citizens in Ireland is strongly mediated by their family status as homemakers; that is, as wives, mothers and daughters (Lewis, 1992, Conroy Jackson, 1993, Sainsbury, 1994b). Strong regimes have historically discouraged women's labour market participation and treat women as homemakers rather than as breadwinners (Lewis, 1992). The remainder of this discussion illustrates this idea through a selective review of key aspects in the historical development of social welfare from the mid-nineteenth century to the present day.

The Poor Law

The origins of the male breadwinner model lie in the very foundations of the social welfare system itself. The system created was essentially foreign in origin, having been transposed from England onto Ireland in the 1830s. The 1834 English Poor Law was imported to Ireland in 1838 under the Poor Law (Ireland) Act. Not only did this Act lay the legislative foundations for a rudimentary system of poor relief provided in workhouses at the local or parish level and based on the principles of deterrence and stigma (Fraser, 1984), but it provided the gendered conceptual framework within which social welfare entitlements have since been framed.

Existing research into the history of social welfare has largely failed to highlight the fact that a rudimentary system of poor relief was operating sophisticated distinctions on the basis of gender (see, for example, the work of O Cinnéide, 1970, Cook, 1983). An exception is Burke's (1987) study of the Poor Law. She documented how women's experiences of the workhouse differed from those of men. Her research findings can be interpreted as evidence of State patriarchy insofar as the workhouses provided a substitute form of protection for women in the event of the absence or failure of men to provide for them. Thus, women were deemed 'deserving' and entitled to indoor relief only by proving that their husbands had either failed to provide for them or had deserted them for longer than twelve months. In effect, the public authorities would only act when the family (that is, husbands) had failed to provide for its members. This was in strict accordance with the principle of subsidiarity. The reality of the pervasive notion of the family as a primary provider of welfare was that women were assumed and expected to be economically dependent on men. It was assumed that the male breadwinner would adequately provide for the female homemaker until otherwise proven. Subsidiarity thus 'contributed to an official ideology of the privatised family' which has served to obscure the distribution of resources within the family (O'Dowd, 1987, p.30).

The efficiency and justness of the family as a means of distributing resources to meet the needs of individual members has been questioned by some (Millar and Glendinning, 1987, Daly, 1989, 1992). Indeed, women have always comprised the majority of the poor, but women's poverty was disguised by marriage (Lewis and Piachaud, 1987). In the Irish context, that marriage did not necessarily protect women from poverty can be seen in the fact that women outnumbered men in the workhouses by three to one (Burke, 1987). Notwithstanding women's over-representation in workhouses, this 'protection' for women through marriage served to place additional obstacles in the paths of impoverished women in accessing public forms of poverty relief compared with men. The prescribed twelve months' wait for married women under the Poor Law ensured that their access to public resources was dependent on their legal relationship to a man but also that the depth of poverty experienced by them would be greater than for men before being judged as eligible for indoor relief.

In 1847 the principle of no outdoor relief was reversed due to unprecedented strains placed on the local workhouse system by the Famine (1845-50). Outdoor relief provided for persons in their home was sanctioned for certain groups of destitute persons. Widows with two or more legitimate dependent children were the first group of people to be removed from the workhouse and entitled to outdoor relief. The distinctions made in order to both enter and remove certain groups of the poor from the workhouse were based on individuals' family status. Thus, although these selection criteria were formally gender-neutral insofar as entry was granted on the basis of a person being deemed 'deserving' or 'undeserving', the criteria were, at the level of administration, clearly gendered. This formed the system for categorising women (as wives and mothers) and relegated their depth of need to a secondary consideration. Thus, since the outset of public forms of poor relief, women have been treated differently and unequally as compared with men by the public authorities for the purposes of relieving poverty.

Social Insurance

Like the Poor Law which founded the basis of the social services and social assistance (Burke, 1987), the emerging system of public welfare and the concept of entitlements in the late nineteenth and early twentieth centuries were determined by British legislation. Although the National Insurance Act (1911) was preceeded by the Workmen's Compensation Act (1871) and the Pensions Act (1908),[2] it is commonly regarded as the cornerstone of the male breadwinner regime.

The National Insurance Act established health and unemployment benefits based on obligatory weekly contributions while in work in return for entitlement to benefit when sick or unemployed. The scheme was initially experimental and restricted to certain industries which were particularly liable to seasonal fluctuations; in 1920 it was extended to cover all employees and apprentices. Although it excluded the majority of the Irish workforce (for example, agricultural workers, the self-employed, employees in private domestic service and workers in non-manual employment whose pay was above a specified ceiling), the National Insurance Act was crucial because it formalised the unequal social value of men and women. The social insurance scheme defined women's labour as inferior to that of men as seen in the unequal rates of contribution and benefit. Figure 1 shows that these rates differentiated between adult men and women and between boys and girls. That the differential rate was applied to male and female children demonstrates that marital status was merely a manifestation of a deeper inequality based on gender. Male labour was accorded a higher social value than female labour.

Figure 1: *Rates of Contribution, Ordinary Rate October 1948*

	FROM EMPLOYER	FROM EMPLOYEES	TOTAL
shillings			
Man	1/0d.	-/11d.	1/11d.
Woman	-/10d.	-/9d.	1/7d.
Boy	-/6d.	-/5d.	-/11d.
Girl	-/5d.	-/5 d.	-/10d.

Source: Report of the Department of Social Welfare (1949).

The scheme also distinguished between different women on the basis of their marital status. Single women contributed as much as men although they were entitled to less benefit than them. Married women were automatically defined as dependants of their husbands and were therefore not entitled to any protection other than that which they derived from their legal relationship to an insured husband. The National Insurance Act set out the organising principles of a wage system designed to ensure that the male breadwinner could provide for his family. This principle can be seen in the following extract:

> Married women living with their husbands need not be included since where the unit is the family, it is the husband's and not the wife's health which it is important to insure. So long as the husband is in good health and able to work, adequate provision will be made for the needs of the family, irrespective of the wife's health, whereas when the husband's health fails there is no one to earn wages. (Government Actuaries, 1910, quoted in Fraser, 1984, p.167)

The principles underlying the National Insurance Act were extended and consolidated in 1921. Amending legislation introduced a system of supplements in the form of adult and child dependant's allowances which were paid as personal allowances to the (male) recipient of benefit in respect of his dependant wife, who was not in employment, and in respect of any children. Again, Ireland was not alone in designing a social protection system based on the principle of women's dependency, but the complex system of personal allowances in social welfare is peculiarly Irish. The treatment of women as dependants was also mirrored in the fiscal system. Tax concessions were calculated on the basis of presumed economies of scale resulting from marriage.[3] Single men and women were treated equally in relation to personal income tax, although single women were entitled to lower rates of allowance than were single men.

The development of the tax and social welfare system thus enshrined women as dependants in the private, familial sphere. The structure of social welfare created disincentives for wives to work and their exclusion from the labour force translated into their exclusion from social insurance schemes. Figure 2 illustrates the long-term consequences of the construction of women as dependants. It shows that women have essentially remained at the margins of the social insurance system throughout the twentieth century. While the proportion of insured women within the insured labour force rose by just over half between 1926 and 1979 (from twenty per cent to thirty-three per cent, respectively), the proportion of insured persons (men and women) within the labour force had more than tripled from nineteen per cent in 1926 to sixty-four per cent in 1979. From this it can be concluded that although the proportion of insured women as a proportion of the female workforce has increased (column 6), the relative gap between women and men in relation to core social insurance schemes has actually widened over the years (columns 3 and 4).

Statehood, Ideology and Social Welfare

The period following Ireland's Independence from Britain in 1921 and the foundation of the Free State in 1922 witnessed a marked strengthening of the

Figure 2: *Women, Unemployment Insurance and the Labour Force, 1926-1979* [1]

YEAR	(1) INSURED POPULATION	(2) INSURED WOMEN	(3) INSURED WOMEN AS A PROPORTION OF THE INSURED POPULATION (%)	(4) INSURED PERSONS AS A PROPORTION OF THE LABOUR FORCE[2] (%)	(5) INSURED WOMEN AS A PROPORTION OF THE LABOUR FORCE (%)	(6) INSURED WOMEN AS A PROPORTION OF THE FEMALE LABOUR FORCE (%)
1926	246,134	50,450	20	19	4	15
1936	411,418	89,474	22	31	7	25
1946	433,427	113,791	26	33	9	34
1951	514,611	138,182	27	40	11	42
1961	629,316	187,842	30	49	15	65
1966	688,410	219,727	32	61	20	76
1971	732,943	262,807	36	65	23	91
1979[3]	820,000	270,000	33	64	21	75

Source: author's own calculations based on the Census of the Population and Statistical Information on Social Welfare Services (Department of Social Welfare)

Notes:

1. 1979 is the last year for which information distinguishing between men and women in relation to Unemployment Insurance was published. Although 1985 was the last year for which information relating to insured persons for unemployment as opposed to persons insured for all benefits, it is not possible to determine the proportion of women and men insured.
2. Labour force size is derived from Census figures: the labour force in 1926 was occupied persons twelve years old and over, in 1946 it included persons aged fourteen years and over, in 1986 it included persons of fifteen years and over. 'Occupied' persons excludes retired persons, students, people who have not yet entered the labour market, people on 'home duties'.
3. Estimated figure for this year.

prescription of women's role as homemakers. Rather than dismantling British institutions and rejecting their operational assumptions, the State built on gender prescriptions and overt forms of discrimination were successively introduced. The Committee of Inquiry into Health Insurance and Medical Services (1925) paved the way for the introduction of the marriage grant and marriage bar. These had the effect of removing women from public sector employment upon marriage and closing their insurance record (women received a one-off payment and were obliged to forfeit their entitlements to insurance benefits). The new government's policy of 'reform pending thorough restructuring' effectively meant that women were excluded from full citizenship in the new Ireland.

The reforms to public assistance and local administration in 1923 abolished workhouses and boards of guardians and loosened the restrictions on outdoor relief, thereby permitting a greater number of people to be provided for at home.[4] Outdoor relief was formally renamed Home Assistance. Two-thirds of the recipients of Home Assistance were women. This proportion increased in subsequent decades as predominantly male workers were lifted out of the class of Home Assistance recipients and incorporated into an expanding system of social insurance. Thus, while men were gradually 'vertically' incorporated into national social insurance schemes, women were 'horizontally' transferred between reformed schemes of local poor relief. Due to their over-representation within the poor law and social assistance schemes and due to the discretionary, social control dimension of these, women are particularly affected by any changes to these structures. In fact, the unwillingness of successive Irish governments to abolish the concept of local poor relief is borne out each time these schemes have come under review. In effect, this 'review' has amounted to relabelling without fundamental overhaul: outdoor relief was renamed Home Assistance in 1923 and again Supplementary Welfare Allowance in 1975. Despite some attempt to ensure uniformity of service and to introduce a right of appeal, the localised, discretionary and stigmatising nature of the poor law tradition has been retained to the present day.

The 1930s was a crucial period in understanding the particular strength of the male breadwinner model in Ireland. This was the period during which the State sought to consolidate its legitimacy (O'Dowd, 1987) through inter alia the expansion of the social welfare system and the development of national schemes in particular. In effect, the development of social rights which marginalised women as dependants was integral to the consolidation of the State and the search for Irish identity (Meaney, 1993). At a cultural level this entailed the exercise of power over women in a variety of spheres, and was reflected in the close scrutiny of the role of women and control over their bodies and sexuality (Meaney, 1993, Mahon, 1995). In this respect, the 1937 Constitution represented a marked break from England by reinforcing the role of married women in particular as homemakers.[5] This is apparent in the clear subordination of women within the emergent social welfare system: the nature of the development of social assistance has consolidated both the sex segregated structure of social welfare and the unequal terms on which women were entitled to payments. Evidence from abroad suggests that such segregation is not a unique Irish phenomenon, but has been a common feature of social welfare across Europe, Australia and North America (Lewis, 1992, Sainsbury, 1993, 1994a). In this respect, the idealisation of women as homemakers in the private sphere is to an extent a reflection of international ideologies which influenced other countries but which were magnified by the social conservatism of Irish political ideology and religion - Catholic nationalism. These ideologies converged on the definition of the family and marriage as the natural sphere of women (O'Dowd, 1987, Nic Ghiolla Phádraig, 1995). The Irish system of sex segregation developed in the 1930s is discussed below in the context of the Unemployment Assistance Act and the Widows' and Orphans' Pensions Act.

The Unemployment Assistance Act (1933)

Having attended to the reform of local social assistance in 1923, the Irish government embarked on the establishment of national programmes of social assistance in the 1930s. A dual structure of social assistance was created, one local and one national. Responsibility for the provision of relief for unemployed people (including agricultural workers) was transferred from local communities (Home Assistance) to the State (Unemployment Assistance scheme). However, the political focus on the structure of social assistance did not extend to a review of its underlying principles which were retained as a model for organising national programmes. A consistent assumption underlying the reforms was that the family was the core institution by which the welfare of individual citizens was ensured. Again, women's legal and social status as wives served to ensure that they would only be entitled to social assistance if their husband was ineligible. Figure 3 illustrates the centrality of family status in determining the social value of citizens. It is this conceptual classification which has both served to devalue women and privilege men. It can be seen that women's rates of payment are consistently lower than men's in comparable categories by three shillings.

Figure 3: *Unemployment Assistance: Rate of Benefit (Borough of Dun Laoghaire, 1947)*

	RATE OF BENEFIT
shillings	
Man, no dependants	16/0d.
Spinster or widow, no dependants	13/0d.
Man with dependant wife	22/6d.
Married woman with dependant husband	19/0d.
Man with dependant wife and one other dependant	25/0d.
Married woman, dependant husband and one other dependant	22/0d.

Source: *Report of the Department of Social Welfare* (1948).

Widows' and Orphans' Pension Act (1935)

The origins of the Widows' and Orphans' Pension Act lay in a concern to upgrade the economic status of deceased workers' wives (who comprised one in three of all of the recipients of Home Assistance and one in two women recipients of Home Assistance). The extent of poverty amongst widows was explained in terms of the incomplete development of the male breadwinner regime which did not provide total coverage of the labour force, rather than by the unequal terms on which entitlements had actually evolved. Although women's poverty was due to the deficiencies and inefficiencies of a social insurance system designed for men, the solution advanced was to extend the male breadwinner logic and create new categories of benefit and assistance for women.

Thus the Widows' and Orphans' Pension Act replicated a two-tiered insurance and assistance structure. Widows' entitlements to insurance benefit were determined by their deceased husband's contribution record. Widows whose husbands had not established a sufficient record were entitled to the social assistance payment. The Act introduced the further condition that if the claimant of insurance or assistance payments either remarried or cohabited she would lose her entitlements derived from her first marriage. This was based on the assumption and prescription of women's dependency on men.

This parallel system removed widows from the body of the poor (that is, from Home Assistance) and up-graded their treatment through the development of a national scheme for them. The fact that widows were the first group of women benefitting from special schemes to improve their standard of living and that they have fared comparatively better than other groups of women (for example, unmarried mothers) does not detract from the general point that these schemes perpetuated women's marginality within social welfare. In effect, policy-makers had attempted to apply the principles of a system based on male patterns of labour market participation in designing a system for a particular group of women. However, as social welfare was designed with men in mind and as women were regarded as a category of the population, the system was only able to accommodate women by grafting on to it a parallel system of categorical benefits which replicated the prescription of women's dependency.

Redistributive Politics in the Post-War Period

The Second World War is often regarded as a landmark in the development of the Welfare State and in the development of women's emancipation. More 'outward-looking' and 'progressive' policies were developed during the 1950s and 1960s in an attempt to raise Irish social welfare services to British and

European standards (Cook, 1983, McCashin, 1985, Maguire, 1986, Breen et al., 1990, O'Connell and Rottman, 1992). The emphasis of the reforms of the Social Welfare Act (1952) was on extending and upgrading the value of social insurance benefits, bringing groups of hitherto excluded groups of workers into existing compulsory schemes and introducing additional insurance benefits. While this may have addressed the exclusion of a substantial proportion of the workforce, it reinforced the gendered principles underlying women's entitlements and their position at the margins of social welfare. Thus, the male breadwinner model retained its dominance as a mode of social organisation through the growing role of the State in social provision.

The Social Welfare Act was central to setting the nature and pace of social welfare development during this period. The commitment to expand social insurance formed part of an overall move to rationalise the administrative and organisational basis of social welfare in an attempt to integrate and simplify the system. The Department of Social Welfare was founded (1947) to centralise and coordinate existing schemes. Resources were channelled into social insurance, thereby automatically privileging men and indirectly discriminating against women (Home Assistance did not benefit from these reforms). The volume of national resources invested in schemes which benefitted men can be appreciated by considering that welfare expenditure increased by thirteen per cent between 1947-1952, while GDP grew by 3.7 per cent over the same period.

Notwithstanding these changes, Conroy Jackson (1993) argues that the transition was marked more by continuity in the treatment of women as homemakers than by change. She notes the 'rigidity and persistence of the state in sustaining and prescribing the place of women and mothers as primarily in the home' (p.73). Women's marginality to social welfare was in fact consolidated by the insurance-based, categorical logic of development underpinning State expansion in social welfare. Indeed, the proportion of women entering the labour market and benefitting from the expansion of social insurance was low. Between 1946 and 1961 while the insured population as a proportion of the labour force rose from thirty-three per cent to forty-nine per cent, the corresponding figures for women rose from nine per cent to just fifteen per cent (Figure 2). Furthermore, between 1935 and 1970, the proportion of women recipients of Home Assistance increased from fifty-seven per cent to sixty-eight per cent, indicating the gradual removal of men from that stream of welfare into an expanding social insurance system.

The post-war Welfare State can be regarded as an historically specific variant of the male breadwinner regime which has progressively enshrined and strengthened women's status as homemakers first as a Kingdom, as a Free State and then as a Republic. The development of social rights in post-war Ireland was a regressive, exclusive and uneven process which directly discriminated against women. For example, Unemployment Insurance was extended to male employees engaged in private domestic service or agriculture in 1953, while thirteen years elapsed before Unemployment Insurance was extended to female employees in the same sectors. Women, higher-paid employees and the self-employed remained largely excluded from the system. The constitutional reverence of women's life within the home ensured their marginalisation from the benefits of economic growth and social welfare development.

The State's practice of categorising and differentiating between women as an integral feature of welfare expansionism accelerated. The Social Welfare Act equalised rates of benefit for single women with those of single men. It is not possible, however, to interpret this as indicative of a narrowing of gender inequality or of an authentic attempt to promote substantive gender equality because women's entitlements still depended on their marital or parental status. Discriminatory practices such as the marriage bar (lifted as late as 1973), the 'marriage grant', 'small stamps' (lower contributions and lower rates of benefit for shorter periods of time) for married women and the payment of adult dependant's allowances in respect of them were all retained.

In other words, the moves towards equalisation through the eradication of a limited aspect of sex discrimination for single women did not counterbalance the overriding commitment to perpetuate women's inequality through developing the male breadwinner model. Indeed, the limited equalisation of rates of benefit ignores the fact that all women were scrutinised as homemakers even when some were incorporated into the male breadwinner system ostensibly as 'equals'. To argue otherwise is to perceive absolute legislative and procedural changes as evidence of a narrowing of gender inequality and to focus on isolated changes rather than the perpetuation of inequality. Further, it is tantamount to regarding substantive sex inequalities in social welfare as a procedural anomaly rather than as an inherent feature of the system's design.

Equal Rights and the Women Only Schemes

The 1960s and 1970s witnessed stronger demands for equality under 'second wave' feminism (Mahon, 1987, 1995, Smyth, 1988). Catalysts for the renewed Women's Movement in the Republic of Ireland were the Civil Rights Movements in the US and Northern Ireland, student rebellion in America and Europe and the resurgence of Republicanism in southern Ireland (Smyth, 1988). Women's organisations, politicians and bureaucrats converged in their concern for inter alia equal rights for women at work and in social welfare.[6] The First Commission on the Status of Women was established in 1970 following the report of an ad hoc committee to investigate discrimination against women in Ireland. An interim report on Equal Pay (1971) and a full report detailing nearly fifty recommendations (1972) were published. In 1973 the Council for the Status of Women was established to monitor the implementation of these recommendations and to coordinate women's organisations (Smyth, 1988).

Smyth (1988) argues that the liberal reformist agenda of the 1968 ad hoc committee paved the way for the ensuing legislative reforms of the early to mid 1970s.[7] In particular, the Employment of Married Women Act (1973) and the Anti-Discrimination (Pay) Act (1974) phased out the marriage bar for public sector female workers and legislated for equal pay. The Employment Equality Act (1977) eliminated discrimination in employment or promotion on the grounds of sex or marital status (Mahon, 1995). A range of 'women's benefits' were also introduced during the late 1960s and early 1970s: Prescribed Relatives' Allowance (1968); Deserted Wife's Allowance (1970); Deserted Wife's Benefit (1973); Unmarried Mother's Allowance (1973); Prisoner's Wife's Allowance (1974), and the Single Woman's Allowance (1974).[8] These were all social assistance payments, with the exception of Deserted Wife's Benefit.

These and other concrete achievements were in part a result of pressure on Ireland from external institutions. The introduction of equal pay was a result of Ireland's accession to the EEC in 1973. As a member state Ireland was obliged to implement article 119 on equal pay for equal work.[9] The Council of Europe Committee passed on recommendations regarding the treatment of unmarried mothers, and the United Nations designated 1974 as the International Women's Year. These external pressures on the State undoubtedly helped legitimate some of the demands made by the Women's Movement (Mahon, 1987).

The phased introduction of these women only schemes subscribe to the broader historical process of the gender restructuring of welfare. They extend the category-based provisions for widows introduced in 1935. This historical process has essentially consisted of a simultaneous and mutually complementary process of the dismantling of one unacceptable form of discrimination against women and the introduction of new structures which reinforce women's status as wives, mothers and daughters, but above all as private unpaid carers. Further, these schemes constitute a remedial measure, patching over the inefficiencies and harsher edges of the system.

The importance of these schemes lies in the fact that they marked the first phase of moves towards 'equality' (Whyte, 1995) and the individualisation of rights. Women formerly entitled only to Home Assistance were eligible for payments in their own right but ultimately on the basis of their family status (as wives, mothers, daughters) rather than on their citizenship. In this sense, although these schemes represented some advance they did not amount to an outright transition from the system of derived rights for women based on their relationship to men to an individual model based on individual and equal entitlement to benefits as citizens (see Sainsbury, 1994b).[10] In effect, the rights and needs of women were addressed by the State only insofar as they coincided with its prescription of female domesticity under article 41 of the Constitution (Conroy Jackson, 1993). The State responded to demands for equal rights for women through incremental reform while firmly retaining the principle of sexual difference and inequality.

The Unmarried Mother's Allowance illustrates this point. Through the introduction of the Unmarried Mother's Allowance the State accepted the right of lone mothers and their extra-marital children to public support. This was viewed as a victory by Cherish (an association of lone mothers). However, its introduction can be explained in terms of protecting the special role of motherhood within Irish society. The British Abortion Act (1967) allowed Irish women (eighty per cent of whom were unmarried) to avail of Britain's abortion facilities. Receipt of the payment prohibited lone mothers taking up paid work and effectively constituted a 'wage' for full-time homemakers. According to Conroy Jackson (1993), it both corresponded to article 41 of the Constitution and offered an incentive for mothers to stay at home; it was 'a form of bonus for those deserving mothers who had continued with their pregnancies' (p.83). In addition, the Unmarried Mother's Allowance dovetailed with the gendered categorical development of social policy for women in Ireland insofar as it created a separate administrative category for a particular group of women.

This introduction of 'new' entitlements for women took place alongside another concerted move to upgrade social insurance. This entailed a move from flat-rate to pay-related benefits in 1974. In the same year, the Abolition of Insurance Limit Act extended social insurance to all private sector employees, but not to self-employed or part-time workers, of which a sizeable proportion were women. Thus, while women were principally affected by reforms to social assistance which further enshrined their role as homemakers, men benefitted from the expansion of work-related social insurance benefits. This has essentially been the history of social welfare development since Independence. When women were transferred into social insurance it was as deserted wives or widows, that is, as women whose husbands had failed to provide for them due to absence or death. 'Equality' thus amounted to reform of the margins of the male breadwinner model; it was in effect procedural equality underpinned by substantive inequality of status. Not only therefore were the categories of restructuring gendered but Ireland retained the Poor Law model in both spirit and structure for its female citizens. Women were still defined in relation to men, and their entitlements, as indicated by the titles of the range of women's benefits, 'depended on the gravity of their status as victims of male sexuality, abandonment and crime' (Conroy Jackson, 1993, p.84).

The emergence of the category of desertion in its own right at this time is particularly revealing. As a concept, it has been present in social welfare since the Poor Law. As under the Poor Law, women applying for the deserted wife's payments had to prove their sexual and moral innocence. In other words, a woman had to prove she had been deserted by her husband for at least three months (under the Poor Law it was twelve months), that she had made all reasonable efforts to be reconciled with him and that she had already attempted to obtain maintenance payments from him. Individualisation merely resulted in the reduction by nine months of the period of desertion; the organising concept remained intact!

Current Developments: The Reconfiguration of Inequality

The 1980s and 1990s have proved in some respects to be a turning point in the social welfare system. Whyte (1995) identifies two phases during this period. The first is the litigious process of the implementation of the EC 1979 Equal Treatment Directive to remove discrimination against married women from social welfare schemes covering work-related contingencies such as sickness, accident and unemployment. Women were legally entitled to claim benefit at the same rate and duration as men and were entitled to claim Unemployment Assistance in their own right. The Irish government's shameful stalling of the Directive's implementation for more than fifteen years testifies to the extent that the granting equal entitlements to married women requires fundamental change and assumptions in the structure of social welfare.

The second phase that Whyte identifies is the abolition of the women's benefits that were introduced in the 1970s. The payments to the various categories of women (widows, unmarried mothers, deserted wives) were extended to men in comparable circumstances. He notes the striking comparison between the Department's reluctance to implement the EC Equal Treatment Directive which benefitted women and the readiness with which the Department undertook 'on its own initiative and without any pressure from the courts' the reforms to eliminate discrimination against men (Whyte, 1995, p.11).

Notwithstanding attempts to eliminate formal sex discrimination against either sex in social welfare, the historical process of categorisation and differentiation of women has continued well into the 1990s. The recent reform of provisions for lone mothers can be understood in this light. In 1990 lone mothers were transferred from the array of women's benefits (Unmarried Mother's Allowance, Deserted Wives payments) into a new unified category, the Lone Parent's Allowance.[11] The different statuses - separated, deserted, prisoner's spouse, widowed, unmarried - were retained for administrative purposes and are used in the enumeration of welfare recipients in the Department's annual statistical reports. Compared with the schemes of the 1970s, the reforms in the 1990s formally distinguished between women who were or who had been wives (deserted and prisoners' wives, widows) and those who are mothers who may or may not also be wives (lone parents). Once again, the State had failed to define women by anything other than by their family status.

Given the Department of Social Welfare's profound resistance to undertake thorough restructuring of the system and its piecemeal approach to reform, the direction taken in the 1990s seems bleak. The divorce referendum appeared to offer the best hope for some moving away from the marital family as the organising basis of social welfare. However, the ideology of dependency which is engrained in policy reappeared during the passage of the Social Welfare Bill No. 2 during 1995. The Social Welfare (No. 2) Bill was introduced in advance of the 1995 divorce referendum. The Bill aimed to 'provide for the necessary changes in the Social Welfare Code so as to ensure that no spouse will be disadvantaged in terms of his or her social welfare entitlements as a result of his or her legal status being changed from married, separated or deserted to divorced' (Explanatory Memorandum). The Bill introduces a new class of claimants as defined by their marital status (divorcee) and ensures equality of status between different categories of claimants whose marriages have broken down (that is, between divorced, separated, deserted women). Under the Bill, for the purposes of the Department of Social Welfare, a divorced woman will be treated as the current wife of her former husband. Thus, a woman may be entitled to claim, for example, Survivor's Pension on her former husband's record. She may qualify for Widow's (non-contributory) Pension if she fails to qualify for the insurance-based Survivor's Pension (cohabitation acts as a bar to entitlement). As there are no restrictions on the number of times men can remarry, the Department is faced with the potential prospect of multiple people claiming benefits off a single contributions record. This may cause severe strain on the finances of social welfare. For all intents and purposes women's entitlements will still be defined by their former legal relationship with men, despite the severing of that relationship by the courts.

Conclusion

The need for an individualised model of social welfare entitlements to replace the current male breadwinner model has never been more pressing. The attempts over the past twenty-five years to introduce more individualised entitlements for women have merely postponed the introduction of an authentic individualised model of social welfare, created enormous political, legal and administrative problems in their wake and perpetuated profound inequalities. The State has continued to operate notions of women as separate and unequal to men, upholding public and private patriarchy through social welfare policy. Yet the State has become a prisoner of its own making, locked into the anomalies and inefficiencies of the male breadwinner logic. Ireland has faced huge problems in reconciling demands for equality from women and from the EU with a system premised on women's inequality.

This historical review has aimed to shed new light on the gendered nature of redistributive politics, on the processes by which men and women have been incorporated as citizens of the State and the centrality of women's welfare entitlements in understanding the overall structure of social welfare. The State has pursued strategies of division, differentiation, categorisation and exclusion. Marginalisation and exclusion has been the price paid by women as the State has sought to affirm its legitimacy. Therefore, it is not evident that sporadic equality measures such as they are presently framed are sufficient to bridge the vastness of the gender division in social welfare. Indeed, the very categories of development and change are gendered. As inequalities have been constructed, dismantled and replaced by new ones, women's inequality has been modified but not fundamentally altered as their structural position remains at the margins of social welfare.

Discussion Topics

1. Discuss how the constitutional prescription of women as homemakers has influenced the development of the Irish social welfare system.

2. To what extent do women's experiences of social welfare in Ireland differ in the 1990s as compared with the mid-nineteenth century?

3. To what extent can the model of equality that the Irish State has pursued be said to be ineffective as a strategy for promoting women's full citizenship?

4. What are the strategic considerations and difficulties to take account of in reforming social welfare with a view to creating gender equality?

Acknowledgement

This article is based on research undertaken by the author while based in the Women's Education, Research and Resource Centre, University College Dublin (WERRC) during 1994-95. The research was part of a comparative research programme entitled 'Gender and European Welfare Regimes', coordinated by Professor Jane Lewis of the London School of Economics and sponsored by the Human Capital Mobility Programme of the DGXII of the European Commission. The author would like to acknowledge and thank the anonymous reviewer of the first draft of this article and in particular Dr. Pauline Conroy Jackson for her support and insights during the course of the research.

Notes

1. Readers interested in understanding how Irish women fared compared with women in other countries are initially referred to the work of Jane Lewis (1992), Nicola Yeates (1995) and Diane Sainsbury (1994a).
2. The Workmen's Compensation Act (1897) established a legally enforceable entitlement to benefit, rendering employers fully liable for accidents to employees while at work and obliged them to compensate certain classes of workers according to fixed scales and rates. The 1908 Pensions Act established the principle of entitlement to support from the state in old age, and did much to remove elderly people over the age of seventy from the workhouse by providing them with a basic pension. The majority of these people were in fact women due to their greater longevity and lower earning capacity. The Pensions Act also advanced the idea of public assistance based on means-testing and some modicum of entitlement, as opposed to discretionary poor relief. It was intended that the pension would supplement rather than replace income and the means of recipients were assessed on a household basis. This meant that the resources of husbands and wives were assessed together rather than individually: it was assumed that a household's resources were equally shared.
3. In the case of dual earner couples (who constituted five per cent of all couples at the time), the husband was responsible for the payment of his wife's tax. This entailed aggregating the couple's incomes to arrive at a taxable joint income; wive's tax allowances could be claimed by the husbands for themselves. This effectively amounted to de facto redistribution from women to men within marriage.
4. Home Assistance was administered by the local authorities. The service consisted of payments made in cash or kind to a person residing at home. Poor relief was subject to changes in the law relating to the operation of local schemes. Local authorities each fixed their own criteria of eligibility and rate of payment, although the Minister of Local Government could amend or alter any scheme to achieve a degree of uniformity. Effectively though there were wide disparities in Home Assistance between counties. The service is administered by locally-based officers, known as Assistance Officers (colloquially, Relieving Officers). Home Assistance was the scheme of the last resort, and the recipients were those who did not fall into existing schemes or for whom existing schemes did not meet their needs fully. See O'CinnÇide (1970) for a full history of the scheme.

5. Article 41.1.1 defined the family as a 'moral institution, possessing inalienable and imprescriptible rights'. Further, that 'by her life within the home, woman gives the State a support without which the common good cannot be achieved' (41.2.1) and that the 'State shall therefore endeavour to ensure that mothers shall not be obliged by economic necessity to engage in labour to the neglect of their duties in the home'.

6. Smyth lists the complete aims of the Irish Women's Liberation Movement as: One Family, one House; Equal Rights in Law; Equal Pay Now; Removal of the Marriage Bar; Justice for Widows, Deserted Wives, Unmarried Mothers; Equal Educational Opportunities and Contraception - a human right (p.335).

7. Evelyn Mahon (1995) notes other legal changes: the Juries Act (1976) made women eligible for jury service; the Family Home Protection Act (1976) ensured that the family home could not be sold without the consent of the partner; the Family Law (Maintenance of Spouses and Children) Act (1976) obliged the spouse to support their partner and children (p.682).

8. Prescribed Relatives' Allowance was paid as a supplement to the pension of the 'caree' rather than the carer. In order to claim the Allowance, prescribed female relatives had to provide full-time care and were prohibited from taking paid employment. It was in effect a replacement for earnings, albeit paid to the caree. Carers were thus dependants of those whom they cared for. The Allowance was not payable in respect of married women as it was assumed that they would be at home providing care for free anyway. New claimants were transferred to the replacement payment Carer's Allowance in 1990. The Prescribed Relative's Allowance still exists, but as a residual category. The Deserted Wife's schemes were open to women who had been deserted by their husbands for a period of more than three months. Desertion was in effect an insurable contingency to cover women against the potential loss of protection resulting from their husbands' flight. Prisoner's Wife's Allowance was a means-tested benefit payable to women aged forty or over whose husbands were imprisoned for more than six months. The Single Woman's Allowance was introduced to provide an income for unmarried women who had not established a contributions record due to their having left the labour force to care for their parents. In effect, it covered the consequences of the Prescribed Relatives' Allowance which prevented women from building up a contributions record. Readers are referred to the past and current versions of the Department of Social Welfare Guide to Social Welfare Services for more details on the qualifying criteria of each scheme.

9. The principle of equal pay for women was reluctantly accepted by the Irish government. In 1973 the government sent a delegation of civil servants to Brussels to obtain a derogation from article 119. This demand was refused by the other member states (Conroy, 1992).

10. Under the individual model women and men would have shared roles as both earners and carers, the individual would be the recipient of benefit and the unit of both benefits and contributions for the purposes of both tax and social welfare. Employment and wage policies would be aimed at both sexes equally (see Sainsbury, 1994b, p.153).

11. The Lone Parent's Allowance was introduced in 1990. Men and women recipients with children were transferred from Deserted Wife's payments and Prisoner's Wife's Allowance to the new scheme, while those without children remained in the existing schemes. It is a means-tested payment and claimants must have at least one dependant child residing with them to qualify and must not be cohabiting. Refer to the Department of Social Welfare's Guide to Social Welfare Services for further information.

References and Further Reading

Breen, R, Hannan, D F, Rottman, D B and Whelan, C T. 1990 *Understanding Contemporary Ireland: State, Class and Development in the Republic of Ireland* Dublin: Gill and Macmillan.

Bryson, L. 1992 *Welfare and the State: Who Benefits?* London: Macmillan.

Burke, H. 1987 *The People and the Poor Law in Ireland* Littlehampton: WEB.

Conroy, P. 1992 *Twenty Years in the European Community: What Now? Boom or Doom*, paper to the 12th Pearse School 10-11 April, Dublin.

Conroy Jackson, P. 1993 'Managing the Mothers: the Case of Ireland' in Lewis J. (ed.) *Women and Social Policies in Europe. Work, Family and the State* Aldershot: Edward Elgar.

Cook, G. 1983 'The Growth and Development of the Social Security System in the Republic of Ireland' *Social Studies* 7(2), pp.127-142.

Cook, G, McCashin, T. 1992 *Inequality, Litigation and Policy Resolution: Gender Dependence in Social Security and Personal Income Tax in the Republic of Ireland* Social Security: 50 years after Beveridge, paper presented to York University Conference.

Cook, G, McCashin, T. 1997 'Male Breadwinner: A Case Study of Gender and Social Security in the Republic of Ireland' in Byrne, A and Leonard, M. (eds.) *Women and Irish Society: A Sociological Reader* Belfast: Beyond the Pale Publications.

Cousins, M. 1995 *The Irish Social Welfare System: Law and Social Policy* Dublin: The Round Hall Press.

Daly, M. 1989 *Women and Poverty in Ireland* Dublin: Attic Press/Combat Poverty Agency.

Daly, M. 1992 'Europe's Poor Women? Gender in research on Poverty' *European Social Review* 8(1) pp.1-12.

Donnelly A. 1993 'Social Welfare Law' in Connelly, A. (ed.) *Gender and the Law in Ireland* Dublin: Oak Tree.

Duncan, S. 1995 'Theorising European Gender Systems' *Journal of European Social Policy* 5(4) pp.263-84.

Evason, E. 1993 'Women and Poverty' in Smyth A. (ed.) *Irish Women's Studies Reader* Dublin: Attic Press.

Fraser, D. 1984 *The Evolution of the British Welfare State: A History of Social Policy since the Industrial Revolution* 2nd edition, London: Macmillan.

Langan, M and Ostner, I. 1991 'Gender and Welfare' in Room G. (ed.) *Towards a European Welfare State?* Bristol: Social Policy Association with School for Advanced Urban Studies pp.127-150.

Lewis, J and Ostner, I. 1994 *Gender and the Evolution of European Social Policies* working paper 4/94, Centre for Social Policy Research, Bremen.

Lewis, J. 1992 'Gender and the Development of Welfare Regimes' *Journal of European Social Policy* 2(3) pp.159-73.

Lewis, J and Piachaud, D. 1987 'Women and Poverty in the Twentieth Century' in Glendinning, C and Millar, J. (eds.) *Women and Poverty in Britain* Hemel Hempstead: Harvester Wheatsheaf.

Maguire, M. 1986 'Ireland' in Flora, P. (ed.) *Growth to Limits: the Western European Welfare States since World War II* vol 2 Berlin: Walter de Gruyter.

Mahon, E. 1987 'Women's Rights and Catholicism in Ireland' *New Left Review* No. 166, pp.53-77.

Mahon, E. 1995 'From Democracy to Femocracy: the Women's Movement in the Republic of Ireland' in Clancy, P, Drudy, S, Lynch, K and O'Dowd L. (eds.) *Irish Society - Sociological Perspectives* Dublin: Institute of Public Administration in association with the Sociological Association of Ireland pp.675-708.

McCashin, A. 1985 'Social Policy: 1957-1982' *Administration* 30 pp.203-23.

Meaney, G. 1993 'Sex and Nation' in Smyth A. (ed.) *Irish Women's Studies Reader* Dublin: Attic Press.

Millar, J and Glendinning, C. 1987 'Invisible Women, Invisible Poverty' in Glendinning, C and Millar, J. (eds.) *Women and Poverty in Britain* Hemel Hempstead: Harvester Wheatsheaf.

Nic Ghiolla Phádraig, M. 1995 'The Power of the Catholic Church in the Republic of Ireland' in *Irish Society - Sociological Perspectives* Clancy, P, Drudy, S, Lynch, K and O'Dowd, L. (eds.) Dublin: Institute of Public Administration in association with the Sociological Association of Ireland.

O Cinnéide, S. 1970 *A Law for the Poor* Dublin: Institute of Public Administration.

O'Connell, P, Rottman, D. 1992 'The Irish Welfare State in Comparative Perspective' in Goldthorpe, J and Whelan, C. (eds.) *The Development of Industrial Society in Ireland* Oxford: Oxford University Press, pp.205-39.

O'Dowd, L. 1987 'Church, State and Women: The Aftermath of Partition' in Curtin, C, Jackson, P and O'Connor, B. (eds.) *Gender in Irish Society* Galway: Galway University Press pp.5-36.

Pascall, G. 1986 *Social Policy: A Feminist Analysis* London: Routledge.

Sainsbury, D. 1993 'Dual Welfare and Sex Segregation of Access to Social Benefits: Income Maintenance Policies in the UK, the US, the Netherlands and Sweden' *Journal of Social Policy* 22(1) pp.69-98.

Sainsbury, D. (ed.) 1994a *Gendering Welfare States* London: Sage.

Sainsbury, D. 1994b 'Women's and Men's Social Rights' in Sainsbury, D. (ed.) *Gendering Welfare States* London: Sage.

Smyth, A. 1988 'The Contemporary Women's Movement in the Republic of Ireland' *Women's Studies International Forum* 11(4) pp.331-341.

Thiele, B. 1992 'Vanishing Acts in Social and Political Thought: Tricks of the Trade' in McDowell, L and Pringle, R. (eds.) *Defining Women: Social Institutions and Gender Divisions* Milton Keynes: Open University.

Whyte, G F. 1995 *Gender Equality in the Irish Social Welfare System* Dublin: Trinity College.

Wilson, E. 1977 *Women and the Welfare State* London: Tavistock.

Yeates, N. 1995 *Unequal Status, Unequal Treatment. The Gender Restructuring of Welfare in Ireland* report prepared under the Human Capital Mobility Programme for the DGXII of the European Commission, Brussels.

Young, G, Fort, L, Danner, M. 1994 'Moving from the 'Status of Women' to 'Gender Inequality': Conceptualisation, Social Indicators and an Empirical Application', *International Sociology* 9(1) pp.55-85.

10.

Male Breadwinner: A Case Study of Gender and Social Security in the Republic of Ireland.

Geoffrey Cook and Anthony McCashin

Introduction

T his chapter seeks to understand the problems of reforming the Irish social security system by removing a patriarchal legacy and the establishment of greater gender equity in the system. The Irish social security system as it was developed in the 1950s through to the 1970s was a very unequal system with often different contribution and benefit rules between men and women and in many cases any entitlement to benefit was contingent on a woman's relationship to a man.

Instead of offering a generic gender based critique of the social security system, this chapter seeks to focus on the ways in which policy makers in the Republic of Ireland responded to the European Community's Directive on Equal Treatment in Social Security. The tortuous process of the implementation of this Directive reveals a great deal about gender assumptions concerning women's economic role and also about the nature of the Irish policy making process.

Social Security in the Republic of Ireland

The modern Irish social security system was established in the immediate post war period and was greatly influenced by the famous British Beveridge Report (Beveridge, 1942). Ireland's system was based on three types of payment. First, social insurance was a flat rate in terms of contributions and benefits and limited to employees earning beneath a specific threshold. Contributions came from employees, employers and the State. Second, social assistance was means tested and was financed by the State, and thirdly, children's allowances (later called child benefit) were State financed and eventually extended to all children in the State.

The social insurance system established in the 1950s was a very limited version of the British system. Middle to high earners were excluded from the

Irish system as were farmers, the self employed and public servants. Also, there was no insurance based old age pension in the initial post war system. In the 1960s, the social insurance dimension to the system was expanded with the introduction of old age pensions, occupational injuries payments and pay related supplements to insurance benefits. Social insurance was eventually extended to all employees including the self employed.

More pertinently, the Beveridge system of social insurance treated married women as a special insurance class.

> All women by marriage acquire a new economic and social status with risks and rights different from those of the unmarried. On marriage a woman gains a legal right to maintenance by her husband as a first line of defence against risks which fall directly on the solitary woman; she undertakes at the same time to perform vital unpaid service and becomes exposed to new risks, including the risk that her married life may be ended prematurely by widowhood or separation (Beveridge, 1942, p.49).

Beveridge acknowledged that some married women would be gainfully employed but he distinguished their earnings status from that of single women and all men in two ways. First, her earnings would be liable to interruptions by childbirth and an expectant mother 'should be under no economic pressure to continue to work as long as she can or to return to it as soon as she can'. Second, Beveridge argued that married women's earnings should be seen as secondary.

> Unless there are children, the housewife earnings in general are a means not of subsistence but of a standard of living above subsistence like the higher earnings of a skilled man compared with a labourer .... In sickness or unemployment the housewife does not need compensating benefit on the same scale as the solitary woman because, among other things, her home is provided for her either by her husband's earnings or benefits if his earning is interrupted (Beveridge,1942, p.49).

This reasoning led Beveridge to propose a lower rate of benefit for married women relative to unmarried women and all men. In Ireland this male breadwinner model was a central feature of the social security system which derived from the Beveridge inspired White Paper A Plan for Social Security (Ireland, 1948) and the truncated version which was implemented as the Social Welfare Act 1952.

On marriage a female contributor to the social insurance system received a marriage grant which closed her contribution record. Any work experience gained after marriage (that was within the scope of social insurance) necessitated the commencement of a new contribution record. The operation of such exclusion rules along with the income limit for social insurance coverage (operative till 1974) meant that many female contributors had patchy and inadequate entitlements to social insurance benefits. Unemployment and disability benefits were paid at lower rates to married women than to single people and payment was made for a shorter period (312 days rather than 390 days). Earnings related benefit was thus paid for a shorter period as this was only paid when flat rate benefit was paid and women usually fared worse than men because their earnings on average were less.

This core male breadwinner treatment of married women was embedded in both Irish and British systems in a wider system of gender differentiation. In Ireland, access to unemployment benefit and unemployment assistance were major areas of discrimination. Unemployment benefit was paid to those who were ready and available for work and when married women sought to claim unemployment benefit, there was usually a detailed scrutiny of the woman's child care and domestic arrangements in order to test availability for work. In the case of unemployment assistance, a widow or single woman applicant was required to have at least one dependant or at least one year's contribution record (to assess attachment to the labour market). A married woman became eligible for unemployment assistance only if her husband was incapable of self-support through physical or mental infirmity and was wholly or mainly maintained by her, or if she had one or more child dependants. Even the legal title to the children's allowance scheme was initially vested in the husband.

To add to this flagrant discrimination, the recognition of women's traditional role was weakly acknowledged in the Irish social security system. Thus, part-time work was excluded from social insurance coverage, and until the late 1980s no formal payment system existed in respect of the caring work performed by women in the home.

This Irish experience of the male breadwinner model in social security may be placed in the broader context of Jane Lewis's typology of welfare states (Lewis, 1992), as in Figure 1. Ireland and Britain are clearly located in the strong male breadwinner category. Such welfare states emphasise women's domestic and family roles and utilise a range of policies, notably labour market and social security policies, to underpin men's role as breadwinners and women's economically secondary role as dependants.

Figure 1: *Gender and Welfare Regimes.*

TYPE OF SYSTEM	EXAMPLE OF COUNTRIES	POLICIES
Strong male breadwinner system	Ireland Britain	Exclusion of women from labour market. Women treated as dependant in tax and social security.
Modified male breadwinner system	France	Generous family policies. Strong horizontal redistribution to families with children. Moderately high female labour force participation.
Weak male breadwinner system	Sweden	Active encouragement for high female labour force participation. Individualisation of rights and benefits in tax and social security.

Source: Lewis, 1992

At the other end of the spectrum lies Sweden with its weak male breadwinner system, which fosters labour market participation for all and confers individual treatment and rights in taxation and social security. Recent large rises in unemployment in Sweden have reduced the potential impact of this system. Between these ends of the continuum lies France with generous and substantive family policies. In this modified male breadwinner system, all families with children are supported by means of high children's allowances, strong employment rights, and maternity provisions for married women, and recognition for child care needs. This system attempts to achieve a more neutral choice for women as between family and work.

Conceptions of Sex Equality in Social Security

The concept of sex equality in social security has not received a thorough review and analysis in the Irish context. Without such an analysis, the incremental reforms of women's rights in the social security system may be seen as more significant in theory than in practice. Adopting the Abel-Smith scheme, several dimensions to sex equality in social security may be discerned (Abel Smith, 1982).

Actuarial sex equality allows the differentiation of the sexes in benefits received because of the differences in the costs of providing such benefits. If women are more likely to be sick or unemployed or to live longer, then lower benefits may be paid to women compared to men, or women may as a group be actuarially required to pay higher contributions to cover their greater risks of claiming. A second type of sex equality is the pooling of risks between men and women producing insurance status sex equality. Thus, men and women have the same rights to benefits based on their contribution records. However, different life and work patterns may preclude many women from building up a contribution record as full as that of many men. Under citizen sex equality, citizenship rights bestowed on women allow them to draw identical benefits to men, although their contribution records may be distinctly inferior. With positive sex equality, special insurance credits are allocated to women in so far as they tend or care for the sick, or children or elderly relatives, yet men may also claim social security credits if they discharge these socially vital roles.

The final category of sex equality is sex role equality which aims to make roles more equal between the sexes. Under sex role equality, the social security system facilitates both men and women in pursuing a career and in caring for children. Paternity as well as maternity benefits are paid and under some schemes men may be obliged to discharge their child care roles by partial retirement from the labour market in order to facilitate women's pursuit of a career. Sex role equality in social security, therefore, represents an attempt not merely to reduce the double burden on women of pursuing a career and caring for children, but of ensuring male responsibility for, and share of the double burden.

The introduction of the old age pension in 1908 in the United Kingdom (which included Ireland) represented a distinct breakthrough for sex equality. As Abel-Smith pointed out, the old age pension was a model of sex equality. The introduction of national insurance in 1911, on the other hand, represented the introduction of actuarial sex equality which intensified as the scope of national insurance broadened and deepened after Irish independence. This actuarial sex equality in social insurance has been modified by various expedients as the Commission on the Status of Women Report (1972) showed. The Directive on Sex Equality from the European Community opened up the prospect of insurance status sex equality and even citizen sex equality.

Some fundamental questions must be asked about the attainment of these latter dimensions of sex equality in social security schemes. First, what type of sex equality do Irish women themselves want in the social security system? Second, what are the best means of attaining the desired goal of sex equality. On the former question, there is an unfortunate dearth of data and information in the Irish context. On the latter question, a critique of existing social security strategies as far as they effect women must be made. As social insurance is employment and contribution based, any inferiority of earnings is directly reflected in levels of benefits. There is also the problem for many women of entry or re-entry to the labour market. Even if paid work is assured, then if there are several and widely spaced pregnancies, there are problems of building up an adequate uninterrupted sequence of contributions to make beneficiary status at all worthwhile. Actuarial sex equality in social insurance schemes would thus seem to reinforce Irishwomen's second class status compared with men, when faced with certain contingencies for which the social insurance system gives a benefit. Insurance status sex equality would still see many women disadvantaged because they would not have the opportunity to build up a significant sequential level of contributions.

The strategy of social assistance, i.e. payments related to means rather than insurance contributions, has not been seen as a useful means of achieving sex equality in social security. Ignorance and stigma associated with means tests are not useful allies in the attainment of positive sex equality or sex role equality in social security. If all women, whatever their economic or marital status, are included in a social security scheme, then the attractiveness of comprehensiveness must be assessed against the disadvantages of high cost and potential disincentive effects. The usual way of blanketing in all women into the social security system is the award of credits, rather than the payment of contributions, for socially useful activities like caring for children or sick relatives. The whole rationale of a credit system is to overcome low market valuation of female labour. Market rates of remuneration do not reflect the social value of women's work. Yet credit systems are obliged to cope with many thorny issues like part-time work and the balance between household duties and paid employment.

The most difficult issue with credits is the question of financing. In fact, there are strong reasons in any credit system for a subsidy from the taxpayer. The credit system represents the social valuation of the privatisation of child-rearing and the social care of dependant relatives. The social valuation must be high enough so that benefits based mainly on credits are adequate in relation to average net take-home pay, but the social valuation of the caring role must not be so excessive that the massive disincentive effects in the contributor workforce are created. While such a system would be very expensive to operationalise, it would overcome, firstly, low levels of benefits to those with patchy earnings and contribution records and, secondly, the dependency of most women on derived rights from their contributor husbands.

The European Community Equal Treatment Directive

The Irish debate about sex equality in social security has not focused on differing conceptions of equality or on ways of achieving greater equality by the utilisation of credits. Rather, the issues addressed have been the most effective and least expensive ways of introducing the European Community Directive on Sex Equality in social security schemes. The EC Directive 79/7 provided for the progressive implementation of the principle of equal treatment between men and women in social security matters in the case of statutory schemes covering sickness, invalidity, unemployment, old age and occupational injuries. The Directive made exceptions in the case of survivors benefits, family benefits and pensionable age, and gave a six year gestation period to member states to implement the appropriate reform.

The Equal Treatment Directive had its roots in an earlier directive on equality in employment and vocational training. The Directive stipulated that in EC member states there should be 'no discrimination whatsoever on grounds of sex either directly or indirectly by reference in particular to marital or family status (see Whyte, 1995 for details). Even after the six year gestation period given by the EC, Ireland had not implemented the Equal Treatment Directive in Social Security schemes.

Ireland's implementation of the Directive was prolonged, controversial and litigious. First, some of the most straight forward inequalities were rectified. Thus, under the Social Welfare Act (No. 2) 1985, reduced rates of benefit paid to women were equalised to the male rates in the unemployment benefit, disability benefit, invalidity pension and occupational injuries schemes. Also the duration of payment of unemployment benefit to married women was made the same as for other claimants. These provisions became operative in May 1986. Married women were allowed to claim unemployment assistance but this only became operative in November 1986 almost eight years after the Directive was issued.

Secondly, the Government attempted to introduce a gender neutral definition of adult dependancy governing entitlements to both adult and child dependancy additions to the payments. In the pre-equality situation (as shown in Table 1), a man could claim the adult dependant payment for his wife irrespective of her employment status, whereas a woman could only make such a claim where (in effect) her husband was incapacitated.

Table 1: *Structure of Pre-equality Social Security Payments in Ireland in 1985. Unemployment Benefit and Assistance.*

	UNEMPLOYMENT BENEFIT	UNEMPLOYMENT ASSISTANCE
IR£ per week.		
Personal rate	39.50	32.75
Adult dependant rate	26.50	23.65
Child dependant addition	9.40	8.15

Source: Department of Social Welfare, Booklet SW19, 1985.

Under the new arrangements to implement the Directive, a more equal application of the concept of dependancy specified that either spouse was now entitled to claim the other as an 'adult dependant' provided that the putative dependant had either no income or an income below a specified threshold (originally £50 per week). Where the spouse's income was above this threshold, the claimant lost the adult dependant payment. Furthermore, only half of the child dependancy payments would be payable, as the second non-dependant adult was deemed to be contributing to the maintenance of the children, and the latter were therefore 'only half-dependent' on the social welfare payment. These provisions resulted in the reduction of the total net incomes of some of the poorest most vulnerable families in Ireland.

To mitigate the losses the Government introduced a transitional scheme whereby a man whose wife earned more than IR£50 per week would have the full child dependancy additions restored to him together with a payment of IR£10. An additional IR£20 per week was payable to a husband on social security whose wife claimed social security in her own right and each parent could claim half the total child dependancy additions.

Special provisions were made under the transitional scheme for men claiming unemployment assistance with a working wife. Thus, for a man claiming unemployment assistance in November 1986 when his wife was receiving a social security payment and where the combined income was reduced by IR£2 per week or more as the result of the implementation of the sex equality Directive and where the couple were paying more than IR£2 per week on rent or mortgage repayments or hire purchase, then this couple qualified for an extra statutory payment equal to the combined reduction in income or the amount of the expenses. The transitional payments were extended for more than one year to cushion the impact on vulnerable families but the transitional payments made available were themselves in breach of the Equality Directive and were legally overturned (see Whyte, 1995).

The long term consequences of this new factual definition of dependancy was to create a marked poverty trap for couples, where one was in receipt of social security and the other earning very low pay. The poverty trap is a situation in which a rise in gross income can result in a fall in net income. As Table 2 shows, for the 1996 tax benefit year, this predicament arises where the impact of the spouse's modest earnings on the unemployment assistance payable is considered. As the spouses earnings increase, this entails reductions in the social security payment and, in particular, the loss of the adult dependant payment and half of the child dependant additions. Figure 2 shows for a couple without children and a couple with two children how the net income line declines precipitately as gross income rises and the family loses the dependancy allowances.

Table 2: *The Poverty Trap: Effect of Spouse's Earnings on Unemployment Assistance and Net Family Income, 1996 (Irish pounds).*

	No Children		Two Children	
Spouse's Gross Earnings	UA paid	UA and net Earnings	UA paid	UA and net Earnings
20.00	103.00	123.00	129.40	149.40
40.00	103.00	143.00	126.90	166.90
60.00	100.50	160.50	119.40	179.40
80.00	52.00	132.00	57.70	137.70
100.00	42.55	141.45	48.25	147.15
120.00	33.10	150.90	38.80	156.60
140.00	23.85	160.35	29.35	166.05
160.00	16.20	167.80	19.90	175.50
180.00	10.75	173.25	12.99	182.41
200.00	7.55	176.45	9.79	185.61

Source: Department of Social Welfare.

The implementation of the Sex Equality Directive has necessitated changes in the procedures for the assessment of means and provision was made for the limitation of the entitlement of married couples to take into account the sharing of household expenses. The Social Welfare Act (No.2) 1985, stipulated that where both of a married couple living together qualified for unemployment assistance in their own right, the overall amount payable to the couple would be limited to what they would receive if only one spouse claimed and received an allowance for the other as an adult dependant.

In this situation each person would receive half of the total married rate of payment. A similar limitation was introduced where one of a married couple was a social insurance recipient or was a means tested old age pensioner and the other was a recipient of unemployment assistance. In this latter case, the amount of unemployment assistance was to be reduced to stay within the limitation. This limitation only applied where at least one of the couples was an unemployment assistance recipient. (In a situation where both partners of a married couple were entitled to a social insurance payment in their own right by virtue of a separate contribution record, each partner would receive the full personal level of payment).

Figure 2a: *The Poverty Trap Diagram – Effect of Spouse's Earnings on Unemployment Assistance and Net Family Income 1996 (Couple, No Children).*

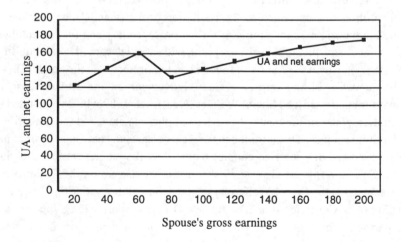

Source: Department of Social Welfare.

Figure 2b: *The Poverty Trap Diagram – Effect of Spouse's Earnings on Unemployment Assistance and Net Family Income 1996 (Couple, Two Children).*

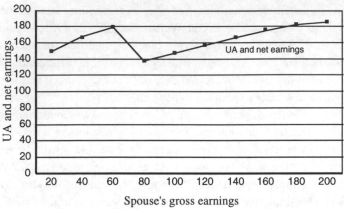

Spouse's gross earnings

Source: Department of Social Welfare.

This intricate and delicate situation became subject to legal review in the Hyland case, where the constitutionality of such arrangements were challenged. In a Supreme Court case, Hyland had successfully shown that these limitation arrangements had discriminated against married partners in comparison with partners who were cohabiting and receiving the full personal rates of payment, and that such discrimination against married partners violated the Irish Constitution's commitment to the institution of marriage. (Under Article 41, 'The State recognises the family as the national, primary and fundamental unit of society, and pledges itself to guard with special care the institution of marriage on which the family is founded and to protect it against attack').

In the wake of the Supreme Court judgement on the Hyland case the Government passed The Social Welfare (No.2) Act, 1989 which re-instated the limitation of the entitlements of married couples and extended the limitation to cohabiting couples. This introduced the legal consistency between the treatment of married and non-married couples required by the judgement in the Hyland case. The Government also established a Review Group on the Treatment of Households in the Social Welfare system to examine the wider implications of the Supreme Court decision. The Review Group's report offered four possible scenarios for the future. One was to retain the payment structure in its present form, while the other options were to abolish the limitation, to extend the limitation, or lastly to structure social assistance around household units. Given the long-term structural changes required to implement some of these scenarios, the Review Group concluded that only two scenarios could be introduced in the short-term: the abolition of the limitation applying to married couples and cohabiting couples, or the extension of the limitation to other categories of claimants (Department of Social Welfare, 1991). Currently the limitations remain in place.

The net outcome of the implementation of the EC Directive is that in social security some degree of gender equality has been achieved – equalisation of payment rates, and similar contribution requirements for social insurance, for example. However, those aspects of the Equality Directive impinging on married women's work participation were badly implemented. Notably, the social security regime may now reinforce marginal labour force status for women married to unemployed men, and institutionalise an acute poverty trap for low income families. It is difficult to find fault with Callender's verdict on the evolution of equal treatment up to 1988:

> What happened, in the end, was an ill prepared attempt to implement the Directive at the least possible cost to the State, followed by an even more panic stricken effort to alleviate the worst effects of this policy (Callender, 1988, p.14).

Since 1988, official policy has deliberately applied the Directive in an 'aggregation' framework. Where this was legally challenged (in the Hyland case), the response was to 'equalise downwards' the rights of non-married couples rather than 'equalise upwards' (and individualise) the rights of married couples. In short, this represented a legalist and minimalist strategy.

Equal Treatment Implementation in Perspective

How does this episode of policy making compare with other relevant episodes? The minimalist delayed response to the directive can be contrasted with the famous case, Murphy vs Attorney General, which was concerned with the tax treatment of married women. Historically, Irish unmarried men and women in Ireland have been equally treated in relation to personal income tax. Gender inequality arose in the treatment of married women. From 1923 to 1951 married men whose spouses were not in employment (the overwhelming majority of situations) received an additional personal allowance for this 'dependant'. The total personal allowances were not double the allowance for a single person reflecting an implicit assumption of economies of scale (Kennedy, 1989). This was the practice for most of the period up to 1980 (with the exception of a brief period during the nineteen fifties).

In relation to dual earner couples, the regime was categorically discriminatory: a married woman's earnings were aggregated with her husband's and the joint income was taxed. A husband claimed a working wife's allowance and was responsible for payment of her tax. This led to a higher tax liability for a married couple relative to two single people at the same aggregate level of income and therefore discriminated against married women in particular.

A constitutional challenge to the aggregation of spouses' incomes was successfully mounted in 1980. The challenge invoked those clauses in the Constitution which promised to guard 'with special care' the institution of marriage. In its judgement the High Court adverted to the fact that married couples or other multi-person households or units were not so treated. What is important to note is that there had been virtually no public or political debate on the underlying issue of principle involved – the unit of taxation – and that the policy change which ensued in the wake of the judgement arose only because of the legal requirement to give effect to the Court's judgement.

How the judgement was implemented in policy terms is of some significance. In the immediate aftermath of the judgement the Government introduced income splitting arrangements: double tax bands and double personal allowances for all married couples, both one earner and dual earners couples. The rationale for this interpretation, in the words of the Minister for Finance, was that the doubling of allowances and bands only to dual income couples would constitute:

> unjustifiable discrimination against the one income family, particularly where a married woman elects to care for the family on a full time basis rather than take up work outside the home (Minister for Finance, Budget, 1980).

The Courts had focused on a comparison between single and married: the policy makers, however, also drew a comparison between dual earner and one earner families. What is not clear from the policy statement at the time is whether or not the policy makers considered that the extension of the double allowances/bands only to dual earner couples would be found unconstitutional. The Irish constitution refers to the woman's 'life within the home' and 'duties in the home', and, arguably, tax arrangements which gave greater allowances or tax bands to 'working' wives as distinct from 'housewives' might also have been challenged constitutionally. There is a distinct contrast between this policy change and the implementation of the EC Directive. Policy was reformed immediately after the Court judgement, and the new 'double' tax allowances were conferred on all married couples – a process of 'levelling up' rather than levelling down. This tax reform, while impinging on all married couples with taxable incomes, disproportionately benefited the rapidly growing number of dual earner couples in middle and higher earner groups.

Conclusion

This chapter has sought to elucidate the complexities of reforming Ireland's social security system in implementing the Directive on Equal Treatment in social security systems. The problems so encountered were particularly severe because Ireland adhered to a post-Beveridgean strong male breadwinner system.

Policy makers in the Irish system baulked at reform and indeed no fundamental progress was made in the six year time period given by the EC Commission. The policy paralysis was compounded by a lack of debate about gender equity in social security and a lack of analysis about the diverse types of sex equality in social security systems. Gender policy debates at this period focused on so called moral issues of access to contraception, the right to life of the unborn foetus, and the lack of civil divorce. The enormous amount of heat generated by such debates completely eclipsed how Ireland should comply with the Equal Treatment Directive.

As has been shown, a very ill prepared attempt to implement the Directive at the least possible cost to the State was followed by a panic stricken effort to alleviate the worst effects of the policy. The net result was a minimalist, least cost strategy which in the end proved expensive when the transitional payment system was itself deemed inequitable.

This chapter has focused on a gender based analysis, but when this approach is supplemented by a class based analysis, then it can be seen that in many respects working class female recipients of the social security system have fared much worse than middle class female tax payers in the Irish system. This conclusion is clearly borne out in a comparison of how the social security system was reformed and the slow speed of the reform in response to the Hyland judgement with how the tax system was reformed and the swift reaction of policy makers to the Murphy judgement.

Not only were policy makers badly equipped for reform in the Irish social security system but the Women's Movement and other pressure groups were not able to obtain a rapid, effective and fair policy response. There were policy alternatives. It was clear in 1978 and 1979 that the adult dependant payments could be the flashpoint of policy difficulty. These payments could have been gradually floated upwards over the transition period. Also, the transition period could have been used to devise a more tapered income definition of dependancy. In fact a rather low cut off might have been accepted in the early period 1978-1981 as unemployment was at a historic low in 1978 and rose rapidly to eighteen per cent in 1986. This lower threshold could have been relaxed upwards as long term unemployment among families escalated. Furthermore, the child additional payments could have been gradually incorporated in a more unified Child Income Support system, which would have greatly ameliorated the poverty trap problem. Such policy options were not given serious consideration and the Irish policy making process meted out rough justice to many of the most disadvantaged women in Irish society.

Discussion Topics

1.   Compare and contrast different types of male breadwinner welfare systems.
2.   Assess the legacy of the British Beveridge Report on the Irish Social Security System.
3.   Assess and review the different types of equality which may be pursued in social security systems.
4.   Compare the policy impact of the Murphy judgement with that of the Hyland judgement.

References and Further Reading

Abel-Smith, B. 1982 'Sex Equality in Social Security' in Lewis, J. (ed.) *Women and Social Policy* London: Croom Helm

Beveridge, W. 1942 *Social Insurance and Allied Services* Cmd. 6404. London: HMSO.

Callender, R. 1988 'Ireland and the Implementation of Divorce 79/7/EEC. The Social, Political and Legal Issues' in Whyte, G. (ed.) *Sex Equality, Community Rights and Irish Social Welfare Law* Irish Centre for European Law, Trinity College Dublin.

Commission on the Status of Women *1972 Report* Dublin: Stationery Office.

Department of Social Welfare 1991 *Report of the Review Group on the Treatment of Households in the Social Welfare Code* Dublin: Government Publications.

European Community Directive on Sex Equality in Social Security Schemes 79/7 EEC.

Ireland. 1948 White Paper. *A Plan for Social Security.* Ireland: Stationery Office.

Kennedy, F. 1989 *Family, Economy and Government in Ireland* Research Series, Paper No. 143. Dublin: ESRI.

Lewis, J. 1992 'Gender and the Development of Welfare Regimes' *Journal of European Social Policy* Volume 2, No. 3 pp.159-173.

Minister for Finance. *1980 Budget* Dublin: Stationery Office.

Whyte, G. 1995 *Gender and Equality in the Irish Social Welfare System* mimeo.

11.

Gendered Citizenship: The Social Construction of Mothers in Ireland

Anne Coakley

Introduction

The relationship between the state, the economy and the family have been considered important components of any analysis of welfare state provision. However the family, the private realm, has been relatively neglected in such analyses. Recent feminist writings have focused more attention on women and the family. In particular they have utilised a social citizenship model as a means of evaluating and comparing social provision for women in different countries. Income maintenance schemes are an important dimension of social citizenship if one defines social citizenship in terms of access to the average standard of living in a society, and to a sense of inclusiveness in the life of the community.

This chapter examines the social construction of married mothers in income maintenance schemes in the Republic of Ireland[1] following the implementation of the EU equality directive on social security[2] (Coakley, 1995). Married women, and in particular, married mothers became a key focus of state social welfare policy both in the lead up to, and in the aftermath of, the directive. The directive had major implications for the social rights of this group. Its objective of granting equal treatment to men and women in social welfare has not been resolved. The directive's aim of individualising married women in social welfare resulted in many contradictions when it was imposed on a familist model that assumed women's dependency within marriage. The first section of this chapter will briefly define social citizenship. It will focus in particular on feminist theories on the gendering of citizenship evident in the structure of social welfare benefits. The next section adopts some of these key concepts to explore how Irish state policy, in the post directive period, reproduced traditional modes of dependency while at the same time introducing some individualisation of social welfare schemes for married women. Finally, the most problematic issues raised by the directive are discussed. The assumptions inherent in the existing structure of social welfare payments, of financial equality in married households, and that childcare is the private responsibility of married mothers is challenged.

Social Citizenship

Marshall's (1963) definition of social citizenship referred to social rights associated with the development of the welfare state in the twentieth century. These included not only the right to economic security but the right of access to the prevailing standard of living. Social rights embodied in social citizenship are central to Esping-Andersen's (1990) comparative analysis of welfare states. The nature of social citizenship varies across countries. If social welfare benefits for example, are to be enjoyed as a social right, benefits should be universal, that is, they should be available to all citizens of a certain age and condition (for example, sickness, unemployment, parenthood). Secondly, his analysis involves de-commodification, i.e. that the individual should be able to enjoy the average standard of living without a dependence on work in the labour market.

While feminists have utilised Esping-Andersen's model they have been critical of his concepts of social citizenship and de-commodification which are based on participation in the formal economy. Work is defined as paid work and welfare as policies that permit, or discourage the de-commodification of labour. Lewis (1992) argues that women disappear from such an analysis when they are not part of the paid labour market. The crucial relationship is between paid work, unpaid work and welfare. In the tripartite relationship between the state, market and family, the family is seen as part of the private realm and is not adequately included in the analysis (Orloff, 1993). However, the family must be acknowledged as a significant provider of welfare and unpaid caring work.

De-commodification is associated with entitlements and social rights that protect the individual from dependence on the labour market. However, O'Connor (1993) argues that this must be supplemented by the concept of personal autonomy. This refers to protection from personal and public dependence and is central to unravelling the relationship between the state, market and family. All groups may not have equal access to the labour market and hence they may not be equally commodified. Services relating to the organisation of daily life may facilitate or hinder women's labour force participation. The level of personal autonomy will vary according to the range of services which protect individuals from economic dependence on family members and/or on state agencies.

A central part of insulation from dependence is the extent to which public services are available as citizenship rights as opposed to a means-tested basis. According to O'Connor social rights not directly linked to the labour market have been relatively neglected in comparative analyses of welfare state regimes. There is a tiered system of access to social rights:

- female stratum of welfare/social assistance (need based)
- male stratum of benefits (labour force based)
- dependants (women and children) stratum of indirect social rights.

Orloff (1993) concludes that in all systems of social provision, claims based on motherhood or marriage often have more stringent eligibility requirements and are associated with lower benefit levels than are work based claims. Welfare state regimes are structured by, and in turn structure, both class and gender (O'Connor, 1993, Orloff, 1993). Both dimensions must be incorporated in an analysis of social provision. Social citizenship has different implications for members of different social classes due to social inequalities, but it also has different implications for men and women due to structured gender inequalities.

Women's position in the family reflects both their reproductive role in the home and their position in the labour market. While the divide between public and private is a key analytical concept in understanding women's position they cannot be rigidly categorised as separate spheres. Rather the public and private are reflected in one another and the boundary between them is fluid and changing. The familist model has supported the breadwinner/dependent form of family in Britain and the Republic of Ireland and has maintained many women in the private sphere and out of public life. It also ensures the availability of women for caring work. The dependency of women is sustained by women's caring work and by women's position in the labour market. Women are dependent because they care for other dependents; for children, and for the sick, the handicapped and the elderly. The price of such caring work is economic dependence (Pascall, 1986).

Irish women have had the lowest labour market participation rate in the EU, and while it has increased considerably it continues to rank low by EU standards (Table 1).

Table 1: *Percentage of Women in the Labour Force in EU Countries*

	1987	1992
EUR 12	39.3	41.0
Belgium	38.5	40.6
Germany	39.5	41.2
Greece	35.8	36.8
Spain	32.9	36.1
France	43.3	44.6
Ireland	32.8	35.4
Italy	35.6	36.8
Luxembourg	35.4	37.5
Netherlands	37.6	40.4
Portugal	41.8	44.4
United Kingdom	42.2	43.3

Source: Eurostat 1995.

The most significant change in the Irish female labour force has been the increased participation rates of married women. Most of this increase has taken place since 1971 with the rate more than trebling from 7.5 per cent in that year to 23.7 per cent in 1989. By 1992, the participation rate for married women in the labour force had increased to twenty-nine per cent (Table 2). Married women as a percentage of the female labour force has increased from 13.6 per cent in 1971 to 41.5 per cent in 1989 (NESC, 1991). Young married women in particular are remaining in the labour market so that they carry dual responsibilities for earning and caring.

Table 2: *Female Participation Rates in the Irish Labour Force (per cent).*

	SINGLE	MARRIED	SEPARATED	WIDOWED
1990	49	25	33	7
1991	47	27	39	7
1992	50	29	40	8

Source: Labour Force Surveys (LFS) 1990, 1991, 1992.

Nonetheless there is a striking continuity in the number of women engaged in home duties. Just under half of all women aged fifteen years and over, forty-nine per cent (LFS, 1991) are engaged in home duties as compared with sixty per cent twenty years ago.

Irish Social Welfare

Class based explanations of the Irish welfare state (Breen et al., 1990, O'Connell, et al., 1992) have been dominant neglecting the importance of women and the family in welfare provision.

> But the choice of family policies in particular also reflect our understanding that a central feature of social policy in developed capitalist countries is to be found in the way it defines and constructs families as sources of informal welfare supply and when families fail as causes of social problems (Cochrane et al., 1993, p.5).

However recent work has classified Ireland in terms of welfare state regimes (Mc Laughlin, 1993) and has examined some of the dimensions of the relationship between women, the family and the labour market (Cousins, 1995). Irish social welfare provision operates a three tier system of income maintenance. Social insurance compensates for absence from the formal labour market and grants clear individual entitlements. Social assistance is means tested and is based on household need. Supplementary welfare allowance, the third tier, is the direct successor to the Poor Law. When it was introduced in 1975, the legal embodiment of the Act was progressive, in that it gave all citizens of the state an entitlement to a minimum income replacing the harsh principles of the Poor Law. Its main importance now is in the delivery of a range of means tested secondary benefits.

The importance of the male worker based social insurance schemes is that they give recipients the status of rights-bearers and hence they can enjoy the social rights of citizenship. Essentially recipients of social assistance are clients and in this context are dependent and are therefore denied the autonomy of social citizenship. Despite changes in the labour market, the post-second world war model of social insurance is still dominant in many EU countries including Ireland. It is based on a continuous typical male work record and was designed to deal with contingencies such as unemployment and sickness on a temporary basis only. Increasingly due to long-term unemployment and the increase in the number of lone parents, means tested social assistance schemes have assumed more importance as a family income. However social assistance has been slow to change and is still moulded by the traditional familist mode of the male breadwinner with wife and children as dependents.

Conroy-Jackson (1993) uses the concept of 'dependent mothers' to describe how the Irish state has historically constructed women. Married women have been seriously discriminated against in their own right and even further if they became mothers (Mahon, 1994, 1995). Leira's (1992) theorisation on welfare state design highlights the gendered nature of social citizenship. If one explicates the assumptions inherent in the structuring of welfare benefits, a distinction can be made between citizen the earner and citizen the carer. Earning and caring give access to different social rights and this leads to a dualism in social citizenship. Earning or paid work in the formal labour market is more valued than caring in the family. The position of women as mothers who combine the role of worker and carer are not adequately recognised in social provision. Leira argues that the interplay of key dimensions in the structuring of welfare state benefits produces gendered citizenship. There is a differentiation of work forms between paid work in the formal economy and unpaid work in the home for purposes of social welfare entitlements. Eligibility conditions for unemployment benefit and assistance are based on a continuous male work record with no caring responsibilities. The welfare state's definition of public/private responsibility for caring places caring for children, the elderly and the sick largely in the private realm. The gendered division of labour ascribes the greater part of unpaid caring work to women. In Ireland the male model of full-time paid work in the labour market grants clear social rights of citizenship in contrast to the lower status of unpaid caring work. The Irish state defines caring for children largely as a private responsibility. Welfare state entitlements are 'structured according to a general set of premises in which formal employment is more favoured than informal caring' (Leira, 1992, p.21).

In Ireland the social construction of the family by the state and in particular the gendered construction of men and women within the family has given rise to a series of policy measures which has produced a dual concept of social citizenship. There are two distinct modes within which mothers are constructed, the familist mode and the individualist mode. Nowhere is this more evident than in social welfare schemes. Married women have historically been constructed by state policies within the familist mode. This mode is underwritten by a male breadwinner as head of household and women and children as dependents of his household. However, this does not explain all of welfare provision in the form of support for lone parents or in the changes since the implementation of the EU equality directive. Married mothers who are working full time outside the home and increasingly lone parents are defined more in the individualist mode. Lone mothers are constructed in an individualist mode and they now can avail of benefits and courses available to unemployed men such as the principal state work scheme, the Community Employment Programme (CEP). They are also granted a childcare and travel allowance if they are in paid work. Married mothers who have a full-time labour market based work record also enjoy the same social rights to insurance based benefits as men. In contrast married mothers who are classified as full-time in the home have been reconstructed in the context of a re-definition of dependency. The familist boundary has shifted somewhat but means tested social assistance schemes have been reproduced on a familist basis.

The EU Directive in Ireland

EU member states agreed in 1978 on the Directive on equal treatment for men and women in social security and countries were given six years to comply. It was finally implemented at the end of 1986 in Ireland. The implementation of the EU Equality Directive in Ireland exposed the manner in which the state socially constructed women within marriage. The Directive's aim of individualising married women in social welfare to ensure equal treatment resulted in many contradictions when it was imposed on a familist model that assumed women's dependency within marriage. It also highlighted the problem of women combining earning and caring.

The implementation of the EU Equality directive in Ireland was contained in the Social Welfare Act (No.2) of 1985. It introduced changes in four key areas:

— reduced rates of benefit payable to married women under unemployment benefit, disability benefit, invalidity pension and occupational injuries benefit schemes were abolished

– payment of unemployment benefit was to be paid for the same duration to married women as all other claimants

– married women could now apply for unemployment assistance subject to a means test

– concepts of adult and child dependents broadened so that both spouses could make a claim for a spouse and children under the social insurance and social assistance schemes.

Individualist Mode

The social construction of wives as dependents before the EU legislation meant that men could claim for them on social insurance regardless of whether the woman was in full time employment or not. Historically, women lost their accumulated entitlement to social insurance benefits on marriage from 1929.[3] It was not until 1973 that women were again granted the right to retain their social insurance record on marriage, but it was at a reduced rate and for a shorter period of time than for other categories of workers.

After 1985, married women who participated in the labour market on the same basis as men were granted the same entitlement to work related social insurance schemes such as unemployment or disability benefit. The equality legislation obliged the state to give equality of treatment and individualised payments to married women who had an adequate work record in the formal labour market. Within the familist mode, these women had been discriminated in the past on the basis of marriage. Social insurance confers clear rights of citizenship and clear entitlements. However, in Ireland, up to this point the state had either blatantly removed the inherent rights contained in the social insurance principle or had granted reduced rights of citizenship to married women who had full insurance records. Individual rights to social insurance for married women in paid work now gain precedence over their marital status. Further, if both spouses are eligible for insurance payments they are paid two full adult rates.

The Familist Mode

The most controversial issue surrounding the directive in Ireland centred on the treatment of married women for unemployment assistance, and in particular, married mothers who were at home full-time. Unemployment assistance, a household means tested payment, is now the most common type of social assistance payment, particularly due to the persistence of long term unemployment.

Two central factors emerged around unemployment assistance payments. Firstly, married couples had their means jointly assessed under the existing familist based mode for purposes of unemployment assistance. A man received a full individual adult rate of payment for himself. In addition he was entitled to a payment for his wife as an adult dependent but it was pitched at only sixty per cent of the adult rate. Secondly, the assumption that child care was a married mother's private responsibility was made more explicit as her newly gained formal rights under the directive conflicted with existing conditions for applying for unemployment assistance.

The issue for the state was how to apply the legislation to married women engaged in home duties, who in theory could now apply as individuals for unemployment assistance. The state's response was to limit the individual entitlements of a married couple to the existing baseline used for a male breadwinner and his wife.[4] The resources of a married couple are aggregated in the assessment for unemployment assistance and supplementary welfare allowance on the assumption of income sharing and economies of household. Reduced rates of payments for married couples are justified on assumed mutual obligations between spouses which sets them apart from other households. Income sharing is assumed and is based on the premise that the husband as the main recipient shares his income fairly with his wife. The second justification for a reduced payment for a couple is based on the notion of economies of household which implies that is less expensive for a couple to manage a household than other individuals who have no legal obligation towards one another.

While the state was obligated by EU law to introduce equality legislation, at the same time it was busy amending and consolidating existing social welfare law to limit the individual entitlements of married women in the home in particular. However cohabiting couples were not affected and were treated as individuals. The Social Welfare (No 2) Act 1989, provided that cohabiting couples would now only be entitled to the same social assistance payment as a married couple. At the same time, the Review Group on the Treatment of Households in the Social Welfare System was established by the state to examine the assessment of married and cohabiting households.

Prior to the introduction of the EU directive, the concept of a married woman as a 'natural' dependent of her husband was an integral part of social welfare policy. The practise of paying a man for his wife regardless of whether or not she had an income of her own was based on the notion that most married women and in particular married mothers stayed at home and did not do any paid work. Further, children were deemed to be dependents of their father regardless of which parent was the main earner. After the introduction of the EU directive an adult dependent and part or all of a child dependent allowance could now be claimed by either spouse. An earnings ceiling of £60 gross per week (1996 rate) was also imposed on married couples where one was claiming social welfare and the other worked. This involved a reconstruction of dependency which shifted the parameters of the familist mode somewhat. While it is assumed that there is no financial advantage to being unemployed as against being an adult dependent, this issue may be important for mothers where there is not an adequate sharing of income within households and if they wished to enter or re-enter the labour market. In addition married mothers who are not 'signing on' the live register are not eligible for the general state training schemes particularly those under the Community Employment Programme (CEP).

Because these changes directly impacted on families with low incomes, the state introduced a transitional payment of between £10 and £20 per week on a reduced basis from 1986 to 1992. This in effect replaced the adult dependent allowance that men had lost. This payment was made to the breadwinner whose income had been reduced and not to women in the same circumstances. From the beginning of the 1980s, women had been actively campaigning for changes in the social welfare code. Women did not initially qualify for adult dependent or child dependent rates from 1984-1986. This discrimination was challenged in the courts in 1992. Women won the right to some payments but the state decided to stop the transitional payments to men when women made a claim for them. A group of married women who challenged these practices successfully won eligible women their right to back payment for these periods in the Courts in March 1995. It was estimated that £260 million was due to 70,000 women in back money for this particular period. It would have only cost a fraction of this had the women been treated in an individualist mode, and in the same manner as their husbands at the time.

The familist interpretation of the Directive was particularly significant for married mothers in Ireland due to the relatively high numbers engaged in home duties. In terms of equity one of the indirect negative effects of equal treatment was that many low income families were worse off. This is why the alleviation payments were introduced for a period. In addition, the £60 earnings limit affected families commonly where the woman had a part-time job. Low paid and part-time workers whose spouses were on social assistance were those most affected or those earning just above the limit (Cook and McCashin, 1992). The manner in which the state attempted to redefine the individualist mode in a familist context made equality a negative issue for many low income families who ended up poorer.

A married mother's role as carer was acknowledged in so far as it could be used to discourage her from the transition from a familist status to an unemployed individual by applying the basic eligibility conditions rigourously. The basic eligibility conditions for claiming unemployment benefit or assistance specify that one must be available for and genuinely seeking work. On the 'availability for work' criteria women were subject to discriminatory questioning and asked about childcare arrangements. They were often refused payment on this basis. Callender (1988) documents that both before and after the directive was implemented, this was a major welfare rights issue that women's groups had lobbied against and several representations were made to the Department of Social Welfare before the matter was formally resolved. As in Leira's classification, welfare state policy genders citizenship. Child care was to remain in the private realm of women and the family, and recognising it as appropriate to the public realm would have challenged the whole basis of the familist mode. Married women at home continue to be discriminated against in return-to-work schemes. Unlike lone parents, who are treated in an individualist fashion for work schemes, married women at home will not generally be eligible.

Equality in Households

The equal treatment of married women in social welfare has not been resolved by the EU equality directive. As in Leira's (1992) theorisation, caring for children remains a private responsibility. Further the continued assessment of married couples on the basis of aggregation of household means assumes an equal distribution of resources in such households. The Commission on Social Welfare (1986) recognised 'that the sharing implicit in the calculation of the basic payment for a couple may not actually take place' (p.197). It proposed that payments should be split where sharing does not take place. It also recommended, contrary to the Social Welfare Act 1985, that where each member of a couple individually applied for either social insurance or social assistance they should be paid two full adult rates.

The concept of treating each member of a couple as individuals was based on the premise that if each experienced a contingency (for example, if a woman who is full-time in the home, whose husband becomes unemployed, becomes available for work and registers officially as unemployed, she should be paid a full individual adult rate), they would qualify in their own right. The notion of contingency has always been based on labour market conditions in so far as if one experiences the contingency of unemployment or sickness, one is entitled to an individual payment based on one's insurance record. Any other situation was in effect outside the realm of the labour market and thus of insurance and hence was defined as need. The concept is now outdated as in practice long-term unemployment has meant that people experiencing a contingency may be means tested on the basis of household need if they no longer have a current insurance record. While the move from insurance to social assistance payments for people is not defined as problematic, the possibility of moving from assistance to insurance payments to include work such as caring has not been seriously considered.

The Government Review Group on the Treatment of Households (1991), in contrast, did not reach agreement on the assessment of men and women in families. It was concerned that if the limitation for couples was abolished it would discriminate against women working in the home and couples who were both unemployed would be treated more favourably. The traditional division between contingency and need is being used here to justify the status quo. Contrary to the spirit of the directive, the Government Review Group assumed that women working in the home would not wish to move to the status of being 'unemployed'. One of the main considerations of the Review Group was the cost implications to the state, if unemployment assistance payments were individualised for married women. Many of the forty-nine per cent of women engaged in home duties would be eligible and would have an added financial incentive to make a claim for assistance. The Review Group was examining the two most important assumptions of the implementation of the equality directive on social security in Ireland; the aggregation of household means of married couples and caring as a private responsibility for married mothers.

On the one hand the report argues in favour of treating married men and women as individual claimants if their claim is based on actual or potential ties to the labour market. However it does not deal with the more problematic issue of women as carers in the home as meriting equal treatment to those in the paid economy. The Review Group did not challenge the division between paid and unpaid work nor between contingency and need. Indeed it argued strongly in favour of social welfare payments reflecting an assumption of household economies and a sharing of income between married couples. It did suggest that the term 'adult dependent' be replaced by the term 'qualified partner'. To this end the Minister for Social Welfare has actually replaced the term 'adult dependent' with the term 'qualifying adult' in the Social Welfare Act 1996. There is however no financial gain for a couple.

Rottman's (1994) study of income distribution within Irish households begins to challenge some of the unresolved issues around married/cohabiting households such as sharing between couples. However, there are considerable problems with his methodological approach which takes a married couple as a consensual unit for granted. The study found that on average only half of income, which is predominantly husband derived, is shared in Irish households. In nearly ninety per cent of homes the wife is given the responsibility of managing the money and buying essentials such as food. In reality, in most houses, husbands control the money as the main earners or as the principal recipients of social welfare payments. This is most evident in both high earning and low income families where there is either a large amount or very little income to be shared. This conforms to Pahl's (1989) findings, that in low income households, women tend to be responsible for the management and spending of money after the husband's allowance is taken out. Women have the greatest say in households in which there is least to control such as low income households particularly 'those dependent on social welfare, and households raising young children' (Rottman, 1994, p.15)

The study showed that only one third of the total income is shared in families dependent on social welfare.

> In general, the results of this study do confirm a fit between family financial management in practice and the fundamental assumption used in formulating social policy that income will be shared (Rottman, 1994, p.107).

It does not really make sense to formulate social policy based on the household distribution patterns of the average family where at least one adult may be working and where long term dependency on social welfare is less likely. Studies in Britain (Brannen and Wilson, 1987) and in particular those that focus on women have shown that while men may be the arbiter of living standards, women are the keeper of living standards in households with children. The preliminary results of a study (Coakley, 1996) of households dependent on social welfare points to the importance of an independent source of income for mothers. This includes not only earned income from paid work but goods and assistance flowing into households in the form of loans, gifts and other resources. These assume particular significance in households where women are not the direct recipients of the main income. Mothers kin and friendship networks are the key to such exchanges. Such findings point to the divergence between the structure and adequacy of existing social assistance payments for two parent families, and the reality of daily life as mothers struggle to reconcile health keeping with housekeeping.

Conclusion

The formal recognition of the traditional family and a married woman as unpaid carer in the home is laid down by the Irish Constitution and is endorsed by current social welfare practise. In Ireland the dual role of women as mothers and carers (Leira, 1992) is not acknowledged. One can either take one role or the other. There is a clear differentiation between caring and waged work in the system of benefits and entitlements. Because of their reproductive and caring responsibilities married women in particular will continue to be excluded from social rights of citizenship. At present, social assistance is tied up with subsistence and with traditional family forms. In order for caring to be valued in society one needs a broadening of the principles of social insurance to include caring as well as earning. In addition, there is a need to restructure child benefit and income and non-income provision for families with children. At present caring for mothers is associated with financial dependency and a subsistence level of income if the family is dependent on state welfare.

One of the fundamental criticisms of EU equality legislation is the restriction of equal rights to the sphere of paid work. It is based on the achievement of adult worker citizenship and on equality of treatment rather than equality of conditions. The substantive inequalities in the division of unpaid work makes it impossible for the majority of women to start on equal terms.

The EU equality directive gave women formal equality (Sohrab, 1994) but in practice it made explicit the unequal treatment of married women in a familist model. In Ireland, the issue has focused on married women's entitlement to assistance based payments particularly in relation to unemployment. In reality, it seems that individual countries can make their own guide-lines in relation to social assistance. The directive only covers social assistance in so far as it is intended to supplement or replace the main work based schemes of sickness, unemployment, occupational benefits, invalidity and old age. The distinction that is traditionally made between contingency (insurance) based schemes and need/household based (social assistance) derives from a conceptualisation of work that is valued as paid work in the formal labour market (production) and the hidden realm of the family/the private sphere where work such as caring is not valued (social reproduction). The familist boundaries have shifted particularly in the reconstruction of dependency but a dualism in social citizenship persists. Mothers who are full time in the labour market and lone parents are defined in the individualist mode for training and welfare. In contrast, mothers who are full time in the home are still largely defined in the familist mode.

Discussion Topics

1. In what way is social citizenship different for men and women?

2. Explain what is meant by the familist and individualist modes in the structure of social welfare.

3. What were the main changes introduced by the EU equality directive for married women in Ireland?

4. How are married mothers at home full-time still discriminated against in the social welfare system?

Notes

1. Hereafter referred to as Ireland.
2. The Third Equality Directive (Council Directive 79/7/EEC, Ref. O.J. 1979 1.6/24) on the progressive implementation of the principle of equal treatment for men and women in matters of social security.
3. The state also introduced a marriage bar in 1929, whereby women on marriage were obliged to give up paid work. The marriage bar was removed in 1973.
4. The income limitation for married couples was provided for by section 12 of the Social Welfare (No.2) Act 1985.

References and Further Reading

Brannen, J and Wilson, G. (eds.) 1987 *Give and Take in Families: Studies in Resource in Distribution* London: Allen and Unwin.

Breen, R, Hannan, D, Rottman, D and Whelan, C. 1990 *Understanding Contemporary Ireland* Dublin: Gill and Macmillan.

Callender R. 1988 'Ireland and the Implementation of Directive 79/7 EEC' in Whyte G. (ed.) *Sex Equality, Community Rights and Irish Social Welfare Law* Dublin: Irish Centre For European Law

Coakley, A. 1995 Unpublished research on *The Social Construction of Mothers in Ireland in Social Welfare* for Ph.D thesis.

Coakley, A. 1996 'The Social Citizenship Of Mothers in Ireland; Perspectives on Paid and Unpaid Work' Paper presented at European conference on The Gender of Rights at the University of Athens, based on unpublished research for Ph.D thesis.

Cochrane, A and Clarke, J. (eds.) *Comparing Welfare States: Britain in international Context* London: Sage

Commission on the Status of Women. *1972 Report to the Minister for Finance* Dublin: Stationery Office

Commission on Social Welfare. 1986 Dublin: Stationery Office.

Conroy-Jackson, P. 1993 'Managing the Mothers: The Case of Ireland' in Lewis J. (ed.) *Women and Social Policies in Europe* Hants: Edward Elgar.

Cook G, and McCashin A. 1992 'Inequality, Litigation and Policy Resolution: Gender Dependence in Social Security and Personal Income Tax in the Republic of Ireland' paper presented at York University Conference on Social Security: Fifty years after Beveridge.

Cousins, M. 1995 *The Irish Social Welfare System : Law and Social Policy* Dublin : The Round Hall Press

Daly, M. 1985 *The Hidden Workers: The Work Lives of Part-time Women Cleaners* Dublin: Employment Equality Agency.

Esping-Andersen, G. 1990 *The Three Worlds of Welfare Capitalism* New Jersey: Princeton University Press.

Eurostat. 1995 *Women and Men in the European Union: A Statistical Portrait* Luxembourg: Office For Official Publications of the European Commission.

Fraser N. 1989 *Unruly Practices: Power, Discourse and Gender in Contemporary Social Theory* Cambridge: Polity Press.

Labour Force Surveys. 1990, 1991, 1992 Dublin: Stationery Office.

Langan, M and Ostner, I. 1991 'Gender and Welfare: Towards a Comparitive Framework' in Room, G. (ed.) *Towards a European Welfare State* Bristol: School for Advanced Urban Studies.

Leira A. 1992 *Welfare States and Working Mothers* New York: Cambridge University Press.

Leira A. 1993 'The "Woman-Friendly" Welfare State?: The Case of Norway and Sweden' in Lewis, J. (ed.) *Women and Social Policies in Europe* Hants: Edward Elgar.

Lewis, J. 1992 'Gender and the Development of Welfare Regimes' *Journal European Social Policy* 2:31 pp.159-173.

Lewis, J. (ed.) 1993 *Women and Social Policies in Europe* Hants: Edward Elgar.

Mahon, E. 1994 'Ireland: A Private Patriarchy?' *Environment and Planning* Vol. 26 July pp.1277-1296.

Mahon, E. 1995 'From Democracy to Femocracy: the Women's Movement in the Republic of Ireland' in Clancy, P, Drudy S, Lynch, K and O'Dowd, L. (eds.) *Irish Society: Sociological Perspectives* Dublin: Institute of Public Administration.

Marshall, T H. 1963 'Citizenship and Social Class' in Marshall, T H. *Sociology at the Crossroads and Other Essays* London: Heinemann .

Meehan, E. 1993 *Citizenship and the European Community* London: Sage.

Mc Laughlin, E. 1993 'Ireland: Catholic Corporatism' in Cochrane, A and Clarke J. (eds.) *Comparing Welfare States: Britain in International Context* London: Sage.

NESC. 1991 *Women's Participation in the Irish Labour Market* Dublin: Government Publication.

O'Connell, P J and Rottman, D B. 1992 'The Irish Welfare State in Comparitive Perspective' in Goldthorpe, J H and Whelan C T. (eds.) *The Development of Industrial Society in Ireland* New York: Oxford University Press.

O'Connor, J S. 1993 'Gender, Class and Citizenship in the Comparitive Analysis of Welfare State Regimes: Theoretical and Methodological Issues' *British Journal Sociology* 44:3 pp.501-518.

Orloff, A S. 1993 'Gender and the Social Rights of Citizenship: the Comparitive Analysis of Gender Relations and Welfare States' *American Sociological Review* 58:3 pp.303-328.

Pahl, J. 1989 *Money and Marriage* London: Macmillan.

Pascall, G. 1986 *Social Policy: A Feminist Analysis* London: Tavistock.

Report of the Review Group on the Treatment of Households in the Social Welfare Code. 1991 Dublin: Stationery Office.

Rottman, D. 1994 *Income Distribution in Irish Households* Dublin: Combat Poverty Agency.

Second Commission on the Status of Women. *1993 Report to Government* Dublin: Stationery Office.

Sohrab, J A. 1994 'An Overview of the Equality Directive on Social Security and its Implementation in Four Social Security Systems' *Journal of European Social Policy* 4 (4) pp.263-276.

Statistical Information on Social Welfare Services. 1987-1993 Dublin: Stationery Office.

Wilson E. 1977 *Women and the Welfare State* London: Tavistock.

Wilson, G. 1987 *Money in the Family* Avebury: Hants.

12.

Women and Poverty: Differences in Living Standards within Households

Sara Cantillon

Introduction

This chapter is concerned with the issue of access to and consumption of resources within the home. The distribution of resources within the household merit attention for at least two reasons: firstly, since the household as a unit of analysis does not allow an accurate view of individual living standards, an internal examination of the household would provide a better measure of the relative poverty risk facing different individuals. Secondly, the use of the household unit has important policy implications. The social welfare system distributes resources on a household basis, largely to an assumed male 'head of household' in the case of married couples. If resources are not evenly distributed to assumed dependants the capacity of the social welfare system to achieve desired living standards is seriously impaired.

Section one discusses the general issue of poverty and gender, the concept of the feminisation of poverty and the use of the household as the unit of analysis. Section two reviews the main contributions to household theory within neo-classical economics and the emerging feminist challenge. It concludes with a review of empirical studies which highlight the limitations of the household as a unit of analysis. These, mostly small scale qualitative studies are primarily concerned with inequality in process as distinct from inequality in outcomes. Section three takes a first, albeit limited, step in assessing differences in outcomes in material living standards between married couples in Irish households. It includes a general discussion of the data, some of the limitations for present purposes and provides results in relation to the relative position of a husband and wife within the same household. These indicate a limited overall imbalance in favour of the husband. The chapter concludes by substantiating the view that the position of individuals within households needs to be studied rather than assumed a priori and that a greater focus on individual living standards is required than that provided under conventional methods.

Gender and the Measurement of Poverty

The topic of resource sharing and women and poverty has been the subject of substantial debate over the last few years with some confusion about the different elements. Even if we take 'women and poverty' as the umbrella, key distinctions can be made, inter alia, between the feminisation of poverty, hidden poverty, outcomes in terms of material standards and processes and control over resources.

Perhaps the most widely cited analysis of poverty and gender is the feminisation of poverty thesis which implies a shift in the burden of poverty from men to women. Pearce (1978) coined the term to refer to a basic contradiction in US society towards the end of the 1970s: despite women's increased financial independence, and greater participation in the labour market, the number of women living in poverty had risen dramatically over the previous twenty years.

The feminisation of poverty thesis has, however, proved somewhat problematic. As Mc Lanahan et al. (1989) show, Pearce's predictions of a continued increase in female poverty have not been borne out. While she was right about the increase between 1954 and 1970, the proportion of the American poor who were women showed a decline between 1970 and 1984. Glenndinning and Millar (1989) also criticise the feminisation of poverty idea arguing that it is not women's share of poverty that is increasing but rather that the share has become more visible. Other studies in the UK (Lewis and Piachaud, 1987) support this view. The relevance of the feminisation of poverty thesis to Ireland has been looked at by McCashin (1993) and Nolan and Callan (1994). These studies suggest that 'the risk of income poverty for female headed households has fallen' (Nolan and Callan, 1994, p.184) The same trend is found across different income cut-offs and alternative equivalence scales which is partly explained by the fact that many female headed households are headed by elderly women and widows whose relative income position improved considerably over the period on account of increases in social welfare rates. There is thus a divergence between the age groups of female headed households with women under thirty-five faring less well. Lone mothers face a high risk of poverty and while this fact is given due recognition in both of these studies, the fact that this category of households is still a small proportion of the population suggest that, to date, there has not been a US-style feminisation of poverty in Ireland.

The feminisation of poverty debate provides a clear example of the tendency for research on poverty and gender to be on particular groups of women that are poor with simple empirical observations made on, for example, the growth in female-headed households, the elderly, or the higher volume of female to male unemployment. Research therefore tends to be of the 'add women and stir' variety rather than a genuine rethinking of the methodology. The existing analytical structure, however, is not sufficient for understanding the gender dimensions of poverty. As Glendinning and Millar argue:

> Women's access to, use of and attitudes towards, resources are radically different from, and cannot be equated with those of men. The conditions under which women obtain access to resources, the levels of those resources, women's control over resources, and the degree of responsibility for the welfare of others in deploying those resources are all factors which make women particularly vulnerable to poverty and which shape women's experience of the impact of poverty (1989, p.369).

Such factors do not come into play in the way that poverty is conceptualised and measured. In most poverty studies, collective units (families, households, tax units), rather than individuals, are used as the unit of analysis. The units do not allow the resources or needs of individual members to be identified so that there is a gap in the picture presented. To treat the family or household as a unit effectively assumes either that there are no conflicts of interest within the family or that the interests of individual family members can be subsumed within the interests of the household head. Thus consensus rather than conflict is the basic premise and the possibility that there might be a real conflict of interests between women and men is sidestepped.

The Theoretical and the Empirical Household

The idea that households make their basic economic decisions as single utility maximising units is the assumption made by most economists. It is, furthermore, the dominant model within policy circles where policy interventions are designed, carried out and evaluated. It is assumed that family income is distributed equitably between the various family members and there is no need to enquire into intra-family equity. Thus the family enters the 'black box' where the interests of women and children become invisible.

Theoretical Defence

Neglect of the issue of distribution within the family has been justified by economists on a number of grounds. Early economists, such as James Mill, justified treating the household as a single unit on the grounds that the interest of women and children were subsumed in the interests of the male household head:

> One thing is pretty clear, that all those individuals whose interests are indisputably included in those of other individuals may be struck off without inconvenience ... in this light, women may be regarded, the interests

of almost all of whom is involved either in that of their fathers or in that of their husbands.[1]

Samuelson (1956) provides a more formal justification with his consensus model of the family which, as Woolley (1993) notes, essentially stresses that 'blood is thicker than water'.

Of modern economists, Becker (1981, 1988) gives the most rigorous defence for the family utility function assumption. Becker's treatise purports to show that the household has a single utility function which is identical to that of the head of household, that is the male income earner and that women and children count only to the extent of their husband's and father's caring. There has been some dissension from the ranks, with both Galbraith and Sen, for example, criticising the idea of the household unit. That all household members with different tastes, needs, preferences should be held in neo-classical theory to be the same individual is, according to Galbraith 'a heroic simplification which leaves all the inner conflicts and compromises of the household unexplored'.[2] Sen (1990) evocatively refers to the conventional model of the family as the 'glued together family'.

Clearly, one of the main problems of the household unit concerns the aggregation of preferences over individual household members. Katz (1991) identifies two distinct ways of conceptualising this aggregation. The first is to assume that altruism exists within the household and that household members 'subordinate their individual inclinations in pursuit of common household goals'.[3] The second option in resolving the aggregation problem is to assume that the joint household utility function is the product of a decision-making process where individual member's preferences were previously assigned particular weights. Thus there are two theoretical approaches, within neo-classical economics, to the concept of the household unit: the 'altruistic' model and the 'bargaining' model. The former ignores the issue of conflict between individual members of the household whereas the latter explicitly incorporates it. It should be, however, noted that the weights assigned to individual member's preferences are exogenous to the model.

Models of Intra Household Resource Allocation

In the new home economics model, households maximise their utility (satisfaction or happiness) subject to a budget constraint. The spending of household income is assumed to both reflect collective preferences and be independent of who actually earns that income. The assumption of altruism within the household means that regardless of whether income is pooled or there is unequal control there are no consequences for spending or consumption. Everyone acts in accordance with the joint household utility function, i.e., everyone thinks of his/

her own utility only in terms of collectivity. In this sense the actual division of resources is irrelevant since no one distinguishes themselves as an individual with desires separate from the whole.

The second approach, the bargaining model (e.g., Horney and McElroy, 1988), perceives the single family utility function as the main weakness of the new home economics model and so replaces it with a Nash bargained objective function. The basic idea is that individuals enter into households and into collective household resource allocation processes only when, by doing so, they can do better than they would on their own, with their own labour, assets and income. The formulation of the household utility function is explicitly conflictual and dependent on the relative 'fall back' positions (or threat point[4]) of the individuals involved. Stronger fall back positions afford the individual more bargaining power. The influence of any individual in the bargaining process which formulates household decisions is determined by that individual's access to economic resources. Changes in the bargaining position are parallel to changes in economic opportunities.

The Feminist Response

The first argument presented by feminists concerns the methodology itself.[5] There is a blatant inconsistency between the basic explanatory device used in neo-classical economics of a rational self-interested individual and the family utility function where all family members act as if they all have the same preferences for food, clothing, and leisure. Economists side-step the inconsistency by colluding in the false division of the private and public spheres, e.g. Becker assumes altruism in the family and selfishness in the market place.[6]

Second, there is little discussion of why conflict is absent from families. A consequence of the family utility function is that conflict within the family cannot be addressed. To paraphrase Katz (1991, p.40) the model begs a theory of the family. Alternatively it assumes a theory of the family in which individuals act unselfishly, and consequently, this theory conflicts with the assumptions on individual behaviour in other spheres of life.

Another feminist criticism (Nelson, 1994) of Becker's model concerns the fact that the head of the household's unique capability is ascribed to his altruism rather than his power over household resources.

> The 'altruist' does not keep all the income for himself it is true, but what makes him the head is that he is the person *who has the power* to transfer general purchasing power *among* all members (net transfers to the altruist are not ruled out) as *he happens to care* about their welfare (p.129, emphasis in the original)

That his position is a function of his power is further emphasised by looking at the position of other family members who may be more altruistically inclined but who do not have the opportunity to act upon it because they lack power (Nelson, 1994).

As for the terminology, Becker protests that his references to the altruistic head as male and to the beneficiaries as women and children are arbitrary and have no connection at all to the fact that it is generally men who have greater access to money. There is absolutely no recognition, let alone, discussion of male power nor the effects of such power differentials within the family. Indeed the whole emphasis seems to be to stress male altruism and by extension the selfishness of women and children. Such assumptions are clearly in need of a feminist critique. Bergman (1987) summarises the general feeling:

> to say that the new home economists are not feminist in their orientation would be as much of an understatement as to say that Bengal tigers are not vegetarians (p.132).

The bargaining model certainly has advantages over the new home economics especially, as Sen says, in capturing the idea of 'the co-existence of extensive conflicts and pervasive co-operation in household arrangements' (1990, p.125). The model is, however, insufficient in many respects.

The most significant deficiency is its assumption that a priori individual household members are equal. It thus fails to incorporate gender and gender relations as significant variables. The pervasive gender inequalities that characterise society are somehow left at the halldoor. Another aspect underlying this view is the assumption that people choose their domestic arrangements freely. Such a view ignores important constraints on choice.[7] Even leaving aside the enormous sociological and feminist literature on gender constraints in relation to marriage and on the compulsory nature of heterosexuality itself (Rich, 1980) this argument has particularly little force when applied to children, ignoring as it does their situation and vulnerability.

Sen's critique of the model emphasises the role of perception in intra-household processes. He argues that the models are particularly negligent of the influence of 'perceived contributions and perceived interests' (1990). Contributions to the household which are the source of bargaining power will not be the same for women and men. Women will not receive the same degree of bargaining power for the same objective resource contribution, whether it be assets, income, time, etc., because of the socially defined gender evaluation of the work of different members of the household. As many authors have noted, no recognition is given for the deployment of emotional resources within the household. Even when that contribution is in the form of wages it tends to be discounted. Yet research indicates that women's earnings contribution to the household, albeit at low pay, cushion the family from the impoverishing impact of male low pay.[8] Furthermore, the wife's earnings contribute towards maintaining or improving the standard of all family members rather than hers alone. With regard to perceived interests or preferences, sociological and feminist research suggests that, due to gender-specific socialisation, women's utility will be much more oriented toward collective goods and men's toward personal goods. And yet such values and beliefs about appropriate gender behaviour continue to underlie the way in which researchers discuss and interpret the experience of poverty. Women's self-sacrifice is rarely considered problematic but instead has been seen as part of a natural feminine altruism and concern for the well-being of others.

Finally, the notion of altruism in the family and selfishness in the market place has serious policy implications. In the conventional model of the altruistic family we are unable to explain, for example, why it might make a difference to pay family allowance payments to mothers rather than to fathers. This failing also applies to the more recent literature centred on a co-operative bargaining model of the family. To conclude, feminist criticism has clearly illustrated that, at the theoretical level, the assumptions underlying the use of the household as a unit are flawed. Empirical evidence accumulated to date substantiates their argument. Such data suggest that the distribution of resources within the household is not necessarily equitable and further, that there is a strong association between control of income and power within marriage.

Empirical Evidence

There are several types of within-household inequality and a useful distinction made by Jenkins (1994) is between inequality of process and inequality of outcome. Pahl's work (1989) on the association between control over household finances and power within the household focuses on the former. This chapter focuses on the latter where outcome is measured in terms of differential access to material resources between men and women within the household.

Rejecting economists' standard assumption that the household is an unproblematic unit raises the question as to whether there can be differences in living standards between husband and wife in the same household, and if so whether these reflect the access of each partner to household resources?

Pahl (1989) illustrated the link between financial arrangements within households and inequalities and showed how particular systems of financial allocation were clearly associated with inequalities in power over decision making. Pahl's research strongly confirms that the position of individuals within households needs to be studied rather than assumed a priori. The male's breadwinner role tends to legitimate, for men themselves, a claim to greater control over the deployment of household resources. On the other hand, although women are less likely to control household income they are more likely to bear responsibility for day-to-day budgeting. Pahl (1989), and Volger and Pahl

(1994) developed a taxonomy of four household allocative systems which profiles the arrangements made between husbands and wives for money management. These four systems are:

1. Whole wage system

(a) Female whole wage system: Husbands hand over wage packet minus personal spending money. Wife takes care of all bills. Wives usually have no personal spending money separate from collective funds. This system is usually found in low income, working class families with a strict division of labour between husbands and wives.

(b) Male whole wage system: Husbands have sole responsibility for managing all household finances, wives have no personal spending money. This system has tended to be prominent in studies of abused women.

2. Housekeeping allowance system: Husbands give wives a fixed amount for housekeeping. The remainder stays under the husband's control and he pays for other items. Wife does not have any personal spending money separate from housekeeping money which is allocated for collective expenditure. This system is common among higher paid workers and middle class couples in which the husband is the only earner.

3. Independent management system: Both partners have independent incomes and neither has access to all household money. Each partner is responsible for specific items of expenditure and the principle of keeping flows of money separate within the household is maintained. Usually associated with dual earner households.

4. Pooling system: in order to produce an accurate picture which included actual as well as perceived management of finances Pahl subdivided this allocative category into three subdivisions. (a) Equal pooling system: both partners have access to all or nearly all household money and both hold responsibility for household finances; (b) the male managed pool: male responsible for management and (c) the female managed pool: female responsible for management. The male and female managed pools are more similar to the male and female segregated systems than to the equal pooling system.

For Pahl the allocative system is a crucial indicator of power within marriage with the dominant partner in decision making being the most likely to control, as opposed to manage, household funds. The orthodox model of households as egalitarian decision-making units, within which resources are shared equally, i.e. where the pool was jointly controlled, applied to only one-fifth of the households in the sample.

A study on the distribution of financial resources within households was also undertaken in Ireland.[9] On the whole, many similarities in the financial management of Irish and British households were found. One noticeable feature of the Irish data is the fact that the equal pool, female dominated pool and the independent management system tended to be used more in Ireland than in Britain when the woman was employed outside the home. This suggests that the employment status of women in Irish households is particularly relevant in terms of adopting a female dominated or an equal pool system.

Table 1: *Distribution of Household Allocative Systems in British and Irish Households (couple households only).*

HOUSEHOLD ALLOCATIVE SYSTEM	BRITAIN	IRELAND
	%	%
Female Whole Wage	25.7	29.5
Male Whole Wage	9.4	4.1
Housekeeping Allowance	12.1	29.5
Independent Management	3.5	4.1
Equal Pool	10.6	14.1
Male Managed Pool	35.3	13.2
Female Managed Pool	3.4	5.6
Total	100	100
(n)	(3299)	(459)

Source: Working Paper No. 64 of the European Scientific Network on Household Panel Studies.

The most distinctive difference between the two countries, however, can be seen in the housekeeping allowance category. Only 12.1 per cent of British households used a housekeeping system compared to 29.5 per cent of Irish households.

A Look at Differences in Living Standards within the Home

This section looks at the distribution of resources within Irish households by means of previously collected, but unused, material from the 1987 ESRI Survey of Income Distribution, Poverty and the Usage of State Services.[10] While a wide range of information was gathered in the survey, the focus here is the indicators of style of living in the individual questionnaire. Attention is given to married persons where both are living in the same household and both completed the individual questionnaire which provides a substantial sample of 1,763 couples. The core of the questionnaire is a list of twenty aspects of standard of living which were taken, for the most part, from previous studies such as Townsend (1987) and Mack and Lansley (1985).

Before looking at the data it is worth noting that this survey has a number of shortcomings as a basis for comparison of men's and women's living standards. Firstly, the research agenda was specifically aimed at measuring the extent and nature of poverty in Ireland. While it gathered data, inter alia, on differences in access to and possession of resources between individual members within the household, it did not set out with this as the primary focus of the research. A related limitation is that the list of the items that comprise a household's standard of living contains many elements that are not obviously related to the consumption of any individual member. The items, for the most part, relate to household or family consumption. Further, the items, for the most part, reflect the living standards of the 'poor' minorities rather than differences in living standards across income levels. Thus minimal clothing levels and eating patterns are emphasised whereas items which reflect differences in the way in which these minima are attained, or which concern leisure activity, are ill-represented.

A second issue is the manner of data collection. The information was gathered by means of interview with the head of household for the full questionnaire and with other adult household members for the individual questionnaire. The interviews are presumed to comprise an assortment of: one-on-one interviews between the interviewer and respondents; the interviewer and one respondent with other respondent present; or a simultaneous interview with a couple. Given the intimate nature of some of the questions asked, the possibility of the presence of a partner/spouse acting as a filter to answers exists, which in turn may have had the effect of minimising the differences. In Pahl's study on inter-household activities she interviewed the couple together first, then separately, at the same time in different rooms, and found that frequently there were wide discrepancies between the husband's and the wife's answers to the same question.

Despite these limitations, the data provides a unique opportunity for an initial glimpse inside Irish households on the basis of a large nationally representative sample. Two specific tasks present themselves: firstly, to investigate whether there is any difference in the responses of partners within the same household, and secondly, to establish if there is a gender imbalance and, if so, which gender it tends to favour.

In order to ascertain the level of consensus and sharing within Irish families, the data set was examined in the following ways:

(1) differences in response by husband and wife,

(2) the deprivation of husband and wife relative to each other within households and the overall gender imbalance across selected items for all households.

Table 2 addresses the first item by showing the percentage of the total sample of households in which the husband and wife gave different answers on access to, or consumption of, each of the twenty items. Given the unambiguously joint nature of the many of the items, (i.e. that are enjoyed by the household as a whole and contribute to the living standards of all its members) the impression of homogeneity between the living standards of husbands and wives is not surprising. It is surprising that there is a difference for items such as the fridge, the bath, or the telephone and it seems reasonable to put such differences down to random error.

However, some differences in other items of joint consumption, although also slight, are a little more difficult to categorise in this manner. While at first glance, it seems reasonable to assume that items such as the telephone, the television or the car are collectively consumed commodities, there could be an uneven allocation in their consumption within the household. Such a discrepancy between husband and wife might concern the extent to which the car or the washing machine for example, is perceived to belong to, and benefit, any one individual or the family. These are not interchangeable items of joint consumption bestowing as they do very different benefits and freedoms. Another potentially problematic item of assumed collective consumption is heating for the living room when it is cold. Graham (1992) cited food and fuel consumption as the two major items of joint consumption in which women, facing severe budget constraints, felt reductions could be made. The cutbacks in consumption were not, however, evenly spread amongst family members.[11]

Table 2: *Percentage of Households in which Husbands and Wives gave Different Responses.*

Life Style Item	Percentage of Total
Refrigerator	0.3
Washing machine	1.2
Telephone	1.2
Car	2.1
Colour television	1.2
A week's annual holiday away from home (not staying with relatives)	11.0
A dry damp-free dwelling	2.8
Heating for the living rooms when it is cold	1.9
Central heating in house	3.0
An indoor toilet	0.3
Bath or shower (not shared with other households)	0.2
A meal with meat, chicken or fish every second day	5.0
A warm, waterproof overcoat	11.1
Two pairs of strong shoes	13.2
To be able to save some of one's income regularly	16.0
A daily newspaper	7.0
A roast joint or its equivalent once a week	8.0
A hobby or leisure activity	23.0
New, not second hand, clothes	7.0
Presents for friends or family once a year	12.0

Source: ESRI Survey of Income Distribution, Poverty and Usage of State Services, 1987.

Finally, in relation to joint consumption, a distinction could be made between access to and actual consumption. Delphy (1984) highlights the question of modes of consumption in relation to food arguing that you cannot serve at the table and be served at the same time. Thus the possibility exists that even in items of joint consumption the observed divergence between some Irish husbands and wives may reflect genuine gender differences as opposed to the 'fridge' input error discussed above.

Returning to Table 2, some of the differences in answers, are quite considerable. Six of the items elicit a different response from over ten per cent of the total sample. These figures suggest that there are some differences in consumption within the household and that this association is stronger on the consumption of items of a more personal nature. For present purposes, which is to highlight any discrepancies in living standards between husband and wife, it makes sense to focus on items of a more personal, rather than familial nature, and which also cover a range of aspects of living standards including food, clothing and leisure. Thus the rest of the analysis focuses on the following ten items: holidays, meat, overcoat, shoes, being able to save, daily newspaper, roast once a week, leisure activity, new clothes and presents.

As Table 2 shows, the greatest discrepancy in the answers of husbands and wives is in relation to a leisure activity with twenty-three per cent of the total sample, giving different responses. Being able to save some money on a regular basis also shows a considerable difference with sixteen per cent of households giving divergent responses. A greater difference in certain items such as meat might, on the results of other empirical work, have been expected. Evidence from the UK (Land, 1983, Kerr and Charles, 1986,) and France (Delphy and Leonard, 1992) suggest that meat is particularly subject to differentiated consumption. Delphy found, from her study of farm workers in rural France, that the distribution of food within families reflects differences in the status of family members with choice foods, i.e., high status foods such as meat, especially reserved for the head of household. Kerr and Charles (1986) also found gender (and age) differentiation in both the quantity and quality of meat consumed.

This sample shows only a slight difference in consumption between husbands and wives. From the question which asks for a 'yes' or 'no' response as to whether the respondent has meat, chicken or fish every second day there are not detailed enough data to ascertain a qualitative difference in consumption. We simply do not know if the wife (and children) consume more lower grade meats (e.g.sausages, fish fingers, burgers) while the husband eats similar quantities but higher grade meats or vice versa. It is worth noting, however, that when the question itself becomes more specific, i.e., from meat every second day to a roast joint once a week, there is an increase in the difference in response between husband and wife.

Table 3: *Differences in Answers by Gender: Percentage of Disagreeing Cases Where Husband Has, Wife Lacks.*

Holiday	51.6
Meat every second day	52.3
Warm overcoat	59.0**
Strong shoes	56.2*
Able to save	8.2
Daily newspaper	57.0**
Roast once a week	59.4**
Hobby/Leisure	62.0**
New Clothes	66.4**
Presents	

** = significantly different from 50% at 5% level.
* = significantly different from 50% at 10% level.

Source: Derived from ESRI Survey of Income Distribution, Poverty and Usage of State Services, 1987.

Table 3 gives a breakdown of the different answers by gender. The cross-tabulation of answers and gender indicates that the differences in access to the items covered are more likely to favour men's consumption than women's.[12] In this table fifty per cent implies that an equal number of men and women in different households have said no, to possession of, or access to, the said item. If the figure rises above fifty per cent that means that there are a greater number of households where the woman is disadvantaged. If the figure is below fifty per cent more men are deprived of the said item. For almost all the items the imbalance favours the husband — the exceptions are presents and being able to save with only a marginal imbalance in the latter. For the former, sixty-seven per cent of wives say they give presents to friends or family once a year as opposed to thirty-three per cent of husbands who say they do. It is difficult to explain this item in the light of the others. It could be the case that the wife does the purchasing and giving on behalf of the husband and family. It could also be argued that the onus on women to participate in such social etiquette, e.g., remembering anniversaries, birthdays, etc is stronger than on men. In any case, the information required to test such an argument is not available. The important point is that the one item which significantly 'favours' women is not an item of personal consumption. Presents represent forms of barter or exchange relating to social obligations. Buying presents does not mean spending money on oneself: it is spent on others. There is a very slight imbalance, in favour of women in regard to saving but the point raised in regard to presents also applies here. Savings may not be used for personal consumption at all. They may be used for collectivistic reasons e.g. family outings, Christmas savings stamps, Communions, etc.

The differences in access to all of the other items favour men's consumption rather than women's. The imbalance for the most part is not dramatic ranging from around fifty-two to sixty-two per cent. On new clothing, however, the imbalance is quite considerable and suggests that wives go longer without new clothing than their husbands. In our sample households, sixty-eight per cent of women, compared to thirty-two per cent of men, say they do not have access to new, rather than second hand clothing. Since new clothing is one of the best examples, available in this range of items, of personal rather than family consumption, the imbalance in favour of the husband is of considerable interest.

While second-hand clothing may be as effective as new clothing in its function of keeping the wearer warm, such clothing may affect a person's sense of confidence, self-respect or morale. Land (1983), for example, relates that several of the mothers she interviewed in her study said that they felt ashamed to visit their children's school in second-hand clothing because they felt that other parents and teachers would look down on them. Given that the wife/mother often acts as the family's 'public representative' in dealings with outside institutions, anything that diminishes her confidence in visiting schools, doctors, on her children's behalf, could in the long-run be to the children's detriment.

Another item in which there is a considerable imbalance in favour of the man is in leisure activities or hobbies. Table 3 shows that husbands and wives do not have equal access to leisure activities or hobbies. Both spouses were asked if they had such an activity, almost a quarter of the total sample, gave different answers. Sixty-two per cent of husbands said they had a hobby or a leisure activity when their wives did not. It is most likely that time and personal spending money play a role in this imbalance with the wife, presumably, having less of both.

Having established the percentage of couples who gave different answers and the gender imbalance in those cases the next step is to ascertain the extent of the imbalance within each household (i.e. the net position of the average husband in relation to the average wife) and the gender imbalance for all households. The matrix, Figure 1, shows the overall position in terms of absence or possession of the ten items. The shaded diagonal area crossing the matrix represents 'equality' on a within household basis. We can follow it diagonally across the items; there are eight households where both the husband and wife have only one item, sixteen households where they both have two, twenty-one where they both have three, etc. The higher number of households are clustered in the bottom right corner indicating that the majority of households possess, or have access to, most of the items. The sum of the cells on the centre diagonal equal 878. While these 878 households thus represent households where the husbands and wives differed in their responses, for every item the wife was deprived of compared to her husband, he was deprived of another compared to her.

Figure 1: *Matrix of Imbalance Across the 10 Items for all Households*

		0	1	2	3	4	5	6	7	8	9	10		Total
	0	5	4		1			1						11
	1	3	8	5	2	3	3	1						25
	2	1	5	16	6	7	4	1		1				41
	3	1	5	4	21	15	12	7	3	2	1			71
	4		2	4	18	28	29	8	6	3	2	2		102
	5	1	1	3	7	20	67	34	26	9	2	1		171
	6			3	6	11	38	91	63	24	8	5		345
	7				2	6	20	49	157	84	22	5		249
	8					1	13	24	59	158	71	23		349
	9							7	24	52	126	51		260
	10							2	2	12	65	201		282
Total		11	25	35	63	91	186	224	341	345	297	288		1,906

Column span header: Man has 'x' number of items. Row span label: Woman has 'x' number of items.

Source: Derived from ESRI Survey of Income Distribution, Poverty and Usage of State Services, 1987.

In a very limited sense the husband and wife could be regarded as equally 'well off' in terms of the numbers of the ten items they have. These are net figures, however, and so no distinction is made between the actual items, as was the case earlier in the analysis, which means that the same weight is being given to each item. This is somewhat problematic in so far as assumptions are implicitly made about one item being 'worth' as much as another, but the picture presented is of interest nevertheless.

Moving out from the central shaded diagonal towards the corners we see the relative deprivation of husbands and wives. The greater area of white in the lower left hand corner confirms what our analysis to date has shown, that the gender imbalance across the items favours the husband.

Looking at the other shaded diagonals in the matrix we can see, for example, there are four households where the man has access to six more items than the woman. These four houses can be found on the diagonal in the top right hand corner of the matrix. This diagonal is where the number of items the man has, less the number of items the woman has, is equal to six. The four households are as follows: in one household the husband has eight of the ten items while the wife has only two of the ten. Eight minus two gives the net position and hence this household's place on the upper diagonal. In a second household the husband has nine of the ten items while his wife has only three. In two households, the husbands have all ten items while their wives have only four of the ten items. Alternatively, we can look at households where the husband is deprived compared to the wife. The shaded diagonal in the bottom left corner of the matrix shows, for example, a household where the wife has five of the ten items while her husband has only one.

Conclusion

There are strong practical reasons for using the household rather than the individual as the unit of analysis insofar as a woman with no income of her own is not necessarily poor while a man with earnings from a full time job can be poor if there are many dependants sharing that income. At the same time any account which perceives families exclusively as units, inevitably minimises the divergence of interest between men and women. A collective unit clearly cannot say anything about individual welfare until this point is explored. Thus there is a gap in the picture. In contrast to the theoretical framework in which families are treated as economic units in which every member is equal, every member has a common purpose and every member gets the same share of resources, an initial glance at the available information suggests that the family is a unit with a hierarchy and that divisions by sex within the family household are not just differences but inequalities.

Discussion Topics

1. Discuss the limitations of existing poverty research for understanding the gender dimensions of poverty.

2. Consider how a theory of power might be incorporated into any reconceptualisation of poverty.

3. Draw out the distinctions between inequality in process and inequality in outcomes in relation to access to and control over resources.

4.   Discuss the practical and theoretical difficulties of focusing on the individual rather than the household in poverty research.

Notes

1. As quoted in Folbre and Hartmann, 1988, p.188.
2. As quoted in 'The Profits in Womanly Virtue', *The Observer Magazine*, 13 April, 1980.
3. Ellis as quoted in Katz (1991, p.39)
4. The threat point in co-operative bargaining models is divorce.
5. See generally Woolley (1993) , Ferber and Nelson (1993) and England (1989).
6. As England (1989) shows altruism can be found within the market place, e.g male collusion to keep women out of 'their' jobs can be thought of as selective within-sex altruism.
7. Jenkins (1994) argues that this justification for using the household unit centres on the revealed preference argument: within household inequalities should be discounted because those affected by the inequalities accept them. Underlying this view is the assumption that people choose their domestic arrangements freely in which case it can be asked why, if they chose to live with inequality, we should be concerned about it?
8. For example, the Royal Commission on the Distribution of Income and Wealth (1978) stressed that 'many families are taken out of the lower incomes category by their wives earnings' (p.147). A DHSS study (1980) estimated that the number of two parent families with a father in employment but whose total income was below supplementary benefit level would have increased four-fold if the mother had not been earning.
9. Heather L, Rose, D, Whelan, B and Williams, J. 'Comparing Household Allocative Systems in Britain and Ireland' Working Papers of the European Scientific Network on Household Panel Studies, Paper 64 University of Essex.
10. For a detailed description of the organisation and content of the Survey the reader is referred to Chapter 4 of Callan et al. (1989)
11. Excerpts from Graham's interviews (1992, p.220) poignantly illustrate the case: 'I put the central heating on for one hour before the kids go to bed and one hour before they get up. I sit in a sleeping bag once they have gone to bed I turn it off when I am on my own and put a blanket on myself. Sometimes we both do but my husband does not like being cold and turns the heating back on'.
12. For an extended analysis of this data that controls for taste see Cantillon and Nolan (1996)

References and Further Reading

Becker, G. 1981 *A Treatise on the Family* Cambridge, Mass: Harvard University Press.
Becker, G. 1988 'The Family and the State' *Journal of Political Economy* No.82 pp.1063-1093.
Bergmann, B. 1987 'The Task of a Feminist Economics: A More Equitable Future' in Farnham C. (ed.) *The Impact of Feminist Research in the Academy* Bloomington: Indiana University.

Callan, T, Nolan, B, Whelan, C and Whelan, B. 1989 *Poverty, Income and Welfare in Ireland* General Research Series No.146, Dublin: Economic and Social Research Institute.

Cantillon, S and Nolan, B. 1996 *Are Married Women more Deprived than their Husbands?* ESRI Working Paper No. 73, Dublin: Economic and Social Research Institute.

Delphy, C and Leonard, D. 1992 *Familiar Exploitations* Cambridge: Polity Press

Delphy, C 1984 'Sharing the Same Table: Consumption and the Family' in *Close to Home* London: Hutchinson.

England, P. 1989 'A Feminist Critique of Rational-Choice Theories: Implications for Sociology' *American Sociologist* Vol.20, I, Spring, pp.14-28.

Ferber, M and Nelson, J. (eds.) 1993 *Beyond Economic Man: Feminist Theory and Economics* Chicago: University of Chicago Press.

Folbre, N and Hartmann, H. 1988 'The Rhetoric of Self Interest' in Klamer, A. (ed.) *The Consequences of Economic Rhetoric* New York: Cambridge University Press.

Galbraith, K. 1980 'The Profits in Womanly Virtue' *The Observer Magazine* 13 April.

Glendinning, C and Millar, J. 1989 'Gender and Poverty' *Journal of Social Policy* Vol.18, No.3 pp.363-381.

Glendinning, C and Millar, J. (eds.) *Women & Poverty in Britain in the 1990's* Brighton: Wheatsheaf Books.

Graham, H. 1992 'Budgeting for Health: Mothers in Low Income Households' in Glendinning and Millar, (eds.) *Women and Poverty in Britain in the 1990s* Brighton: Wheatsheaf Books.

Heather, L, Rose, D, Whelan, B and Williams, J. 1991 *Comparing Household: Allocative Systems in Britain and Ireland*, Working Papers of the European Scientific Network on Household Panel Studies, Paper 64 University of Essex.

Horney, M and McElroy, M. 1988 'The Household Allocation Problem' *Research in Population Economics* Vol.6 pp.15-38.

Jenkins, S. 1994 *The Within-Household Distribution and Why it Matters: An Economist's Perspective*, University College of Swansea Discussion Paper Series No.94-05.

Katz, E. 1991 'The Myth of Harmony' *Review of Radical Political Economics* Vol.2 23, pp.37-56.

Kerr, M and Charles, N. 1986 'Servers and Providers: The Distribution of Food within the Family' *Sociological Review* Vol.34, 1, pp.115-157

Land, H. 1983 'Poverty and Gender: The Distribution of Resources within the Family' in Brown, M. (ed.) *The Structure of Disadvantage* London: Heinemann.

Lewis, J and Piachaud, D. 1987 'Women and Poverty in the Twentieth Century' in Glendinning, C and Millar, J. (eds.) *Women and Poverty in Britain* Brighton: Wheatsheaf Books.

Mack, J and Lansley, S. 1985 *Poor Britain* London: Allen and Unwin.

McCashin, A. 1993 *Lone Parents in the Republic of Ireland* Broadsheet Paper No 29, Dublin: Economic and Social Research Institute.

McLanahan, S, Sorensen, A and Watson, D. 1989 'Sex Differences in Poverty' *SIGNS* Autumn, pp.102-122.

Nelson, J. 1994 'I, Thou and Them', *Papers and Proceedings of the American Economic Association American Economic Review* May 1994, pp.126-131.

Nolan, B and Callan, T. (eds.) 1994 *Poverty and Policy in Ireland* Dublin: Gill and Macmillan.

Pearce, D. 1978 'The Feminization of Poverty: Women, Work and Welfare' *Urban and Social Change Review* 11 February pp.131-157.

Pahl, J. 1989 *Money and Marriage* London:Macmillan.

Rich, A. 1980 *Compulsory Heterosexuality in Blood, Bread and Poetry* London: Virago.

Samuelson, P. 1956 'Social Indifference Curves' *Quarterly Journal of Economics* Vol.52, pp.211-249.

Sen, A K. 1990 'Gender and Co-operative Conflicts' in Tinker, I. (ed.) *Persistent Inequalities: Women and World Development* New York: Oxford University Press.

Townsend, P. 1987 'Deprivation' *Journal of Social Policy* Vol.16, 2.

Volger, C and Pahl, J. 1994 'Money, Power and Inequality within Marriage' *The Sociological Review* Vol.42, No.2 May, pp.263-288.

Wilson, G. 1987 *Women and Money: The Distribution of Resources and Responsibilities in the Family* Aldershot: Gower.

Woolley, F. 1993 'The Feminist Challenge to Neo-Classical Economics' *Cambridge Journal of Economics* Vol.17, No.4 pp.485-500.

Section 4:
Women and Mental Health

Women in the Republic of Ireland have the lowest life expectancy of all women in the EU; they are disproportionately represented amongst the poor and the disadvantaged and are consequently more likely to suffer ill-health (Second Commission on the Status of Women, 1993). A national plan for women's health was recently published (Department of Health, 1995) and the Commission on the Status of Women has recommended that all health proposals are examined for their gender related implications. Women's mental well-being is also a matter of concern, particularly the mental health of married women. Married women are more likely to suffer from depression and are more likely to become mentally ill than married men or single men and women (Gaffney, 1991). The Commission concluded that

> there are strong grounds for believing that the incidence of depression among women is a direct consequence of social and environmental factors related to the lesser financial and social status of women, isolation and inadequacies in the built environment. In particular, the negative effect of dependency may be inferred from the mental health statistics (Second Commission on the Status of Women, 1993, p.349).

The mental health status of women has received little research attention to date. The two authors in this section of the text provide an historical overview and contemporary insights into women's mental health issues.

Historically, writers have interpreted the madness of women as connected to the reproductive cycle, women's irresponsibility, melancholy and unmanageability. The confines of marriage and expectations of conformity may be unbearable for some women — an explanation that was also used for the higher incidence of mental illness among women. Are women more prone to mental illness? Or are they more likely to be diagnosed and labelled as mentally ill? Are some women more likely to become mentally ill than others? Women, in general, are over-represented in European and US psychiatric statistics, but until recently this was not the case in Ireland. The debate on gender and mental illness is treated in the two contributions in this section.

Ireland was one of the first countries in Europe to set up an asylum system for the lunatic poor and by the close of the nineteenth century, a total of twenty-three asylums were established countrywide. Those who were disruptive to the social order, the poor, the criminal and those of unsound mind were incarcerated, often for indefinite periods. Pauline Prior's research on women in the asylum system in nineteenth century Ireland reveals that though women were slightly less at risk of psychiatric labelling than men (a pattern that continues to characterise Irish psychiatric admissions), women represented forty-five per cent of the general asylum population and twenty per cent of the criminal lunatics. Most of the women who were incarcerated in district asylums were poor, with little or no education. Some were abandoned by families who could not support dependent women. Unsound mind and lack of means often went hand in hand. Prior cites witnessed reports of the extreme deprivation and poverty of women imprisoned within the asylum system. Women labelled as 'insane prostitutes' also found their way into lunatic asylums, though one medical superintendent thought it more appropriate that 'females of abandoned habits of life' be placed within the prison system. Prior's research includes those who were sentenced to the criminal lunatic asylum for serious crimes caused by loss of control. While most men were confined for murdering their wives, most women were confined for infanticide. Women who committed infanticide tended to be poor, largely unmarried and to have murdered one child only. The justice system was usually sympathetic on the grounds that women who killed their own offspring were 'attacked by puerperal mania'. Prior presents three cases of women who committed serious crimes, arguing that the label of mental illness and asylum incarceration were convenient solutions to deeply rooted and unexamined social problems.

Sociological and feminist explanations on women and mental illness are reviewed by Anne Cleary. Depression is given as the main reason for female admission to psychiatric institutions, the female rate being twice the male rate. Depression is also used more frequently as an admissions category in the private hospital system compared to the public system. Irish statistics are based on in-patient figures and we know little about why people present for treatment in the first place. Cleary's own research contributes to our understanding of this process. Early studies of women and depression seemed to indicate that being married was more stressful for women than men, but the exact relationship between marital role and mental health is more complex. Other studies found that women who worked outside the home were less likely to present for depression, but more recent research points to the adverse effects on mental health of multiple roles inside and outside the home for women, but not for men. Women are more likely to be stressed, it is argued, due to the roles they occupy and/or to socialisation which sensitises them to distress in personal and familial relationships. Factors in the woman's past and present life have also been used in research studies to understand why depression occurs. Marital violence or the presence of parental mental ill-health or a lack of maternal care in the woman's own life could cause depression. In an examination of a specific community in an Irish urban setting, Cleary examines both the prevalence and the social and psychological factors associated with the development of depression. Latest trends now indicate that an excess of women over men are being admitted to Irish psychiatric hospitals, which is more in line with European patterns. Her findings provide much evidence that a system of domination continues to burden many women and her work points to new areas of research and activism for women.

References

Department of Health. 1995 *Developing a Policy for Women's Health*, Dublin: Government Publications.

Gaffney, M. 1991 *Glass Slippers and Tough Bargains* Dublin: Attic Press.

Second Commission on the Status of Women. 1993 *Report to Government* Dublin: Government Publications.

13.

Women, Mental Disorder and Crime in Nineteenth Century Ireland
Pauline M Prior

Introduction

T he relationship between gender and mental disorder is of interest not only to academics, but to the many thousands of people whose lives have been affected by encounters with the psychiatric system (Busfield, 1986, Showalter, 1987, Ussher, 1991, Russell, 1995, Prior, 1996). Although the discourse surrounding the individual experience of mental distress and its treatment has changed radically over the past one hundred years many of the issues raised by historical material are highly relevant today. These are issues related to the labelling of certain behaviours as mental illnesses, the vulnerability of certain individuals to hospitalisation, the use of the insanity plea to avoid culpability in cases of serious crime and the undeniable social control elements in mental health policy. The aim of this chapter is to explore some of these issues by focusing on women who found themselves within the asylum system (public, private and criminal) in nineteenth century Ireland with a view to offering some enlightenment on social attitudes to mental illness, to gender roles and to serious crime.

Methodology

Historical research on mental disorder in Ireland is very rewarding because of the availability of a wealth of documentation. The main sources for this particular discussion include the annual reports (1845-1920) of the Inspectors of Lunacy on asylums in Ireland; the case registers (1850-1900) of the Criminal Lunatic Asylum (now the Central Mental Hospital), Dundrum, Dublin; the report of the 1843 Select Committee (HL) on the Lunatic Poor; convict records from the office of the Chief Secretary for Ireland held at the National Archives, Dublin; and finally patient records from district asylums in Northern Ireland, held in the Public Record Office, Belfast. These were supplemented by historical writings on mental disorder and by newspaper accounts of particular crimes.

Theoretical Debates

There are two distinct views on the relationship between women and madness. On the one hand, one can see madness as 'one of the wrongs of women' or, on the other, as 'the essential feminine nature, unveiling itself before scientific male rationality' (Showalter, 1987, p.3). These perspectives have been associated by Pugliesi (1992) with two distinct research traditions.

> The *social causation* perspective contends that women are more vulnerable to distress, depression and other mental health problems than are men. Social constructionists focus on psychiatric theory and practice and suggests that women are more likely to be identified as having mental health problems by professionals such as epidemiologists and practitioners (Pugliesi, 1992, p.44).

Both research traditions rest on the assumption that women outnumber men in psychiatric statistics. MacDonald (1981) in his research on the seventeenth century doctor Richard Napier, found that women patients were twice as likely to show signs of mental disorder than men. Research in Britain (Showalter, 1987) and France (Ripa, 1990) has also shown that from the middle of the nineteenth century if not before, there were more women than men in the public asylum system in both countries, a pattern which had been predicted by the Scottish alienist (medical specialist in mental disorder), WAF Browne, in his most famous publication What Asylums Were, Are, and Ought to Be: 'in the case of a public asylum, a larger proportion of the building should be allotted to females, as their numbers almost always preponderate' (Browne, 1837, reprinted in Scull, 1991, p.184).

Explanations for the over representation of women in psychiatric statistics have included arguments about the intolerable constraints involved in traditional female roles, the acceptability of illness as a mode of protest and attention-seeking for women, and the inability of a male dominated society to accept creative but different female behaviour (Skultans, 1979, Showalter, 1987, Ripa, 1990, Shorter, 1990, Ussher 1991). Interestingly, Browne, writing in 1837, had already examined the relationship between marriage and mental disorder. He suggested that marriage was for a man 'a shield against himself and his passions' and a source of 'joy, solace and support', though not so for women. He blamed the education of women for this.

> The education of females is however, more imperfect and vicious than that of men; it tends to arrest the development of the body; it overtasks certain mental powers, it leaves others untouched and untaught; so far as it is moral it is directed to sordid and selfish feelings, and substitutes a vapid sentimentalism for a knowledge of the realities and duties of life. From such a perversion of the means of training, what can be expected to flow but sickly refinement, weak insipidity, or absolute disease (Browne, 1837, reprinted in Scull, 1991, p.67).

Discussions continue today on the relationship between marriage, gender and psychiatric admission. Research in the UK and the USA has consistently confirmed the fact that marriage while being protective for men, is a risk factor for women (Belle and Goldman, 1980, Pilowsky et al., 1991). Even in Ireland, where the overall rate of admission to psychiatric hospitals has always been higher for men than for women, the rate for married women is consistently higher than for married men. One can conjecture as to the reasons for this. Is marriage itself destructive to the mental health of women, or do women trapped in unhappy marriages find in mental illness a socially acceptable method of protest and of escape?

Historical accounts of women with mental disorders focus on the inherent irrationality, weakness and mysteriousness of the female psyche. The visual image of the delicate and beautiful young girl appeared in plays and paintings, for example, in Shakespeare's Ophelia and in Robert Fleury's painting of Pinel freeing the insane. A different kind of woman, crazy and sometimes dangerous, appeared in late nineteenth century fiction reminding the reader of the unpredictability of women. Modern feminists find in these women images of anger and revolt against family and societal constraints (Gilbert and Gubar, 1979). For some, the revolution was against family tyranny (of husband or father) and for others it was against state tyranny. In nineteenth century France, for example, political activity by women was seen not only as unnatural, but as a symptom of insanity (Ripa, 1990, p.25). The image of this kind of woman is not of a delicate Ophelia or a Crazy Jane, but rather of a strong woman who attempted to assume the masculine role of political or intellectual leadership. Just as the delicate woman features in the historical literature on women and madness, so too does the strong woman who knows her own desires and wishes to follow them even when doing so will bring her into conflict with social norms. This was most apparent in the area of sexual desire. In the eyes of a Victorian psychiatrist, excessive sexual desire in a woman (defined sometimes as 'erotomania' and 'nymphomania') was a clear sign of insanity. Treatments ranged from harmful procedures such as the cliterodectomy to disciplinary regimes which included the elimination of meat from the diet and the boring repetition of laundry work (Showalter, 1987, pp.74-84). All were aimed at eliminating unruly desires and wild behaviour and restoring the female patient to piety, passivity and peacefulness.

Women in Irish Asylums

The process of institutionalisation of criminals, lunatics, vagrants and paupers throughout Europe during the nineteenth century has been attributed largely to the growth of capitalism (Foucault, 1967, Cohen and Scull, 1983). Although not highly industrialised, Ireland was one of the first countries to establish a centrally controlled network of asylums for the lunatic poor. According to Finnane (1981, p.20), this was due to a combination of factors:

> ...the absence of a Poor Law in Ireland; the scarcity of any special confinement for lunatics; and finally the state of rural Ireland, its economic backwardness, the poverty and vulnerability of its rapidly growing population, the affront that these conditions gave to those who wished to improve Ireland, and the challenge that they offered to the maintenance of social order.

The process began with the appointment of a Select Committee on the Relief of the Lunatic Poor in Ireland in 1817 and culminated in the passing of the Lunacy (Ireland) Act 1821 [1 & 2 Geo. iv, c. 33], which provided the legal basis for the twenty three asylums established throughout Ireland between 1825 and 1899 (Prior, 1993, p.25). By the first decade of the twentieth century these asylums offered a total of almost 17,000 places for people of unsound mind (Finnane, 1981, p.227).

An examination of the gender composition of both staff and patients reveals a picture which accords to some extent with the situation in similar institutions in England. The administration of the system was predominantly in the hands of men. Each asylum had a Board of Governors, made up of the 'great and good' from the surrounding county. Rarely, if ever, did a woman feature on these Boards of Governors. Except for the position of matron, all the top staff positions (resident medical superintendent, clerk, storekeeper) were held by men. However, the role of the matron was a very important one because of the strict division between men and women patients and staff.

> She shall reside in the Asylum, and shall exercise immediate superintendence over the female department, but in position and authority subordinate to the Resident Medical Superintendent, to whom she is to report daily its condition, and any irregularity or misconduct that may occur within it (Lunacy Report, 1874, p.273).

Some matrons were extremely powerful and treatment regimes on female wards were often controlled by them rather than by the Medical Superintendent. Elizabeth Malcolm, in her research on St Patrick's Hospital, Dublin (a private asylum), found that Jane Gill (matron 1853-85) was so well regarded by the Governors that they 'entrusted her with the entire management of the institution' and that visiting medical officers consulted her about patient treatment and her advice was often sought on building plans (Malcolm, 1989, p.160). However, as Malcolm notes, this was not a normal state of affairs and had more to do with the shortcomings of the Medical Superintendent of that time than to any enlightened management structure. In Ireland as in Great Britain, lay managers of asylums were replaced by doctors as the century progressed and the role of matron declined in status. By the 1870s, there was only one husband and wife team in charge of an asylum, Dr Robert Stuart and his wife Mary in the Belfast Asylum (Lunacy Report, 1874, pp.224-8). Unlike the moral managers of earlier times, medical managers did not wish to engage socially with asylum staff or patients, an attitude which extended to wives and family members.

> The circumstances of the superintendent's wife acting as matron involves a sacrifice of social position injurious if not fatal to success. It is above all things indispensable that medical superintendents of asylums should be educated gentlemen; and if that is to be the case, their wives cannot be matrons (J M Granville 1877, *The Care and Cure of the Insane*, quoted in Showalter, 1987, p.103).

Women staff in the asylums were drawn from uneducated families living in the locality. In his evidence to the Select Committee on the State of the Lunatic Poor in Ireland in 1843, the manager of the Clonmel Asylum complained: 'I may here mention that the Difficulty in procuring educated females as assistants and nurses is also a sad Calamity'. However, in most asylums there were no such complaints and (as with their male colleagues) physical strength and height were considered more important than education or intelligence.

In examining the gender composition of the patient population, simplistic feminist arguments about the mysogynistic nature of the asylum system are inadequate. In contrast to England and France, men dominated Irish asylum statistics throughout the nineteenth century (Finnane, 1981, pp.130-2). Men had higher admission rates in almost all age groups, and though many asylums tried to keep the bed allocation equal, men generally exceeded females in annual statistics. For example, in 1873, out of a total number of 9,417 patients treated in the asylum system, fifty-four per cent were men and forty-six per cent were women (Lunacy Report, 1874, p.182) and while the admission rate (per 100,000 of the population) for women aged between thirty and thirty-nine years rose from forty-six in 1861 to 147 in 1901, the rate for men in the same age bracket rose from forty-seven to 180 (Finnane, 1981, p.135). The predominance of men in psychiatric statistics continues to distinguish Ireland from other western countries. Finnane's research seems to support the argument that those who are the most marginalised in society will find their way into the psychiatric system. In nineteenth century Ireland these were single, landless, young men who by definition had no economic or familial support. The reasons given for current admission patterns have more to do with the higher risk of alcoholism among men combined with the ease with which those suffering from alcohol related problems are admitted to the Irish psychiatric system. This pattern may change under the new mental health legislation as the appropriateness of the treatment of alcoholism within psychiatric hospitals is challenged.

Among the women who found their way into the asylum system, one group was clearly unwelcome.

> Re-committal of Insane Prostitutes: With reference to the admission of a class of persons committed to prison by the city divisional magistrates for drunkenness, insubordination and violence in the public streets, and altogether comprising females of abandoned habits of life, utterly regardless of every principle of morality... It is no doubt a matter of some difficulty to decide how far habits of profligacy, intemperance and depravity in its every form may be regarded as more correctly indicative of criminality or insanity (Lunacy Report, 1874, p.89).

The Medical Superintendent of the Richmond Asylum who wrote the report, went on to suggest that some of these women were not insane and would be better placed within the prison system. Other women found their way into asylums because of health difficulties surrounding childbirth, grief at the death of a loved one, or financial hardship brought on by changed circumstances. Dependent women were often committed by male members of the family (brother, father, uncle) when 'distress of mind' was compounded by poverty. For example, Eleanor Story, a forty-one year old single woman from County Cavan, was committed to St Patrick's in 1843 by her brother because of her 'lack of means' and 'unsoundness of mind' (Malcolm, 1989, p.147). Her discharge four months later had more to do with the unwillingness of the family to pay the required fee than to her recovery. Others were less fortunate and remained confined for years.

However, while women abandoned by family in the private asylum system seemed to be treated with dignity, many of those in the public system were not so fortunate. Some district asylums were well regulated and a significant number of patients recovered their mental stability through work rather than medical treatment.

> The tranquil and convalescent males are occupied under the Gardener and Keeper... many are engaged in the Weaver's shop, tailoring, pumping water and similar occupations. The tranquil and convalescent Females are also occupied in knitting, spinning, Kitchen, Laundry and Ward Duties (Select Committee 1843, Evidence of Clonmel Asylum).

Other asylums, however, were not so well managed. Dr Frances White, Inspector of Lunacy, presented a shocking picture of the Cork Asylum, in his evidence to the same committee.

> In the Female Division, there were Four Patients, confined in dark ill-ventilated Cells, who were described as being of the Refractory or more Violent class. On opening their cell doors, they presented a most Wretched and Deplorable Appearance... one of these unfortunate beings was sitting in her bed of loose Straw and only half clothed... Another patient, an aged woman was rolled up in a Blanket without even a chemise on her, huddled

up in some loose straw, she had not been out of her cell for some Length of time (Select Committee 1843, Evidence 21 July).

These descriptions of extreme deprivation became more common as the century progressed and as the public asylum system in Ireland expanded and provided an escape route for people whose lives were precarious both emotionally and financially. People committed within this system were not necessarily social outcasts, though the stigma attached to the asylum was indeed potent and destructive. Families could and did receive some of these patients home. However, those who found themselves in the Central Criminal Lunatic Asylum rarely returned to a normal lifestyle after this experience.

Women in Dundrum

The Central Criminal Lunatic Asylum at Dundrum, County Dublin was opened in 1850 to cater for criminals from all over Ireland who developed a mental disorder when already within the prison system, or who committed serious crimes and were found to be insane at the time of the crime or of the trial. Of the 823 people admitted between 1850 and 1900, only 21 per cent were women. This is not an unexpected finding, as historical and current research has confirmed the under representation of women in crime statistics (Morris, 1987, Naffine, 1987, d'Orban, 1993, Daly, 1994). An interesting feature of the Dundrum records is the fact that, although fifty-five women were committed to Dundrum between 1850 and 1900 for killing a person, only a very small minority had killed adults, all of whom were women. This was in contrast to the men, who not only killed their wives but other women in their households. This trend was clear within the first decade of the establishment of Dundrum and was documented by the Inspectors of Lunacy.

> The most frequent kind of homicide among the men is wife murder... This fact, at first sight might seem to argue less constancy, fidelity and tenderness with the male sex; but there are strong causes to explain away, or, at least, reduce the force of the conclusion; for it is well known, that, occasionally among the first and most marked symptoms of the disease with lunatics may be reckoned a mistrust and aversion to members of their own family, and to those particularly with whom they had been united by the strongest ties of affection (Lunacy Report, 1854, p.19).

Though the reason given by the Inspectors for the prevalence of this crime among men may have seemed feasible to them at the time, it is obviously flawed when one considers that this pattern of behaviour might also be expected to show itself among women. However, this was not the case.

> On the other hand, we have no record of a female killing her husband, the most common mode of destruction among women being infanticide...

Great commiseration is, no doubt, due to many who come within this category; for we can fully imagine how shame and anguish must weigh on an unfortunate and betrayed female, with enfeebled system, what strong temptations induce her to evade the censure of the world in the destruction of the evidence of her guilt, by a crime that outrages her most powerful instinct, maternal love of her offspring (Lunacy Report, 1854, p.19).

Lest there be any confusion on this point, it is not argued here that women in Ireland were never involved in killing men, but rather that they did not find their way into the criminal lunatic asylum. At the time of going to press there is no published research on women who killed men in nineteenth century Ireland. Therefore one can only surmise that those who did were not successful in using the insanity defence to avoid responsibility for their actions.

In contrast, a significant number of women who killed children found their way into Dundrum. Although these killings took place in very different circumstances some patterns are evident. All of the women were poor, most were unmarried, most murders involved one child only, and rarely were other people involved in the act. The following discussion will focus on three women whose lives show clearly the social pressures of the time and whose cases illustrate some of the medico-legal debates surrounding crime and mental disorder as they relate to women.

Infanticide

Hannah Sullivan, a seventeen year old single servant from Cork was indicted in 1895 for the murder of her newly born illegitimate child. Her explanation of her crime was that she did not know what was happening as she did not realise that she was expecting a child. According to her, the child's head was caught in the lavatory seat as she gave birth. The official account of the crime was that she had killed the baby 'by cutting off its head in the loft of her master's premises at Tralee' (Female Casebook 1893-1920, p.145, Case F946). Hannah was admitted to Dundrum in 1895, showed no signs of insanity and was discharged to her mother's care in 1896. This is a very typical story of nineteenth century female life. Though infanticide was not unusual in traditional societies as a method of controlling the population, it was legally outlawed in Ireland as in other countries since the seventeenth century. Even the concealment of the death of an illegitimate child was suspect (Hoffer and Hull, 1981). In Scotland it was a capital offence to conceal a pregnancy if the baby died (Bluglass, 1990, p.524). Though there was great ambivalence about the crime, as shown by the fact that only a minority of cases were reported to the authorities (Mc Loughlin, 1996), women in situations like Hannah found understanding and leniency among judges and jurors alike. Smith (1981, p.143) has attributed this to the view of women held by the medical and legal profession, a view that included notions of 'passivity, emotion, and irresponsibility'. During the second half of the century particularly, medical discourse on female disease and illness (especially mental illness) linked abnormality of behaviour with the reproductive system. Within this context, puerperal insanity was seen as sufficiently powerful to remove all responsibility for her actions from the new mother, even if this action involved the destruction of her own child. Requests for early discharge were often couched in the following terms.

> A young woman of respectable condition and the mother of three children, who, from fright at her last confinement, was attacked by puerperal mania, and destroyed her infant. She is now and has been for about eighteen months restored to reason, her husband and family are urgent for her liberation (Lunacy Report, 1852, p.16).

The unquestioning acceptance of the fact that a woman must be ill (and therefore not responsible for her actions) if she kills her own child is disappearing in modern times. The ease with which the legal system and the media could move to a position of condemnation towards a woman who had killed her baby because of social or emotional difficulties surrounding the birth, was shown in Ireland during the 1980s at the trial of Joanne Hayes (more widely known as the Kerry Babies trial) and in the USA in 1995 at the trial of Caroline Beale, the English girl found guilty in New York of the manslaughter of her new-born baby. Both cases demonstrate the newer (and harsher) morality of adult responsibility which rejects any social or psychological explanation for the killing of a child. However, compassion extended to individuals in nineteenth century Ireland was not helpful for women in general. It confirmed the prevailing view of women as unpredictable, prone to madness and in need of protection from themselves and thus prevented a public examination of a pattern of behaviour that was becoming more and more common as the century progressed. Statistics on the Irish situation are unreliable because of under reporting (Mc Loughlin, 1996), but one would expect them to be similar to England, where in the mid-nineteenth century sixty-one per cent of all homicide victims were under one year old (Bluglass, 1990, p.524). In other words, infanticide was a significant method of population control. However, it did not fit easily with notions of maternal love which should prevail even in situations of hardship. It was easier for society to accept that a woman was mentally deranged rather than rational at the moment of destroying her baby.

Destroying a Family

For some women, the only escape from an intolerable marital situation was an attempt to abandon life by killing their children and attempting to kill themselves.

For Sarah Mc Allister and Catherine Wynn, the unfaithfulness of their husbands did not lead to crimes of passion against husband or lover (more prevalent today), but rather to acts of self destruction. Mc Allister, a thirty-three year old married woman from Antrim, was admitted to Dundrum in 1892, having been indicted for the murder (by poisoning) of her two youngest children (Female Casebook, 1893-1920, p.81, F861). She said that she had become depressed because of her husband's infidelity and that she wanted to kill herself, but denied killing her children. A year later, she was still determined to die: 'We have great trouble getting her to eat food... she wants to starve herself'. Dr G Revington, Resident Medical Superintendent, wrote of her

> A very interesting case, extremely acute, rapidly passing from mania into melancholia, with lucid intervals followed by severe relapses. Resembles what is known as Folie Circulaire. Her health has improved very rapidly, but the mental recovery has not kept pace (Lunacy Report, 1893, p.63).

Although her symptoms abated during the years that followed, Sarah died in Dundrum, unwanted by her husband and four remaining children or indeed by her family of origin.

Catherine Wynn, a thirty-five year old woman from Sligo, also expressed anger against her husband by destroying her children. She was indicted in 1893 for the murder of her three children, aged ten months, four and five years (Female Casebook, 1893-1920, p.85, F868). She had drowned them in a bath of boiling water and had attempted to kill herself by putting her head into the water. The circumstances leading up to the crime included a confession of infidelity by her husband and a declaration of his intention to abandon her. She recovered physically but not mentally from this terrible tragedy. Described in 1899 as 'mentally a hopeless case', she spent the remainder of her life in Dundrum. As Smith (1981, p.159) argues in relation to the case of Mrs Brough (convicted in 1854 for the murder of her six children) it makes little sense to ask now if these women were really 'mad'. Regardless of their mental state, their anger against their husbands was wrongly directed towards children who had no control over the relationships within which they found themselves. The label of mental illness was easily attached to behaviour which challenged not only the deeply held values of motherhood but also exposed the powerlessness of every married woman. These women were accepted as 'mad' rather than 'bad'.

Destroying a 'Changeling'

The focus of the final discussion has a particularly Irish flavour. Joanna Doyle, a forty-five year old mother of eight children from County Kerry, was indicted in 1888 for the murder of her thirteen year old 'epileptic, idiot' son. Dr

Revington, Resident Medical Superintendent at Dundrum, described her as follows.

> A wild Kerry peasant, scarcely able to speak English intelligibly. It appears that she, her husband and a number of their children all became insane at once and jointly murdered one of the sons, an imbecile idiot (Female Casebook, 1893-1920, p.29, F772).

So excited by the case was Dr Oscar Woods, the Medical Superintendent of the Killarney Asylum, that he presented a paper on it to a meeting of the Irish branch of the Medico Psychological Association. In psychiatric terminology, this was a case of *Folie a Deux*, or 'communicated insanity' in five members of one family. Joanna, her three daughters and one son (aged between fifteen and twenty-four) had all been admitted to Killarney asylum after the crime. The boy, Patsy, had been killed by Joanna in the farm yard (using a hatchet) while the rest of the family watched. When the police arrived, Patsy was dead and the family members were 'all evidently insane, jumping about and shouting in an excited way'. Dr Woods suggested that the outbreak of group insanity was caused by a combination of factors.

> No doubt the hereditary taint and the strong superstitious ideas instilled into their ignorant minds by the old country women, acting on people whose bodily health was somewhat undermined by bad food and loss of rest, had much to say to the cause of the attack (Woods, 1889).

Joanna, according to Woods, had become insane first and had communicated her condition to the rest of the family. The explanation given by Joanna was logical in its own terms and reflects the folklore of the time.

> On Saturday night at cock-crow I took that fairy Patsy — he was not my son, he was a devil, a bad fairy, I could have no luck while he was in the house — carried him out of the house and threw him into the yard, and then got a hatchet and struck him three blows on the head. I then came back, and we all prayed and went to Heaven (Woods, 1889, p.536).

In the days following the crime, when the immediate excitement had begun to subside, Joanna's children agreed that they believed that Patsy was a fairy because they had heard their mother and other people saying it. The story of the 'changeling' was not uncommon at the time and had led three years earlier to the murder of a woman by her husband and a group of relatives (Folklore, 1895). In a case which became known as the 'witch-burning at Clonmel', Michael Cleary and eight others were found guilty to varying degrees of the manslaughter of his twenty-six year old wife Bridget. There was no insanity defence in Cleary's case and he was sentenced to twenty years penal servitude. In contrast, Joanna was found 'not guilty on the grounds of insanity'. Her children were discharged quickly from Killarney asylum but she spent the remainder of her life in Dundrum. Once again we see society's acceptance of the female as passive, superstitious and prone to insanity. The descriptions given by those who committed both crimes were similar but Michael Cleary was viewed as a rational man, responsible for his actions and deserving of punishment. Again we see the easy acceptance of the female as 'mad' rather than 'bad'.

Conclusion

In examining some of the issues in relation to the incarceration of women within the expanding asylum system in Ireland during the last century, we have found many patterns relevant to current debates on women and mental illness. Unlike other countries, women in Ireland were less at risk of psychiatric labelling than men although they represented over forty-five per cent of the general asylum population and over twenty per cent of criminal lunatics; poverty and low educational standards featured in the majority of cases; mental illnesses were often associated with the reproductive cycle; financial dependency on male relatives often led to rejection and consequent institutionalisation; and frustration and anger were often wrongly directed by women against children, the only people over whom they had power and control. While the district asylums provided shelter for those who were both emotionally and financially vulnerable, the criminal lunatic asylum was the acceptable escape route for both men and women who committed serious crimes under conditions that the public understood as reasonable grounds for the loss of control. In current terms, the asylum system provided both a solution and a cloak for many human and social problems. In doing so, it hindered public debate on problems which were deeply rooted in social structures. Mental health policy and provision may look very different today but it still caters for those in society who are the most dependent, socially isolated and poor, as well as providing women with an acceptable way out of difficult situations.

Discussion Topics

1. What do you understand by the term 'mental illness'?

2. Discuss the situations in which you think insanity might be used to excuse an individual from culpability for a serious crime?

3. Is infanticide ever socially or morally acceptable?

4. Does historical research on mental illness help us to understand current attitudes to mental health in Ireland?

References and Further Reading

Allen, H. 1986 'Psychiatry and the Construction of the Feminine', in Miller, P and Rose, N (eds.). *The Power of Psychiatry* Cambridge: Polity Press.

Belle, D and Goldman, N. 1980 'Patterns of Diagnoses Received by Men and Women', in Guttentag, M et al. (eds.) *The Mental Health of Women* New York: Academic Press.

Bluglass, R. 1990 'Infanticide and Filicide', in Bluglass R and Bowden P. (eds.) *Principles and Practice of Forensic Psychiatry*. Edinburgh: Churchill Livingstone.

Busfield, J. 1986 *Managing Madness: Changing Ideas and Practice* London: Hutchinson.

Cohen, S and Scull, A. (eds.) 1983 *Social Control and the State: Historical and Comparative Essays* Oxford: Martin Robertson.

Daly, K. 1994 *Gender, Crime and Punishment* New Haven: Yale University Press.

d'Orban, PT. 1993 'Female Offenders', in Gunn J and Taylor P (eds.) *Forensic Psychiatry: Clinical, Legal and Ethical Issues* London: Butterworth and Heinnemann.

Female Casebook 1893-1920 Central Criminal Lunatic Asylum. (Held at the Central Mental Hospital, Dundrum, County Dublin)

Folklore 1895 'The Witch Burning at Clonmel', *Folklore: Transactions of the Folklore Society*, Vol.VI: 49 (Dec) pp.373-84.

Finnane, M. 1981 *Insanity and the Insane in Post Famine Ireland* London: Croom Helm.

Foucault, M. 1967 *Madness and Civilization* London: Tavistock.

Gilbert, S and Gubar, S. 1979 *The Madwoman in the Attic: The Woman Writer and the Nineteenth Century Literary Imagination* New Haven, Connecticut: Yale University Press.

Harris, R. 1989 *Murders and Madness: Medicine, Law and Society in the 'fin de siecle'* New York: Oxford University Press.

Hoffer, P and Hull, N E. 1981 *Murdering Mothers: Infanticide in England and New England 1558-1803* New York: University Press.

Lunacy Report 1852 *6th Report on the District, Criminal and Private Lunatic Asylums of Ireland*, Parliamentary Session 1852-3 (1653) XLI. 353.

Lunacy Report 1854 *7th Report*. Parliamentary Session 1854-5 (1981) XVI. 137.

Lunacy Report 1874 *23rd Report*. Parliamentary Session 1874 (c.1004) XXV11.363

Lunacy Report 1893 *42nd Report*. Parliamentary Session 1893-4 (c.7125) XLVI. 369.

Mac Donald, M. 1981 *Mystical Bedlam: Madness, Anxiety and Healing in Seventeenth Century England* Cambridge: Cambridge University Press.

Malcolm, E. 1989 *Swift's Hospital* Dublin: Gill and Macmillan.

McLoughlin, D. 1996 'Infanticide in Nineteenth Century Ireland' in Mc Loughlin D (ed.) *Field Day Anthology of Irish Women's Writing* Dublin. (forthcoming)

Morris, A. 1987 *Women, Crime and Criminal Justice* Oxford: Basil Blackwell.

Naffine, N. 1987 *Female Crime: The Construction of Women in Criminology* Sydney: Allen and Unwin.

Pilowsky, L, O'Sullivan, G, Ramana, R, Palazidou, E, and Moodley, P. (eds.), 1991 'Women and Mental Health', *British Journal of Psychiatry* 158: Supplement 10.

Prior, PM. 1993 *Mental Health and Politics in Northern Ireland* Aldershot: Avebury.

Prior, PM. 1996 'The Dark Side of Goodness: Women, Social Norms and Mental Health', *Journal of Gender Studies* 5(1) pp.27-37.

Pugliesi, K. 1992 'Women and Mental Health: Two Traditions of Feminist Research', *Women and Health* Vol. 19(2/3) pp.43-68.

Ripa, Y. 1990 *Women and Madness: the Incarceration of Women in Nineteenth Century France* Cambridge: Polity Press.

Russell, D. 1995 *Women, Madness and Medicine* Cambridge: Polity Press.

Scull, A. (ed.) 1991 *The Asylum as Utopia: W A F Browne and the Mid Nineteenth Century Consolidation of Psychiatry*, London: Tavistock/Routledge.

Select Committee 1843 *Report of the Select Committee of the House of Lords on the State of the Lunatic Poor in Ireland* Parliamentary Session 1843 (625) X p.439.

Shorter, E. 1990 'Mania, Hysteria and Gender in Lower Austria 1891-1905', *History of Psychiatry*, 1:3-31.

Showalter, E. 1987 *The Female Malady: Women, Madness and English Culture 1830-1980* London: Virago Press.

Skultans, V. 1979 *English Madness: Ideas on Insanity 1530-1890* London: Routledge and Kegan Paul.

Smith, R. 1981 *Trial by Medicine: Insanity and Responsibility in Victorian Trials* Edinburgh: Edinburgh University Press.

Ussher, J. 1991 *Women's Madness: Mysogyny or Mental Illness?* London: Harvester Wheatsheaf.

Woods, O. 1889 'Notes of a Case of Folie a Deux in Five Members of One Family', *Journal of Mental Science* Vol. XXXIV p.148 (Jan).

14.

Madness and Mental Health in Irish Women
Anne Cleary

Introduction

An interest in the concept of madness can be traced to the origins of sociology as a discipline. A key issue of sociology - the relationship between the individual, self and society, prompted Comte, and later Durkheim, to analyse the link between society and madness. In the twentieth century we have witnessed a variety of sociological theories of madness, some associated with paradigmatic shifts in the discipline, while others have arisen within the sub-discipline of medical sociology. Definitions of madness at the beginning of the twentieth century were at first closely allied to medical definitions, but from the 1960s onwards sociological interest has centred on re-evaluating the basis of the concept 'madness' and in recent times attempting to dismantle it altogether. In contemporary debate, many sociologists share the view that madness is a socially constructed category that varies across time and in different cultures. However, basic differences in perspective remain. Some theorists work within a general medical framework in that they accept diagnostic categories and then analyse the social implications of these categories. Labelling theorists (a perspective dominant in the 1960s and 1970s) focus on the deviant role and identity while social constructionists such as Foucault (1967) deny the ontological existence of the concept. Over the past three decades a new feminist framework has emerged which has borrowed from all these perspectives and yet added a new dimension to the analysis of madness. This new framework – 'the feminisation of madness' – is based on the idea that there is a link between conceptions of femininity and madness. The idea has been developed by a number of writers beginning with Chesler (Chesler, 1972) and continuing through the 1980s with Showalter's book 'The Female Malady' (Showalter, 1987). Much feminist interest in this area is prompted by a consistent finding in the research literature that more women than men are, or at least are diagnosed as being, mentally ill or more specifically as suffering from depression

(Dohrenwend and Dohrenwend, 1976, Kessler et al., 1993, Weissman et al., 1993, Prior, 1997).

The apparent over-representation of women in mental health statistics is questioned on both theoretical and empirical grounds. The research on which these findings are based is criticised at many levels from the underlying assumptions to the study design, to the interpretations. Thus, it is said, over-representation may be due to more women being diagnosed as mentally ill because medical discourse is patriarchal (Broverman et al., 1970, English and Ehrenreich, 1976, Busfield, 1982). There is also evidence that women are more likely to recognise (Dohrenwend, 1977) and report psychological symptoms (Rogers et al., 1993). Another factor which might be implicated in higher rates for women is the type of research instrument used to measure symptoms such as depression. A wide variety of methods have been used and the criticism here is that the presumed excess of female depression is merely an artefact, the result of including a wide spectrum of signs and symptoms, whether of a prolonged or transient nature, within the category 'depression' (Newmann, 1984). A final criticism is that much of the evidence for this apparent over-representation is based on patient statistics which provide information only on those who use the mental health services and is therefore not a precise indicator of prevalence. Another potential problem is that most of the research emphasis in this area has tended to focus exclusively on women. Joan Busfield's recent book is a departure from this general trend (Busfield, 1996). It may be that at least part of the discrepancy between male and female figures for depression could be due to the fact that men may show symptoms of distress or depression differently to women. Thus the high figures for alcoholism among men may be indicative of a more culturally acceptable manifestation of depression in men.

Women and Depression

Although the methodological difficulties discussed above must be borne in mind in any discussion on gender and mental health there is a good deal of evidence to suggest that more women than men seek help for psychological problems, particularly depression. This finding is based on both hospital and community studies in different cultural settings (Weissman et al., 1993). There are however, exceptions to this general finding. In some countries such as India (Anath, 1978), prevalence and treatment rates for all types of mental disorder show an excess of men, and studies in Uganda (Orley and Wing, 1979) show no gender differences in treated rates. Similarly, a number of studies carried out among Black Americans did not find an over-representation of women (Comstock and Helsing, 1976, Dressler and Badger, 1985). Ireland (at least up to the

1980s) was also a possible exception to this trend in that treated rates in rural Ireland showed that more men than women sought treatment for depression (O'Hare and O'Connor, 1987). If one accepts the research evidence that more women than men suffer from mental ill health, then the focus of interest changes to the possible causes of this over-representation. The classical medical interpretation emphasises a biological, hormonal role in female depression and other similar conditions but there is a close connection between some medical and sociological explanations. Thus, one sociological theory of female depression rests on medical constructs in that it accepts the medical diagnosis and the inquiry then focuses on the social factors that might give rise to mental health problems in women. The general orientation of this research work is that it is the difficulties that women encounter in their daily lives that cause them to be mentally ill and both sociological and feminist based research has followed this line of inquiry. Other theoretical and empirical work on this topic represents different strands of feminist thinking. An important point of division here is that some writers refuse to accept the validity of any diagnostic category in that they view all mental illness as a social construct. In this way, labelling/constructivist approaches, as illustrated by Chesler's work, focus on how women's behaviour is defined, interpreted and treated (Chesler, 1972). This explanation is based on the idea that patriarchal authority is responsible for mental ill health in women. This may be operating at a general level in society in that, as Chesler and others have claimed, there is a double standard of mental health operating for men and women. There is, she says, a tendency to pathologise female behaviour and women may be defined or labelled as mentally ill when they conform, or fail to conform, to stereotypical gender roles. Another more specific form of sexism may be operating within the medical profession in that doctors/psychiatrists may be imposing patriarchal values by treating women in stereotypic ways thereby reinforcing inequality (Penfold and Walker, 1983).

Usshers' (1991) and Showalter's (1987) work represents a further elaboration of the feminist stance. Both claim a more fundamental link between women and madness which according to Showalter '... goes beyond statistical evidence or the social conditions of women' (Showalter, 1987, p.3). Madness, Showalter claims, is symbolically represented as feminine, even when experienced by men. To prove her theory, Showalter uses English nineteenth century in-patient statistics and cultural representations such as paintings and photographs. However, the theoretical and statistical foundations of her analysis, as Busfield (1994) and Prior (1997) have shown, are doubtful if not inaccurate. Ussher (1991) has addressed the theme of madness among women as a form of misogyny, which along with its historical predecessor witchcraft, she claims is used as a means of regulating and controlling women. Symptoms, she maintains, are the only possible manifestations of protest in a situation of oppression and the label 'mad' is an attempt to silence that protest.

Theorists and researchers who view mental disorder among women to be the result of difficulty or oppression in women's lives have followed various lines of inquiry. Feminist writers have been particularly interested in the possible association between depression and powerlessness in women while sociological inquiry has examined a number of social factors in the women's past and present lives (Weissman and Paykel, 1974, Brown and Harris, 1978, Aneshensel et al., 1981, Simon, 1995). Early interest centred on the social role of women, particularly that of married women, since more married than single women sought treatment for depression (Bernard, 1972, Gove and Tudor, 1973, Radloff, 1975). Initial theories hypothesised that the apparent mental health disadvantage experienced by women is a result of the limited number and types of roles they possess relative to men (Gove and Tudor, 1973) and this type of research concentrated on the effects of the 'housewife role'. Subsequent research has not always supported this theory. This general approach now appears too simplistic, as the exact relationship of social role to psychological ill health is more complex (Thoits, 1995). Some studies have found that employment outside the home benefits women while other studies have found no mental health advantage for women from such employment (Ross and Mirowsky, 1995, Brown and Bifulco, 1990, Cleary and Mechanic, 1983, Brown and Harris, 1978). More recent research has shown that holding multiple roles (both inside and outside the home) may not necessarily be beneficial psychologically because of the so called 'double burden' involved (Thoits, 1986, Simon, 1995). Women, even if they work outside the home, usually have the prime care and work responsibilities within the home, therefore working outside may increase their overall workload and hence increase rather than diminish stress in their lives. In this way, some researchers have investigated factors such as the division of household labour and labour market inequality, both of which are rooted in traditional gender norms and expectations (Kessler and McRae, 1982, Rosenfield, 1989). This work has indicated the complexity of the issue and emphasised the importance of examining the characteristics of roles (and interactions between roles) in order to specify the conditions under which combining work and family roles is beneficial or harmful for women (and men). But this type of research still does not explain sufficiently why, or under what circumstances, women find multiple roles stressful and the focus has now turned to cultural factors and investigating the different meanings that work and family roles have for men and women (Thoits, 1995, Simon, 1995). A possible clue to this has emerged from recent research which has shown that combining multiple roles appears to result in negative self-evaluations for women but not for men and for this reason multiple roles appear to be more protective for men (Simon, 1995).

Another possible explanation might lie in the link between stressful events and situations and women's psychological well-being (Lin and Ensel, 1989, Coyne and Downey, 1991, Aneshensel, 1992, Thoits, 1995, Turner et al., 1995). Studies into the effects of these stresses or life events have indicated that the emotional impact of undesirable life events may be particularly significant for women (Kessler and McLeod, 1984). Women, it has been suggested, are inherently more susceptible to stress because of the way they are socialised (Choderow, 1974), and/or because of the social roles they usually occupy (Bardwick, 1971, Brown and Prudo, 1981). The key point here is the woman's central position in the caring network of the family which, it is said, exposes her to situations of stress. In addition, it is claimed, women may be more susceptible to such stress because they are more attuned to the interpersonal environment surrounding them (Scarf, 1981). Stressful events can be long or short term and certain long term stresses have been identified as important, particularly marital disharmony and violence (Coyne and Downey, 1991, Brown et al., 1993). Similarly, research has pointed to certain adverse factors in the woman's childhood as important in terms of adult depression. These factors include maternal lack of care, violence, parental mental ill health and serious marital disharmony (Kessler and Magee, 1993, Brown and Harris, 1993). Brown and his co-workers have incorporated a number of these strands into a model which links depression to factors in the woman's past and present life. These factors are seen to operate together to bring about depression (Brown and Harris, 1978). Present life stresses are divided into 'life events' (short term acute changes) and difficulties (non-discrete problems operating over a longer time period), which act to trigger an episode of depression (Brown and Harris, 1978). The other element in the model, the presence of 'vulnerability factors' (e.g. early loss of mother, presence of young children, lack of employment outside the home, lack of a confiding relationship and lack of community integratedness), produces an underlying susceptibility to depression (Brown and Harris, 1978).

Gender and Mental Health in Ireland

In Ireland, figures relating to the prevalence of mental illness are almost entirely confined to in-patient data. This is due partly to our historical over-dependence on an institutionally based service as well as the underdevelopment of community linked research. Recent data in relation to psychiatric admissions (Keogh and Walsh, 1995) demonstrate that Irish figures reflect international findings in terms of gender differences and psychiatric morbidity.[1] In Ireland, more men than women are admitted to psychiatric hospitals and units overall (male admissions represent fifty-five per cent of all admissions). However gender differences vary in terms of diagnostic category (Keogh and Walsh, 1995). Female admissions predominate for the diagnostic category of depressive disorders with a rate of 243.5 per 100,000, compared to 161.7 for males. Males predominate in the category of alcoholism with a rate of 243.7 per 100,000 compared to 70.0 for females (Keogh and Walsh, 1995). In-patient figures give some indication of how many Irish women and men seek help for mental health problems although, as already mentioned, use of service statistics are poor indicators of actual prevalence. Community studies which include out-patient attendance offer a more comprehensive image of who attends the psychiatric services, but such studies are rare in this country. One such study carried out in Ireland in the 1980s by O'Hare and O'Connor raised interesting questions about the gender distribution of those seeking psychiatric help (O'Hare and O'Connor, 1987). They found that the male incidence of depression was higher in rural areas of Ireland, while, in Dublin, female rates were twice those for males. This study appeared to show a different gender pattern in rural Ireland compared to other countries, but recent data has indicated that figures are now more in line with international trends (Health Research Board/Unpublished).

Women and Depression – The Results of an Irish Study

The study reported here was an attempt to examine the topic of mental health, particularly depression, among women in Ireland. The main objective was to investigate the extent of the condition and to look at the possible causes, as no research information existed on the topic (other than in-patient figures). The overall research framework was based on Brown and Harris's multifactorial model but research instruments were expanded to allow for cultural differences. The study had two specific aims: firstly to establish the prevalence of depression among women in a specific community and secondly to investigate social and psychosocial factors associated with its development. Briefly, the methodology of the prevalence study involved screening a random sample of seventy-five women from a Dublin city community for psychiatric symptoms using the Present State Examination (PSE) (Wing et al., 1974). To investigate the relevant social factors a consecutive sample of fifty women attending the district psychiatric hospital was compared with fifty-four women from the community study who had minimal or no symptoms. All those selected were between eighteen and sixty-five years. The Bedford College Life Events Schedule (Brown and Harris, 1978) and a social and demographic questionnaire were then administered to the women. The interviews were extensive – lasting from two to six hours and all the interviews were carried out by the author. The interviews were tape recorded to facilitate the interview process and to allow independent rating (by a psychiatrist trained in the use of the PSE). The overall response rate was ninety-three per cent (eighty-eight per cent for the community prevalence study and one hundred per cent for the hospital sample). The women appeared to speak freely about their lives and experiences and for these reasons, plus the high response rate, this study provides a reasonable picture of how a particular group of women experienced depression.

The Prevalence of Depression among Irish Women

The first major finding of the study was that the prevalence of depression (i.e. the total number of women with a diagnosis of depression) among women in an urban Irish setting is at least as high as similar environments in other countries (Brown and Harris, 1978). The one-year period prevalence figure for depression, as defined by the PSE (Wing et al., 1974), was eighteen per cent of the population at risk (women aged eighteen to sixty-five years). This relatively high rate may be attributed to a number of general factors, in particular the nature of the study area. The district was an economically disadvantaged area and some writers have suggested that living in such an environment involves specific stresses which are associated with higher rates of mental disorder (Rutter and Quinton, 1975). Secondly, the pattern of help-seeking for psychological problems might be important. Ease of access might influence the 'illness behaviour' in the district and in this respect the area had a higher than average ratio of psychiatrists to population because a long established psychiatric hospital is situated in the area. This might contribute to a lessening of stigma which would further increase utilisation of the service.

Present Adversity and Stresses

The study examined a number of factors in the present lives of the women which had emerged as important in similar research. These factors included age, marital status, employment outside the home and the quality of intimate relationships. Age at onset of the depression emerged as a significant factor only in relation to married women. The majority of both the patient group and the comparison group were married but there were more single women (thirty-four per cent in contrast to seven per cent) as well as single parents (ten per cent in contrast to two per cent) among the patient group. When marital status and age were considered together it emerged that the married group had two periods of increased risk, late twenties and late forties. Single women appeared to be relatively free from depression until a later stage in their lives (fifty to fifty-five years). Another finding was that both the patient and comparison groups had married and become mothers at approximately the same age but more of the patient group were either pregnant or had children when they married (twenty-one per cent of the patient group in contrast to eight per cent of the non depressed group). Having young children at home did appear to be important when only women under forty years were considered (ninety per cent of this patient subgroup had children less than or equal to fourteen years compared to twenty-seven per cent of the comparison subgroup). Unlike Brown's work (Brown and Harris, 1978) working outside the home was not found to be a significant factor in terms of preventing depression. In terms of employment, an interesting difference between the two groups was the fact that the comparison group had a more stable job history.

Significant differences however, emerged between the two groups in terms of marital difficulties. Marital difficulties were extensive among the patient group. Thirty per cent of the married depressed group in contrast to six per cent of the married comparison group (p<0.01) had experienced violence in their marriage and a third had been separated at some point in their marriage (this was in contrast to four per cent for the comparison group p<0.01). Alcoholism was also more common among spouses of the patient group (twenty-four per cent in contrast to four per cent for the comparison group, p<0.01). The depressed women also subjectively viewed their marriages as unhappy. Only twelve per cent of this group said they had a happy/fairly happy marriage in contrast to almost three quarters (seventy-four per cent) of the non depressed group and one third of the married patients (in contrast to ten per cent of the comparison group) said that they regretted their marriage. In addition, two thirds of the patient group had considered separation at some point in the marriage in comparison to only ten per cent of the comparison group. It could be argued that depressed mood influenced these womens' attitude to their marital situations but this is unlikely to account for the very large difference between the patient and comparison groups. Furthermore, the 'objective evidence' of marital disharmony provided by the data on violence and separation, plus the fact that these marital difficulties had, in general, predated the episode of depression, tend to support the validity of the findings.

The seventeen single women in the patient group fell into three distinct groupings. The first group of seven women were over fifty years, the second group (three) were in their mid to late thirties and the last group (five) were twenty years or younger (the remaining two women were in their late twenties). Among the older group, four had first developed symptoms after the loss through death, or hospital admission, of an elderly parent for whom they were the chief care giver. The problems expressed by the second group primarily involved difficulties forming and maintaining relationships with men. The third group of single women all lived in the parental home despite a pattern of interactional difficulties with their parents. Four of the five women in this latter group were sexually active but were not using contraceptives. Two of the women were single parents (another women subsequently became pregnant soon after interview).

The impact of more specific or discrete life events and difficulties in the lives of the women was also examined and this was based on Brown's framework (Brown and Harris, 1978). The importance of life events – especially severe events – was confirmed as precipitators of depression. The patient group experienced more severe life events in the short term, *ie* in the four week period before the onset of depression. Nineteen per cent of the patient group in contrast to two per cent of the patient group experienced at least one severe event (p<0.01) during this time. Long term stress factors, or 'difficulties' as defined by the Brown criteria, were also found to play an important role in the development of depression. Difficulties were common in the lives of all the respondents but severe, prolonged difficulties were a more frequent occurrence in the patient group. Twice as many of the patient group (sixty-three per cent in contrast to thirty-two per cent of the non-depressed women, p<0.01), reported at least one severe long term stress factor in their lives.

Positive factors such as support from family and friends have been shown to counteract negative event situations and the women were therefore questioned about support. A minority of the patient group (thirty-eight per cent in contrast to sixty-five per cent of the comparison group) said that they had close or confiding relationships. Reflecting the marital difficulties found in the depressed group, less than one third of the married patient group (thirty per cent) reported a close relationship with their husbands (in contrast to sixty-three per cent of the comparison group, p<0.02). Another possible source of support, religion, was examined and the depressed women were found to be irregular or non-churchgoers. Eighty per cent of the comparison group attended church regularly in contrast to fifty-two per cent of the patient group (p<0.01). In terms of housing, which has also been implicated by Brown et al. (Brown and Harris, 1978) as linked to support or isolation, more (fifty per cent) of the patient group lived in rented flat accommodation in comparison to the non-depressed group (thirty-nine per cent). When an index of low support and poor social integration was constructed from four factors, absence of daily confidant, no regular social activity, rented flat accommodation and low rate of church attendance, over half (fifty-six per cent) of the patient group had two or more of these factors, and this was in marked contrast to the non-depressed women (twenty-six per cent). The women who were depressed therefore emerged as a more socially isolated group.

Childhood Adversity Factors

It was in this section of the study that perhaps the most significant findings emerged. Table 1 shows some of the important childhood adversity factors identified. As the table indicates the women who were depressed showed a history of significant disadvantage and deprivation in their backgrounds. Lack of parental care, rather than loss of parent due to death, was more significant in terms of developing depression. Physical absence of father or mother appeared to have little detrimental effect on the psychological health of the woman (in fact, more of the non-patient group had a father absent from home during childhood). However, another aspect of separation appeared to have some influence in that more of the patients (thirty per cent of this group in contrast to thirteen per cent) were hospitalised as children and this difference was significant (p<0.05). In terms of material disadvantage, the patient group were more affected by prolonged paternal employment in that approximately a fifth of the patients' fathers had been unemployed for at least half of their childhood compared with only two per cent of fathers of the comparison group. Severe parental disharmony (involving violence) was also significantly more common among the patient group. In addition, more of the patient group were affected by parental alcoholism (thirty per cent in contrast to eleven per cent) and the difference in the levels of paternal alcoholism was statistically significant (p<0.05).

Table 1: *Childhood Adversity Factors.*

	PATIENT GROUP	COMPARISON GROUP
	%	%
Parental Psychiatric Illness	32	8*
Parental Marital Disharmony	26	2*
Long-term Unemployment	21	2*
	N=50	N=54*

* P<0.01

The findings in relation to parental psychiatric illness revealed important differences between the two groups in that significantly more of the patient group had a parent with a psychiatric problem. This parent was more commonly the mother (twenty-four per cent of patients in contrast to six per cent of the comparison group reported their mothers as having had psychiatric problems during their childhood) and this included four patients both of whose parents suffered from a psychiatric condition. A finding which appeared to substantiate the effect of this was that psychiatric symptoms were also common among the siblings of the patient group. A third of the patient group (thirty-six per cent in contrast to seven per cent, p<0.001) had at least one sibling currently receiving treatment for psychiatric problems and female siblings were more commonly affected. In addition, depression was the most common condition in that forty per cent of the patient group had at least one female sibling who had depression presently or at some time in the past (in contrast to seven per cent for the comparison group, p<0.001). The number of female family members in the patient group who suffered from depression was particularly high. In fact, overall forty per cent of patients' siblings and mothers were presently affected by this condition or had been in the past in contrast to nine per cent for the comparison group (p<0.001).

Significantly more of the patient group described their childhoods as unhappy (thirty per cent in contrast to two per cent). When they were asked to give reasons for this childhood unhappiness they identified parental disharmony, parental illness, a poor relationship with one or both parents or lack of parental affection as important factors. Problematic relationships with parents during childhood were much more common among the patient group. Over twice as many of the patient group said they had had a difficult relationship with their mothers (twenty per cent in contrast to eight per cent). The same percentage of patients reported difficult relationships with their fathers but as very few of the comparison group had experienced this particular problem the difference between the groups was significant (twenty per cent in contrast to two per cent, p<0.01). An index was constructed from the most important of these childhood deprivational factors (parental alcoholism, parental marital disharmony with violence and paternal long-term unemployment). This index showed that over half (fifty-four per cent) of the women in the patient group experienced at least one factor in contrast to fifteen per cent of the comparison women (p<0.001). Furthermore, those scoring higher on the index appeared to develop depression at an earlier age (as measured by age they first presented to the psychiatric services).

Discussion

This study demonstrated that certain social factors are significantly implicated in the development of depression in women. Those with depression experienced more stresses, both long and short term, in their lives than the non-depressed group. Short term stresses ('life events'), according to Brown's model (Brown and Harris, 1978), were found to be important in terms of precipitating the onset of depression, in that they clustered in the period prior to onset. Again, using Brown's formulation (Brown and Harris, 1978), long-term stresses or 'difficulties' were much more common among the patient group. In the married group of depressed women, stresses such as severe marital disharmony were particularly prevalent and this is in line with research findings elsewhere (Coyne and Downey, 1991). However, the findings indicate that present life stresses are merely part of the overall picture and any account of the development of depression in a woman must include factors in her past life. In this respect a life span approach, as suggested by some researchers in the area (Coyne and Downey, 1991, Brown et al., 1993) offers a more comprehensive picture of this process. The study also confirmed another element of Brown et al.'s model (Brown and Harris, 1978) i.e. the importance of a confiding relationship. Nevertheless, the study did not find support overall for Brown's model of depression (Brown and Harris, 1978) and this perhaps points to some of the inherent problems in his approach. In this respect, Brown and his co-workers have experienced difficulties in replicating some of the components of the model (Brown and Prudo, 1981).

In terms of childhood adversity the study found the patient group to be significantly disadvantaged, and this is consistent with research literature on the topic (Weissman et al., 1987, Birtchnell, 1988). Furthermore, certain deprivational factors, already indicated in similar research (Kessler and Magee, 1993), clustered in the lives of the depressed women. These key factors included parental psychiatric disorder, alcoholism and severe marital disharmony (Kessler and Magee, 1993). The mechanism through which individual deprivational factors affect children is complex and, as Rutter (Rutter, 1989) has said, the pathways from childhood to adult life involve a complicated set of linkages over time. Furthermore, as he points out, the analysis of these connections needs to take account of the context and meaning of transitions for each individual and the way these transitions are negotiated. Single adversity factors may not be important in themselves but what does seem to be significant is an interactive effect in that experiencing certain negative factors increases the possibility of experiencing other negative factors. In this respect, Brown et al. (1986) have shown a link between poor parental care in childhood and high risk of pre-marital pregnancy and later marital difficulties and Rutter has shown an association between poor schooling and later difficulties (Grey et al., 1980). The present study provided some evidence for this thesis. The women who became depressed did appear to have difficulty negotiating key stages in their lives. They tended to leave school early and their work life demonstrated an erratic pattern both in terms of number of jobs worked and time spent working. Again, although those who married did so at approximately the same age as the comparison group a number of them were pregnant or already had children when they married. Additionally, because all of the married women made the transition directly from family home to marital home – directly exchanging the daughter role for the role of wife – it is unlikely they had time to develop an independent adult identity. Failure to do this may make women vulnerable to marital problems, since self esteem and identity, as Bardwick (1971) and others (Bernard, 1972) have noted, is often achieved for women primarily within the marital relationship. In terms of the present study it may be said that some of the depressed women failed to break the sequence of continuing disadvantage within the marital situation.

Although Rutter (1989) and others have attempted to describe the possible developmental pathways linking childhood and adult life, it is more difficult to pinpoint the mechanisms involved in this process. However, a number of studies have emphasised the centrality of self esteem in this process (Brown et al., 1986, Miller et al., 1980). Childhood adversities, it is felt, may create a vulnerability to later depression because they lead to diminished self-esteem and sense of self-efficacy and Brown has postulated self-esteem as one of the mechanisms mediating the link between lack of affectionate care in childhood and vulnerability to depression in adult life (Brown et al., 1986). Another related element may be the learning of mastery and controllability (Mirowsky and Ross, 1990). As indicated in this study, deprivational factors may operate against the child in her attempts to develop mastery and control of her environment. Another factor which might be important here for women is having a depressed mother as a role model and this was experienced by a number of women in the study. As Weissman (Weissman et al., 1987) has said, the lack of parental care which is often implied here is likely to increase the mental health risk for the children and there is some confirmation of this from another Irish study (Leader et al., 1985). More specifically, Choderow (Choderow, 1974) has claimed that such an upbringing can have psychological consequences for the female child as the mother is unlikely to impart a strong sense of self to her daughter. That a depressive response can be learned in this way is perhaps indicated from the number of siblings (particularly female siblings) of the depressed group who also suffered from depression. A competing theory would implicate genetic factors in this process but there is no convincing evidence for this (Barlow, 1988).

Conclusion

The findings of this study indicate that the women who developed depression had experienced more adversity in their childhood and this may have created a vulnerability in the negotiation of later transitions and difficulties. This vulnerability, it is proposed, has its origins in the women's poor foundation in self esteem. The concept of 'learned helplessness' (Seligman, 1975) is useful here but is only part of the explanation (Greene, 1989). In this study many of the women lived in extremely difficult situations which would be distressing for most people, and what was particularly difficult about these situations was that the prospect of amelioration was slight. This reflects the findings of other similar studies, that many of the problems encountered by such women were largely beyond their control (Pearlin, 1991). Such a situation may be objectively hopeless and a psychological feeling of hopelessness or powerlessness may be a rational response. This point may also be linked to the relative powerlessness of women's lives.

Finally, these findings must be interpreted in the light of current theoretical frameworks. This study has focused on women but does not exclude the possibility of similar explanations for depression in men. The study has adopted to a large extent a social causation model of explanation but this does not exclude other explanations. Busfield (Busfield, 1988) has rightly pointed out that the dominant explanations relating to women and mental health do not have to be oppositional. Examining such a multifaceted phenomenon as depression in women (or indeed men) requires a more complex approach. This study looked at the possible social factors associated with depression for a particular group of women with a research diagnosis of depression.

However, a wider framework needs to be employed to illuminate the context in which these issues are operating. There is very real evidence, as this paper has shown, that many women seek out and receive help for depression and much of this help is sought within a system of health care where the discourse is predominantly male. Furthermore, many of the difficulties of women's lives could ultimately be traced to the patriarchal dominance of society and the implications of this. At the same time, other dominant systems such as class and ethnicity must be considered therefore general theories based on a notion of 'women' as a unitary group are hardly realistic. Some women are more likely to become depressed than others and the reasons why some women become depressed vary across class and culture and race. In addition, there are different reasons why individual women become depressed and this relates to the meaning of events and experiences for each woman. This study has presented a picture of why one particular group of women became depressed.

Discussion Topics

1. Examine the various competing theories explaining the higher rates of depression among women. Which theory offers the most 'realistic' account?

2. Discuss the idea that madness is a form of controlling women.

3. Discuss the methodological problems involved in this area of study. Could they account for the higher rates of mental disorder among women?

4. Do men and women show distress in different ways? Is it more socially acceptable for men in this country to develop alcoholism rather than depression?

Notes

1. Data here refers to admissions to public and private hospitals and units in the twenty-six counties.

References and Further Reading

Anath, J. 1978 'Psychopathology in Indian Females' *Social Science and Medicine* Vol.12, No.3B pp.177-178.

Aneshensel, C, Frerichs, R, and Clark, V. 1981 'Family Roles and Sex Differences in Depression' *Journal of Health and Social Behaviour* Vol.22 pp.379-93.

Aneshensel, C. 1992 'Social Stress: Theory and Research' *Annual Review of Sociology*, Vol.18 pp.15-38.

Bardwick, J. 1971 *The Psychology of Women* New York: Harper and Row.

Barlow, D H. 1988 *Anxiety and Its Disorders* New York: Guildford Press.

Bastide, R. 1972 *The Sociology of Mental Disorder* London: Routledge and Kegan Paul.

Bernard, J. 1972 *The Future of Marriage* New Haven: Yale University Press.

Birtchnell, J. 1988 'Depression and Family Relationships: A Study of Young Married Women on a London Housing Estate' *British Journal of Psychiatry* Vol.153 pp.758-69.

Broverman, D, Clarkson, F, Rosenkratz, P. 1970 'Sex Role Stereotypes and Clinical Judgements of Mental Health' *Journal of Consulting and Clinical Psychology* Vol.34 pp.1-7.

Brown, G W, Harris, T. 1978 *The Social Origins of Depression* London: Tavistock.

Brown, G W and Prudo, R. 1981 'Psychiatric Disorder in a Rural and Urban Population. Aetiology of Depression' *Psychological Medicine* Vol.11 pp.581-99.

Brown, G W, Andrews, B and Harris, T. 1986 'Social Support, Self-Esteem, and Depression' *Psychological Medicine* Vol.16 pp.813-31.

Brown, G W and Bifulco, A. 1990 'Motherhood, Employment and the Development of Depression. A Replication of a Finding?' *British Journal of Psychiatry* Vol.156 pp.169-79.

Brown, G W, Harris, T and Eales, M. 1993 'Aetiology of Anxiety and Depressive Disorders in an Inner-City Population. Comorbidity and Adversity' *Psychological Medicine* Vol.23 pp.155-65.

Brown, G W, Harris, T and Eales, M. 1993 'Aetiology of Anxiety and Depressive Disorders in an Inner-City Population. Early Adversity' *Psychological Medicine* Vol.23, pp.143-54.

Busfield, J. 1982 'Gender and Mental Illness' *International Journal of Mental Health* Vol.11 pp.46-66.

Busfield, J. 1988 'Mental Illness as a Social Product: A Contradiction in Feminists' Arguments?' *Sociology of Health and Illness* Vol.10 pp.521-42.

Busfield, J. 1994 'The Female Malady? Men, Women and Madness in Nineteenth Century Britain' *Sociology* Vol.28, No. 1 pp.259-77.

Busfield, J. 1996 *Men, Women and Madness* London: Macmillan.

Chesler, P. 1972 *Women and Madness* New York: Doubleday.

Choderow, N. 1974 'Family Structure and Feminine Personality' in Rosaldo, M and Lamphere, L *Women, Culture and Society* Stanford, California: Stanford University Press.

Cleary, P and Mechanic, D. 1983 'Sex Differences in Psychological Distress Among Married People' *Journal of Health and Social Behaviour* Vol.21 pp.111-21.

Comstock, G W and Helsing, K J. 1976 'Symptoms of Depression in Two Communities' *Psychological Medicine* Vol.6 pp.551-63.

Coyne, J and Downey, G. 1991 'Social Factors and Psychopathology: Stress, Social Support, and Coping Processes' *Annual Review of Psychology* Vol.42 pp.401-25.

Dohrenwend, B and Dohrenwend, B S. 1976 'Sex Differences and Psychiatric Disorders' *American Journal of Sociology* Vol.81, No.6 pp.1447-54.

Dohrenwend, B and Dohrenwend, B S. 1977 'Sex Differences in Mental Health Illness: A Reply to Gove and Tudor' *American Journal of Sociology* Vol.82 pp.1336-41.

Dressler, W W and Badger, L W. 1985 'Epidemiology of Depressive Symptoms in a Black Community: A Comparative Analysis' *Journal of Nervous and Mental Diseases* Vol.173 pp.212-20.

Durkheim, E. 1970 *Suicide* (Translated by Spaulding, J A and Simpson, G.) London: Routledge and Kegan Paul.

English, B and Ehrenreich, D. 1976 *Complaints and Disorders: The Sexual Politics of Sickness* London: Writers and Readers Publishing Cooperative.

Foucault, M. 1967 *Madness and Civilisation: A History of Insanity in the Age of Reason* (Translated by Howard, R.) London: Tavistock.

Greene, S. 1989 'The Relationship Between Depression and Hopelessness' *British Journal of Psychiatry* Vol.154 pp.650-59.

Grey, G, Smith, A and Rutter, M. 1980 'School Attendance and the First Year of Employment' in Hersov, L and Berg, I. (eds.) *Out of School: Modern Perspectives in Truancy and School Refusal* Chichester: Wiley.

Gove, W and Tudor, J. 1973 'Adult Sex Roles and Mental Illness' *American Journal of Sociology* Vol.78 pp.812-35.

Health Research Board. Unpublished figures.

Harris, T, Brown, G W and Bifulco, A. 1986 'Loss of Parent in Childhood and Adult Psychiatric Disorder: The Role of Adequate Parental Care' *Psychological Medicine* Vol.16 pp.641-59.

Keogh, F and Walsh, D. 1995 *Activities of Irish Psychiatric Hospitals and Units 1994* Dublin: Health Research Board.

Kessler, R, McGonagle, K, Swartz, M, Blazer, D and Nelson, C. 1993 'Sex and Depression in the National Comorbidity Survey 1: Lifetime Prevalence, Chronicity and Recurrence' *Journal of Affective Disorders* Vol.29, No.2+3 (Special Issue) pp.85-96.

Kessler, R and McRae, J. 1982 'The Effect of Wives' Employment on the Mental Health of Married Men and Women' *American Sociological Review* Vol.47 pp.217-27.

Kessler, R and McLeod, J. 1984. 'Sex Differences in Vulnerability to Undesirable Life Events' *American Sociological Review* Vol.49 pp.620-31.

Kessler, R and Magee, W. 1993 'Childhood Adversities and Adult Depression: Basic Patterns of Association in a US National Survey' *Psychological Medicine* Vol.23 pp.679-91.

Leader, H, Fitzgerald, M and Kinsella, A. 1985 'Behaviourally Deviant Pre-School Children and Depressed Mothers' *Irish Journal of Medical Science* Vol.154 pp.106-9.

Lin, N and Ensel, W. 1989 'Life Stress and Health: Stressors and Resources' *American Sociological Review* Vol.54 pp.383-99.

Miller, P, Kreitman, N B, Ingham, J G. 1980 'Self-Esteem, Life Stress and Psychiatric Disorder' *Journal of Affective Disorders* Vol.17 pp.65-76.

Mirowsky, J and Ross, C. 1990 'Control or Defense? Depression and the Sense of Control Over Good and Bad Outcomes' *Journal of Health and Social Behaviour* Vol. 31 pp.71-86.

Newmann, J P. 1984 'Sex Differences in Symptoms of Depression: Clinical Disorder or Normal Distress?' *Journal of Health and Social Behaviour* Vol.21 pp.33-42.

O'Hare, A. and O'Connor, A. 1987 'Gender Differences in Treated Mental Illness in the Republic of Ireland' in Curtin, C, Jackson, P and O'Connor, B. (eds.) *Gender in Irish Society* Galway: Galway University Press.

Orley, J and Wing, J K. 1979 'Psychiatric Disorder in in two African Villages' *Archives of General Psychiatry* Vol.36 pp.513-20.

Pearlin, L. 1991 'The Study of Coping: An Overview of Problems and Directions' in Eckenrode, J. (ed.) *The Social Context of Coping* New York: Plenum.

Penfold, S P and Walker, G A. 1983 *Women and the Psychiatric Paradox* Montreal and London: Eden Press.

Prior, P. 1997 'Women, Mental Disorder and Crime in Nineteenth Century Ireland' in Byrne, A and Leonard, M. (eds.) *Women and Irish Society: A Sociological Reader* Dublin: Attic Press.

Radloff, L. 1975 'Sex Differences in Depression: The Effects of Occupation and Marital Status' *Sex Roles* Vol.1 pp.249-65.

Rogers, A, Pilgrim, D and Lacey, R. 1993 *Experiencing Psychiatry: Users' Views of Services* London: Macmillan.

Rosenfield, S. 1989 'The Effects of Women's Employment: Personal Control and Sex Differences in Mental Health' *Journal of Health and Social Behaviour* Vol.30 pp.77-91.

Ross, C and Mirowsky, J. 1995 'Does Employment Affect Health?' *Journal of Health and Social Behaviour* Vol.36 pp.230-43.

Rutter, M and Quinton, D. 1975 'Psychiatric Disorder: Ecological Factors and Concepts of Causation' in McGurk, H. (ed.) *Ecological Factors in Human Development* Holland: New Amsterdam.

Rutter, M. 1989 'Pathways from Childhood to Adult Life' *Journal of Child Psychology and Psychiatry* Vol.30 pp.23-51.

Scarf, M. 1981 *Unfinished Business: Pressure Points in the Lives of Women* Glasgow: Fontana/ Collins.

Seligman, M E P. 1975 *Helplessness* San Fransisco: W H Freeman.

Showalter, E. 1987 *The Female Malady* London: Virago.

Simon, R W. 1995 'Gender, Multiple Roles, Role Meaning and Depression' *Journal of Health and Social Behaviour* Vol.36 pp.182-94.

Thoits, P A. 1995. 'Identity-Relevant Events and Psychological Symptoms: A Cautionary Tale' *Journal of Health and Social Behaviour* Vol.36 pp.72-82.

Thoits, P. 1986 'Multiple Identities: Examining Gender and Marital Status Differences in Distress' *American Sociological Review* Vol.51 pp.259-72.

Thoits, P. 1995 'Stress, Coping, and Social Support Processes: Where Are We? What Next?' *Journal of Health and Social Behaviour* Extra Issue pp.53-79.

Turner, J, Wheaton, B and Lloyd, D. 1995 'The Epidemiology of Social Stress' *American Sociological Review* Vol.60 pp.104-25.

Ussher, J M. 1991 *Women's Madness: Misogny or Mental Illness?* London: Harvester Wheatsheaf.

Weissman, M, Bland, R, Joyce, P, Newman, S, Wells, E and Wittchen, H. 1993 'Sex Differences in Rates of Depression: Cross-National Perspectives' *Journal of Affective Disorders* Vol.29, No.2+3 (Special Issue) pp.77-84.

Weissman, M and Paykel, E. 1974 *The Depressed Woman* London: University of Chicago Press.

Weissman, M, Gammon, G D, John, K, Merikangas, K R, Warner, V, Prusoff, B A and Scholomskas, D. 1987 'Children of Depressed Parents: Increased Psychopathology and Early Onset of Major Depression' *Archives of General Psychiatry* Vol.44 pp.847-53.

Wing, J K, Cooper, J E and Sartorius, N. 1974 *Measurement and Classification of Psychiatric Symptoms: An Instruction Manual for the PSE and Catego Program* Cambridge: Cambridge University Press.

Section 5:
Women and Reproduction

For feminists, the issue of who should control reproduction and how, has always been closely tied to efforts to improve the situation of women. Motherhood and reproduction can entail a measure of oppression for the women concerned. Traditionally, motherhood has been glorified as women's chief vocation and the definition of women primarily as child rearers was not only taken for granted but was idealised as the basis for moral and family reform. However, Mitchel (1966) warns that when motherhood is used as a mystique, it becomes an instrument of oppression. Feminists have tried to demystify aspects of motherhood by documenting the unfavourable conditions within which childbirth is largely controlled by the male dominated medical profession. This is not to deny the considerable advances in medicine which have made childbirth a much less hazardous process for both the mother and the child. However, such advances have been accompanied by male doctors having considerable control over women's lives and in the process, women's control as professionals and as mothers has been eroded. Since childbirth and mothering are to a large extent controlled by the male medical profession, women are often unable to make informed choices during pregnancy and childbirth. The way in which medical men view women is a powerful element in the control of their female patients. As Oakley (1984) points out reproduction and motherhood have become a male medicalised domain. Giving women more control over their bodies is central to increasing women's control over their own lives.

The authors of the five chapters in this section outline the ways in which the experience of reproduction and motherhood impinges on women's lives and suggest ways in which male control of reproduction and motherhood can be eradicated. Their collective aim is to challenge the conditions within which reproduction and motherhood can be oppressive.

Sandra Ryan outlines the medicalised nature of childbirth in Ireland. She charts the gradual removal of midwives from their traditional role as the primary carers of women in childbirth. The simultaneous development of obstetrics as a 'science' masculinised childbirth and male experts increasingly viewed women as reproductive machines which required their intervention to ensure that they function efficiently. So persuasive has the male control of childbirth been that the Republic of Ireland's medically managed childbirth model has been exemplified as a model method of delivery and exported to Britain and elsewhere. Yet, despite this worrying trend, Ryan outlines ways in which women can regain influence in childbirth. She points to research which indicates that more and more women are choosing to have their babies at home thus undermining the supremacy of obstetric care in large centralised impersonal units.

Ryan suggests that feminist critiques of health care should be incorporated into the third level courses increasingly undertaken by nurses and midwives in order to highlight the patriarchal nature of the medical profession and to demonstrate alternative models of healthcare which treat women as women rather than as mere reproductive machines.

Jocelyne Rigal's chapter reminds us not to treat women as a homogeneous group linked simplistically through gender but emphasises that women have different histories and cultural backgrounds and sometimes these can intersect to produce and perpetuate particular kinds of disadvantage. Rigal illustrates the cultural barriers between female health professionals and Traveller women. She suggests that while gender is instrumental in enabling female health professionals gain access to Traveller women, nonetheless, their contrasting backgrounds and different educational attainments lead female health professionals to consider themselves superior to Traveller women. These differences produce asymmetrical power relationships between both groups and this is illustrated throughout the chapter in the interactions between female health professionals and Traveller women. By controlling access to information regarding contraceptive methods, female health professionals hinder the choice and control of Traveller women over their reproductive lives. The female professional health workers in Rigal's study decided the most effective means of birth control for the Traveller women and their decisions were often based on moral rather than medical judgements. Rigal effectively reminds us that there is no one generalisable, identifiable, collectively shared experience of motherhood. Social class, ethnicity and economic status impinge upon the social conditions of mothering for individual women and differentially influence their experiences.

The control of women's fertility is also the subject of Abbey Hyde's research. In this case, the perceived control of fathers over their daughters' sexuality. The concept of patriarchy which refers to the rule of the father over his wife and children is used to effectively illustrate the extent to which men continue to exert power and authority within families. Hyde provides a qualitative analysis of the differing responses of mothers and fathers to news of their daughters' non-marital pregnancies. While mothers lamented the possible lost life chances of their daughters as a result of untimely pregnancies, nonetheless, they were generally supportive of their daughters. Fathers, on the other hand, were more concerned with how they and their patriarchal position in society was affected by their daughters' pregnancies. Fathers felt that daughters, in their apparent inability to control their fertility, had exposed them as failures and as inadequate protectors of their daughters' sexuality. Hyde traces the origins of this view to traditional transfers of women between males in elementary societies. She suggests that the contemporary form of these exchanges is to be found in marriage where fathers 'give away' daughters and newly married women interchange their fathers' surname for that of their husbands'. Part of this process involves symbolically transferring the sexual protection of daughters to other approved men through marriage.

Feminist discussions of reproduction and motherhood not only focus on questions of choice and external conditions but also look closely at women's experiences as mothers. This is the theme of the chapter by Marie Leane and Elizabeth Kiely. They explore the reality of lone motherhood based on the subjective accounts of four mothers. While the sample is undoubtedly small, nonetheless, the 'lived experiences' of the women effectively challenge new right rhetoric on single lone motherhood. The women in Leane and Kiely's study did not become pregnant to gain access to welfare benefits and housing accommodation. Rather, their accounts vividly portray the inadequacy of welfare benefit entitlements and the poverty experienced by lone mothers. Their research indicates that lone mothers are more likely to be suffering economic hardship, poor housing and are unlikely to be able to exercise much choice over employment. Yet, despite these difficulties, the women in Leane and Kiely's study viewed motherhood as a positive and rewarding experience. Their main problems related to the ideological and practical barriers surrounding reconciling childcare responsibilities with paid employment. By illustrating state policy towards working mothers in Sweden, Leane and Kiely suggest various ways in which the Irish State could promote and facilitate the labour market participation of single lone mothers. Their research counteracts the notion that most people live in nuclear families and that mothers always have husbands to support them. Like the previous chapter, Leane and Kiely's research demonstrates that for an increasing number of women, parenthood does not necessarily mean marriage.

State policy towards motherhood is taken up by Patricia Kennedy in her chapter which examines the impact welfare policies have on women's experiences as lifegivers, carers and earners in both parts of Ireland. In terms of maternity entitlements, women in the North fare better than women in the Republic of Ireland, although both regions fall behind the provision available in many other European countries. Kennedy demonstrates how entitlements to maternity benefits are closely linked to women's participation in formal employment. This reduces non-working women to passive consumers of health services and the state which dictate to employed women how long they can remain absent from the labour market. Within the context of the European Union, Kennedy suggests the rights of pregnant women in the Republic of Ireland are likely to be enhanced under the Social Protocol of the Maastricht Treaty. However, this will remain a shallow victory for women in Northern Ireland as the United Kingdom is not party to the Social Protocol.

By challenging the invisibility of women's own experiences of reproduction and motherhood and the role of the state in defining motherhood, the chapters in this section illustrate the extent of the patriarchal control of women's bodies and argue for women to take control of the most intimate aspects of their own lives.

References and Further Reading

Mitchel, J. 1966 'Women: The Longest Revolution' *New Left Review* No.40 pp.11-37.
Oakley, A. 1984 *The Captured Womb* Oxford: Blackwell.

15.

Interventions In Childbirth: The Midwives' Role

Sandra Ryan

Introduction

Childbirth in Ireland, as in many western countries, has become a highly medicalised event. Women no longer have control over how, where, when and with whom they give birth. I will argue that this is the result of two mutually reinforcing patriarchal phenomena; the masculinisation of childbirth, and the effects of colonial legislation. This chapter focuses on the developments of midwifery in Ireland within these constraints. Midwives at present are unable to offer women-centered childbirth care because their autonomy is impaired by their position as a subordinate occupational group. However, midwives in Ireland have not yet followed the 'professionalisation' route of their counterparts in Britain. The final part of this chapter will suggest that this is positive for Irish midwives, and women in childbirth, because there is an opportunity to move childbirth in Ireland towards a feminist paradigm.

The Masculinisation of Childbirth

The developments in childbirth practices over the last century have resulted in childbirth being taken out of the control of women. This situation can be explained by the influence of professional power and patriarchy in many societies. In order to explain the masculinisation of childbirth it is necessary to consider two inter-related factors which enabled the appropriation of childbirth by obstetricians. The first is the inter-occupational relationship between midwives and doctors, which has resulted in the removal of midwives from their traditional role as the primary carers of women in childbirth; the second is the development of obstetrics as a 'science', whereby doctors have conceptualised women as reproductive machines which require interventions to ensure that they function efficiently.

The Erosion of Midwifery

Historically it has been predominantly women who have cared for the vulnerable and dependent in their own homes. Midwives have long been associated with the gender specific task of caring for pregnant women and their social role was significant in many ways. Midwives practised family health care by the use of traditional medicines such as herbs and other empirically tested strategies (Oakley, 1993). They were also associated with witchcraft, but because early Europeans recognised 'good' witches and 'bad' witches, midwives were seen as good witches or 'wise women' (which remains the French term for midwife today). This association with witchcraft is important because this 'taint' played a part in Church and State attempts to curtail the power of women and restrict the practice of medicine to the new university trained male medical practitioners later in the nineteenth century.

Childbirth became the target for control by the emerging medical profession of obstetricians. The demise of the midwives' role can be directly linked to the rise in professional power of physicians. One of the tactics used by physicians during this period was to discredit the worth and capabilities of midwives. One notable accusation was made in an American obstetrics textbook:

> Midwives do harm not only through their lack of obstetric knowledge, their lack of antiseptic precautions, and their tendency to conceal undesirable features, but most of them are the most inveterate quacks... The institution of midwives is a remnant of barbaric times, a blot on our civilisation which ought to be wiped out as soon as possible (Garrigues, 1902, p.211).

It is interesting to note that in order to establish themselves as the providers of care for women in childbirth, obstetricians discredited midwives rather than prove their own value. The significance of gender in the growth of the professions cannot be over-emphasized. The professional ideal was immersed in a culture of masculinity and the sexual division of labour. Masculine traits such as objectivity, competitiveness, individualism and predictability were lauded over the culturally feminine traits such as nurturance, intuition, and personal interaction (Davies, 1995). This prevailing culture hampered midwives in their inter-occupational struggles with obstetricians. The response of midwives was to attempt to recover some autonomy by adopting their own professionalising strategies, such as the registration of practitioners. Ann Witz (1992) has provided a neo-Weberian account of the struggle for midwives in Britain to gain registration during the late 19th century. Obstetricians had gained their dominant position by excluding female midwives from certain areas of childbirth and by regulating their practice on 'normal' childbirth. Their tactics entailed:

> The encirclement of women within a related but distinct sphere of competence within a division of labour, and invariably, precisely because these

occupations are gendered, involve their subordination to a male occupation. (Witz, 1992, p.197).

The midwives' response to this position of subordination was to play the doctors at their own game. Witz argues that the registration campaign was part of a female 'professional project' that involved a 'dual closure strategy'. On the one hand they were attempting to usurp some autonomy and control from physicians. On the other they were attempting to raise their market value by seeking to restrict entry to their own occupational group to suitably trained midwives.

Although midwives succeeded in gaining registration by 1902, this did not prevent obstetricians from ensuring that their status was reduced to that of an adjunct occupation – that is an occupational group which is allocated a lesser role than the dominant profession and yet provides a service that the dominant profession could not proceed without. Consequently the role of the midwife changed from an independent practitioner who accrued a salary from her own clients, to one who attended women in uncomplicated labour under medical control and supervision.

The Rise and Rise of Obstetric Power

Obstetrics as we know it today derived from the growth of the lying-in hospitals of the eighteenth century. Male involvement in birth came in the form of 'man midwives' who originated from the barber-surgeons of this time. The significance of these roots is that from the outset obstetrics was established as a surgical speciality (Porter, 1995). This background reinforced the prevailing 'rational' 'male' 'scientific' view that those who cared for childbearing women could only do so by viewing the female body as a machine which needed to be controlled and interfered with by technical means. As Ann Oakley pointed out:

> In the absence of understanding, control and management were important-childbirth and women had to be 'mastered'. The masculine gender of this word is highly significant. The male role in obstetrics paralleled the male cultural role; socialised to be masters of their own fates, families and environments, the same kind of impulse possessed the men who first took over childbirth from the traditional carers of women, midwives (Oakley, 1993, p.71)

In addition to its claim over scientific rationality the medical profession of obstetrics completed its domination over childbirth by two other related means, the increasing removal of childbirth from home and the use of technology on all women in childbirth.

Hospital Birth

In Ireland 99.5 per cent of births currently take place in hospital despite a lack of compelling evidence that it is safer than at home (Campbell and MacFarlane, 1990, O'Connor, 1995). These statistics show an almost complete reversal of the situation less than one hundred years ago. At the beginning of this century hospital births were only for the very poorest of women where they were at grave risk of contracting puerperal or 'childbed' fever which was due to a lack of handwashing by physicians. In Ireland, puerperal fever accounted for fifty per cent of maternal deaths in 1925. Records of home and hospital delivery in Dublin in the 1920s and 1930s indicated that home was the safer place to give birth (O'Connor, 1995).

Since the Health Care Act of 1970, women have been entitled to care in childbirth at home. However, despite the growing demand, those who wish to do so face difficulties in getting professional help or support from midwives or general practitioners. Some professionals go so far as to accuse women of risking their baby's life in an effort to browbeat them into accepting hospitalisation (Katz Rothman, 1982, Doyal, 1995, O'Connor, 1995). In Ireland the disempowering and pathological effects of hospitalised childbirth are exacerbated because services are concentrated in large centralised obstetrician-run hospitals.

The Use of Technology

One of the outcomes of childbirth taking place in hospital is that it has become a highly medicalised event involving the use of technologically advanced equipment. There has been such a dramatic change in technology and obstetric practice over the last century that childbirth is no longer seen as part of the natural cycle of life. Birth is viewed as a pathological process that is only 'normal' retrospectively (Oakley, 1993, Doyal, 1995, O'Connor, 1995). Such change has had a profound effect on the lives of women and how they view childbirth themselves (Arney, 1985, Garcia et al., 1990, Oakley, 1993).

It is difficult to assess fully the impact of a 'high tech' birth on women. Research in a number of countries indicates that it tends to deny women the emotional support, information and control that they require during childbirth (Kitzinger, 1978, Oakley, 1979, Reid and Garcia, 1989). Women globally are beginning to register objections to the many routine and unnecessary practices that surround hospital births. Two examples of the most common 'routine' medical procedures in hospital childbirth are episiotomy and induction of birth. The feminist challenge to these procedures is that they are unproven practices developed in a masculine model of health care which damage women physically and emotionally.

Episiotomy

Described as the Western world's version of genital mutilation (Kitzinger, 1989, 1995), episiotomy is the most common surgical procedure carried out in North America and several other European countries (Doyal, 1995). Episiotomy involves cutting women from the vagina towards the anus in order to widen the 'birth canal'. Foetal distress is often given as a reason for carrying out an episiotomy, the rationale being that it will hasten labour. It is always performed when a surgical delivery is to be carried out (often as a result of an induced labour or following epidural pain relief). However, there is no evidence to indicate that routine episiotomies do anything to improve either delivery or post-childbirth recovery (Chalmers, et al., 1989). In fact, many women are unaware that it is being carried out and undergo a surgical procedure without informed consent (Banta and Thacker, 1982, WHO, 1986).

Induction of Labour

Induction of labour became fashionable in obstetrics in the early 1970s (Oakley, 1993). Whether induced by rupturing membranes or by an intravenous drip, induced birth is painful. Inch (1982) has shown that induced labours can lead to a cascade of interventions that in some cases leads on to emergency caesarian section. There are of course some genuine reasons for induced birth, involving the well-being of either the mother or child. However, the rationale for induced birth is often rather more spurious. For example, Macfarlane (1978) noted a distinct pattern of induced births on Tuesdays, Wednesdays, Thursdays and Fridays. Few births occurred on Sundays or public holidays. That women can be exposed to such unnecessary danger and pain simply in order to convenience the working routine of obstetricians, is a stark example of their disempowerment.

It is fair to say that following consumer and media pressure the high induction rates of the seventies were addressed (Oakley, 1993). However, in Ireland, the domination of what has become known as 'actively managed labour' may well cause an increase in induced births once more (Ryan et al., 1995).

The 'Active Management of Labour'

Ireland has become a major exporter of a particular style of care in childbirth. The 'Active management of labour' was pioneered in the National Maternity Hospital, Holles St Dublin. This approach to childbirth is an exemplar of the dominance of a male model of childbirth, and the subsequent reduction of midwifery to an adjunct role. It has become the mode of practice in many countries (O'Connor, 1995) and in Ireland is the practice in approximately seventy-three per cent of maternity units (Irish Association for Improvements in Maternity Services (IAIMS, 1995).

Developed primarily for first time mothers in order to prevent 'prolonged and difficult' labours, this method ensured that obstetricians could have a role in all births and not just the complicated ones (O'Connor, 1995). This type of highly managed childbirth does not allow women giving birth in hospitals the freedom to choose the way they would like their labour to progress. In the centres practicing actively managed births a protocol of care is routinely followed:

> Progress is assessed, initially at one hour after admission. Artificial rupture of membranes is now performed... Progress is assessed for the second time at two hours after admission. An oxytocin infusion is started unless significant progress... has been made since the previous examination... Progress is assessed for the third time at three hours after admission. Further progress is assessed at intervals not exceeding two hours. (O'Driscoll et al., 1993).

Active management of labour was founded on the unproven assumption that first time mothers suffered from inefficient muscle activity of the uterus. The appeal to women in labour of this highly managed birth is the guarantee that they will deliver their babies within twelve hours of admission to hospital. The natural and individual process of birth is interfered with from the outset, and obstetricians have a standardised yardstick by which to measure each woman's progress in labour and assess that progress according to the protocol.

The active management of labour appears to be the culmination in the shift over the last century from home and natural delivery to completely medicalised birth. It reduces birthing women from the status of autonomous subjects to that of objects in a routinised and mechanistic process, where medico-technical considerations are all that matters. It also undermines any authority of the midwife in attendance. She is there to carry out a pre-determined protocol of 'care' which does not allow for any individual clinical decisions on her part.

Historically, childbirth was a women only affair. Other women were the necessary and welcomed persons who cared for women in childbirth. Recent research has shown that this social support (in this case by midwives) had measurable positive outcomes including; babies above normal birthweight; an increased likelihood of spontaneous onset of labour and delivery; babies who were healthy at delivery and afterwards and better post-partum physical and psychological health of the mothers (Oakley, 1993). Yet the masculinisation of childbirth has led to the erosion of the midwives' role and as a consequence women are being denied their right to the support of other women.

Midwifery in Ireland

Historically the change in Ireland's provision of maternity services has shadowed that of England. This is hardly surprising given that until recently Ireland was an English colony. The patriarchal model which dominated the development of midwifery as we know it today, was transposed to Ireland by dint of colonial rule. Midwifery in the North of Ireland remains under the jurisdiction of the British National Health Service (NHS). So Ireland's model of childbirth in its present form is the result of a combination of patriarchal domination of health care delivery and colonial rule. The practical implications of these two factors can be demonstrated by examining the move from women-centered childbirth to hospital based obstetric care.

At the beginning of the century midwives were employed as part of the district dispensary service set up primarily for the poor. Some midwives also practiced privately and, as in England, became a threat to general practitioners whose charges were more expensive. Irish physicians were able to use the colonial powers from England in the form of legislation to protect their claims over childbirth. For example in 1902 the Royal College of Physicians extended its 'Midwives and Health Visitors Act' to Ireland. By alleging that unlicensed 'handy women' were responsible for the high maternal death rates, physicians succeeded in giving control of training and registration of midwives in Ireland to the London-based Central Midwives Board. The colonial control of childbirth did not cease with independence, the act remained in force until 1952 when An Bord Altrainas took over midwifery training.

In rural Ireland, up until the 1950s, birth was still considered a natural event which took place at home and involved only women. In 1956 thirty-one per cent of all births took place at home and yet by 1966 the figure had fallen to only ten per cent. By this stage the Maternity and Infant Care Scheme was established which allowed for hospital delivery on the payment of a small fee. O'Connor (1995) suggests that the cultural attitude which prevailed at the time was that care which required payment was superior. In 1976 Comhairle na n-Ospideal echoed the British Peel report which recommended that all births should take place in hospital. The consequences of such legislation can be seen in the current level of home births which stands at 0.5 per cent.

Ironically the current decline of British influence comes at a time when feminist voices are beginning to have an influence on British maternity services. Yet this influence has not been transposed to the North of Ireland. Some of the positive changes recommended following the British 'Changing Childbirth' document, for example the promotion of midwife/GP-led birth centres, has been blocked by obstetrician- led objections in the North of Ireland.

Even more worrying, the South of Ireland has become the centre of influence in medically managed childbirth and exports it elsewhere, including Britain (midwives in some centres in the North of Ireland gain training in this style of labour management by educational visits to Dublin). So, just as Britain was relinquishing its control over Irish midwives, the 'active management of labour', hailed as a landmark in obstetrics, became well established. The adverse effect of this is that midwives in Ireland have not had an opportunity, between colonial rule and the power of medicine, to reclaim their position as experts in women-centered childbirth.

There remains a close link between Irish and British maternity policy; midwives and obstetricians have been able to train and practice in either country without restriction. However, unlike their counterparts in Britain, Irish midwives still do not have their own regulatory body (O'Connor, 1995). In the remainder of this chapter I will point to the positive side of this situation, in that Irish midwives have not yet entered the divisive 'professionalisation' race. It may not be too late for midwives in Ireland to follow a different route.

Towards a Feminist Paradigm for Midwifery?

There are some positive signs in the move towards regaining childbirth for women. To begin with, Marie O'Connor's (1995) research shows that women are demonstrating their disapproval of the quality of obstetric care in the large centralised units by voting to stay at home and give birth. In doing so, they face a tide of disapproval and pressure from professionals along with an absence of adequate birthcare support in the community. In a national survey carried out by the Economic and Social Research Institute (ESRI), seventeen per cent of lower income women and thirteen per cent of higher income women stated they would like to have a home birth (Dwyer, 1994). In their most recently published booklet, the Irish Association for Improvement in Maternity Services (IAIMS) provide information about the services available, and the intervention rates, in a county by county breakdown. Information about interventionist childbirth practices is useful. While on its own it will not change such practices, it at least gives women the opportunity to become informed about hospital practices in their area.

There is a dearth of midwifery literature relating to Ireland (McCrea, 1995). However in midwifery journals used on this side of the Atlantic, a return to the traditional skills of women-centred midwifery care is being actively promoted. The British Government's 'Changing Childbirth' document is a direct result of consumer pressure. However, midwives remain concerned that their role as experts in non-interventionist care has been eroded during the years of 'high tech' childbirth. Katz Rothman (1982) describes how American midwives had to reconceptualise their understanding of childbirth from a masculine medical model back to a women-centered model. Katz Rothman describes the process by which midwives suddenly realised that the medical model fought against women's natural impulses in childbirth, instead of working with them, as 'radicalisation'. This radicalisation involves the recognition by midwives of the value of care, support and partnership with birthing women.

Midwives: Professionals or Partners?

There is now a growing feminist literature which has challenged the gender-blindness of much of the sociological analyses of professions. Alongside the feminist critiques of the professions, the undervalue of care and care work has been subject to sustained examination (Ungerson, 1983, Pascall, 1986, Parker, 1992). Developments in both of these subject areas have direct relevance for birthing women, midwives and feminist scholars interested in women's health.

We know that much of the midwifery practices and regulation of training in Ireland has mirrored Britain. However, midwives in Ireland may be in a better position to develop women-centered midwifery care than their colleagues in Britain who have already followed the female professional projects route described by Witz (1992). Critiques of the professionalisation of 'female' occupations have centred around the fact that such developments create two tier organisations which relegate some women workers to a peripheral role influenced by race, class (Robinson, 1992) and domestic commitments (Robinson, 1993) and at the same time move the professionals-to-be further away from relationships with clients (Salvage, 1992, Davies, 1995, Sandall, 1995). Irish midwives do not yet appear to have engaged the 'professionalisation' race in that they have yet to be regulated as a group separate from nursing (O'Connor, 1995). This gives them time to develop a relationship with the very vocal pressure groups in Ireland such as IAIMS, and form partnerships with women which will reject the professional project model in favour of a feminist one. One way of achieving this is to make sure that women have access to the ample studies which demonstrate that midwives are the appropriate health workers to support women in 'normal' childbirth (see next section for examples). Another is by the inclusion of feminist critiques of health care in the ever increasing third level courses taken by nurses and midwives (MacWhannell, 1994). These two activities will have two outcomes; the first is that nurses and midwives become alerted to the power differences in patriarchal institutions which curtail their ability to function independently. The second is the realisation that the present western, male-dominated view of health care is only one side of the story.

The Effectiveness of Womens' Care

Turning the spurious scientistic rationale of obstetrics on its head, Ann Oakley has demonstrated that women and midwives can make use of the 'scientific' model of research in the shape of randomised control trials and 'prove' the value of love and caring in childbirth (Oakley, 1993). Love and care appear to be two immeasurable constructs, however, they can and have been measured in what Oakley describes as social intervention studies.

One such study (Olds et al., 1986) set out to enhance women's informal support systems by the use of home visiting nurses. A similar study among Asian families (Dance, 1987) showed how the use of a link worker had a positive effect on pregnancies, for example, fewer medical problems; more happiness; shorter labours; less use of analgesia in labour; higher mean birthweight and fewer feeding problems. Using a different approach, Nelson et al. (1980) showed how maternal expectation of a pleasant delivery (in this case the Leboyer method) can effect the length of labour. A Scottish study showed how the community based as opposed to large centralised services facilitated close social interactions between midwives and women. The setting plays an important part in women's ability to relax in childbirth as Klein et al. (1984) demonstrated by the significantly lower use of medication and instrumental delivery in women who were cared for in 'birth rooms' rather than the traditional labour ward. A British study the 'Know your midwife' scheme carried out by Flint and Poulengeris in London (1987) showed that the women in the scheme felt more confident to ask questions in the ante-natal period, had a higher percentage of spontaneous onset of labour, felt in control during labour, had little or no analgesia, had few episiotomies, slightly bigger babies that needed less resuscitation, were more likely to be breastfeeding at six weeks and found it easier to be a mother.

Although the above studies were carried out in the 1980s in Britain, they are of relevance to Ireland today. They demonstrate that positive change can slowly be brought about. As Oakley points out:

> Love-caring — is as important as science — technical knowledge, monitoring and intervention- in the maternity services today. Rather than being the soft option, it is a fundamental necessity. For those who wish to concern themselves with scientific proof, this can be demonstrated from published studies examining the effects of social support as distinct from clinical care. Consequently the goals, of satisfying mothers and producing healthy babies, which are often deemed by obstetricians to be at odds with one another, are in reality the same goal. The definitions of caring given by midwives on the one hand and obstetricians on the other, have been very different and opposite... *Midwives must do everything to reclaim this concept of care (and the rest of us must do everything we can to help them)*, both for the sake of women and babies and for the sake of themselves (Oakley, 1993, p.77 my emphasis).

Conclusion

Childbirth in Ireland remains an obstetric-led masculine model of care. Yet there is the opportunity for women and midwives to form alliances that will begin the slow process of reclaiming childbirth for women. This opportunity may arise because of two reasons. First because of the increase in pressure groups led by women who want to have their babies on their own terms; and second by the fact that Irish midwives have not yet gone down the cul de sac of professionalisation (Davies, 1995) like their counterparts in Britain. While this at present leaves midwives in the unchanged position of being an adjunct occupation to obstetricians, it gives them time to listen to what Irish women want, take note of the research available which valorises their position as true partners for women in childbirth, and join in the battle to reclaim childbirth.

The last word to an Irish sociologist whose groundbreaking work on home birth gives some indication that women in Ireland are beginning to fight back against the seemingly unremitting tide of obstetric-led childbirth:

> Home birth reminds us that women can do it, in, and out, of hospital, away from the birth machines. Listening to women's stories, birth becomes more ordinary and less frightening. It becomes more down to earth, yet more precious, than we could possibly have imagined (O'Connor, 1995, p.287).

Discussion Topics

1. Why do obstetricians hold such a powerful position in Irish health care?

2. What range of birth choices are available to women in contemporary Ireland? Do women really have a choice?

3. Why do you think more women choose to have their babies in hospitals rather than at home?

4. Helping mothers to have a positive childbirth experience conflicts with producing healthy babies. Discuss.

References and Further Reading

Arney, W R. 1985 *Power and the Profession of Obstetrics* Chicago: University Press

Banta, D and Thacker, S. 1982 'The Risks and Benefits of Episiotomy; A review' *Birth*, Vol.9 (1) pp.25-30.

Campbell, R and Macfarlane, A. 1990 'Recent Debate on the Place of Birth' in Garcia, R Kilpatrick, R and Richards, M. (eds.) *The Politics of Maternity Care* Oxford: Oxford University Press

Chalmers, I, Enkin, M and Keirse, M. 1989 (eds.) *Effective Care in Pregnancy and Childbirth* Oxford: Clarendon Press.

Comhairle na n-Ospideal. 1976 'Development of Hospital Maternity Services: A Discussion Document' Dublin.

Dance, J. 1987 'A Social Intervention by Linkworkers to Pakistani Women and Pregnancy Outcome', Unpublished: cited in Oakley, A. 1993 *Essays on Women Medicine and Health* Edinburgh: Edinburgh University Press.

Davies, C. 1995 *Gender and the Professional Predicament in Nursing*, Basingstoke: Open University Press.

Department of Health, 1993 *Changing Childbirth Part 1: Report of the Expert Maternity Group* London: HMSO.

Doyal, L. 1995 *What Makes Women Sick?: Gender and the Political Economy of Health* London: Routledge.

Dwyer, M. 1994 *National survey on womens' health needs*, Economic and Social Research Institute, Unpublished paper.

Flint, C and Poulengeris, P. 1987 *The Know Your Midwife Scheme*, report published by authors: London.

Garcia, J Kilpatrick, R and Richards M. 1990 *The Politics of Maternity Care*, Oxford: Oxford University Press.

Garrigues, H J. 1902 *A Textbook of the Art and Science of Midwifery* Philadelphia: Lippencot.

Inch, S. 1982 *Birthrights*, London: Hutchinson.

Irish Association for the Improvement of Maternity Services, 1995 *A Guide to Maternity Units in Ireland* Dublin: IAIMS

Katz Rothman, B. 1982 *In Labour: Women and Power in the Birth Place* London: Junction Books.

Kitzinger, S. 1978 *Women as Mothers* London: Fontana.

Kitzinger, S. 1989 'Childbirth and Society' in Chalmers, I, Enkin, M and Keirse, M. (eds.) *Effective Care in Pregnancy and Childbirth* Oxford: Clarendon Press.

Kitzinger, S. 1992 'Birth and Violence Against Women: Generating Hypotheses from Womens' Accounts of Unhappiness after Childbirth', in Roberts, H. (ed.) *Womens' Health Matters* London: Routledge.

Kitzinger, S 1995 'Preface' to O'Connor, M. 1995 *Birth Tides: Turning Towards Home Birth* London: Pandora.

Klien, M, Papageorgio, A, Westreich, R, Spector-Dunsky, L, Elkins, V, Kramer, M S and Gelfand, M M. 1984 'Care in the Birth Room Versus a Conventional Setting: A Control Trial' *Canadian Medical Association Journal* 131 pp.1461-1466.

MacFarlane, A. 1978 'Variations in Number of Births and Peri-Natal Mortality Rates by Day of the Week in England and Wales' *British Medical Journal* 2 pp.1670-1673.

MacWhannell, D. 1994 'Health and Caring in a Feminist Context' in Davies, S, Lubelska, C and Quinn, J. (eds.) *Changing the Subject: Women in Higher Education* London: Taylor and Francis.

McCrea, H. 1995 'The Role of Midwives in a Teaching Hospital in the Republic of Ireland' *British Journal of Midwifery* Vol.2 (9) pp.407-408.

Nelson, N M, Enkin, M W, Saigail, S, Bennett, K J, Milner, and Sackett, D L. 1980 'A Randomised Clinical Trial of the Leboyer Method of Childbirth' *New England Journal of Medicine* March 20, pp.656-686.

Oakley, A. 1979 *Becoming a Mother* Oxford: Martin Robinson.

Oakley, A. 1993 *Essays on Women Medicine and Health* Edinburgh: Edinburgh University Press.

O'Connor, M. 1995 *Birth Tides: Turning Towards Home Birth* London: Pandora.

O'Driscoll, K, Meagher, D, and Boylan, P. 1993 *Active Management of Labour* (2nd ed) London: Bailliere Tindall.

Olds, D L, Henderson, C R, Tatelbaum, R, and Chamberlin, R. 1986 'Improving the Delivery of Prenatal Care and Outcomes of Pregnancy: A Randomised Trial of Home Nurse Visitation' *Paediatrics* 77 pp.16-28.

Parker, G. 1992 *With Due Care and Attention; A Review of Research on Informal Care* London: Family Policy Studies Centre.

Pascal, G. 1986 *Social Policy: A Feminist Analysis* London: Tavistock.

Porter, S. 1995 *Sociology in Practice: Health For All?* London: Distance Learning Centre.

Reid, M and Garcia, J. 1989 'Women's Views of Care During Pregnancy and Childbirth', in Chalmers, I, Enkin, M, and Kierse, M, (eds.), *Effective Care in Pregnancy and Childbirth* Oxford: Clarendon Press.

Robinson, S. 1990 'Maintaining the Independence of the Midwifery Profession', in Garcia, J, Kilpatrick, R and Richards, M. (eds.), *Politics of Maternity Care* Oxford: Oxford University Press.

Robinson, K. 1992 'The Nursing Workforce: Aspects of Inequality' in Robinson, J, Gray, A and Elkan, R. (eds.) *Policy Issues in Nursing* Buckingham: Open University Press.

Robinson, S. 1993 'Combining Work with Caring for Children: Findings from a Longitudinal Study of Midwives Careers' *Midwifery* 9, (4), pp.183-196.

Ryan, S, Harisson, S, Parker M, and Magee, S. 1995 *Interventions in Labour of Primigravid Women: The Midwives Role*, Unpublished report, University of Ulster.

Salvage, J. 1992 'Empowering Patients or Empowering Nurses?' in Robinson, J, Gray, A and Elkan, R. (eds.) *Policy Issues in Nursing* Buckinghamshire: Open University Press.

Sandall, J. 1995 'Choice, Continuity and Control: Changing Midwifery Towards a Sociological Perspective' *Midwifery*, 11, pp.201-209.

Ungerson, C. 1983 'Women and Caring: Skills, Tasks and Taboos in Garmarnikow', E, Morgan, D and Purvis, J. (eds.) *The Public and the Private* London: Heinman.

Witz, A. 1992 *Professions and Patriarchy* London: Routledge.

World Health Organisation, 1986 *Having a Baby in Europe* Copenhagen: WHO regional Office for Europe.

16.

Family Planning for Irish Traveller Women: Gender, Ethnicity and Professionalism at Work

Jocelyne Rigal

Introduction

For a long time, feminists have claimed that only by having control over their reproductive capacities, could women exercise choice and control over their lives. But more recently, they have argued that women's choice was limited by a male-dominated medical profession who controlled access and information on contraception through gender and status asymmetry (Roberts, 1981, Fisher and Todd, 1986). For women belonging to minorities or living in the developing world, it has been argued that their reproductive freedom is even more endangered by biases pertaining to contraception, abortion and sterilisation, which reflect eugenic and social control purposes. Quite precisely, distortion and/or denial of information, or even abuse of informed consent, have been revealed in practices which amount to manipulation of these vulnerable women by fertility control providers (Bunkle, 1984, Bryan et al., 1985, Pearson, 1985, Donovan, 1986, Phoenix, 1990). Thus feminists such as Rothman (1984) and Richardson (1993) have argued that the extent of a woman's choice depended upon her race, ethnicity, class and sexual orientation, and that the same reproductive technology can be used for or against women - depending on their background. They also realised that women's attitudes to childbearing and motherhood varied and could clash with wider structures, and then defined a truly liberating reproductive politics as one which legitimised any woman's choice.

This analysis pertains to Irish Traveller women. As they live in appalling conditions and have the highest fertility rate in the European Community, health policies have encouraged them to adopt family planning.[1] This paper will focus upon the implementation of family planning among these women, through an analysis of interactions between female health professionals and Traveller women, and will examine the implications of such counselling. Quite precisely, I will assess whether this counselling was motivated by an allegiance to gender on the part of the nurses, or whether it reasserted their allegiance to professionalism and, from there, to their own community. It follows that the nurses' intervention could enhance, or impede, Traveller women's choice in their reproductive life.

The data was collected through participant observation conducted from October to November 1990 in the mobile clinic run for the Travelling People by the Eastern Health Board.[2] Fieldnotes were recorded to describe interactions taking place between Traveller women and the two nurses, and, to my regret, I was not allowed by the nurses to tape record any of these interactions, for they argued that tape recording would inhibit Traveller women. But private conversations between the nurses were recorded. For the purpose of confidentiality, the informants' names have been altered, and the nurses will be referred to as Laura and Patricia throughout this chapter.

Why Look at Family Planning for Irish Traveller Women?

I have documented elsewhere (Rigal, 1993) the evolution of Irish Traveller women's mothering, and quite specifically, the rise of an ideal family size among this population, with their subsequent use of contraception. The research revealed the role of health workers among Traveller women in urging them to use contraception, thus encouraging them to discard their traditional high fertility and their mothering norms and behaviours.

Feminists who analysed medical consultations dealing with women's health issues (Fisher, 1982 and 1986, Fisher and Todd, 1986, Davis, 1988, Todd, 1989) have concluded that the choice of women is not enhanced, but restricted by male health professionals who have control over information and over the range of options they offer, in a pattern of asymmetrical interactions arising from their gender and professionalism. Further, this exercise of power by male health professionals has been interpreted as an attempt to control women's sexuality and lifestyle in the interest of the social order.

These studies have given little space to medical interactions involving poor and minority women, even though they have asserted that these social parameters do impact upon the course of interactions, and lead to poorer treatment (Todd, 1989). Similarly, it has been voiced that black women were given poor treatment in British maternity services, and encouraged to limit their fertility (Sheffield Black Women's Group, 1984, Bryan et al., 1985, Pearson, 1985, Donovan, 1986, Phoenix, 1990).

Thus, family planning programmes targeted at Traveller women are to be related to the controversial debate on the worldwide implementation of family planning among black and minority women. Such intervention among Traveller women has never been analysed.[3] In the course of my fieldwork conducted in the mobile clinic operated by the Eastern Health Board for Traveller women and their children living in County Dublin, I have analysed the tenets of this implementation through interactions taking place between Traveller women and the staff, and whether they increase, or restrict, the choice and control given to these minority women in their reproductive lives.

Cultural Conflict

Contraceptive counselling in the mobile clinic often yielded to a misunderstood, but substantial, cultural conflict between settled health professionals and Traveller women. Interviews I conducted with older Traveller women have shown that family planning is alien to their traditional experience of motherhood, a feature once shared by Irish settled women. Consequently, contraception is a new element of young Traveller women's experience of motherhood. In this sense, Traveller women's cultural specificity regarding childbearing arises out of a temporal lag with their settled counterparts. The novelty of contraception and the taboos still surrounding sexuality among Traveller women were indicated by the fact that they never broached this topic when talking with the nurses; it was brought to their attention by the nurses.

A conversation I heard between Laura and a thirty-four year-old Traveller woman who was expecting her tenth child vividly illustrates cultural conflicts which surround family planning issues between both populations.

Laura: Were you using something?

Traveller woman: No.

Laura: So, it was planned?

Traveller woman: Yes.

Laura: That's great.

[fieldnotes 20/11/1990]

In this extract, Laura suggests that not using contraception necessarily means (see her use of 'so') planning a pregnancy, when for the Traveller woman, it might mean fatalism or lack of control. Meanwhile, Laura reinforces the idea that pregnancy is an event that should be planned, by saying 'that's great,' reflecting an increasingly prevailing norm from the settled society.

The cultural barriers between Traveller women and contraception were confirmed further by a conversation Laura had with Nan, a twenty-five year-old mother with seven children, who came to have her three-month-old baby examined.

Laura: Is it the pill or the coil?

Nan: Nothing.

Laura: Is it because he doesn't like it?

Nan: No, it's me who doesn't like it.

Laura: But if you don't do anything, you're gonna keep on having more and more.

[fieldnotes 7/11/1990]

At this point, Nan said that she was using the safe period, which was explained to her at the maternity hospital where she had her last baby.

Laura: And what did they tell you?

Nan: Not to make love between the tenth and the twentieth day after my periods.

Laura: That's right.

[fieldnotes 7/11/1990]

Laura then produced a booklet on natural family planning which showed a circle representing the different phases of the menstrual cycle. Laura told Nan that if she wanted to be absolutely safe, she should refrain from sex on a somewhat longer period which she indicated on the circle.

Nan: It's working till now.

Laura: And it might work for years. You can keep this booklet.

I: You must have a cooperative husband.

[fieldnotes 7/11/1990]

Granted that dislike of contraceptive technology has been expressed by mainstream women, including feminists, and that natural family planning was the second most prevalent contraceptive method among the settled Irish (Wilson-Davis, 1982), the fact that Nan disliked artificial means of contraception is not unique, but it might suggest their foreign character for some Traveller women. The dislike could demonstrate her resistance to the medicalisation of sexuality (unlike natural family planning, the methods she rejected involved devices or drugs which were beyond her control and/or her comprehension). In this vein, Nan's refusal of modern contraception can be interpreted as a resistance to the growing impact, and control, of medicine upon her life.

The following account of a contraceptive counselling session documents another implication of cultural conflict between Traveller women and health professionals.

This discussion took place in a training centre for Traveller females where the staff of the mobile clinic had brought samples of the different contraceptive methods with them. It turned out that a young mother, Bernadette, was interested in the intra-uterine contraceptive device and apparently wanted one. We were sitting around a table with other young Traveller mothers who also became involved in the interaction.

Patricia showed the different devices she had: diaphragm, condoms, pessaries and intra-uterine device. The diaphragm elicited her remark: 'But you would not use one of those'. One of the mothers replied by shaking her head negatively. Patricia proceeded to explain this method while this young mother was listening with an apparent interest. I noticed that Patricia did not use the word 'vagina' in her explanation but used the term 'passage' instead.

During all this conversation, I noticed that the Traveller mothers were giggling and smiling out of embarrassment, especially when the devices were taken out of their case. We then talked about the intra-uterine device with Bernadette. Patricia showed it to her and said that she should check regularly for the thread, to make sure the device was still in place. Bernadette answered that she would not do that. She then asked how and where she could get this device, to which Patricia replied that she should make an appointment in a family planning clinic. Bernadette then asked these questions about its insertion:

Bernadette: Is it painful?

Patricia: No, it's not.

Bernadette: It's a bit embarrassing, like?

Patricia: The doctor is only interested in putting it in right. He doesn't even look.

I: You can ask for a woman doctor if you want.

Bernadette: Is there a chance that the doctor would assault you?

Patricia: Oh no, he would not insult you.

Bernadette: I meant assault you.

Patricia: There would always be a woman in the room with you, you would not be left alone with a doctor.

Bernadette: Could it be put in by the nurse working here?

Patricia: No, it's got to be inserted by an especially trained doctor; just ask the nurse to phone for you when you have your periods.

Bernadette: [with a smile] I keep on praying.

[fieldnotes 19/11/1990]

All these questions related to the insertion itself, while Bernadette never inquired about how this device worked or what were its possible contra-indications or side effects. This single focus shows how inhibited this young Traveller woman was about this procedure, and her lack of concern for the other aspects of her contraceptive choice. Her questions reveal her perception that this insertion was not a medical service but was of a sexual nature. In addition, her hope for a nurse she already knew revealed her preference not only for a female professional, but for a personal contact.

In the course of this interaction, the dichotomy between Traveller women and health professionals is maintained. No advice was based on personal experience and no communication or nuance produced gender commitment. Further, as Patricia mis-heard 'assault' and denied that male doctors might sexually assault their female patients, she displayed her professional loyalty to them. And when later, I commented to this nurse that she did not use the word 'vagina' with these young Traveller women, she replied: 'It's a word they don't use; you have to go down to their level.' This remark explicitly points to a discrepancy between this nurse's attitude on and off duty in regard to her interactions with Traveller women. While in the course of this interaction, she treated Traveller women with an apparent respect, her phrasing in private reveals a more condescending attitude. This condescension on the part of the nurses, and their professionalism, both betray the asymmetry between the protagonists. Such asymmetry is not based on gender since all protagonists were women, but arises out of different educational attainments and contrasting backgrounds. The nurses portray themselves as professional and educated, while Traveller women are perceived as lay and uneducated. Such asymmetry has been described as implicit in all medical interactions (Waitzkin, 1979, Fisher, 1982, Fisher and Todd, 1986, Borges, 1986, Davis, 1988).

The asymmetry structuring this encounter between Traveller mothers and health professionals is not only confirmed by Patricia's later comment but also by their interaction during which one party was asking information, the other, based on professionalism, was providing it. Thus, it furthered the dichotomy between both populations and confirms my analysis on the nurses' control over information on contraception.

Control of Information

That health professionals have control over medical information is not to be unexpected in interactions dealing with contraception or other issues. It is not necessarily problematic either, if professionals are prepared to share their knowledge with their clients. But what the health professionals' control over contraceptive information can yield to is their restricting the range of options they propose to their clients if not actually manipulating the information. Such practices clearly hinder the choice and control of Traveller women in their reproductive life, and are thus clearly detrimental to these women. The following section will document the occurrence of such practices in the course of my fieldwork.

This asymmetry between Traveller women and health professionals when talking about contraception was further exemplified by the access to information Traveller women were given. When explaining the different contraceptive methods, the nurses limited their explanation to the pill and the intra-uterine device, which they called by its lay name, the 'coil'. This limitation could be explained by the fact that the nurses knew it was unlikely Traveller women would adopt another method, because of their taboos or because of their husbands' attitude towards contraception. But this limitation also represents control over access to information about the full range of contraceptive methods.

Restricting information on contraceptive methods has been highlighted in other contexts, such as in conversations between physicians and middle-class American women (Fisher and Todd, 1986). My findings reinforce their conclusion :

> Patients are systematically denied the information they need to participate actively in their contraceptive decision, yet this decision making has the potential to affect their lives. (Fisher and Todd, 1986, p.8)

But in this context, the patients can double-check the information they get from their physician. This possibility is beyond the reach of most Traveller women because of their illiteracy.

This incomplete information was extended to another contraceptive method, Depo-Provera. This is an injectable drug stopping ovulation which is administered every three months. I observed on one occasion a Traveller woman asking how 'The shots were working'; Laura simply replied: 'It's like the pill, but then it's not a pill'. This answer would surely strike most as dubious. It might be justified since Depo-Provera works very much like contraceptive pills, as it suppresses ovulation by the administration of hormones in the body. However, Laura's reply, in my opinion, meant that this Traveller woman left the mobile clinic with the very same vague notion about how 'the shots' were working, as when she entered. This incomplete information in the case of Depo-Provera could yield to an attempt at manipulation. A controversy surrounds its use: it has never been accepted as safe by the American Food and Drug Administration and therefore it has never been marketed in the United States and other countries. But it has been given to women in the developing world where regular check ups to assess potential side effects do not usually take place. Even though recent medical research suggests that Depo-Provera does not present any immediate danger to women's health (WHO, 1990), and given that women in the developing world might consider Depo-Provera safer than childbearing and its side effects negligible in a context of chronic ill health (MacIntyre, 1993), there is an accusation that these populations have been used as guinea pigs for testing this drug (Rakusen, 1981, Bunkle, 1984). In western countries where it has been distributed, its use continues to be problematic. Depo-Provera is mostly used by ethnic minorities, like Black women in Britain, who are not always given full information or whose consent is not always sought (Bryan et al., 1985, Pearson, 1985, Sheffield Black Women's Group, 1994).

When Traveller women were asking about 'the shots', the nurses never alerted them to the polemic surrounding this method and its side effects. On one occasion, Teresa, a Traveller mother, precisely asked if 'the shots' were dangerous. To this, Laura replied: 'If they were, they would not be available'.

Teresa's case was difficult. At the age of twenty four, she had five children and was expecting her sixth. Her attempts to control her fertility had been obvious failures. There was a potential for future duress if this woman kept on having children. In this context, Laura might have done a risk analysis and reached the conclusion that Depo-Provera was less risky for this woman than continual childbearing. Thus, it could be argued that my concern for Traveller women's right to know of the polemics about Depo-Provera bypassed any real appreciation of their circumstances, in contrast to the nurses. This clash between the nurses' attitudes and mine might in turn reflect a clash between pragmatism and feminist medical sociology. Nonetheless, Laura's reply was not accurate. Overall though, the restriction and the manipulation of information given by doctors have been described as mechanisms engendering and perpetuating asymmetry in doctors-patients interactions (Waitzkin, 1979, Fisher and Todd, 1986, Davis, 1988).

Social Control

Further, the controversial provision of Depo-Provera among vulnerable women such as Travellers was conveyed to me in a comment I heard from Patricia. One day, I saw Winnie watching the video tape on ante natal care, and thus learned that she was 'in the family way', to repeat Patricia's expression. I spoke to Winnie, as I had known her for a few years. I asked her when she was due, and how she felt about having a new baby. To this, she replied: 'I don't mind', and mentioned that her youngest child was five. I then replied: 'It's a bit of a break'. I stayed with Winnie and watched the rest of the video tape with her. Then, the mobile clinic had to leave, and I sat in the ambulance next to Patricia.

Patricia had noticed that I knew Winnie, and I explained how I met her. Patricia then told me that Winnie was supposed not to get pregnant again, because she started to develop cervical cancer a few years before. The hospital staff told her then that another pregnancy would put her health at risk. Perhaps Winnie had been inadequately warned. Perhaps she underestimated the risk she was taking by having another baby. An outsider could also interpret this situation as a failure to advocate contraception successfully. 'She just told me that she did not mind having a new baby' I said in conclusion. Patricia shook her head disapprovingly, and said: 'They should have given her the shots'.

This last statement can be interpreted as a good intention to help a Traveller woman to fight off a serious disease. But it is also a frightening utterance when it comes to the lack of control over one's body assumed by this nurse. This remark lacks any appearance of caring for powerless women, and it shows that this nurse did not work with an empowering model in mind. It is hard also to ignore the asymmetrical relation implied by the actual phrasing, in that it clearly opposes 'they' to 'her': 'they' sanctions the anonymity of the hospital staff. The contrast between these plural and singular pronouns also reinforces Winnie's vulnerability. The verb 'given' is imbued with a repressive intervention. Winnie was perceived by this nurse to be as irresponsible and unreliable as a child. Accordingly, she suggested a solution appropriate for a child, verging on a punishment.

No doubt, this account testifies once more to the cultural conflict which exists between Traveller mothers and settled health professionals. Winnie's new pregnancy had been brought on by the traditional passivity and fatalism held by Traveller women to their fertility. But for Patricia, it was a sign of irresponsible failure in dealing with contraception. What this cultural conflict over contraception between Traveller women and settled health professionals points to is the different meanings of childbearing and fertility for different women. When confronted by such conflicts, health professionals misunderstand the cultural component of Traveller women's behaviour and blame them for failing to attain what they expect from them.

While one could argue for the positive outcomes of family planning for Traveller women, this case study shows that it can yield to very ambivalent results when it is brought to them by a dominant population. Quite specifically, by attempting to introduce Traveller women to family planning, health professionals try to dismiss their traditional norms and behaviours of childbearing to replace them by their own which they consider superior. In other words, they try to regulate their experiences. In my fieldwork, this attempt occurred in a pervasive way, in that it took the form of a 'hidden agenda'. It was not overtly acknowledged by the nurses, but performed by them unconsciously. But in its most extreme form, their intervention has a potential for repression. This potential was also obvious in another research context, when one Traveller informant told of a sterilisation performed on a Traveller woman without her consent.

Such practices yield to the social control of Traveller women's mothering, which is grounded in its problematisation by health professionals, and in their ignorance of the cultural dimension in Traveller women's behaviours. In the face of such conflicts, a critical analysis cannot fail to interpret them as an attempt by health interventionists to implement social control over the mothering norms and behaviours of Traveller women. This interpretation coincides with Foucault's description of medicine as an institution performing social control upon body-related norms and behaviours of individuals. But to refine Foucault's theory for its relevance to our field, I ought to mention that this writer has neither addressed gender, nor minorities issues.

Conclusion

The analysis of interactions taking place between the female staff of the mobile clinic and Traveller women has shown that gender is operational for the nurses to have access to these minority women and then to discuss intimate topics with them. However, in their interactions with their clientele, these nurses ignore any allegiance based on gender and employed their status and resources in a pattern of asymmetrical power relations with Traveller women.

Medical professionalism generates assessable devices to perpetuate Traveller women's subordinate position, and as illustrated the nurses from the mobile clinic controlled access to resources and information. But they also hold norms and behaviours in relation to fertility which they attempt to implement among Irish Traveller women, as their professionalism reflects the ideology and the culture of the majority population.[4] Further, such professionalism is subject to the negative perception that the settled community, at large, has of Traveller women as mothers. While interacting with them, settled health professionals might put these stereotypes aside, but these often re-emerge after their encounters, in their discussions and decision making. These stereotypes are often prompted by Traveller behaviours of which much of the cultural content passes unrecognised and are therefore misinterpreted and problematised, a bias certainly fostered by intervention policies and programmes targeted at this minority group.[5]

Medical interactions between Traveller women and female nurses from the majority population present the same structure as economic transactions between Irish Travellers and settled Irish (Gmelch, 1974). Interactions are always instrumental and restricted to a narrow range of role relationships, in accord with Barth's analysis (1969) on interactions across ethnic boundaries. As both Traveller and settled women maintain personal distance as they meet in the mobile clinic, Traveller women's ethnicity emerges as a boundary phenomenon which is perpetuated in spite of acculturation (Barth 1969). However, we have highlighted the role that power, through the nurses' control over information and their regulation of mothering norms and behaviours, plays in perpetuating the ethnic boundary with their Traveller visitors (Abramson et al., 1989).

Thus, professionalism and ethnicity converge to produce asymmetrical interactions between Traveller mothers and settled health professionals. Their impact clearly overrides that of gender, in contradiction of West's conclusions on the lesser asymmetry of medical interactions involving a female physician (West, 1984, West, 1990). It is precisely because of ethnicity, as an additional barrier standing between settled health professionals and Traveller mothers, that 'sisterhood' is negated.[6] Female health professionals from the majority population reinforce their professional status, and thus their allegiance to their own community. In the process, they dissociate themselves from Traveller women so that their stigma will not 'spill over' them (Goffman, 1976). Such analysis questions the mono-cultural and mono-ethnic construct of Irish society and reveals the strength of cleavages between Irish women, which surpass any convergence of interest based on gender. Ultimately, by aligning themselves with a male-dominated medical profession and intervention policies targeted at Traveller women, female health professionals from the settled community further the oppression of these 'other' women from Ireland.[7]

Discussion Topics

1. Does contraception increase women's control over their lives?

2. How do you think contraceptive counselling provided to Traveller women and to Irish working-class women is likely to be different and alike? How is the gender of the providers going to influence this counselling?

3. Is the uptake of contraception among Irish Traveller women likely to be different from the uptake among settled women living in the Republic of Ireland?

4. Can you propose suggestions for improving the delivery of contraceptive counselling to Traveller women?

Notes

1. The high fertility of the Irish Travellers has been widely documented (Gmelch, G. 1977, Report of the Travelling People Review Body, 1983, Rottman et al., 1986, Forde and O'Nuallain, 1992). In 1989, Barry et al. revealed that their fertility rate reached 5.3, more than double the national average and the highest in the European Community.
2. In view of the Travellers' difficult access to conventional medical services, the Report of the Travelling People Review Body (1983) expressed the need for specific family planning services to reach this minority. This concern led the

Eastern Health Board in 1985 to set up a mobile clinic, one of whose objectives was to provide contraceptive counselling to Traveller women.

3. Recently, and for the first time in the history of intervention policies targeted at the Irish Travellers, the Report of the Task Force on the Travelling Community (1995, p.282) has reckoned the differential impact of intervention policies according to gender in the following quote: 'The Task Force recognises the need to examine the way in which each of the areas discussed in this Report affects Traveller women and to specify the gender impact of the various recommendations in preparation for their implementation.'

4. Similarly to us, the Dublin Travellers Education and Development Group argues: 'Traveller women are particularly vulnerable to cultural stress because it is they who interact with health care providers and who consequently are often put under pressure to conform to the cultural values of the dominant society, thereby creating additional anxiety and stress for them.' (DTEDG, 1993, p.17)

5. It is only recently that the provision of health care to Irish Travellers has been recognised by policy makers as a cross-cultural endeavour, as shown by the research commissioned by the Task Force on the Travelling Community to the Centre for Health Promotion Studies.

6. Thorton Dill (1987, p.160) defines this concept in the following terms 'a nurturant, positive feeling of attachment and loyalty to other women, which grows out of a shared experience of oppression', before she acknowledged, along with the American feminist movement, the challenge to the emergence of 'sisterhood' of differences - racial, ethnic, cultural and economic- surpassing a convergence of interest based on gender.

7. That the medical profession is male-dominated has been amply documented (Fisher, 1986, Fisher and Todd, 1986, Todd, 1989). As for the policy makers involved in the recent Task Force for the Travelling Community (1995), out of eighteen members, eleven were men, in spite of a female chairperson.

References and Further Reading

Abramson, H, Hannan, D, Tovey, H. 1989 *Why Irish? Irish Identity and Irish Language* Dublin: Bord na Gaeilge.

Barry, J, Herity, B and Solan, J. 1989 'Vital Statistics of Travelling People, 1987' in *The Travellers Health Status Study*, Dublin: The Health Research Board.

Barth, F. 1969 'Introduction' in Barth F. (ed.) *Ethnic Groups and Boundaries The Social Organization of Cultural Difference* London: Allen and Unwin.

Borges, S. 1986 'A Feminist Critique of Scientific Ideology: An Analysis of Two Doctor - Patient Encounters' in Fisher S and Todd A. (eds.) *Discourse and Institutional Authority: Medicine, Education, and Law* Norwood: Ablex.

Bryan, B, Dadzie, S and Scafe, S. 1985 *The Heart of the Race: Black Women's Lives in Britain* London: Virago.

Bunkle, P. 1984 'Calling the Shots? The International Policy of Depo-Provera' in Arditti, R, Klein, R D and Minden S. (eds.) *Test Tube Women What Future for Motherhood* London: Pandora Press.

Centre for Health Promotion Studies 1995 *Health Service Provision for the Travelling Community in Ireland* Unpublished Study Commissioned by the Task Force on the Travelling Community.

Davis, K. 1988 *Power Under the Microscope*, Dordrecht: Foris Publications.

Donovan, J. 1986 *We Don't Buy Sickness It Just Comes Health, Illness and Health Care in the Lives of Black People in London* Aldershot: Gower.

Dublin Travellers Education and Development Group 1993 *Submission to Department of Health in Relation to Proposed National Health Strategy* Dublin: Pavee Point Publications.

Fisher, S. 1982 'The Decision-Making Process: How Doctors and Patients Communicate' in Di Pietro R. (ed.) *Linguistics and the Professions* Norwood: Ablex.

Fisher, S. 1986 *In the Patient's Best Interests: Women and the Politics of Medical Decisions* New Brunswick, NJ Rutgers University Press.

Fisher, S, and Todd, A. 1986 'Friendly Persuasion: Negotiating Decisions to use Oral Contraceptives' in Fisher, S and Todd, A. (eds.) *Discourse and Institutional Authority: Medicine, Education, and Law* Norwood: Ablex.

Forde, M, and O'Nuallain, S. 1992 *Changing Needs of Irish Travellers: Health, Education and Social Issues* Galway: Woodlands Centre.

Foucault, M. 1973 *The Birth of the Clinic An Archeology of Medical Perception* London: Tavistock Publications.

Foucault, M. 1977 *Discipline and Punish, The Birth of the Prison* London: Allen Lane.

Gmelch, G. 1977 *The Irish Tinkers: The Urbanization of an Itinerant People* California: Menilo Park.

Gmelch, S. 1974 *The Emergence and the Persistence of an Itinerant Ethnic Group* Unpublished Ph.D Thesis, University of California Santa Barbara.

Goffman, E. 1976 *Stigma: Notes on the Management of a Spoiled Identity* London: Harmondsworth.

MacIntyre, M. 1993 'Fictive Kinship or Mistaken Identity? Fieldwork in Tubetube Island, Papua New Guinea' in Bell, D, Caplan P, and Wazir-Jahan Begum, K. (eds.) *Gendered Fields: Women, Men and Ethnography* London: Routledge.

Pearson, M. 1985 *Racial Equality and Good Practice Maternity Care Training in Health and Race*, Centre for Ethnic Minorities Health Studies.

Phoenix, A. 1990 'Black Women and the Maternity Services' in Garcia, J, Kilpatrick, R, and Richards M. (eds.) *The Politics of Maternity Care* Oxford: Clarendon Press.

Rakusen, J. 1981 'Depo-Provera: The Extent of the Problem' in Roberts, H. (ed.) *Women, Health and Reproduction*, London: Routledge and Kegan Paul.

Report of the Travelling People Review Body 1983 Dublin: The Stationery Office.

Report of the Task Force on the Travelling Community 1995 Dublin: The Stationery Office.

Richardson, D. 1993 *Women, Motherhood and Childbearing*, London: MacMillan.

Rigal, J. 1993 'The Emergence of Fertility Control Among Irish Travellers', in *Irish Journal of Sociology*, Vol.3, pp.93-108.

Roberts, H. 1981 'Male Hegemony in Family Planning' in Roberts, H. (ed.) *Women, Health and Reproduction* London: Routlege and Kegan Paul.

Rothman, B K. 1984 'The Meanings of Choice in Reproductive Technology' in Arditti, R, Duelli Klein, R and Minden, S. (eds.) *Test Tube Women What Future for Motherhood* London: Pandora Press.

Rottman, D, Dale Tussing, A and Wiley, M. 1986 *The Population Structures and Living Circumstances of Irish Travellers : Results from the 1981 Census of Traveller Families*, Dublin: The Economic and Social Research Institute.

Sheffield Black 'Women's Group. 1994 Black Women: What Kind of Health Care Can We Expect in Racist Britain?' in Kanter, H, Lefanu, S, Shah, S and Spedding C. (eds.) *Sweeping Statements: Writings from the Women's Liberation Movement* London: The Women's Press.

Thornton Dill, B. 1987 'Race, Class, Gender: Prospects for an All Inclusive Sisterhood' in Deegan M J, and Hill M. (eds.) *Symbolic Interaction and the Study of Women* London: Allen and Unwin.

Todd, A. 1989 *Intimate Adversaries: Cultural Conflict Between Doctors and Women Patients*, Philadelphia: University of Philadelphia Press.

Waitzkin, H. 1979 'Medicine, Superstructure and Micropolitics', in *Social Science and Medicine*, Vol.13, no.6, pp.601-611.

West, C. 1984 'When the Doctor is a Lady, Power, Status and Gender in Physician-Patient Conversation' in *Symbolic Interaction*, Vol.7, no.1, pp.87-106.

West, C. 1990 'Not Just Doctors Orders: Directive Response Sequences in Patients' Visits to Women and Men Physicians' in *Discourse and Society*, Vol.1, no.1, pp.85-11.

Wilson-Davis, K. 1982 'Fertility and Family Planning in the Irish Republic', 1975, in *Journal of Biosocial Science*, Vol.14, pp.343-358.

World Health Organisation 1990 *Injectable Contraceptives Their Role in Family Planning Care* World Health Organization.

17.

Gender Differences in the Responses of Parents to Their Daughters' Non-marital Pregnancy

Abbey Hyde

Introduction

This paper will present data on the experiences of fifty-one unmarried pregnant women in disclosing news of their pregnancies to their mothers and fathers. An argument will be presented suggesting that patterns of disclosure to mothers and fathers, and their responses to news of the pregnancy, differed along gendered lines. Mothers' and fathers' differing responses suggest divergent priorities with regard to their daughters' role in society - for mothers, their daughters needed to experience life beyond the traditional mothering role, while fathers were primarily concerned that their daughters would subscribe to the traditional social arrangement in which reproduction is embedded, and which supports patriarchal structures.

A small number of Irish studies on non-marital childbearing have included parental involvement in a daughter's pregnancy in relation to parents' awareness of the pregnancy, their initial responses to news of the pregnancy and the level of support they offered (Creegan, 1967, Rynne and Lacey, 1983, Darling, 1984, O'Hare et al., 1987, Flanagan and Richardson, 1992). In general, findings indicated that mothers tend to be informed more frequently and at an earlier stage than fathers. Where parents' initial reactions to the pregnancy have been investigated, these have often been limited by analysing mothers' and fathers' responses collectively (Creegan 1967, Darling, 1984) or mothers' responses only (Rynne and Lacey, 1983). This obviates an understanding of gender differences in responses that might arise between mothers and fathers. In terms of parental support, where levels have been analysed separately for mothers and fathers (Rynne and Lacey, 1983, Flanagan and Richardson, 1992), mothers were found to be marginally more supportive than were fathers.

No studies were located, either nationally or internationally that offered a qualitative analysis of the differing responses of mothers and fathers to news of their daughters' non-marital pregnancy. This obscures any gender differences that might arise between each parent's reaction, and the basis for such differences. This paper will focus on how parents' responses took on a specific gendered character. The gendered character of disclosure of and responses to the pregnancy was cross-cut by social class, which impacted on the extent to which non-marital pregnancies were problematised by participants' parents. However, it is beyond the scope of this chapter to include a class analysis here.

Methodological Stance

The present study is part of a larger project investigating unmarried women's experiences of pregnancy and the early weeks of motherhood. Fifty-one women were selected from the pre-natal clinic of a major maternity hospital in Dublin. The criteria for entry to the study were that potential participants would be unmarried to the father of the foetus and be first time mothers-to-be. The women's ages ranged from sixteen to thirty-six; twelve of the women were under twenty when they gave birth. The social class background of participants varied; however the majority were working-class. While variations in age and social class enhanced the richness of data, qualitative samples of this kind do not aim to generalise to the wider population, but rather aim to provide an understanding of events which may then be compared with findings from other contexts.

The process of selection was as follows: at the pre-natal clinic, midwifery staff invited potential participants to meet me and discuss the study. Women were informed that the decision to partake or not need only be made after they had spoken to me and acquired details of the study. In all, ninety women were invited to take part in the study, of which seventy-eight agreed. Fifty-one women were eventually interviewed; this wastage rate compares well with similar studies where participants were interviewed in their own homes (Phoenix, 1991). Participants in the present study were interviewed on two separate occasions; firstly in the later stages of pregnancy, and secondly, approximately six weeks after the birth. The interviews were conducted during 1992 and 1993.

In order to understand the experiences of participants, a qualitative approach from a pluralist feminist standpoint position was adopted. This feminist standpoint is based on the notion that human activity structures and sets limits on understanding (Harding, 1989). Underpinning the standpoint position is the view that the dominance of conceptual schemes based on male perspectives of the social world has meant a partial and distorted understanding of events, which can only be redressed by uncovering an understanding of the world from the perspective of women's activities. Earlier theoretical models of patriarchy as a universal oppression were later seen to understate differences among women's experiences in terms of class, race, sexual identity and so forth. This has prompted writers such as Gelsthorpe (1992, p.215) to argue for a pluralist standpoint position - while women have a particular vantage point as women, their characteristics and circumstances vary, giving rise to a range of 'uniquely valid insights'.

Data were analysed using a style of qualitative analysis resembling 'grounded theory', first introduced by Glaser and Strauss (1967), and later developed and refined (Glaser, 1978, 1992, Strauss, 1987, Strauss and Corbin, 1990, 1994). Grounded theory has been described as 'a qualitative research method that uses a systematic set of procedures to develop an inductively derived grounded theory about a phenomenon' (Strauss and Corbin, 1990, p.24), where theoretical insights are developed by the researcher from the data, although at a certain level of abstraction from such data. In the present study, as data collection progressed, questions about topics became increasingly more focused around theoretically relevant issues. One of these issues is the subject of the present chapter - the impact of gender on disclosure of the pregnancy to parents and their differing responses to it.

Patterns of Disclosure and Responses along Gendered Lines

The structure of participants' immediate families varied, and this may have had some bearing on the pattern of disclosure to parents. While only one participant's mother was dead, ten participants' fathers were deceased. A further nine had parents who lived separately and in another case the father was in prison. Nonetheless, both parents were told together in only seven cases. Where parents were told separately, in all but one instance mothers were informed first, and, although the immediate dread for most participants on discovery of the pregnancy was telling the mother, most had greater difficulties with telling the fathers when the time came to do so. As has been noted in other studies referred to earlier, mothers were almost always informed about the pregnancy prior to fathers.

Mothers - Disclosure and Responses

All but seven participants informed their mothers of the pregnancy directly themselves. In eight cases, mothers (though not fathers) were aware at the early stages that their daughters thought they might be pregnant and were either waiting for the results of a pregnancy test, or were considering getting one done. There was little or no inhibition here, on the part of mother and daughter in discussing the possibility of a pregnancy.

Mothers responded in a variety of ways to news of their daughters' pregnancies. These responses are summarised as follows:[1]

In seven cases, expressions of pleasure and delight at the news were voiced, and the pregnancy was expressed as something positive. Typically the response here was:

> *Lorna:* She welled up, and it was great ... She was delighted. (Twenty-nine-year-old sales person)

In ten instances, negative views of the pregnancy were not forthcoming, yet pleasure at news of the pregnancy was not expressed. The pregnancy was constructed as acceptable and not, for the most part, seen as a problem. An example of this type of response was:

> *Rebecca:* I had to get me sister to tell ma because I felt I was letting her down, but ma didn't feel like that.
>
> *AH:* What did she say?
>
> *Rebecca:* She said it was grand. It was okay. (Twenty-two-year-old unemployed)

The pregnancy was seen by eighteen mothers as negative, but the mother was calm and supportive. The mother concentrated on providing support for the daughter in what she perceived to be a difficult situation, without dwelling on the circumstances in which the pregnancy arose, as in Celine's case:

> *Celine:* She says, 'Right, it's something we'll have to deal with now. There's nothing we can do now. It's happened.' She was very calm. (Seventeen-year-old leaving certificate pupil)

In fifteen instances, the mother was openly negative about the pregnancy and the circumstances in which it arose, as exemplified by Trish's mother:

> *Trish:* But like she was very upset and she says, 'I can't believe this is happening,' - like this, 'this is like a nightmare.' She was upset because she didn't think I'd be that stupid, this that and the other. 'How could you?' and bla bla bla. (Twenty-two-year-old receptionist)

Overall, the responses indicated that some women had little or no misgivings about approaching their mothers with news of the pregnancy, even at the stage where the pregnancy had not yet been confirmed, suggesting a considerable degree of openness. Furthermore, while the vast majority of mothers were less than delighted with the news, a sizeable minority indicated acceptance.

Fathers – Disclosure and Responses

In the case of fathers, the pattern of disclosure differed from that of mothers. Participants were far less likely to reveal news of the pregnancy directly to their fathers. Of the thirty-seven fathers in question (ten were deceased, and four had no contact with their daughters), only fourteen women told their fathers directly, and in seven of these cases, participants told both parents together.

Only four fathers expressed pleasure that their daughter was pregnant, and just six fathers indicated acceptance of the pregnancy where neither pleasure nor displeasure was expressed. In situations where the pregnancy was defined as problematic, seven fathers were calm and supportive, while sixteen fathers were initially overtly negative about the pregnancy. Negative responses were proportionately higher among fathers than mothers since there were fewer fathers involved. More significantly, fathers' negative responses tended to be expressed far more strongly than those of mothers, and fathers took longer to 'recover' from the news than did mothers.

Where mothers had conveyed news of the pregnancy to fathers, in five cases the fathers never, throughout the entire pregnancy, directly acknowledged their awareness of the pregnancy to their daughters. In some cases, fathers withdrew from all interactions with their pregnant daughters for days and sometimes weeks after the fathers became aware of the pregnancy. In other situations where fathers openly responded to news of the pregnancy initially, a period of social disengagement with their daughters followed in some instances. In Frances' case below, the father withdrew from interaction with the entire family (who showed support for Frances) for three weeks:

> *Frances:* But for about three weeks, he didn't speak - it wasn't only me. He didn't speak to anybody in the house. He had to come to terms with it in his own way. And like no matter what anybody says to him, you're not going to change him. You have to let him rant and rave. (Twenty-six-year-old nurses' aide, engaged prior to the pregnancy)

In another case a father withdrew from interaction immediately on discovering news of the pregnancy before openly expressing his views but made these known when he resumed interaction with his daughter some time later.

The Basis of Concern - Mothers

Where mothers and fathers expressed negative reactions to news of the pregnancy, their distress was usually rooted in different factors. Participants' accounts suggest that mothers often voiced misgivings about the lost life opportunities and life difficulties that the daughters might experience as a result of the pregnancy, especially if the participant was an adolescent or in her early twenties:

> *Jenny:* You see I was over in Germany for two years and I had all these goals. I was going to do this and I was going to do that ... I think it [mother's response] was worse than crying, the words that she said, 'How could you let yourself down?' It wasn't so much, 'You let me down,' or, 'God, what

will the neighbours think?,' but, 'How could you let yourself down?' - more concerned about me, what's going to happen in my life. In a way, she tries to live her life through mine. She wants me to have everything that she didn't have. (Twenty-three-year-old, unemployed)

AH: How was your mother about it?

Orlaith: Very upset, cause my brother was born before she got married and she got a lot of hassle from people and getting money and sent here and there so ... just, she didn't want it for me. (Seventeen-year-old waitress)

AH: What was it that annoyed her most about the pregnancy?

Martina: She feels that the I've thrown away my life, that I'm far too young, and could have got on. (Sixteen-year-old school pupil)

A small number of mothers were concerned about practicalities, such as where their daughter and her baby would live, especially if the parental home could not easily accommodate another inhabitant, although, regardless of how overcrowded the house was, all mothers offered to accommodate their daughters. The primary concern in the short-term for at least five mothers was how their husbands would respond to the news. In such instances, mothers shared with their daughters the anxiety about disclosure, and this seemed to preoccupy them more than concerns about the pregnancy. Interestingly, according to participants' accounts, the specific issue of the daughter not being married did not tend to be expressed as a high priority for concern by most mothers, although there were accounts where mothers' disappointment in relation to the daughters' unmarried status was in evidence. Where mothers' responses were strongly openly negative, they tended to be voiced more so in relation to how the daughters' lives would be affected by the pregnancies, rather than their (the mothers') own sense of personal hurt.

The Basis of Concern - Fathers

Fathers' responses took a different tone than those of mothers. Fathers were rarely reported to have voiced concerns, as respondents' mothers did, about how a daughter's life would be affected by the pregnancy. Where fathers were informed directly or where they acknowledged their awareness of the pregnancy to the daughter, negative reactions were almost always expressed in terms of the father's own personal hurt and disappointment. In Stephanie's case, her father made her feel that the pregnancy was deliberately planned specifically to agitate him. In Frances' case, the father was much more explicit in his contention that the pregnancy arose intentionally in order to undermine his authority:

Stephanie: Me da was very hurt over it. That's what he kept telling me that he was very hurt. I felt very guilty over that. It was like I had went out and done it purposely, you know, just to get at him, but it wasn't like that at all, but it was kind of the way he started making me feel. (Twenty-three-year-old, unemployed, engaged prior to the pregnancy)

Frances: He said, 'I heard about you. I'm very disappointed in you.' ... He said [to the sisters] I'd planned it. They [sisters] told me all this afterwards - I planned the pregnancy, that I was a selfish bitch and I always did what I wanted anyway. Em, basically he said everything, he couldn't possibly have said anything worse, you know. I had done it to get the better of him. (Twenty-six-year-old nurses' aide, engaged prior to the pregnancy)

Mary below, admitted to her father that she had actively planned the pregnancy, and this deliberate deviance was interpreted as less acceptable to the father than an unanticipated pregnancy would have been:

Mary: I told him, you see, that I really wanted a baby anyway, and I said that if it wasn't with [partner] I'd probably have a baby with somebody anyway ... You see, I think the fact that we had planned it was even worse like, that if we had 'got caught', that that might have been acceptable, but the fact that here I was telling him that this is what I want [laughs]. (Thirty-three-year-old public relations officer, engaged prior to the pregnancy)

In two cases, fathers focused on their daughters' moral character, implying that the pregnancy was a consequence of the daughters being sexually loose women, who liberally made themselves available to men:

AH: What sort of things did he [the father] say?

Marie: 'You're a slut. You'd open your legs to anything.' ... 'Got yourself plugged.' (Twenty-year-old, unemployed)

AH: What kind of things did your father say when you told him?

Trish: It was really, 'Oh how could you let yourself do this,' and, 'You'd go off with anyone like that,' and, 'How long are you going out with him? You don't even care do you? You could have been with anyone.' Trying to make out I was some bloody whore. (Twenty-two-year-old receptionist)

The possibility of marriage before the birth was raised in six cases. In four instances, fathers asked their daughters if they intended to marry, implying that they ought to marry. In two cases, mothers raised the issue; in one such case the participant, who was engaged prior to becoming pregnant, suspected that the topic was raised by the mother to appease the father:

Frances: The only thing she [mother] said to me was, 'Are you getting married before the birth?' I said, 'No,' and she said, 'But sure, you were going to get married anyway before you knew you were pregnant.' ... I think from her meself that if she thought she could turn around and say to me father, 'Hold on - they're getting married,' it would have eased the blow on him maybe. (Twenty-six-year-old nurses' aide, engaged prior to the pregnancy)

In another instance, a father lamented that the passage to motherhood would mean that his daughter could not now marry in the way he had intended for her. The symbolic 'giving away' of his daughter's sexuality to another man at marriage was contaminated for the father since her sexual activity was now exposed:

Pauline: I came home, me dad was upstairs in bed sobbing ...

AH: What did your father say?

Pauline: He said, 'All the things I had planned for you.' And I said, 'What do you mean by that?' and he said, 'A wedding and everything.' And I said, 'That can't change, you know', and he said, 'No, it's different now.' (Twenty-year-old secretary)

Similarly, Mary felt that marriage after the birth of the baby would come too late to negate her father's disappointment, while her mother was seen to be more likely to adapt to the situation:

Mary: Even if we do get married eventually, it won't make a lot of difference because of the fact that we have had a baby. I think my father would have more of a problem getting over it than my mother ... But at the end of the day, like, mothers and daughters ... they can empathise, and they can feel more for them, whereas fathers tend to be more proud ... When I got engaged he felt I would get married sometime, but I think he feels at this stage that we'll probably never get married, and I don't know that it would redeem [partner] in his eyes even if we did. (Thirty-three-year-old public relations officer, engaged prior to the pregnancy)

When asked what they thought it was about the pregnancy that upset their fathers so much, a number of women (especially the younger ones) mentioned that to their fathers, they still represented young girls on whom the fathers doted:

Annie: My father dotes on me. I'm his favourite. There's no favourites in the family, but I'm the youngest. I'm the baby to him. (Twenty-year-old secretary)

Emma: To me da, I'm still his baby cause I'm the oldest girl. He'll never let me go like ... My da couldn't believe it like. He kept on saying, 'No, she's not.' Like, 'My little girl,' like ... He was disgusted with me and he was upset and he was crying. (Nineteen-year-old machinist)

Mothers were mentioned far less often with regard to moving from the 'little girl' status to that of adult. Sharpe (1994, p.85) has noted fathers' need to preserve their daughters' innocence, and the sense in which daughters 'belong to fathers twice over, as children and as females'. This issue of patriarchal control by fathers over daughters will be expanded on in the discussion section.

Discussion

A central theme in the preceding data was that the pattern of disclosure to, and responses of parents to a daughter's non-marital pregnancy took on a specific gendered character. I argued that where concerns were expressed by mothers and fathers in relation to the pregnancy, such concerns were rooted in differing perspectives on women's position in relation to their reproductive functions.

In an attempt to understand the differing responses to news of their daughter's pregnancy by mothers and fathers, it is useful to draw on the work of anthropologists who have explored the ways in which tribal kinships are structured around marriage based on the exchange of women. The marriage system that existed in Ireland in the earlier part of this century is explored and linked to the gendered responses noted in the present study.

Claude Levi-Strauss (1969, p.497) in The Elementary Structures of Kinship suggested that the transfer of women between males establishes the 'supreme rule of the gift'. In this sense the daughters (the 'gifts') are exchanged from their fathers to their husbands on marriage. As 'gifts', they are seen to act as mechanisms that defuse hostilities between male exchangers and are thus instrumental in developing networks of relationships among groups of people.

Boose (1989) suggests that daughters incorporate what the anthropologist Victor Turner (1969, p.85) described as the attributes of those in liminal situations and roles, or 'liminal personae' ('threshold people')[2] within their culture, insofar as daughters are located in intermediate positions in cultural space. 'Liminal personae' are located in necessarily ambiguous positions, according to Turner, because such persons remain outside of the network of classification that usually confers states and positions within a society. Turner (p.95) contended that individuals in liminal roles are likely to manifest themselves as 'dangerous and anarchical' to those involved in the maintenance of 'structure' within that society. Turner (p.95) defines this threat as 'the powers of the weak'. The 'betwixt and between' (Turner, 1969, p.81) positions that daughters occupy make them a threat to family and community members while they remain unmarried (Boose, 1989). Boose (1989, p.67-68) explains why this is so in the following quotation:

> Inside patriarchal construction, community and family can be rescued from their own potential violence only when daughters become wives - when the liminal danger of virginal menstruation shed within the paternal house is countered by the antidote of hymeneal blood shed inside the husband's. It is therefore not the daughter's passage to adolescence that receives the ritual of community sanction. The ritual that legitimates the daughter is the same one that eradicates her daughterhood and relocates her dangerous fertility inside the authorised status of wife/mother.

Within the traditional family structure, the daughter was thus viewed as 'the temporary sojourner within her family, destined to seek legitimation and name outside its boundaries' (Boose, 1989, p.21), and in an ambiguous position until she did so.

Since the famine period in the 1800s until the early half of the twentieth century[3] the position of unmarried adult daughters in the Irish situation bore more than a passing resemblance to the system within tribal groups explored by anthropologists presented above. What occurred was the transfer of women from their fathers to their husbands at marriage in exchange for a dowry, which was paid by the bride's father. This system of exchange centred around 'match-making',[4] which is vividly described by anthropologists Arensberg and Kimball (1968) in County Clare in the 1930s. In spite of possible doubts about the validity (Gibbon, 1973, Peillon, 1982) and representativeness (Brown, 1985, Fitzpatrick, 1985) of the accounts presented by Arensberg and Kimball, it has been acknowledged that their depiction of life in rural Ireland bears a strong resemblance to records of rural life reported elsewhere in Ireland at that time (Brown, 1985).

In the contemporary period, both sons and daughters were subjected to the father's power until well into adulthood (and for males often well into middle age)[5] and each could be described as 'liminal personae' in Turner's (1969) sense until they married, or for the duration of their lifetimes if they remained single. Because of the large numbers of men and women who remained unmarried throughout their lives after the famine until the 1960s, the sexualities of these 'liminal personae' were kept in check by the strict doctrines of the Catholic Church, who persistently preached about the 'dangers of sex' (O'Faolain, 1954). Judging by relatively low levels of non-marital births from the time of the famine to the 1970s, it appears that people generally behaved as priests advised (Connell, 1968). The chastity of unmarried peasant Irish women was described variously as, '"remarkable", "ferocious", "complete and awful", a virtue no longer, but a "blight", [and] a "dreadful evil"' (Connell, 1968, p.138). These definitions correspond well to Turner's (1969, p.95) description of 'liminal personae' as frequently regarded to be 'dangerous, inauspicious, or polluting to persons, objects, events, and relationships that have not been ritually incorporated into the liminal context'.

The marriage norms operating in Ireland described above, bear some similarities to Levi-Strauss' notion of gift exchange within kinships, insofar as the traffic of women was practised in both contexts. Gayle Rubin (1975, p.174) has critiqued Levi-Strauss' structuralist perspective on kinship arguing that, since it is women who are being transferred, they do not benefit from the 'quasi-mystical power of social linkage' that stems from such exchanges. Rubin locates the roots of women's oppression in the system of exchange of women through marriage. She further suggests that the 'exchange of women' concept is very powerful because it locates women's oppression in the traffic in women instead of in the exchange of merchandise. If this exchange of women is central to women's oppression as Rubin suggests, then non-marital childbearing, in circumventing the traditional male-dominated transactions in women, has wide-ranging implications for male and female power relations.

There are clear threats to patriarchal structures when a breakdown in traditional relations between men and women occurs, and the daughter's 'dangerous fertility' (dangerous for patriarchy) bypasses the male-controlled route of marriage. Even in contexts of more liberal rules of conduct governing marriage than occurred earlier this century, marriage continues to serve the interests of patriarchy through the expropriation of female labour in the domestic mode of production (Walby, 1990), the maintenance of female dependency, and the male appropriation of biological children irrespective of the father's role in parenting (Chesler, 1991).

Conclusion

At the time when data were collected for the present study, we were only a few generations beyond the 'exchange' of women for a dowry through arrangements made by their fathers, although marriage norms had changed dramatically compared with those described by Arensberg and Kimball in the 1930s (Whelan and Fahey, 1994). There remain the remnants of the traditional system in the 1990s where fathers 'give away' their daughters in marriage, and newly married women interchange their father's surname for that of their husband's. It is being argued here that the differing responses of participants' fathers and mothers to news of a daughter's pregnancy explored within this chapter, arise as a residue of the kinship system where fathers controlled the exchange of their daughters to other men in marriage, and ensured the smooth reproduction of patriarchal relations from one generation to the next. Evidence provided here suggests that fathers continued to rely on their daughters to sustain the social organisation of reproduction which they (the fathers) were dominant in defining.

When a pregnancy arose, fathers were often deeply personally hurt and disappointed, in some cases openly crying at the news. It appears that, as the fathers saw it, in their inability to control fertility, daughters had in turn failed and exposed their fathers as inadequate protectors of the daughter's sexuality, and had upset the established social arrangement for reproduction. With changing attitudes to sex outside marriage, fathers were likely to be aware that to expect their daughters to remain virgins until marriage was unrealistic in the changing cultural climate towards sexuality. A father could, however, still look forward to symbolically 'giving away' his daughter to the sexual protection of another approved man through marriage, without the need to know much about her sexual career prior to this.

Participants' mothers' concerns about the pregnancy differed from those of fathers, and instead centred on the lost life chances their daughters might experience as a consequence of what they (the mothers) felt to be inappropriate staging of the pregnancy. What this suggests is that participants' mothers were concerned that their daughters would not be in a position, as a consequence of the pregnancy, to avail themselves of opportunities in life beyond the traditional role of mother, such as developing career and life chances, which many of the mothers themselves had forfeited to their childbearing functions. Fathers, on the other hand, were concerned that their daughters were moving away from women's traditional role vis-a-vis men, that is, being wives before they became mothers. Thus, at a broad level, where concerns were expressed by parents, what the differing apprehensions of mothers and fathers represent are differing perspectives on the role of women in society.

Discussion Topics

1. In what ways do the traditional marriage ceremony and associated rituals reflect male dominance?

2. Why do you think that more women are choosing to become mothers but not wives?

3. What advantages and disadvantages does legal marriage have for women and men?

4. How do you explain the different responses of mothers and fathers to their daughters non-marital pregnancy?

Notes

1. In order to protect the anonymity of participants, all names have been changed and some less common occupations have been altered to similar ones within the same socio-economic group according to the current Irish six-point scale.
2. The notion of 'liminal phase' of rites de passage was first defined by Arnold van Gennep (1960). The liminal phase was seen as an intervening period after which an individual had detached from an earlier fixed position in the social structure, or set of social conditions, but had not yet re-aggregated, or reincorporated into a new well-defined and 'structural' type.
3. The analysis here will confine itself to this period. The marriage customs before the famine did appear to differ from those which followed, but were nonetheless strongly patriarchal (see Connolly, 1985).

4. A 'match' has been defined as a 'contractual marriage made by the parents of families of the marrying parties and involving the disposal of property' (Arensberg and Kimball, 1968, p.105). This definition, however, obscures the differing degrees of control exhibited by mothers and fathers over the arrangement, which will be discussed later in this chapter.

5. Males, it seems, were as likely to suffer as females, would be called 'boys' until they married, which was often well into their middle years and were strongly subjected to their fathers' control (Connell, 1968). However, after they married, they became the patriarchs who in turn controlled their children's lives until well into adulthood.

References and Further Reading

Arensberg, C M and Kimball, S T. 1968 *Family and Community in Ireland* (second edition) Massachusetts: Harvard University Press.

Boose, L E. 1989 'The Father's House and the Daughter In It: The Structures of Western Culture's Daughter-Father Relationship' pp.19-74 in Flowers, L E and B S. (eds.) *Fathers and Daughters* Baltimore: The John Hopkins University Press.

Brown, T. 1985 *Ireland: A Social and Cultural History 1922-1985* London: Fontana Press.

Chesler, P. 1991 'Mothers on Trial: The Custodial Vulnerability of Women' *Feminism and Psychology* Vol.1, No.3, pp.409-425.

Connell, K H. 1968 *Irish Peasant Society: Four Historical Essays* Oxford: Claredon Press.

Connolly, S J. 1985 'Marriage in Pre-Famine Ireland' in Cosgrove A. (ed.) *Marriage in Ireland* Dublin: College Press.

Creegan, M F. 1967 *Unmarried Mothers: an Analysis and Discussion of Interviews Conducted in an Irish Mother and Baby Home* Unpublished M.Soc.Sc. Thesis University College Dublin.

Darling, V. 1984 *And Baby Makes Two* Dublin: Federation of Services for Unmarried Parents and their Children.

Fitzpatrick, D. 1985 'Marriage in Post-Famine Ireland' in Cosgrove A. (ed.) *Marriage in Ireland* Dublin: College Press.

Flanagan, N and Richardson, V. 1992 *Unmarried Mothers: A Social Profile* Dublin: University College Dublin.

Gelsthorpe, L. 1992 'Response to Martin Hammersley's paper "On Feminist Methodology"' *Sociology* Vol.26, No.2. pp.213-218.

Gibbon, A. 1973 'Arensberg and Kimball Revisited' *Economy and Society* Vol.2, No.4. pp.479-98.

Glaser, B and Strauss, A. 1967 *The Discovery of Grounded Theory: Strategies for Qualitative Research* Chicago: Aldine Publications Co.

Glaser, B. 1978 Theoretical Sensitivity Mill Valley: California: Sociology Press.

Glaser, B. 1992 *Basics of Grounded Theory Analysis Mill Valley*, California: Sociology Press.

Harding, S. 1989 'Feminist Justificatory Strategies' in Garry, A and Pearsall, M. (eds.) *Women Knowledge and Reality: Explorations in Feminist Philosophy* Mass: Unwin Hyman.

Levi-Strauss, C. 1969 *The Elementary Structures of Kinship* (Translated by Bell, J H, von Sturmer, J R and Needham, R.) Boston: Beacon Press.

O'Faolain, S. 1954 'Love Among the Irish' in O'Brien, J A. (ed.) *The Vanishing Irish: The Enigma of the Modern World* London: W.H. Allen.

O'Hare, A, Dromey, M, O'Connor, A, Clarke, M and Kirwan, G. 1987 *Mothers Alone?: A Study of Women who Gave Birth Outside Marriage* Dublin: Federation of Services for Unmarried Parents and their Children

Peillon, M. 1982 *Contemporary Irish Society: An Introduction* Dublin: Gill and Macmillan.

Phoenix, A. 1991 *Young Mothers?* Cambridge: Polity Press.

Rubin, G. 1975 'The Traffic in Women: Notes on the Political Economy of Sex' in Reiter, R R. (ed.) *Toward an Anthropology of Women* New York: Monthly Review Press.

Rynne, A and Lacey, L. 1983 *A Survey of 249 Irish Women Interviewed while Pregnant Out of Wedlock between September 1982 and July 1983* Unpublished Report.

Sharpe, S. 1994 *Fathers and Daughters* London: Routledge.

Strauss, A L. 1987 *Qualitative Analysis for Social Scientists* Cambridge: Cambridge University Press.

Strauss, A L and Corbin, J. 1990 *Basics of Qualitative Research: Grounded Theory Procedures and Techniques* London: Sage.

Strauss, A and Corbin, J. 1994 'Grounded Theory Methodology: An Overview' in Denzin, N and Lincoln, Y. (eds.) *Handbook of Qualitative Research* London: Sage.

Turner, V. 1969 *The Ritual Process: Structure and Anti-Structure* Harmondsworth: Penguin.

van Gennep, A. 1960 *The Rites of Passage* (Translated by M B Vizedom and G L Caffee) London: Routledge and Kegan Paul.

Walby, S. 1990 *Theorising Patriarchy* Oxford: Basil Blackwell.

Whelan, T and Fahey, T. 1994 'Marriage and the Family' in Whelan, C. (ed.) *Values and Social Change in Ireland* Dublin: Gill and Macmillan.

18.

Single Lone Motherhood – Reality Versus Rhetoric

Maire Leane and Elizabeth Kiely

Introduction

In Irish society there are growing numbers of young single women who are rearing children on their own.[1] Births outside marriage in the Republic of Ireland have risen from 5.4 per cent of all births in 1981 to 19.7 per cent of all births in 1994 (Department of Health, 1981, 1993). For a multitude of reasons society has and continues to perceive these women in a negative way. They have been castigated, punished, stigmatised, ignored, labelled and controlled. The Irish Constitution continues to disenfranchise family units established outside the institution of marriage.

The myths and stereotypes which negate the reality of the lives of single lone mothers are reflected in the current neo-conservative backlash against them. Political commentators in the USA and the UK have cast these women as welfare scroungers breeding pathological children in non-viable social and economic units (Murray, 1993, Toomey Jacksonville, 1994). In recent times concern about rising numbers of single lone mothers has been articulated by an Irish politician (McNally, 1996).

At the most rudimentary level research has documented the link between lone parenthood and social problems such as poverty, homelessness, failure to thrive, poor educational achievement and delinquency (Crellin et al., 1971, Madge, 1983, McAnarney and Henee, 1989). Most research in Ireland has documented the objective conditions of single lone mothers as an oppressed and socially disadvantaged group (Darling, 1984, Millar et al., 1992, McCashin, 1993, O'Grady, 1993, Magee, 1994). This chapter presents single lone mothers' subjective analyses of their experiences of motherhood in a patriarchal, capitalist society, in which motherhood is only recognised within the institution of marriage.

The chapter written from a feminist perspective, utilises a qualitative methodological approach. The potential of qualitative methods conducive to the expression of women's views and experiences, has been recognised in feminist epistemological discourse (Graham, 1983, Oakley, 1981). The value of this approach for social policy planning has also been identified (Finch, 1991). The research protocol based on the notion of objectivity has been challenged by Oakley who argues that such objectivity is not only unrealistic, but also ethically indefensible when interviewing women (Oakley, 1981). She calls for the establishment of a non-hierarchical, non-objectifying approach to interviewing which is in keeping with feminist principles. The fact that one of the researchers in this project had previously worked as a facilitator with the study group, meant that a relationship of trust had been established, which enhanced the expression of personal opinion. The material provided by the women in the study group will be used to examine the prevailing negative characterisations of single lone motherhood created by previous research. It will be argued that problems often attributed to the individual pathological characteristics of single lone mothers are in fact created by structural factors.

Irish Single Mothers: A Demographic and Social Profile

In recent years there has been a rapid increase in births to single women. In 1981, 5.4 per cent of all births were outside marriage, this had increased to 12.6 per cent by 1989, and to 19.7 per cent by 1994. The number of women claiming Unmarried Mothers Allowance, now known as Lone Parent Allowance, rose from 12,039 in 1986 to 45,779 in 1995 (Department of Social Welfare, 1986).[2] However it has to be acknowledged that not every non-marital birth will result in the formation of a new lone parent family, as the mother may subsequently marry, she may already be a lone parent; the child may be placed for adoption or the mother may be cohabiting (Treoir, 1995).

Lone parent households have a higher than average risk of poverty (Callan et al., 1989). The 1987 Household Budget Survey revealed that eighty-eight per cent of households headed by single lone parents are in the lowest socioeconomic group as compared with fourteen per cent of households headed by two parents. Unemployment rates among single parents are high with ninety per cent of single lone parent households being dependent on social welfare payments for four fifths (or more) of their total income in 1987 (Household Budget Survey, 1987). Relative to other categories of lone parents, single lone parents have low rates of economic activity. McCashin (1993) estimated that in 1987 about twelve per cent of single lone parents were employed compared with thirty-four per cent of separated lone parents and thirty-nine per cent of widowed lone parents. He suggests that the relatively low rate of economic activity among single lone parents may relate to the ages of their children who would most likely be of pre-school age.

Another indicator of low income is eligibility for a medical card. In 1992, ninety-three per cent of single lone parents had full medical card entitlement (Treoir, 1995). Despite the existence of poverty among single lone parents,

O'Grady (1993) claims there is no evidence of the emergence of an Irish 'underclass' in which long-term welfare-dependent single lone mothers predominate. His research revealed that only forty per cent of mothers who first applied for Unmarried Mothers Allowance in 1985 were still in receipt of the allowance at the end of 1990, while only twenty-six per cent of those who had first applied for the allowance in 1980 were still receiving it at the end of 1990. O'Grady's work also indicated that those who were younger at the time of the first claim of the allowance tended to remain claiming for a longer period.

Single Lone Mothers and the New Right

The family has become a focus for much critical analysis and debate in political circles in the US and UK. Commentators associated with conservative or right wing political factions have highlighted the 'moral malaise' which is afflicting modern families (Dennis, 1993, Davies et al., 1993, Murray, 1994, Gingrich, 1995). This malaise, they suggest is apparent in the emergence of an underclass characterised by increasing numbers of lone parent families, growing levels of educational under-achievement and unemployment, coupled with soaring crime rates. They argue that the expansion of the rights and benefits accorded to individuals through the welfare state has led to a decline in personal and family responsibility. To a large extent the debate about responsibilities has centred around moral issues and single lone parents in particular have been targeted for condemnation. Murray (1993, p.14) referring to the British context, claims that:

> a single woman with a small child is not a viable economic unit and not being a viable economic unit, neither is the single woman and child a legitimate social unit

It has also been suggested that single lone mothers become pregnant to gain entitlement to housing and welfare benefits. Redwood (1995) warns of the danger of the assumption that:

> the illegitimate child is the passport to a council flat and a benefit income.

While concern regarding declining family values has been expressed in Ireland, issues such as homosexuality, abortion and divorce have been to the fore. Single lone parenthood has received less attention as a family values issue in the Irish political arena. However, the traditional stigmatisation of single lone parents in this country does nothing to instill confidence that the New Right rhetoric will not gain ground in the Irish context. For example, a recent quote from *The Irish Times* (McNally, 1996) states:

> It seems to me we've gone from one extreme to the other in the space of twenty years, from one of complete intolerance towards single mothers to completely un-questioning acceptance. And I think it's time we asked a few questions. (McNally, 1996)

Solutions being put forward to address the 'problem' of single lone parenthood, are rooted in the belief that the traditional two parent family is best and must be re-engineered. Overhauling the welfare system so as to return to the nineteenth century form of relief which would exclude single lone parents as claimants is central to this re-engineering process. So too is the reconstruction of social stigma to turn the tide so that women would have to choose between marriage, adoption, or abortion, to avoid the socially unacceptable status of single lone motherhood (Murray, 1993, Bush, 1994, Redwood, 1995). There is widespread consensus between right wing commentators that the revival of social stigma is dependant on the withdrawal of social benefits (Murray, 1993, Morgan, 1995). As Bartholomew (1995) states:

> The money comes before the morality. It is because of the money paid to lone parents that we no longer regard illegitimacy as immoral.

This New Right rhetoric has not gone unchallenged (Riley and Shaw, 1985, Acock and Demo, 1994, Fox Piven, 1994, Rodger, 1995, Timmins, 1995). A growing body of empirical research has shown that social problems are not endemic to lone parent families and that normal child development is possible outside the two parent family model. However, yet again this research is dominated by what Phoenix (1991) has dubbed 'the outsider perspective'. The social construction of single lone motherhood has remained largely in the confines of political and academic debate where outsider views predominate. The absence of an 'insider perspective' (Phoenix, 1991) represents a lacuna in this field of research which this chapter seeks to address by documenting the lived experience of single lone motherhood in Ireland.

Single Motherhood: The Lived Experience

The study group consisted of four women who were members of a Women's Group run in Newbury House, a Family Centre in Mayfield, in the Northside of Cork City. The majority of the group members were single lone mothers and group discussion of the issues faced by these women, provided the background information which instructed the development of the interview schedule and informed the analysis and interpretation of the data. All of the respondents were single lone mothers at the time of their first pregnancy, one has subsequently married and has since separated. At the time of interview in July 1995, the women were aged between nineteen and twenty-four and had given birth to their first child between the ages of fifteen and nineteen, with none of them having more than two children. At the time of their first pregnancies all were either living in their family home or with their partners and all were employed, in full-time education or on an employment training course. At the time of interview all of the women were living either at home or in local authority accommodation in the Northside of the city, and all were dependent on lone parent allowance as their main source of income.

The analytical framework of the study was constructed around the investigation of key themes in the New Right rhetoric on single lone motherhood. These themes include; motivation for pregnancy, morality and social stigma, irresponsibility and welfare dependency and non viability of single lone parent family units.

Motivation for Pregnancy

New Right rhetoric argues that single women become pregnant to gain entitlement to benefits and housing (Redwood, 1995). There is no evidence from this study to support such a claim. None of the women spoke of making a conscious decision to become pregnant. Their initial reactions to learning of their pregnancy were ones of shock and fear, as is clearly evidenced by the following comments.

> I know it's very naive to say but at the time I really didn't know what ... I knew about the facts of life and this and that but I didn't think just one time it could happen to you. Do you know what I mean? I was very naive. I was really only experimenting, so was my boyfriend at the time, like, but it happened, you know what I mean.

> At the beginning it was a shock.

> At first it was okay but as the months went on I got more afraid.

> I didn't want it, my first reaction was petrified. When I went to the hospital I was thrilled and then I wanted it more.

> I was terrified, scared and upset. I was afraid to tell my parents.

Many of the respondents held negative perceptions about single lone parenthood prior to their pregnancies and did not perceive it as a status which would enhance their life chances.

> I always thought they were stupid. How could you get pregnant! You're stuck for life, but then when I got pregnant myself I had more respect for them. I didn't think they were dirt or anything.

> I just wondered how they coped. I thought it was easy to rear them, I helped my mam ... a friend of mine had one at 17 and I wondered how she coped, she was living at home, her mother and father weren't helping her. It's hard like.

Research suggests that the instance of women becoming single lone mothers by choice is rare (Cashmore, 1985, Close, 1985, Renvoize, 1985, Rickford, 1992). Furthermore there is evidence from both the US and UK that young women do not become pregnant for instrumental reasons such as housing and benefits (Clark, 1989, Phoenix, 1991). One UK study revealed that:

> few young single women had deliberately got pregnant — let alone knew about their rights to housing and benefits. Most did not know they were

pregnant until some months into pregnancy and then believed their boyfriend would become the knight on the white charger and rescue them. None had become pregnant in order to live on their own with a child (Slipman, 1994).

The aspirations held by the women in the study group prior to becoming pregnant make it clear that they had no wish to assume the role of a dependent single lone mother. As one woman explained:

> I wanted my own place, my own job and then maybe settle down and have a child.

Similar sentiments were expressed by other women:

> ... I was doing a FAS course for two years in catering and I worked in X (Hotel) and the Y (Hotel) and I would like to be a chef or I would like to be a secretary in an office, if I had my time over again I would have a good job.

> I never wanted (planned) my kids, I wanted my freedom, I wanted to be a secretary.

The New Right belief that entitlement to welfare benefits is a core motive for single women to become pregnant is not supported by the findings of this work. In reality the single lone mothers interviewed expressed difficulty even in determining what their social welfare entitlements were.

> I didn't get pregnant just to have money, d'you know what I mean ...

> I remember like that on my first baby, when I went up she (Community Welfare Officer) wouldn't give me nothing. She said do it yourself, you are living at home with your mother, I hadn't a clue about social welfare so I just went off.

> I was told (informally) you should get a cheque every month towards clothes, but you are not told that, I found it out three weeks ago.

Morality and Social Stigma

While the New Right call for the return of social stigma as a means of stemming the rise in single lone parent families, the statements of the women in the group would suggest the social stigma is still a factor in the Irish context.

> Some people would look down on us and call us stupid fools, they wouldn't give a second thought about us.

> I used to have to go to one (Community Welfare Officer) and I wasn't treated very well. It's your problem and she was getting rid of you. But I feel that we weren't on the same level, that's the way I feel. You're not stuck with children, ye have ye're own life, we have to look up to ye, you know what I mean.

> I've been called those names myself, I've resented it and even fought people when I was younger, that's because I wasn't one ... it was just a mistake ...

> People do treat you different when you're not married and have kids. They have less time for you.

I remember when I was in having F. (child), I was 17 and all the nurses, even the student nurses, treated me like a piece of shit ... The Sister came along one day and she saw how the staff were treating me and she did back me up as if to say 'don't treat her like that' ... They do have their priority patients, married women and their husbands and we are children over there. No matter what age we were, we were treated terrible which was very wrong.

The New right argument that single lone parents are of weak moral character or lacking in positive moral influence was refuted by the assertions of the interviewees. The reaction of the women's parents suggests that they did not take the issue of their daughter's pregnancies lightly:

My parents didn't talk to me for five or six months and I just couldn't cope with that and then eventually they did, I am the youngest in the family.

My mam killed me at first but then after a while it was okay. She was thrilled, she knew I had no one else and she supported me.

... the way I was brought up by my Nan was not strict as such, but she had her morals in place, not to have sex before marriage, so when I had J.(child) I felt very guilty, I felt I was after breaking one of my Nan's rules and my Nan was after dying a year before.

Irresponsibility and Welfare Dependency

In contrast to the New Right rhetoric that single lone mothers are irresponsible, evidence from this work suggests the opposite to be true. The women viewed their mothering role in positive terms and gave first priority to the perceived needs of their children:

I am rearing my kids the best I can, I keep them clean and I look after them the best I can and that is all I can do.

You'd show off the children ... we'd dress them up and show that we could look after them. Every mother does it just to prove everybody wrong.

I love my kids and I adore the ground they walk on ...

... if you have money left over for yourself, you go along and then you see something for the kids and you buy it

I think I'm doing a pretty good job of it, I don't know like, really and truly, I just take one day as it comes, hop over the hurdles as they appear like, do you know. I have a lot of support as I said, from my parents and my Dad, I think everything is ok so far.

These assertions find parallels in the work of Phoenix (1991) and Acock and Demo (1994). These studies found that single lone mothers had positive views about their role as mothers, defended themselves against negative stereotypes and shared the parenting values held by mothers in all family types.

The inadequacy of welfare payments to single lone parents and the poverty they experience belie the New Right claim that generous welfare payments entice young women to become mothers. The unsatisfactory rate of welfare benefits provided to Irish single lone parents is reflected in the responses of the study group:

> I want the child to go off the baby food and onto the table food, I might have more money then.

> I have my name down for another place (apartment) but I haven't got the money for it.

> You can't go out, you haven't got the money. You have to buy milk and nappies and that's your money. I can't go out I haven't got it.

> We get a certain amount ... and then they (government) are going to give us an extra £1.50, I don't know what they expect us to buy.

Furthermore the single lone mothers reported negative experiences in their interactions with social welfare officials particularly in relation to discretionary payments:

> They give whatever they feel like giving, if they don't like you, you don't get anything, if they like you, you might get something, but no one gets the proper rate.

> You are entitled to a certain amount, but I hate going up asking for it...

> You are entitled to a lot of things but you mightn't get it.

> It is very upsetting and it makes you angry... I think the way it works up there (Social Welfare Office) is the more money they don't give out, the more money they get at the end of the week.

Contrary to the New Right belief that single lone mothers are complacent welfare dependents, the single lone mothers in this study wished to avail of job and educational opportunities which would provide greater financial independence. These ambitions have been thwarted by the orientation of Irish social policy provision for single lone parents, which reflected a 'benefits at home' model (Millar et al., 1992). More recently steps have been introduced to facilitate single lone parents to return to work or education on a part-time or full-time basis. Such measures include continued entitlement to social welfare payment and secondary benefits, for single lone parents returning to education. Travel and childcare expenses incurred by single lone parents who are returning to employment, are allowed against their earnings and a standard earnings disregard of £25 and £6 per dependent child is also permitted for the purpose of the calculation of means. The Back to Work Allowance scheme enables a lone parent to keep seventy-five per cent of her/his weekly social welfare payment for twelve months and fifty per cent of earnings for the following twelve months, in addition to any earnings from their employment. They also continue to receive any secondary benefits they were entitled to before participating in the scheme.[3] Reconciling work and caring responsibilities is an issue for all parents however it can be a huge challenge for single lone parents. This fact has been emphasised by the Working Group on Childcare Facilities for Working

Parents who made a range of recommendations outlining the need for greater provision of childcare facilities in this country. While the policy changes outlined above are welcome, the following comments from the study group suggest that many obstacles exist for single lone parents wishing to return to education or employment:

> I was working when I became pregnant first, it was a full time job and they took me back on after as well like, but I couldn't hack it.

> I'd love to go out there and find a job and get off it (welfare) but I haven't enough qualifications for work, there is not enough support for somebody my age to go back to school like, and the childcare costs forty or fifty pounds a week, d'you know, and that's just for one child, so I think there are a lot of people out there who are willing to help themselves, they have no way of figuring out how to because they are left short at the end of the week if they do and the government are just not willing to help them.

> There is no mother could go out and work and rear her child, 'cause you would be up all night, you couldn't go to work and you couldn't afford a baby sitter in the first place.

> He (child) is thirteen months. I went for a job and they told me it would be too hard for me.

> I would love to do my inter-cert... people say you could do these courses, but I wouldn't be able to do these courses anyway.

> I put my name down in here (Newbury House) to do a course but I couldn't do it.

New Right rhetoric identifies marriage as a desirable solution to the 'problem' of single lone motherhood. Marriage was not considered to be a positive option by the majority of the women interviewed.

> I got married, I felt a lot better before I got married, a lot of things have changed.

> I have a boyfriend at the moment, like he could be there today and he could go away, and I would be stuck with two kids all on my own, in my eyes I'm on my own anyway cause I can't rely on him, fellas can do what they want, which is very wrong, they should have some sort of responsibility ... it is all on our shoulders, it is very wrong, the system is fucked up. It is hard not to be able to rely on your partner.

> P (Partner) gives me all his money, but some times he could go on a binge and I wouldn't see a penny and he is bad, what happens is he is so good and then snap!, it would be alright if he stayed the same all the time, then I would know what to expect, but when he doesn't it is very hard.

> I always wanted my child to have his dad, I felt I was taking something away from him (Child), but why I left him was that I could envision F. (Child) sitting in a corner and his dad beating me and that wasn't on at all.

Only one woman saw marriage as a desirable option, expressing a wish to have a partner:

> I'd like somebody with me now, even though I'm so young I know that there is plenty of time but I am after going through two kids in four years so

you know what I mean, I just need somebody more than friends and family.
But whether I will meet him tomorrow ... nobody knows.

Along with the unreliability of partners the women's disillusionment with
marriage stemmed from negative experiences of marriage which they had
witnessed in their own families:

...every marriage I knew ended, my mam, my uncle, every body's, everyone
I know, being married doesn't do anything for you ...

Co-habitation was also viewed negatively by the study group however it was
seen to have certain advantages, such as a greater sense of freedom and
independence which did not apply to marriage:

There are girls living with fellas now and the only difference is the ring.

You have your own money, you are more independent like, when you get
married on dole, you don't get that kind of money (individual payment)...
it's not worth it, getting money off your man... I couldn't stand that crap.

While marriage is not, for the most part, seen as a desirable option, the lack of
a supportive partner creates difficulties and some worries for single lone
mothers:

We have to grow up quicker, I was seventeen going on forty, because I was
rearing a child on my own.

Before you go out you have to think of everything first. Getting someone in,
getting them fed, make sure you have a few pound going out, there are so
many things, it's very hard.

It's harder alright like, you have to organise babysitters if you want to go
out, you have to organise childminders if you want to work, you have to
arrange with certain people if you want to work, like social welfare, things
like that ...

You didn't realise how much work was involved, you're changing nappies
constantly and the first year is the hardest, with teething ... it's much easier
now.

Really my fear is raising the kids the best I could like without a father, even
though they have a grandfather and three uncles... I know that's a lot of
male ... what do you call it.. (influence?) yeah, but sometimes I feel it that
they haven't a fatherly influence living with them when there is other
people around them that have.

Phoenix (1991) in her study of teenage mothers found primarily negative
attitudes to marriage with young males with few employment opportunities
proving to be unattractive marriage partners. Slipman (1994) referring to lack
of permanent employment for young men suggests that while they have lost
their traditional breadwinner role, they have not yet assumed joint caring roles
within the family. The strain of single lone mothering as identified by the
women in this study is reiterated in the findings of Acock and Demo (1994,
p.20) who concluded that:

...the pressures of coping alone rather than being able to delegate family responsibilities to a partner, albeit only limited amounts, contribute to the role strain experienced by continuously single mothers.

Given the above findings it is not unreasonable that single lone mothers choose to maintain their single status.

The insider perspective outlined in this study draws into question many of the New Right assumptions regarding single lone motherhood and highlights the inappropriate nature of many New Right solutions.

Single Lone Parents and Social Policy

A variety of policy models have been developed internationally to address the needs of single lone mothers (Roll, 1992). These policy initiatives reflect varying degrees of reliance on earnings, social transfers and private transfers. Such initiatives bifurcate into those which assume the labour market participation of single lone mothers and those which assume their dependence on state support. This provision of state support has been castigated by New Right commentators who call for greater levels of self sufficiency among single lone parents (Murray, 1993, Gingrich, 1995). The policy approach traditionally pursued in Sweden has facilitated the labour market participation of lone parents. Over ninety per cent of women in Sweden aged between twenty-five and fifty-five, are in the labour force, with almost equal levels of participation between married and solo mothers (Gornick, 1992).[4] The structure of the Swedish tax system, the provision of daycare places and parental leave favour working mothers. Hobson (1994) in a study of solo mothers and social policy regimes in five countries, found that solo mothers in Sweden were less likely to experience poverty than their counterparts in the Netherlands, the UK, Germany, and the USA. This would suggest that policy regimes which promote and facilitate the labour market participation of single lone mothers can prove effective in alleviating poverty among this group. Adoption of such a policy regime is dependent on the existence of certain conditions. These include availability of work, provision of public childcare facilities, attitudinal acceptance of working mothers, and compatible tax and benefit systems. These conditions have not been cultivated in Ireland. The traditional assumption that mothers should work-full time in the home is still influential; unemployment rates are high, especially among women whose work is mainly concentrated in the service sector and is characterised by low pay and part-time hours; levels of childcare provision are inadequate and the tax/benefit system is structured in such a way that a single lone parent can even become financially worse off by taking employment (Treoir, 1995). The existence of many such unfavourable conditions in the UK, the USA and Ireland, highlight the impracticality of New Right demands for economic self sufficiency among single lone parents.

Scheiwe's (1994) study of poverty among mothers in the UK, Belgium and Germany indicates:

> a very weak commitment in Britain to what might be regarded as the building blocks of good family policy: strong institutional support for mothers' labour market chances, socialised childcare facilities, cash benefits subsidising the costs of children and importantly, a welfare rather than punitive response to the breakdown of marriage. (Rodger, 1995, p.7-8).

Schram (1994, p.67-68) documents similar findings from the USA:

> Policies geared toward women with children tend to offer inferior benefits or are lacking in commitment to the services and strategies, like child care and pay equity, that women need in order to become self-sufficient ... Rather than the growth in female-headed families causing poverty, it is the persistent lack of adequate paying jobs, the deterioration of needed services and, most especially, the low value of public assistance for women with children which are the major contributing factors to their poverty status.

The UK Commission on Social Justice (1995), recognises the need to support families, acknowledging that:

> the best escape route from poverty is paid work, supported by a minimum wage, decent training opportunities, stronger anti-discrimination legislation and good quality, affordable childcare, as well as the higher level of child benefit. (Lister, 1995, p.11).

Schram (1994) and Rodger (1995) reinforce the need for a policy approach which does not censure, but supports families irrespective of their structure. Schram (1994, p.81) suggests:

> By emphasizing how income support can help families develop capacities for self-sufficiency and by making such assistance available to all families regardless of structure and relationship to the labor market, such policies can overcome popular resistance and gain political credibility.

This study among others, (Phoenix, 1991, Burghes, 1993) provides clear evidence that single lone mothers aspire to gain employment but identifies many barriers to achieving this goal, barriers which New Right discourse fails to acknowledge. Shortsighted policies which seek to force welfare recipients into a non-receptive labour market can only exacerbate the problems faced by single lone mothers. Limited training and work opportunities confine many single lone mothers to the margins of the labour market, in jobs which do little to alleviate their risk of poverty. The idealisation of the home-based mother in Irish society may be internalised by the single lone mother seeking to confirm her standing as a 'good' mother. This may create an ideological barrier to her engagement in paid work. Conflicts surrounding the reconciliation of paid work and care responsibilities are commonplace in the experiences of women. This issue has been recognised in feminist analyses of gender and social rights (Ungerson, 1990, Orloff, 1993). To develop a social policy regime which provides women with viable choices regarding caring and paid employment, is a challenge which requires a fundamental re-think of the way in which systems of care and work are structured in Western society. The experiences and needs of single lone mothers must be viewed in the context of the inequality of women's position in society and the lack of 'non-controlling help' (Fox Harding, 1996) provided to families. Acquiescence with the New Right demand that support be removed from single lone parent families will result in,

> either the over-burdening of the family, or the finding of permanent alternative care. A more supportive style of intervention might enable the original family structure to continue, if that is what those involved want. (Fox Harding, 1996, p.197)

This chapter by documenting the experiences of single lone mothers has challenged the validity of New Right rhetoric which stigmatises lone mothers. It further underlines the need for an approach to social policy which supports all families, regardless of their structure, and in a manner which does not collude in the oppression of women.

Discussion Topics

1.   Why are single lone parent families at risk of poverty?

2.   Why do you think the New Right rhetoric has gained popularity in the UK and USA?

3.   In your opinion what social policy reforms are likely to be most effective in addressing the needs of single lone parent families?

4.   What is a 'good' mother?

Acknowledgement

The authors wish to sincerely thank all of the women who took part in the research.

Notes

1.   Throughout this chapter the term 'single lone mother' is used to refer to mothers who have never married. The term 'lone parent' denotes any adult parenting on their own.
2.   Information regarding the number of Lone Parent Allowance claimants for 1995 was received on request from the Department of Social Welfare. These figures are not yet published.
3.   This information is contained in a Fact Sheet for Lone Parents, available on request from the Department of Social Welfare.
4.   The term 'solo mother' is used to refer to any category of woman parenting on her own.

References and Further Reading

Acock, A and Demo, D. 1994 *Family Diversity And Well-Being* London: Sage.

Bartholomew, J. 1995 'Don't Take Single Parents For Granted: Stop the Hand-Outs', in *The Daily Telegraph* 23/8/95.

Bryan, A, 1992 in Langan M, and Day L. (eds.) *Women, Oppression and Social Work* London: Routledge.

Burghes, L. 1993 *One-parent Families : Policy Options For The 1990s* York: Joseph Rowntree Foundation.

Bush, J. 1994 Cited in 'Jeb — One From Central Casting' in *The Sunday Times* 30/10/94.

Callan, T, Nolan, B, Whelan, B J, Hannon, D F, Creighton, S. 1989 *Poverty, Income And Welfare In Ireland* Dublin: E.S.R.I.

Cashmore, E. 1985 *Having To: The World Of One Parent Families* London: Allen and Unwin.

Clark, E. 1989 *Young Single Mothers Today: A Qualitative Study of Housing And Support Needs* London: National Council for One Parent Families.

Close, P. 1988 'Family Form And Economic Production' in Close P, and Collins R. (eds.) *Family And Economy In Modern Society* London: Macmillan.

Crellin, E, Pringle, H, and West, P. 1971 *Born Illegitimate* London: National Children's Bureau.

Darling, V. 1984 *And Baby Makes Two* Dublin: F.S.U.P.C.

Davies, J, Berger, B and Carlson, A. 1993 *The Family: Is It Just Another Lifestyle Choice?* London: Institute Of Economic Affairs.

Dennis, N. 1993 *Rising Crime and The Dismembered Family* London: Institute of Economic Affairs.

Department of Health. 1981, 1993 *Vital Statistics* Dublin: Stationery Office.

Department of Social Welfare. 1986, 1994 *Statistical Information on Social Welfare Services* Dublin: Stationery Office.

Federation of Services For Unmarried Parents And Their Children. 1995 *National Anti-Poverty Strategy Submission* Dublin.

Finch, J. 1991 'Feminist Research And Social Policy' in Maclean M and Groves D. (eds.) *Women's Issues In Social Policy* London: Routledge.

Fox Harding, L. 1996 *Family, State and Social Policy* London: Macmillan.

Fox Piven, F. 1994 Cited in *It's A Family Affair* Leicester: National Youth Agency, p.9.

Gingrich, N. 1995 Cited in 'Teenage Mums: An Idea Out Of Control' in *The Independent* 15/8/95, p.11.

Gornick, J. 1992 cited in Hobson, B. 1994 'Solo Mothers, Social Policy Regimes and The Logics of Gender' in D Sainsbury *Gendering Welfare States* London: Sage

Graham, H. 1983 'Do Her Answers Fit His Questions? Women And The Survey Method' in Gamarnikow, G, Morgan, D, Purvis, J and Taylorson, D. (eds.) *The Public And The Private* London: Heinemann.

Gustafasson, S. 1990 'The Labour Force Participation And Earnings Of Lone Parents. A Swedish Case Study With Comparisons To Germany' in *Lone Parent Families* The Economic Challenge Paris: OECD.

Hobson, B. 1994 'Solo Mothers, Social Policy Regimes and The Logics of Gender' in D Sainsbury *Gendering Welfare States* London: Sage.

Lister, R. 1995 'Social Justice: Radical Plan Or Washout?' *Poverty* 90 Spring 1995 pp.8-11

Madge, N. 1983 *Families At Risk* London: Heinemann.

Magee, C. 1994 *Teenage Parents — Issues Of Policy And Practice* Dublin: Irish Youthwork Press.

McAnarney, E R, Henee, W R. 1989 Adolescent Pregnancy and its Consequences *A M A*, July 7, 1989, 262(1).

McCashin, A. 1993 *Lone Parents In The Republic Of Ireland: Enumeration, Description And Implications For Social Security* Dublin: ESRI Paper No. 29.

McNally, F. 1996 'Rise And Rise Of The Welfare Mother' in *The Irish Times* 6/3/96.

Millar, J, Leeper, S and Davies, C. 1992 *Lone Parents, Poverty and Public Policy in Ireland: A Comparative Study* Dublin: Combat Poverty Agency.

Morgan, P. 1995 Cited in 'The Ethnic Time Bomb' in *The International Express*, 16-22 August, 1995 p.2.

Murray, C. 1993 'Keep It In The Family' in *The Sunday Times*, 14/11/93.

Murray, C. 1994 *The Underclass: The Crisis Deepens* London: Institute Of Economic Affairs.

Oakley, A. 1981 'Interviewing Women: a Contradiction in Terms?' in Roberts H. (ed.) *Doing Feminist Research* London: Routledge and Kegan Paul.

O'Grady, T. 1993 *Married To The State* Dublin: Department of Social Welfare.

Orloff, A S. 1993 'Gender And The Social Rights Of Citizenship: State Policies And Gender Relations In Comparative Research' *American Sociological Review*, Vol.58, No.3, pp.303-328.

Phoenix, A. 1991 *Young Mothers?* Cambridge: Polity Press.

Redwood, J. 1995 Cited in 'Teenage Mums: An Idea Out of Control' in *The Independent* 15/8/95, p.11.

Redwood, J. 1995 Cited in 'MPs Go To War On Lone Parents' in *The International Express* 16-22 August, p.2.

Renvoize, J. 1985 *Going Solo: Single Mothers By Choice* London: Routledge and Kegan Paul.

Rickford, F. 1992 'Baby Boom' *Social Work Today*, 5/11, p.10

Riley, D and Shaw, M. 1985 *Parental Supervision And Juvenile Delinquency* London: Home Office Research Study, No.83, H.M.S.O.

Rodger, J. 1995 'Family Policy or Moral Regulation?' in *Critical Social Policy* Issue 43, Summer, 1995.

Roll, J. 1992 *Lone Parent Families in the European Community* London: European Family and Social Policy Unit.

Scheiwe, K. 1994 cited in Rodger, J. 1995 'Family Policy or Moral Regulation?' in *Critical Social Policy* Issue 43, Summer, 1995.

Schram, S F. 1994 'Postindustrial Welfare Policy: Just Say No To Women And Children' *Review of Radical Political Economics* Vol.26, No.1, pp.56-84.

Slipman, S. 1994 Cited in *It's A Family Affair* Leicester: National Youth Agency, pp.19-20.

Timmins, N. 1995 'Teenage Mums: An Idea Out Of Control' in *The Independent* 15/8/95.

Toomey Jacksonville, C 1994 'Jeb — One From Central Casting', in *The Sunday Times* 30/10/1994.

TREOIR. 1995 *Lone Parents In Ireland — Summary Report* Dublin: The Federation of Services for Unmarried Parents and their Children.

Ungerson, C. (ed.) 1990 *Gender and Caring: Work and Welfare in Britain and Scandinavia* New York: Harvester Wheatsheaf.

Working Group on Childcare Facilities for Working Parents. 1994 *Report to the Minister for Equality and Law Reform* Dublin: Stationery Office.

19.

A Comparative Study of Maternity Entitlements in Northern Ireland and the Republic of Ireland in the 1990s.
Patricia Kennedy

Introduction

> ... Even though not all women personally experience motherhood, hardly any woman in present day welfare states is unaffected by its potentiality, and most women actually do become mothers. Considering, too, that the gender-differentiated family is a central character of welfare state design, an investigation of welfare state motherhood also sheds light on the welfare state approach to women more generally. (Leira, 1992, p.3)

This paper introduces a study of one aspect of the relationship between the welfare states of the Republic of Ireland (from here on referred to as Ireland) and Northern Ireland and women as they experience pregnancy and the first year of motherhood. It is an exploration of the interplay between the welfare state and mothers (including pregnant women under the definition of motherhood). This will contribute to an understanding of the relationship between the welfare state and all women, as women are commonly perceived in society as potential mothers.

The aim of this paper is twofold. Firstly, to introduce a model of motherhood which encompasses women's three intertwined roles as carer, as earner and as lifegiver. Secondly, it will compare the social construction of motherhood in Ireland and Northern Ireland, utilising statistical data on women as mothers and maternity entitlements.

A New Paradigm: The Three Dimensional Model of Motherhood

This paper presents a paradigm developed by this author which encompasses mothers' three dimensional role as earner, as carer and as lifegiver. An examination of the welfare state treatment of mothers as earner, carer and lifegiver means in effect an examination of welfare policies, health policies and labour policies where they intersect, which is the point where the public and private domains meet and where women tend to live their lives. A close look at this intersection will illuminate the welfare state's construction of motherhood.

Social theorists examining the relationship between the welfare state and mothers have tended to view mothers in their role as carer (Beveridge, 1942) or at best in the dual role of carer and earner (Titmuss, 1963, Pinker, 1979, Johnson, 1987). This has been to the neglect of the very crucial area of biological reproduction. Parsons (1955, 1960) offers a theory of motherhood as being functional to society. He views motherhood as serving the needs of the family while simultaneously serving the needs of capitalism. Role differentiation, he accepts as beneficial to all concerned, that is, to the male breadwinner and to the female carer/dependent. The 'naturalness' of these roles coincides with reproductive functions, both biological and social. Parsons argues that because women bear and nurse children, there is a strong assumption that the father who is exempted from biological reproduction should specialise in the '... alternative instrumental direction ...' (Parsons, 1955, p.13).

Alongside these functional theories of sociology, there developed psychological theories propounded primarily by Bowlby (1953). His infamous theory of maternal deprivation (for a critical appraisal see Rutter, 1972) suggests the child who does not enjoy a warm, intimate and continuous relationship with his mother or permanent mother-substitute, would suffer from maternal deprivation. He minimises the father's role, emphasising an infant's need for an intense, continuous relationship with his mother in order to prevent the child suffering from emotional deprivation and growing up to be a damaged adult who would similarly damage his own offspring. Mother's own needs are ignored as she is shackled to her child. Bowlby claims that leaving any child under three years should be avoided at all costs (1953).

Pascall indicates the enduring influence of the maternal deprivation thesis as an intrinsic part of social policy, claiming that state policies for young children reflect this belief in the need for continuous care by mothers. Pascall argues that

> ... the idealisation of this-historically somewhat peculiar-intimate and isolated relationship underpins the place of women in domestic life and therefore in public life too... (Pascall, 1986, p.84).

Other feminist theorists have strongly criticised Bowlby's and Parsons' theories which are linked very much to a belief in biological determinism. Oakley (1974, 1979, 1989, 1992) indicates the social construction of motherhood, examining differences in social practices cross-culturally. Eisenstein (1979, 1983) distinguishes between the 'biological' and 'political' aspects of motherhood. Biological aspects encompass acts determined by women's biological capacity to conceive, give birth, lactate, while political aspects encompass the gendered role of caring, nurturing and social reproduction.

Rich (1977) in a determined backlash against theories of biological determinism, distinguishes between the biological nature of motherhood and motherhood as an institution. She distinguishes between two meanings of motherhood, the potential relationship of any woman to her capacity to reproduce, and the institution of motherhood which she charges with ensuring that all women shall remain under male control. Rich argues that the institution of motherhood 'has been a keystone of the most diverse social and political systems ...' (Rich, 1977, p.13).

A succession of feminist writers have taken up the 'domestic labour' debate (Barrett, 1980, Hartmann, 1981, and Eisenstein, 1979) and have attempted to explore the dual role of women in society, that is as carer and as earner. They have brought together the public and the private arenas of production and reproduction (Wilson, 1977, Barrett and McIntosh, 1991). Pascall (1986) emphasises the importance of reproduction for feminist theory. She argues that reproductive labour is characteristically women's labour and an examination of it is the best hope of understanding male dominance.

The issues of social reproduction, associated with caring, paid and unpaid have been analysed in terms of sociology and psychology. Graham (1983) has very usefully designed a model of caring work as being both an activity and an identity, and women's work as 'a labour of love'. This model is very illuminating in terms of the welfare state as it questions at a very fundamental level woman's caring role. Looking more specifically at mothers, Leira (1992) takes a two pronged view of mothers as carers and as earners. This is an invaluable approach as so often mothers have been rendered invisible. They have been viewed one-dimensionally, either as carers or as earners, dividing the private realm of unpaid work from the public realm of paid work.

Leira argues that any analysis of motherhood has to take place within a broad context which illuminates the different ways the welfare state has dealt with economic and caring provision.

While Leira has developed a very useful model for understanding mothers' relationship to the welfare state, this paper argues that a third dimension is essential. Introduced here is a model which will contribute to the creation of a more thorough understanding of the relationship of the welfare state to women's experience of pregnancy and motherhood. While women primarily find themselves in the role of carer and many juggle this with the role of earner, this study argues that both of these roles can be passed on to other parties, be it the State, other women, friends or relations. However, there is another dimension to women's role as mother which cannot be passed on, this being the biological element of motherhood and nurturing.

Lifegiving

The period from conception to childbirth is a period in a woman's life which reflects the public/private divisions of women's lives. Conception is a result of an intimate private act. However, the nine months following conception is a long journey for a woman as she travels in and out of the public world of hospital appointments and the public gaze and comments as her body blooms and grows, and the private, silent world of morning sickness, exhaustion and feelings of loneliness, isolation and at other times ecstasy and for some the private loss of miscarriage. The journey into the male controlled world of medicine and eventually birth for the majority of women takes place in a very public, male controlled labour ward (Oakley, 1992, Tew, 1995, O'Connor, 1992, 1995). On the way to this ward, women undergo a period of socialisation and education as they attend ante-natal appointments and classes (Mason, 1994).

It is only woman who can conceive, lactate and give birth. It is only the biological mother who is caught in the grips of labour pain. It is only the biological mother who experiences abortion, suffers the pain of a miscarriage or the experience of childbirth. It is only the biological mother who lactates. These are the very basic elements which the mother has to balance with her role as carer and earner and these are the most prudent issues ignored by social policy analysts. This is the area of a woman's life deemed as private and as such outside the sphere of social policy. At the same time, such essentially private areas as contraception and abortion have been commandeered by the media, legislators and the Church and become public issues in both Northern Ireland and in the Republic (Smyth, 1992).

Women as Mothers in Northern Ireland and Ireland
The male breadwinner model

Jane Lewis in developing a gender analysis of welfare regimes, argues that there exists 'male breadwinner' models of welfare regimes. She indicates that Ireland and Britain are examples of historically strong male breadwinner states and that this in part explains the high incidence of women's part-time labour market participation, under developed child care services, poor maternity rights, and differential access to social security for men and women (Lewis, 1992).

The welfare state of Northern Ireland has traditionally been viewed in relation to Great Britain. McLaughlin claims that for the most part public policy in Northern Ireland for over twenty years has been guided by two principles. The first, is to appear to do something about the sectarian conflict and the second, to achieve parity of provision with Great Britain (McLaughlin, 1991). Perhaps it is now time to view Northern Ireland in relation to Ireland, as two states on the periphery of Europe sharing a common history. A comparative examination of maternity entitlements in the two welfare states will give an insight into some similarities and differences in their relative social policies in relation to mothers. Perhaps our geographical location, together with the strength of the institutionalised Churches will lend itself to comparison.

McLaughlin indicates that women in Northern Ireland are '... particularly oppressed by the influence of conservative religious ideologies and by the parochial or inward-looking nature of life in a divided and troubled society ... (McLaughlin, 1991, p.6)

Barrington's reference to the historical power of the Catholic Church in the Republic of Ireland '... and brooding behind every aspect of Irish life is the church ...' (Barrington, 1987, p.2) reflects Evason's references to the power of the Churches in Northern Ireland. Evason claims '... Northern Ireland remained a deeply oppressive, conservative society, with a rigid perception of women's role and duties. On the one side there was the Catholic Church- fast becoming the most reactionary branch of Catholicism in Western Europe and on the other an equally conservative Protestantism ...' (Evason, 1991, p.14)

In this context, this paper presents a profile of mothers on this island. It is vital to acknowledge the effects of the political conflict in Northern Ireland on women. Eileen Evason indicates that women in Northern Ireland, '... have taken the bulk of the strain and hardship produced by Northern Ireland's political and economic problems...' (Evason, 1991, p.13).

Statistical Profile of Mothers

Utilising statistical data, this section of the paper, illustrates who are the women experiencing motherhood in Ireland today. The population of Ireland (1991 Census) is 3,525,719, with women making up 1,772,301 of this number (1991 Census), while the 1991 Northern Ireland Census shows respective figures of 1,601,000 and 820,000. However, an estimate of the number of women actually of childbearing age will give a more concise number of the women directly affected by those policies pertaining to pregnancy and the first year of motherhood. Recent statistics on birth rates in Ireland (Deptartment of Health, 1993) show a total of 49,456 births. Equivalent figures for Northern Ireland show a birth rate of 26,236 (Annual Abstracts of Statistics, 1993). The age range fifteen to forty-five is the most common age of mothers of young children in Ireland and Northern Ireland. The number of women in the fifteen to forty-five age group is 777,176 in the Republic (Census 1991) and 332,319 in Northern Ireland (Census 1991). This gives an estimate of the number of women directly effected by maternity policies.

Table 1: *Age breakdown of females in Republic of Ireland and Northern Ireland 1991.*

AGE	IRELAND	AGE	NORTH
1 - 15	457,726	1 - 15	190,400
15 - 20	163,618	15 - 20	60,900
20 - 25	130,193	20 - 25	64,100
25 - 30	125,661	25 - 30	62,900
30 - 35	126,903	30 - 35	59,600
35 - 40	118,724	35 - 40	51,700
40 - 45	112,077	40 - 45	48,700
45 - 50	93,319	45 - 50	47,600
50 - 55	79,880	50 - 55	39,900
55 and over	368,834	55 and over	197,700

Source: *Census of Population 1991*, Government Publications, Dublin. *72nd Annual Report of the Registrar General* 1993, Belfast, HMSO.

Comparative statistics for Ireland and Northern Ireland for live births from 1926-1993 indicate a steady decline in fertility rates in both parts of the island but with a lower rate of birth in the Republic.

Table 2: *Live births per 1,000 of population for selected years Northern Ireland and Ireland.*

YEAR	NORTHERN IRELAND	IRELAND
1926	22.5	20.6
1937	19.8	19.2
1951	20.7	21.2
1961	22.4	21.2
1966	22.5	21.6
1971	20.6	22.8
1981	17.8	21.0
1987	17.7	16.5
1988	17.6	15.4
1989	16.5	14.8
1990	16.7	15.1
1991	16.4	14.9
1992	15.8	14.6
1993	15.3	13.9

Source: *Census of Population 1991*, Government Publications, Dublin. *72nd Annual Report of the Registrar General 1993*, Belfast, HMSO.

Figures show an increase in non-marital births in both parts of the island with that in the North exceeding that of the Republic.

Table 3: *Non-marital birhts as a percentage of total births in Northern Ireland and Ireland 1981-1992.*

YEAR	NORTHERN IRELAND	IRELAND
1981	6.96	5.4
1982	7.81	6.2
1983	8.74	6.8
1984	10.12	8.0
1985	11.56	8.5
1986	12.72	9.6
1987	14.27	9.7
1988	16.08	10.7
1989	16.92	12.8
1990	18.76	14.5
1991	20.20	16.6
1992	21.91	18.0
1993	21.91	19.5

Source: Department of Health Statistics. *72nd Annual Report of the Registrar General 1993*, Belfast, HMSO.

Patterns for the North of Ireland and Ireland show similar decline in the birth rate but an increase in non-marital births.

Maternity Entitlements

Health, welfare and labour policies intersect at an important point for women. Mothers come into contact with health services as healthy people rather than sick people, as pregnancy is not an illness. Looking at maternity policies, that is, maternity leave and entitlements for women on leave from paid work and for those outside the paid labour market indicates the value of examining motherhood in terms of carer, earner and lifegiver. An evaluation of maternity entitlements gives a vision of how motherhood is dealt with in both the North of Ireland and Ireland.

318   *Women and Irish Society*

Table 4: *Maternity Entitlements Northern Ireland and the Republic of Ireland.*

NORTHERN IRELAND	REPUBLIC OF IRELAND
Statutory Maternity Pay (SMP)	**Maternity Benefit**
Payable if a woman has been in employment without a break for at least six months by her 26 week of pregnancy and has been paying NI. Two rates: 1. For a woman working at least 16 hours a week full-time for at least two years, or at least eight hours a week part-time for at least five years. The first six weeks are paid at ninety per cent of average earnings. The remaining 12 weeks are paid at a lower rate of £52.50 (1995). 2. For a woman in same employment between 26 weeks and two years lower rate is paid for the whole period.	Payable to women who satisfy certain PRSI contributions on their own insurance record. To qualify, must have at least 39 weeks PRSI paid in the 12 months immediately before the first day of maternity leave. Or, 39 weeks PRSI paid since you first started working and 39 weeks PRSI paid or credited in the relevant tax year. Payment is 70% of average earnings in relevant tax year, subject to maximum and minimum limits. Rate of maternity benefit will be compared to the rate of disability benefit which would be payable in your case and the higher of the two will be paid automatically. For those in receipt of lone-parents allowance, widows pension, deserted wives benefit, deserted wives allowance, prisoners wives allowance, half is paid.
Maternity Allowance	**Maternity Allowance**
Payable by local security office for up to 18 weeks to someone who has changed jobs or become self employed, if the standard rate NI payments have paid for at least 26 weeks in the 52 weeks leading up to the 26th week of pregnancy. Less than lower rate of SMP. £52.50 if paying NI contribution (earning over £58 per week). Otherwise lower rate of £45.55.	The general Maternity Allowance payment was abolished in 1992.
Maternity Payment	**Maternity Grant**
Paid from the social fund and is payable if the mother or partner are getting income support or family credit. Full amount payable only if savings are less that £500. From 11 weeks before the birth to three months after the birth. For adopted baby up until one year old.	This means tested payment of £8 is the only payment available to mothers who are not in employment.
Other entitlements	**Exceptional Needs Payments**
Free milk; dental treatment, free to all pregnant and nursing mothers (up to one year after confinement); free health care under the NHS and free prescriptions during pregnanct and up until child's first birthday for mother and 18 years for child.	Means tested payments towards maternity expenses under the exceptional needs payments of the supplementary allowance scheme. Under the Mother and Infant Health Scheme free health care for the mother during pregnancy and for mother and infant up to six weeks after the birth.

Source: Kennedy, P. Unpublished PhD thesis in progress.

Earning, Caring and Lifegiving

In Ireland, maternity leave was introduced in 1981 under the Maternity Protection of Employees Act but the most recent legislation is the 1994 Maternity Protection Act. This introduced measures to encourage improvements in the safety and health at work of pregnant workers and workers who have given birth or are breast feeding. The period of maternity leave available to employed workers is fourteen weeks, four of which has to be taken before the expected date of delivery and four weeks after. The woman has the freedom to avail of an additional four weeks unpaid leave. This is a two-tier system with women who are able to afford a four week unpaid period availing of a longer period than those constrained by financial considerations. This has implications for women who wish to breastfeed because they are generally unable to unite paid work with breast feeding. A woman who nurses her baby is faced with time constraints and has few options concerning such an important issue. Returning to full time work after three or four months has other implications. Tiredness is an issue for many women, from pregnancy and childbirth, but also from adjusting to a new routine. There is also the issue of finding suitable child care and coping with the emotions associated for many women with returning to work and leaving such a young baby. There is no acknowledgement of the responsibility for home duties assigned to women who work both in and outside the home.

In Northern Ireland the longer period of maternity leave of eighteen weeks is beneficial as is the choice to take up to twenty-nine weeks unpaid leave. However, it militates against those unable to afford to remain unpaid for a twenty-nine week period and assumes the existence of a male breadwinner. In Northern Ireland the rate of statutory maternity benefit is less overall than in the Republic. While the first six weeks is paid at a rate of ninety per cent of salary, the remaining twelve weeks is paid at a rate of £52.50 per week. While maternity allowance is paid at a rate of £52.50 to those who have paid sufficient National Insurance contributions (must be earning in excess of £58 (1995 rate), others receive a lower payment of £45.55.

It is only women who can give birth and experience pregnancy and lactation. This very role guarantees certain life experiences. In Northern Ireland and Ireland, it would appear that the State clearly dictates how much time a woman can take away from the paid labour market. As regards the welfare system it would appear that women outside the paid labour market (including women who work below a certain number of hours each week) are largely ignored in terms of finance. In Ireland there is a meagre means tested grant of £8. Other than this payment women receive no extra assistance except for those who can negotiate a discretionary payment under the Exceptional Needs Scheme.

Women experiencing pregnancy and the early weeks of maternity are only acknowledged by the welfare system in their role as paid workers in the paid labour market. It is women as paid workers who are partially compensated for taking time off paid work to give birth while at the same time they are in fact penalised for the very fact that it is only women who can give birth. This is reflected in the Social Security system. Cousins indicates how developments in the 1980s and 1990s have seen maternity protection becoming much more closely linked to participation in the paid labour force with the abolition of both maternity grants and allowances for women outside paid employment (Cousins, 1995).

Hinds refers to the system in the United Kingdom as '... essentially one of unpaid child care leave for women, a system which promotes traditional patterns of domestic responsibility once a reasonable period for childbirth and maternal health has ended' (Hinds, 1991, p.97). This is also true for Ireland.

Women in Ireland and in Northern Ireland are short-changed by the welfare state when they become pregnant. Women outside the paid labour market are in reality, non- existent to the welfare state except as patients availing of maternity healthcare service. Setting aside the debate about the colonisation of the birth process by the male medical profession, and merely looking at entitlement to health care for pregnant women, mothers and their infants, women in Northern Ireland fare far better than their southern sisters. Women in the Republic of Ireland, under the Maternity and Infant Care Scheme can only avail of free medical care during pregnancy and for six weeks after delivery. After this time eligibility criteria must be satisfied, and in fact only fifty-four per cent of women in the sixteen to forty- four age group are eligible for medical cards in the Republic (Deptartment of Health, 1993). Recent research indicates this is totally inadequate (Glazener, C M A et al., 1995). The lack of support services (statutory) and also emotional support (paternity leave) in reality implies that women must get on with the task of motherhood drawing on very limited fiscal and social supports.

While labour legislation has improved in recent times as regards maternity leave entitlement, both the Republic of Ireland and Northern Ireland fare very badly when compared with other European member states. The time a woman is allowed to take off from work is significant as it dictates such issues as whether or not a woman can breastfeed her baby and when she has to start to wean her baby. This has serious implications for the child's welfare. The woman who wants to share the early months of her child's life is denied flexibility and choice and in reality is forced to return to work or to depend on welfare payments or on a male breadwinner, and to pay somebody, usually another woman to care for the new baby. The total absence of paternity leave in Ireland and the very limited five days in the North of Ireland reinforces traditional patterns of parenting and enforced responsibility on the mother.

In this context parental leave is an important issue, and one which the EU has recognised. The Council of Social Affairs Ministers adopted a Directive on Parental Leave on 29 March 1996. This was the first measure to be agreed under the social protocol of the Maastricht Treaty. It gives legal approval to the Framework Agreement on Parental Leave drawn up by the Social Partners in December 1995. The member states have a minimum of two years in which to implement the Directive. It will not apply to Northern Ireland as the United Kingdom is not party to the Social Protocol. However, in Ireland, it has been welcomed as an important milestone in that it will give all working mothers and fathers a right to three months leave from work on the birth or adoption of a child.

Conclusion

This comparative study of maternity rights for women in Ireland presents a three dimensional model of motherhood on this island. The intersection of health, welfare and labour policies defines women's role as mother within the welfare state. In the context of a male-breadwinner state a woman is expected to reproduce and is allocated a certain amount of time to proceed through the various stages from conception to the end of lactation. The woman who is a part of the paid labour force is expected to juggle pregnancy and motherhood while the woman outside the paid labour market is expected to depend on a male breadwinner or the state for financial support. Within the confines of the present study a first step has been taken to compare welfare state motherhood in Ireland with that of Northern Ireland and pessimistically calls to mind the words of Mary O'Brien (1981) as she refers to reproduction as '... nature's bitter trap ...'

Discussion Topics

1. Are all women viewed as 'potential mothers' within Irish Society?

2. What type of policies do you feel need to be implemented to improve women's experiences of welfare state motherhood?

3. Discuss the arguments in favour of paternal leave.

4. How does Jane Lewis's male breadwinner model contribute to a clearer understanding of motherhood?

References and Further Reading

Barrett, M. 1980 *Women's Oppression Today the Marxist/Feminist Encounter* London: Verso.

Barrett, M and McIntosh, M.1991 *The Anti-Social Family* London: Verso.

Barrington, R. 1987 *Health, Medicine and Politics in Ireland 1900-1970* Dublin: Institute of Public Administration.

Beveridge, W. 1942 *Social Insurance and Allied Services*, Cmnd. 6404, HMSO, London.

Bowlby, J. 1953 *Child Care and the Growth of Love* Harmondsworth: Penguin.

Central Statistics Office *Census of Population 1991* Dublin: Government Stationery Office.

Central Statistics Office, 1991 *Northern Ireland Census Summary report* Belfast: HMSO.

Central Statistics Office, 1993 *Annual Abstracts of Statistics* London: HMSO.

Cousins, M. 1995 *Social Welfare and the Law in Ireland* Dublin: Macmillan.

Davies, C and McLaughlin, E. (eds.) 1991 *Women, Employment and Social Policy in Northern Ireland a Problem Postponed?* Belfast Policy Research Unit QUB and UU.

Davies, B M. 1991 *Community Health and Social Services* London: Edward Arnold

Department of Health, 1994 *A National Breast feeding Policy for Ireland* Dublin: Government Stationery Office.

Department of Health, 1993 *Health Statistics 1993*, Dublin: Government Stationery Office.

Edgerton, L. 1986 'Public Protest, Domestic Acquiescence: Women in Northern Ireland' in Ridd, R and Calloway, H (eds.) *Caught up in Conflict: Women's Responses to Political Strife* Basingstoke: Macmillan in association with the Oxford University Women's Studies Centre.

Eisenstein, Z. (ed.) 1979 *Capitalist Patriarchy and the Case for Socialist Feminism* New York: Monthly Review Press.

Eisenstein, Z. 1983 'The State, the Patriarchal Family and Working Mothers' in Diamond, I. (ed.) *Families, Politics and Public Policy* New York and London: Longman.

Evason, E. 1991 *Against the Grain, The Contemporary Women's Movement in Northern Ireland* Dublin: Attic Press.

Glazener, C M A et al. 1995 'Postnatal Maternal Morbidity: Extent, Causes, Prevention and Treatment' in *British Journal of Obstetrics and Gynaecology* April, Vol.102, pp.282-287.

Graham, H. 1983 'Caring, A Labour of Love' in Finch, J and Groves, D. (eds.) *A Labour of Love*, London: Routledge and Kegan Paul.

Hartmann, H. 1981 'The Unhappy Marriage of Marxism and Feminism, Towards a More Progressive Union' in Sargent, L. (ed.) *Women and Revolution* Boston: South End Press.

Hinds, B. 1991 'Child care Provision and Policy' in Davies, C and Mc Laughlin, E *Women, Employment and Social Policy in Northern Ireland: Problem Postponed?* Policy Research Institute, Q U B and U U.

Johnson, N. 1987 *The Welfare State in Transition* UK: Harvester Wheatsheaf.

Leira, A. 1992 *Welfare States and Working Mothers* Cambridge: Cambridge University Press.

Lewis, J. 1992 'Gender and the Development of Welfare Regimes' in *Journal of European Social Policy*, 2(3) pp.159-173.

Mason, M. 1995 *Towards Woman Centered Childbirth Through Childbirth Education* Unpublished M A (Womens Studies) Thesis Dublin: University College Dublin.

Mayo, M and Weir, A. 1993 'The Future for feminist Social Policy' in *Social Policy Review* 5.

McLaughlin, E. 1991 'Introduction: A Problem Postponed' in Davies, C and McLaughlin, E. *Women, Employment and Social Policy in Northern Ireland a Problem Postponed?* Belfast Policy Research Unit QUB and UU Belfast.

O'Brien, M. 1981 *The Politics of Reproduction* London, Boston: RKP.

O'Connor, J. Gender, 'Class and Citizenship in the Comparative Analysis of Welfare State Regimes: Theoretical and Methodological Issues' in *British Journal of Sociology* Vol. 44, Issue 3 Sept 1993 pp.501-518

O'Connor, M. 1992 *Women and Birth a National Study of intentional home births in Ireland* Study conducted under the aegis of the Coombe Lying in Hospital and the Dept of Health, Dublin.

O'Connor, M. 1995 *Birth Tides* London: Pandora.

Oakley, A. 1974 *The Sociology of Housework* London: Martin Robertson.

Oakley, A. 1979 *Becoming a Mother* London: Martin Robertson.

Oakley, A. 1980 *Women Confined* London: Martin Robertson.

Oakley, A. 1992 *Social Support and Motherhood* Oxford: Blackwell.

Orlaff, A. 'Gender and the Social Rights of Citizenship: the Comparative Analysis of Gender Relations and Welfare States' in *American Sociological Review* 1993, Vol 58 June pp.303-328.

Parsons, T. 1955 'The American Family, its Relations to Personality and to the Social Structure' in Parsons, T and Bales, R *Family, Socialisation and Interaction Process* Glencoe, Illinois: The Free Press.

Parsons, T. 1960 'The Stability of the American Family System' in Bell N W and Vogel E F. (eds.) *A Modern Introduction to the Family* Glencoe, Illinois: The Free Press.

Pascall, G. 1986 *Social Policy A Feminist Analysis* London: Tavistock.

Pinker, R. 1979 *The Idea of Welfare* London: Heinemann.

Registrar General *71 Annual Report* Belfast, HMSO, 1992.

Registrar General *72 Annual Report* Belfast, HMSO, 1994.

Rich, A. 1977 *Of Women Born, Motherhood as Experience and Institution* London: Virago.

Rutter, M. 1972 *Maternal Deprivation Reassessed* London: Penguin.

Smyth, A. (ed.) 1992 *The Abortion Papers* Dublin: Attic Press.

Tew, M. 1995 *Safer Childbirth, a Critical History of Maternity Care* London: Chapman and Hall.

Titmuss ,R. 1963 *Essays on the Welfare State* London: Allen and Unwin.

Ungerson, C. (ed.) 1985. *Women and Social Policy, A Reader* London: MacMillan.

Williams, F. 1989 *Social Policy a critical Introduction, Issues of Race, Gender and Class* Cambridge: Polity.

Wilson, E. 1977 *Women and The Welfare State* London: Tavistock.

Section 6:
Women and Violence

V iolence against women can take many forms. It encompasses more than actual physical assault and includes all behaviour designed to control and intimidate women. The two chapters in this section concentrate on one form of violence - domestic violence. The term itself is a contentious one. Some feminists argue that by emphasising the word domestic, violence in the family is seen as a private affair, something to be sorted out between husband and wife rather than needing intervention by the police and other welfare agencies. Smith (1989) suggests that this attitude leads to a lack of help received by battered women from doctors, social workers and the police. The two chapters in this section are a sobering reminder of the extent to which intimate relationships between men and women can be conditioned by patriarchy and violence.

The main focus of the two chapters in this section is on responses to violence against women. Joan McKiernan and Monica McWilliams concentrate mainly on the responses of clergy to victims of domestic violence while the chapter by Rosie Meade outlines the work of community activists in responding to assaults on women. The chapter by McKiernan and McWilliams is based on in-depth interviews with thirty-one Catholic, twenty-two Protestant and three Traveller women's experience of domestic violence. McKiernan and McWilliams explore the influence of church representatives on women's decisions to remain with or leave abusive partners. Forty-four per cent of the Catholic women and thirty-six per cent of Protestant women had approached their clergy for help during their abusive relationships with their partners. However, in many instances, clergy were far from supportive. McKiernan and McWilliams state that clergy responses fell into four main categories: supportive; negative; blaming women and rationalising or minimising the violence. By failing to support women in abusive relationships, McKiernan and McWilliams suggest that the clergy uphold a religious ideology based on rationalising and legitimating women's subordinate position in society. One third of the sample stated that the responses of the clergy had affected their own responses to domestic violence. This figure was higher for Catholics, particularly over the age of thirty-five.

In contrast to the largely unsupportive role of the clergy in responding to domestic violence, Meade's chapter outlines the importance of community groups in supporting and helping the victims of domestic violence. Her chapter is based on the work of Cork Women's Support Group (CWSG) set up in 1994 to create a greater awareness of women's experiences of separation and domestic violence. The research is based on a focused interview with nine members of the CWSG aimed at identifying what group members felt were the most important issues in relation to domestic violence and effective responses to it. While several clergy in McKiernan and McWilliams' study were keen to pass judgement on incidents of domestic violence, the community activists in Meade's study were wary of giving advice preferring to support rather than influence victims' decisions.

Meade suggests that victims of domestic violence have not been well served by professionals and this is borne out by McKiernan and McWilliams' research. Often professionals are motivated by a desire to 'restore the equilibrium of family life' and in the process, the powerlessness of women in violent relationships is upheld and legitimated. This is why self-help groups are so important. They can provide help in those areas where state agencies have been particularly inadequate. Although frequently underfunded, feminist orientated community groups constitute an important intervention in dealing with violence against women. Feminist groups emphasise the notion of 'survivor' rather than 'victim' and highlight the strategies women adopt to enable them to cope with their ordeals and emphasise how women are able to develop tactics of resistance. By advocating women-centred responses to domestic violence, Meade suggests that feminist orientated community activists can empower women to reach their own decisions about whether to remain in or terminate violent relationships.

References and Further Reading

Smith, L. 1989 *Domestic Violence: An Overview of the Literature* London: HMSO.

20.

Women, Religion and Violence in the Family
Joan McKiernan and Monica McWilliams

Introduction

Domestic violence is not something new. On the contrary, there is a long history of the church's acquaintance with this subject. As far back as the fourteenth century, reference was made to a woman who presented herself at an ecclesiastical court, seeking refuge from her abusive husband (Freeman, 1979). She did not find that refuge. Domestic violence was left untouched and protected by church and state as part of the private sphere of family life. Despite attempts in the late 19th century to have domestic violence recognised as a crime, victims had relatively few rights until the mid 1970s. In the past twenty years there has been an explosion of legal reform and social service intervention, the development of refuges and helplines and extensive coverage of trials and front page headlines in media reports. All of this has led to a recognition of domestic violence as a 'public harm'.

The first refuge for abused women in Ireland opened over twenty years ago. Since that time there has been a growth in refuge provision, particularly in the North. Alongside this, there has been an increase in public education campaigns and considerable research pointing to the seriousness of domestic violence in contemporary Irish society (Evason, 1982, Montgomery and Bell, 1986, Casey, 1989, Ruddle and O'Connor, 1992, McWilliams and McKiernan, 1993, Kelleher, Kelleher and O'Connor, 1995 and McWilliams and Spence, 1996).

There has, however, been much resistance to change. Although domestic violence has evolved from a 'private' to a more 'public' issue, it has remained a divisive issue. Abuse which occurs in the context of people's own homes is deeply threatening. It challenges our most fundamental assumptions about the nature of intimate relations and the safety of family life. By seeing such abuse as 'private' we affirm it as a problem that is individual, that only involves a particular male-female relationship, and for which there is no social responsibility to remedy.

This recognition of the need to change and, at the same time, a resistance to change was one of the issues addressed in a research study carried out with Protestant and Catholic women in Northern Ireland. The influence of religious and societal values on victims of domestic violence, on members of their families and on church representatives is an important factor in facilitating or obstructing such change. Through the examination of responses to the issue of domestic violence, it is possible to show how religion can act to contain or confront domestic violence on the one hand and reinforce or liberate women from their position as victims on the other.

Religion, Domestic Violence and Control of Women

Feminist literature on domestic violence provides a well-developed analysis illustrating how throughout the centuries men's use of violence as a form of control over women has been maintained and endorsed by legal, political and economic institutions. Historically, women have been confined to the home and excluded from positions of power and status outside the family. While structural constraints have limited women's ability to change or influence the social order, religious ideology has rationalised and legitimised the subordinate position of women, ensuring the acceptance of that order by both men and women (Fiorenza, 1985).

Feminist scholarship in religion has uncovered the role of Christianity in encouraging and legitimatising violence against women (Brown and Bohn, 1989). Researchers have also commented on the pervasiveness of domestic violence in other cultures (Levinson, 1989) and in other religions (Hoffman et al., 1994). However, given the focus on domestic violence in Irish society, we concentrate here on the Christian churches.

Dobash and Dobash (1979) comment on how Christian ideology, through the ages, has been used to condone the use of violence by men to maintain the subordinate position of women in the family. For example, in the 1500s John Calvin's advice for an abused woman was to 'bear with patience the cross which God has seen fit to place upon her.' He further instructed that she should not deviate from her duty which was 'to please her husband, but to be faithful whatever happens' (McClure, 1994).

Feminist literature has shown that Christianity is replete with characterisations of women as the inferior, weaker sex responsible for male wrongs (Rossi, 1991). Christian women have been inundated with models which encourage submissiveness, modesty and suffering as Christian virtues (Young, 1993). The early Christian model is the abused wife St. Monica who advised other abused women to endure in silence. Maria Goretti is the twentieth century example. She was canonised because she forgave her rapist murderer. Traditional theology of Jesus as the Suffering Servant has also been used to encourage abused women to stay within violent marriages (Daggers, 1995). Feminists have argued that even if Christians have not directly advocated wife beating, support for the subordination of women can contribute to blaming abused women while condoning male violence as an appropriate response to women's insubordination (Daggers, 1995).

Although the Bible has often been used to support the patriarchal subordination of women (for example, Eph. 5:2; Col. 3:18), some have argued for new readings or alternative theological scripts, reflecting the desire for change from within the church (Fiorenza, 1985, Witherington, 1992). O'Dowd (1987) and Inglis (1987) show how the churches in Ireland have resisted such change, retaining traditional views about family life. In their opposition to married women working outside the home and in their obsession with issues of morality, the churches have made a common stand in restricting women's role outside the home. For example, the 1945 Catholic Bishops' Lenten Pastoral was supported by Unionist MPs at Stormont in arguing that nursery provision for children destroyed 'the natural and divinely ordained traditional family' (cited in McShane, 1987). In spite of the increase in marital breakdown, lone parenthood and the participation of married women in the labour market, the influence of the churches in matters relating to the family continues. Challenges to the male right to dominate and to abuse women have come only in very recent history.

The Troubles

Religious domination and its impact on women must also be set in the context of Northern Ireland's political conflict, more popularly known as the 'Troubles'. The ability of women to challenge traditional attitudes, the view of 'acceptable' violence, and the definition of social problems for policy makers all impinge on the recognition of domestic violence as a problem. There are differing views on the impact of the Troubles on women's ability to challenge male domination. Some, such as Fairweather et al. (1984), argued that the political conflict made women stronger and that women questioned institutions which had been taken for granted.

Others, though, have suggested that the Troubles reinforced the religious hold on society by the development of a communal identity based on religion. Ridd and Calloway (1986) suggested that conflict in societies such as Northern Ireland, while aimed at social change, may also be an inherently conservative agent. The sense of insecurity that accompanied disturbances reflected strongly upon women, particularly where they were represented as the custodians of society's cultural values.

The popular views of Mother Ireland and the religious/political images on Belfast's walls symbolising women as the suffering mothers of 'martyred' sons may have presented a challenge for women who wished to contest such victimised positions or to confront the imagery of themselves as self-sacrificing individuals.

Edgerton (1986) argued that women were worried in case they would be perceived as betraying their religion by bringing issues such as domestic violence out into the open. For these women raising questions about the Catholic church's control of family morals may be interpreted as letting their side down. According to Edgerton it was easier for women in nationalist areas to confront the harassment of the British army than to disclose their personal struggle with domestic violence.

In recent years there has been much community activism amongst women in Northern Ireland which has created space for a more radical agenda. Women activists working within the framework of feminist politics have argued that women should no longer be subjected to the unending control of abusive partners or to the control of those to whom they turn for help. Women have been challenging the more laissez-faire responses to domestic violence by police officers. They are also seeking ways to hold accountable those who are resisting any change in the gender specific cultural beliefs and practices which permit men's use of violence to dominate and control women in intimate relationships. Those in the positions of providing help have also been encouraged to move away from their advocacy of simple explanations for domestic violence and to locate the causes of the violence within a wider cultural framework. The importance of religious attitudes within this cultural framework was a central focus of the research and it is to this that we now turn.

The Research

The research involved in-depth interviews with fifty-six women who had experienced domestic violence in Northern Ireland. The research design included two sample areas, one rural and one urban. The women were contacted through refuge workers, community activists, social workers and solicitors. At the time of the interviews twenty-two of the women were living in refuges.

Twenty-eight women had already ended their relationships and were resettled in the community while six of the women were still living with their partners. Almost half of the women had lived in violent relationships for over five years.

The sample included women from the two largest communities in Northern Ireland, Protestant (twenty-two) and Catholic (thirty-one), and a smaller group from the Traveller community (three). The women, whose ages ranged from eighteen to fifty-two years, were predominantly working class but women from middle class or professional households and farming families were also represented in the sample. Most of the women came from large towns, but a small number of women living in rural areas were also interviewed.

The Violence

During the interviews women told of horrific injuries which they sustained at the hands of their partners. They described violent acts which would not be tolerated in any context other than the home. Over half said they needed medical treatment for their injuries, while almost a quarter of the women required hospital treatment at least once. Over a third were hit while they were pregnant and two women suffered miscarriages. One woman recalled how she had 'buried a baby because of him'. A number of women spoke of marital rape.

Several women reported that they had sex when they did not want to and others had given in just to please their partner. Marital rape was one of the problems that women were most reluctant to disclose and they included this point almost as an afterthought in the interviews. Often women saw no escape from the brutality except by inflicting harm on themselves or by attempting to end their own lives.

Violence as Control

The research findings from this study support the theories developed in feminist literature which show that domestic violence is best understood as a reflection of the wider unequal power relationship of men and women in society. This has provided the most expansive area of the literature and is an approach adopted by sociologists (Pagelow, 1981, Pahl, 1985, Dobash and Dobash, 1979, 1992, Hanmer and Maynard, 1987, Yllo and Bograd, 1988, Kelly, 1988, Edwards, 1989), criminologists (Stanko, 1985) and medical practitioners (Stark, Flitcraft and Frazier, 1979).

The inequality between men and women is enshrined in the image and support for the male dominated nuclear family. Rather than viewing violence as sporadic, the result of family rows, alcoholism or individual personality traits, it is argued that violence is used by men to assert their authority in the family and maintain women's subordination. The theory of violence as control is used to explain both the personal violence of men towards women and children as well as the process by which women become victimised when attempting to seek help.

The women's stories supported this view that men use violence to maintain their power in the family and to control their partners' behaviour. In their descriptions of physical and emotional abuse, the women told of many ways in which their partners had controlled their lives (see list).

Women's Descriptions of Gendered Power and Control

he put me down	I was brainwashed
I felt good for nothing	he was jealous
he always had to have the upper hand	he was possessive
he disagreed with anything I said	he was domineering
he alienated friends and family	he was powerful
I was not allowed to work	he was terrifying
he controlled my movements	I had to obey
he treated house and me as his possessions	he picked my clothes
he followed me everywhere	I was kept a prisoner

The descriptions illustrate a number of aspects of emotional abuse which men used, such as restriction of women's movements and the severance of social networks. The women also experienced a process of confidence reduction and a withering away of their self esteem, what many called brainwashing or thought control. One said, 'It was as if I didn't have a personality. He had sort of brainwashed me as if I was hopeless and nobody else would want me.'

Traditional attitudes towards women's role in the home prompted much violence. One woman said that early in the marriage she realised that 'if I stepped over a certain line outside these parameters of behaviour, he could be violent.' The attempt to assert control over every aspect of women's lives, even the reproductive process, was illustrated by the man who instructed his wife to 'have a son or else' as she went off to hospital to have their second child.

Women who challenged the traditional male attitudes by going to work or gaining education met with abuse. One woman said that the violence began when she started work as a secretary. 'He didn't want me to work. I should be at home looking after the children — that's what his mummy had always done.' Another found things got worse when she went back to university. 'That was stepping outside the bounds.' She felt her husband, a teacher, thought he was the only one that was allowed to be educated.

Though only a minority of the women in our sample were in regular employment, it was an ordeal for them to keep their jobs because of the attitudes and violence of their partners. One woman's business was destroyed and other women told of being followed to work regularly. Deprived of access to social networks for support and an independent means of gaining their own income, it was more difficult for these women to leave the relationship and live on their own.

Clergy in the Decision Making Process

The interviews included questions about contacts with clergy in order to examine the extent to which religious attitudes in Northern Ireland impinged on women's decision-making process. Forty-one per cent (23) of the women said they had approached clergy at some time for support. The response rate was affected by the number of women who felt they were able to predict the response of the churches.

> The Catholic church are very pro-marriage... I know my priest would probably try to talk you round... you have to stay in there no matter what. I don't want them to tell me that because I've done that for too long.

There were differences in the level of response. Catholic women had a higher level of contact with forty-four per cent (fifteen) responding to this question compared with thirty-six per cent (eight) of Protestant women. There were twenty-five different contacts with clergy, but only seven were seen as helpful. Women went to their clergy at different stages of the relationship. Those who went during their relationship wanted the clergy to 'do something about their husbands' or to give them some advice or information on what they could do themselves. Others wanted support when they were trying to leave their partners. One woman went to her priest because she had no family to turn to and preferred not to involve the neighbours.

> I thought maybe the priest could give me some guidance, not spiritual guidance, but put me in the right lines to talk to somebody or give me some sort of moral support, or make me realise that I was doing the right thing ... I wanted just somebody to say 'you are doing the right thing', but he didn't.

Clerical Responses

Supportive

Some clergy were helpful by accompanying a woman to a refuge or maintaining contact with the woman afterwards. 'He phones me up to check if I'm all right. He told my sister to always believe me ... So when the crisis came my sister knew that I was telling the truth although everyone else thought my husband was a gentleman.'

One woman commented on a particularly supportive priest who, after years of intervening and talking to her violent husband, suggested she should leave. In this case, however, the woman had endured years of abuse and it was only after she had tried everything, including numerous consultations with the priest, that she was given this advice. She felt she had proved herself honourable and worthy as a good mother and, having done so, was eventually advised to leave. Another priest privately recommended that the woman get a better solicitor, but then said, 'As a priest, I'll pray for you.' His actions appeared to be governed by a professional orientation as he made a distinction between his role as a priest which was strictly religious and his role as a help-provider. He accepted limitations on his power to support and advise in this serious, but private, matter.

Negative/'Maintain the Family' Responses

While officially the churches have been reluctant to intervene in the private sphere of the family in any way that could be perceived as undermining the institution of marriage, clergy are quite ready to intrude when that institution is threatened. Most of the Catholic women had particular difficulty because of the Catholic church's support for the nuclear family and opposition to divorce and remarriage.

Several women were told to stay with their husband — no matter what. Some priests tried to convince women who had left their husbands to go back to them. Several of the priests supported women in leaving their partners, but maintained that 'you'll still be married'. One woman was told, 'If you want to leave him, then leave him, but you'll still be married, and he has these rights.' The priest emphasised that the man had his marital rights — that he was still married to the woman in the eyes of God. This exemplifies the confrontation between the sacred and the secular in that despite the availability of judicial separation and divorce, the emphasis was on the permanency of the marital vows.

Catholic women who considered getting annulments found the process a difficult one. A woman who had stayed in a violent marriage for over twenty years was still told by her priest, 'marriage is for life until death do you part. And no matter what happens in that marriage, you're married for the rest of your life.' When she finally left and wanted to start a new relationship she wanted to do things 'properly by the church,' but she found the priests unresponsive. She was told that she would have to write down every event in her long marriage and then wait three or four years for an annulment. 'The marriage by all circumstances has to continue,' she reports she was told. These responses, which include the denial of sacraments to women who have entered new relationships, caused enormous pain to religious women and made it much more difficult for them to make a fresh start after years of violence.

Blaming Women/Supporting Husbands

Men also went to the churches. However, rather than seeking help to change their violent behaviour, they looked to the church to maintain their dominant position in the family. In her study of women and the family, McLaughlin (1989) argues that the church acts as one of the sources of support for the moral authority of the husband/father role in the family. Most of the time this moral authority is taken for granted, but the church is called upon when a wife's behaviour 'appears unreasonable in the context of male authority'. In her Derry based study McLaughlin found many women were familiar with the 'I'll get the priest to you' threat from their husbands. In our research we found this was not an idle threat. When a priest came out at the behest of one husband, the priest only spoke to the woman's father who then convinced her to take the husband back. Although the priest and the father knew about the violence, the priest did not talk directly to the woman. In this instance, three men made decisions about how to control a dreadfully abused woman. In the several cases of mixed marriage in the sample, husbands would not go to the cleric of their own religion but to their wife's priest or minister in order to put pressure on her. One Catholic man sent a minister to visit his partner in a refuge. The minister, she reported, had said that 'God is making all these things happen to me, to stop living in sin. God is punishing me.' She felt the minister particularly disapproved of her cohabiting relationship because she was involved with a Catholic.

Rationalising/Minimising the Violence

Alongside the defence of men, the refusal to believe women was another common response. Sometimes other transgressions committed by the husband made more of an impression. For example, in one case a woman noted that it was only when her partner became publicly involved in an adulterous relationship that the priest changed his opinion of her husband who had been until then a 'fine, upstanding member of the parish.'

Other ministers and priests tried to rationalise the husband's behaviour explaining 'he's insecure', 'he has a drink problem'. However some made promises on behalf of the man, 'he won't do it again' despite his history of violent behaviour. The Traveller women found a regular response involved the priest getting husbands to take the pledge. However, this was a temporary solution for as soon as the time limit for the pledge was up, the husbands would go on a binge and the beatings would start again.

These examples point to the need for training in the various churches as such promises can lure women back into abusive relationships. This is a particularly inappropriate response at a time when women have taken the difficult step to seek help. Such promises may be dangerous and constitute a potential threat to a woman's life since research has indicated that violence escalates at the point when men realise that their partners are preparing to leave (Marzuk et al., 1992).

Attitudes

Direct involvement of the clergy was only one aspect of the barriers imposed by religion. Women's decision making processes illustrated the barriers imposed by social and religious attitudes in Northern Ireland. Women were asked if there were any religious beliefs or social attitudes which had affected their decisions in responding to the violence. Only a third of the women said religious beliefs had made a difference. But forty-five per cent of Catholic women said that religion had affected their decisions. There were also differences based on age. Forty-four per cent of women over thirty-five years compared with thirty-one per cent of women under twenty-five years of age said religious beliefs made a difference.

There was a much higher response when women were asked if other people's attitudes made them reluctant to take action about the violence. Half of the women said attitudes did make a difference. Again this was more important to Catholic women, sixty-one per cent of whom pointed to societal attitudes. Attitudinal influence declined by age, but a significant number of young women, thirty-nine per cent of women under twenty-five years, still felt the impact.

Religious Beliefs

The most common religious belief that affected women's decisions was the idea that marriage is forever. 'You make your bed, you lie in it,' was a view repeated over and over again. Specific objections to divorce were mentioned by several women, 'I suppose being brought up a Catholic, I felt when I got married, that was it. You know, it was an awful thing to break up your marriage, and maybe subconsciously, that was probably maybe why I did hang in for so long.'

Others separated and went back because of their opposition to divorce.

> This is going to lead to divorce, I can't do this. So I went back and took more abuse, just because I didn't want a divorce. I'm still pretty anti-divorce, but I can't see any other way out any more.

Attitudes of women's families to divorce also placed limits on the decisions they could make. One mother encouraged her daughter to leave her alcoholic husband, saying 'God wouldn't want you to live like that.' When the woman expressed her fears that she would never get another 'fella', her mother objected, saying she couldn't live with someone else because she was married: 'you're not allowed to do that.' Both Catholic and Protestant women had problems because of the religious beliefs of their families. Their stories illustrated the role of families, particularly fathers, in policing the women in the family. Although Protestant clergy are not expected to be as interventionist as Catholic clergy in matters of individual morality, Protestant fathers and husbands are expected to take on the role of moral guide for the family. One woman still suffers from her Protestant father's condemnation of her because he is opposed to divorce. Four years after her marriage ended he still believed that she should return to the marital home in spite of the violence.

Catholic fathers intervened as well. One Catholic man was more upset when his abusive son-in-law told him that his wife, the man's daughter, was using birth control than he was about the husband's abusive behaviour. The daughter had just had her first child, was being abused by her husband, and only used contraception so that she could concentrate on caring for her dying mother. None of these explanations could convince her father to support her. The reactions of these fathers were painfully disappointing because they were coming from a parent from whom the daughters had expected protection and support.

Marriage is for Life

Religion was not always the basis of the objection to divorce. As one woman explained, 'Well I believe that marriage is for life and you worked at it. Religion wasn't a lot to do with it. I never believed in divorce. I thought it was an easy option. I thought it was just other people's way of moving from one relationship to another. I never seen myself getting a divorce. Maybe being widowed...'

For many women then, religious or not, marriage was serious and you had to work at it.

During the interviews, the very high value that women placed on their marriages and their expectations for a happy future through marriage was evident. Because they wanted to make their marriages work, the women would try again and again and hope for change. One woman thought it was the way women were brought up.

> I wouldn't call it religious beliefs. You're grown up adults, and you make your wee houses and you believe in rose coloured houses. A lot of that. It's the way we're brought up. You play with the dolls.

When all of this was shattered, women felt they were exposed to public view.

> I felt as if I was standing naked in the middle of Belfast. That I was completely stripped to the bone, after having a happy family, sort of people thinking that, I was completely naked, and everybody could see into my very soul, because it had all fallen down around me.

The attachment to marriage and the family was also strongly emphasised by Traveller women. They said a woman's life centred around her children, 'All we believe in is our home and children.' One woman explained, 'Travelling women have a very strict life with the one husband. When we get married, that's for life. It's not easy to separate. It's not because it's Catholic, it's the Travellers way. A very strict way'.

The concept of nakedness epitomises for these women, both Traveller and settled, the extent to which they have internalised the religious and social attitudes which stress the central importance of the family for women's lives. These attitudes play a crucial role in curtailing women's opportunities to change their situation. It is not surprising that those working with survivors of domestic violence have highlighted the difficult task facing women who struggle to challenge the abuse within the restrictive confines of religious and societal attitudes.

Conclusion

The issue of domestic violence has slowly moved from the private world of the family to the arena of public policy. There is evidence that a substantial number of women are taking steps to reject the abuse that has been inflicted upon them. Increasing numbers of women come to Women's Aid for support, obtain legal exclusion and protection orders against abusers, and initiate separation and divorce proceedings. However, there is much individual and societal resistance to this process of rejection. Women's central identities as wives and mothers, their lives in privatised families which brook no interference from the outside world and the shame and stigmas women face provoke much resistance to change.

This resistance is linked to societal attitudes which sustain the subordinate position of women within the family. Religious attitudes and clerical responses can also support the power differences within marriage. Given that many women are faced with choices which they view as determined by their religion, abusive partners may be in a more powerful position because they know that women may not pursue help from outside the family. It is clear that some abused women have endured a process of triple victimisation. This process involves not only the perpetrator of the assaults but also those from within the religious community as well as the institutions of church and state. The responses and attitudes of these groups often minimise or rationalise the abuse. Such collusion with the abuse sends gendered stereotyped messages with the result that the abuse itself is maintained for longer by the perpetrators and endured for longer by the victims.

Churches and other institutions could respond differently. An example of good practice that could be used by churches in Ireland is the special kit produced by the Canadian Church Council on Justice and Corrections. This kit, 'Family Violence in a Patriarchal Culture: a challenge to our way of living,' has been developed to help church officials and churchgoers better understand how abuse flourishes within a pattern of values and beliefs. Public awareness on this issue, such as Women's Aid Zero Tolerance and No Fear Campaigns in Ireland should contribute to informing church policy. There is some indication that churches are beginning to respond to the message of these campaigns. An invitation to Women's Aid to speak at Masses in Dublin is one example. Women's Aid posters and help-line cards have been distributed in some church centres and discussion has been initiated on a more caring pastoral response to domestic violence. A Catholic Bishops' meeting in Maynooth in March 1995 approved the following recommendation from the Women in the Church Working Group of the Irish Commission for Justice and Peace:

> That the Episcopal Conference would request priests throughout the country to call attention in the course of the Sunday homily to the problem of violence against women in society.

In any such homilies women's coping and resistance strategies also need to be acknowledged. Many women have shown their strength by the various strategies they had used to maintain their marriages and care for their children in spite of the violence. The juxtaposition of women as totally active agents capable of leaving violent relationships or as totally passive victims who stay with abusive partners needs to be unpicked by those working from inside the church. It may take time for women to find ways to overcome the physical and psychological damage and to become empowered to re-take control over their lives. As a result of the dominant ideology which governs the responses to the violence both women's ability to resist and the process of building a new life can be made more difficult.

Some church representatives and activists are beginning to recognise that in order to make domestic violence unacceptable, the conditions and the attitudes in which it thrives first need to be changed. Support networks which enable women to make decisions within a framework of choice are essential. Such networks could provide a forum for the community to become involved in discussions around gendered power and masculinity. Young people's projects which challenge the gender inequities within relationships should be expanded. These also need to socialise young men into ways of resolving conflict without resorting to violence and abuse.

In their imaginative ways women activists in Northern Ireland are beginning to create an alternative cultural environment within their local communities — one that will put in place a more democratic set of structures to ensure that women are written into, and not out of, the multiplicity of national narratives that take place after periods of conflict. They are as insistent, in the same way as Eleanor Roosevelt once was when she helped to draft the United Nations Declaration, that a family life free from violence is a fundamental human right. In recognising that domestic violence infringes on the human rights of women and children, the clergy in Ireland need to be part of this new cultural environment and to move from a position of disbelief, indifference and exclusion to one of empathy, support and advocacy. Churches in Ireland still remain a focal point for much community activity and, as we have seen, they can help or hinder challenges to combat domestic violence.

Discussion Topics

1. In the context of domestic violence, what do you understand by the term 'gender-specific cultural beliefs'? To what extent does religion have a role to play in maintaining or changing these beliefs?

2. Discuss the elements of a 'gendered power and control' model in the context of domestic violence. How might an understanding of this model enable church leaders and other help-providers to respond more appropriately to abused women?

3. Although domestic violence has evolved from a private to a more public harm, there has been much resistance to this. Discuss, using examples to highlight your answer.

4. To what extent have community and church activists been successful in challenging attitudes which lend support to the subordination of women within the family?

References and Further Reading

Brown, J and Bohn, C. 1989 *Christianity, Patriarchy and Abuse: A Feminist Critique* New York: Pilgrim Press.

Casey, M. 1989 *Domestic Violence Against Women: The Women's Perspective* Dublin: Social Psychology Research Unit, UCD.

Daggers, J. 1995 'Domestic Violence Against Women in Theological Perspective: Implications for Pastoral Care' *Contact* 116.

Dobash, R E and Dobash, R. 1979 *Violence Against Wives* New York: The Free Press.

Dobash, R E and Dobash, R. 1992 *Women, Violence and Social Change* London: Routledge.

Edgerton, L. 1986 'Public Protest, Domestic Acquiescence' in Ridd, R and Callaway, H. (eds.) *Caught up in Conflict* London: Macmillan.

Edwards, S. 1989 *Policing Domestic Violence* London: Sage.

Evason, E. 1982 *Hidden Violence, A Study of Battered Women in Northern Ireland* Belfast: Farset Press.

Fairweather, E, McDonagh, R, and MacFadyean, M. 1984 *Only the Rivers Run Free* London: Pluto Press.

Fiorenza, E S. 1985 *Bread Not Stone: The Challenge of Feminist Biblical Interpretation* Boston: Beacon Press.

Freeman, M D A. 1979 *Violence in the Home* Farnborough: Saxon House.

Hanmer, J and Maynard, M. (eds.) 1987 *Women, Violence and Social Control* London: Macmillan.

Hoffman, K, Demo, D, and Edwards, H. 1994 'Physical Wife Abuse in a Non-Western Society' *Journal of Marriage and the Family* No. 56, pp.113-146.

Inglis, T. 1987 *Moral Monopoly: The Catholic Church in Modern Irish Society* Dublin: Gill and Macmillan.

Kelleher, P, Kelleher, C, and O'Connor, M. 1995 *Making the Links: Towards an Integrated Strategy for the Elimination of Violence Against Women in Intimate Relationships with Men* Dublin: Women's Aid.

Kelly, L. 1988 *Surviving Sexual Violence* Cambridge: Polity Press.

Levinson, D. 1989 *Violence in Cross-Cultural Perspective* Newbury Park: Sage.

McClure, M. 1994 'God's Providence for Battered' Women *Horizons*, September/October.

McLaughlin, E. 1989 'In Search of the Female Breadwinner: Gender and Unemployment in Derry City' in Donnan, H and McFarlane, G. (eds.) *Social Anthropology and Public Policy in Northern Ireland* Aldershot: Avebury.

McLaughlin, E. 1991 'Introduction: A Problem Postponed' in Davies, C and McLaughlin, E. (eds.) *Women, Employment and Social Policy in Northern Ireland: A Problem Postponed* Belfast: Policy Research Institute.

McShane, L. 1987 'Day Nurseries in Northern Ireland 1945-1955' in Curtin, C, Jackson, P and O'Connor, B. (eds.) *Gender in Irish Society* Galway: Galway University Press.

McWilliams, M. 1991 'Women in Northern Ireland: an Overview' in Hughes, E. (ed.) *Culture and Politics in Northern Ireland 1960-1990* Milton Keynes: Open University Press.

McWilliams, M. 1992 'Women, the Churches, and Social Justice' in Kilroy, P. (ed.) *Women and Religion in Northern Ireland Conference Report*, Coleraine: Centre for Research on Women, University of Ulster.

McWilliams, M and McKiernan, J. 1993 *Bringing it Out in the Open, Domestic Violence in Northern Ireland* Belfast: HMSO.

McWilliams, M and Spence, L. 1996 *A Criminal Justice Response to Domestic Violence in Northern Ireland* Belfast: HMSO.

Marzuk, P, Tardiff, K and Hirsch, C S. 1992 'The Epidemiology of Murder-Suicide' *Journal of American Medical Association* 267 pp.3179-3183.

Montgomery, P and Bell, V. 1986 *Police Response to Wife Assault: A Northern Ireland Study* Belfast: Women's Aid Federation.

O'Dowd, L. 1987 'Church, State and Women' in Curtin, C, Jackson, P and O'Connor, B. *Gender in Irish Society* Galway: Galway University Press.

Pagelow, M. 1981 *Women-Battering: Victims and their Experiences* Newbury Park, CA: Sage.

Pahl, J. (ed.) 1985 *Private Violence and Public Policy* London: Routledge and Kegan.

Ridd, R and Callaway, H. (eds.) 1986 *Caught up in Conflict* London: Macmillan.

Rossi, M A. 1991 *The Legitimation of the Abuse of Women in Christianity* Madison: Women's Studies Research Center.

Ruddle, H and O'Connor, J. 1992 *Breaking the Silence — Violence in the Home: The Women's Perspective* Limerick: Mid-Western Health Board.

Stanko, E. 1985 *Intimate Intrusions. Women's Experience of Male Violence* London: Routledge and Kegan.

Stark, F, Flitcraft, A and Frazier, W. 1979 'Medicine and Patriarchal Violence: The Social Construction of a Private Event' *International Journal of Health Services* 9 pp.461-493.

Witherington, B. 1992 *Women in the Earliest Churches* Cambridge: Cambridge University Press.

Yllo, K and Bograd, M. (eds.) 1988 *Feminist Perspectives on Wife Abuse* London: Sage.

Young, K Z. 1993 'The Imperishable Virginity of Saint Maria Goretti' in Bart, P and Moran, E. (eds.) *Violence Against Women, The Bloody Footprints* Newbury Park: Sage.

21.

Domestic Violence: An Analysis and Response from Community Activists

Rosie R Meade

Introduction

In recent times Irish academic and popular discourse has been more open to debate on issues of 'Domestic Violence'. A recent discussion document on women's health referred directly to the need to 'expand the services for women who are victims of rape and domestic violence' (Dept. of Health, 1995, p.53). The statement can be interpreted as a victory for women who have struggled through the years to raise awareness amongst Irish legislators about issues of domestic violence. These efforts to highlight Irish women's experiences of domestic violence have been complemented by the work of researchers who have estimated the extent and severity of the problem in this country (Casey, 1989, Kelleher et al., 1995). The Kelleher *et al* study was commissioned by Women's Aid and

> provides the first systematic data on violence against women in the home in the Republic of Ireland, as well as an account of the response of services at area level to women who have experienced violence (Kelleher et. al., 1995).

Likewise, in 1993, McWilliams and McKiernan published a study which evaluated the effectiveness of statutory and voluntary supports for women experiencing abuse in Northern Ireland.

As a contribution to the growing body of 'domestic violence literature', this chapter discusses the principal concerns of the Cork Women's Support Group (CWSG). These issues, some of which have been identified previously by other researchers, are introduced by comments which were recorded during a focus group interview with CWSG members. The issues raised include, a de-construction of the terminology which names 'domestic' abuse, an argument for a broad inclusive definition of violence, and a brief look at research which estimates the incidence of that violence. A feminist analysis which locates male violence against women in the context of a patriarchal social order is favoured by the group. Members argue that men abuse women in order to assert power over them and that male violence reflects the unequal treatment of women and men in society. Therefore, instead of asking why women remain in abusive relationships, the social factors that make it difficult for women to leave are identified.

The second section of the chapter focuses directly on the experiences of the CWSG. It explores the origins and rationale of this group which was established in response to the problem of domestic violence. It highlights the members' expectations of community activism and argues that community activists should strive to effect social change. However, social change can prove elusive, particularly if volunteer activists cannot mobilise easily or cannot sustain their involvement. These difficulties have been faced by the CWSG and are indicative of the difficulties which limit the potential of community work in Ireland.

Methodology

This study has been written with the assistance of the CWSG of which the author is a member. The arguments presented in it draw support from two principal sources; existing research on domestic violence and information from focus group interviews. US, UK, Northern Irish and Irish studies have used a variety of research methods to examine, women's experiences of and societal responses to domestic violence (Levinson, 1989, Dobash and Dobash, 1992, McWilliams and McKiernan, 1993, Kelleher et al., 1995). The current study draws on feminist explanations (Dobash and Dobash, 1979: Stanko, 1985) of abuse and the patriarchal oppression of women.

In November 1995 the author conducted a focus group discussion with other members of CWSG. The participants discussed their perceptions of the causes and consequences of domestic violence and why they believe it is a feminist issue. They expressed concern at the limitations of state intervention and support which causes extra hardship for victims. The women explained their reasons for becoming active in the CWSG and highlighted some of the costs associated with participation.

A focus group methodology was used because it was believed that research participants would effectively use the group process to express and explain their views. The nine members of the CWSG have worked together since May 1994. Their familiarity with the author and each other enhanced their willingness to respond honestly in the discussion. As the author introduced general themes for discussion, the participants engaged with each other and used their own language to identify what they perceived as key issues. Thus, the research process was designed to be empowering and the feminist concern with democratizing research was addressed (Kelly et al., 1994). The findings of one focus group interview cannot be used to make more general claims about the experiences of all Irish victims of violence or all Irish community activists.

Focus groups are useful when it comes to investigating what participants think, but they excel at uncovering why they think as they do (Morgan, 1988). Therefore, this chapter explains the activism of CWSG by referring to the members understanding of domestic violence and locates the analysis in the context of a rich body of feminist research.

Definition of Terms

The members of the CWSG unanimously agree that language describing the violence women experience in their homes, should reflect the gravity of the offence. They favour the use of the evocative word 'abuse' because, as one woman asserted:

Abuse is always cruel, always damaging and always wrong.

Another woman doubted the usefulness of the term 'domestic violence'. She said:

Domestic Violence! It almost makes it sound cosy. Like Domestic Science or something. What we are talking about is rape, mental torture and abuse.

Feminists have long expressed concern with the limitations of language and acknowledge that terminology is always value laden (see Maynard, 1993). Prizzey (1974) notes that the term 'battered wife' had entered popular discourse by the early 1970s. However, the term equates abuse with physical assaults and the suggestion that victims must be married to their aggressors is problematic. In 1995 Women's Aid estimated that at least twenty-four per cent of their callers were cohabiting with, or were sisters, daughters, mothers of the men who abused them (Women's Aid, 1995(b), p.4).

Nevertheless, Dobash and Dobash (1979) argue that terms like 'domestic violence' and 'family violence' are inadequate also. This terminology distorts and de-politicises the debate because it fails to acknowledge that men are more likely to be the aggressors and women are more likely to be the victims of abuse. Words like 'family' and 'domesticity' have an attendant ideological significance and are an important social cement (Weeks, 1981). Therefore, use of the feel-good word 'domestic' subtly discredits any assertion that 'real' violence is possible within the home, and a distinction between domestic and 'more criminal' types of violence is made. Buzawa and Buzawa (1990, p.43) identify a 'police bias against arrest' and argue that men who are violent in their own homes are not sanctioned as severely as those who are violent in public.

The expression 'domestic violence' has been accorded statutory recognition in the Domestic Violence Act, 1996 and it is unlikely that it will be dropped from public discourse. However, it is possible that with repeated usage, the term 'domestic violence' may force society to re-examine the myth of egalitarian family life. Such a re-examination might be precipitated by campaigns such as

'Zero Tolerance' which was organised by Women's Aid during 1995. If it does encourage a more widespread questioning of social attitudes continued usage of the term may be considered worthwhile.

The Nature and Extent of the Problem

The CWSG argues that violence is not always experienced physically and favours a comprehensive definition of violence. Therefore the group has identified three particular forms that violence can take; physical, psychological and sexual (CWSG, 1994). Physical attacks include punching, kicking, mutilating, burning and even murder. Statistics from other countries show how severe these attacks can be. One Swedish woman is murdered by her husband every week and battering by male intimates is the most common cause of injury to American women (Bunch and Carillo, 1992, O'Connor, 1994). Psychological abuse includes; insults, exclusion, withholding money, erratic mood changes, silence, intimidation, isolation and threats. Group members stressed the severity of this type of abuse.

> When you are mentally or physically abused your confidence takes a nose dive.

> Insult after insult, like mud being thrown at you. Some of it is bound to stick.

Research shows that this form of abuse has long term consequences such as, depression, fear for children, low self esteem and feelings of isolation (Kelleher *et al*, 1995).

The CWSG describes 'sexual abuse' as, unwanted touching, sexual harassment, rape with objects and forced sexual practices. Evidence suggests that sexual attacks are frequently practised by abusers, often in conjunction with other forms of abuse. At least 400,000 American women a year, it is estimated, are forced to have sexual intercourse either before, during or after a beating (Kramarae and Treichler, 1992). However, it is only within the last five years that the concept of 'rape within marriage' has been given statutory recognition in Ireland. This legal 'oversight' reveals how wives were expected to submit without question to the sexual aggression of their partners.

The CWSG is busy with the task of setting up a help-line and support centre for women experiencing such violence. However, there is concern within the group that the real extent of the problem in Cork is not known and members fear that some 'victims' might be too terrified to disclose abuse or use the service. One woman explained this fear as follows,

> There is the stigma. Maybe it is breaking down, but there are many women who would be afraid to talk about it.

The group members fear that disclosure of abuse might result in 'revenge' attacks by the abusers.

> One deterrent to the women using the centre would be the fear of their husbands finding out.

> Some women are so frightened they would make up excuses to cover up for their absence from the house.

Therefore the members of the CWSG interpret the under-reporting of violence as a consequence of the power-imbalance within abusive relationships. Abusers effectively silence their 'victims' with threats and acts of violence. Women often adopt coping strategies - withhold objections, mask bruises, feign happiness - in order to 'appease' abusers or avoid detection by outsiders (Walker, 1989). Group members agreed that some women do not disclose abuse because they believe they are at fault somehow. As one woman explained,

> Women often take on the shame of being beaten and the blame. But in reality the blame is with their husbands.

As the abusers insidiously shape their consciousness, 'victims' down-play the gravity of the abuse, or accept that it is their 'badness' that precipitates it (see Stanko, 1985, McWilliams and McKiernan, 1993). These beliefs are supported by the prevalence of myths (Women's Aid, nd 1), through which society attributes blame to the victims rather than the aggressors. Women are expected to take responsibility for male violence and consequently victims who could use and benefit from support services do not disclose abuse.

Under-reporting means that the scale of the problem is underestimated and it is difficult to measure the effectiveness of responses. This limits the credibility of activists who are attempting to create awareness or establish support services. Funders usually emphasise the importance of 'measurable results' when funding community projects and groups must provide evidence to convince funders that the cause is urgent enough to merit financial assistance. Social scientists have attempted to gather this evidence by measuring the prevalence of abuse in this and other societies. However, along with the issue of under-reporting already discussed, methodological and theoretical issues mean that the accuracy of many of these studies has been questioned (McWilliams and McKiernan, 1993 for summary). However, even taking these controversies into account,

> studies suggest that from one fifth to one third of all women will be physically assaulted by a partner or ex-partner during their lifetime ... In Great Britain research suggests that violence against women in the home occurs in between one in four and one in ten relationships (McWilliams and McKiernan, 1993, p.15).

The results of a national random sample survey in Canada which involved interviews with approximately 12,300 women indicated that one quarter had experienced violence at the hands of a current or former partner (Kelleher *et* *al,*1995). In 1995 a study conducted for Women's Aid revealed that at least eighteen per cent of women had been 'subjected at some time to violence by a current or former partner' (Kelleher et al., 1995, p.14). Although, these figures may underestimate the extent of the problem (as the filtering of memories and the limitations of the self-administered questionnaire allow incidents to go unrecorded), the data clearly shows that domestic violence in Ireland is a serious problem.

Causes of Abuse

There are a variety of conflicting explanations of abuse (see Gelles, 1987, Levinson, 1989, Dobash and Dobash, 1992), some of which were discussed by members of the CWSG during the interview. All agreed that abusers must take responsibility for their actions and could not blame factors such as alcohol or stress for their actions. As one woman commented,

> If they are so out of control because of the drink, how come they don't attack the barmen or other customers?

During the 1970s, some researchers argued that psycho-pathologies such as drunkenness, poor impulse control or stress, precipitated abusive behaviour (See Fennell, 1974, Steele and Pollock, 1974). However, critics such as Dobash and Dobash (1979, 1992) argue that this literature excuses male violence and does not adequately explain it. Attention is deflected from the abuser's behaviour to his 'condition' and it is assumed that he has little or no control over his actions. CWSG members also dispute that violence is caused by poverty or is a working-class phenomenon. One woman, referring to her help-line experience, said,

> Callers come from all walks of life and all social classes.

These views are supported by other studies, which argue that experiences of violence are neither class nor place specific (Kelleher et al., 1995). Indeed, theorists argue that culture and socialisation ensure that violence is an integral feature of masculinity and is not the preserve of certain socially excluded groups (Ferguson and Synnott, 1995). Many of these standards of 'acceptable' masculine behaviour were set down during the nineteenth century. Victorian writings frequently referred to the 'emotionalism and weakness' of women and men were encouraged to develop 'physical characteristics' or demonstrate 'pure willpower' (Weeks, 1981, p.40). Members of the CWSG believe that these stereotypes still persist today and that the acceptance of unequal male-female relationships legitimates the use of force between men and women.

Therefore the CWSG recognises the links between domestic violence and all male violence. As one woman explained,

Every woman has experienced psychological abuse. The fact of being a woman means we are afraid to walk the streets at night. The threats are always there.

The consensus within the group is that violence, is caused by power inequalities and helps to reinforce those inequalities.

Abuse shows us that women are seen as not having a separate identity, to be treated as possessions.

If a woman has been beaten she will be frightened. Fear stops us talking out.

This analysis is consistent with feminist theory which acknowledges that factors within the family unit and at a societal level make violence a probability. The resilience of gender inequalities ensures that men still dominate and that domination is supported by the threat of violence. Maynard argues that domestic violence, rape, child sexual abuse, pornography and sexual harassment form part of a spectrum of male violence against women and children and facilitates the exercise and enhancement of male power (1993, p.114).

Millet describes the 'family' as the chief institution of patriarchy which 'effects control and conformity where political and other authorities are insufficient' (Millett, 1970, p.33). The family unit has rarely offered women either equality or security and historical evidence suggests, that 'wife abuse' has been tolerated and even encouraged in society. Biblical texts warn women that motherhood and domestic obligation are amends to be made for Eve's transgression; woman's participation in the family is implicitly punitive (Gelles and Cornell, 1990). The (usually) dependent status of women within the family is often exploited by abusers who wish to keep them subordinate. With only a minority officially in the paid labour market, many Irish women have reduced control over the money that enters the household. The Irish constitution supports this economic dependency of women on men. The autonomy of many women is thus curtailed and their financial security is determined by their partners. Indeed, Levinson in his cross-cultural study concluded that,

wife beating was more likely to occur and more likely to be frequent in societies in which men control the family wealth and adults often solve conflict by resorting to physical violence (Levinson, 1989, p.89)

Violence is often used to stifle women's resistance to male oppression. Giddens claims that men may turn to violence as a way of 'shoring up disintegrating systems of patriarchal power' (Giddens, 1994, p.239). In other words, because women's activism has exposed gender inequalities, abusive behaviour may be a last ditch effort by men to maintain a decaying system. Nevertheless, it would be unwise to assume that all violence can be interpreted as a reaction to the emancipation of women. As already noted, abuse was common even when women's rights were more derisory. In truth, incidents of domestic violence remind us that, despite the considerable successes of the Women's Movement, equality of power continues to be elusive.

The Social Response to Violence

Many psychologists have tried to explain why it is that women often seem to tolerate abusive relationships (Gelles, 1987). This issue also came up during the group discussion and participants identified clearly some of the factors which make it difficult for women to end violent relationships. One member explained the predicament as follows,

> Women may be trying to find a reason for staying there because the consequences of leaving are too great.

Another participant referred to emotional ties which make women 'work' at or persevere with abusive relationships.

> He tells her he loves her. Who wants to live alone in a refuge?

One woman referred to women who have few contacts and whose isolation convinces them that violence must be suffered alone. She said,

> Often they may think they are the only ones going through it.

CWSG members agree that victims' economic dependency on their partners influences their decision to stay. This dependency is felt more acutely when there are few alternative social supports for victims.

> The pressure from the man, the financial, housing, social pressure, they all work together.

Therefore members fear that for many women who leave abusive relationships, circumstances become worse, not better:

> Although you get relief from the mental or physical torture, you may be moving to more abuse; abuse from the state including poverty, neglect and isolation.

The under provision and (sometimes) poor quality of refuges is indicative of this neglect and abuse of women. Women's Aid highlights the lack of suitable services, reminding us that within the Republic of Ireland there are only seventy-nine family spaces, and only fourteen in Dublin (Women's Aid, 1995(a), p.4). Between November 1991 and 1992, of the 529 women who sought refuge in the Rathmines Refuge (Dublin), only 149 could be accommodated (Women's Aid, nd 2). Certainly, refuges differ in terms of their quality and ideologies but they can give women the type of specialist attention and support that is not available in alternative accommodation. CWSG members agree that the absence of refuge spaces means that women are more reluctant to walk away from abusive relationships and one woman asked,

> Where can she go if there are no systems to support her?

Many of the refuges that do exist are neither guaranteed long term funding nor a high priority for receipt of monies. A study of the Limerick refuge argued that,

> No organisation involved in such important work should have to be so dependent on voluntary contributions (Lyons *et al*, 1991, p.v).

Faludi reveals that, with the backlash against women's activism in the US, federal funding for refuges was withheld and one-third of the women seeking such shelter found none (Faludi, 1992). There is some evidence which suggests that women experiencing domestic violence are not well served by social work professionals. Social workers tend to, privatise or personalise problems and work 'to restore the equilibrium of family life' (Lupton, 1994, p.68). McWilliams and McKiernan (1993) found that the social workers they interviewed had little pre-vocational or in-service training on domestic violence and usually only came upon cases because children were involved.

Women who experience physical or psychological injury as a result of violence may disclose to medical personnel. However, it is evident that many women receive unsympathetic and critical responses when they do disclose. The development of 'training protocols' for medical professionals who treat women presenting with violence-related injuries has been stressed (SEHB, 1993). These protocols enhance professionals' ability to identify women and children who have been abused and may even make voluntary disclosure by the woman more likely (Cronin and O'Connor, 1993). It also encourages a more diligent collection and preservation of evidence. This evidence can then be used by women who wish to prosecute the abuser.

Ineffectual legal sanctions on male violence inhibit women's capacity to end abusive relationships. Theoretically the law makes no distinction between domestic and other instances of violence as all assaults are criminal offenses. However, it is unusual for cases of 'domestic violence' to be dealt with in the criminal courts and when they are, they are 'frequently down-crimed' (Edwards, 1989, p.473). Likewise the arrest 'option' is usually under-utilised by police. In the Women's Aid study, only twenty per cent of the women who had disclosed, did so to the police. Reasons for not reporting include, fear of revenge (eighty-two per cent), and fear that it would do no good (sixty-two per cent) (Kelleher et. al., 1995, p.23).

CWSG members agree that the law does not offer women adequate protection. Two women remarked,

> Violence in the home; it's just not treated the same. Crimes like kickings and beatings that happen on the street are given so much more attention.

> The Law gives the man a clear message - You won't be prosecuted.

Until recently, the Family Law (Protection of Spouses and Children) Act 1981, was the principal statute providing civil protection for women in abusive relationships. It permitted spouses to apply for Barring and Protection Orders if their safety within the home was under attack. Breaches of either order were punishable by arrest and imprisonment. These orders were very limited in their scope and revealed statutory unwillingness to recognise relationships not based on marriage. Orders offered no protection to cohabitees because the law explicitly stated that only spouses could apply. At best cohabitees could take out an injunction, 'a more complex and expensive legal process and...a lot less effective in its enforcement procedures' (SEHB, 1993, p.33).

Women seeking barring orders are required to provide substantial evidence, eg. medical records, to support their claims of abuse. However, barring orders are rarely made on the basis of a single incident of violence, unless the possibility of a re-occurrence is clearly established (see Duncan and Scully, 1990). Women become aware of an appalling paradox; the violence should continue for there to be a real possibility of release from it. Even when a barring order is granted, it is usually time limited. When it lapses, fresh evidence is required to secure another. One group member remarked on this anomaly,

> It's crazy! What's the woman supposed to do? Let him in for another go at her.

The Domestic Violence Act (1996) extends to cohabitees the right to apply for Safety and Barring Orders (Sections 2 and 3). Unfortunately, only those who are living as husband and wife for at least six months can apply and the status of those who are not living as 'husband and wife' is unclear. While the act does improve the quality of legal protection and is a significant victory for campaigners, the effectiveness of this legislation can only be measured in time.

In general, society's efforts to sanction abusers have been half- hearted, and there has been only a lukewarm commitment to the provision of support services for women. Many of these responsibilities are now assumed by voluntary groups - including the CWSG - which receive erratic state assistance. It is obvious that Irish social policy is limited by economic and social conservatism and this conservatism greatly impedes the work of community activists. Some of the difficulties activists encounter are discussed in the following section.

The Response of the CWSG

The CWSG, formally established in May 1994 owes its origins to a vigorous tradition of community activism in Ireland. The group is an offshoot of the Cork Women's Action Group (CWAG) which has been active in Cork for the last ten years. During this time the CWAG has created a greater awareness of women's experiences of separation and domestic violence. Activists have responded practically to community needs by establishing a help-line to support women going through the court system. Members of the CWAG also worked to set up a unique university course for existing or potential women community activists. The aim of the course is to encourage political reflection and social analysis while stimulating community activism. Some of the women who participated in this course were directly involved in the establishment of the CWSG.

While the development of a help-line provides tangible evidence of the group's success, the CWSG asserts that its achievements cannot be evaluated solely on the basis of the provision of the service.[1] The quality of that service is of greater concern. Therefore, the group stresses respect for the autonomy of callers and disapproves of influencing their behaviour by giving advice. Two group members explained this philosophy,

> We don't want to force women to leave, it's their choice. We will support them in making that choice.

> We don't want to tell people what to do, because then we are just replacing one type of force or pressure with another.

Through activism the group is collectively redefining social problems, developing imaginative responses and contributing to the 'development of a new sense of solidarity and strength among women' (Dominelli, 1990, p.36). Activism shows that women are not intrinsically passive or dependent and it may give heart to abused women who tend to under-estimate their own worth. One member of the group who had herself experienced abuse emphasised the importance of,

> letting women know that you can survive if you leave an abusive partner, thrive even.

Even within a small group such as this, it is possible to identify a variety of motivations which move women to act. This is not surprising since history of Irish activism shows no homogeneity of approach. Activists differ according to their understanding of causes of problems and their prescriptions for solutions. During the group discussion the women talked about their personal motivations for getting involved and one woman explained her participation as follows,

> I am involved to support women going through the trauma because it is so horrific.

Another woman said,

> I am here because I want to be involved in making some small but real change for women and children.

All CWSG members agree that abuse can only be explained by reference to the wider social context. Therefore, they stress the importance of campaigns for appropriate social improvements. These improvements include increased funding for support services, greater legal protection for women and improved welfare provision. In order to highlight the social causes and consequences of domestic violence, the group also hopes to run education programmes in schools, youth clubs and community centres. Through these activities, the CWSG engages with other community members to stimulate a greater understanding of women's experiences of oppression.

The development of MOVE (Men Overcoming Violence) groups, in Ireland shows that some men are concerned with reducing the incidence of domestic violence. MOVE programmes, hold men responsible for their violent behaviour, identify skills which help abusers to control violence and demand that men respect the rights of their partners (Ferguson and Synnott, 1995, MOVE, nd). While the CWSG welcomes programmes which encourage men to re-shape their roles and conduct, it asserts that women cannot rely on abusive men to change themselves on our behalf. In other words, it is not enough for the abuser to have 'a change of heart', society must cease to tolerate and encourage their abuse.

Obstacles to Progress

The CWSG has already encountered many challenges to successful community organisation and one woman referred to these when she said,

> It takes a tremendous effort to get a group working. There are so many demands on our time - child-care, work and all our family responsibilities.

The demands society makes of women accentuate our oppression and marginalisation, by making it difficult for us to collectively organise and protest. Women make many sacrifices to participate and even then are faced with a never-ending struggle for resources (See Crickley and Devlin, 1989, Daly, 1989).

> We have committed women who will staff the centre, the difficulty is getting the other basic resources needed to make it work.

> We have spent the last nineteen months trying to find suitable premises. Now that we have got the loan of a space for a couple of evenings a week, we are having difficulty finding money for insurance, postage and telephone.

These difficulties show how the indifference and lack of empathy which characterise social responses to victims of violence, also characterise state relations with community groups. Working in this 'cold climate' (Tucker, 1989) activists find that they must,

> shout and struggle to be heard and that struggle goes on and on.

Conclusion

This chapter has described and explained the rationale of the CWSG. Both in terms of the analysis of oppression and the nature of its activism the group is explicitly feminist. Group members, either through personal or work experience, have become acutely aware of the social consequences of domestic violence and insist that this type of violence is symptomatic of the oppression experienced by all women in Irish society. Irish laws, social policies and popular assumptions about male-female relationships create a social context within which violence is tolerated and even encouraged. In such a damaging and inhospitable social environment women, particularly women who experience systematic violence, become increasingly alienated and isolated from one another.

The activism of the CWSG challenges this trend because it shows that changes can be won when women express solidarity with one another. Practical benefits include services such as refuges and help-lines which alleviate the distress of women who have been abused. The CWSG may also 'inspire' other women to become active because it shows that women can and do react effectively against injustices. However group members have found it difficult to sustain their enthusiasm for the task at hand. State agencies continue to offer only piece-meal supports to community projects and the CWSG is beset by persistent worries about its future. This is especially frustrating because members believe that essential services should not be dependent on the good will of community women. Nevertheless they continue to invest their energies in a project that would not survive without their commitment.

Acknowledgement

The author would like to acknowledge the co-operation and support of the other members of the Cork Women's Support Group. She would also like to thank Dr Mary E Mulcahy and Fiona Blaney for their advice.

Discussion Topics

1. Do you agree that 'domestic violence' is a feminist issue? Why? Is the abuse of men an important issue too?

2. Identify the policies, you think, would reduce the prevalence of violence and best meet the needs of 'victims' of domestic violence?

3. What terminology should be used to name 'domestic violence'? Is it appropriate to use the term 'victim' when referring to women experiencing abuse?

4. Do you think that the development of groups which encourage men to challenge their violent behaviour is to be welcomed?

Notes

1. The Cork Women's Support Group was formally established in Cork city during May, 1994. The nine members of the group come from a variety of backgrounds and experiences, but each is committed to the principles of collective action and mutual aid. The CWSG is aware that there is a dearth of resources for women in Cork and argues that women and children who experience violence in their homes are particularly marginalised. The group hopes to establish a resource centre which will serve as a point of contact for women in need of support. Members have engaged in lobbying and fund-chasing in order to secure suitable premises, but as yet their efforts have not been successful. However the group has managed to secure use of a community centre and provides a confidential help-line service for victims of abuse. This service is an extension of an existing help-line in Churchfield, Cork. The group is very committed to education and awareness raising and is already networking with other community based women's groups.

References and Further Reading:

Bunch, C and Carillo R. 1992 *Gender Violence: A Development and Human Rights Issue* Dublin: Attic Press.

Buzawa, E and Buzawa, G. 1990 *Domestic Violence: The Criminal Justice Response*. California: Sage.

Casey, M. 1989 *Domestic Violence Against Women: The Women's Perspective* Dublin: Social and Organisational Psychology Research Unit, University College Dublin.

Cork Women's Support Group (CWSG). 1994 *Aims and Objectives* Unpublished document.

Crickley, S and Devlin, M. 1989 'Community Work in the 80s - An Overview' in Combat Poverty Agency (ed.) *Community Work in Ireland* Dublin: Combat Poverty Agency.

Cronin, J and O'Connor, M. 1993 *The Identification and Treatment of Women Admitted to an Accident and Emergency Department as a result of Assault by Spouses/ Partners* Dublin: Women's Aid.

Daly, M. 1989 *Women and Poverty* Dublin: Attic Press.

Department of Health 1995 *Developing a Policy for Women's Health* Dublin: Stationery Office.

Dobash, R and Dobash, R. 1979 *Violence Against Wives* New York: Free Press.

Dobash, R and Dobash, R. 1992 *Women, Violence and Social Change* London: Routledge.

Dominelli, L. 1990 *Women and Community Action* Birmingham: Venture Press.

Duncan, W R and Scully, P. 1990 *Marriage Breakdown in Ireland* Dublin: Butterworth.

Edwards, S. 1989 *Policing Domestic Violence* London: Sage.

Faludi, Susan. 1992 *Backlash: The Undeclared War Against Women* London: Vintage Press.

Fennell, N. 1974 *Irish Marriage - How Are You?* Dublin: Mercier Press.

Ferguson, H and Synnott, P. 1995 'Intervention into Domestic Violence in Ireland: Developing Policy and Practice with Men Who Batter' in *Administration* Vol.43, No.3 pp.57-81.

Gelles, R. 1987 *Family Violence* California: Sage.

Gelles, R and Cornell, C P. 1990 *Intimate Violence in Families* California: Sage.

Giddens, A. 1994 *Beyond Left and Right* Cambridge: Polity Press.

Kelleher and Associates and O'Connor, M. 1995 *Making the Links* Dublin: Women's Aid.

Kelly, L, Burton, S and Regan, L. 1994 'Researching Women's Lives or Studying Women's Oppression? Reflections on what Constitutes Feminist Research' in Maynard M and Purvis J. (ed.) *Researching Women's Lives from a Feminist Perspective* London: Taylor and Francis.

Kramarae, C and Treichler, P A. 1992 *Amazons, Bluestockings and Crones* London: Pandora.

Levinson, D. 1989 *Family Violence in Cross-Cultural Perspective* California: Sage.

Lupton, C. 1994 'The British Refuge Movement' in Lupton, C and Gillespie T. (ed.) *Working With Violence* Hampshire: Macmillan.

Lyons, M, Ruddle, H, O'Connor, J and O'Brien-Kelly, M. 1991 *Seeking Refuge from Violence - The Adapt Experience* Dublin: National College of Industrial Relations.

Maynard, M. 1993 'Violence Towards Women' in Richardson D and Robinson V. (ed.) *Introducing Women's Studies* Hampshire: Macmillan.

McWilliams, M and McKiernan, J. 1993 *Bringing it Out in the Open* UK: HMSO.

Millett, K. 1970 *Sexual Politics* London: Virago Press.

Morgan, D. 1988 *Focus Groups as Qualitative Research* California: Sage.

MOVE Information Fact Pack - *Draft Document* MOVE Dublin and Cork.

O'Connor, M. 1994 'Violence Against Women - A Challenge for Community Workers' in *Newsletter* Community Workers Co-op, Dublin.

Piven, F F and Cloward, R A. 1977 *Poor People's Movements* New York: Pantheon.

Prizzey, E. 1974 *Scream Quietly or the Neighbours will Hear* Middlesex: Penguin.

South Eastern Health Board (SEHB) May, 1993 *Report of the Kilkenny Incest Investigation* Dublin: Stationery Office.

Stanko, E. 1985 *Intimate Intrusions; Women's Experiences of Male Violence* London: Unwin Hyman.

Steele, B and Pollock, C. 1974 'A Psychiatric Study of Parents who Abuse Infants and Small Children' in Helfer R and Kempe C. (ed.) *The Battered Child* Chicago: University of Chicago Press.

Tucker, V. 1989 'Community Work and Social Change' in Combat Poverty Agency and Community Workers Co-op (ed.) *Community Work in Ireland* Dublin: Combat Poverty Agency.

Walker, L. 1989 'Psychology and Violence Against Women' in *American Psychologist* Vol.44, No.4, pp.695-702.

Weeks, J. 1981 *Sex, Politics and Society* Essex: Longman.

Women's Aid. nd 1. *Myths About Violence Against Women* Dublin: Women's Aid.

Women's Aid. nd 2. *Women's Aid: One of the First Points of Contact for Battered Women* Dublin: Women's Aid.

Women's Aid 1995(a) *Zero Tolerance - A National Strategy on Eliminating Violence Against Women* Dublin: Women's Aid.

Women's Aid 1995(b) Press Release: *He Gave Her Flowers, Chocolates and Multiple Bruising* Dublin: Women's Aid.

Section 7:
Rural Women and Farming

A considerable amount of sociological material has been compiled on the subject of families and family life in rural Ireland (see for example McNabb, 1964, Arensberg and Kimball, 1968, Messenger, 1969, Brody, 1973). Many of these studies of rural family life do not question or challenge either the gendered nature of agriculture and rural development or the family farm structure. More recently however questions relating to rural women's personal, social and family lives have begun to be addressed by researchers and activists (Kilmurray and Bradley, 1989, Shortall, 1992, O'Hara, 1994, Byrne, 1995, Owens and Byrne, 1996). Issues including women's marginal position in rural development policy and practice, the isolation experienced by rural women and their remoteness from basic physical and social infrastructures, their subordinate status on the labour market, their unpaid contributions to family and community, their under-representation in agricultural and other organisations, the particular difficulties of farm women and the lack of funding for women's initiatives are all matters of research investigation and concern. The contributions in this section of the text are concerned with gender and farming in particular. Prevalent beliefs, ideologies and farming structures consolidate the view of the male as 'the farmer', entitled to ownership of the land and the person who makes all of the farming decisions.

While not all women living in the countryside are farm women, most of the research on rural women has been concerned with the situation of women on farms. All of the contributors in this section have employed innovative feminist methodologies and analyses in studying the position and roles of farm women in contemporary rural Ireland. Their studies have placed women at the centre of the family farm and see farm women as playing a crucial role in the restructuring, not only of family farming, but of rural society as a whole. Patricia O'Hara's research examines farm family relations, assessing the extent of patriarchal power within the farm family. The unitary conception of the farm family is challenged and a diversity of inequalities in relationships are revealed. Interviewing sixty Irish farm wives in the Republic of Ireland, O'Hara seeks to

357

unveil the nature of women's involvement in family farming and women's own understanding of this involvement. Many women become part of the farm family on marriage and are usually economically dependent on their husbands. In her study, O'Hara found that less than one-fifth of the farms were in joint ownership, but that women seemed largely unconcerned about this. The family home however was in joint ownership in forty per cent of cases and was associated with women working outside the home. Their lack of independence, caring for a large number of children, being involved in hard physical labour with few domestic comforts, all contributed to a sense of powerlessness amongst the older women interviewed. Women were at the bottom of the patriarchal hierarchy of the farm and farm family. But are farm women as subordinated as they appear to be? Younger farm wives are perceived by the older women as having more freedom, being more financially independent and having better marital relationships. O'Hara argues that the re-shaping of familial relationships by farm wives may prove to be essential to the future of family farming in the Republic of Ireland.

Northern Ireland is the setting for the study of farm wives by Deirdre Heenan and Derek Birrell. They found no evidence of a move towards more egalitarian relationships on the family farm, but rather that fundamental inequalities found by researchers in Ireland in the 1940s (Arensberg and Kimball, 1968) 'have remained almost totally intact'. Using interviews with eighty farm wives, Heenan and Birrell discuss household work, caring work, farm administrative work, farm manual work, off-farm work, decision-making and budgeting. Quotations from interview material illustrate many inequalities between the farm couple as well as the staggering amount of work done by farm wives. For example, women are entirely responsible for all domestic work which is distinctly different from domestic work in an urban context as the farmhouse includes workplace and family residence. Women are also the primary carers of children on the farm. Almost all of the women are involved in 'keeping the books' and farm administration. Three-quarters of the women interviewed reared livestock. However most of the decision-making on the farm is made by men and Heenan and Birrell conclude that a clear gendered division of labour is in operation on farms in Northern Ireland.

Sally Shortall, in contrast, argues that women are becoming more visible in the public space of farming, presenting three case studies illuminating a variety of strategies for change. There is no doubt that the patriarchal culture of farming shapes women's experiences but Shortall's work shows that women can bring more egalitarian influences to bear on that culture. Interviewing farm women and agricultural advisers in Northern Ireland, working with the Canadian Farm Women's Network and using the extensive literature on farm women in Norway, Shortall shows the varying circumstances in which women have moved into the public sphere. The state is responsible in Norway for changing the law of inheritance which allows the eldest woman or man to inherit land. Through altering patrilineal inheritance policy, formal equality for farm women is established. Legal changes may be limited, but they can represent a first step for more widespread social change. In Canada, a farm women's network achieved greater visibility for women through lobbying and campaigning. In Northern Ireland, the agricultural service started a number of farm women's groups to provide agricultural training for women. Each of these strategies empower women and contest farm women's marginalisation in the home and on the farm. Issues of equality for women in the countryside provide a focus for urgently needed social science research.

References

Arensberg, C M and Kimball, S T. 1968 *Family and Community in Ireland* Harvard: Harvard University Press.

Brody, H. 1973 *Inishkillane – Change and Decline in the West of Ireland* London: Allen Lane.

Byrne, A. 1995 'Making Development Work for Women' in Byrne, P, Conroy, J, Hayes, A. (eds.) *UCG Women's Studies Centre Review*, Vol.3 pp.201-213.

Kilmurray, A and Bradley, C. 1989 *Rural Women in South Armagh* Derry: Rural Action Project.

Messenger, J. 1969 *Inis Beag* New York: Holt, Rinehart and Winston.

McNabb, P. 1964 *Demography and Social Structure in Newman, J (ed.) Limerick Rural Survey, 1958-1964* Tipperary: Muintir na Tire Publications.

O'Hara, P. 1994 'Constructing the Future: Cooperation and Resistance Among Farm Women' in Whatmore, S, Marsden, T, Lowe, P. (eds.) *Gender and Rurality*, London: David Fulton.

Owens, M and Byrne, A. 1996 'Family Work and Community – Rural Women's Lives' in Hayes, A, Lyons, A, Ní Léime, A and Shaughnessy, L. (eds.) *UCG Women's Studies Centre Review* Vol.4, pp.77-94

Shortall, S. 1992 'Power Analysis and Farm Wives: An Empirical Study of the Power Relationships Affecting Women on Irish Farms' *Sociologia Ruralis* XXXII 4 pp.431-451

22.

Women in Farm Families:
Shedding the Past and Fashioning the Future
Patricia O'Hara

Introduction

Ireland[1] is one of the most agrarian countries in the European Union and virtually all Irish farms are family farms. Indeed the ideological commitment to farming as a family enterprise is so strong that Article 45.2.v of the Constitution requires state policy to ensure that as many families as practicable shall remain on the land. Farm women, as wives and as mothers, are clearly at the heart of farm families, yet family farming as a social form and agriculture as an economic activity have a distinctly male appearance. The visible representation of the family farm is usually that of the male farmer who owns the land, represents the family in farming organisations, is subject to taxation and entitled to social security. Moreover, the public world of agriculture and agribusiness is perhaps one of the last remaining sectors in which women seem almost entirely absent or invisible.

Women's marginality in agriculture as an economic activity has its roots in the patriarchal character of family farming itself. Women may be integral to the farm family, but it is almost invariably men who inherit the land. The continuity of family farming as a social form is based on the patrilineal system of succession, involving the transfer of the farmholding intact to a son in preference to a daughter. Since access to farming is mostly through gift or inheritance rather than the purchase of land, this effectively excludes farm daughters from the occupation of farmer. Thus, women generally become involved in farming, not primarily by choosing farming as an occupation but through their relationship to a male landowner, most commonly through marriage. Irish farming then has a gendered structure in which the interests of men (fathers and sons) supersede those of women and daughters. This is reinforced and legitimated in rural Ireland by the weight of culture, tradition and family ideology which identifies farming as a family activity based largely on male ownership and control of the land (the patrimony). At the same time it is obvious that women are indispensible to family farming as a social form since its very endurance rests on the successful creation and intergenerational transfer of the farm business. Indeed, those with only a passing knowledge of farming in Ireland will be aware of farm women's immense, if largely unheralded and undocumented, influence within farm families. This has perhaps been more widely acknowledged in Irish literature (prose and drama) than in popular or academic discourse. In the latter, farm families are usually conceptualised as 'units' of production and consumption in which a consensus of interests among the members is assumed or implied. Such an assumption of consensus is unwarranted in a patriarchal social form divided on the basis of gender. It obscures the fact that women are apparent subordinates whose invisibility and uncertain status in the 'private' world of the family farm is paralleled by their marginalised status or lack of prominence in the 'public' world of agriculture and rural development.

The purpose of this chapter is to examine some of these issues by focusing on farm wives on family farms. This involves shifting attention from the farm to the farm family so that the starting point is farming as a social form rather than as an economic activity. It also means investigating how farm women fare within an apparently patriarchal institution, rather than how they contribute to the farm enterprise. In the next two sections some recent research on women in family farming is reviewed and discussed, distinguishing between studies which have focused mainly on the farm as the unit of analysis and those which have concentrated more specifically on the farm family. This is followed by an examination of two different, but related, aspects of farm wives' predicament: firstly the gendered ownership of family resources and secondly the relationship between farm wives' subordination and the ideology of family farming, particularly the way in which gender ideologies shape, and are shaped by, farm women's actions. In the latter section I draw on a study of farm families in the west and east of Ireland which generated both quantitative and qualitative data through detailed interviews with farm family members.[2] The approach taken in the analysis is to examine the gendered nature of family farming, not by conceiving women as passive victims of patriarchal structures, but rather by viewing them as social actors who can shape and construct the world around them even within the confines of constraining patriarchal structures.

Women on Family Farms – Revealing What Was Invisible

Until relatively recently, social scientists largely ignored gender as an issue in family farming (indeed in families generally) and it is only in the past two decades that farm women's status and their invisibility have begun to receive attention from rural sociologists and agricultural economists. The predominant focus of this research has been on the work of women on family farms, largely in an attempt to make their contribution to farming more visible. Research in different countries has documented farm women's involvement in farm work, pointing out in particular the extent to which this work is ignored and under-represented (Reimer, 1986, Gasson, 1980, 1992, Keating and Little, 1994, Alston, 1995). In England, Gasson (1992) has shown that most farm wives are involved in the farm business and that their work input is very significant, particularly on small and medium sized holdings where there is no hired labour. Similar levels of involvement have been found in France (Berlan Darque, 1988), Spain (Garcia-Ramon, 1988) and Switzerland where Rossier (1993) found that the Swiss farm woman spends an average of twenty hours per week on farm work. Farm women there have a high degree of involvement in the more labour-intensive systems such as dairying and wives are responsible for the administrative and financial management aspects of the farm operation. In a study of part-time farmers in Ireland, Higgins (1983) found that more than half (fifty-six per cent) of their wives worked on the family farm, contributing an average of forty-one weeks of labour per year. While there is much variation across Europe, the common experience is of farm women's very substantial involvement in farm work but relatively little ownership of land. For instance, a 1987 study of some 6,000 farm households across twenty areas in the EU (including two in Ireland) revealed that forty-nine per cent of farm wives were working regularly on the farm. Only thirteen per cent of farm operators in the formal, legal sense were women and the majority of these were actively running their farms (Bell et al., 1990).

The problem of farm women's invisibility is compounded by the tendency to undervalue their work by considering all married women's non-market work as 'unproductive'. Fahey (1990) has pointed out that Irish labour statistics ignore work carried out in the family. For instance, the work which was carried out in the past by farm workers or domestic servants is no longer considered as 'economic activity' once it is carried out unpaid by farm wives. The basic unit of analysis in agrarian studies and agricultural statistics is the family farm as an entity, or the farmer as an occupational category. In so far as individual family or household members are considered, it is within the context of the labour or decision-making requirements of the farm business. The occupational classifications associated with farming are: 'the farmer' taken to mean the registered holder of the land; and 'relatives assisting' designed to include family members other than the farm wife who may be working on the farm. Since farm women are in the first place wives and any farm work that they do is regarded as unpaid, they are relegated to the same category as 'housewives'. Thus begins a tautology allowing the work that women do on farms to be ignored since women themselves are not categorised as farm workers. The work that men do becomes synonymous with farm work and since women's work is not important, farm wives can be dismissed as unimportant (Hill, 1981, p.373).

In 1991 some minimal recognition was afforded to farm wives when the Census of Agriculture disaggregated farm family labour on farms on the basis of sex and marital status for the first time, including women if they were involved in 'farm work'. According to this Census, there were then 91,431 female family members on family farms in Ireland. Of these, more than two thirds (seventy per cent) were the spouses of male farm holders. Only 16,414 women were categorised as farm holders, just under ten per cent of the total. Women accounted for thirty per cent of all family workers on farms and contributed twenty-eight per cent of all family labour; farm wives contributed twenty per cent of family labour and seventy-four per cent of them said farming was their sole (sixty-four per cent) or major (ten per cent) occupation.

Even though these data represent an advance on the earlier statistics which ignored gender differences, it is important to recognise that they do under-represent women's contribution to the farm, as the definition of farm work on which they rely is often restricted to manual work and the more visible managerial tasks such as account keeping. Many tasks associated with the farm business such as running errands, dealing with callers and involvement in farm decisions are not considered as farm work. This is a common problem in labour statistics across the world. (Boulding, 1980, Waring, 1988, Fahey, 1990, Alston, 1995). It has been specifically addressed in the 1995 Report of the United Nations Development Programme (UNDP) which points out that the restricted definition of economic activity to market work means that much of what women do on farms, in the household and in the family is unrecognised and unrewarded.

The studies and statistics mentioned above have provided much-needed information about the significance of the work of women on family farms, the division of labour between spouses and how it is changing, but most have adopted a rather narrow definition of work and have focused on the farm (rather than the farm family) as the unit of analysis. Official reports which have addressed the status of farm and rural women from a policy perspective have also pointed out the dearth of information about farm women and the relationship between the structures of family farming and farm women's subordinate status as well as their under-representation in the more recent structures of rural development (see Second Commission on the Status of Women, 1993, Report of the Oireachtas Committee on Women's Rights, 1994, Braithwaite, 1994, European Parliament, 1994). But while such reports are clearly important in highlighting the difficulties associated with women's status in agriculture and rural development, they cannot address the very complex set of relations which lie inside the farm family 'unit' which is structured along gender lines.

Women in Farm Families

Recent sociological work on farm women, much of it influenced by feminist theory, has adopted a perspective which begins from the concept of gender as a social division within farm families so that social divisions, inequalities and power relations which constrain women can be addressed (Bouquet, 1982, Stratigaki, 1988, Berlan Darque, 1988, Blanc and McKinnon, 1990, Whatmore, 1991, 1994, Brandth, 1994). At least three main themes can be identified in this work. The first of these has involved examining what farm women do by moving beyond the measurement of work and the delineation of work roles to consideration of labour on family farms as a dynamic negotiated process, involving complex interactions between family members. This has led to the reconceptualisation of the family labour process as fundamentally gendered and has raised significant issues which go far beyond the confines of family farming, including the interrogation of such conceptual dichotomies as 'market' and 'non-market', 'productive' and 'reproductive'. Whatmore (1991), for instance, has put forward a theory of domestic political economy to capture the relationship between women's 'productive' and 'reproductive' work in farm families. Her study of family farming in Britain reveals how patriarchal gender relations operate in the organisation of family work and capital and she concludes that the labour process is a major instrument of subordination of women.

A second related theme has involved consideration of changing gender roles associated with agricultural modernisation and the increases in pluriactivity among farm families. The focus here has been on the renegotiation of gender roles associated with, inter alia, a shift to part-time farming, the establishment of on-farm businesses such as agri-tourism and farm women's participation in off-farm work and its effects on gender relations within the farm household. Berlan Darque (1988) in France and Elbert's work in America (1988) have shown how women find ways of contesting patriarchal structures through negotiation within farm families. Working off the farm, for instance, can put women in a much stronger position to challenge patriarchal structures, particularly if their income is crucial for the continuance of the enterprise. It can allow them to negotiate a more egalitarian distribution of work roles or to retain greater control over day to day consumption (O'Hara, 1994b).

Thirdly, a few theorists, most notably Whatmore (1991), have analysed the construction of gender identities and the ideological processes which shape and reinforce gender inequalities, including the acceptance of the patriarchal farm family as normative. According to Whatmore, the farm family is suffused with ideologies of 'wifehood' which legitimise patriarchal labour relations so that women themselves undervalue or discount aspects of their work as not 'proper' work. Related to this is the idea of the family itself as the primary site of women's oppression. Delphy (1984), and more recently Delphy and Leonard (1992), have used the case of women in family farms to explore the family as a patriarchal institution, showing how the gendered structure of family farming subordinates farm women not just in the labour and decision-making processes but also in the way that consumption and inter-generational transmission favour men over women.

All of this work has provided rich theoretical insights into the nature of family farming which have implications for the way this social form is conceptualised in rural studies generally. Perhaps its most important achievement is its challenge to the idea of the 'unity' of the farm family and its de-construction of the farm family unit into constituent elements of kinship, household and familial ideology (Whatmore, 1994). This has allowed for a conceptualisation of farm women as agents actively constructing, contesting and transforming the social structures in which they are enmeshed (O'Hara, 1994b).

In Ireland, relatively few studies have focused specifically on farm women (see O'Hara 1987a, 1987b, 1990, 1994a, Duggan, 1987, Shortall, 1991, 1992), but the farm family itself has received quite a lot of attention, although not from a feminist perspective. This work was stimulated by Arensberg and Kimball's (1968) classic study of Irish farm families in the 1930s which, although functionalist in theoretical orientation, provided a detailed account of a highly segregated gender division of labour and family interaction on peasant farms in which women were clearly subordinate. Later studies (McNabb, 1964, Messenger, 1969, Brody, 1973, Scheper Hughes, 1979) provided important insights into intra-family processes in farm families.

Most notable among the successors to Arensberg and Kimball is the work of Hannan and Katsiaouni (1977) who examined the task and decision-making involvement of farm husbands and wives (by interviewing both in great detail) in order to establish changes in family patterns since Arensberg and Kimball's time. Their work has been taken to task for failing to question the significance of the gendered division of labour and the reasons for the origins and existence of the status attached to gender roles in farm families (Shortall, 1991). However, it is important to recognise that Hannan and Katsiaouni drew attention to farm women's dissatisfaction with their roles and pointed out the relationship between this and changing ideologies of marriage in favour of more egalitarian relationships. Even without a gender analysis, they made explicit the significance of husbands' power (or wives' powerlessness) over the pattern of family interaction. Their assertion that the quality of the affectional relationship between spouses is a crucial variable in explaining task roles implies that it is not just what women on farms do that is important, but the relationship within which they do it and their understanding of the significance of their work for the family farm. Hannan and Katsiaouni's assertion that family roles are nowadays negotiated rather than culturally prescribed, and that clashing role expectations between spouses result in a high degree of dissatisfaction among farm wives, implies a degree of resistance and agency among farm women sometimes absent from more recent feminist studies.

Analyses of women in farm families have effectively challenged the idea of the farm family as a unity and pointed out the inequalities within it which are structured on the basis of gender. Recent studies informed by a feminist perspective have also broadened the concept of women's work to include non-market work such as childcare, housework and food preparation as indispensable foundations for the continued existence of the family farm (Redclift and Mingione, 1985, Whatmore, 1994). Feminist analyses have also pointed out that, while the work that women do and the relations in which they work are central to understanding farm women's situation, the gendered nature of consumption and reproduction in patriarchal family farming is also a source of subordination. However, the labour process and the ownership and control of resources on the family farm are not just the nexus of patriarchal power relations; they are also part of a complex arena of negotiation involving women in different sets of relationship with the family farm (O'Hara, 1994b). Thus, the nature of women's involvement and their understanding of it, will reflect not just the outcome of social relations which subordinate them, but also their responses to subordination through cooperation and resistance.

Gendered Ownership of Family Farm Resources

The terms on which each member of the farm couple enters farming are quite different and unequal. Women usually enter farming by marrying a man who has acquired (or will eventually acquire) the family patrimony by gift or inheritance. This creates the basis for an uneven distribution of resources so that gender as a social division within farm families structures farm women's access to family resources. Unless farm wives have a separate income source outside of the family farm, they are in a materially different situation from their husbands. They are perceived as dependants of male farmers and are categorised as such in the taxation and social welfare codes. (See Second Commission for the Status of Women Report, 1993, for a detailed discussion).

When a woman marries a farmer she does not receive, as of right, any proprietary entitlement in respect of the farm holding or family home during the couple's lifetime.[3] Only in the event of the death of the landholder is the farm wife legally protected in terms of rights to her husband's estate.[4] This arrangement is indeed ironic – not until after his death is a husband required by law to share his property with his wife, regardless of her input to the family enterprise. Even then, her ownership is usually considered as a temporary arrangement before eventual transfer to one of the couple's children. There are in fact no legal barriers to the establishment of partnerships or other legal arrangements between spouses, however such arrangements are comparatively rare.

Women then enter the family farm on a different basis from the men that they marry. For the most part they remain in this situation throughout their married life as there is no legal requirement for husbands to share property, capital or income with them. Unless they have an independent income in their own right, farm wives' access to money and other family assets in this situation can be wholly dependent on the negotiation of satisfactory sharing arrangements with their husbands. Their bargaining power is dependent on their status inside the family and the farm business as well as the nature of the conjugal contract. Moreover, their capacity to use the ultimate sanction of leaving the marriage has been to date constrained by the non-availability of divorce. Since Ireland does not yet have legal provision for divorce, marriage is looked upon as a permanent arrangement.[5] This further reduces the options available to women. Ironically, if they do find their position intolerable and seek a legal separation, the Judicial Separation and Family Law Reform Act 1989, provides for a kind of deferred community property. This Act allows the court, when deciding a judicial separation, to order a division of property to take into account, inter alia, the contribution of the wife to the welfare of the family, and the effect on her earning capacity of having taken on marital responsibilities. The decision to leave a marriage will however also depend very much on the alternative options. Farm wives who see little possibility of being able to earn an independent income outside the farm family are more likely to remain within it even if they feel powerless and subordinated through not being rewarded or recognised for their contribution. Marriage is also much more than just an economic arrangement so ideologies of family and of wife/motherhood in family farming will also structure women's action and the way they view their situation. Indeed the shifts in the ideology of marriage and family in Ireland which stress sharing and mutual obligation, tend to underplay the material aspects of marriage which were much more explicit in the days of the arranged 'match'.

In the author's recent study of farm wives' involvement in family farming referred to above, only eighteen per cent of the farms studied were in joint ownership. The majority of these were in the west where husband and wife were joint owners in twenty-seven per cent (8/30) of cases. The transfer to joint names was a deliberate decision taken after marriage in just three of these cases. In two of the remaining five farms, the husband had 'married in' to the wife's farm. In a further two cases the farm had been handed over as a gift to the couple at marriage. In the remaining instance the land had been purchased by the couple after marriage. In the east, a mere ten per cent (3/30) of farms were owned jointly by the farm couple. One of these was where the land was acquired after marriage; in a second the husband had 'married in'; and in the other the woman herself purchased the land after marriage (with money which was a gift from her father) and was effectively the farmer. Joint ownership occurred then only in situations where the couple had a strong commitment to sharing as in the three instances in the west, or where land was purchased after marriage. The association of ownership with the male 'farmer' and the patrilineal system is so strong that even in cases where the husband 'marries in' to his wife's family farm, the land is put into joint ownership rather than retained solely in her name.

Generally though, as long as their husbands are alive, farm wives appear unconcerned about the issue of ownership of land even where they are making a very significant labour input to farm production. Their awareness of the possibility of being in a difficult predicament in the event of their husband's death however, means that having a will made is regarded as an important insurance against future insecurity:

> The house and farm are in H's name ... Sometimes I think about it ... if something happened, but I would get it anyway as he has a will made. I have my name on the cheque book. That is important, it makes business straightforward.

> The house and farm are in H's name but he has a will made, he is very proper like that. I don't mind at all. God between us and all harm, but if he died it is mine.

> Women don't think about their name on the farm, unless a situation crops up, they just drift along. They don't think of these things. I never thought of it myself until a neighbour died suddenly.

Forty per cent (24/60) of family homes were jointly owned, forty-three per cent in the west and thirty-seven per cent in the east. In the west, eight homes were on farms which were jointly owned. In one case the home, but not the farm, was in both names. In the remaining four cases, the houses had been recently built or renovated. Building a new home was more significant as a reason for joint ownership in the east where nine out of the eleven jointly owned homes were new. Older houses which were part of the husband's patrimony, or built before his marriage, were more likely to be registered along with the land, solely in his name.

Among the families studied then, the farm remained firmly in the hands of husbands in most cases. In the east in particular, ownership of the land would also include other capital assets such as buildings, animals and machinery. Rarely are substantial proportions of such assets assigned separately to the farm wife, although it is not uncommon for various members of the family to own animals, particularly a son who might be a potential successor. Joint ownership was the exception and it is difficult to detect any significant movement towards a more egalitarian regime. Ownership of land on family farms is structured by gender and the requirements of the patrilineal system of inheritance. Even widow's ownership of land is regarded as a temporary stage until ultimate transfer to a male successor. Women's apparent unconcern about this may owe as much to a recognition of the impregnability of the system as to anything else, but it may also be rooted in their sense of being an outsider, of 'marrying in' to their husband's family property and therefore not having any 'rights'. Only joint purchase of a farm or their husbands' explicit recognition of their contribution can alter the pattern of male dominance. The essentially patriarchal nature of ownership of family property is apparent in the fact that the situation does not appear to hold in reverse. When men 'married in' they became joint owners. The fact that joint ownership was much less common in the east suggests a stronger commitment on the part of male farm owners there to maintaining the gendered structure of ownership on larger, more commercial farms.

The pattern of home ownership indicates a trend towards separation of ownership of farm and home with younger couples building new homes which are jointly owned. Joint ownership of the family home is related to farm wives' involvement in paid employment. More than half the wives who were joint owners of new homes were working off the farm. Working wives may pay the mortgage or spend much of their earnings on furnishings for the new home but, as we shall see below, joint ownership also represents an ideological shift where modern marriage is considered to involve shared ownership of the family home.

Ideology and Equality

As Friedmann (1986) has pointed out, there is an inherent tension between women's equality and the ideology of family farming. Gender roles are institutionalised in the legal code but the contradiction between women's equality and the ideology of family farming rarely becomes explicit. In Ireland, a recent example of this tension between ideology and women's status was the fear, widely expressed during the debate prior to the divorce referendum, of the fragmentation of farm holdings which might result from the introduction of divorce legislation. Farm wives' legal entitlement to land or family assets, in the event of divorce, were seen as potentially threatening to the stability of family farming in Ireland. A further example is the documented reservation of the representative of the Irish Farmers Association to one of the recommendations on community property in the Second Commission on the Status of Women. The reservation to Recommendation 1.5.6 advocating the immediate introduction of a regime of community property in marriage reads:

While in general terms equal share rights are certainly desirable, in cases such as family farms maintaining the viability of farm holdings must also be considered and the need for equity between parents and family members. In this regard, while a 50:50 split may be reasonable in families of one or two children, where there are more than two children it might be more practicable to maintain the one-third legal share provided in the Succession Act, 1965 (Second Commission on the Status of Women, 1993, p.58).

For most farm women, marriage to a farmer usually means entry to a farm which has been controlled by his family. She enters a family system with sets of values, norms and practices which are well established before her arrival. Since the majority of women who marry farmers themselves come from farming backgrounds (two-thirds of the women in the present study), they are entering a familiar situation, having watched their own mother in the role of farm wife:

> My mother worked in the fields. She had eighteen children and was deprived of a lot ... She had a baby in a cradle and used to leave it with the old man [her father-in-law] while she went out and worked. There is no work now compared to that. People complain today but they don't understand what people like her had to do.

> There were sixteen in the family on forty acres. Seven or eight of them are now outside Ireland. My mother didn't believe in birth control and did all the outside work because my father was working [off the farm]. I didn't wonder at farming because I was brought up with it. My sisters in England think I'm mad.

Many of the older women interviewed (now aged over fifty) had a strong sense of the subordination associated with their incorporation into the family farm and how it was sustained by ideologies of marriage and 'wifehood':

> I was reared on a farm and never liked it. I saw my mother slaving and said this is not for me and yet I ended up here. I thought I'd have longer before coming back to the farm from England but my husband talked me into it. There was nothing else in my husband's life only farming ... We had to start from nothing, the place was a wilderness with the old house, two rooms and a kitchen, no electricity, no water, no tongs even which was very important in those days.

Their sense of powerlessness regarding the size of their families, of their lack of freedom and independence, particularly in the early years of their marriage is allied to a sense of being part of a wider set of structures and ideologies which set the terms of their existence. The fact that these ideologies are changing and that farm wives' material dependence on their husbands can be lessened by engaging in paid work are perceived by these older women as lessening farm women's subordination. They see themselves as the last generation who were willing to accede to such an extent to the demands of family and farm. Such women see marriage into farming as completely different for modern women who are gradually being freed from many of the strictures which constrained themselves:

> Everything has changed – going out to work, having fewer children, keeping on their jobs after marriage, having a social life as well as the men, becoming more equal. I think it is a good thing.

> Women have more independence, they don't have to work as hard in the fields, with cows and hens and chickens and rear children at the same time, it is much easier for my daughters.

> Modern women let the men know how they feel, it is fifty-fifty all the time. They make them [the men] share in everything and let them know how they feel. We were brought up to feel that the woman was the heart of the home and that it was her job to keep him happy. It's only fair for women, why should we be slaves.

Younger farm women reflect these changes and bring different expectations to marriage and family which stress 'modern' values, a new home and a desire for a higher material standard of living. They articulate an aspiration for a different kind of marital relationship involving the idea of sharing within the marriage and autonomy for the couple, whereby the husband's behaviour is seen as, and expected to be, new and different from that of his (or her own) father:

> The old people had certain ideas about what to do. For instance my mother-in-law was here one day and I said something about H getting his own dinner and I could see she was shocked ... Men are changing too, H is not the same as his father. In his house the women did the running for the men. The men worked and the women took care of them. That is all changing and farmers are more outgoing. If I suggest holidays to H he says we'll go. The old people had their own ways and that was it.

> The family revolved around the father before, now it revolves around the children. Men are changing ... women have changed the men, they are not putting up with as much, not prepared to be servants any more ... We were always told, don't make noise, you'll disturb your father. Children were to be seen and not heard. Even though he brought us places on Sundays and all that and was very good, he was the man of the house.

These changing ideologies are also an important reason why younger women remain in, or return to, paid work after marriage – to maintain a sense of financial independence and the family's standard of living. It can also be a way of asserting the farm wife's independence and distancing herself from the farm operation. Such women are quite clear about what differentiates them from the older generation of farm wives. As one young farm wife put it:

> There is now a new generation of farm women. Women married farmers in the past to be a farmer's wife. That doesn't happen any more. Most of the

young women have jobs and work for money, although I'm sure most get job satisfaction too ... I don't know what would make me give up work now. I can't think of anything that would, I'd hate to be at home all day.

Conclusion

The public world of agriculture and rural development and the private world of family farming are among the most resilient domains of almost complete male dominance in modern societies. Over the past two decades, studies of women's involvement in family farming have addressed a range of issues which have provided insights into the predicament of all women. Most fundamentally, studies of women's work on family farms have provided an important context for addressing wider issues of how all non-market work is to be understood and how it is conceptualised and represented in official statistics. Studies of farm families have challenged ideas of the farm family as a unity and shown that it is deeply divided along gender lines. Deconstruction of the farm family into constituent elements of household, kinship and ideology has provided important insights into how patriarchal family structures are maintained and reinforced. Examination of the predicament of farm women has also raised important issues about the link between public and private patriarchy and whether it is possible for women to make significant advances in the public arena while they are enmeshed in a patriarchal social form such as family farming.

The empirical evidence from a study of Irish farm wives cited in this chapter suggests that, while women on family farms are enmeshed in a social form which is structured on the basis of gender, they are nevertheless creating room to manoeuvre by constructing ideologies of farm wifehood which stress egalitarianism and sharing. The constraints which older farm wives have felt in their own lives prompt them to endorse and help create new ideologies of privacy, sharing and financial independence which were unavailable to themselves. Younger women live out these new images of family life by insisting on what they consider to be a 'modern' marriage. The importance of ideologies of gender roles in shaping the reality and meaning of farm women's lives is clear and not unexpected, given Hannan and Katsiaouni's (1977) earlier findings. Farm wives are not powerless and without influence but are actively shedding the past and fashioning the future by, inter alia, responding to the constraints of ideology and culture by trying to change them, if not for themselves, at least for their daughters. While they have had limited success in breaching male dominance of the occupation of farmer or patriarchal character of family farming, they are re-fashioning the role of farm 'wife' so that her complicity and unquestioning commitment to a social form in which women are subordinated can no longer be assumed or taken for granted. Thus, farm women's actions are, and will be crucial in determining the evolution of family farming as a social form in Ireland.

Discussion Topics

1. Discuss the links between women's apparent subordination on family farms and their lack of prominence in the public world of agriculture and agribusiness.

2. Discuss the differences between older and younger farm women's lives. What is the future of family farming in Ireland likely to be?

3. Discuss the connections between the status of women in family businesses and the way in which their work is conceptualised and represented.

4. Discuss ways of addressing the problem of Irish women's under-representation in the public world of agriculture and rural development.

Notes

1. Ireland, throughout this chapter, refers to the Republic of Ireland.
2. This material is drawn from a wider study of farm families in the west and east of Ireland carried out between 1989 and 1991. The study generated both quantitative and qualitative data which will be reported in detail in a 1997 publication (O'Hara, P. Women, Farm and Family in Contemporary Ireland Oxford: Berghahn Books). The material used here is based on detailed interviews with sixty farm women carried out during 1991. The interviews covered a wide range of issues, with the emphasis on uncovering how women themselves make sense of their 'place' in family farming. The quotations in the text are taken from different women across a variety of farm situations. The letter 'H' denotes references to 'husband' throughout.
3. The Family Home Protection Act 1976 only provides women with a right of veto on the sale of the family home.
4. The Succession Act 1965 provides for a minimum entitlement to part of the estate to widows.
5. In a national referendum in 1995, the Irish people voted by a narrow margin to remove the constitutional ban on divorce. Legislation providing for divorce is due to be introduced in late 1996.

References and Further Reading

Alston, M. 1995 'Women and their Work on Australian Farms' Rural *Sociology* Vol.60 No.3 pp.521-532.

Arensberg, C M and Kimball, S T. 1968 *Family and Community in Ireland* Harvard: Harvard University Press.

Bell, C, Bryden, J M, Fuller, A M, MacKinnon, N and Spearman, M. 1990 'Economic and Social Change in Europe, Participation by Farm Women in the Labour Market and Implications for Change' in European Commission Childcare Network, *Childcare Needs of Rural Families,* Brussels: Seminar Report Commission of the European Communities.

Berlan Darque, M. 1988 'The Division of Labour and Decision-Making in Farming Couples: Power and Negotiation' *Sociologia Ruralis* Vol.28 No.4 pp.271-92.

Blanc, M, and MacKinnon, N. 1990 'Gender Relations and the Family Farm in Western Europe' *Journal of Rural Studies* Vol.6 No.4 pp.401-5.

Boulding, E. 1980 'The Labour of US Farm Women: A Knowledge Gap' *Sociology of Work and Occupations* Vol.7 No.3 pp.261-90.

Bouquet, M. 1982 'Production and Reproduction of Family Farms in South-West England' *Sociologia Ruralis* Vol.22 No.3-4 pp.227-41.

Braithwaite, M. 1994 *The Economic Role and Situation of Women in Rural Areas European Commission,* Special Issue of Green Europe, Brussels.

Brandth, B. 1994 'Changing Femininity. The Social Construction of Women Farmers in Norway' *Sociologia Ruralis* Vol.XXXIV No.2/3 pp.127-49.

Brody, H. 1973 *Inishkillane: Change and Decline in the West of Ireland* London: Allen Lane.

Bunreacht na hEireann (Constitution of Ireland). 1937 Dublin: Government Publications.

Central Statistics Office. 1991 *Census of Agriculture* Dublin: Government Publications.

Delphy, C. 1984 *Close to Home* London: Hutchinson.

Delphy, C and Leonard, D. 1992 *Familiar Exploitation: A New Analysis of Marriage in Contemporary Societies* Cambridge: Polity Press.

Duggan, C. 1987 'Farming Women or Farmers' Wives? Women in the Farming Press' in Curtin, C, Jackson P and O'Connor, B. (eds.) *Gender in Irish Society* Galway: Galway University Press.

Elbert, S. 1988 'Women and Farming: Changing Structures, Changing Roles' in Haney, W G and Knowles, J B. (eds.) *Women and Farming: Changing Roles, Changing Structures* Boulder: Westview Press.

European Parliament Working Paper. 1994 *Situation, Status and Prospects of Women in Agriculture* Luxembourg: European Parliament Directorate General for Research.

Fahey, T. 1990 'Measuring the Female Labour Supply: Conceptual and Procedural Problems in Irish Official Statistics' *Economic and Social Review* Vol.21 No.2 pp.163-191.

Friedmann, H. 1986 'Family Enterprises in Agriculture: Structural Limits and Political Possibilities' in Cox, G, Lowe, P and Winter, M. *Agriculture: People and Policies* London: Allen and Unwin.

Garcia-Ramon, M D and Canoves, G. 1988 'The Role of Women on the Family Farm: The Case of Catalonia' *Sociologia Ruralis* Vol.28 No.4 pp.271-92.

Gasson, R. 1980 'Roles of Farm Women in England' *Sociologia Ruralis* Vol.20 No.3 pp.165-180.

Gasson, R. 1992 'Farm Wives – Their Contribution to the Farm Business' *Journal of Agricultural Economics* Vol.43 No.1 pp.74-87.

Hannan, D F and Katsiaouni, L. 1977 *Traditional Families?* Dublin: Economic and Social Research Institute.

Higgins, J. 1983 *A Study of Part-time Farmers in the Republic of Ireland* Dublin: An Foras Taluntais.

Hill, F. 1981 'Farm Women: Challenge to Scholarship' *The Rural Sociologist* Vol.1 No.6 pp.376-82.

Keating, N C and Little, H M. 1994 'Getting into it: Farm Roles and Careers of New Zealand Women' *Rural Sociology* Vol.59 No.3 pp.720-36.

McNabb, P. 1964 'Demography' and 'Social Structure' in Newman, J. (ed.) *The Limerick Rural Survey 1958-1964* Tipperary: Muintir na Tire.

Messenger, J. 1969 *Inis Beag – Isle of Ireland* New York: Holt, Rinehart and Winston.

National Farm Survey. 1990 Dublin: Teagasc, Rural Economy Research Centre.

O'Hara, P. 1987a 'Farm Women: Concerns and Values of an Undervalued Workforce' UCD Women's Studies Forum, Working Paper No.2, University College, Dublin.

O'Hara, P. 1987b 'What Became of Them? West of Ireland Women in the Labour Force' in Curtin, C, Jackson, P and O'Connor, B. (eds.) *Gender in Irish Society* Galway: Galway University Press.

O'Hara, P. 1990 'Prospects for Farm Women' in *Women and the Completion of the Internal Market* Dublin: Department of Labour.

O'Hara, P. 1994a 'Out of the Shadows: Women on Family Farms and their Contribution to Agricultural and Rural Development' in Plas, van der L and Fonte, M. (eds.) *Rural Gender Studies in Europe* The Netherlands: Van Gorcum, Assen.

O'Hara, P. 1994b 'Constructing the Future: Cooperation and Resistance Among Farm Women in Ireland' in Whatmore, S, Marsden, T and Lowe, P. (eds.) *Gender and Rurality* London: David Fulton.

Redclift, N and Mignione, E. (eds.) 1985 *Beyond Employment: Household, Gender and Subsistence* London: Basil Blackwell.

Reimer, B. 1986 'Women as Farm Labour' *Rural Sociology* Vol.51 No.2 pp.143-55.

Report of the Oireachtas Committee on Women's Rights. 1994 *Women and Rural Development* Dublin: The Stationary Office.

Rossier, R. 1993 'The Farm Woman's Work Today' paper to *15th European Congress of Rural Sociology*, The Netherlands: Wageningen.

Scheper-Hughes, N. 1979 *Saints, Scholars and Schizophrenics: Mental Illness in Rural Ireland* California: University of California Press.

Second Commission on the Status of Women. 1993 *Report to Government* Dublin: Government Publications.

Shortall, S. 1991 'The Dearth of Data on Irish Farm Wives: A Critical Review of the Literature' *Economic and Social Review* Vol.22 No.4 pp.311-332.

Shortall, S. 1992 'Power Analysis and Farm Wives: An Empirical Analysis of the Power Relationships Affecting Women on Irish Farms' *Sociologia Ruralis* Vol.32 No.4 pp.431-51.

Stratigaki, M. 1988 'Agricultural Modernisation and the Gender Division of Labour: The Case of Heraklion, Greece' *Sociologia Ruralis* Vol.23 No.4 pp.248-62.

United Nations Development Programme (UNDP). 1995 *Human Development Report 1995* Oxford: Oxford University Press.

Waring, M. 1988 *If Women Counted: A New Feminist Economics* London: Macmillan.

Whatmore, S. 1991 *Farming Women: Gender Work and Family Enterprise* London: Macmillan.

Whatmore, S. 1994 'Theoretical Achievements and Challenges in European Rural Gender Studies' in Plas, van der L and Fonte, M. (eds.) *Rural Gender Studies in Europe* The Netherlands: Van Gorcum, Assen.

23.

Farm Wives in Northern Ireland and the Gendered Division of Labour

Deirdre Heenan and Derek Birrell

Introduction

Following the huge upsurge of interest in the area of gender a number of studies have noted that the work and contribution of the farm wife has been consistently overlooked and undervalued (Sachs, 1983, Whatmore, 1988, Gasson, 1992). Shortall (1991) lamented about 'the dearth of data' available on Irish farm wives and she noted that there was a 'paucity of knowledge and statistical data' available on these women. Much of the existing literature has been gleaned from early Irish anthropological studies (Arensberg and Kimball, 1940, Harris, 1972, Brody, 1973). When women were mentioned in these studies it was as wives and mothers but never as workers or partners. The obvious gender divisions within the operation of the farm were not deemed worthy of a mention.

Given that Northern Ireland society has been the focus of so much academic study since 'the troubles' began it is important to note that women on farms have received little attention. Indeed one could be forgiven for assuming that all women in Northern Ireland resided in the Province's two cities. The few existing studies on Irish farm wives have been based in the Republic of Ireland (Matthews, 1981, O'Hara, 1987, Shortall, 1991). The experiences of farm wives in Northern Ireland have been completely overlooked and disregarded. It was thought valuable therefore to produce contemporary data on the lives and work of farm women. The extensive and exhaustive nature of the work of the farm wife was examined in an empirical study. Included in this use of the term work is their role in both farm decision making and household budgeting.

Literature Review

The patriarchal nature of the Irish farm family was first detailed by Arensberg and Kimball (1940). They noted that men dominated and controlled the farm family, their superior status in the community was taken for granted. They described the farm wife as a woman who 'serves' her man. She prepared all the meals on the farm and could not sit at the table until the men had eaten. Over thirty years later the Irish rural family was described as uncompromisingly patriarchal by Brody (1973). Within the household the male was dominant. He controlled the lives of his family and they remained in a subservient position until they married. The patriarchal nature of Northern Irish rural society and the inferior position of farm women were evident in a study by Harris (1972). She noted that the men were entirely responsible for decision making on the farm, and women were rarely consulted. This view was echoed by Leyton (1975) who described the man as the head of the household. He was seen as a symbol of wealth and authority and was afforded great status in the community. Women were expected to sacrifice their life for their children and were described as less significant. The situation appeared to have changed somewhat when Hannan and Katsiaouni (1977) carried out their study of family interaction in rural areas. They asserted that modern families made up over one-third of all families. These modern families had joint decision making roles and husband and wife made an equal contribution.

There was a clear and rigid sexual division of labour in rural Ireland. Arensberg and Kimball (1940) described the sexual division of labour in the rural family as clearly defined and deeply institutionalized. Women's work revolved around the farmyard and farmhouse. Their work was less visible and therefore not deemed as important as the work of the men. The sexual division of labour meant that women worked extensively inside and outside the farmhouse but men's work did not extend into the farmhouse. Harris (1972) noted that this sexual division of labour varied slightly depending on the social status of the farm families. Women from more prosperous farms were very seldom involved in field work while those from poorer farms assisted their husbands with certain field tasks.

The social life of the farm couple was marked by a large degree of separation, with the farming couple rarely socializing together. Brody (1973) noted that after evening tea, the male went out visiting or invited his friends and neighbours to his house. Harris (1972) stated that women were not allowed to sit at the fireside if her husband had local men visiting. She described the social life of rural men as varied. They were often members of local organizations such as the GAA or the Orange Order. They visited their friends and neighbours and frequented the local pub. The women in contrast were limited to occasionally visiting their kin. This dependence on kin for social contact meant that women were often isolated.

These Irish studies of rural life are somewhat limited as they provide only descriptive accounts of Irish farm women's lives. The studies provide snippets of information and are not located within a framework which would allow a deeper understanding of women's lives. The farm wife has however been the subject of an increasing number of research projects in Britain and the USA. From the late 1970s onwards researchers have attempted to create a typology of women's roles in agriculture. These typologies classified farm women into various distinct role types. Following work by Pearson (1979) and Craig (1979), Gasson (1981) identified three distinct roles commonly assumed by English farm women. Firstly, the working farm wife who regularly assisted her husband in manual and managerial tasks on the smaller family farm. Secondly, the farm housewife who was less involved in the running of the larger labour-employing farm and who was primarily involved in family or off-farm activities. Thirdly, the woman farmer who was an equal or dominant partner in the family business who was extensively involved in farm decision making. These typologies have however been criticized as it is claimed that they do not provide a comprehensive picture of the work of the farm wife. Her work in the farm household and her responsibility for child care has been overlooked (Whatmore, 1988).

The Survey

Agricultural land in Northern Ireland is divided into two categories, Lowland and Less Favoured Areas. Over sixty-nine per cent of land in the Province is described as Less Favoured, which typically provides a lower than average agricultural return (Magee, 1990). Structurally the agricultural industry is characterised by small owner-occupied family farms with working owners and high levels of input from all family members. The average area of a working farm in 1993 was 35.1 hectares which is low in comparison to other regions in the UK. For the purposes of this study it was decided to carry out in-depth interviews with eighty farm wives, forty from the Lowland area and forty from the Less Favoured area. A study area was wanted which could be seen as broadly representative of Northern Ireland's agricultural land use. Secondly the study area would have to include Lowland and Less Favoured farming areas. Finally the study area chosen would have to be fairly compact and accessible to the researcher. After some exploratory work it was decided to base the study in Co. Down as it could fulfil the research criteria. Unfortunately the Department of Agriculture in Northern Ireland was unable to release any information on the composition of farm families in the study areas. Therefore a stratified sample designed to get access to farm women of different class backgrounds proved impossible. The researcher was able to get a list of names and addresses of farm households in the area. This list was reduced to farms which had a farm wife under the age of sixty-five living on the farm. From this list forty names from each study area were picked out using random number tables. It was hoped that this sample would allow the researcher to ascertain the importance of locational factors.

Household Work on the Farm

One thing that is extremely clear is that work in the home is still viewed almost exclusively as 'women's work'. The extent to which men are involved in this work is minimal. As in the majority of urban households men were generally only involved in occasional household tasks that were undertaken on a cyclical basis (Montgomery and Davies, 1991). An important aspect of women's domestic work is that it often varies significantly from the domestic work in the average urban household. The fact that the workplace is not separate from the household and the distinction between consumption and production is often blurred means domestic work usually includes work for the farm (Little 1987, Fahey 1992). As one thirty-eight year old woman explained:

> It would be all right if I could just get on with the housework and get it done. But it's never like that. I'm usually in the middle of something when meal will have to be mixed for the calves. Or somebody will call and have to be fed.

Another forty-five year old farm wife complained about the repetitive nature of farm domestic work.

> I'd say on average I wash this (kitchen) floor about six times a day. I'll just have it clean and then they just march all over it looking for something, boots and all. It would be great if you could just wash it once and leave it at that. Nothing is that easy here you clean and cook constantly, you can't say there that's it finished.

With the growth of consumerism and advances in technology, one could be forgiven for assuming that household appliances such as vacuum cleaners, washing machines and dishwashers would have considerably lightened the load of the farm wife. Yet for many of the women this was not the case. They claimed that these gadgets had resulted in higher standards and as a result they actually increased their workload. A fifty-seven year old woman explained that although the automatic washing machine had seemed too good to be true it now seemed as if it had actually doubled her work.

> I can remember the day that we got it and I thought it couldn't possibly do the washing itself. With the twin-tub Monday was the washing day and it took all day. But do you see since we got that thing our ones want the clothes washed after they've had them on two minutes. At least on Tuesday the wash bin used to be empty but not now. Needless to say they expect all these clothes to be ironed before they put them on.

It would be easy to overemphasize the importance of household technology in reducing the workload involved in housework (Cowan, 1983, Fahey, 1992). So-called labour saving devices have in fact often increased the workload of women, as they have resulted in them being caught up in a 'senseless tyranny' of spotless shirts and immaculate floors (Cowan, 1983).

Caring Work

Child care is seen as an extension of domestic labour and is almost entirely the responsibility of the farm wife.

Table 1: *Husbands' Involvement in Child Care in the Less Favoured Area.*

	REGULARLY		OCCASIONALLY		NEVER	
	No.	%	No	%	No.	%
Taking children to and from school	1	2.7	7	18.9	29	78.4
Help with homework	-		3	8.1	34	91.9
Liaise with schools	-		-		37	100.0
Changing nappies	-		-		37	100.0
Put children to bed	-		-		37	100.0
Getting children up	-		1	2.7	36	97.3
Babysitting	1	2.5	12	32.6	24	64.9
Taking children to leisure activities	1	2.7	9	24.3	27	73.0

Source: Survey of Farm Wives 1992.

Table 2: *Husbands' Involvement in Child Care in the Lowland Area.*

	REGULARLY		OCCASIONALLY		NEVER	
	No.	%	No.	%	No.	%
Taking children to and from school	7	17.5	9	22.5	24	60.0
Help with homework	5	12.5	4	10.0	31	77.5
Liaise with schools	2	5.0	3	7.5	35	87.5
Change nappies	-		6	15.0	34	85.0
Put children to bed	1	2.5	8	20.0	31	77.5
Getting children up	-		5	12.5	35	87.5
Babysitting	2	5.0	15	37.5	23	57.5
Taking children to leisure activities	-		18	45.0	22	55.0

Source: Survey of Farm Wives 1992.

Ninety-six per cent of the farm wives had children and there was an average of three children in each family. Over ninety per cent of the women claimed that their husbands had never changed a nappy. Just three of the women who were all from the Lowland area had paid help with the child care. The vast majority of the women relied on their family for assistance. These farm wives overwhelming responsibility for child care supports Whatmore's assertion that where there are children in the farm household, it is the women who are the primary carers (Whatmore, 1991). Furthermore in the thirteen households where there were elderly relatives living with the family it was an unquestioned assumption that their care would be the women's responsibility. A forty year old woman explained that this caring role could often be quite difficult and stressful.

> This house was my husband's parents home and for the first ten years of our marriage my mother-in-law lived with us. It is the done thing on farms, where else would she go? She wasn't bad or anything like that but it was just hard, I always felt that I was being judged. The house was always more hers than it was mine.

In many cases this additional caring role meant that the women were practically housebound. The physical and mental demands of the job meant that they had to be available twenty-four hours a day. It was difficult to leave the house as these relatives needed constant care and attention. Living in a rural area meant that there were practically no support services and no prospect of respite care (Cecil et al., 1987).

Farm Labour

Farm labour can be broadly divided into two separate categories, farm administrative work and farm manual work (Whatmore, 1991). Farm administration is usually centred around the farm house. A large part of this work relates to the paperwork of the farm, keeping farm records, and completing grant forms were typical of this work. Commonly the farm wife was the first point of contact on the farm dealing with enquiries, salesmen and deliveries. All of the farm wives were regularly involved in farm administration but none of them had received any training to help them with the farm administration. Over eighty per cent of the women reported that they were responsible for 'keeping the books'. This level of involvement was high when compared to similar studies in other areas of the United Kingdom.

Table 3: *Farm Administration Work Undertaken by the Farm Wife.*

	REGULARLY		OCCASIONALLY		NEVER	
	No.	%	No.	%	No.	%
Office work/book keeping	65	81	12	15	3	4
Keeping financial records	64	80	13	16	3	4
Dealing with businessphone calls	58	73	17	21	5	6
Contacting vet	56	70	19	24	5	6
Providing meals for employees	55	69	18	22	7	9
Contacting AI man	51	64	20	25	9	11
Dealing with salesmen	47	59	17	21	16	20
Dealing with deliveries	36	45	29	36	15	19

Source: Survey of Farm Wives 1992.

In her study of farm wives in the South of England, Whatmore (1991) stated that book keeping was undertaken by sixty-five per cent of the women and only forty-two per cent of these were involved on a regular basis. It was suggested by Hastings (1987/88) that the farm wife played only a supporting role in the farm business. In their study of the role of the farm wife in the management of the farm business, Buchanan et al. (1982) suggested,

> The wife in the farm house is often strategically placed to act as the hub of the communications network especially where there is no farm office.

They reported that forty-two per cent of farm wives were regularly involved in office type work. This relatively low level of involvement in farm administration may have in part been due to the presence of a farm secretary on some of the farms included in their survey.

Driving for the farm was also seen as a responsibility of the farm wife. This included driving to collect spare machinery parts, driving to collect farm workers, driving to scattered fields with tea and refreshments for those working there, and driving to collect drugs and foodstuffs for animals. Over seventy per cent of the women reported that they were expected to be available to help in an emergency. However as one woman explained the term emergency was used very loosely on the farm.

> Every day brings its own emergency on this farm. Cattle are always breaking out or coming down with something. It just means that you can never relax and forget about it. The car might be needed, you might be needed, you never know what you are coming back to and it takes away all the pleasure of getting out.

When examining this aspect of the farm wife's role it is important not to obscure the difference between farm administration and farm financial management. Farm administration was seen as a 'feminine task'. Book-keeping and form filling were tedious and monotonous and therefore willingly left to women. None of the farms included in this study employed a farm secretary. However when farm administration became farm financial management it was almost always taken over by the men. Farm financial management meant deciding to apply for loans and grants and meeting with the farm accountant and bank manager. Farm administration simply meant preparing and documenting the relevant paperwork.

There were significant differences in the women's levels of involvement in farm administration in the two study areas. Farm wives in the Less Favoured area were more regularly involved in all areas of farm administration. This lower involvement in the Lowland area was thought to be related to the fact that farm owners in the Lowland area were more likely to employ an accountant, who took over some of the farm administration work.

Farm Manual Work

Typically this involved rearing farm animals and field work such as planting, ploughing and harvesting. Almost all of the farm wives (eighty-five per cent) reported that they were involved in farm manual work. Only four farms had a full-time employee and twelve had regular part-time work. This farm manual work was subject to a clear gendered division of labour. Approximately three-quarters of the women were regularly involved in rearing livestock while in striking contrast just 7.5 per cent of the women were involved in ploughing. The rearing of young animals was seen as suitable work for the farm wife. This work which revolved around the farm yard was unskilled, mundane and repetitive, while the 'real work' of the farm was the skilled, technical field work which was almost exclusively the work of men.

Importantly, though when the men were employed full-time off the farm this gendered division of labour is discarded and it is assumed that the women will be both willing and able to undertake all the farm work. Twelve of the farm wives reported that they were entirely responsible for the day-to-day management of the farms as their husbands worked off the farm. None of these farms were dairy farms and of the twelve, eight were in the Less Favoured area. The assumption that some 'heavy' and 'skilled' work is not suitable for women is disregarded when it is no longer useful (Bradley, 1989). All twelve of these women were extensively involved in field work but as one forty-seven year old woman explained this was only acceptable as there was no alternative.

> I work at the planting and ploughing because my husband works full-time and so he can't be expected to do it. Mind you I didn't do it before he started working, or we'd have been the talk of the country.

The vast majority of these farm households adhered to traditional norms and only in exceptional circumstances was the traditional division of labour challenged.

Eleven farms had some form of farm diversification ranging from agritourism to breeding specialist herds. In all cases this diversification was managed by the farm wife. This female preponderance in farm diversification lends weight to the suggestion by Owens (1992) that farm diversification could result in the further exploitation of women. Obviously whether the involvement of women in farm diversification inevitably entails exploitation depends on whether women have control over the extra earned farm income. In five of the eleven cases of farm diversification the women reported that they had a degree of control over the money generated from the farm diversification. None of the women felt that the money was theirs to dispose of how they pleased.

When the two study areas were compared there were notable differences in the amount and type of manual work undertaken by the women. Overall farm wives in the Less Favoured area were more involved in farm manual labour. The fact that farm wives involvement in farm tasks declines when the farm size increases has already been documented (Gasson, 1981, Buchanan et al., 1982). This decrease in involvement in farm work was also related to the sexual division of labour. Farm wives in Lowland areas were restricted to a more rigid division of labour. They were excluded from tasks that were not deemed suitable. These women claimed that their husbands took pride in the fact that they did not 'work like navvies' in the fields. When farms became more prosperous female field labour was replaced by paid help. Eight of the twelve women who managed the farms were from the Less Favoured area.

Off-farm Work

When the farm wives worked off the farm their earnings were often an important part of farm finances and in some cases were essential in order to keep the farm enterprise viable. The dependence of farm families on off-farm work is often underestimated as Ghorayshi (1989, p.581) explained,

> By reducing financial constraints, farm wives with off-farm work may help male operators to concentrate their efforts full-time on the farm.

The importance of off-farm earnings was also noted by Kilmurray and Bradley (1989) who described them as a 'major contribution' to farm households. Given the farm wives extensive involvement in all areas of farm work it was inevitable that the numbers who had off-farm employment would be relatively small. Twenty-four per cent of the women had paid employment and of those thirteen per cent worked part-time. This off-farm work was quite varied. Five of the women undertook secretarial related work. A further five were professionally qualified as either teachers or nurses. The remaining women were in service employment. Significantly over ninety per cent of the women who worked off the farm reported that they were responsible for childcare. This supports McWilliams' (1990) contention that regardless of the fact that women in paid employment do reduce the time spent on housework they continue to carry the domestic burden. Additionally over eighty per cent of the women reported that they remained responsible for farm administration and were still involved, although to a lesser extent, in farm manual work. Previous studies on women's paid work (Abbott and Wallace, 1990, Montgomery and Davies, 1991) have highlighted the fact that women in paid employment usually have a 'double burden' as they remain responsible for domestic work. This study demonstrates that many farm wives who have off-farm employment have in fact a 'triple burden' as they are expected to remain responsible for domestic work and also a range of farm work.

The Farm Decision-making Process

Only nineteen per cent of the farm wives were regularly involved in making the day-to-day decisions on the farm, while twenty-four per cent were involved in the long term decision-making. Day to day decision-making was often deciding what work should be undertaken while long-term decision-making included assessing what new machinery was needed, future numbers of stock and land use.

Table 4: *Farm Wives' Involvement in the Farm Decision-Making Process.*

	Never		Emergency		Occasionally		Regularly	
	No.	%	No.	%	No.	%	No.	%
All farms								
Day-to-day management decisions	28	35	7	9	30	37	15	19
Long-term management decisions	27	34	5	6	29	36	19	24
Less Favoured Area								
Day-to-day management decisions	12	30	3	8	16	40	9	22
Long-term management decisions	15	38	2	5	13	33	10	25
Lowland Area								
Day-to-day management decisions	16	40	4	10	14	35	6	15
Long-term management decisions	12	30	3	8	16	40	9	22

Source: Survey of Farm Wives 1992.

When asked about making final farm decisions only fifteen per cent of the women claimed that they would be confident about making a final farm decision without consulting their husbands. This was in stark contrast with their husbands' role in final farm decision-making. All of the women reported that their husbands often made final farm decisions that they knew nothing about. One fifty-two year old woman from the Lowland area explained the difficulties of the farm decision-making process.

> Many's a time he has come home and said well I've done this or that. If he meets somebody in the town or in the saleyard, then the decisions are made there and then. It's like that in farming.

Another forty-two year old woman explained that this exclusion from final farm decision-making was unavoidable in farming.

> If somebody offers him a good price for the lambs or the sheep, he's not likely to say hold on 'till I ask the wife. If the offer is made then it has to be taken or turned down there and then. If he thinks the price is good enough then I won't argue.

Other women though clearly felt aggrieved by this male domination of the decision-making process. A thirty-seven year old woman explained:

> God it really maddens me, but he does it anyway. I rear the calves and I have a good eye for them. He wouldn't know the first thing about them. Yet he comes back from the saleyard either having decided to sell them or worse still he's bought more calves that I wouldn't have looked at.

Farm decision-making was controlled by the men. The farm wives' participation was sporadic and final farm decisions were overwhelmingly the remit of the men. Having a legal interest in the land did not automatically assign the women a place in the farm decision-making process. Salamon and Keim (1979) suggested that women's power in the farming community was related to their ownership of land. But in Ireland women rarely have any ownership rights and traditionally farms are inherited by males. Twenty-two of these farm wives were legal partners in the farm business but there was no relationship between being a legal partner and being involved in the farm decision-making process. Undoubtedly the process of farm decision making is a complex one, as women can be involved in, participate in, consulted on, or asked for advice on decision-making. There was a small difference between types of agricultural area in relation to decision-making. The farm wives in the Less Favoured area were more likely to be involved in the day-to-day farm decision-making than the long term decision-making while in the Lowland area the results were reversed. This is not surprising as the women in the Less Favoured area were more involved in the farm manual work and were therefore more likely to be forced to make day-to-day operational decisions when their husbands were unavailable.

The women in the Lowland areas were however more likely to be considered as partners and were therefore more involved in the long-term decision-making process.

Household Budgeting

The way in which money is distributed within the household is related to the power relationships within the household. Previous studies on women's responsibility for controlling and spending the family finances have focused on urban women (Hunt, 1980, Pahl, 1980, Whitehead, 1981, Graham, 1984). Consequently it was deemed important that the study should explore the relationship between farm wives and money management. This relationship was a complex and complicated one due to the nature of payment on farms. In order to gain some understanding of this difficult and hitherto unexplored subject it was decided to compare methods of money management on farms with an urban based typology suggested by Pahl (1980). She identified four main patterns of money management:

1.   The whole wage system where one partner was responsible for managing all of the household expenses.

2.   The shared management system where both partners had access to all of the household money and they were jointly responsible for money management.

3.   The allowance system where the husband gave his wife a set amount of money and she was expected to pay for agreed items of expenditure.

4.   The independent management system where both partners had an income and neither had access to all of the household money.

It was decided to divide the whole wage system into whole wage controlled by man and whole wage controlled by woman, in order to make it clear which partner was responsible for the money management. The dominant pattern of money management in farm households was shared management but as Table Five shows it still accounted for the method of money management on less than half of the farms.

Table 5: *Types of Money Management Systems.*

	LESS FAVOURED AREA	LOWLAND
	%	%
Shared management	42.5	42.5
Allowance system	25.0	20.0
Whole wage (wives)	20.0	25.0
Whole wage (husbands)	7.5	22.5
Independent management	5.0	0.0

Source: Survey of Farm Wives 1992.

In the shared management system the women claimed that they had joint control of the family finances. Yet when this shared management was analyzed, in the vast majority of cases it meant that the farm wives were responsible for the management of the family finances but the real financial control remained with the men. Just six of the women who reported that they had joint financial control had joint bank accounts with their husbands. The official meetings with the bank manager were viewed as men's business. Women were usually consulted about these meetings but were rarely present. Their role was generally limited to less official bank business such as withdrawing petty cash for the farm. A farm wife from the Lowland area explained that this was seen as the most suitable arrangement.

> I don't have my name on the cheque book but I don't think that really matters. If I need money he gives it to me. It's not as if I am kept short or anything.

Conversely another woman from the Lowland area claimed that having a joint bank account was very important.

> For me there was no two ways about it. I have always had a bank account and when we got married it was automatically a joint account. There's nothing worse than having to ask for money when you need it. Why should I? It's as much mine as it is his.

Shared financial management translates into different meanings for the farm couple. For the men it usually means having the ultimate financial control, while for the women it means administering the financial affairs of the household.

The inequalities between the farming couple were again evident in the allowance system. In all instances of this financial management system it was the woman who was given an allowance by the man. In the majority of cases where this system had been adopted the women had no say in the rate of this allowance. This was however more a feature of the Less Favoured area than the

Lowland area. In the Less Favoured area eight of the women claimed that the allowance was set by their husbands, while in the Lowland area three of the women were given a set allowance. For these women their husbands' control of the allowance was generally unquestioned.

> There never really has been any discussion about what the allowance should be. He gives me what he thinks should be enough.

> I've never really had any say on how much the allowance is. It's up to him to decide what we can afford to spend. Sometimes if we have done well I might get a bit extra.

The allowance system was usually adopted when the men were working off the farm. Ten of the twelve men who worked off the farm paid their wives a monthly allowance.

Women who were responsible for the whole wage system were overwhelmingly managers of poverty. Similar to the situation in working class urban households, this system of financial management was related to lower levels of income. Of the fourteen women who were responsible for the management of the family finances, eleven described it as a 'chore' and an added 'burden'. Typically when the farm income was irregular and relatively low the women were responsible for household budgeting. Many of the women described how this responsibility did not afford them extra status on the farm but was a hardship.

> It really is a headache, the money just goes no length. It just gets harder and harder there's more and more to be paid out and no more money to do it with.

These women talked about 'getting by' and 'robbing Peter to pay Paul'. Money and expenses were a constant source of worry and stress and the pressure of this financial management was not always shared with their husbands.

> He just thinks that I should be able to manage. We'll get enough to do us is his answer but he doesn't know the half of it.

It might be expected from the work of Pahl (1980) that the middle income level would be associated with a change to an allowance system, as this was seen as a more egalitarian method of money management. However, in this study relatively high income levels are associated with the whole wage system managed by the men. Regular relatively high incomes on dairy farms were associated with the man managing all of the family finances. In ten of the twelve cases were there was a whole wage system managed by the man the families were living on dairy farms. A woman in the Lowland area explained that her husband had always managed the farm accounts.

> He did it before we were married and he just continued to do it. I get spending money every month and he does the rest.

Conclusion

In some of the existing rural based literature there has been a tendency to assume that the farm wife is no longer involved in farm production. It has been suggested that the modernization and mechanisation of agriculture has led to an erosion of her traditional role. Crozier (1985) noted that farm women were no longer responsible for farm manual labour. The 'final removal' of women from agricultural production was described by Bouquet (1984) in her study of farm women's roles in the South-West of England. She asserted that women were no longer involved in farm work as changes in British farming had the effect of relieving women of farm work. In their study of rural life in Ireland, Hannan and Katsiaouni (1977) claimed there had been a considerable shift away from a rigid sexual division of labour on farms. They described a more egalitarian farm family and completely ignored the fundamental inequalities. The importance of the farm wife's contribution was glossed over. It has been suggested by Duggan (1987) that farm literature has deliberately 'reconstructed' the farming woman as the farmer's wife, resulting in the underestimation and devaluation of her work. This study has shown that the life of the Irish farm wife has changed little since it was described in Arensberg and Kimball's (1940) anthropological study of rural life. The fundamental inequalities that were evident in that study have remained almost totally intact. There is a clear gendered division of labour on the farm. The farm wife is almost entirely responsible for the unpaid domestic labour and child care. There was no move towards a more egalitarian distribution of this work, indeed her levels of domestic responsibility had in some cases increased. Men on farms were even less likely to assist with domestic work than their non-farming counterparts. Even when the woman was in paid employment she still carried the bulk of domestic responsibility, often re-organizing the domestic work to evenings and weekends.

Usually the farm wife acted as an unpaid secretary dealing with the administrative work on the farm. She was also extensively involved in the farm manual work which often included responsibility for a number of enterprises. There was still a high degree of specialization of chores on the farm, with the farm wife restricted to mundane repetitive work. Her work was usually thought of as unskilled while men's work was seen as highly skilled and of economic importance to the farm enterprise.

The farm wife's extensive involvement in farm labour did not automatically afford her involvement in the farm decision-making process. This was controlled by men with only a small number of women regularly involved. The farm wives were expected to work on the farm but had little or no control over the conditions or results of their work. The methods of money management within the farm family provided another illustration of the inequalities between the farming couple. The farm wives were often managers of poverty on the farms. They did not have equal access to the household resources and were only responsible for the household finances when it involved budgeting. When examining the social life of the farm couple the similarities with Arensberg and Kimball (1940) are striking. Rural social life was still marked by a large degree of separation, with the farming couple rarely socializing together. The farm wife's social activities tended to reinforce rather than offer an alternative to her traditional role.

A major aim of feminist research is to make the invisible visible and it is hoped that by highlighting the role and status of farm women their marginal position will be recognized. A major step towards making the term 'farmer' less synonymous with men, would be for official statistics to count the labour contribution of women. A broader definition of farm work needs to be adopted as the current narrow definition means that much of the work of the farm wife remains concealed and unacknowledged.

Discussion Topics

1.   Discuss the importance of Irish anthropological studies in providing an understanding of the work and lives of farm wives.

2.   Discuss the significance of the fact that family farming means that the workplace and the household are not separate.

3.   Discuss the main ways in which budgeting on a family farm differs from urban household budgeting.

4.   In what ways could the state or society generally help to make the term 'farmer' less synonymous with men?

References and Further Reading

Arensberg, C A and Kimball, S J. 1940 *Family and Community in Ireland* Harvard: Harvard University Press.

Abbott, P and Wallace, C. 1990 *An Introduction to Sociology: Feminist Perspectives* London: Routledge.

Bouquet, M. 1984 'Women's Work in Rural South-West England', in Long, N. (ed.) *Family and Work in Rural Societies* London: Tavistock.

Bradley, H. 1989 *Men's Work, Women's Work. A Sociological History of the Sexual Division Of Labour in Employment* Oxford: Polity Press.

Brody, H. 1973 *Inishkillane: Change and Decline in the West of Ireland* London: Allen Lane.

Buchanan, W I, Errington, A and Giles A. 1982 *The Farmer's Wife: Her Role in the Management of the Business* Study No.2, Farm Management Unit, University of Reading.

Cecil, R, Offer, J and St Leger, F. 1987 *Informal Welfare* Alershot: Gower Press.

Cowan, R S. 1983 *More Work For Mother: The Ironies of Household Technology from the Open Hearth to the Microwave* New York: Basic Books.

Craig, R A. 1979 *Down on the Farm: Role Conflicts of Australian Farm Women* Paper presented at National Conference of Women in the Country, Victoria: Macmillan Rural Studies Centre.

Crozier, R M. 1985 *Patterns of Hospitality in a Rural Ulster Community* Unpublished Ph.D. thesis, Dept of Social Anthropology, The Queen's University Belfast.

Duggan, C. 1987 'Farming Women or Farmers Wives? Women in the Irish Farming Press', in Curtain, C, Jackson P and O'Connor B. (eds.) *Gender in Irish Society* Galway: Galway University Press.

Fahey, T. 1992 'Housework, the Household Economy and Economic Development in Ireland since the 1920's' *Irish Journal of Sociology*, Vol.2 pp.42-69.

Gasson, R. 1981 'Roles of Women on Farms: A Pilot Study' *Journal of Agricultural Economics* Vol.32, No.1 pp.11-20.

Gasson, R. 1992 'Farmers' Wives - their Contribution to the Farm Business' *Journal of Agricultural Economics*, Vol.43, No.1 pp.74-87.

Ghorayshi, P. 1989 'The Indispensable Nature of Wives' Work on the Farm Family Enterprise', *Canadian Journal of Sociology and Anthropology*, Vol.26 pp.571-595.

Graham, H. 1984 *Women Health and the Family* Brighton: Wheatsheaf.

Hannan, D and Katsiaouni, L. 1977 *Traditional Families? From Culturally Prescribed to Negotiated Roles in Farm Families* Paper 87, Dublin: Economic and Social Research Institute.

Harris, R. 1972 *Prejudice and Tolerance in Ulster: A Study of Neighbours and Strangers in a Border Community* Manchester: Manchester University Press.

Hastings, M. 1987-8 'Farming Wives as Business Managers' *Farm Management* Vol.6, pp.309-315.

Hunt, P. 1980 *Gender and Class Consciousness* London: Macmillan.

Kilmurray, A and Bradley, C. 1989 *Rural Women in South Armagh: Needs and Aspirations* Derry: Rural Action Project.

Leyton, E. 1975 *The One Blood: Kinship and Class in an Irish Village* Newfoundland: St John's Institute of Social and Economic Research, Memorial University of Newfoundland.

Little, J. 1987 'Gender Relations in Rural Areas: the Importance of Women's Domestic Role', *Journal of Rural Studies* Vol.3, No 4 pp.335-342.

Magee, S A. 1990 *A Statistical Review of Agriculturally Less Favoured Areas of Northern Ireland* Belfast: D.A.N.I.

Matthews, A. 1981 'Women in the Farm Labour Force', *Irish Farmers' Monthly*, March.

Montgomery, P and Davies, C. 1991 'A Woman's Place in Northern Ireland', in Stringer P and Robinson G. (eds.) 1991 *Social Attitudes in Northern Ireland* Belfast: Blackstaff Press.

McWilliams, M. 1990 *Housework and Women in Ireland in 1990's* Report of conference organised by the Worker's Education Authority, Women's Studies Branch.

Owens, M. 1992 *Women in Rural Development: A Hit or Miss Affair?* European Centre for Information and the Promotion of Rural Development, University College, Galway.

O'Hara, P. 1987 *Farm Women: Concerns and Issues of an Undervalued Workforce* Report No.2, Women's Studies Forum, University College Dublin.

Pahl, J. 1980 'Patterns of Money Management Within Marriage', *Journal of Social Policy* Vol.9 pp.313-335.

Pearson, J. 1979 'Note on Female Farmers', *Rural Sociology* Vol.44, No.1 pp.189-200.

Sachs, C. 1993 *Invisible Farmers. Women's Work in Agricultural Production* New Jersey: Rhinehart and Allenherd.

Salamon, S and Keim, A M. 1979 'Landownership and Women's Power in a mid-stream Farming Community', *Journal of Marriage and the Family* Vol.41 pp.109-119.

Shortall, S. 1991 'The Dearth of Data on Irish Farm Wives: A Critical Review of the Literature', *The Economic and Social Review* 22 pp.311-332.

Shortall, S. 1992 'Power Analysis and Farm Wives: An Empirical Study of the Power Relationships Affecting Women on Irish Farms', *Sociologia Ruralis*, Vol.22, No.4 pp.431-451.

Tovey, H. 1992 'Rural Sociology in Ireland: A Review', *Irish Journal of Sociology* Vol.2 pp.96-121.

Whatmore, S J. 1988 *The 'Other Half' of the Family Farm: An Analysis of the Position of Farm Wives in the Familial Gender Division of Labour on the Farm*, Unpublished Ph.D. thesis, University of London.

Whatmore, S J. 1991 *Farming Women. Gender, Work and Family Enterprise* London: Macmillan.

Whitehead, A. 1981 'I'm Hungry Mum: The Politics of Domestic Budgeting' in Young, K, Wolkowitz, C and McCullagh, R. (eds.) *Of Marriage and the Market* London: CSE.

24.
Gender, Power and Farming:
Northern Ireland, Canada and Norway Compared
Sally Shortall

Introduction

Recent research has illustrated the difficulties of conceptualising the role of women on family farms. Their farm work is frequently not counted, they are under-represented in farming organisations, and they rarely own land. They are 'invisible' (Sachs, 1983). While international research has documented this situation, there are a number of concurrent instances over the last two decades of farm women becoming increasingly visible in the public space of farming. One such instance is Northern Ireland. This chapter will examine the case of Northern Ireland and compare it with two other examples of women moving into the public space of farming in Norway and Canada. In each case the extent to which farm women have come to the fore is different, as are the circumstances which facilitated the social change. In Norway, the State played a key role. In Canada, the mobilisation of farm women was key, and in Northern Ireland, agricultural advisers were the main impetus.

In Northern Ireland, interviews with agricultural advisers and farm women in the training groups were carried out in 1994/1995. This is described in greater detail elsewhere (Shortall, 1996). Work with the Canadian Farm Women's Network was conducted between 1990-1992 (Shortall, 1993, 1994). The Norwegian case is developed from the extensive literature that is available on farm women in Norway. The unusual events in Norway render it an invaluable comparative case.

Women and Farming: An Overview

Thorough reviews of the literature on women and farming do exist, one of the most comprehensive is Sarah Whatmore's recent work (1994). This section will confine itself to identifying those aspects of the literature on women and farming which relate to the three case studies. These are: inheritance and entry to farming, defining farm work, the farming media, involvement in farming organisations, and participation in agricultural training.

Inheritance and Entry to Farming

The patrilineal line of inheritance is pervasive in the industrialised world, and for example, it has been documented for Ireland (Shortall, 1991, 1992, O'Hara, 1994), Britain (Gasson, 1984, Whatmore, 1991), Australia (James, 1982, Alston, 1990), Canada (Reimer, 1986, Ghorayshi, 1989) and the United States (Sachs, 1983, Rosenfeld, 1985). The typical passing of land from father to son is considered one of the key sources of inequalities in gender relations in agriculture (Gasson et al., 1988). The patrilineal line of inheritance is a central social structure in agriculture which powerfully reinforces the image of farming as a male occupation (Shortall, 1992). For the majority of women on farms, their entry is through marriage. Farming practice fashions sons rather than daughters as family 'successors' (Whatmore et al., 1994). Where women do own land, it is an important dimension of power (Salamon and Keim, 1979), however the patrilineal line of inheritance makes this an unusual event. Inheritance laws in Norway are unique, and considered in depth further on.

Defining Farm Work

The farm work that women do is probably the most researched topic in the literature on farm women. Research has shown that the typical definition of farm work is too narrow and does not cover all of the work essential to the farm business. Much of the work that is not covered by the usual definition is work carried out by women (Gasson, 1984, Reimer, 1986, Alston, 1990, Shortall, 1992). Some aspects of the work women do are difficult to quantify, such as running errands for the farm (Shortall, 1992). In many cases it is the continual presence of women who can be called on when necessary that is most important (Gasson, 1984). It is the virtual impossibility of separating productive and reproductive work roles on the farm which make it difficult to conceptualise the farm work done by women (Elbert, 1988). Typologies like those developed by Whatmore (1991), and Rosenfeld (1985) illustrate that women also do non-agricultural work which may be essential for the farm business (i.e., either on or off farm employment that supports the farm). It is frequently the case that women have to tabulate and prove the farm work they do in a way that is not necessary for men (Alston, 1995).

The Media and Farming

Farming tends to be represented in the media as a male occupation. Until quite recently, women rarely featured in farming television programmes, and farming newspapers reinforce 'farmer' and 'farm wife' work roles (Duggan, 1987, Bell and Pandy, 1989, Shortall, 1992, Alston, 1995). More recent research has analysed how tractor advertising reinforces images of masculinity (Brandth, 1995). Brandth points out, and media studies more generally have noted, representations are not merely reflections of their sources, but contribute to the shaping of them.

Farming Organisations

In general, there are few women in longer established farming unions and farming associations (Shortall, 1992, Teather, 1996). In some cases, organisations have specific committees for women or the farm family. For example, the Ulster Farmers' Union (UFU) executive of eighty is all male, and they have recently formed a farm family committee to deal with family and women's issues (The Farmers' Journal, March, 1996). These committees however, tend to be somewhat ghettoised and have a lower profile than the organisations mainstream activities. Many women on farms lack farming networks, especially with other women, and women are enthusiastic about any formal or informal opportunities to network (MacKenzie, 1992, Shortall, 1994, Teather, 1996). Gender segregation raises more general sociological and feminist questions about whether organisations confirm stereotypes and reinforce difference by this approach, or whether it provides space for both men and women to participate, and pursue different agendas. Within farming, it is argued that the involvement of women in farming organisations alters the representation of farming through the visible involvement of women, and also through the broadened understanding of farming issues which seems to follow. Women tend to bring issues concerning the farm family, succession and inheritance, and stress and isolation to the fore (Teather, 1994, Shortall, 1994). It becomes more difficult to understand family farming as essentially a productive activity, and easier to acknowledge it as a social form.

Agricultural Education and Training

The participation of women in agricultural education and training has changed over time. In the past, particular areas of farm work, notably dairying and poultry, were considered women's work. Agricultural education and training was targeted at women, and many participated (Bourke, 1993, van der Burg, 1994). In Northern Ireland, one of the three colleges was previously a college for women. As production became more commercialised, these areas moved into the male domain and training was targeted at men. Currently, few European farm women are trained (EC, 1988). Training for agriculture is vocational, and usually it is not undertaken unless the person knows they will own a farm. It is not surprising then that few young women undertake training, as they are unlikely to inherit a farm. After they have entered farming through marriage, education and training is directed at the 'farmer', and procedures of advertising and organising training illustrates that women are not expected to attend (Shortall, 1992). Frequently notification of short courses are addressed to the men on farms. Women who are not from a farm background have greater difficulty performing tasks on the farm as familiarity with farming is their main source of knowledge (Alston, 1995). Even those women brought up on farms are likely to have been socialised away from particular types of work as children. The lack of a general agricultural education restricts women's effectiveness in taking initiatives and implementing new approaches (van der Burg, 1994).

In addition to the low participation rates of women, the content of educational programmes may exclude women. Agricultural education has been described as gender specific education, oriented toward farm men's fields of labour (van der Burg, 1994). Even if women participated to a greater extent in educational courses, the training they receive will only partially relate to the work they do on farms. Women's involvement in agricultural education and training raises constitutive questions about training, and the understanding of farming for which it caters. In other words, if we consider the training farm women require, it necessitates a questioning of what is commonly understood as farming.

The feminist study of farm women has broadly followed more general trends in feminist studies. It has progressed from identifying the work and activities of farm women, to illustrating that the gender divisions in farming have cultural rather than biological foundations (Whatmore, 1994). Each of the areas reviewed; inheritance, farm work, the media, farming organisations and agricultural training are organised on cultural rather than biological principles. The three case studies Norway, Canada and Northern Ireland exemplify different attempts to question the legitimacy of the way these areas are organised. We begin with Norway and the patrilineal line of inheritance.

Three Case Studies

(1) Norway

State intervention in the farm sector occurs nearly entirely on behalf of the enterprise (Meyer and Labao, 1994). It tends to deal with farm business matters rather than farming culture. It is not surprising that the state which did dramatically intervene in customary farming practice was a social democratic Nordic state; Norway. Norwegian social policy has been underpinned by a commitment to equality throughout most of this century. The state is responsible to provide and guarantee adequate levels of welfare for all members of society.

Norway's welfare state, like that of all social democracies, is couched within a broad egalitarian ideology (Esping-Andersen, 1988, p.170).

Farm Women and Ownership of Land

A strong cultural commitment to gender equality brought forward a law of succession, the allodial law, which gives the right to take over the farm intact to the eldest child irrespective of gender (Haugen, 1994, Jodahl, 1994). In spite of strong male resistance to the new law, the state brought it forward as a matter of principle (Blekesaune et al., 1993, Haugen and Brandth, 1994).

Law however, is only one social force that influences norms and cultural behaviour (Voyce, 1994). Although the law has changed, there is 'an ideological lag' in farming practice, and it is questionable whether state policy is enough to alter the gendered structure of agricultural social relations (Haugen, 1994). Children and teenagers on farms continue to experience gender socialisation, such that boys are supported to take up their allodial right to inherit the farm, and girls are more often socialised to relinquish it (Haugen, 1994). Formal equality now exists, but different attitudes, practices and expectations based on gender specific roles persist. In addition, farming remains a male occupation, and women entering farming in a professional capacity conform with the provisions that already exist for men (Haugen and Brandth, 1994).

There is no doubt that formal political equality is of limited value if the traditional practice of unequal gender relations persists. Even so, legal changes may constitute the first step (Haugen, 1994). The allodial law has changed the context of women on farms in Norway, through challenging the patrilineal line of inheritance. It questions the basis of legitimacy of traditional gendered farming practice. This challenge came from the State.

(2) Canada

Canada has a relatively active and visible feminist movement. It was influenced by the development of the American feminist movement in the 1960s, and the Canadian feminist movement has occasionally been more successful at achieving legal reform than its southern counterparts (Backhouse and Flaherty, 1992). The farm women's movement developed in the 1970s. While it did not develop out of the more general Canadian feminist movement, the organisation of farm women was no doubt facilitated by its existence.

The first farm women's group in Canada was formed in 1975, and by 1991, there were forty two new farm women's groups (Shortall, 1993, 1994). Three key factors set the scene for the farm women's groups to develop. Firstly, women initially organised because of their concern about the 'farm crisis';

increased farm bankruptcies, financial difficulties and cutbacks in rural social services. Secondly, the women's movement meant that increasing attention was paid to the concerns and views of women, and increased state funding was provided for projects dealing with women's issues. Thirdly, a high profile divorce case, Murdoch v. Murdoch, caused a great deal of public debate about the value of farm women's work. Irene Murdoch worked on her husband's farm, and after an arduous legal battle, she was awarded one quarter of the ranch's value. More high profile cases followed the Murdoch case, and also raised questions about the appropriate division of land on divorce. This caused public debate about the value of the work women do on the farm and in the farm house (MacKenzie, 1992).

The farm women's groups then, came into being in a context where women and farm women received increased attention. The Canadian Farm Women's Network (CFWN), a National umbrella organisation for the scattered farm women's groups was formed in 1985. It is the CFWN, not the Canadian State which has provided the main impetus for change regarding the status of farm women through lobbying, providing networks and proposing alternatives.

Farm Women and Ownership of Land

While ownership of farm property is an issue that the CFWN have acted on, it is in a very different way to the Norwegian case. An Ontario women's group published (1987) and later revised (1994) a manual titled; Cover Your Assets: A Guide to Farm Partnerships (MacKenzie, 1992, Teather, 1996). This booklet details both the benefits for the farm (tax advantages, loan entitlements), and the necessity for women of legalising their stake in their business partnership. The patrilineal line of inheritance is not questioned, rather women are encouraged to safeguard their legal position after entering a farm business, usually through marriage.

Representation in Farming Organisations

Farm women quickly realised that they met few women in farming organisations, in government farming bodies and committees, or on marketing boards. When they raised this issue, they were often told no suitably qualified women existed (Shortall, 1994). The CFWN decided to form a 'talent bank' of farm women; this is a directory of qualified farm women who can be proposed as vacancies arise in farming organisations. Provincial networks provide training for women who wish to sit on boards and councils. This strategy has had some limited success. Nonetheless, women continue to struggle to ensure adequate representation (Farm Living, 9 November, 1995). Farm women have noted too that it is more difficult to include women in traditional grass-root type farming organisations, rather than in federal or provincial government farming organisations, boards and committees (Farm Living, 23 October, 1994). The CFWN has called for changed regulations regarding membership, and has also urged farming organisations to deliberately recruit, support and develop women at grassroots, district and regional levels.

The Canadian Farm Women's Network highlights the limited number of women in farming organisations. Through their talent bank and lobbying of organisations, they actively try to increase the representation of women. In doing so they are questioning both previously taken for granted farming norms, and the legitimacy of institutions that are unrepresentative on a gender basis.

The Farming Media

The CFWN, and most provincial farm women's networks, issue regular newsletters. This provides an alternative source of farming information for women. It also provides a forum where women can discuss and debate issues of particular relevance to women, such as partnership arrangements, the availability of credit for women operators, and the status of women's farm work. In addition, the farm women's networks provide training for farm women's groups to deal effectively with the media. Women have received training on public speaking and drafting press releases. In recent years many provincial newspapers with farming supplements carry regular articles about the farm women's networks, and short pieces written by farm women.

The farm women's newsletters have a wide circulation amongst members. Although modest, there is increased representation of women in more mainstream farming media. Again, the farm women's movement have acted as a key force bringing about change through providing an alternative form of communication, and training women to effectively deal with the general farming media.

Defining Farm Work

A key concern of the CFWN is how to define farm work and how to ascertain the value of farm women's work. It is a frequently discussed topic in the newsletters and at farm women's conferences. Since 1990, editorials in the CFWN newsletter have urged women to make their farm work visible by changing the title of their work so that it can be counted in the census of agriculture (Shortall, 1994). Newsletters feature articles by farm women that say discussion and dialogue has raised their appreciation of the often invisible and unrecognised work they do (OFWN newsletter 3,4, 1991). One of the most significant achievements of the farm women's network was their successful lobbying of Statistics Canada to change the Census of Agriculture questionnaire. Prior to 1991, it was only possible to cite one person as farm operator. Women argued that in instances of partnerships between men and women, it was usually the man who was cited in the census form as the farm operator, thus rendering women invisible. This practice was changed in 1991, and now up to three operators can be named. It is generally accepted that the change came about because of effective lobbying by the farm women's network (Farm Women's Bureau, 1996). The change only increases the visibility of women in terms of the typically 'male' farm work that they do, but nonetheless, it marked a very important triumph for the farm women's network.

(3) Northern Ireland

Northern Ireland has been a contested region of the United Kingdom since the partition of Ireland in 1922, and the establishment of the Irish State. The political cleavage between unionism and nationalism has defined political economic and social life since the 1920s (Rooney, 1995). Reference to fair employment and equality in Northern Ireland typically refer to Protestants and Catholics rather than men and women (Davies et al., 1995).

Women of many insecure societies are stifled by the social and sexual conservatism typical of such societies (Meaney, 1993). Northern Ireland is considered profoundly unstable (Rooney, 1995), and both the church and state in the North have shaped conservative ideology and the traditional thinking behind major institutions (McWilliams, 1993). The women's movement in the North also reflects political and religious tensions. Many feminist issues are political, and divide women along political lines (Meaney, 1993). Many women (and nationalist women in particular) feel that feminism has taken a back seat to the political struggle (Connolly, 1995).

Northern Ireland then, is a conservative region, where political and religious divisions are of paramount importance. Unlike Norway, where gender equality is a key political goal, in the North the key political issue is equality of the religious communities. Unlike Canada, where state funding for women's groups (including farm women's groups) is widely available, women's groups in Northern Ireland receive less funding than in the rest of the UK (McWilliams, 1993). Gender issues are not of the same priority as political and religious issues. The role of the state, and of the women's movement in mobilising farm women then, is likely to be more restricted.

Agriculture in Northern Ireland

The farming structure in the North and Republic of Ireland are similar for historical reasons. In both, practically all farms are owner occupied. In Britain, about thirty per cent of farms are worked by tenant farmers (NIEC, 1989). The average size of farm is thirty five hectares, also closer to the average in the Republic (23ha) than the rest of the UK (71ha) (NIEC, 1994). The structure of farming reflects global patterns with a decline in the number of full-time farmers, an increase in part-time farming and a concentration of holdings (NIEC, 1989). There is considerable variation in the size of farms within Northern Ireland. The larger, more prosperous farms tend to be protestant and these are typically the farms with whom the agricultural advisory service have most regular contact (PAFT, 1996).

Women in Agriculture

Almost all women on farms in Northern Ireland 'married into' their occupation. Few women farm independently, although some women have sole responsibility for the farm if their spouse has off farm employment. The women interviewed reported considerable involvement in their farms, for example; milking on a full time basis, harvesting potatoes, rearing calves and pigs, doing farm accounts, and influencing farm business management and development.

The participation of women in agricultural education and training is low. For the year 1994/1995, 1151 people enrolled in full and part-time agricultural courses in the three agricultural colleges in the North. Women accounted for between one and four and a half per cent. On-going training is provided for adults in farming, consisting of short courses and discussion groups. Again attendance is almost entirely male, and the discussion groups are known colloquially as 'the men's groups'.

The Formation of the Farm Women's Groups

Four of the forty two agricultural advisers in Northern Ireland are women. One of these felt that farm business plans would be improved if women were more vociferous in stating their opinions and ideas when farm business plans were discussed. She was also aware that women were doing farm accounts and would benefit from a more complete understanding of the financial state of the farm. Despite repeatedly asking the women to come along to existing training provisions, women did not participate. She decided to organise some training specifically for women, and discussed the idea with two of the other women advisers. Then they actively solicited women on the farms with which they had contact. These three women advisers are responsible for the creation of the five farm women's groups.

The advisers formed the groups in response to a practical, technical problem. They thought that the farms with which they had contact would be more effective if the women on those farms were trained. In other words, the formation of the groups was not motivated by political, moral or feminist considerations. Clearly there is a gender factor involved in the fact that it was women advisers who recognised the lack of training for women as problematic.

The Farm Women's Groups

Women have received training on such topics as calving, lambing, filling out forms, farm accounts, producing quality milk, business development, planning for succession, inheritance and tax, computer skills, and they have had sessions with vets and representatives of meal companies. They have also had sessions on leadership skills, chairing a session, farm safety and dealing with stress. The women were very positive about the farm women's groups, and see them as a new departure. One woman said:

> there have always been discussion groups for men but not for women. You could go but you would stick out like a sore thumb. I would go to those if they were more fifty: fifty (men and women).

Another woman said:

> I'd never been at anything like this before - I would rather join something I know something about rather than something I know nothing about.

In addition to the knowledge gained, women spoke about the validation of their knowledge as a result of participating in the groups:

> I don't doubt myself so much when I go to do something machine wise. Instead of asking, I have the confidence to just go and do it now.

Another woman described how training had allowed others, including her husband, to accept her views and opinions more easily as valid and informed. The women spoke favourably about the opportunity to spend time with other farm women. Women on farms do not have a public space where they can meet other farm women on the basis of a shared occupation. One woman put it like this:

> We are all in the same boat, we all have it (farming) in common - if you go into town and say something about farming, they look at you and have no idea what you are talking about.

Women pass on information and support each other. It is their first opportunity to participate in a formal occupational network.

Women spoke about how they were encouraged to attend the training groups by the women advisers. For many, this represented a real change in the way they were approached by an organisation they previously considered disinterested in them. Many felt they would be out of place at mainstream training provisions. This is reflected in the following quotes:

You find it's your husband gets the invite.

You would be lucky if there was one other woman at a talk.

Betty encouraged me to go along.

This illustrates that organisational culture is influential. Even without the wider context of state direction, or a women's movement, organisational behaviour can include or exclude farm women. It is misleading however to present the changed approach to the farm women as a change in organisational culture. It does not run that deep. Colleagues of the women advisers continue to have difficulty accepting the training as such rather than as an additional provision for women. This relates to the difficulties conceptualising women's work roles. In order to recognise the value of training, it is necessary to recognise the work. The training is gendered, it is for farm women, and no doubt this exacerbates the problem as training for men, which is no doubt taken as the norm, is overtly organised around types of farming (dairying, tillage, etc.) and the virtual gender exclusivity is not formally stated. The advisers recounted the views of senior colleagues:

I was asked 'are we becoming Women's Institute organisers now?'

The view of many people is it's all very nice but so what? What is it going to do to develop the farm?

Key individuals within an organisation have made a difference. However, it is difficult to assess how sustained, or extensive an exercise this can be without a wider frame of support.

Some Comments About Farm Women's Groups in Northern Ireland

The agricultural advisers were not concerned about changing the system of agricultural training, but rather with assisting farm women to gain access to training. This leaves the existing model, based on the idea of the male farmer, intact. The provision for women is additional, and it leads to some irrational practices like duplicating sessions with the vet and meal representative for the women's groups and the men's discussion groups.

The training groups illustrate that women will participate in training if they are given the opportunity, and encouragement to do so. The groups consist of eighty women, which may seem like a small number. What is significant, is that nearly all of the women approached by the advisers attended, and the small size is more reflective of the limited effort given to the initiative within the agricultural service.

In the last few years in Northern Ireland, forms of inequality and discrimination other than religious are receiving increased attention (McWilliams, 1993). A recent policy has brought all government departments under scrutiny to see if their policies are discriminatory under five headings, one of which is gender (PAFT, 1996). This may provide a wider context of support for the farm women's groups. The groups are highlighted as one of the department of agriculture's provisions for women. This may not result in a great deal of change in gender and training patterns however. Frequently, existing programmes are elevated for reasons of political expediency. The training groups were formed to provide women with access, not to question the gendered nature and structure of agriculture training. In addition, the provision as it stands, only reaches a particular group of women. On a more positive note however, the formation of the training groups has flagged training for farm women as an issue, and in the current political climate it is possibly one that will receive increased attention.

Conclusion

In this chapter, three attempts to bring farm women into the public space of farming are examined. Each case has a different initial basis, or motivation for this change; in Norway, it is part of a wider societal commitment to gender equity, in Canada, it is farm women's concern about the farm family business and their own exclusion by a patriarchally organised occupation, in Northern Ireland, it is women agricultural advisers' concern with a technical problem - women on farms are untrained. Each case tackles particular aspects of farming culture that contribute to the absence of women from the public space of farming; in Norway the main emphasis is on inheritance of the farm, in Canada, women have focused on the definition of farm work, the farming media and representation in farming organisations, and in Northern Ireland the focus is on women's participation in agricultural education and training. Together, these case studies illustrate the multifaceted way in which farming culture affects the situation of women. They also illustrate the many processes by which change can occur; state action and state support, the mobilisation of women, and the attitudes of key individuals in contact with the farm. All of these overlap to a varying degree in each situation. In Norway and Canada, there is a more overt questioning of the patriarchal nature of farming and gender equity than in Northern Ireland. In Northern Ireland this was not the objective of the groups, rather it was to provide agricultural education and training for women. But by doing so, the formation of the groups tackles an aspect of farming culture that shape women's experience. Each case in its own way questions the basis of legitimacy of the image and culture of farming. This opens the door for greater change in the future.

Discussion Topics

1. Is state intervention enough to change the power structures of agriculture?

2. How important is feminism in changing our perception of farm work?

3. How does networking help to bring about change in farm women's lives? Is it the most effective and reliable strategy?

4. The political struggle in Northern Ireland is responsible for the low priority given to training for farm women. Discuss.

References and Further Reading

Alston, M. 1990 'Feminism and Farm Women' *Australian Social Work* 43 pp.213-234.

Alston, M. 1995 'Women and Their Work on Australian Farms' *Rural Sociology* 60 3 pp.521-532.

Backhouse, C and Flaherty D. (eds.) 1992 *Challenging Times: The Women's Movement in Canada and the United States* Montreal: McGill-Queen's University Press.

Bell, J and Pandy U. 1989 'Gender-role Stereotypes in Australian Farm Advertising' *Media Information Australia* 51 pp.45-59.

Blekesaune, Haney,A and Haugen M S. 1993 'On The Question of the Feminisation of Production on Part-time Farms: Evidence from Norway' *Rural Sociology* 58 1 pp.111-129.

Bourke, J. 1993 *Husbandry to Housewifery - Women, Economic Change, and Housework in Ireland, 1890-1914* Oxford: Clarendon Press.

Brandth, B. 1995 'Rural Masculinity in Transition - Gender Images in Tractor Advertisements' *Journal of Rural Studies* 11 2 pp.123-133.

Connolly, C. 1995 'Ourselves Alone? Clar na mBan Conference Report' *Feminist Review* 50 pp.118-127.

Davies, C, Heaton, N, Robinson, G and McWilliams M. 1995 'A Matter of Small Importance? Catholic and Protestant Women in the Northern Ireland Labour Market' Belfast: The Equal Opportunities Commission.

Duggan, C. 1987 'Farming Women or Farming Wives? Women in the Farming Press' pp.54-70 in Curtin, C, Jackson, P and O'Connor B. (eds.) *Gender in Irish Society* Galway: Galway University Press.

Elbert, S. 1988 'Women and Farming: Changing Structures, Changing Roles' in Haney, W and Knowles J. (eds.) *Women and Farming - Changing Roles, Changing Structures* New Jersey: Rowman and Allanheld.

Esping-Andersen, G. 1988 *Politics Against Markets* New Jersey: Princeton University Press.

European Commission. 1988 *Women in Agriculture Supplement to Women of Europe*, Brussels.

Farm Living, 1994 October 23.

Farm Living, 1995 November 9.

Farm Women's Bureau 1996 *Circular* March Vol.1 no.1.

Farmers' Journal, The. 1996 March

Gasson, R. 1984 'Farm Women in Europe: Their Need for Off Farm Employment' *Sociologia Ruralis* 24 3/4 pp.16-229.

Gasson, R, Crow, G, Errington, A, Hutson, J, Marsden, T and Winter D M. 1988 'The Farm as a Family Business: A Review' *Journal of Agricultural Economics* 39 pp.1-41.

Gasson, R. 1992 'Farmers' Wives: Their Contribution to the Farm Business' *Journal of Agricultural Economics* 43 pp.74-87.

Ghorayshi P. 1989 'The Indispensable Nature of Wives' Work for the Farm Family Enterprise' *The Canadian Review of Sociology and Anthropology* 26 4 pp.571-595.

Haugen, M and Brandth R. 1994 'Gender Differences in Modern Agriculture. The Case of Female Farmers in Norway' *Gender and Society* 8 2 pp.206-229.

Haugen, M S. 1994 'Rural Women's Status in Family and Property Law: Lessons from Norway' pp.87-101 in Whatmore, S, Marsden, T, and Lowe P. (eds.) *Gender and Rurality* London: David Fulton Publishers Ltd.

Haugen, M S. 1990 'Female Farmers in Norwegian Agriculture - From Traditional Farm Women to Professional Farmers' *Sociologia Ruralis* XXX 2.

James, K. 1982 'Women on Australian Farms: A Conceptual Scheme' *The Australian and New Zealand Journal of Sociology* 18 3 pp.302-19.

Jodahl, T. 1994 'Northern Europe: Farm Women in the Nordic Countries' pp.21-27 in van der Burg M and Endeveld M. (eds.) *Women on Family Farms - Gender Research, EC Policies and New Perspectives* Wageningen; Circle for Rural European Studies.

MacKenzie, F. 1992 '"The worse it got, the more we laughed": A Discourse of Resistance Among Farmers of Eastern Ontario' *Society and Space: Environment and Planning Development* D 10 6 pp.691-714.

McWilliams, M. 1993 'The Church, the State and the Women's Movement in Northern Ireland' pp.79-100 in Smyth A. (ed.) *Irish Women's Studies Reader* Dublin: Attic Press.

Meaney, G. 1993 'Sex and Nation: Women in Irish Culture and Politics' pp.230-245 in Smyth A. (ed.) *Irish Women's Studies Reader* Dublin: Attic Press.

Meyer, K and Labao L M. 1994 'Engendering the Farm Crisis: Women's Political Response in USA' pp.69-86 in Whatmore, S, Marsden, T, and Lowe P. (eds.) *Gender and Rurality* London: David Fulton Publishers Ltd.

Northern Ireland Economic Council. 1989 *Agriculture and the Rural Economy in Northern Ireland* Report 76

Northern Ireland Economic Council. 1994 *The Impact of CAP Reform on Northern Ireland* Report 109

O'Hara, P. 1994 'Out of the Shadows - Women on Family Farms and Their Contribution to Agriculture and Rural Development' in van der Burg M and Endeveld M. (eds.) *Women on Family Farms - Gender Research, EC Policies and New Perspectives* Wageningen; Circle for Rural European Studies.

Ontario Farm Women's Network *Newsletter.* 1991 3, 4.

Osborne, R., Gallagher, A., Cormack, R. and Shortall, S. 1996 'The Implementation of the Policy Appraisal and Fair Treatment Guidelines in Northern Ireland' in McLaughlin, E. and Quirk, P. (eds.) *Policy Aspects of Employment Equality in Northern Ireland*, Belfast: Standing Advisory Commission on Human Rights (SACHR) pp. 127-152.

Reimer, B. 1986 'Women as Farm Labour' *Rural Sociology* 51 2 pp.143-155.

Rooney, E. 1995 'Political Division, Practical Alliance: Problems for Women in Conflict' *Journal of Women's History* 6 7 pp.40-49.

Rosenfeld, R. 1985 *Farm Women: Work, Farm and Family in the United States* North Carolina: University of North Carolina Press.

Sachs, C. 1983 'The Invisible Farmers: Women' in Haney, W and Knowles J. (eds.) *Women and Farming - Changing Roles, Changing Structures* New Jersey: Rowman and Allanheld

Salamon, S Keim A M. 1979 'Land Ownership and Women's Power in a Midwestern Farming Community' *Journal of Marriage the Family* 41 pp.109-119.

Shortall, S. 1991 'The Dearth of Data on Irish Farm Wives: A Critical Review of the Literature' *The Economic and Social Review* 22 4 pp.311-332.

Shortall, S. 1992 'Power Analysis and Farm Wives: An Empirical Study of the Power Relationships Affecting Women on Irish Farms' *Sociologia Ruralis* XXXII 4 pp.431-451.

Shortall, S. 1993 'Irish and Canadian Farm Women: Some Similarities, Differences and Comments' *The Canadian Review of Sociology and Anthropology* 30 2 pp.172-191.

Shortall, S. 1994 'Farm Women's Groups: Feminist or Farming or Community Groups, or New Social Movements?' *Sociology* 28 1 pp.279-291.

Shortall, S. 1996 (Forthcoming) 'Training to be Farmers or Wives? Agricultural Training for women in Northern Ireland' *Sociologia Ruralis*

Saskatchewan Women's Agricultural Network (Swan). *Newsletter* 1995 Fall.

Teather, E. 1994 'Contesting Rurality: Country Women's Social and Political Networks' pp. 31-49 in Whatmore, S, Marsden, T, and Lowe P. (eds.) *Gender and Rurality* London: David Fulton Publishers Ltd.

Teather, E. 1996 'Farm Women in Canada, New Zealand and Australia redefine their Rurality' *Journal of Gender Studies* Vol.12 No. 1 pp.1-14.

Whatmore, S. 1991 *Farming Women: Gender, Work and Family Enterprise* London: Macmillan.

Whatmore, S. 1994 'Theoretical Achievements and Challenges in European Rural Gender Studies' in van der Burg M and Endeveld M. (eds.) *Women on Family Farms - Gender Research, EC Policies and New Perspectives* Wageningen: Circle for Rural European Studies.

Whatmore, S, Marsden, T, and Lowe P. 1994 *Introduction: Feminist Perspectives in Rural Studies* pp.1-11 in Whatmore, S, Marsden, T, and Lowe P. (eds.) 'Gender and Rurality' London: David Fulton Publishers Ltd.

van der Burg, M. 1994 'From Categories to Dimensions of Identities' pp.121-135 in van der Burg M and Endeveld M. (eds.) *Women on Family Farms - Gender Research*, EC Policies and New Perspectives Wageningen; Circle for Rural European Studies.

Voyce, M. 1994 'Testamentary Freedom, Patriarchy and the Inheritance of the Family Farm in Australia' *Sociologia Ruralis* XXXIV 1 pp.71-84.

Section 8:
Hidden Lives

One of the enduring objectives of the Women's Movement has been to make visible the realities of women's lives. While 'the personal is political' has been a catch cry of the movement it also represents the emancipatory objectives of feminism. Women's experiences of struggle in the everyday world have been the focus of feminist research. Feminist scholars and activists have aimed to reveal the many hidden and conflictual aspects of women's private and public lives. Talking, researching and writing about women's lives has greatly contributed to our knowledge and theorising about women in certain areas - for example, this volume contains research on women and welfare, domestic violence, the nature of women's work, education and women's health - all of which have important policy implications. While there are many problems attached to funding and resourcing feminist and Women's Studies research and researchers themselves come from a variety of backgrounds, it is evident that some level of gender-based research is being generated in Ireland. However, there are many neglected aspects of the personal that still require public attention, and the chapters in this section seek to make visible under-researched areas of women's experiences. Revealing hidden processes shows up the depth of gender inequality in our society and the deficiencies in our knowledge about it.

Social scientists in the past produced knowledge which we would now regard as 'gendered'. They often generalised from the male experience of the world and excluded women from their analysis. Those who did attempt to understand women's lives did so in the context of their relationship with men - as daughters, wives and mothers. This is evident from Anne Byrne's representation of Irish sociological writing in the 1940s and 1950s on never-married women. In the first half of the twentieth century Ireland had a high proportion of people who remained single - not out of choice, but of necessity. Byrne reviews the variety of explanations for postponed marriage and permanent celibacy in this period, questioning some explanations produced by sociologists about single women. The prejudices and stigmatising attitudes of Irish society in relation to the

411

'spinsters' of this period are evident in the sociological accounts of the time as is the absence from them of single women's own voices and perspectives on their lives.

Prejudice and discrimination are also features of lesbian and gay existence in Irish society. Geraldine Moane considers that in spite of rapid social change in the past thirty years, homophobia is apparent in the Irish psyche and society. Moane provides an understanding of lesbian existence in Ireland, an existence which often remains hidden from public view. Systematic research on lesbians is complex, as the population remains hidden and few women publicly acknowledge their lesbian sexual orientation. Moane presents findings from the few Irish-based research publications on lesbians and gays, touching on issues of coming out, poverty, harassment and discrimination. She also emphasises the importance of activism to combat homophobia and to build a celebratory lesbian community.

Women's drinking behaviour is the focus of Tanya Cassidy's research. Women are often left out of research studies on alcohol use. Traditionally, it was thought that most women largely abstained from alcohol or at least did not consume alcohol in public or in the company of men. However, socio-economic changes in the past thirty years have seen a decrease in female abstinence. Cassidy discusses the alliance between the Catholic Church and mothers in maintaining familial sobriety. She presents her own research findings which suggest that women are more likely to drink at home and mothers are especially concerned to control their drinking, even on 'girls' nights out.

E Maria Lohan addresses another aspect of invisibility and reveals yet another dimension of inequality within households in her examination of women's use of the telephone. The domestic telephone is regarded as a feminised medium of communication. Women's friendships are created and maintained through phone calls, but often 'women's talk' is ridiculed by and then hidden from other family members. Women use the phone as a work tool for managing the household, keeping in contact with family and friends as well as organising events, care of children or gathering and giving information. But Lohan points out that while women use the phone to manage the domestic space, men own and control the phone. Her research reveals that women often feel guilty about bills, sometimes hiding them, at other times not making calls in order to economise. Women's control of the phone has also been limited by recent price restructuring which make daytime private calls more expensive. Yet the private domestic space is the setting for much of women's labour and the phone an essential work tool. Patriarchal conceptions of the public and private can create great difficulties in women's lives.

The social, spatial and symbolic implications of the separation of the public sphere of production and the private sphere of reproduction are discussed in

Wendy Saunderson's chapter on gender and urban space. In the first comprehensive research of its kind, Saunderson interviewed one hundred and twenty men and women who were involved in planning the city of Belfast and who lived in the city. The research took place in the context of political unrest and instability in Northern Ireland. Notwithstanding 'the troubles', she found that while both men and women have strong, positive urban identities, based on a conception of Belfast as modern and sophisticated, certain aspects of the built environment were a cause of concern and conflict. Most of the women interviewed (eighty-seven per cent) were not at all satisfied with the public transport system, compared to only three per cent of men dissatisfied. Women's need for safe, frequent, reliable and affordable public transport was not being met. Saunderson argues that feelings about public transport were most likely to compromise women's identities as users of the city. The night-time city also was a matter of much concern. Many women did not go into Belfast at night because of fear of sexual harassment or attack. This is in contrast to men; although just over half did fear personal attack, the remainder were more concerned about being caught up in sectarian violence. Saunderson's research clearly shows that women are not full participants in the urban setting and the built environment is not built for women.

The final chapter on hidden lives brings attention to yet another research area that has been overlooked by social scientists in the Republic of Ireland - the lives of women with disabilities. Disability has been acknowledged within feminist debate, pointing to the double exclusion of women with disabilities in society. Barbara Murray and Audrey O'Carroll identify the dearth of data on disability in Ireland. It is not possible to give an accurate count of the number of women and girls with a disability at present. There is no published information on the number of people with disability in the labour force, in educational institutions, as users of the health services, rape crisis centres and women's shelters. Murray and O'Carroll discuss the invisibility of women with disabilities in research on vocational training, employment and on adolescence. Equality of opportunity is denied to many young women with disabilities, as they are not encouraged to participate in state examinations or to pursue third-level education. While access difficulties limit life choices, so do disabilist attitudes which assume that women with disabilities are sexless and roleless. In education, vocational training and other services, many obstacles prevent women from meeting potential partners. Murray and O'Carroll challenge researchers to chart the lives and experiences of women with disabilities and to introduce a disability dimension, similar to the gender dimension, into research agendas.

The contributions in this section continue the tradition of revealing aspects of women's experiences which are problematic and about which little is known. While the existence of inequality is a recurrent element, it is evident that there are many kinds of inequality brought about by poverty, discrimination, misrepresentation. Not only one's gender, but one's sexual orientation, intellectual and physical ability, marital status and class can give rise to multiple forms of inequality. To know the forms, dimensions and variety of effects of inequalities is a necessary prerequisite for social change. Exploring and witnessing the responses of those who know and experience inequality provides greater motivation for those working for change within the social services in general and feminism in particular.

25.

Single Women in Ireland:
A Re-Examination of the Sociological Evidence.
Anne Byrne

Introduction

This chapter examines sociological writing about single women in Ireland in the first half of the twentieth century. Historically, Ireland has had an exceptionally high proportion of people who remained single; yet we know little of the fabric and feel of their lives. What was it like to be a single person in a marriage-oriented and familistic society? There has been no sociological study of the lives of single women in Ireland to date, though single women are mentioned in some community studies. Most social scientists, writing about Irish society in the 1940s and 1950s, have at least by default, cast single women as marginal, unimportant and leading largely miserable lives. This chapter details the few sociological accounts which touch on the lives of single women, presenting a variety of interpretations of their situation. The accounts, in the main, demonstrate a distinctive lack of analyses taking the specificities of gender into consideration. The absence of rich ethnographic data and the sound of women's own voices, talking about their experiences, means that we have little alternative but to re-examine what sociological evidence there is on single women's lives.[1]

Since the mid-nineteenth century, Irish society has experienced great change in terms of the political and social life of the country, in population structure, forms of livelihood, migration patterns, government systems and changes in values and attitudes. In the period before the Great Famine of the 1840s right up to the 1960s, the structure of Irish society altered from a traditional to a modernising society. The population fell from approximately eight million to three million through famine and emigration. A 'flight from the land' reduced the number of smallholders. Agriculture shifted from labour-intensive tillage to capital-intensive rearing of livestock and the cultivation of pasture land. An intensive effort to improve the standard of living and lifestyle of the Irish people became a major objective, and part of the ideology of the Irish Free State in 1922. In the late nineteenth century and early twentieth century relative prosperity was achieved through a form of population control in rural Ireland – encouraging people either to postpone marriage or to be permanently celibate. We know little about the consequences of this policy on the lives of those on which it was acted out.

Permanent Celibacy and Postponed Marriage

Marriage patterns in Ireland after the famine have been the subject of much interest, since compared to most other Europeans, Irish people have tended to be older on marriage and Ireland has had the highest proportion of people who remain permanently single. Kennedy (1970) noted a rise in postponed marriage after the Great Famine in the 1840s, a second rise in postponed marriage in the 1870s, an increasingly greater discrepancy between the sexes in permanent celibacy after the 1880s (more bachelors than spinsters), then a decline (in the 1970s) in postponed marriage and permanent celibacy. Kennedy's work has made a significant contribution to what we know about the extent of singlehood in Ireland in the first part of the twentieth century. The term 'postponed marriage' refers to the proportion single of those aged twenty-five to thirty-four years, while 'permanent celibacy' refers to the proportion of the never married aged forty-five years and over. However, there is dispute both about the interpretation and origins of postponed marriage and permanent celibacy. Hajnal (1965) described a distinctive historical West European marriage pattern consisting of late age at first marriage (bridal age twenty-five to twenty-six) and a high proportion of the population who never marry (between ten and twenty per cent). In western Europe, up to twenty per cent of the female population never married. This is in contrast to Eastern European patterns of almost universal and youthful marriage.

Connell (1968) asserted that Irish population growth in the late eighteenth century can be accounted for by a fall in the age of female marriage. Dickson (1991) rejects this argument and shows that prior to the Cromwellian period (pre-1640), the mean age of marriage among women was twenty-two to twenty-three years; he also found a difference of five years between male and female mean ages of marriage. He suggests that the male age of marriage was closer to the European norm (older), but that this was not the case when it came to women. In the late seventeenth century, 'servants and maids, female and male were very numerous and, it seems, largely celibate in non-gentry households in mid-seventeenth century Ireland' (Dickson, 1991, p.232). By the eighteenth century, however, unmarried servants living in the household were much less common and tended to be younger. The shift can probably, for the most part, be accounted for by changes in the nature of work (textile work and similar work brought with it the possibility to earn cash) which allowed more poor women to consider parenthood, which in turn could account for accelerated population growth.

When did a high rate of singleness come to be a feature of Irish demographic life? Is it a new development or a continuation of an older pattern? From the 1850s onwards permanent celibacy amongst Irish women and men increased every year up to the 1960s (Table 1). While the Irish rates were much higher than the English rates, the same pattern of increase can also be discerned in England and Wales. However permanent celibacy in England began to decrease after 1921, while in Ireland by 1936 thirty-four per cent of men and twenty-five per cent of women between forty-five and fifty-four years were single or 'permanently celibate' (Table 2). What are the explanations for these patterns? Why did they persist in Ireland? From which class in society did they emerge and how widespread was the adoption of these marriage patterns? What were the effects of postponed marriage and permanent celibacy on the young women and men concerned and the consequences for society? How was the change in marriage patterns brought about? Some of these questions have been partially debated in Irish sociological writing.

Table 1: *Percentage Single and Ever Married, 1901-1992*

	25-34 YEARS		35-44 YEARS		ALL 15 YEARS +	
YEAR	FEMALE	MALE	FEMALE	MALE	FEMALE	MALE
	S/ M	S /M	S /M	S /M	S/ M	S /M
1901	53/47	72/28	28/72	38/62	49/51	57/43
1951	46/54	67/33	28/72	41/60	43/57	53/47
1961	37/63	58/42	23/77	36/64	39/61	48/52
1971	26/74	41/58	18/83	92/71	36/64	46/54
1981	22/78	34/66	11/89	19/81	34/66	43/57
1986	26/74	38/62	11/89	18/82	34/66	43/57
1992	32/68	44/56	12/88	18/82	35/65	43/57

S = Single
M= Married
Source: Census of Population, Various Years.

There are two main types of argument explaining singleness – those that focus on ideological explanations and those that are substantially founded on material concerns. The range of arguments claiming to explain the historic high rates of singleness in the population include the nature of Irish Catholicism, the drive to improve familial and individual standards of living, the stem family system, emigration and labour-force activity of single women. Throughout all

Table 2: *Percentage Single in Certain Age Groups, 1936-1991.*

	AGE GROUP						
	15-19	20-24	25-34	35-44	45-54	55-64	65+
MALES							
1936	99.9	96.2	73.8	44.2	33.5	28.2	23.6
1946	99.8	95.0	70.4	43.0	32.1	30.0	25.4
1951	99.9	94.9	67.4	40.5	31.0	28.8	26.6
1961	99.8	92.5	58.0	36.2	29.7	28.1	26.7
1966	99.7	89.6	49.8	33.4	29.1	27.7	26.8
1971	99.5	84.6	41.3	28.9	28.1	27.1	26.8
1979	99.3	81.6	34.1	21.1	25.3	26.6	26.3
1981	99.4	82.4	34.2	19.4	23.9	26.3	26.0
1986	99.8	88.7	38.3	17.7	20.2	25.1	25.3
1991	99.9	93.9	43.5	17.8	16.7	22.1	24.4
FEMALES							
1936	99.1	86.4	54.8	30.2	25.1	23.7	22.7
1946	98.4	82.5	48.3	30.0	25.6	24.4	23.3
1951	98.9	82.3	45.6	27.6	25.7	24.7	23.7
1961	98.9	78.2	37.1	22.7	23.1	25.0	24.3
1966	98.4	74.8	31.0	20.4	20.8	24.4	24.8
1971	97.9	68.9	25.7	17.5	18.8	22.0	25.1
1979	97.3	66.3	21.5	12.3	15.7	18.9	23.8
1981	97.7	67.7	21.9	11.4	14.6	18.2	23.2
1986	99.0	77.6	26.4	10.7	12.1	16.5	21.7
1991	99.9	86.2	31.7	11.5	10.2	14.2	19.8

Source: *Census of Population*, Various Years.

of these arguments, the emphasis is on the male experience, with women included in generalisations that are more pertinent to men. A gender analysis is missing. In the ideologically-based arguments, where the experience of women is touched upon, it is as if women are to blame for not marrying and must bear responsibility for the surfeit of men in rural Ireland from the 1900s onwards. In later accounts women are regarded as causing permanent celibacy amongst men, as mothers and as reluctant wives. In materially-based arguments, women are written about as useful labour units but are also cast as dependent burdens and spinster sisters when an inheriting brother wants to marry.

Conflicting arguments abound. There is evidence showing that women were urged to marry by the Catholic Church, to stay at home and have babies and were not encouraged to emigrate. Others opine that mothers actually educated their daughters specifically for emigration, using the threat of lifelong singlehood at home as encouragement. What is not in doubt is that church, state and family colluded in shaping the life choices of generations of Irish women and men, limiting and constraining their sexual and marital relationships. There is little evidence of the emotional and non-material preparation for the single life in a society which had such a high rate of singleness – apart from preparation for the religious life. The lack of visible ethnographic material on women's experiences in this period of Irish social history causes me to question the evidence presented to date.

Irish Catholicism and Remaining Single

Commentators dispute the extent to which Irish Catholicism can account for the high rates of singleness in the population (Connell, 1968, Kennedy, 1970, Hynes, 1978). Evidence is cited demonstrating great reverence for the holy, moral celibate life which both attracted vocations and provided a model for lay people to follow (O'Brien, 1954). Sex was seen as largely immoral, and therefore, the argument goes, to lead a good moral life, it is preferable to remain celibate and therefore single. The lack of widespread divorce, the prohibition on birth control and the preference by the Catholic Church that married women should not work are all examined as potential deterrents to marriage. Kennedy, however, argues that the Catholic Church differentiated between lawful and unlawful sex. Lawful and compulsory sex with your spouse was condoned but sex amongst the unmarried was prohibited. Kennedy shows that permanent celibacy did not vary by religion, as non-Catholics also had a high rate of singleness in the 1940s. This points to other factors in the population, according to Kennedy, such as the material and social aspirations of the Irish rather than the nature of Catholicism itself to explain the high levels of permanent celibacy and postponed marriage.

In a study of Irish Catholicism after the famine, Hynes explained the 'devotional revolution' as part of the embourgeoisement of the rising farmer class, who at all costs had to control ownership and consolidate land.

> Thus strenuous efforts were made to gain and keep control over land and such efforts involved the regulation of its members by each family and a lot of sacrifice and long range planning. In other words, like modernisation elsewhere, modernisation in Ireland, involved a growth in discipline (Hynes, 1978, p.147).

Celibacy, postponed marriage and emigration were all essential aspects of this discipline. Hynes argues that women in particular took to the new Catholicism, which emphasised sexual purity and control of sexual urges. Their interest in the supernatural was purely instrumental, according to him.

> In the case of women, they knew that to stay in the marriage market with a realistic chance of getting a husband they had to keep their reputation. Sex

was dangerous to their aspirations and this helps explain why they were receptive to the puritanical elements in the Catholic teachings available to them. Their goal of an acceptable living standard led them to postpone marriage until they were older and ... reduced their fertility more than did those who married early (Hynes, 1978, p.149).

Religious regulation did seem to triumph at this period and could be construed as a strong ideological system which explains the prevalence and acceptance of singleness in the population. But to understand the role of Catholicism and its priests in either causing or perpetuating permanent celibacy and postponed marriage, the role of the State and of economic and social conditions also need to be examined.

Single for the Sake of Society?

From the 1840s onwards, there was a concerted attempt by rural dwellers to improve their standard of living. While there is dispute amongst commentators as to the timing of this attempt (pre- or post Famine?) and its relative prevalence amongst cottiers, labourers or tenant farmers, it is apparent that the means of achieving material well-being was consolidation of land and the reduction, in the long term, of the number of dependants on the holding. In order to prevent the further fragmentation of holdings, which was a typical pattern before the Famine, only one child from each family would inherit the land, marry and produce the next generation. This is the idea in its most simple form and it is known as the 'stem family system' as opposed to the 'joint family system' where property was held in common. Most social scientists who concern themselves with this period in Irish development see permanent celibacy and postponed marriage as consequences of the stem family system.

Singleness and the Stem Family System

The consequences of this system of impartible inheritance were immense, not only on the social structure but on the community and the family, and most particularly on individuals. My concern here is with the latter, and especially with the lives of never-married single women. However, it is extremely difficult to know from sociological accounts of the period how the stem system affected the lives of these women. The stem system was based on three-generational farm households, in which any son could inherit, first or last. In the absence of sons, daughters could also inherit. This was the period of the arranged marriage or 'match' of heirs, based on the scarcity of land and the overall objective of improving the living standards of the family. While the heir could marry, he had to ensure that dependent siblings were provided for if they remained on the land, or he had to assist in their emigration or further education. One daughter in the household might possibly marry, if she had a dowry and if she could find an acceptable mate in the community – acceptable in terms of financial and land security and in the number of dependants in her prospective groom's household. The remaining daughters and sons had few options – they could remain on the land and work as 'relatives assisting' or they could try to emigrate. Within the stem family system, there is a continual tension between the status of family members as labour units and as dependants to be cared for by the heir (see Varley, 1983). In the case of non-inheriting sons, there was little chance that their fathers could buy additional land for them, but in some cases they might inherit a smallholding from a bachelor uncle. But setting up a family on a smallholding was a very risky business and most small holders (with under five acres) chose to keep all of the income from the holding for their own personal use, rather than share it with a potential wife and children (Kennedy, 1970).

Those who did marry under this system, tended to do so later rather than earlier. And again, there is dispute about the extensiveness of the stem system and whether it was a new adaptation or simply a continuation of a practice begun by the rising tenant farmer classes before the Famine. There is no doubt however, about the tendency of both females and males to marry in their late twenties and mid-thirties respectively. This was due in the main to the reluctance of the father to either name the heir until the latest possible moment (often as he lay dying) or to hand over the property in his later years. Once the heir was named, he had to secure a marriage partner and care for his dependants, who might be numerous. If the heir was female, often she had to wait until both parents died to inherit, which made her less attractive or acceptable as a potential child bearer and producer of a male heir. Descriptions of the Irish country divorce are particularly poignant in this scenario. Curtin and Varley comment:

> Not to have children in 1930s Clare exposed the woman (who was considered the culpable party) to possible verbal or physical abuse at the hands of her husband, or even to being returned in disgrace to her natal home under the then-disappearing procedure known as the 'country divorce'. Such a separation allowed farm ownership to be transferred to the heir's brother, in the hope that this man's marriage would result in the birth of a male child and the desired generational continuity (Curtin and Varley, 1984, pp.31-32).

The stem family system ensured the preservation of property and family lines of inheritance, at all costs.

The Status and Treatment of the Unmarried

There is an ambivalence in the literature on the status of the unmarried in the population. While bachelors certainly get a little more attention from sociologists (Brody, 1973, Curtin and Varley, 1984), the unmarried single female, where she is considered, is conceptualised as marginal, on the perimeter in the community and is written out of accounts with statements that many single women emigrated. Sex, rather than marital status was a prior determinant of one's position in the local community. Single women, compared to single men, were at the very bottom of the social hierarchy with low social status and little solidarity amongst them. The marginalisation of single women and the lack of serious consideration of the nature of their lives by social commentators is rather ironic considering the collective effort to keep women single for as long as possible. Bachelor drinking groups, on the other hand, were regarded as part of the maturation process for single males and socialised young men into prolonging singlehood.

> The bachelor group is in revolt against responsibility, and at the same time is a refuge against loneliness. Its members, perhaps unconsciously, create a subtle, psychological ambience, which arises out of a poignant contrast between age and youth, between the past and the present, and which intensifies the feeling that youth is short and must not be trammelled (McNabb, 1964, p.224).

This was part of 'marriage avoidance' strategies condoned by the community, necessary in order to keep the stem family system intact. McNabb noted in his study of a small community in County Limerick in the early 1950s that while people accepted in the course of time that one would marry, marriage was seen as a limitation on male freedom. He describes the opinion of the community as likening marriage to old age – a process which is inevitable and which one would like to defer as long as possible.

> The community is not opposed to marriage – it is something in the course of nature and one accepts its philosophically – but each individual avoids it as long as possible, just as one tries to avoid old age. When such an attitude to marriage reigns, the institution has low status. It may be a personal ideal, but it is not a social ideal, nor is it a positive goal for the majority of the community (McNabb, 1964, pp.223).

The community which controlled marriage, is described by McNabb (1964) as 'favouring' the single person. He does not exactly describe what is meant by this term, but writes that

> ... the large number of single people in the community has weighted it against marriage and gives the family poor representation. Community life favours the single...The higher percentage single, even in the older age groups, means that there is no stigma attached to the single state. This is supported to a great extent by a celibate clergy...lay people aim at celibacy in the same sense as does the clergyman. Where the single state is an acceptable one, and where the higher proportion of the adult population are single, it is inevitable that the society will be organised primarily for their benefit (McNabb, 1964, p.224).

It seems to me very doubtful the society was organised for the 'benefit' of the single; rather they were the unwitting and perhaps unwilling victims of a system which subsumed individual interests, needs and aspirations to familial, communal and societal goals of economic prosperity. McNabb does comment earlier in his account that the marriage-makers were perhaps aware of the deficiencies in this system – but that for the sake of the family and prosperity, the tradition must endure.

> The parents have the depressing spectacle of many unhappy bachelors and spinsters in the neighbourhood, and have no wish to see their children in the same plight....They are quite conscious of the defects in the old system, but cannot see that there is any reasonable alternative (McNabb, 1964, p.221).

Hynes' (1978) reading of the status of the unmarried is quite different. The single in a rural community were generally both without land and children – the two requirements for the continuation of the economic system for which families struggled to maintain.

> The stem family system required many people to marry late, if at all, and in the community these unmarried men and women – because they were neither married nor controlled property – had very low status (Hynes, 1978, p.148).

The unmarried, both male and female, were the losers in this system which gave preferential economic treatment to heirs, who could then marry. Hynes sees the bachelor drinking role as one of the devices which men used to cope with their situation, while women chose to emigrate, if they could.

Single Women and Rural Life

The unimportance of unmarried females in rural society is apparent from accounts of studies of small communities. Brody (1973) and McNabb (1974) used schematic models of the communities which they observed, consisting of a series of concentric circles with men at their centres and women on the perimeters. Both place unmarried women on the absolute outside of the communal circle.

> In our community, the model is as follows: the centre and larger area represents the bachelors: the next circle represents male children; outside that again is the circle of married people, and the extreme circle is of unmarried adult females (McNabb, 1964, p.224).

Brody (1973) uses a similar model in describing Inishkillane. 'At the centre of this society are bachelors and family men; at its outer perimeter are the women' (Brody, 1973, p.161). He goes on to draw a diagram, with men at the centre, and unmarried women on the outside, those whom he assumes are 'least committed to life in farming society' (Brody, 1973, p.161). He does not pause here, to reflect that perhaps the women (whom he says were unduly influenced by magazines, films and newspapers) may have been thoroughly dissatisfied with their treatment within the family and saw no future for themselves in rural Ireland.

Kennedy's (1970) work on mortality and living standards among the Irish at the beginning of this century gives us some insight into the treatment of young women and girls in rural Ireland. Using census data, he shows quite clearly that up until 1950 female mortality is greater than male, reaching a peak in the decade 1901-1910, when the female death rate for those aged ten to fourteen years was one hundred and forty per cent of the male death rate. Most of these girl children would have been living as daughters in their parents' own homes and one can only conjecture that hard physical labour combined with a lack of nourishing food contributed to these shockingly higher death rates for females. The decade of high female mortality was also the decade of the greatest transfer of land. Kennedy surmises:

> Could there have been other expenses associated with land ownership which resulted in some of the more land-hungry farmers buying fields with money taken away from the support of their families? (Kennedy, 1970, p.61).

Viney (1968) provides a grim description of life in rural Ireland for women on small farms or in labouring families in the 1950s and 1960s – much of it confined by hard physical labour, in houses with few material comforts, with no opportunities for leisure and poor relations between husband and wife, fathers and children. Marital fertility on the other hand was high, with no opportunity and no permission for women to limit the number of children, as contraceptives were not widely available and were forbidden by the Catholic Church. Mothers did not encourage daughters to marry farmers but according to Viney a mother might give 'the girls an education that will enable them to make their way in the world away from any other farm' (Viney, 1968, p.338). Nursing, teaching and typing were the favoured occupations. But single women who stayed at home had to 'work as hard as their mother did, and in return are given pocket money, their keep and an occasional lump sum for clothes' (Viney, 1968, p.338). Pocket-money instead of wages was seen as preferred for family members who worked on the farm so as not to confuse them with 'that despised being, a "servant girl" – a term still used for female help' (Viney, 1968, p.339). The servant girl however had the possibility of financial independence, an option not available to the spinster sister who stayed at home. McNabb also described the labour of young women which included household chores, looking after younger children and heavy farm work.

> When a daughter reaches sixteen, if she remains on the farm, she must do a full day's work, and too often her life is one of unrelieved drudgery. There is almost an Oriental attitude to girls. They are favoured neither by father or mother and accepted only on sufferance (McNabb, 1964, p.230).

McBreen's Heifer[2] – or How Much is a Woman Worth?

Hynes (1978) considered the impact of modernisation on single women in rural society, but mainly in terms of their economic value. The single woman's worth as labourer (albeit unpaid) steadily decline and this in turn affected not only her marriage prospects, but her very survival. Changing patterns of agriculture, from a labour-intensive system to capital-intensive system reduced women's economic input both as labourers and as producers. Their value in the economic exchange system was decreased. In the marriage market, as only one son could seek a bride, but all women were potential brides, supply far outweighed demand and 'reduced the value of any particular woman' (Hynes, 1978, p.149). In order to improve her position in the rural marriage market, the single woman was dependent on either her father or her brother to provide her with a dowry. She was constrained no matter which way she turned, as she was economically dependent on the family whether she stayed at home on the farm or wanted to marry.

McNabb also acknowledged women's poor position in the marriage market, but attributed it to their lack of importance in all aspects of community.

> ... the girl is subservient to all other members of the family and shares no confidences either with her parents or her brothers. Her only right is to a dowry if she marries with her parents' consent...The females play a weak role in community life and cannot be said to have any direct influence on the marriage pattern (McNabb, 1964, pp.224-231).

Marriage, according to McNabb's account, is men's business and women have no input or rights in the conduct of marital affairs. He does, however, note that some women were not happy with these arrangements and are 'beginning to lay down conditions and are setting their faces against being pawns in property transactions' (McNabb, 1964, p.224). Women's disenchantment with rural society is also explained by their disenchantment with rural men.

> The modern country girl is turning away from the land. The wealth of the prospective husband, although still important, is not so decisive as his personal appearance, his manners and the kind of home he can provide. She objects to the 'muck and dirt' of the farm life and would prefer to marry a professional man or even a white collar worker...The status of the farmer has gone down considerably in the eyes of the female population (McNabb, 1964, p.221).

Hynes hypothesises why women may have been dissatisfied, and, though he does not name it, he describes patriarchy.

> ... the falling status of women together with the increasing separation of the sexes, both results of the triumph of the stem family system, would make the people receptive to beliefs which stressed the authority of the male and the different, complementary but ultimately subordinate contributions of the female in society and especially in the family (Hynes, 1978, p.149).

An insider's view of the situation is passionately present in the letter below written in response to a newspaper competition for the best account of how wives met their husbands. A very annoyed person (signed as 'cut the coddin') wrote:

> Nothing irritates me more than your idiotic series 'How I met my Husband'. Every honest woman in this country will tell you that she met her husband

through the amount of money or property she happened to posess ... there is no sentiment in your 'sahool' (sic) Irishman when it comes to taking a wife. She must have a fortune or he is not interested. Incidentally, Irishmen make the worst husbands in the world. They are mean, selfish, lazy and with absolutely no respect or consideration for women (Times Pictorial, October, 1952).

Single Women and the Flight from the Land

Given the constraints on marriage and the poor prospects for unmarried women who remained on the land, the dominance of the family in economic and social affairs and the allegedly poor relations between the sexes, it is not surprising that as soon as they were able, single women fled from rural Ireland. This can be read as rebellion or at the very least resistance to the patriarchal constraints that sought to control and restrain their lives. It could be argued that rather than submit to the exigencies and constraints of rural life, single women created alternatives for themselves, and sought new strategies for economic, social and personal survival. This however is not the view presented at the time.

Single women, unlike married women, participated in the labour market but conditions in the 1940s were so unfavourable and wages so low, that work did not confer any social status of importance (see O'Dowd, 1987). Single women chose to migrate and emigrate in the face of poor working conditions, long hours, low wages and few career prospects. Ireland at this time had one of the highest rates of female migration and emigration in the Western world (Jackson, 1987, Rudd, 1988). However, commentators of the period, writing in the 1950s up to the late 1970s, do not regard emigration as rejection or as a form of rebellion. Single women were seen as agents of decline in rural Ireland, rather than as agents of change in the conditions and circumstances of their own lives. For example, Brody's central thesis on population decline and consequent demoralisation in the community of Inishkillane seems to rest on women's shoulders. He states that decline is inevitable as women have rejected rural life.

> The decline has not been halted, and is unlikely to be halted in the near future, precisely because country girls have refused to marry into local farms. So long as they reject life in the parish, no new generation can emerge and no check to the downward trend can be effected (Brody, 1973, pp.98-99).

Single women were blamed for their anti-rural attitudes for denigrating life on the land and were described as guilt-free deserters, who left home and family without as much as a backward glance (O'Brien, 1954, McNabb, 1964, Viney, 1968, Brody, 1973). Most commentators were simply not interested in the single woman's experience or her plight, and the single woman was described as leaving rural Ireland for the attraction of the cities whether at home in Ireland, England or the US. Female migration, is only looked at in terms of the consequences for the surfeit of males left behind – postponed marriage or permanent celibacy. McNabb asserts that it was the more vital and less conservative people in the community who emigrated. He described the girls (sic) who remained '...as rather passive and not likely to go out of their way to be attractive to men or to help them over their diffidence in the face of new responsibilities' (McNabb, 1964, p.220). Women were blamed for leaving, succumbing to the lure of the city and if they stay behind they were further vilified as somehow inferior and dullards. McNabb's unsympathetic interpretation of single women's motivation to emigrate or not greatly compromised his ability to understand and represent the female experience at the time.

Because of their increasingly marginalised position in rural communities, single women certainly had more to gain by moving to the large towns and cities of the US and England and they continued to leave in a steady stream right up to the 1960s. The preponderance of single women in Irish towns also meant that there were not enough urban males available for marriage.

> The result was the degree of permanent celibacy among females was higher in urban than in rural areas, at least between 1926 and 1966. The fact that spinsterhood was more characteristic of Irish urban than rural residents needs to be emphasised to counter the general impression that permanent celibacy in Ireland was primarily a rural phenomenon (Kennedy, 1970, p.170).

Kennedy has interpreted both emigration and remaining single as alternative ways of securing 'respectable adult status' for men and women in Ireland, though he admits it was more difficult for single females to achieve if they remained in rural Ireland, due to women's subordinate role in the countryside. Being single and independent in an urban context was the only way single women could secure respectable adult status.

> ... many Irish women preferred urban over rural lifestyle, even if it meant the possibility of becoming a spinster...since 1961 in Irish rural areas there have been about twenty four bachelors for every ten spinsters (Kennedy, 1970, p.72).

In a letter to the *Times Pictorial*, Miss S B Henderson asks why marriage rates are so low and expresses her opinion of city men:

> Can it be that only in the city one sees a pretty girl or are men so mean that they will not share what they can earn with anyone else? Or can it be that the girls do not think that the men are good enough for them? In any case, I think that most of the young men in Dublin are a poor, scruffy, badly groomed, untidy lot (*Times Pictorial*, 12 July, 1952).

Walsh (1985) interprets these patterns quite differently, asserting that since 1926, women had a better prospect of marriage than men, as in general the numbers of men far outweighed the numbers of women, right up to the 1960s. But there is little evidence that women preferred marriage in rural Ireland to being single and independent in the towns and cities. As many commentators noted, if the women were looking for husbands they were going in the wrong direction.

The Vanishing Irish?

By the end of the 1950s much anxiety began to be expressed about late marriage and the high rate of singleness in the population. The Commission on Emigration noted with concern:

> A profoundly adverse effect on the psychology of the people must be produced where so many do not marry at all, or else postpone marriage to ages higher than are customary elsewhere or are desirable or natural. There is something gravely wrong in a community where there is such widespread frustration of a natural expectation, and in our considered view, the low marriage rate is one of our two great population problems – the other being emigration...' (Commission on Emigration and other Population Problems, 1948-54, Majority Report, para 164, in Walsh, 1985, p.32).

Irish marriage patterns were described as the 'strange enigma of a race that believes passionately in family life and yet produces more old bachelors and more old maids than any race in the civilised world' (O'Brien, 1954, p.220). In his concern for the vanishing Irish, O'Brien described

> The most pathetic aspect of the whole tragic situation is that the women of Ireland, who crave wifehood and motherhood as much as, if not more than the women of other races, are pulled willy-nilly into a spinsterhood not of their own choosing. Is it any wonder, that after enduring their plights for decades they are now fleeing from the island of bachelors so that Eire has now one of the lowest proportion of women to men of any country in the world? (O'Brien, 1954, p.221).

While the accuracy of O'Brien's demographic statistics may be questioned, the postponement of marriage and celibacy – a strategy to improve familial and national prosperity – was now interpreted as a national tragedy. From the 1950s onward a concern about rural depopulation and the flight from the land is reflected in public pleas in newspapers and in radio broadcasts by politicians aimed at workers to return from England and engage in labour at home (see Times Pictorial, 7 January, 1950 reference to radio broadcast by Taoiseach Costelloe) and in exhortations to young Irishwomen to stay in rural Ireland and marry the surfeit of bachelors in order to repopulate the land (O'Brien, 1954). At this point, public discourse certainly changes from supporting celibacy and postponed marriage to actively encouraging marriage and high fertility within marriage.

Therefore, by the late 1950s, in spite of initially poor economic conditions, the generations who matured after the second world war, started to marry at a higher rate and at a younger age. There was a steady increase in the marriage rate and a decrease in the age of brides and grooms, along with a reduction in the differences in age between men and women on marriage. But as the marriage rates increased, marital fertility decreased, giving some credence to the notion that the lack of availability of contraceptives and the consequent difficulty in limiting family size may have been a deterrent to marriage in the past. Rising incomes and a period of relative prosperity in Ireland, combined with decreasing prospects abroad, may also have been important factors in pushing up the marriage rate in the 1960s.

These patterns continued until the late 1970s and early 1980s when the marriage rate began to decline and the proportion single in the population began to increase. Walsh describes this increase in the proportion single for the age group fifteen to thirty-four years as significant and marks the end of decline charted since 1936 (Walsh, 1985, p.148). The economic recession of the late 1970s and 1980s then had an effect on marriage rates and average age of marriage, witnessing a return to deferred marriage and a later marrying age. Whether this is due to economic forces alone or disenchantment with the institution of marriage can only be determined by time, more precise census information and further research.

Conclusion

Traditionally high rates of male celibacy have been explained in terms of an agricultural economy, impartible inheritance, the excess of males over females, female migration and urbanisation. The cohort of Irish women who have never married has however been overlooked by sociologists in a manner which unfairly reproduces the prejudices of society. In her own words, Imelda from Dublin writes:

> The women of Ireland are a sorely tried lot. Virtue is preached at them from every corner – and I am not talking here about the church – but what national happiness can one expect if the women of the country are being frustrated. This frustration is being elevated to the status of a national mission, and the state is slowly dying. The few young men who want to live their lives free of hide bound restrictions are going away, and the girls are going away also because they cannot find the emotional outlet so dear to all women in this country. I pity the poor Irish women over forty and fifty who are unable to make a new start in life; they must remain behind with the gummy old chaps, who are grand fellows in their own way, but would fly from marriage, like the devil from a paraffin torch placed to his posterior (*Times Pictorial*, quoted in O'Brien, 1954, pp.230-231).

Discussion Questions

1. What are the most convincing explanations for the persistence of the high rate of singleness in Ireland in the first part of the century?

2. Is there any stigma attached to being a single woman in Irish society today?

3. Can you recall the life and circumstances of any female or male relative who never married?

4.   What images are evoked by the words 'spinster' and 'bachelor'?

Notes

1. This chapter is background material to work on the lives of never-married women in contemporary Irish society being conducted by the author.
2. In a song by Percy French, a man deliberates whether to marry 'Pretty Kitty' or 'Plain Jane'. Jane, though she had a 'face that the divil designed' would be accompanied by a heifer and thus the attractiveness of the marriage bargain is increased.

References

Brody, H. 1973 *Inishkillane – Change and Decline in the West of Ireland* London: Allen Lane.

Connell, K H. 1968 *Catholicism and Marriage in the Century After the Famine in Irish Peasent Society* Oxford: Clarendon Press.

Curtin, C and Varley, A. 1984 'Children and Childhood in Rural Ireland: A Consideration of the Ethnographic Literature' in Curtin, C, Kelly, M, O'Dowd, L (eds.) *Culture and Ideology in Ireland* Galway: Galway University Press.

Dickson, D. 1991 'No Scythians Here: Women and Marriage in 17th Century Ireland' in MacCurtain, M and O Dowd, M (eds.) *Women in Early Modern Ireland* Edinburgh: Edinburgh University Press.

Fitzpatrick, D. 1983 'Irish Farm Families Before the First World War' *Comparative Studies in Society and History* Vol.25, No.2, April pp.339-374.

Hajnal, J. 1965 'European Marriage Patters in Perspective in Glass', DV and Eversley, DE (eds.) *Population in History* London: Edward Arnold.

Hynes, E. 1978 'The Great Hunger and Irish Catholicism' *Societas,* Vol.VIII, No.2, Spring pp.137-156.

Jackson, P. 1987 *Migrant Women: The Republic of Ireland* Report to the Commission of the European Communities Feb. 10, 1987, V/139/89-EN.

Kennedy, R E. 1970 *The Irish – Emigration, Marriage and Fertility* California: University of California Press.

McNabb, P. 1964 'Demography' and 'Social Structure' in Newman, J (ed.) *Limerick Rural Survey, 1958-1964* Tipperary: Muintir na Tire Publications.

O'Brien, J A. 1954 *The Vanishing Irish* London: WH Allen.

O'Dowd, L. 1987 'Church, State and Women in Curtin' C, Jackson, P and O'Connor, B (eds.) *Gender in Irish Society* Galway: Galway University Press.

Rudd, J. 1988 'Invisible Exports: the Emigration of Irish Women this Century' *Women's Studies International Forum* Vol.11 No.4 pp.307-311.

Times Pictorial Weekly, various years.

Varley, A. 1983 'The Stem Family in Ireland Reconsidered' *Comparative Studies in Society and History* Vol.25, No.2, April pp.381-391.

Viney, E. 1968 'Women in Rural Ireland' *Christus Rex* Vol.XXIX, pp.333-342.

Walsh, B M. 1985 'Marriage in Ireland in the Twentieth Century' in Cosgrove, A (ed.) *Marriage in Ireland* Dublin: College Press.

26.

Lesbian Politics and Community
Geraldine Moane

Introduction

The phrase 'rapid social change' has become almost a cliché to describe economic, social and cultural changes in Ireland over the last 30 years, indeed, over the last decade. Often, the phrase has connotations of tremendous progress, of the sweeping away of the old restrictions and prejudices of the past, and with them, the psychological inhibitions. Yet rapid social change does not necessarily imply marked psychological change. In the case of homosexuality, for example, it is apparent that fear and prejudice is alive and well in Irish psyches and society, despite important legislative changes, unprecedented inclusion of lesbians and gay men in progressive social agendas, and increasing depictions of lesbians and gay men in art and culture.

Understanding Lesbian Existence – Conceptual Issues

The continued existence of prejudice, despite rapid social change, is one of the many paradoxes of lesbian and gay existence. These include an existence marked on the one hand by prejudice and discrimination (homophobia), and on the other by celebration and community solidarity (lesbian and gay pride). Coming to awareness of lesbian or gay sexuality occurs even where there is total silence about lesbian and gay existence. Lesbians and gay men are spatially dispersed, yet have developed a strong sense of community and culture. Homosexuality has been a criminal offence, yet government funding has been provided to lesbian and gay groups.

Variety and complexity is another feature of lesbian existence which must be acknowledged. Indeed, it would be impossible for one writer to provide a comprehensive account of lesbian existence, or more specifically, of lesbian politics and community in Ireland. As Patricia Prendiville (1996) points out, lesbian politics and community are embedded in a changing social context and hence are constantly undergoing change themselves (Prendiville, 1996). What follows is a necessarily selective overview of concepts which have illuminated lesbian existence over time, followed by a review of research, and then discussion of some of the goals and ideals of lesbian politics and community.

There are a multiplicity of theories which have been applied to homosexuality, including biological, medical, psychological and sociological theories. Many of these theories have viewed homosexuality as either a deficit or failure in the development of heterosexuality, or as a form of disorder or deviance. Indeed, textbooks in Psychology still discuss homosexuality, or, more recently, sexual orientation, in their chapter on 'abnormal psychology', while textbooks in Sociology will often include the topic in chapters on deviance. These 'deficit or deviance' approaches have posed considerable problems for lesbians and gay men, and along with religious views have been a primary source of prejudice and discrimination (Kitzinger, 1987, Hyde, 1994).

There are also, of course, theoretical analyses which have developed out of the women's liberation movements, and the lesbian and gay liberation movements. Radical feminists, for example, analyse the construction of sexuality in a patriarchal context, regarding lesbian existence as on the one hand a defiance of heterosexuality, and on the other an embracing of a woman-centred existence (woman-identification) (Humm, 1992). Queer theory challenges the categories of gender and of homosexuality, emphasising the diversity of sexualities, and their construction as social and cultural forms in specific contexts (Abelove et al., 1993).

Even these theoretical analyses have difficulty with the paradoxes of lesbian and gay existence, and in particular of lesbian existence, which is more likely to be hidden. In *The Mystery of Lesbians*, Julia Penelope asks: 'How, without guidance, encouragement, accurate information, images and words to nurture us, do we manage finally to conceive ourselves? How, in spite of derision, incarceration, violence and poverty, do we find the courage to create ourselves?' (1984, p.93). Terry Castle (1993) coins the phrase 'The Apparitional Lesbian' to capture the pervasive though ethereal presence of lesbians in Western culture.

An understanding of lesbian existence is further complicated by the tendency to place lesbians in the 'lesbian and gay' category, or in the 'women' category. While obviously lesbians and gay men have much in common, there are also enormous differences and sometimes conflict between the two groups. Joni Crone writes that 'the vast majority of lesbians and gay men in Ireland experience life very differently. This is not due to any lack of solidarity, but to our gender differences' (1995, p.61). Lesbians experience the same difficulties as other women in terms of education, training, employment, reproductive rights and cultural representations, but, even within the context of the women's movement, are faced with prejudice and discrimination on the basis of sexual orientation.

Indeed Mary McDermott suggests that the limits of modern liberation movements need to be examined closely in an Irish context, where 'the 3C's – of colonialism, catholicism and celticism' raise questions about the efficacy of identity politics and the power dynamics of contemporary bureaucracies (McDermott, 1996, p.5).

The words 'homophobia' and 'heterosexism' have been coined to refer specifically to prejudice and discrimination on the basis of sexual orientation, drawing parallels to concepts like racism, sexism, and xenophobia. Their manifestations include ignorance, fear, anger, hatred, and rejection, sometimes amounting to extreme violence as the killings of homosexuals in many countries uncovered by Amnesty International (1994) illustrates. The most notorious example of this in the Irish context was the so-called Fairview Park murder in 1983, when a gang assaulted and killed a gay man. The gang were found guilty but given suspended sentences, following which they held a victory march in Fairview Park. While this clearly involved homophobia at many levels, it also resulted in a mobilisation of public opinion in support of a protest march organised by the Dublin Lesbian and Gay Men's Collective (Dublin Lesbian and Gay Men's Collective, 1986).

A further complication in understanding lesbian existence is the acknowledgement that categorisation into heterosexual or homosexual is problematic. Sexual orientation may not be a fixed entity, but rather a fluid and changing continuum. The idea of a sexual continuum was developed by Alfred Kinsey during his pioneering research on sexual behaviour based on interviews with thousands of women and men (Kinsey et al., 1948, 1953). Kinsey built on Freud's view that humans are fundamentally bisexual, i.e. can experience erotic feeling for both sexes. He argued that there is a continuum from exclusively heterosexual to exclusively homosexual, with a middle range indicating bisexuality. He developed a six-point scale where a score of four, for example, would indicate a primarily homosexual (where six means exclusively homosexual) interest or experience but with substantial heterosexual experience or interest as well (Kinsey, 1948, 1953). Sex surveys and other research suggest that between eighty per cent and ninety per cent of individuals regard themselves as heterosexual, with the remainder varying between bisexuality and homosexuality (Hyde, 1994).

Adrienne Rich developed the concept of lesbian continuum to capture the range and diversity of lesbian experience. Lesbian continuum refers to 'a range – through each woman's life and throughout history – of woman-identified experience, not simply the fact that a woman has had or consciously desired genital sexual experience with another woman' (Rich, 1980, p.463). She points out that the experience of being lesbian varies not only across an individual's own lifetime, but also across different cultures and backgrounds. Depending on cultural conditions, lesbian existence has been completely underground, or has flourished openly.

In Western Europe it is only in the late nineteenth and twentieth centuries that some women gained enough economic independence to be openly lesbian. Penalties for being openly lesbian have included execution, mutilation, ostracisation and exile, making it extremely difficult to find evidence from history of women who were openly sexual with each other. However, there is considerable evidence of women passing as men, and of passionate relationships between women (Faderman, 1981, Donoghue, 1993). Examples of the latter from Irish history include the Ladies of Llangollen, and Somerville and Ross. The Ladies of Llangollen were Eleanor Butler and Sarah Ponsonby, who eloped with each other and lived their lives in Llangollen in Wales. Somerville and Ross, best known as the authors of *Memoirs of an Irish R.M.*, are Edith Somerville and Violet Martin (who wrote under the pen name Martin Ross), who were devoted to each other over their lifetimes (Faderman, 1981).

The variety and complexity of lesbian existence also makes inadequate any single definition of lesbian. Discussions of lesbianism have viewed it as: (1) a sexual preference or orientation, which focuses on the sexual aspect of being lesbian; (2) a lifestyle, which regards lesbianism as one of many lifestyles; (3) primary emotional or affective involvement with a woman or with women, which focuses on the emotional aspect of being lesbian; (4) an identity based on culture and politics, which broadens the focus beyond the purely personal or interpersonal; (5) woman-identification, which involves the casting of erotic, emotional, social, political, intellectual and spiritual allegiances with women (Raymond, 1986, Kitzinger, 1987, Allen, 1990, Hyde, 1994). It is noteworthy that these themes barely articulate with cultural stereotypes of lesbians as man-hating – they represent lesbianism as an orientation towards women, rather than away from men. There is also, of course, considerable diversity in demographic and other background variables.

Systematic research on lesbians is difficult in any culture, given the difficulties of contacting a hidden population, and lack of resources provided for such research. However, over the last twenty years research in Psychology and Sociology, particularly in the USA, has illuminated a number of aspects of lesbian existence, including the coming out process, sexuality, love and relationships, lesbian culture and community, lesbian health, lesbian mothers and their children, and the impact of ethnicity, race and disability on lesbian existence (Greene and Herek, 1994, Hyde, 1994). By definition, most research involves lesbians who have 'come out', that is, acknowledged their lesbian sexual orientation. A considerable amount of research is still based on patient populations in medical and psychological settings, which obviously creates enormous problems of representativeness. While it is beyond the scope of the present chapter to review this research, it is worth mentioning that research on many different samples has long ago refuted the idea that homosexuality is a form of mental illness, or is associated with high levels of mental illness or disturbances of personality (Bell and Weinberg, 1978, Hyde, 1994).

Overview of Irish Research

Unfortunately, there has been very little published research on Irish lesbians and gay men. The most comprehensive is the study commissioned by the Gay and Lesbian Equality Network (GLEN, 1995), which was government funded, and which will be discussed in detail below. This absence of research is an outcome of the lack of funding resources, and contributes to the invisibility of lesbians and gay men, who are generally omitted from Irish academic discourse in Sociology and Psychology. In the absence of research, for example, it has been difficult to include coverage of lesbians and gay men in two recent Irish publications in Sociology and Psychology (Clancy et al., 1995, and Halliday and Coyle, 1995).

There are a number of books, articles, theses, and research reports which provide discussions by lesbians and gay men of the Irish context. The first book was published by Dublin Lesbian and Gay Men's Collective in 1986, and contained a wide range of articles on coming out, relationships, marriage and children, health, violence, work and politics. Since then there have been a number of publications on civil rights (ICCL, 1990), lesbian and gay politics and culture (Rose, 1994, O'Carroll and Collins, 1995), coming out (Byrne and Larkin, 1994) and family issues (Wardlaw, 1994). There are also, of course, lesbian and gay writers, musicians and artists (see O'Carroll and Collins, 1995), and publications which cover lesbian and gay issues such as Belfast *Women's News*, *MsChief*, and *Gay Community News*.

Sexual Orientation and Psychological Health

The first published study of 'Irish homosexual and heterosexual males and females' was published in 1984 by Helena Carlson. Carlson administered standardised measures of sex-role orientation, self-esteem and depression to 112 Irish women and men, including twenty-three lesbians, forty-nine gay men, seventeen heterosexual women and twenty-three heterosexual men, all of whom were recruited through word of mouth and participated on a voluntary basis. There were no significant differences between heterosexual and homosexual respondents on measures of depression and self esteem. Both lesbians and gay men were found to be more androgynous (i.e. having characteristics traditionally assigned to both sexes) than heterosexual respondents. Carlson argued that androgyny has been repeatedly found to be associated with higher levels of well-being, and that the higher levels of androgyny in lesbians and gay men would counterbalance the loss of self esteem and increased stresses caused by prejudice and intolerance (Carlson and Baxter, 1984).

Coming Out and Making Contact

Insights into coming out in the Irish context are provided by the experience of Dublin Lesbian Line (Dublin Lesbian Line Collective, 1991), whose records were analysed over a nine-year period (1984-1993) by Cathy Corcoran (Corcoran, 1993). Coming out is defined by Greene (1994) as 'the realisation of one's gay or lesbian sexual orientation and the subsequent disclosure of that orientation to others' (p.6). The difficulties of disclosure are manifested in silent calls, whose frequencies ranged from eight per cent to fourteen per cent over the time examined, while a further nine per cent to twenty-six per cent of calls were hang-ups. The interpretation of many of these calls as coming out calls is supported by the fact that many callers who make contact reveal that they had earlier made silent or hang-up calls in which they were literally dumbstruck by fear and embarrassment.

Between nine per cent and sixteen per cent of calls were classified as 'seeking help', mostly because of isolation and depression related to coming out or being closeted, or because of problems such as fear about coming out to parents or friends. Between five per cent and nine per cent of callers were seeking a meeting with a volunteer on the line who would accompany her to the 'coming out' discussion group (First Out) or a lesbian social venue. Meeting with a volunteer from lesbian line or attending the First Out discussion group (both of which involve trained volunteers with agreed policies regarding confidentiality, sexual relationships etc.) is often a major first step for women who are coming out (Dublin Lesbian Line Collective, 1991).

A substantial number of phone calls to Dublin Lesbian Line (and to other lesbian lines) are thus made by women who are dealing with coming out issues – women who, it should be noted, are of diverse ages and backgrounds, and include mothers and married women. The majority of calls were information calls, which constituted between twenty-six per cent and forty per cent of calls received. These callers include women seeking information on upcoming social events, on lesbian and gay social venues, on friendly accommodation, on political activities and support groups. They also include callers seeking lesbian friendly doctors, counsellors, solicitors and other services, or the names of interesting books, magazines and videos.

In discussing her findings, Corcoran noted firstly that there was an increase over the years in the number of phone calls from younger women, and from married women, which she linked to a more progressive social climate. There has been a consistent decline in hang-up calls and in silent calls, again suggesting a reduction in fear and embarrassment about lesbian issues. The overall number of phone calls increased in the early 1990s, and also showed increases when issues related to lesbians and gay men received media coverage. The phone is continuously busy during operation hours, and it is apparent that there is a need for expanded services. New developments in Dublin include the setting up of a 1550 lesbian information line and the availability of information and advice from Lesbians Organising Together (LOT), which will presumably change the profile of callers to Dublin Lesbian Line.

Poverty and the Effects of Discrimination

The continuing reality of prejudice and discrimination is documented most thoroughly in a study published by the Combat Poverty Agency in 1995. This study was undertaken by NEXUS research co-operative and Gay and Lesbian Equality Network (GLEN). The study 'set out to explore how discrimination and fear of discrimination impacts on the levels of poverty and exclusion amongst lesbians and gay men and to establish the needs of those most at risk of experiencing poverty' (GLEN and NEXUS, 1995, p.xi). It aimed to be as inclusive as possible, while acknowledging the difficulties of accessing what is a largely hidden population. It combined qualitative and quantitative techniques and employed a snowball sampling methodology to gain access to respondents. The published report was based on a sample of 159 respondents, eighty-five women and seventy-four men, biased in favour of younger people (fifty-three per cent were aged under thirty years). While no claims to representativeness were made, every attempt was made to obtain a diverse sample in terms of class and regional distribution. The authors point out that the results may be most informative about those who are out (to themselves and/or to friends, family etc).

Respondents were judged to be in poverty if they were unemployed or had incomes less than seventy per cent of average household income and did not have access to at least one of a list of items such as heating or fuel judged to be essential for a normal standard of living. The study was also concerned with the ways in which the lives of lesbians and gay men can be impoverished. Impoverishment refers to the cumulative effect even on those who are not economically deprived of difficulties in areas such as education, training, employment, housing and neighbourhood safety which are brought about by fear, discrimination and harassment in relation to sexual orientation. The questionnaire contained 252 questions covering education, employment and income, support from family and friends, provision of services, and harassment and violence.

The results in the published study are broken down by poverty and non-poverty groups, rather than by gender, making it impossible to differentiate findings for lesbians. However, it can be borne in mind that most poverty studies find considerably higher levels of poverty among women than among men. Whether these gender differences are exaggerated or mitigated in the case of lesbians and gay men remains to be ascertained.

The extent of poverty is illustrated by the finding that, based on the definition discussed above, twenty-one per cent of respondents were found to be living in poverty. Most of these (ninety-four per cent) were unemployed or on FAS (employment training) schemes, and ninety-one per cent said that they had difficulty making ends meet. Over half (fifty-seven per cent) of all respondents said that they found it difficult to make ends meet. One third (thirty-one per cent) of respondents said they had had to leave home without knowing where they could live, highlighting the risk of homelessness, especially for young lesbians and gay men.

Experiences of discrimination included difficulties at school (fifty-seven per cent), physical assault (twenty-five per cent) and threats of violence (forty-one per cent), discrimination in pubs, restaurants and hotels (thirty-nine per cent), and harassment at work (forty per cent). Even higher percentages of respondents believed that they would experience discrimination in these and other areas if they were to disclose their sexual orientation. Many respondents said they avoided work for which they were qualified (twenty-one per cent) or certain categories of work (thirty-nine per cent) because of experiences of harassment and fear of discrimination.

Social isolation and social exclusion can be brought about through rejection by family and friends, fear of coming out or of being identified as gay or lesbian, lack of social venues for lesbians and gay men, and costs of socialising. Many respondents, for example, did not attend discos (fifty-one per cent) or get involved in sports (fifty per cent) while at school because of their sexual orientation, and of those who went to college, around forty per cent experienced difficulties socially. The majority of the sample (eighty-two per cent) were out to some extent to their family, but sixty-one per cent indicated that they had had some problems with their families as a result. Problems were also experienced coming out to friends (fifty-four per cent), including embarrassment, rejection, and gradual breakdown of some relationships. In spite of these difficulties, the vast majority of those who had come out said that it had improved their lives considerably. Very few respondents who had difficulties were willing to talk to official sources of help because of lack of support for their sexual orientation, preferring instead to contact services provided by the lesbian and gay community.

The findings presented so far obviously provide strong evidence for the existence of prejudice and discrimination towards lesbians and gay men. As the executive summary states: 'The survey results clearly show that there are significant cumulative and interlocking processes of discrimination operating in Irish society that increase the risk of poverty and exclusion for lesbians and gay men. These processes further disadvantage those already living in poverty' (p.xii). The findings also vindicate the emphasis in lesbian and gay activism on combating homophobia, on providing services, and on building a supportive and celebratory community.

Lesbian Politics and Community – Goals and Ideals

Lesbian politics and lesbian community encompass an enormous range of activities and viewpoints with varying levels of interconnectedness. Politics range from radical separatist to reformist, with numerous autonomous groups and individuals operating with or without articulated philosophies and ideals. Discussions about community range from questioning its very existence to aspirations about care, togetherness, tolerance, mutual responsibility, support for the less able, creativity and celebration (Moane, 1994). One of the important functions of lesbian and gay pride events, in addition to the celebratory function mentioned above, is to bring together the disparate strands. The rainbow has recently been adopted as a symbol to reflect the combination of unity and diversity inherent in lesbian and gay politics and community.

Historical Background

It has already been mentioned that lesbian lives are lived in a context marked by prejudice and discrimination on the one hand, and by celebration and pride on the other. These and other themes discussed above are evident in the social and political organising of lesbians over the last twenty years. It should be noted here that of course lesbians have also been active in every area of concern to the women's movement, and also in trade unions, nationalism, socialism, traveller's rights, disability rights, ecology, and other progressive movements (Moane, 1995).

Writers in O'Carroll and Collins (1995) provide detailed overviews of many aspects of lesbian and gay organising since the 1970s. During the 1970s and 1980s the general trend for lesbians was one of ebbing and flowing, with some groups such as lesbian mothers forming and disbanding, while others, particularly lesbian lines, remaining continually active. While lesbians were active in the women's movement and the lesbian and gay rights movement right from the beginning, it was only in 1978 that lesbians acting explicitly on behalf of lesbians began to mobilise. In that year the first lesbian conference was held in

Trinity College Dublin, and Dublin Lesbian Line Collective was formed (Crone, 1995).

From the beginning, Dublin Lesbian Line operated on a collective basis, and along with other lesbian lines around the country formed a cornerstone of the lesbian community. There was an emphasis among lesbians on forming a supportive and celebratory community, and this found expression over the years in the organisation of events such as the annual Cork Fun Weekend, the Wild and Wonderful Women's Weekend in Dublin, and the Irish Women's Camp. The variety of social events include discos, cabarets, quizzes, sports, lectures, workshops, readings, and film festivals. Support groups have formed around such areas as coming out, health, religion, and motherhood.

Lesbian activism received a further boost in 1987 when the Third International Interdisciplinary Congress on Women, with its accompanying Festival of Art and Culture was held in Dublin. Lesbians from around the world met with Irish lesbians, stimulating the desire for further political activism, and for national and international networking. Much of this activism continued to be channelled into lesbian lines, who extended their activities into Public Relations and media work, and into providing resources and meeting spaces for lesbians. Lesbian culture continued to develop through writing, art, culture and a range of other activities.

In 1991, Dublin Lesbian Line, Dublin Lesbian Discussion Group (now First Out), and Cork Lesbian Line made written submissions to the Second Commission on the Status of Women (1993), which was followed by an oral presentation to the Commission by Dublin Lesbian Line. The submission from Dublin Lesbian Line asserted the right of lesbians to participate as full and equal members in all areas of society. Proposals for change involved four broad areas: (1) provision of resources, in particular funding for an office or meeting place; (2) legislative reforms, especially the inclusion of lesbians in anti-discrimination legislation (and of course the decriminalisation of homosexuality); (3) an education programme which would include realistic portrayals of lesbians and education about lesbians in all areas of education and training (including youth, education and health professionals); (4) positive action to promote open lesbians into positions of power in the private and public sector (Dublin Lesbian Line Collective, 1991). Cork and Dublin Lesbian lines have also been active in the National Women's Council of Ireland, and recently, the delegate from Dublin Lesbian Line Collective became the first representative of a lesbian organisation to be elected to its executive.

In its report, the Commission acknowledged that those with a homosexual orientation constitute a substantial although largely underground minority, and wrote that 'there is no doubt that there is a powerful taboo in operation' (p.174). The Commission recommended: (a) the decriminalisation of homosexual acts between consenting adults; (b) the inclusion of sexual orientation in the Unfair Dismissals Act; (c) the inclusion of a module on homophobia in the proposed sex and relationship education course in second-level schools; (d) consideration of lesbian groups for funding from the Department of Social Welfare (Second Commission on the Status of Women, 1993). This last recommendation laid important groundwork for lesbian groups to receive government funding.

In 1991 a co-ordinating group Lesbians Organising Together (LOT) was formed at a meeting in the offices of Dublin Lesbian Line Collective, involving the various groups and individuals who were active at the time. The initial aim of LOT was to provide co-ordination, support and resources for lesbians in Dublin. Since its formation, groups and activities associated with LOT include: Dublin Lesbian Line and coming out discussion groups; campaigns for legislative protection for lesbians and gay men; the education of the public through outreach, publishing and media work; the provision of resources and social spaces for lesbians; support for lesbian mothers and young lesbians. Groups associated with LOT generally operate independently and have access to the resources provided by the LOT co-ordinating group. LOT has been involved for the last three years in organising the annual 'Lesbian Lives' conference with the Women's Education Research and Resource Centre in UCD. Over the years LOT has received funding from many agencies as well as from its own fundraising. Recently it received core funding from the Department of Social Welfare, the first lesbian group to do so. This decision attracted considerable negative media attention. LOT has also been the first lesbian group to receive NOW funding for an outreach and education programme (Lesbian Education and Awareness – LEA). LOT also runs a CE (Community Enterprise) programme which staffs an office and a drop-in centre (LOT, 1992-1995).

Lesbians have also been involved with gay men in lesbian and gay organising, particularly in campaigning for legislative changes. Up to 1993 homosexual activity was a criminal offence under what David Norris referred to as 'the lingering shame of British imperial statute' (1995, p.14) – the 1861 Offences Against the Person Act. This law remained in place despite the fact that work codes in government agencies included a statement of intolerance of discrimination on the basis of sexual orientation, and the Prohibition of Incitement to Hatred Act (1989) included sexual orientation in its title. In campaigning for law reform, it was argued not only that homosexuality should be decriminalised, but that the principle of equality should apply to lesbians and gay men (Robson, 1995). In 1993 homosexuality was decriminalised, and the new law introduced an equal age of consent, which makes Ireland a welcome exception to many European countries, where the age of consent for homosexuals is higher than for heterosexuals.

It is thus accepted that there should be legislative protection against discrimination on the grounds of sexual orientation, and sexual orientation has been included in the Unfair Dismissals Act (1993), the Employment Equality Act (1996) and the forthcoming Equal Status Act. However, the latter two acts allow for exemptions on the grounds of religion, and as the Lesbian Equality Network (LEN) pointed out in its submission to the Department of Equality and Law Reform, this exemption is particularly problematic for lesbians and gay men as they are the only group for whom the very basis of their identity (homosexuality) is considered to be immoral (LEN, 1994).

This necessarily selective historical overview has emphasised the remarkable progress which has been made even in the last few years. However, it should be borne in mind that the changes so far have had the most impact on those who are already out and comfortable with their sexuality. Unfortunately, as the GLEN survey illustrates, negative attitudes towards homosexuality and towards lesbians and gay men continue to prevail. Indeed the Catholic Church still argues that homosexuality is a disorder, and can be a basis for discrimination (Congregation for the Doctrine of the Faith, 1992).

Ideals and Goals of Lesbian Organising

The above discussion highlighted some of the goals of lesbian organising. At a practical level, the main priorities have been firstly to diminish the immediate impact of homophobia by providing support for coming out lesbians and secondly to build a supportive and celebratory community. The main groups providing such support for coming out lesbians are lesbians lines, which, as discussed above, provide a telephone and meeting service. There are also discussion groups aimed at those coming out or exploring their sexuality. The provision of an office and drop-in centre with resources and information has also been an important goal which has been achieved in Dublin through the work of LOT. Education, outreach, and legislative reform are among the goals of lesbian organising discussed above.

At the more abstract level of ideals, there has been considerable discussion of the kind of communities that lesbians want or aspire to. Many ideals have been expressed in lesbian culture, including romantic fiction, music and music festivals, art, poetry, literature, celebration, and woman centred spirituality. In Ireland, events such as the Irish (formerly Galway) Women's Camp, the Cork Fun Weekend, and the Dublin Wild and Wonderful Women's Weekend explicitly aim to enact these ideals.

Two important ideals are those of equality and inclusiveness, which are interconnected, and are also connected with other ideals such as lesbian pride, and ideals about lesbian relationships and sexuality. Both equality and inclusiveness require new ways of organising. Hierarchical structures and inaccessibilty through financial or other (e.g. attitudinal) barriers are seen as reproducing inequality and exclusivity or elitism. The structures which have evolved to incorporate these ideals include collective organisation, decision-making by consensus, and rotation of responsibilities. Lesbian Lines in Ireland have been organised in this way since their foundation. A fundamental principle is that 'each member of the group has an equal say at all levels of decision-making' (Galway Lesbian Line, 1993, p.2). The recently formed Lesbian and Bisexual Youth Group (which can be contacted through LOT), for example, adopted this approach based on some members' experience in Dublin Lesbian Line Collective.

The concept of autonomy has also been central to much lesbian political organising. Each lesbian line, for example, operates as an independent and autonomous group, and this principle was maintained in the formation of a national network of lesbian and gay lines. Another example involving the principle of autonomy is the Dublin-based group Lesbians Organising Together (LOT). As noted above, this was formed as a co-ordinating structure, and now has nine affiliated groups. For the most part groups operate completely autonomously, although some policies are commonly agreed. LOT's mission statement includes the aspiration: 'To enable lesbians, bisexual women, and women exploring their sexuality to participate as full and equal members of society', and states that 'LOT strives to work with the values of: equality of opportunity; awareness of diversity; inclusion; visibility and accessibility; pride; friendliness; competence; autonomy of activism' (LOT, 1996).

Many of the groups discussed so far are women only, which is itself a principle of organising. This is a form of separation, or of separatism, a practice which is common to many subordinate or minority groups ranging from African Americans to nationalist groups. It is based on the understanding that empowerment requires separating from those who practice domination, or from situations that involve domination (Moane, 1996). This can provide the ground on which a separate identity and culture can develop, and a basis, where desired, for entering into coalitions.

These ideals, and others, are often aspirations which are difficult to implement, and which sometimes themselves create difficulties. Difficulties arise from the inevitable features of political organising which include lack of resources, power struggles, personality clashes, and frustrations and defeats. A particular challenge for lesbian organising in the 1990s arises out of the increased availability of funding and bureaucratisation in the area of voluntary and community work. The organisational demands that this creates are very much at odds with the values and ideals of lesbian organising discussed above. Hopefully the diversity and vibrancy of lesbian community and politics will help to create innovative solutions to this and other challenges.

Discussion Topics

1. Would you agree with the ideas of Kinsey and Rich about the sexual continuum and the lesbian continuum? What are the implications of this for an understanding of sexuality generally?

2. Would you agree that lesbians experience prejudice and discrimination? Why do you think this is? Is there anything unique about the prejudice and discrimination experienced by lesbians?

3. Do you think lesbians do well in achieving the two goals of supporting women who are coming out, and building a supportive and celebratory community? What aspects of lesbian organising do you think are particularly important?

4. Do you think lesbian organisations should receive financial support for providing services for lesbians? Should lesbian groups be treated like other groups, or should they be given special consideration?

References and Further Reading

Abelove, H, Barale, M A and Halperin D. (eds.) 1993 *The Lesbian and Gay Studies Reader* London: Routledge.

Allen, J. (ed.) 1990 *Lesbian Philosophies and Cultures* New York: State University of New York Press.

Amnesty International. 1994 *Breaking the Silence: Human Rights Violations Based on Sexual Orientation* New York: Amnesty International.

Bell, A P and Weinberg, M S. 1978 *Homosexualities* New York: Simon and Schuster.

Byrne, S and Larkin, J. 1994 *Coming Out* Dublin: Martello.

Carlson, H and Baxter, L. 1984 'Androgyny, Depression, and Self-Esteem in Irish Homosexual and Heterosexual Males and Females' *Sex Roles*, 5, pp.157-467.

Castle, T. 1993 *The Apparitional Lesbian* New York: Columbia University Press.

Clancy, P, Drudy, S, Lynch, K, and O'Dowd, L. (eds.) 1995 *Irish Society: Sociological Perspectives* Dublin: Insitute of Public Administration.

Congregation for the Doctrine of the Faith. 1992 *Some Considerations Concerning the Catholic Response to Legislative Proposals on the Non-Discrimination of Homosexual Persons* Rome: The Vatican.

Corcoran, C. 1993 *Breaking the Silence: An Analysis of the Dublin Lesbian Line Telephone Archives*, April 1984-June 1993 M.A. Thesis, University College Dublin.

Crone, J. 1995 'Lesbians: The Lavender Women of Ireland' in O'Carroll, I and Collins, E. (eds.), *Lesbian and Gay Visions of Ireland* London: Cassells.

Donoghue, E. 1993 *Passion Between Women, British Lesbian Culture* London: Scarlett Press.

Dublin Lesbian and Gay Men's Collective. 1986 *Out for Ourselves, the Lives of Irish Lesbians and Gay Men* Dublin: Women's Community Press.

Dublin Lesbian Line Collective. 1991 *Submission to the Second Commission on the Status of Women* Dublin: Dublin Lesbian Line.

Faderman, L. 1981 *Surpassing the Love of Men* New York: Quill.

Galway Lesbian Line. 1993 *Annual Report* Galway: Galway Lesbian Line.

GLEN and NEXUS. 1995 *Poverty among Lesbians and Gay Men* Dublin: Combat Poverty Agency.

Greene, B. 1994 'Lesbian and Gay Sexual Orientations: Implications for Clinical Training, Practice and Research' Greene, G and Herek, G M. (eds.) *Lesbian and Gay Psychology* New York: Sage Publications.

Greene, B and Herek, G M. (eds.) 1994 *Lesbian and Gay Psychology* New York: Sage Publications.

Halliday, A and Coyle, K. (eds.) 1994 'The Irish Psyche.' Special Issue of *The Irish Journal of Psychology* Dublin: Psychological Society of Ireland.

Humm, M. 1992 *Feminisms: A Reader* London: Harvester.

Hyde, J S. 1994 *Understanding Human Sexuality (Fifth Edition)* New York: McGraw Hill.

ICCL. 1990 *Equality Now for Lesbians and Gay Men* Dublin: Irish Council for Civil Liberties.

Kinsey, A C, Pomeroy, W B and Martin, C E. 1948 *Sexual Behaviour in the Human Male* Philadelphia: Saunders.

Kinsey, A C, Pomeroy, W B Martin, C E and Gebhard, P H. 1953 *Sexual Behaviour in the Human Female* Philadelphia: Saunders.

Kitzinger, C. 1987 *The Social Construction of Lesbianism* London: Sage.

LEN. 1994 *Submission to the Department of Equality and Law Reform* Dublin: LEN.

LOT. 1992-1995 *Annual Reports* Dublin: Lesbians Organising Together.

LOT. 1996 *Information Leaflet* Dublin: Lesbians Organising Together.

McDermott, M. 1996 *How 'Liberating' is the Gay Liberation Movement?* Paper presented to the Centre for the Study of Homosexuality, Bremen, Germany.

Moane, G. 1994 *A Lesbian Feminist Perspective on the Family* Presentation on 'The Family and Community', organised by Dublin Lesbian and Gay Pride Week Committee and Women's Education Research and Resource Centre, UCD.

Moane, G. 1996 'Legacies of Colonialism for Irish Women: Oppresive or Empowering?' *Irish Journal of Feminist Studies* 1 pp.100-119.

Norris, D. 1995 'Criminal Law (Sexual Offences) Bill 1993, Second Stage Speech' in O'Carroll, I and Collins, E (eds.), *Lesbian and Gay Vision of Ireland* London: Cassells.

O'Carroll, I, and Collins, E. (eds.) 1995 *Lesbian and Gay Visions of Ireland* London: Cassells.

Penelope, J. 1984 'The Mystery of Lesbians' *Lesbian Ethics*, 1, 86-97.

Prendiville, P. 1996 Introduction *LOT Resource Manual* Dublin: Lesbians Organising Together.

Raymond, J. 1986 *A Passion for Friends, Toward a Philosophy of Female Affection* London:The Women's Press.

Robson, C. 1995 'Anatomy of a Campaign' in O'Carroll, I and Collins, E. (eds.), *Lesbian and Gay Visions of Ireland* London: Cassells.

Rose, K. 1994 *Diverse Communities: The Evolution of Lesbian and Gay Politics in Ireland* Cork: Cork University Press.

Rich, A. 1980 'Compulsory Heterosexuality and Lesbian Existence.' *Signs: Journal of Women in Culture and Society,* 15, pp.459-485.

Second Commission on the Status of Women. 1993 *Report to Government* Dublin: Stationery Office.

Wardlaw, C. 1994 *One in Every Family: Myths about Lesbians and Gay Men* Dublin: Basement Press.

27.

Sober for the Sake of the Children: The Church, The State and Alcohol use amongst Women in Ireland

Tanya M Cassidy

Introduction

In Ireland[1] there is a popular belief that, in the past, women did not drink alcohol, at least not 'good' women, and not in public. Ireland had the largest percentage of abstainers amongst the twelve EU countries. Moreover, in all countries, including Ireland, women were more likely to be abstainers than men (Hupkens et al., 1993). However, in the last thirty years, the percentage of abstainers, particularly women, has been dropping in Ireland (Walsh, 1980, Conniffe and McCoy, 1993). A recent 'Eurobarometer' survey (an annual EU attitudinal survey) indicates that the ratio of female to male abstainers is closer in Ireland than in any other EU country. Moreover, there is evidence that, prior to the famine, Irish men and women commonly consumed alcohol with each other in public (Pritchard, 1985).

Over the last thirty years Ireland has undergone major socio-economic changes which have had far-reaching social effects. During this same time period, alcohol consumption has been increasing (Walsh, 1980, Conniffe and McCoy, 1993). It has been argued that a significant proportion of this increase is due to the drop in total abstainers in Irish society, especially female abstainers (Conniffe and McCoy, 1993). Other evidence, such as increased hospitalisation rates, indicate that alcohol consumption amongst women has increased. This increased female consumption is not unique to Ireland, but has been argued to be associated with development in nations (Shaw, 1980). Moreover, it has been seen as the 'price' of social emancipation and equality.

Recently, feminists have been presenting interesting social structural arguments pertaining to questions about why modernisation and employment have not lead to levels of equality (Goldin, 1990, Pyle, 1990, Skocpol, 1992). In general, these authors have argued that historical state structures and relationships need to be considered when talking about issues related to inequality amongst the sexes. Ireland is somewhat unusual since the level of labour force participation of married women is low, although participation rates are increasing steadily. It is important to recognise the role of the Catholic Church in any discussion of the Irish state and women. Not only are women defined by the state as the keepers of the family, but they are also defined this way by the Church.[2] It is my contention that the Catholic Church's position towards female abstinence in particular has been influenced by their vision of the role of mothers in society.

In an attempt to understand changes in women's drinking practices in Ireland we need to consider not only social customs in pubs and the socio-economic conditions of the nation, but also issues surrounding abstinence, the Catholic Church and the family.

Women and the Uneasy Case of Irish Inebriety

On my first trip to Ireland, my partner (a native Corkman) was showing me the sights of Cork City. An elderly woman, who was obviously intoxicated, spotted our camera and asked us to take her picture. My partner, who viewed the woman as 'harmless' and pleasant, was happy to oblige. It occurred to me that the stereotypical Irish caricature of a drunk was most often male, not female, and therefore this interaction stood out.

Another image which was contrary to the stereotypical image of the drunken Irishman was the high level of abstinence in Irish society. One of the first things I noticed after arriving in Cork City was a prominently located statue in the centre of the main business thoroughfare. Known locally simply as 'The Statue', it is arguably the most frequently used landmark in Cork conversation. Erected in 1864, it is an imposing figure of Father Mathew, the celebrated temperance leader of the 1830s. Father Mathew in his crusade administered oaths to large numbers of Irish people to abstain from the use of alcohol. Later I was to learn that a large percentage of Irish society currently abstains from the use of alcohol, particularly women, and many of them have done so for their entire lives. I had been unaware of this dichotomy in Irish drinking behaviour, and I was motivated to delve deeper into the puzzle of Irish drinking.

First I turned to the seminal works of Bales (1946, 1962, 1980 [1944]). Bales concentrated on male drinking in Ireland, although he said 'the Irish child of the nineteenth century saw a great deal of drinking, on the part of both males and females, older and younger' (1980, p.163). This unsupported observation of consumption by Irish women is linked, by Bales, to issues surrounding childcare. Bales goes on to quote an 'episode' which originally appeared in one of Carleton's (1869) often negative nineteenth century stories about the peasantry.[3] In the story, a father, Larry, hits his son, Dick. His mother, Sally, comes in and releases a great wail:

> And to make a long story short, they sat down, and drank the bottle of whiskey among them. Larry and Sally made it up, and were as great friends as ever, and Dick was made drunk for the bating he got from his father (Carleton, 1869, pp.95-96).

The only other example of drinking amongst Irish women that Bales specifically mentions is a report that ether drinking, prevalent in Northern Ireland during the nineteenth century, was practised 'among both sexes' (1962, p.162). Once again, however Bales links this image with children through his source whom he quotes as saying that the Irish 'mother may be seen with her daughters, and maybe a neighbour-Irishwoman or two, at a friendly ether "bee"' (Kerr, 1894, p.131).

Generally, however, Bales gives the impression that drinking in Ireland was an almost exclusively male domain. In an interesting reinterpretation and expansion of Bales' work, Stivers (1976) showed that many of the Irish drinking practices were also common amongst the English and Scottish. Similar to Bales, however, Stivers only briefly pondered the question of drinking amongst Irish women, whom he said 'were excluded from rural pubs,' but 'were allowed and even expected to imbibe on such special communal occasion as weddings' (1976, p.177). Stivers went on to say that Irish women who drank on any other occasions, regardless of the amount, would be considered 'deviant', 'a fallen women or an alcoholic', and '[e]xtreme degradation was her lot' (1976, p.177).

Within Ireland, Perceval (1955) remarks that Irishmen and women had different beverages preferences, with the former being partial to whiskey and stout, whereas the latter, along with youths, favoured port wine or sherry which were considered 'teetotaller drinks'. Perceval says that rural pubs are often shops, and so women, particularly during the day, would be present, but 'it is very rare to see women drinking' (1955, p.148). Rural pubs are not suited for women, Perceval contends, because they lack entertainment and comfort, whereas a man might take a women for a drink in a 'good class hotel' which has either a 'lounge bar or a private bar' (1955, p.148). In cities, on the other hand, he says there has been a large increase in the number of lounge bars, specifically intended to attract female customers. He adds '[t]here has been a definite increase in drinking by women – particularly young women – in these lounges and also in all good class hotels, and it is now quite usual for a man and his wife or "girl friend" to spend a good deal of time and money on drinking, especially at week-ends' (1955, p.148).

Over the last thirty years, consumption rates have been rising in Ireland, a large percentage of which researchers contribute to falling abstinence rates amongst women and youths (Walsh, 1980, Conniffe and McCoy, 1993). Although drinking amongst young people in Ireland has been the focus of many studies (O'Connor, 1978, Grube and Morgan, 1986, 1990), the study of drinking amongst Irish women has tended to focus on alcoholics or problem drinkers (O'Connor, 1987, Corrigan and Butler, 1991, Ward, 1993, Corrigan, et al.,

1995). Although these studies are important, alcoholics or problem drinkers are a very small percentage of the drinking population in any society. Studies of alcoholic women indicate they are most likely to be married, a fact that other studies in Ireland have found to be false for males (Walsh, 1968). Moreover, researchers say that three-quarters of drinking amongst alcoholic Irish women occurs in the home and alone. Conniffe and McCoy point out 'that young unmarried women are more likely than other women to be heavy drinkers' (1993, p.76). Furthermore, in one of the earliest studies on drinking amongst Irish youths (Fitzpatrick, 1970a, 1970b), it was reported that the vast majority of males drank beer, stout, or lager (92.5 per cent), whereas the majority of females drank vodka (35.6 per cent) or beer (32.8 per cent); vodka is also the spirit with the largest consumption increase between 1965 and 1971, thus suggesting that a large part of the increase in consumption amongst Irish youths is associated with females.

The Institutionalisation of Abstinence

The most important factor influencing drinking in Ireland since the late eighteenth century until relatively recently seems to have been the various temperance and abstinence movements. For at least two hundred years, two ideal types of drinkers have co-existed in Irish society: heavy drinkers and abstainers. Both Bales (1980, 1962) and Stivers (1976) recognised the role of these two groups in Irish society, but neither discussed the relationship with the sexes.

Beginning in the 1780s, we see the origins of the first wave of the Irish temperance movement, mainly driven by the Protestant ascendancy, who became particularly vocal in 1829, the year of Catholic emancipation (Bretherton, 1991). The 'enlightened' wealthy believed that the consumption of whiskey caused and exacerbated poverty among the lower classes. While the upper classes continued to enjoy such beverages as wine, the poor were encouraged to switch to beer.

This early campaign failed to enlist any substantial part of the vast Catholic population. Even Bishop James Doyle, the only member of the Catholic hierarchy who supported this early Protestant temperance movement, doubted its success. In a letter in 1829, he said 'I am not prepared to express to others a confidence which I do not feel, that such societies in this country at this time, with our present laws and social government, can be productive of any great, or extensive, or permanent good' (Malcolm, 1986, p.84).

Things were to change dramatically with the advent of the second wave of temperance supporters. In the 1830s anti-alcohol sentiments were to harden, as they had in many other countries, to the advocation of total abstinence (Bretherton, 1991). This seems to have been spearheaded by people of humbler means who saw the earlier paternalistic movement of the Protestant ascendancy as hypocritical, and designed to allow the rich to continue to enjoy their wine. In Cork, this movement was not to become popular until 1835 when William Martin, a Quaker who founded the Cork Total Abstinence Society, enlisted the help of Father Theobald Mathew. Father Mathew acted more as an individual than as a representative of the Catholic Church, and he went to great efforts to avoid sectarianism within the temperance movement. However, the movement became linked to O'Connell's repeal campaign, especially after O'Connell took the pledge, even though he had to give it up shortly afterwards, due to doctor's orders. Thus despite Father Mathew's efforts to remain neutral, his movement lived and died with Irish sectarian politics, and he is probably most remembered for saying 'Ireland free is Ireland sober, and Ireland sober is Ireland free.'

Several bishops, such as Higgins and McHale, 'even though they had no theological or practical objections to teetotalism', were in open opposition to Father Mathew (Quinn, 1992, p.545). Mathew was seen as being overly zealous, and in close co-operation with Protestants (Malcolm, 1986). Thus the 'unusual step was taken' to overturn the parish priests' recommendation of Father Mathew for Bishop of Cork, and take the bishops' alternate recommendation since they believed that 'the appointment of Mathew would jeopardise the Church's independence' (Quinn, 1992, p.552).

In the third wave of temperance, however, Father Mathew's name was to be resurrected and used for its charismatic qualities. The Sacred Heart Pioneer Total Abstinence Association (known simply as 'Pioneers') movement was originally organised in 1898 by Father James Cullen and four non-drinking women (Mac Greil, 1993). Most of the Pioneer literature concentrates on Father Cullen, and only briefly mentions 'his four like-minded associates, Mrs M L Bury, Mrs A Egan, Miss L Bower, and Mrs A M Sullivan, who were already non-drinkers' (Mac Greil, 1993, p.7), and few ever mention that the movement was originally only for women, although men were later allowed to join (O'Connor, 1978, Malcolm, 1982). The previous abstinence movements in Ireland, like those in other countries, had been mainly associated with men. However, during the time of the formation of the Pioneers, an international female-centred abstinence campaign with religious connections which operated under the umbrella term of the 'World's Woman's Christian Temperance Union' (World's WCTU), was gaining momentum in both America and Britain.

Originally the Woman's Christian Temperance Crusade (1873-1874) 'was the largest nineteenth-century protest movement by women,' whereas its successor, the American WCTU, 'institutionalised temperance women's independence from male control' (Blocker, 1985, p.461). In 1885, at the centenary celebrations of temperance, 'Frances Willard, the dynamic and charismatic president, told her adoring followers that the "second temperance century" would witness the export of temperance reform around the globe, spearheaded by her recently created World's Woman's Christian Temperance

Union' (Tyrrell, 1991, p.217). Willard had established the World's WCTU a brief two years prior to this address, and there was already a declared membership of over half a million. By 1920, membership rose to over a million and the organisation was present in forty-two countries. Moreover, the movement in both America and Britain became linked with women's issues, particularly suffrage (Blocker, 1985). Even though the temperance campaigners 'avoided the suffrage issue, the Crusade was widely regarded, by both opponents and male supporters, as a movement for women's rights' (Blocker, 1985, p.463).

In Ireland, on the other hand, the Pioneers' movement quickly allowed males to join. Moreover, the Church dominated the movement, and thus enforced their vision of the role of Irish women. This role, from the middle of the nineteenth century, defined mothers as 'the organisational link between the Catholic Church and the individual' (Inglis, 1987, p.188). In his interesting discussion of relationship between the Church and the Irish mother, Inglis says:

> It was she who carried through the new moral and civil code from the church and school into the home ... It was she who, through a variety of subtle strategies and practices, persuaded her children to emigrate, postpone marriage, or not to marry at all. It was she who, through inculcating these practices and a rational regulation of life in her family, provided the vital force necessary for the restructuring of Irish rural life in the late nineteenth and early twentieth centuries (Inglis, 1987, p.188).

Moreover, it was she who encouraged temperance; however, she received her 'moral power in and through the Church' (Inglis, 1987, p.188).

Pioneers totally abstain from alcohol, and pray for reparations for the sins committed by excessive drinkers. Since women drink less than men, and were primarily responsible for the family, it seems reasonable to suggest that Father Cullen's original vision might have been that women might be more receptive to the concept of doing penance for their drunken husbands, sons and/or fathers. Moreover, the power of this perception of female abstinence might have contributed to the social stigma attached to female drinking, a stigma which seems to have been the norm for many decades prior to the most recent socio-economic changes.

Moving Drinking Out of the Domestic Sphere

One of the most distinctive features associated with drinking in Ireland is its public nature. Most people in Ireland drink in a public drinking establishment rather than in their homes (Conniffe and McCoy, 1993, Morgan and Grube, 1994, see Table 1.1 below). Consequently, Irish drinking is highly visible, whereas home consumption is reserved for guests and holiday occasions, especially Christmas.

Table 1: *Home Consumption of Beer as Percentage of Total Sales, 1990.*

COUNTRY	% OF TOTAL SALES
Denmark	74
France	65
The Netherlands	62
West Germany	60
Italy	57
Portugal	37
Belgium	31
Spain	25
UK	20
Ireland	6

Source: Thurman (1992).

This state of affairs was not always the case. The Irish public house is a relatively modern construction. Prior to the eighteenth century and modern commercialisation of the brewing and distilling industries in Ireland, production of alcohol was part of the domestic sphere and was mainly conducted by women (Joyce, 1913, Cullen, 1991). Brewing was also connected with the production of bread, as the yeast on the surface of the beer was used for this purpose (Cullen, 1991). Thus it is not surprising that ale was the staple drink and was consumed primarily in the home, particularly with meals. It is important to remember that during this time water, particularly in the cities, was highly contaminated, and until later in the nineteenth century, tea was a drink of the wealthy (MacLysaght, 1939). Milk was a common beverage consumed more in the countryside, but this beverage seemed to act more as a protein substitute (Chart, 1910). Distilled spirits were associated with medicinal use, as well as with feasts and markets, although imported wine was also popular on such occasions (McGuire, 1973, p.93).

The production of both brewed and distilled alcohol seems to have commercialised in the seventeenth and eighteenth centuries. However, Irish whiskey was a major export product long before. By contrast, ale was perishable but easy to produce, and thus was more appropriate for home consumption. The nineteenth century in Ireland saw an increased commercialisation of beer, which was more complicated to produce but less perishable than ale. This change had happened much earlier in England but in Ireland was hampered by the lack of an efficient transportation system until the spread of the rail network (Lynch and Vaizey, 1960, McGuire, 1973). Thus in Ireland, production of ale often varied in quality, inspiring the following ballad about Irish beer from 1725 called 'The old Cheese':

This beer is sour-thin, musty, thick and stale,
And worse than anything except the ale.

In addition to home brewing, it seems that many publicans would have produced their own ale, and that a substantial number of publicans were women. Laurence (1994) estimates that in seventeenth century England a quarter of licensed ale-houses were run by women. It seems reasonable to suggest, particularly since Ireland was under English rule at the time, that Irish women were also substantially involved in the ale-houses. Moreover, it is an often forgotten fact that a *síbín* – pronounced sheebeen – the Irish term that is now used to refer to an unlicensed drinking house, once referred to 'weak small-beer, taplash' (Dineen, 1927) or 'ale which had not paid duty, hence shebeen houses or shebeens where such ale was sold' (McGuire, 1973, p.159). Furthermore, in the sixteenth century 'one of the commonest legal charges brought against women' was the keeping of an unlicensed alehouse (Laurence, 1994, p.151).

In the nineteenth century things were to drastically change. With the widespread commercialisation of both the brewing and distilling industries, and growing class distinctions in drinking habits, as well as the introduction of organised temperance movements, 'the drinking place became less like a home, more like a shop' and women were less and less welcome (Harrison, 1971, p.46). More and more, the home became the woman's domain, whereas drinking in the pub served as 'the chief social life of the men and the chief means of getting them out of homes dominated by their women' (Fontaine, 1940, p.32, also quoted in Bales, 1962, p.171).

In my historical research, I found the following memo written by a Beamish and Crawford's sales representative to his superiors on 11 April, 1884. He states:

> It is a curious fact that the extra stout is used only by the men, and the houses near the markets to where the women are the principal customer cannot sell it at all.

This memo indicates that in the nineteenth century some Irish women, in Cork City at least, would drink in pubs which were located in the market area or shopping district, and these women drank differently from their male counterparts.

Not all women who drank in Ireland, however, would go to a pub, even these specially designated ones. There is a popular story in Ireland of the grandmother who would almost daily send her grandchild to the pub to fetch two pints of porter with instructions to inform the barman that it was needed to bake a porter cake, although it was local common knowledge that she did not mix most of this beverage with flour.[4]

In my research in Cork City, several of my respondents told me that up until about thirty years ago, Irish women were mainly confined in many pubs to drinking in an area known as a 'snug'. A snug was a small room, often with a fireplace and comfortable chairs, that was set off from the main bar-room (usually one entered it by going through a side door just inside the main entrance of the pub; thus, one did not have to go through the bar to reach the snug or vice versa). Men did not drink in the snug, unless they were accompanied by women or children. There also seems to have been several social restrictions placed on women who drank alcohol. For instance, some pubs refused to sell women pint measures of beer, instead requiring that they purchase it by the half-pint glass. In my research, I found one pub which still practised this distinction.

Drinking in Contemporary Ireland

Throughout the 1960s and the 1970s, the Irish government instituted several policies that have resulted in, or have been accompanied by, numerous economic and social organisational changes. The decision to steer the Irish economy away from its mainly agricultural base toward an expanded emphasis on light industry was a planning development in step with the later acceptance of membership in the European Economic Community, now the European Union. In addition, the introduction (after 1968) of free second-level schooling provided a more educated work force, one more suited both to rapid urbanisation and greater exposure to external cultural products, such as western feminist notions. Some examples of policy decisions specifically addressing women and employment which have been passed are the removal of marriage bars (1973), the Anti-discrimination Act (1974), the Employment Equality Act (1977), and the provision of maternity leave (1981). In addition, the availability of contraceptives has progressively increased, from 1979 when they were made available by prescription for 'genuine family planning purposes', to 1993 when vending machine sales of condoms were legalised. Moreover, a referendum was passed very recently (November 1995) to remove the Irish constitutional ban on divorce, although by a wafer-thin margin.

The Irish constitution is unique in the western world in so far as it specifically guarantees rights for the family. The recent amendment of Article 41 continues this tradition by specifically guaranteeing rights to the spouse and children of the first marriage. The rights of the family were the prime legal consideration in the High Court decision (1980) that tax-free allowances and tax bands for married people should be raised so that they are exactly double those of single people. However, Pyle (1990) has cited these familial rights as one indication of the discrimination against women present in Irish social institutions.

Pyle (1990) attempts to understand why so many married Irish women leave the labour force. In many other countries which have undergone, or are undergoing, similar social changes associated with modernisation we see increased participation of women, especially married women, in the workforce. Statistics in Ireland indicate that married women's participation in the labour force has increased three-fold, from 5.2 per cent in 1961 to 17.4 per cent in 1981 (Beale, 1987, p.144). In comparison to other Western countries, however, Ireland has one of the highest percentages of women who drop out of the labour force after marriage (Pyle, 1990). In general, Pyle asserts that 'the type of approach that best explains the change in female labour force activity during economic growth is one that focuses on gender inequality in major social institutions, such as the firm, the household, and the state and the manner in which state policy reinforces (or, alternatively alleviates) male domination in both of them' (Pyle, 1990, p.120).

Pyle's observations about the inherent patriarchal characteristics of the state are interesting and important. However, she fails to recognise, at least in Ireland, the historical role of the Church, particularly in relationship to women and the positions taken by the early Irish state which I discussed above. Moreover, Pyle does not consider the cultural meanings associated with the role of women in the family. Fine-Davis in her research on attitudes towards women and work in Ireland, found that a large majority (seventy-eight per cent) of her overall sample of both men and women felt that 'being a wife and mother are the most fulfilling role any women could want' (1983, p.9). This perception may be a holdover from the past but it can be argued that, Irish women, unlike Irish men, have an acceptable alternative to unemployment, namely being a mother, a role which accords much higher status than being on the 'dole' (dependant on social welfare). It should also be noted that Pyle is relying on older statistics and there are recent indications that female workforce participation in Ireland has continued to increase, and it remains to be seen if her assertions still hold true. Currently the Irish economy is one of the fastest growing in Europe and during the period 1987-90, total female employment grew by 7.4 per cent (Rubery and Fagan, 1993, p.134). In fact, preliminary 1995 figures for Ireland indicate that the proportion of female employed labour force participation has reached thirty-seven per cent.

Along with this increased female workforce participation, Ireland has seen large increases in alcohol consumption rates, particularly amongst women (Walsh, 1980, Conniffe and McCoy, 1993). Ireland is not unique in its increased consumption rates following the Second World War (Room, 1984). Researchers have pointed out that increased 'modernisation' in a society results in increased consumption (Bacon, 1945). More recently, socio-economic studies have argued that alcohol consumption rates are directly related to income. Specifically people, and especially women, from higher income brackets are less likely to abstain from drinking (Lawrence and Maxwell, 1962, Conniffe and McCoy, 1993, Smart, 1989). In Ireland, between 1960 and 1990, real disposable income per adult, as well as consumption rates, have almost doubled (Conniffe and McCoy, 1993). However, incomes and alcohol expenditure are influenced by household structure. In fact, regardless of income level, households with children spend less on alcohol, which Conniffe and McCoy argue is due to 'reduced discretionary income, so that a couple with children with an equal income to a single adult, actually have much less allocatable income' (1993, p.xiv).

Furthermore, studies on leisure have found that the leisure patterns of men and women are tied to life cycles, and that this seems to be especially true for women (Parker, 1976). Specifically it seems that, after women marry, and especially after they have children, their leisure activities change. Moreover, cross-cultural studies have shown that women are the providers of drinks in many societies (Bjeren, 1992, Stewart, 1992), and that the procurement and/or production of alcohol beverages are often a part of the domestic chores. As a consequence, female drinking most often seems to be within the domestic context, usually at family celebrations, when guests are visiting, or during all-female visits (Gefou-Madianou, 1992). '[I]t seems that for women's same-sex gatherings the drinking of alcohol is not of central concern' in many European countries (Gefou-Madianou, 1992, p.16). It has been argued that these get-togethers

> are largely 'productivity bound'. That is to say, women participating in these gatherings are at the same time busy embroidering, crocheting, needle pointing, or preparing or selling foods, agricultural or other goods. In that important respect, these gatherings contrast with the unproductive and at time anti-productive nature of all-male drinking gatherings, for in the bars, taverns and coffee-houses men will be found drinking, gambling, or simply passing the time (Gefou-Madianou, 1992, p.15).

During the summer and winter of 1992, I returned to Ireland to talk to people in Cork City about drinking. I interacted with and interviewed fifty individuals from twenty-five families throughout Cork City.[5] In an attempt to meet the criterion of procuring willing respondents from several neighbourhoods around the city,[6] I utilized a non-randon snowballing technique.[7] Respondents were asked about their own drinking patterns, as well as about the drinking patterns of their parents and of, when appropriate, their spouse and adult children. Thirty-five of the respondents indicated they drank alcohol, whereas fifteen said they did not, which is consistent with national figures of the percentage of abstainers in Irish society (O'Connor and Daly, 1983).

Contact time with each of these families varied, and was guided by a questionnaire that I had previously developed. This process took a minimum of an hour and a half to complete. Most of the time I spoke to people in their own homes. I spoke with more women (thirty-two) than men (eighteen). I also tried to visit several drinking establishments, especially those my respondents had mentioned. Though permission was routinely obtained to use a tape recorder from the respondents, I made a conscious effort not to draw their attention to the machine. Every attempt was made to make the interviews comfortable, like a 'conversation' or 'chat'. Eye contact was maintained with the respondent as much as possible, and I believe this helped maintain informality in the interaction. Only brief notes were needed and these were later expanded using the recordings.

The majority of my non-drinking respondents were women (ten out of fifteen), most of whom were over thirty years of age, and all but one of these women had never had alcohol in their lives, except in a 'sherry trifle', as one elderly woman pointed out. Research has shown that over the last thirty years there has been a drop in abstinence rates in Ireland, particularly amongst young people and women (Conniffe and McCoy, 1993). Although none of the non-drinking women I spoke with formally identified themselves as belonging to the Pioneers, they all recognised the organisation. One women, in her mid-sixties, told me that her husband, at one time a heavy drinker, said she should get herself a gold pin from the Pioneers since she had never drank 'a drop' in her life.

Amongst my drinking respondents in Cork, I found that women, as compared with men, often drank less which is consistent with previous research. Age and life-stage was also significant amongst my drinking respondents. Several of my female drinking respondents talked about how their patterns of drinking changed after they were married, and particularly after they had children. One of my female respondents, Mrs Murphy,[8] a married middle aged homecare provider with a long-term unemployed husband, told me that while she and her husband were courting they would often go out to a pub and drink. After they got engaged, she said, they would go out on Saturday nights for 'a few drinks' with both of her parents. This practice continued until after the birth of their first child at which time, as she pointed out, someone had to stay at home with the children.

Mrs Murphy went on to say she rarely went out after the children were born, the exception being some kind of occasion like a christening, an engagement, a wedding, a funeral, or a twenty-first birthday celebration. Often these events were held in a pub or a hotel, and alcohol was always present. Later, Mrs Murphy pointed out that when her older children were able to take care of the younger ones, she started going once a week to the local bingo, which is held at the local Gaelic Athletic Association (GAA) club. Within this club is a bar for club members. The bingo is held in a separate room where alcohol is not supposed to be served. Nevertheless, she said that it is a regular and accepted practice amongst the women (who are generally married) to go to the bar, get a drink, and bring it back to the room where they play bingo. She went on to say that it is also a common practice after the game for many of these women to cross the road to the local pub for a couple of drinks. She does not consider this 'going out', because she goes out for the bingo, and the fact that they go to a pub is secondary to this:

> We'd go into the pub after bingo, and we'd have a drink, one or two, or a couple. I used to never bother with it when I was single. It is since I got married I kinda go to it. The one I go to, that's a bar then as well, that's a club. They'd all have a drink, they'd have lager. – Would you have a drink yourself? – Now and then I would, but sometimes then I wouldn't because I find you mightn't be marking the books so well with too many.

Mrs Murphy's stressed that she was going for the bingo and the company, but not for the drink itself. Several of the women I spoke with in Cork, like Mrs

Murphy, suggested when they drank alcohol in all-female gatherings drink was not that important, which is similar to what researchers in other cultures have called 'productivity bound' drinking.

Researchers in other cultures have also found that female alcohol consumption often occurs within the domestic context (Gefou-Madianou, 1992). As noted before, Ireland, when compared with any other European nation, is unusual in the high percentage of alcohol consumed outside of the home (Thurman, 1992). Thus the majority of female alcohol consumption in Ireland also occurs outside the home, often in a pub or a club, as with Mrs Murphy and her bingo nights. My research in Cork however, indicates that Irish women, particularly married Irish women, are more likely than Irish men to drink in the home, although these drinking experiences are still usually productively orientated.

Mrs Casey, a forty-two year old stay-at-home mother of four children, the eldest of whom is in his early twenties and the youngest is ten years old, told me that she rarely would go out to a pub, only around Christmas and similar special occasions. Her husband, a self-employed businessman, rarely drinks, and thus they rarely go out to drink together. Mrs Casey said she drinks most often with her friends, but not in a pub, although they do so regularly:

> My friends, we get together every Monday night in each other's houses, and we might bring a can or something, and just have a drink, and make popcorn, and watch a video. The "Big M" it's called. It's just all women. Women only!

These Monday night all-female gatherings are Mrs Casey's main source of entertainment, but similar to Mrs Murphy with her bingos, Mrs Casey sees drink as not very important in these gatherings. The important point of the gatherings is to be out for the night with 'the girls'. Researchers have argued that cross-culturally women are more likely to drink privately in an attempt to 'seek to maintain their image as good mothers, sisters, wives, caretakers, in short as "good women"' (Gefou-Madianou, 1992, p.15).

Research suggests that even women who work outside the home will choose to drink at home (Park, 1990). Mrs O'Keefe, another of my respondents and a well-educated mother of four who works outside the home as a teacher, told me she would go to a pub for her lunch with people from work, but no one drinks. She would also go to a pub to celebrate the end-of-term, and on these occasions she would drink alcohol. Most often, she would drink in a pub when she and her husband go for one or two drinks before or after going out to the theatre, or for dinner. Mrs O'Keefe drinks lager in a pub, but not at home which is the place she drinks most often, where she prefers whiskey.

Mrs O'Keefe and her husband regularly have wine with their meals, especially at the weekend and when they have company. Also, at least three or four evenings a week, especially at weekends, Mrs O'Keefe will have a measure (shot) of whiskey. Since she likes whiskey, and feels she can tolerate it better than other people she knows, she fears this competence is an indication of potential problems:

> I would like to have a drink every day. I'm saying I would like, and my body is sort of telling me to have a drink every day. And I don't want to have a drink every day because I would be afraid that if I have a drink every day, then I might want two drinks, and I might go along the path of insidious alcoholism.

Despite her concerns, Mrs O'Keefe finds the consumption of alcohol relaxing and pleasant. Her desire to remain in control of her drinking is reminiscent of Mrs Murphy's desire to be able to continue to play a game of bingo efficiently. Mrs Casey, on the other hand, said she does not really like the taste of most alcohol, particularly beer, and would prefer something sweet, which she said made it harder for her to drink in excess. These concerns about a need to be in control of one's alcohol consumption are expressed also by other Irish people, but they seemed to be a necessary expression for Irish mothers.

Conclusion

Ireland is often cited as an example in cross-cultural research on alcohol use. However, many studies fail to recognise that international comparisons of consumption rates suggest that Ireland is comparatively low overall, even when we correct for the abstainers (Walsh, 1980, Conniffe and McCoy, 1993). Moreover, in many studies, the drinking habits of Irish women are rarely mentioned.

Future research needs to look at both contemporary and historic relationships amongst various groups of women, as well as in relationship to their male counterparts. For instance, some studies have indicated that aggression is less likely to occur in mixed-sex drinking groups (Graham, *et al*, 1980). Moreover, Hunt and Satterlee have suggested that through playing darts 'working class women sought to gain greater access to their pub' (Hunt and Satterlee, 1987, p.597). Visions of drinking in Ireland which ignore women give not only an incomplete picture, but an inaccurate one. The dichotomy of heavy drinker and abstainer, or male and female levels of consumption, coexist in Irish society and in turn are mutually influential.[9]

Discussion Topics

1. Outline the changes in women's drinking practices in Ireland.

2. What role did women play in the Irish temperance movement?

3. Are pubs in Ireland for 'men only'?

4. Leisure patterns of men and women in Ireland are tied to life cycles. Discuss and illustrate with reference to case study material.

Notes:

1. Unless otherwise stated, Ireland refers to the Republic of Ireland.
2. Unless otherwise stated, I shall use the term 'the Church' to refer to the Irish Catholic Church. Figures from the 1991 census indicate that approximately ninety-two per cent of the people in the Republic of Ireland identify themselves as Catholic.
3. Bales acknowledged the criticism of Carleton as highly critical of the Catholic clergy, but he also accepted that Carleton's vision of the Irish peasant was 'life-like-reality' (1980, p.164).
4. For a version of this story, see John B Keane's entertaining account of a rural pub entitled Letters of an Irish Publican (1992).
5. I sought to interview both the husband and wife in a given family. Then I networked out within the family to interview a person from a previous generation (a parent of either of the spouses) and a later generation (a child who was at least eighteen years of age). Only three individuals from the 'grand-parent' generation were interviewed due to the fact that the majority of families grandparents were deceased. However, relevant information for this part of the design was obtained through reports of the later generation.
6. Cork City is divided geographically, socially and economically into three areas: the city centre, the Southside and the Northside. In addition, both the Southside and the Northside are each subdivided into several neighbourhoods. The River Lee splits into two channels (the North and South Channels) which later rejoin. The city centre is essentially the area trapped between the channels, and so is not part of either side of the city – it is considered 'neutral'. Cork's city centre, which is extremely compact due to geographical constraints, would be termed the business district in classical urban analysis. The residential neighbourhoods, approximately eight on either side, branch out and up from this centre. The Northside, the smaller and older side, is generally recognised as the poorer part of town.
7. Snowballing refers to the technique of making use of previous interviewees to help with contacts for future interviews.
8. This and all subsequent names in this paper are pseudonyms to protect the anonymity of my respondents.
9. I compare these two groups in more detail in a previous paper, Irish Drinking Worlds: A Socio-Cultural Reinterpretation of Ambivalence, 1996.

References and Further Reading

Bacon, S D. 1945 'Alcohol and Complex Society' in *Alcohol, Science and Society; twenty-nine lectures with discussions as given at Yale Summer School of Alcohol Studies* New Haven: Quarterly Journal of Studies on Alcohol.

Bacon, S D. 1962. 'Alcohol and Complex Society.' in Pittman, D J and Snyder, C R. (eds.) *Society, Culture and Drinking Patterns.* New York: John Wiley.

Bales, R F. 1946 'Cultural Difference in Rates of Alcoholism' *Quarterly Journal of Studies on Alcohol* Vol.6, pp.480- 499.

Bales, R F. 1962. 'Attitudes towards Drinking in Irish Culture' in Pittman, D J and Snyder C R (eds.) *Society, Culture and Drinking Patterns.* New York: John Wiley.

Bales, R F. 1980 (1944) *The 'Fixation Factor' in Alcohol Addiction: An Hypothesis Derived from a Comparative Study of Irish and Jewish Social Norms* New York: Arno Press.

Beale, J. 1987 *Women in Ireland.* Bloomington: Indiana University Press.

Bjeren, G. 1992 'Drinking and Masculinity in Everyday Swedish Culture' in Gefou-Madianou, Dimitra, (ed.) *Alcohol, Gender and Culture* London: Routledge.

Blocker, J S Jr. 1985 'Separate Paths: Suffragists and the Women's Temperance Crusade' *Signs* 10(3) pp.460-76.

Bretherton, G Cornell. 1991 'Against the Flowing Tide: Whiskey and Temperance in Making Modern Ireland' in Barrows, S and Room, R *Drinking: Behaviour and Belief in Modern History* Berkeley: University of California Press.

Cassidy, T M. 1996 'Irish Drinking Worlds: A Sociocultural Reinterpretation of Ambivalence' *International Journal of Sociology and Social Policy* (To appear in a special issue on alcohol research).

Carleton, W. 1869 *Traits and Stories of the Irish Peasantry* London: William Tegg.

Chart, D A. 1910 *Ireland from the Union to Catholic Emancipation: A Study of Social, Economic and Administrative Conditions 1800-1829* London: J M Dent and Sons.

Conniffe, D and McCoy, D. 1993 *Alcohol Use in Ireland: Some Economic and Social Implications* General Research Series Paper No. 160, Dublin: The Economic and Social Research Institute.

Corrigan, E M and Butler, S. 1991 'Irish Alcoholic Women in Treatment: Early Findings' *The International Journal of the Addictions* Vol.26(3) pp.281-292.

Corrigan, E M, Butler, S, and Camasso, M J. 1995 'Outcome of Treatment for Irish Alcoholic Women' *Irish Journal of Psychological Medicine.* Vol.12(2) pp.48-52.

Cullen, N. 1991 'Women and the Preparation of Food in Eighteenth-Century Ireland' in MacCurtain, M and O'Dowd, M (eds.) *Women in Early Modern Ireland.* Dublin: Wolfhound Press.

Dawson, W R. 1911 'The Presidential Address on the Relations Between the Geographical Distribution of Insanity and That of Certain Social and Other Conditions in Ireland' *Journal of Mental Science* Vol.57 pp.538-597.

Dinneen, P S. 1927 *Foclóir Gaedhilge agus Béarla: an Irish English Dictionary* Dublin: Educational Company of Ireland.

Eurobarometer 37.07.37.1. 1992 *The Drug Prevention Program* Brussels: INRA (Europe).

Fine-Davis, M. 1983 *Women and Work in Ireland: A Social Psychological Perspective* Dublin: Council for the Status of Women.

Fitzpatrick, J. 1970a *Drinking and Young People: A Sociological Study* Unpublished M.Soc.Sc.thesis, National University of Ireland.

Fitzpatrick, J. 1970b *Drinking and Young People: A Sociological Study* Report to the Irish National Council on Alcoholism, Dublin.

Flanagan, L. 1995 *Bottle, Draught and Keg: An Irish Drinking Anthology.* Dublin: Gill and Macmillan.

Fontaine, E de la. 1940 'Cultural and Psychological implications in Case Work Treatment with Irish Clients' *Cultural Problems in Social Case Work* New York: Family Welfare Association of America.

Foster, R F. 1988 *Modern Ireland: 1600-1972.* London: Butler and Tanner.

Gefou-Madianou, D. 1992 'Introduction: Alcohol Commensality, Identity Transformations and Transcendence' in Gefou-Madianou, D (ed.) *Alcohol, Gender and Culture* London: Routledge.

Goldin, C. 1990 *Understanding the Gender Gap: An Economic History of American Women.* New York: Oxford University Press.

Graham, K, Rocque, L La, Yetman, R, Ross, T J, and Guistra, E. 1980 'Aggression and Barroom Environments' *Journal of Studies on Alcohol.* Vol.41(3) pp.277-292.

Grube, J W and Morgan, M. 1986 *Smoking, Drinking and Other Drug Use Among Dublin Post-Primary School Pupils* Paper No. 132, Dublin: The Economic and Social Research Institute.

Grube, J W and Morgan, M. 1990 *The Development and Maintenance of Smoking, Drinking and Other Drug Use Among Dublin Post-Primary Pupils* General Research Series, Paper No. 148, Dublin: The Economic and Social Research Institute.

Harrison, B. 1971 *Drink and the Victorians: the Temperance Question in England, 1815-1872* London: Faber and Faber.

Hunt, G and Satterlee, S. 1987 'Darts, Drink and the Pub: the Culture of Female Drinking' *The Sociological Review* Vol.35 pp.575-601.

Hupkens, C L H, Knibbe, R A, and Drop, M J. 1993 'Alcohol Consumption in the European Community: Uniformity and Diversity in Drinking Patterns' *Addiction* Vol.88 pp.1391-1404.

Inglis, T. 1987 *Moral Monopoly: The Catholic Church in Modern Irish Society* Dublin: Gill and Macmillan.

Joyce, P W. 1913 *Social History of Ancient Ireland* 2nd Edition, 2 Volumes. Dublin: M H Gill and Sons.

Keane, J B. 1992 *Letters of an Irish Publican* Cork: The Mercier Press.

Kerr, N. 1894 *Inebriety or Narcomania* London: H K Lewis.

Laurence, A. 1994 *Women in England, 1500-1760: A Social History* London: Weidenfeld and Nicolson.

Lawrence, J J and Maxwell, M A. 1962 'Drinking and Socio-Economic Status' in Pittman, D J and Snyder, C R *Society, Culture, and Drinking Patterns* New York: John Wiley.

Lynch, P and Vaizey, J. 1960 *Guinness's Brewery in the Irish Economy 1759-1876* London: Cambridge University Press.

Mac Greil, M. (ed.) 1993 *Final Report: Toward a Second Century* Dublin: Pioneer Total Abstinence Association.

McGuffin, J. 1978 *In Praise of Poteen* Belfast: The Appletree Press.

McGuire, J R. 1973 *Irish Whiskey: A History of Distilling, the Spirit Trade and Excise Controls in Ireland* Dublin: Gill and MacMillan.

MacLysaght, E. 1939 *Irish Life in the Seventeenth Century* Cork: Cork University Press.

Malcolm, E. 1982 'The Catholic Church and the Irish Temperance Movement, 1838-1901' *Irish Historical Studies* Vol.23(89) pp.1-16.

Malcolm, E. 1986 *'Ireland Sober, Ireland Free': Drink and Temperance in Nineteenth-Century Ireland* Dublin: Gill and MacMillan.

Morgan, M and Grube, J W. 1994 'The Irish and Alcohol: A Classic Case of Ambivalence' *The Irish Journal of Psychology.* Vol.15, 2-3 pp.390-403.

Nicholls, K. 1985 'Two Islands, One Street, Article 11' *The Cork Examiner* Wednesday, 13 March.

O'Connor, A. 1987 'Female Alcoholism in Ireland: A Follow-Up Study' *The Irish Journal of Psychiatry* Vol.8(1) pp.13-16.

O'Connor, J. 1978 *The Young Drinkers: A Cross-National Study of Social and Cultural Influences* London: Tavistock Publications.

O'Connor, J and Daly, M. 1983 *The Smoking Habit* Dublin: Gill and Macmillan.

O'Curry, E. 1873 *On the Manners and Customs of the Ancient Irish* London: Williams and Norgate.

Park, J. 1990 'Only "Those" Women: Women and the Control of Alcohol in New Zealand' *Contemporary Drug Problems* Vol.17(2).

Parker, S. 1976 *The Sociology of Leisure* London: George Allen and Unwin.

Perceval, R J. 1955 'Alcohol and Alcoholism in the Republic of Ireland' *International Journal on Alcohol and Alcoholism* Vol.1 pp.146-55.

Pyle, J L. 1990 *The State and Women in the Economy: Lessons from Sex Discrimination in the Republic of Ireland* Albany: State University of New York Press.

Pritchard, D. 1985 *Irish Pubs* Ireland: Real Ireland Design Limited.

Quinn, J F. 1992 'The "Vagabond Friar": Father Mathew's Difficulties with the Irish Bishops, 1840-1856' *The Catholic Historical Review* Vol.78 pp.542-56.

Room, R. 1984 'A "Reverence for Strong Drink": The Lost Generation and the Elevation of Alcohol in American Culture' *Journal of Studies on Alcohol* Vol.45 pp.540-6.

Rubery, J and Fagan, C. 1993 'Occupational Segregation of Women and Men in the European Community' *Social Europe, Supplement* 3/93 Luxembourg: Office for Official Publucations of the European Communities.

Ryan, J C. 1992 *Irish Whiskey* The Irish Heritage Series: 71. Dublin: Eason and Son.

Shaw, S. 1980 'The Causes of Increasing Drinking Problems Amongst Women: A General Etiological Theory' in *Cumberwell Council on Alcoholism Women and Alcohol* New York: Tavistock Publications.

Skocpol, T. 1992 *Protecting Soldiers and Mothers: The Political Origins of Social Policy in the United States* Cambridge, Massachusetts: The Belknap Press of Harvard University Press.

Smart, G G. 1989 'Is the Post-War Drinking Binge Ending? Cross-national Trends in per capita Alcohol Consumption' *British Journal of Addiction* Vol.84 pp.743-748.

Stewart, M. 1992 '"I can't drink beer, I've just drunk water": Alcohol, Bodily Substance and Commensality among Hungarian Rom' in Gefou-Madianou, D. (ed.) *Alcohol, Gender and Culture* London: Routledge.

Stivers, R A. 1976 *A Hair of the Dog: Irish Drinking and American Stereotype.* University Park: The Pennsylvania University Press.

Thurman, C. 1992 'Drinking Patterns in Europe' *The Professional Statistician* Vol.11(8).

Tyrrell, I. 1991 'Women and Temperance in International Perspective: The World's WCTU, 1880s-1920s' In Barrows, S and Room, R. *Drinking: Behavior and Belief in Modern History* Berkeley: University of California Press.

Walsh, B M. 1980 *Drinking in Ireland: A Review of Trends in Alcohol Consumption, Alcohol Related Problems, and Policies Towards Alcohol* Broadsheet No. 20, Dublin: The Economic and Social Research Institute.

Walsh, D. 1968 'Alcoholism in Dublin' *Journal of the Irish Medical Association.* Vol.61 pp.153-156.

Ward, Y. 1993 *A Bottle in the Cupboard: Women and Alcohol* Dublin: Attic Press.

28.

The Feminisation of the Phone Space: Women and Domestic Telephony in Ireland
E Maria Lohan

Introduction

The lives of women are cinematically mapped onto the lines of telephone communication. It highlights their encounters with 'the built environment', (Wajcman, 1993) problems of relative isolation and their unequal access to private transport. Telephone usage also reflects the blurred lines between women's work and leisure in the home. The telephone, for many women is a work tool, but women's work is frequently also keeping in contact with family, friends and neighbours. The telephone is a crucial line running through the lives of Irish women.

There are, however, significant controls on women's usage of the domestic phone. Within the home, men own the phone economically. The phone is most often in their name, as head of the household, and frequently this control is extended over the telephone bill. In addition, men own the phone culturally, since women's talk on the phone is popularly ridiculed as gossip. This paper is the result of research (including sixty detailed questionnaires and twelve in-depth interviews) with women's groups affiliated to the Western Women's Link[1] and a smaller number of women living in urban Dublin, six months after the effective implementation of metered local calls.[2] This policy is exemplary of how a state-supported commercial policy disproportionately affects women and other groups in the home.

Though the telephone has been coined the 'neglected medium', fallen between the stools of interpersonal and mass media research (Fielding and Hartley, 1987), a recent proliferation of studies on the usage of, and attitudes to, the telephone have begun to address the paucity of research in this area. These studies suggest that the domestic telephone, in terms of usage, has become a feminised medium of communication. Consistently, reports show considerably greater usage of the domestic phone by women over men (Schabedoth et al., 1989, Dordick and La Rose, 1992, Lange, 1993, Perin, 1994). A French study reported that women use the telephone up to twice as much as men (Claisse,

1989) whilst Lange concluded that the telephone was emphatically 'feminine' (Lange, 1993, p.210).[3] Other studies have spoken of a 'pervasive feminine culture of the telephone' (Moyal, 1989).

Furthermore, particular types of telephony are regarded as more feminine than others. Recent studies have classified calls in terms of their purpose into categories such as: instrumental vs. intrinsic (Moyal, 1989); person oriented vs. object oriented (Claisse, 1989); or functional vs. socio-affective/relational (Perin, 1994).

In common with traditional functionalist ideology, women have come to be associated with expressive person-oriented calls and men with instrumental or business calls and this in turn is borne out as an experiential reality in the data.

In this chapter, I draw on my own recent research on women and the domestic telephone in the Republic of Ireland in which I attempt to answer two questions. Firstly, why is the domestic telephone feminised? Here I will be assessing some of the reasons for women's predominant usage of the domestic telephone in an Irish context outlining contributing factors from my data such as the home and neighbourhood as work environments, and women acting as 'linchpins' in families.[4] The second question pertains to the strong association between women, femininity and domestic telephony. This apparent association has arguably led sociological and media researchers to theorise in one direction only, overshadowing questions of whether there might also be substantial barriers to female telephony. The data I present here uncovers significant cultural and economic control over the phone in the home. The second question I am therefore posing is whether the domestic telephone needs to be further feminised?

The potential for the feminisation of the phone space in Ireland needs to be understood within the complexities of the gendering of technologies. Technologies are not just gendered in the production stage, at which point they generally reflect the values and aspirations of their makers, but also in the consumption phases where technologies can be redefined again. In this chapter, I will be suggesting that the gendering of the domestic phone is conditioned by the position of men and women within the domestic space.

How Feminine is the Telephone?
The Significance of the Telephone to Women in Ireland

Early malestream writing about the telephone can be clearly located within the wave of technological determinism, claiming that the telephone has the power to overcome time and space, and make unequals equal (Ball, 1968; McLuhan, 1964). Such theories of human freedom through technology were oblivious to (though co-extant with) feminist theories on the restrictive nature of women's lives. A popular theme of feminist writing in the sixties and seventies was the isolation experienced by women within their own homes, associated with increased industrialisation and the suburbanisation of women (Lopata, 1971, Oakley, 1974).

Uniting these two strands of thought then, the question might be asked whether the problem of women's isolation can be solved, or even alleviated, by communication technologies?

The greater presence of women in the home during the day is undoubtedly a major contributing factor to women's reliance on the domestic telephone and in interviewing such women for this study, I did, in fact, perceive a relative sense of isolation which was expressed through their usage of the telephone.

> I find the telephone is like an extension of my thoughts, I use it to check on someone that I've been thinking about or to ask someone a question. If you are alone in the house the phone helps you from going crazy (Hilda, a full-time mother/housewife living in a rural area, forty, very involved in local community organisation).

> The phone is like a magnet. Every time you pass it you just want to reach out and call someone (Bernie, Grand-mother/housewife living in a small town, fifty-five).

A relative sense of isolation is perhaps most poignant for disabled women, who though they may receive day-time visits and care, the telephone remains an important means for them to initiate sociability. One of my interviewees (Maura), for example uses the telephone for joining in radio quizzes by asking one of her young daughters to dial the local radio station before going to school. Maura, then uses the re-dial button to access the number during the day.[5]

Yet in a feminist study of the telephone, there is a need to critique theories of technological determinism which assume the telephone, as a form of technology, can unshackle itself from controlling social forces such as capitalism or patriarchy and thus liberate people. In addition, a feminist study of the telephone must confront women's power of social agency in the construction of networks and thus challenge the implicit association of isolation with the domestic sphere. Recent feminist studies of the telephone have addressed the former but not the latter.

For example, Rakow's study of women and the telephone in a small American town questions the notion that the telephone has rescued women from the loneliness of the household and instead reminds us that it facilitated the positioning of women to that very domain through the telephone's role in the re-organisation of social and economic life, reinforcing the division between private and public spheres (Rakow, 1992, p.79). Likewise, Mattelart makes the point that women are responsive to means of communication that make their 'exile more gentle' but which can 'reproduce their exile and effectively generate the conditions of their isolation' (1976, p.296). This is what Martin refers to as the 'contradiction between the privatisation and socialisation of women's communication' (1991, p.165).

When we ask why women are more confined to homes then it becomes clear that women's usage of the domestic telephone is a symptom of their position within families. Cross-culturally, women have unequal access to resources such as money, private transport and employment opportunities. Care of the elderly, the young and the home environment invariably falls to women. The distance between home and work is great and those in the home often have inadequate access to public transport.

The Home as a Connected Work Environment

What remains unquestioned in former studies of telephony though is the assumption that it is the domestic sphere per se which is isolated and isolating. The (artificial) division of the private and public and the notion of women being socially isolated plays down women's work in the home, the neighbourhood as a work environment and the telephone as a work tool. It also underplays the power of social agency explicit in women's construction of their own networks. The telephone as one of the main locations of this interaction makes these processes visible.

We associate the domestic phone with women of leisure and leisurely chat but in this study amongst Irish women, and other international studies (Claisse, 1989, Schabedoth et al., 1989, Adler, 1993), such calls were clearly in the minority.[6]

The home phone is used in a very work-like manner for managing the household and household members' lives. Calls by women most frequently involved co-ordinating transport for themselves or children, organising children's activities, calls to financial and insurance services, calls organising events in their communities and information-seeking on behalf of themselves and their families. Using the car for errands was the other option if, firstly, it was available to women, and secondly, if children or elderly relatives in women's care could be accommodated. It was those who had neither access to a phone nor a car whose lives were most dependent upon sympathetic neighbours.

Similar to studies on the division of labour in the home, (e.g. Leonard, 1992, Gregson and Lowe, 1993, Morris, 1993), domestic telephony studies show that the employment of women outside the home does not radically alter the division of calls (Claisse, 1989, Schabedoth et al., 1989).

Apart from women's usage of the telephone to save time and money in daily tasks, some of the women in my study found the medium of the telephone more satisfactory for doing business. Women spoke of having much more confidence in speaking to strangers by phone than face-to-face.

It's fantastic I've found. Say, if you were behind with a bill, I'd ring and I'd say you will get your money, the money is on its way and then I'd pay within a week or so. That's much easier than going in face-to-face and feeling like a beggar And it's very acceptable. Well I've only discovered it recently. People love to get this phone call, they appreciate the call to say that you're coming in to pay them. It's keeping the lines of communication open. Once you keep that open it's not a problem it's when you ignore it completely you start getting in the solicitors letters etc (Monica, early thirties, married, recently moved to a new housing estate in a semi-urban area).

The Neighbourhood as a Work Environment

Not only is the home an important site of (women's) work but Irish women's descriptions of their usage of the telephone construct the neighbourhood as a work virtual environment in which women have many colleague-like relationships with their neighbours and other women within their local area network code. Most particularly the work of organising children's activities, often brings woman and children together.

Frequently, friendships are built up through this telephone contact and perhaps because of this, women's work in the home again becomes blurred as does the conventional heuristic distinction between calls which are work/task oriented and calls which are sociable/person oriented. In general there has been a reluctance to consider the instrumental nature of friendships or the extent of material reciprocity involved (Allan, 1989, O'Connor, 1992) except in the case of working class communities where they are used to offset poverty (Richards 1990).

The women in this study were involved on a daily basis with a network of locally based women and institutions forming a kind of *interface work* which connects the household to formal services such as schools, shops and churches and informally to advice and information, transport sharing and other resource pooling.

Women have also developed less predictable usages for the telephone. One of the most interesting things that emerged was the usage of the telephone in a newly built suburban neighbourhood to create acquaintances and friendships. More usually predictions about the usage of the telephone (McLuhan, 1964 and Ball, 1968) and studies of telephony (for example Claisse, 1989, Rakow, 1992) describe the telephone in the sociable senses as a means of maintaining friendships already established. A part-time nurse, wife and mother who recently moved to a new suburb explained how she had introduced herself to all her neighbours by telephone. I asked her if she would ring up an absolute stranger and she replied:

> Yes, that's how we all got to know one another around her . I'm living in a
> place where a lot of new people are moving in and it's handy. Otherwise
> you are always passing. They are your neighbours whom you've never ever
> been formerly introduced to. It's nearly nosier or more imposing to go
> knocking on the door (Monica, early thirties, married, recently moved to a
> new housing estate in a semi-urban area).

She explained that a lot of the women in the area were employed, some part-
time, and on their day-off or when on holidays, they would ring around to see
who was there to ask them over for a coffee morning or something. Someone
would know everyone's number and you'd just ring around.

> It's really great because it is not as if it goes on every week or anything or
> that anyone is under any pressure to do anything (Monica, as above).

In this case the telephone had become a form of doorbell used to request/invite
entry into a sociable network which was then sustained by a mixture of face-to-
face and telephone interaction.

Women as the Linchpins of Family

Three quarters of the sample agreed/strongly agreed that the telephone was the
strongest communications link with their families. Families lived too far away
for frequent visits and the convenience of the telephone facilitated regular
communication.[7] The telephone, it would appear is a vital 'umbilical chord'
(Claisse, 1989) running through matrilineal lines in Irish families and is a
considerable factor in the feminisation of the domestic phone space. These
sometimes invisible lines could be mapped out on telephone bills where
interviewees described how their bills might be particularly high some months
due to (minor) crises in the family, for example grandchildren being sick or
daughters experiencing health or marital difficulties. In other cases, telephone
support was more on-going, for example, to an elderly relative living on their
own.

> You might go one day and ring the following. It's nice to have the follow up
> call to keep the communication going (Margaret, mid-forties, living in a
> rural town).

The telephone very clearly played an important part in the well-being of
women. The sound of the telephone is 'like the sun coming up' (Mary, mid-
fifties living in a rural town). Not realising it, the women in this study regularly
reified their own generosities of caregiving and listening as characteristics of
the technology instead. The telephone has a sense of immediacy they said and
'power' as a medium of information on how a person *really* is.

> You can tell by a person's voice if they are OK or not and you wouldn't be
> able to detect that in a letter (Roisin, thirty-five, mother, employed part-
> time).

Daughters too, confirmed that lines of communication within families were largely feminised lines. Though fathers sometimes initiated calls, and thus legitimated them, women were the primary communicators within the family network. From a daughter's perspective, they reported to me a distinct reticence by fathers on the phone. Their fathers were more comfortable with the medium as a messaging system as opposed to a medium for social or personable chat. In the next section I will explicate this further and suggest that it can be partly explained by the association of the domestic phone with chat and with women, along with a mixture of cultural and economic reasons.

> My Dad will always ring if he has something specific to ask. My Mother will maybe ring me for a chat but my father will always ring me with something specific in mind (Geraldine, twenty-five, married, urban area, secretary).

> Certainly, I found with him (father) he'd be inclined to just say one or two things and then pass the phone onto somebody else. I think that's mainly for reasons of economy. He's very aware of the phone bill more than anything else (Rachel, twenty-five, single, employed, and living in Dublin).

The Need for the Feminisation of the Domestic Phone Space: Barriers to Female Domestic Telephony

It is clear that there are compelling reasons also for the telephone to be interpreted as 'feminine' within the Irish context. However, in this section I argue that the feminine culture of the telephone is curtailed by the parameters of private and public patriarchal control over the telephone.[8] This renders the telephone 'masculine' and hence the need for the feminisation of the domestic phone space. Women might *love* to use the telephone but men *own* the phone. This ownership is asserted culturally and economically.

The concoction of masculine and feminine identities which the domestic telephone has been imbued with, is partly due to its enigmatic state as neither being completely a 'brown good' or a 'white good' (Cockburn and Ormrod, 1993). Loosely based on the colours of these machines, brown goods, such as televisions, hi-fi systems and video-recorders are largely entertainment machines and tend to be controlled by male members of the household (Cockburn and Ormrod, 1993, p.15). By contrast, white goods such as fridges and washing machines are connected to housework, and therefore feminine. Men own the phone in the home economically, as principle 'head of the household'. The telephone is most often in *his* name and it is *his* name which is most often used in telephone directories.[9] Traditionally too, men have enjoyed more financial authority over the home.[10]

Even when men are not the principle bill-payers they frequently act as authorisers of such bill paying. Interviews with Irish women were full of illustrations of this point. One woman was, 'waiting for the right time to bring out the phone bill' (Urban Mother in her 40s). High bills were glued up with pritt-stick or burned whilst smaller bills were left around, reminiscent of children with high and low grades. The telephone caused gender specific rows like no other bill:

> I think it's because it's considered a luxury. Your light [electricity] bill can be any amount. It's there and that's it, but with the phone, nobody used it and certainly not I (Juliet, recently married, thirty, employed, semi-urban).

Few could explain the phenomenon of guilt, but it seems to be connected with women's primary *responsibility* for the domestic environment as opposed to authority over the domestic environment.

> You have lots of bills coming into the home, light bill etc. but there is something about the phone bill ... There is something about the phone bill that gets everyone's back up ... It's always someone else's fault (Margaret, forty-five, employed, semi-urban area).

> I think it causes rows in the house. You feel that you're a bad manager, that you haven't monitored the kids or something (Ann, fifty, semi-urban small town).

Women were, however, managing their telephone expenses in very clear ways. For example, one woman told me how she had to make a lot of calls to her sister as she had two very sick children and stated that she would have to off-set this by not making calls that she would normally make.

Cultural Ownership of the Telephone

Private patriarchy was also expressed as cultural control over the telephone which manifested itself as a 'big brother' watching over women's friendships and women's conversation. Women's ties and the significance of women's ties have largely remained invisible, often occurring only when male partners are not there.

> Sometimes they (men) are inclined to sit by supervising and saying to you afterwards: why did you say that, it was daft (Sarah, forty-five, housewife, semi-urban).

> We can't chat as easily when the men are there because we can't talk about them. You can't let off steam; You can't criticise them (Annmarie, forty-five, housewife, semi-urban).

> I often have my friends in but I'm lucky: my husband goes to bed early, thanks be to God. I'd be delighted when he's gone to bed (Bridie, sixty, semi-urban).

Women's friendships and women's talk is constantly in a 'less than' equation in relation to men's. Men's friendships belong in the Big World and speak the language of Big Talk (Semiotic Solutions, 1992). Women's friendships, by contrast are associated with the small world or the domestic, the traditional place of women's friendships, and sit in the shadow of the ideologically dominant male-female relationship (Dobash and Dobash, 1980, Oliker, 1989, O'Connor, 1992). The language of women's friendships is frequently constructed through a vocabulary of feelings and emotions but women's engagement with relationships is frequently trivialised as gossip. Consequently, women find it difficult to claim a space for their telephony particularly following marriage and motherhood. According to Allan 'female ties are usually seen as a personal luxury having no wider relevance' (1989, p.131) and there was considerable evidence in my study that women were willing to forego the maintenance of friendships with other women when they conflicted with family commitments and when the economic cost of that communication became more onerous. One woman interviewee said that she had lost touch with her friends since she got married.

> Oh definitely, well especially if you get married. I think it has to, to a certain extent, because you have made a commitment to a person and most of my friends are involved and they are getting on with their lives. It is true, like, your friends are more important to you in your teens/early twenties but when men come on the scene then your priority is switched to that relationship and your relationship with him becomes more exclusive (Geraldine, twenty-five, married urban area, secretary).

Public Patriarchal Control of the Telephone

The current re-structuring of the telecommunications industry, and particularly the recent price re-structuring of domestic telephone services has copper-fastened patriarchal control over the telephone by reinforcing private patriarchy already extant in the home. The difficulties women have been experiencing in constructing a space for their friendships and talk has been exacerbated by the reduction in the overall telephone space available to them, due to the increased cost of day-time calls. Day-time calls have become a luxury that most women can't afford or are subject to a greater rationalisation process.

> I just make short quick calls and I only phone when I have a reason to when I really have to (Eilis, thirty, employed, semi-urban).

Secondly, the telephone price-restructuring imposes a male time-frame by assuming that women have equal access to leisurely calls in the evening time. This, however, is rarely the case for married women or mothers.

> And its ridiculous to say that you can do it after six o'clock, that's when their families are home, and you're cooking the tea. I voted Labour last year

but I'll never forgive Labour for not objecting to do these phone charges (Paula, Disabled woman, married, seventy, living in a rural area).

In another group, a woman said:

I can't phone people after six o'clock because I feel guilty about it and I can't phone people during the day because I can't afford it. My bill has been halved but I'm not happy with it (Roisin, thirty-five, mother, employed part-time).

The Importance of the Local Area Network

In addition, the recent price re-structuring steam-rolled over the feminine culture of the telephone by under-estimating the importance of the local area network for women. Women mentioned that the cheap weekend calls were indeed helpful especially for relatives in other parts of Ireland. Yet they expressed doubt over this being an incentive to initiate contact with relatives with whom they were previously not in regular contact. The phone pattern which had existed was more likely to be maintained though the duration of calls might be longer. Younger and single women, who maintained a wider geography of networks, did especially welcome cheaper long-distance, yet they too felt this might well diminish over time:

But sometimes I think there is no point. I'm not going to see them for ages. They were friends I had when I lived near them. It's when the telephone combines with meetings that it's most fun (Ursula, student, single, early twenties, living in Dublin).

The reasons for the importance of the telephone in women's lives are grounded in the local area network and must question Giddens' (1991) discussion of the reduced significance of locality within modernity. One woman who was born in England, now living in a rural area in Galway with friends dispersed in both England and Ireland put it like this:

I liked making local calls because it was an ordinary thing to do; It was a relaxing thing to do. You said what you needed to say. There was no stress involved (with the telephone) except a little if you were making a long distance call. The general thing with the phone was it was a friendly thing. You could pick up the phone and have a chat with it. That's changed now. There's stress involved in all of it. Even though it's cheaper now to make long distance calls, there is still a bit of stress involved because it's long distance. Before the phone was a friendly thing (Veronica, married, unemployed, thirty-five, living in a rural area).

This was echoed by a middle-aged woman from another group.

The advantage of long-distance calls [being cheaper] is hideous. They are rare calls. You think a lot before making such calls. Local calls are more normal and necessary (Hilda, housewife, forty, rural area).

Conclusion

The domestic telephone has been feminised by women in Ireland for the pursuits of home, work, family and friendships but in a way which is limited by men's overall control of the technology within the household and beyond it. In some senses, the telephone is a metaphor for matrifocality (McLauglin, 1993) within which women gain considerable pleasure and power but is nonetheless under the rubric of patriarchal control.

Women caught between restraints on their material resources and demands on their affective resources use the domestic telephone as an important means of pushing out their personal space.

In addition, women's feminine culture of the telephone questions the malestream division of the private/public (sustained by the industry's division of business and private lines). Modern societies view the private as 'a space of personal leisure and enhancement, thereby denying the salience of the household as a site of domestic labour for women' (Walby, 1994, p.383). The lines of women's telephone communication weave in and out through these domains, even within the one call.

Domestic telephone culture however needs to be further feminised. Women's feminine culture of the telephone remains invisible to the technologically driven telephone industry who are sacrificing universal residential telephony and the value of POTS (plain old telephone services) for the sake of investment in hi-tech PANS (picture and network services).

Women's feminine culture remains invisible to the Irish State, despite the savings to the State accrued from women's caring and community work, within which the telephone is pivotal.

Finally, the feminine culture of the telephone remains invisible to their families, although women's usage of the telephone is the site of valuable interface work essential for lubricating the work of the domestic economy. Frequently too, women's friendships are kept out of sight and out of mind from the cultural sensitivity of the importance of the family. Women's telephone calls might not only be regarded as superfluous but also subversive.

Discussion Topics

1. Men and women relate to technologies differently. How do sociologies of technology critique this belief?

2. Can technologies take on gendered personas, and if so, how?

3.   Is access to a private telephone essential for citizenship and social participation in modern Ireland?

4.   Is the telephone an important national resource?

Notes

1.   I'd like to extend my sincere gratitude to all the women who participated by interview or questionnaire, and to the WWL, of which I am a member, for access to other groups within the organisation. The research was carried out between April and June 1994 and involved a detailed questionnaire followed by interview. Some of the interviews were group interviews within the women's group meetings, others were individual interviews which largely took place in the interviewees' homes. Names of interviewees have been replaced with fictional names. It is my hope that future Telecom policies will more adequately reflect the needs of women and I am grateful to British Telecom for sponsoring this project.

2.   Telecom Eireann restructured their telephone charges from un-metered to metered local calls on 15 January 1993. This was substantially revised from 1 September 1993. Local calls now cost 11.17p for three minutes daytime (8am-6pm) and 11.17p for fifteen minutes evening time excluding VAT. VAT @ twenty-one per cent was passed onto the consumer from 1 April 1994. At the same time, the local calling area was enlarged outside of Dublin and the cost of national and international calls was reduced. Weekend national calls were reduced to the local economy rate (11.17p for fifteen minutes excluding VAT). It is perhaps the cheap weekend calls and expensive day-time calls which are the largest changes.

3.   This was as a result of a national study of telephone usage in which women were found to participate in 70.4 per cent of all calls with only 29.6 per cent of all calls involving men. And of those respondents who could be classified as 'extremely frequent callers' 89.2 per cent were women.

4.   In 1992, the total activity rate for Irish women was 36.8 per cent compared to fifty-one per cent in the UK (Eurostat, 1994). In particular, the labour market activity rates for married women in Ireland is low at 29.1 per cent (1991 figure); (Lewis, 1993, p.9). Approximately, forty per cent of my sample were full-time housewives.

5.   I am particularly grateful to members of the Galway women's Multiple Sclerosis group who shared with me their stories of the role of the telephone in their lives.

6.   Respondents were asked for the primary reason for their last call made which produced the following result: To organise something (thirty-six per cent); To request or provide information (thirty-five per cent); To see how somebody was (nineteen per cent); To chat (seven per cent); To ask or receive advice (four per cent). Though these results are broadly consistent with international studies, I felt that emphasis on the instrumentality of their calls was part of the economic rationality forced upon them by the rise in phone charges.

7.   Family with whom they do not live.

8.   This is based on Sylvia Walby's (1990, p.20) definition of public and private patriarchy. Private patriarchy is maintained by women's economic dependence on

men in the home whilst public patriarchy is maintained by the state and inequality in the workforce.

9. More recently, the latter has also been regarded as a safety precaution.

10. At best in dual career households, women are entitled to joint-say over financial management (Gregson amd Lowe, 1993) Although female management of finances is prevalent amongst low-income families, it is likely to be management of 'his money' (Morris, 1993, Mc Laughlin, 1993).

References and Further Reading

Allan, G. 1989 *Friendships, Developing a Sociological Perspective* London: Harvester Wheatsheaf.

Adler, J. 1993 'Telephoning in Germany: Callers, Rituals, Contents and Functions' *Telecommunications Policy* May/June 1993 pp.281-296.

Ball, D. 1968 'Towards a Sociology of Telephone and Telephoners' in Truzzi, M. (ed.) *The Sociology of Everyday life* NJ: Engelewood Cliffs.

Bell L and Ribbens, J. 1994 'Isolated Housewives and Complex Maternal Worlds - The Significance of Social Contacts between Women with Children in Industrial Societies' *Sociological Review* 42, pp.227-261.

Claisse, G. 1989 'Telefon, Kommunication und Gesellschaft Daten Gegen Mythen' in Lange U (ed.) *Telefon und Gesellschaft: Beitrage zu einer Soziologie der Telefonkommunikation, Forschungsgrupe Telefonkomunikation* (Hrsg) Vol. 1 Berlin: Volker Speiss.

Cockburn, C and Ormrod, S. 1993 *Gender and Technology in the Making* London: Sage.

Di Leonardo, M. 1988 'The Female World of Cards and Holidays: Women Family and the Work of Kinship' in Thorne, B and Yalom, K (eds.) *Feminism and the Family: Two Decades of Thought* Boston: North Eastern University Press.

Delphy, C and Leonard, D. 1992 *Familiar Exploitation.* Cambridge: Polity Press.

Dobash, R, Emerson, and Dobash R. 1980 *Violence against Wives: A Case Against the Patriarchy* London: Open Books.

Dordick, H and La Rose, R. 1992 *The Telephone in Daily Life: A Study of Personal Telephone Use* Philadelphia: Temple University.

Eurostat 1994 Statistics Office of the EC Luxemburg, Dublin.

Fielding, G and Hartley, P. 1987 'The Telephone: The Neglected Medium' in Cashden, A and Jordin, M. (eds.) *Studies in Communication*, Oxford: Basil Blackwell.

Giddens, A. 1991 *Modernity and Self-Identity: Self and Society in the Late Modern Age*, Cambridge: Polity Press.

Gregson, N and Lowe, M. 1993 'Re-Negotiating the Domestic Division of Labour? A Study of Dual Career Households in North-East and South-East England' in *The Sociological Review* 1993. pp.474-505.

Kramarae, C. 1988 'Gotta go Myrtle, Technology is at the Door' in Kramarae C. (ed.) *Technology and Women's Voices* London: Routledge and Kegan Paul.

Lange, U. 1993 'Telefonkommunikation im Privaten Alltag und die Grenzen der Interpretation' in Meyer, S and Schulze, E. (eds.) *Technisiertes Familienleben Blick zurück und nach Vorn.* Berlin: Sigma.

Leonard, M. 1992 'Ourselves Alone: Household Work Strategies in a Deprived Community' *Irish Journal of Sociology* 2: pp.70-84.

Lewis, J. 1993 'Introduction to Women, Work, Family and Social Policies in Europe' in Lewis J. (ed.) *Women and Social Policies in Europe* England: Edward Elgar.

Lopata, H. 1971 *Occupation, Housewife*, New York: Oxford University Press.

Martin, M. 1991 *'Hello Central' Gender, Technology and Culture in the Formation of Telephone Systems* Montreal; London: Mc Gill, Queens University Press.

Matrix Book Group. 1984 *Making Space Women and the Man Made Environment* London and Sydney: Pluto Press.

Mattelart, M. 1976 'The Feminine Voice of the Coup d'Etat' in Nash, J and Icken S. (eds.) *Sex and Class in Latin America* New York: Praeger.

McLaughlin, E. 1993 'Women and the Family in Northern Ireland, A Review' in *Womens Studies International Forum* Vol. 16, No.6, pp.553-568.

McLuhan, M. 1964 *Understanding Media - the Extension of Man* London: Routledge and Keegan Paul.

Morris, L. 1993 'Household Finance Management and the Labour Market: A Case Study in Hartlepool' in *The Sociological Review* pp.506-535

Moyal, A. 1989 'The Feminine Culture of the Telephone' in *Prometheus*, Vol.7, No.1. June pp.5-31.

Oakley, A. 1974 *Housewife* Harmondsworth: Penguin.

O'Connor, P. 1992 *Friendships Between Women: A Critical Review* London: Harvester Wheatsheaf.

Oliker, S. 1989 *Best Friends and Marriage: Exchange Among Women*, California: University of California Press.

Perin, P. 1994 'Consumer Telephone Usage' paper given at COST 248 meeting, Lund Sweden, March.

Rakow, L F. 1992 *Gender on the Line, Women, the Telephone and Community Life* Urbana and Chicago: University of Illinois Press.

Richards, L. 1990 *Nobody's Home: Dreams and Realities in a New Suburb* Australia: Oxford University Press.

Schabedoth, E et al. 1989 'Der Kleine Unterschied', Erste Ergebnisse einer repräsentiven Befragung von Berliner Haushalten zur Nutzung des Telefons im privaten Alltag in Lange U (ed.) *Telefon und Gesellschaft: Bertrage zu einer soziologie der Telefonkommunikation* (Hrsg) Vol. 1, pp.101-116.

Semiotic Solutions. 1992 British Telecom Management Summary of Semiotic Analysis.

Wajcman, J. 1993 *Feminism Confronts Technology* Cambridge: Polity Press in association with Blackwell Publishers.

Walby, S. 1990 *Theorizing Patriarchy* Oxford: Basil Blackwell.

Walby, S. 1994 'Is Citizenship Gendered?' *Sociology* Vol. 28 No. 2. May pp.379-395.

29.

Women, Cities and Identity: The Production and Consumption of Gendered Urban Space in Belfast

Wendy Saunderson

Introduction

By the year 2000, seventy-five per cent of all Europeans will be living in cities (Jones, 1988). Currently, of the thirty per cent of Northern Ireland's population who live in the Belfast Urban Area, and the twenty-six per cent of Southern Ireland's population who live in the Greater Dublin Area, fifty-two per cent are women. However, of the architects and town planners who plan and design our cities, the vast majority are men. What does this suggest for urban women, as the majority of city dwellers; and for women architects and planners, as the minority of landed professionals? Do women and men identify differently with city living? What lies at the interface between urban production and consumption?

This chapter reports a recently completed research project (Saunderson, 1995a) aimed at uncovering the position of gender in the processes and outcomes of urban production and consumption; and exploring social, spatial, and symbolic representations of the city, by focusing on the urban identities of the women and men who produce and consume the built environment of Belfast. An overview of the genesis and development of feminist perspectives on the city is followed by an introduction to the research, and a small selection of the findings. Conclusions and recommendations are offered about the position of gender in the social, spatial and symbolic structures, processes and outcomes of urban production and consumption.

Women and Cities: Genesis and Development of a Research Area

The specificity of women's relationship to the built environment has been on feminist research agendas in North America since the early 1970s. In Britain, however, it is only within the past ten to fifteen years that published literature specifically concerned with such issues has appeared, and that British town planning has acknowledged and begun to respond to its androcentricity and to its failure to consider women's position in the production and consumption of urban planning and design. In Ireland, feminist perspectives on urban social process and spatial forms remain conspicuous by their absence (Saunderson, 1994).

Beginnings of this research area in the 1970s paralleled and were spurred on by major change and development in the disciplines within which urban research was mainly situated. In urban sociology, there was a spawning of radical conflict theories. In environmental/architectural psychology, interest, activity and funding for person-environment research was at its peak, as the discipline took its first steps towards theory development. In human geography - in the wake of the quantitative revolution of the 1960s, and as a critical reaction to the crisis of capitalism - radical perspectives dominated. It was during this time that feminist perspectives gained ascendancy, feminist geographers being the first to take up the mantle of research on women and the urban environment. Initially, a spate of work by this feminist caucus of the Institute of British Geographers highlighted women's and men's different perception and experience of the city, particularly emphasising spatial constraints experienced by women. Soon after, women's spatial constraints in the city were paralleled with their gender role constraints. These accounts, however, remained largely at the descriptive level (for a review of this early work, see Zelinsky et al., 1982).

Nascent directions for this research area in Britain were grounded in an encyclopedic corpus of foundational texts from North America (Stimpson et al., 1981, Hayden, 1984). In the early 1980s, there was an important shift away from women as the focus of inquiry and from accepting gender roles as natural and given, to conceptualising unequal gender relations as the root of women's subordination in the city, transforming the status of the perspective from a 'geography of women' to a 'feminist geography'. There followed a substantial body of literature emphasising the institutionalised structures - mostly social and spatial - creating and perpetuating women's disadvantage in the built environment. One popular and enduring paradigm has been the implications for women of the social, spatial and symbolic separation between the public sphere (of production) and the private sphere (of reproduction) (cf. Siltanen and Stanworth, 1984).

The last half of the 1980s saw the development and refinement of a feminist approach to understanding the role of gender divisions in environmental change and development (cf. Little et al., 1988). Debates about patriarchy had taken hold (Foord and Gregson, 1986). It was time to take the needs of urban women seriously. Assertions abounded. In response, prescriptive contributions appeared from both academics and practitioners on both sides of the Atlantic, towards better planned and designed cities for women. Such prescriptions for women-centred planning were also hatched in Ireland at this time: both in Belfast (CTA, 1988) and in Dublin (Barrett et al., 1986, Caffrey and Eanaigh, 1990).

Development of the research area in the 1990s has (in line with developments in so many disciplines) often fractured and fragmented out of disciplinary boundaries, and into a pastiche of 'cultural studies'. Following the line of the post-structuralists (Lacan, Derrida, Kristeva, Foucault), postmodernism (and its discontents) has been the arena in which some feminist perspectives on the city have been sited (McDowell, 1990). Indeed, in the mid-1990s, postmodernism, 'characterised by the crumbling of overarching theories and an unprecedented eclecticism and combination of thought, taste and culture' (Hague, 1995, p.211), is often as evident in the literature about the city as it is in the city itself.

Many of these developments have produced (and have been produced by) a welcome concern with issues of subjectivity and sexuality (Colomina, 1992, Valentine, 1993). 'Space' is central. Theorisations of the significance of space and place (as they intersect with gender, class, race, sexuality and culture) are used to map out the geographies of women's lives within and between spaces and places, and to explore gendered socio-spatial relations across the life course (Katz and Monk, 1993, Ardener, 1993). Explorations of the role of spaces and places in the performance of gender and sexuality, and the concept of space and place in contextualising gender relations, are *de rigueur* in the mid-1990s (Bell and Valentine, 1995, Betsky, 1995, Duncan, 1996). This literature introduces a wealth of approaches to ways in which gender relations and the 'old' paradigms (for example, of public-private dichotomies) can be re-contextualised and re-conceptualised within the ever-changing social landscapes and the ever-increasing complexities of contemporary culture and life in urban milieux.

Still though, into the 1990s, there is a flourishing literature from both academics and practitioners, offering sustained feminist analyses of planning for women (Little, 1994, RTPI, 1995, OECD, 1995), and of women in planning (Greed, 1992, 1994). However, regarding much academic research on the city, 'urban scholars are greatly unaccustomed to thinking about gender, let alone uncovering cities as sites of institutionalised patriarchy' (Garber and Turner, 1995, p.xv).

Women, Cities and Identity: the Study

An understanding of the position of gender in the structures, processes and outcomes of urban production and consumption begins with the simple but central questions of 'who plans?' and 'for whom?'. Women comprise only twenty-three per cent of urban planners and only nine per cent of urban designers (WDS, 1993), but fifty-two per cent of the population. A central aspect of the research problem was revealed as the specificity of women's relationship to the built environment, arising from women's social role as the primary carers of dependants (children, elderly, disabled) in our society, and often, from women's dual role as mother and worker. Women's gender role-related disadvantage of physical constrictions over time and space is underpinned and 'endorsed' by gendered ideologies embedded in the social, economic and political structures and processes of the city. Such structures and processes, in turn, enable gender relations which effectively institutionalise women's dependency. As Garber and Turner (1995, p.xi) see it:

> Women's dependency is effectively institutionalised by (a) welfare, job training, housing, and child care policies that label as pathological women who do not rely on men for material support or social and self worth; (b) public safety services, public transportation, and streetscapes that render women physically vulnerable; and (c) economic development strategies that produce jobs of marginal benefit to the majority of female heads of households. Hence, the local state induces, even though it might not force, gender compliance.

The implications of such institutionalised dependency are axiomatic to the specificity of women's relationship to the built environment.

Conceptualising, Accessing and Measuring 'Urban Identity'

In general terms, 'urban identity' is defined here as 'the sense of oneself as a participant in the urban milieu'. It is the 'portion' of self-identity that focuses on relatively conscious, personally held beliefs, interpretations, and evaluations of oneself as a participant in urban milieux. Using an urban sociopsychological approach (relating psychological perception to social situations within the city) and an urban psychophysical approach (relating subjective perception to objective physical attributes of the city), urban identity is conceptualised, accessed and 'measured' as a type of place-identity (Proshansky et al., 1983); and as a substructure of self-identity (Pronshansky, 1978). This conceptualisation of urban identity is couched within the metatheoretical framework of 'Identity Structure Analysis' (ISA, Weinreich, 1989), a formal system of concepts of identity which may be operationalised via ISA's Identity Exploration (IDEX) computer software (cf. Saunderson, 1995a for methodological details).

To *access* urban identity, detailed and lengthy sensitising procedures were carried out: personal accounts of city living were collected from male and female architects and town planners at their work places, and from men and women in the cafes, bars, shops, bus stops and benches of Belfast. These 'internal, covert and reflective elements of social behaviour and experience' (Denzin, 1978, p.252) were used to design an ISA 'Identity Instrument' containing salient aspects, artefacts and personal constructions of urban life.

The 'administration' of the Identity Instrument to 120 of Belfast's male and female urban producers (most of whom were directly involved in planning Belfast), and urban consumers (randomly sampled from the 1991 Electoral Register, Ward 26/19 Malone), elicited some 56,000 separate judgements and some 200 hours of audio tape. As regards 'measuring' urban identity, the IDEX software facilitated the transformation of almost purely idiographic, qualitative information about city life into normalised quantitative indices of identity.

In acknowledging our possession of 'multiple realities' (Schutz, 1967), ISA facilitates the investigation of 'situated identities', that is, self as situated in different social contexts. Situated identity is explored here in terms of Belfast's urban dwellers' construal of self, others and the city, in the three situated identity contexts of personal self ('me as I am now'), *urban-user self* ('me as a user of the built environment') and, for architects and town planners, *urban-professional self* ('me as a producer of the built environment'). This facility allows comparison of identification patterns in several situated identities, both within and between the groups of men and women as producers and consumers of Belfast's built environment.

Belfast: A Contested City?

The empirical investigation was carried out in Belfast, an urban area of sixty square miles, housing just under half a million people - almost one-third of the Northern Ireland population. Belfast is well known as a contested city: as a city of contrasts. Frequently paralleled with Beruit by the international media; often referred to as a 'pariah' city; and well known as the capital city of one of the most deprived regions of the United Kingdom - indeed, Belfast's status as a contested city is exemplary (Saunderson, 1995b).

Since the mid-1980s, however, Belfast city centre has clearly undergone something of a revival, largely due to concerted efforts towards its re-imaging through physical planning linked to the Belfast Urban Area Plan (BUAP) 2001. The purpose of the BUAP 2001 is to establish physical development policies for the Belfast Urban Area up to the year 2001. Geared towards the reflation, reclamation and reinvigoration of Belfast's population and urban core, the plan's emphasis in such 'spatial eugenics' (Greed, 1994) is on investment in the post-industrial sectors of retailing, leisure and tourism. So, harnessed to the commercial thrust of the BUAP 2001, Belfast's planners, policy-makers and politicians alike, are under pressure to put 'image-building' at the centre of urban development: to diminish the old symbolism of the depressed 'city under siege' and to project Belfast city centre as an oasis of normality and indeed as a symbol of a normal Northern Ireland (Neill, 1995).

Further to a mere projection of normality, the 'new' Belfast effortlessly provides a parallel with the London Docklands, displaying in built form, the values of Thatcherism, corporate identity and functional anonymity (Edwards, 1993, pp.17-18). It is here, in the 'hyper-reality' (Baudrillard, 1988) of Belfast's new imaging, that 'post-modern capitalism thrives on the symbolic in the processes surrounding consumption' (Bocock, 1993, p.114). And it is here, that we can 'buy' collective and individual identities: where ideas are being consumed as much as objects. But there is a fragility about it. All the while, the old symbolism of Belfast squats uncomfortably underneath: 'it is a condition of visual schizophrenia ... a case of "lipstick on the gorilla"' (Neill, 1992, p.9). Certainly, the experience of the 1980s, the decade of entrepreneurial urban mercantilism and aggressive place-marketing, is that urban regeneration is not impossible, but it is uneven and partial (Parkinson, 1989).

That Belfast's reinvigoration is led by consumption rather than production (Neill, 1995) and that women are more concerned with issues of consumption than production (Little, 1994), is accurate. Less accurate, perhaps, is the view from within the DOE(NI)'s Belfast planning office that 'women's consumption of the city is no different to men's' (HPTO, 1992). This view was directly reflected in the BUAP 2001, despite community objections to the Plan's exclusion of women's transportation needs; of the needs of the family, particularly women and children; and of women's need for safety in the city.

While there exists no circular or White Paper giving specific guidance on gender issues in town planning, as Greed (1993) submits, the relevant statutory authority is required by law to take gender issues into account in the provision of public facilities (under the Sex Discrimination Act, 1975); and the Royal Town Planning Institute's Code of Professional Conduct (1986) makes it illegal to discriminate on the basis of race, sex, creed or religion - this alone should govern individual planners' conduct (Greed, 1993, p.238). The BUAP's failure to recognise women's issues amounted to indirect discrimination (Blackman, 1991, p.98).

The Production and Consumption of Gendered Urban Space: The Results

The selected portions of empirical findings reported here suggest, in brief, that Belfast's re-imaging has been 'successful'; and that (like men) women in Belfast have generally strong and positive urban identities, but that (unlike men) women's urban identity is laid vulnerable by several particular aspects of urban life when the women construe themselves as users of the built environment. Women working as architects and town planners in Belfast appear to have fully absorbed a 'malestream' professional identity; and lastly, incongruities lie at the interface between urban production and consumption in Belfast, particularly regarding the ownership of professional knowledge and the democratisation of urban production.

Women's Positive Self-Image in the City

Urban women in Belfast possess generally strong and positive urban identities. In other words: the qualities women attribute to the city centre are congruent to their 'ideal' qualities for self (high 'idealistic identification'); women perceive a strong similarity between attributes of their own self-image and those of the city (strong 'empathetic identification'); and, their strong 'ego-involvement' with the urban core renders it a highly salient feature of their urban lives. Therefore, core urban identity, as the organising nexus of the individual in the city, is strong and positive for urban women (and men) in Belfast.

A particularly prominent and positive feature in the identity structures of urban women (and reinforcing earlier assertions about Belfast's re-imaging) is Castlecourt Shopping Mall. Often referred to as Belfast's 'heart transplant', Castlecourt was consciously designed as a symbol of a stylish, sophisticated, cosmopolitan consumer culture of a 'new look' Belfast: another Cathedral of Consumerism (Fiske, 1989) in which we are invited to 'buy' or create a social identity for ourselves (cf. Bocock, 1993). Castlecourt is a very salient feature in the urban lives of Belfast's women. Not only does it exemplify all they aspire to in terms of aesthetic pleasure, safety, congeniality and accessibility, urban consumers see themselves as personally 'sharing' the very desirable, sophisticated and thoroughly modern characteristics that Castlecourt epitomises for them. One woman asserted:

> Well, when you walk into it, you just get a buzz (sic): it's big, modern, trendy, I like Debenhams myself. And you feel really safe, especially with the kids. It's just a really good place to be; you could be anyone, in any big city in the world - and you can forget about what's going on outside.

For Belfast's urban consumers, both women and men, Castlecourt clearly reinforces and enhances a desired self-image in the city, contributing to and supporting a strong and positive urban identity. While other aspects of city living such as city parks and the day-time city centre generally support confident urban identities, certain urban aspects create sharp vulnerability in the identity structures of Belfast's urban women.

Women and Vulnerable Urban Identity

When urban women are asked to think of themselves as actually using the built environment, certain aspects of the city give rise to strong conflicts in identification coupled with low self-esteem, contributing to a highly vulnerable identity state. Identification conflicts arise when one perceives similar attributes in oneself and another, while simultaneously wishing to dissociate from the other's attributes, thus creating an 'uncomfortable' psychological state. Urban women experience strong identification conflicts with aspects of the city closely associated with the tasks and demands of their social role as primary carers (e.g. children's public play areas); and with the people responsible for providing such aspects (i.e. town planners and city councillors). Their strongest identification conflicts are with public transport and the night-time city.

Public Transport

The specificity of women's relationship to the built environment involves distinctive and demanding spatial activity arising from their social role as the primary carers of children and other dependants, and often, their dual role as mother and worker. Such spatial activity gives rise to women's particular mobility needs, often, for short, multi-purpose, multi-stage journeys, and always, for safe, frequent, accessible, reliable and affordable transport provision. However, public transport is a highly contested aspect of urban women's lives. That eighty-seven per cent of women are 'not at all satisfied with public transport in Belfast' (compared with three per cent of men) suggests that women's particular mobility needs in the city are not being met. Further, of all aspects of city life, women's highest identification conflicts are associated with public transport, rendering it the strongest contributor to vulnerabilities in urban women's identities as users of the city. Public transport creates no such vulnerability in the urban identities of men, for whom it is not a contested aspect of the city.

The Night-time City

Ease of movement in the city is as much psychological as it is physical. If a woman perceives personal danger or threat, then fear results. Whether this fear is 'justified' or not, is immaterial with regard to the consequences it will have in influencing subsequent movement, avoidance or encounter. When urban women in Belfast construe themselves as using the built environment, their identifications with the night-time city immediately parallel percepts of personal danger and insecurity, and become highly conflicted (unlike those of men in this identity context). Many women, particularly urban consumers, said they simply did not go into Belfast at night; some said they would, but only if they were accompanied, were in a car, or had booked a return taxi. One woman submitted:

> You don't go into the city at night if you know what's good for you - it's no place for women late at night. Anyway, I can never be blamed for being caught in 'the wrong place' at 'the wrong time' if I stay at home in my own space - at least I can control what goes on here.

Such protestations and indications of an implicit curfew on women using the night-time city reinforced the contention, again and again, of gendered and contested urban space. Clearly, for women in Belfast, fear for personal security in the night-time city adds a very undesirable dimension (socially, spatially and symbolically) to their urban lives.

But what do urban dwellers in Belfast *mean* by personal safety and security? Safety from what? This was a particularly pertinent question in the context of the politically distressed 'pre-ceasefire' climate of Belfast. Of urban men, fifty-three per cent feared personal attack in the city (being robbed/mugged or personally threatened), while forty-seven per cent felt their personal safety threatened by sectarian violence (being 'caught up' in terrorist bombs or shootings). In contrast, *all* urban women referred to personal safety in terms of being safe from sexual harassment or direct sexual attack (twenty per cent of women also fear, amongst other things, sectarian activity, but only at night). So, it would appear that even in the face of the exceptionally 'troubled' political climate of Belfast, issues of women's personal safety in the city remain very much in the arena of sexual politics, not sectarian politics.

What does all this suggest about urban identity, gender, and contested urban space in Belfast? Urban identity, 'the sense of oneself as a participant in the urban milieu', is generally strong and positive for both women and men. However, insofar as urban identity may be conceptualised as an 'indicator' of social, spatial, and symbolic representations of the city; for many women, the consumption of particular aspects of urban living (such as public transport provision and the night-time city) renders Belfast as highly contested space - socially, spatially and symbolically - along the lines of gender.

Women as Urban Producers: Contested Identities?

Historically and contemporarily, patriarchy and the professions have been seen as largely synonymous. The questions of 'who designs the designers?' and of whether women design differently to men, remain largely rhetorical ones. Women in the urban planning and design professions are interviewed, accepted, trained, examined, judged competent, referred, interviewed again, then employed, and indeed promoted, almost exclusively, by men. Certainly, the landed professions of architecture and town planning reflect a male-oriented ethos, praxis and pedagogy. But how does women's enculturation into the landed professions affect their identity? Does their identity modulate between personal self ('me as I am now') and professional self ('me as an architect/town planner')? Or do they 'absorb' the male-oriented ethos of their professions?

The findings suggest that women's enculturation into the particular socio-cultural matrix of the landed professions does not result in a modulation (i.e. contest) of identity between personal and professional self. Rather, the particular and pervasive processes of professionalisation appear to result in women's identifications in the personal self being *modified* to those of the professional self. Such modification, rather than modulation, of identity between these facets of self reveals that personal and professional self are largely coexistent for urban-professional women in Belfast, just as they are for their male colleagues. These findings may be contrasted to Wager's (1993) study of academic women which demonstrated a distinct modulation between identifications in the personal 'feminine' self, and the professional 'feminist' self, of female university lecturers in Finland.

However, even though female producers' personal and professional identities appear 'harmonious', this is not to give the impression of satisfaction amongst the women who plan and design Belfast. On the contrary, the empirical findings reveal that many women architects and town planners are acutely aware of, and often adversely affected by, both structural inadequacies in city planning and their minority position as women in male-dominated professions.

Tensions at the Urban Production-Consumption Interface

Considerable tensions characterise the broad interface between urban production and urban consumption. There is, of course, not only one interface between urban production and consumption, but as many interfaces as there are social representations of the systems that regulate the relationships between the production and consumption of the city defined on the basis of gender, age, class, race, sexuality, and culture (Saunderson, 1995b). The production-consumption interface to which the following empirical findings respond, is that of the value and belief systems of the women and men who 'produce' and 'consume' Belfast.

Findings reveal that the most central 'core' value of urban designers is 'attractiveness and aesthetic pleasure', and that for urban consumers, it is 'being satisfied with the way things are'. These core evaluative criteria by which Belfast's producers and consumers most readily and consistently appraise self, others and the city, underpin the fundamental thrust of the empirical study. Such dominant evaluative dimensions of identity suggest the different 'orientations' of Belfast's urban producers and consumers, which, if reflected in the built environment itself, suggest a basic incongruence between the representation of producer and consumer interests and aspirations in the city. So, regarding questions of 'who plans?' and 'for whom?', incongruities between the sets of beliefs, value systems and symbolic frameworks of urban producers and consumers clearly suggest contested space at the production-consumption interface.

The 'contest' is about the ownership of professional knowledge and decision-making power in the city. This is especially pertinent in the Northern Ireland context, where town planners possess the unique status of both 'poacher' and 'gamekeeper'. The importance of the public's ability to access and openly question professional judgements about the city is a core evaluative dimension of identity for the majority of urban consumers: it is only a secondary evaluative criterion of identity for the majority of architects and town planners. Clearly then, the value of public participatory planning is more central to the urban consumer culture than to the urban design culture.

The concept of who 'owns' urban-professional knowledge is also deeply gendered, especially amongst urban consumers. Of the urban consumers who aspire towards participatory planning as a core evaluative dimension of identity, eighty-three per cent are women. It therefore appears that any impetus from urban consumers to address the contested ownership of professional knowledge at the producer-consumer interface is going to come largely from women. Further, since ninety-three per cent of female architects and town planners favour the democratisation of urban planning (albeit, as a secondary evaluative dimension of identity) - it also appears that there is considerable support for such an impetus from women within the landed professions.

Conclusions and Recommendations

This was an ambitious study. As an attempt to conceptualise, access and 'measure' the urban identities of women and men who produce and consume the built environment of Belfast; and to uncover the position of gender in the processes of urban production and consumption; this chapter is a battle report, not a victory salute. Much more remains to be done to further uncover and understand the relationship between gender, social processes, and spatial form in the production and consumption of urban space. Empirical findings presented here, though, indicate that the identities of all urban women in Belfast (whether producers or consumers) are in an arena of stress when they construe themselves and the city in terms of using the built environment.

For women as consumers of the built environment, needs, preferences and aspirations are marginalised by gendered urban structures and processes (not least, the male-dominated planning system) that effectively institutionalise women's dependency. The vast majority of our care-providers (to children, the elderly and the disabled) are women: the vast majority of those responsible for planning the physical (and social, and economic) facilitation for such care, are men. So, while the urban identity of women in Belfast is largely supported (even enhanced) by 'the city' in general, it is sharply challenged and rendered vulnerable by certain aspects (particularly structural deficiencies) of city life related to the tasks and demands of their social role as primary carers.

For women who work as architects and town planners in Belfast, the alignment of their personal identity with their professional identity presents itself as a reflection of their 'absorbtion' into the male-dominated ethos, praxis and pedagogy of the planning and design professions in Northern Ireland. For these urban-professional women, prominence of position and professional aspirations are often marginalised by the numerical domination of their professions by men. Further, the ownership of professional knowledge is clearly a contentious issue for Belfast's urban women. There exists a strong desire for the democratisation of urban planning and design, both from women in the landed professions and women as urban consumers.

This study not only provides much-needed empirical research on urban women, but it also reveals ample evidence to suggest the specificity of women's relationship to the city, and certainly, a sufficient amount to warrant a response from planning practice. City-wide strategies should be formulated to incorporate women, not as a homogeneous group, but as an aggregate, taking full account of the complex inter-relations between the many facets of their public and private lives in the city. In particular, ways of improving public transport and women's perceptions of safety in the night-time city should be prioritised. Women are not, and should not be treated as, a 'special needs' group: they constitute fifty-two per cent of the population. As part of a wider commitment to dissolving inequalities within the built environment, planning must make a conscious effort to relate its activities to creating links between different policy areas (housing, transport, childcare, retailing and leisure) and other divisions such as class, race, age, sexuality and culture, but particularly to gender, which subsumes all such divisions.

Women working within the planning system are uniquely placed to address the situation. If professional women's groups within architecture and town planning institutes maintain a high profile and strong impetus, women's issues in Ireland's cities can be kept to the fore and pressed towards recognition and change. Also, expression of urban consumers' ideas and aspirations should be facilitated via properly open consultation exercises and public inquiries, where technical language and specialist frameworks are dispensed with in favour of accessible, non-intimidatory forums for discussion. Further, more planning and design professionals should work with women at grassroots level, which will increase understanding of each other's constraints in relation to both city planning and city living, and will sensitise professional considerations and planning interventions to community experience and preferences.

More *empirical* research is needed: not only into precisely how women's full participation in urban milieux is hindered, but also, into the values and attitudes underlying the praxes and pedagogy of urban planning in Ireland, and how these are reflected in gender relations both inside and outside the planning system; into ways of improving academic-practice links between the two Northern Irish universities and the DOE(NI); and into the nature and extent of gender bias in planning education itself. Research proselytising the incorporation of women's needs in urban planning should be both interpretable by practitioners, and applicable to planning practice. Research-based ideas are more helpful than research *per se*. Further, feminist research needs to concentrate its efforts on planning theory as well as planning practice.

The built environment, whether construed as a product or a process, is a function of many complex forces. A polysemantic notion (Mazza, 1995) such as 'design' compounds such complexities. That design problems are multifariously rooted in personal, social and cultural aspects of life, means there exists no objective context for formulating solutions or judging their 'correctness' at any given historical moment or in any given place or space. Clearer though, is the position of gender in the processes and problems of urban production and urban consumption. Such a position reflects, reinforces, and is shaped by, layers of institutional structures, processes and outcomes that shape urban gender relations, themselves shaped by broader societal gender relations. Although valuable beginnings are discernible (cf. Charles and Hughes-Freeland, 1995, Walby, 1997, forthcoming), it is these broader gender relations that need to be addressed before any meaningful change can be made - socially, spatially and symbolically - at the level of women's lives in cities, as producers and/or consumers of the urban environment.

Discussion Topics

1. What, in your view, is the most contentious issue concerning women's relationship to urban space? Contextualise and discuss this issue in terms of its social, spatial, and symbolic relevance to women's urban lives.

2. Towards redressing the male-oriented ethos, praxis and pedagogy of the urban planning and design professions, is the case for more women entering the landed professions stronger than the case for strengthening the position of those women already in these professions?

3. 'Since the 1970s increased attention has been focused on gender in relation to planning practice, but not to planning theory' (Sandercock and Forsythe, 1992). In what ways and to what end can feminist theory contribute to planning theory?

4. What suggestions do you have that would improve women's urban lives? Is the city a safe place for women?

Reference and Further Reading

Ardener, S. 1993 *Women and Space: Ground Rules and Social Maps* Oxford: Berg.

Barrett, M, Boothman, G, Caffrey, C, Doyle, A, McCambley, S, McElwee, D, McKeown, G, O'Shee, M and Sheridan, A-M. 1986 *Submission to Dublin Corporation for City Development Plan Review* Dublin: Women and Planning Group.

Baudrillard, J. 1988 *Selected Writings* Cambridge: Polity Press.

Bell, D and Valentine, G. (eds.) 1995 *Mapping Desire: Geographies of Sexuality* London: Routledge.

Betsky, A. 1995 *Building Sex: Men, Women, Architecture, and the Construction of Sexuality* New York: William Morrow.

Blackman, T. 1991 *Planning Belfast* Aldershot: Avebury.

Bocock, R. 1993 *Consumption* London: Routledge.

Caffrey, C and Eanaigh, C. 1990 *Toilets, Babycare and Creche Facilities in Shopping Developments* Dublin: Women and Planning Group.

Charles, N and Hughes-Freeland, F. (eds.) 1995 *Practising Feminism: Identity, Difference Power* London: Routledge.

Colomina, B. 1992 *Sexuality and Space* New York: Princeton Architectural Association.

CTA (Community Technical Aid). 1988 *Objections to BUAP 2001 Draft Plan* Belfast: CTA.

Denzin, N. 1978 *The Research Act* Chicago: Aldine.

Duncan, N. (ed.) 1996 *Bodyspace: Destabilising Geographies of Gender and Sexuality* London: Routledge.

Edwards, B. 1993 'Deconstructing the City: The Experience of London Docklands' *The Planner*, Feb.1993, pp.16-18.

Fiske, J. 1989 *Reading the Popular* Boston: Unwin Hyman.

Foord, J and Gregson, N. 1986 'Patriarchy: Towards a Reconceptualisation' *Antipode*, 18, 2, pp.186-211.

Garber, J A and Turner, R S. (eds.) 1995 *Gender in Urban Research* London: Sage.

Greed, C. 1992 'Women in Planning' *The Planner*, 78, 13, pp.11-13.

Greed, C. 1993 *Introducing Town Planning* London: Routledge.

Greed, C. 1994 *Women and Planning: Creating Gendered Realities* London: Routledge.

Hague, C. 1995 'Texts on Urban and Regional Planning: A Review Article' *Town Planning Review* 66, 2, pp.207-212

Hayden, D. 1984 *Redesigning the American Dream* London: Norton.

Higher Professional Technical Officer (HPTO). 1992 *Personal Interview with a male Higher Professional Technical Officer* Belfast: Town and Country Planning Service.

Jones, D. 1988 'Foreword' in Sherman, B. *Cities Fit to Live In* Whitley: Good Books.

Katz, C and Monk, J. (eds.) 1993 *Full Circles: Geographies of Women Over the Life Course* London: Routledge.

Little, J. 1994 *Gender, Planning and the Policy Process* Oxford: Pergamon.

Little, J, Peake, L and Richardson, P. 1988 *Women in Cities* London: Macmillan.

Mazza, L. 1995 'Technical Knowledge, Practical Reason and the Planner's Responsibility' *Town Planning Review*, 66, 4, pp.389-409.

McDowell, L. 1990 'Gender Matters: Feminism/Postmodernism in Glasgow and Toronto' *Area*, 22, 4, pp.387-90.

Neill, W. 1992 'Re-imaging Belfast' *The Planner*, 78, 18, pp.8-10.

Neill, W. 1995 'Lipstick on the Gorilla? Conflict Management, Urban Development and Image Making in Belfast' In Neill, W, Fitzsimmons, D and Murtagh B. (eds.) *Reimaging the Pariah City* Aldershot: Avebury.

OECD. 1995 *Women in the City: Housing, Services, and the Urban Environment* Paris: OECD.

Parkinson, M. 1989 'The Thatcher Government's Urban Policy, 1979-1989: A Review' *Town Planning Review*, 60, 4, pp.421-440.

Proshansky, H M. 1978 'The City and Self Identity' *Environment and Behaviour* 10, 2, 147-169.

Proshansky, H M, Fabian, A K and Kaminoff, R. 1983 'Place-identity: Physical World Socialisation of the Self' *Journal of Environmental Psychology*, 3, pp.57-83.

Royal Town Planning Institute (RTPI). 1995 *Planning for Women Practice* Advice Note No. 12 London: The Royal Town Planning Institute.

Sandercock, L and Forsythe, A. 1992 'A Gender Agenda' *Journal of the American Planning Association*, 58, 1, pp.49-59.

Saunderson, W. 1994 'Gendered Narratives in an Irish Urban Milieu: Belfast's Urban Design Culture, Urban Consumption, and Urban Identity' Paper presented at the *Gendered Narratives in Ireland* Conference, University of Ulster Magee College, 25th-27th March, 1994.

Saunderson, W. 1995a 'A Theoretical and Empirical Investigation of Gender and Urban Space: The Production and Consumption of the Built Environment' D.Phil. Thesis. University of Ulster, Coleraine.

Saunderson, W. 1995b 'The Production and Consumption of Gendered Urban Space: Social, Spatial, and Symbolic Representations of the City' Paper presented at the British Sociological Association's Annual Conference, *Contested Cities: Social Process and Spatial Forms*, Leicester, 10th-13th April, 1995.

Schutz, A. 1967 *Phenomenology of the Social World* Illinois: Northwestern University Press.

Siltanen, J and Stanworth, M. 1984 'The Politics of Private Woman and Public Man' in Siltanen, J and Stanworth, M. (eds.) *Women and the Public Sphere* London: Hutchinson.

Snitow, A. 1990 'A Gender Diary' in Hirsch, M and Fox Keller, E. (eds.) *Conflict in Feminism* New York: Routledge.

Stimpson, C, Dixler, E, Nelson, M and Yatrakis, K. (eds.) 1981. *Women and the American City* Chicago: University of Chicago Press.

Valentine, G. 1993 'Managing and Negotiating Multiple Identities: Lesbian Time-space Strategies' *Transactions of the Institute of British Geographers* 18, pp.237-48.

Wager, M. 1993 'Constructions of Femininity in Academic Women: Continuity Between Private and Professional Identity' D.Phil. Thesis University of Ulster, Jordanstown.

Walby, S. 1997 (forthcoming) *Restructuring Gender* London: Routledge.

Weinreich, P. 1989 'Variations in Ethnic Identity: Identity Structure Analysis' in Leibkind K. (ed.) *New Identities in Europe* Aldershot: Gower.

Women's Design Service (WDS). 1993 *Training for Building Design and the Construction Industry*. Broadsheet No.6. London: Women's Design Service.

Zelinsky, W, Monk, J and Hanson, S. 1982 'Women and Geography: A Review and Prospectus' *Progress in Human Geography* 6, 3, pp.317-66.

30.

Out of Sight, Out of Mind? Women with Disabilities in Ireland

Barbara Murray and Audrey O'Carroll

Women with disabilities have tended to be overlooked by social researchers in the Republic of Ireland, as well as in feminist debate. The virtual exclusion of disabled women from both of these agendas is a reflection of their widespread social exclusion and the fact that many of them lead hidden lives, often prevented from active social participation by a combination of physical, organisational, financial and attitudinal barriers.

While little research on this issue has been undertaken in this country, evidence from research in the United States and the United Kingdom shows that women with disabilities are more isolated from the larger socio-economic system than men with disabilities and non-disabled women. Their low average participation rates are linked firstly to the fact that they are *women*: some of the obstacles they face are also faced by non-disabled women, although overcoming them may be more difficult for women with disabilities. Their exclusion is also linked to the fact that they have a *disability*: the obstacles in this case are likely to be faced by disabled men, although once again, the process of overcoming them may involve different measures and strategies for women with disabilities (Campling, 1981, Croxen-John, 1988, Morris, 1989, Moran, 1992). Some researchers have even suggested that the double disadvantage which women with disabilities experience may be compounded into a 'female/disabled "plus" factor' (Hanna and Rogovsky, 1991), implying that some of the obstacles which they have to face are not faced either by non-disabled women or men with disabilities, making it more difficult for them to lead the life of their choice in society.

Because some scholars have only recently begun to document this topic in an exploratory way, it is necessary to set the discussion of the small number of Irish-based research projects on women and girls with disabilities against the backdrop of research carried out elsewhere. This review will highlight the issues which have been identified and the topics which need to be researched if a comprehensive profile of the status of women with disabilities in the Republic of Ireland is to be compiled.

Women with Disabilities – An Invisible Group

There is no comprehensive information on the number of people with disabilities in the Republic of Ireland, so that it is not possible to say, with accuracy, how many women and girls with disabilities there are in the country today. Based on the World Health Organisation's assumption that ten per cent of the population has some form of disability, there were an estimated 177,230 women and girls with disabilities living here in 1991. Basing the estimate on the prevalence rate reported by the Office of Population Censuses and Surveys (OPCS) in Northern Ireland (13.8 per cent), the number would be higher, at 244,577. It would be higher still if the prevalence rate recently reported in the United States (almost twenty per cent) was used. These differences are largely due to varying definitions of disability and differences in methodology between the different surveys.

The only current empirical data on the prevalence of disability among people of working age is given by the census category of people over age fifteen who are 'unable to work due to permanent sickness or disability'. In 1991, there were 28,792 women in this category, representing thirty-six per cent of all people in this category and two per cent of all women aged fifteen and over. It is likely that this figure underestimates the number of women with disabilities who are unable to work, since many of these women are likely to be included in the census as 'on home duties'. This is indicated by the differing proportions of married women and men in this category – married women made up a third of the women unable to work due to permanent sickness or disability, while married men made up fifty per cent of the men.

Further information in the number of women unable to work due to disability can be obtained from statistics on disability-related allowances. In 1995, 37,219 women with disabilities received either a disability benefit or an invalidity pension, and an estimated 25,000 women received the Disabled Persons' Maintenance Allowance (DPMA), giving a total of approximately 62,219 women receiving these disability-related allowances. This estimate gives a more accurate picture of the number of women with disabilities over age fifteen than the census data, including as it does those who have worked at some stage (those qualifying for social insurance allowances) and those who have not (those receiving Health Board allowances).

There is no information on the number of people with disabilities in the labour force, making it impossible to establish definitive employment/ unemployment rates. It is generally believed, though, that the unemployment rate among women and men with disabilities is much higher than among the population at large, with estimates of up to seventy per cent being cited.

It would be an important first step in putting girls and women with disabilities on the research and policy agenda in the Republic of Ireland if these gaps in statistical information were to be filled. It would help, for example, if the Census of Population were to include a question on disability. While there would be difficulties with the self-definitional approach which this would involve, it would provide an empirical base on which further work could be carried out. It would also help reduce the current invisibility of women with disabilities and represent a step towards recognition of this group as having specific requirements in terms of service provision, if organisations and agencies as diverse as schools, colleges, universities, health boards, training providers, social welfare, rape crisis centres and women's shelters published information on the extent to which women with disabilities avail of their services.

Different Disabilities – Different Experiences

Even if it were possible to be clear about the number of females with disability living in the Republic of Ireland, this would only be a first step in identifying the issues which they face and the services they require. This is because women with disabilities make up a very heterogeneous group, including as it does women and girls with learning disabilities, physical disabilities, sensory disabilities and mental health difficulties. Further differences arise from the fact that some of these women were born with a disability, while others acquired their disability in the course of their lives through an accident or the onset of a disease or illness. Depending on the severity of their disability and the level of impairment associated with this, these women may experience quite different obstacles when it comes to participating in society.

Women who acquire a disability in the course of their lives have to adjust from a non-disabled lifestyle to one in which they have to come to terms with a disability. This may arise from an accident or the onset of a disease such as multiple sclerosis or because of the emergence of mental health difficulties, conditions which require constant readjustments because of their cyclical or progressive nature. For these women, the process of readjustment and the development of strategies to help them to live with their acquired disabilities is likely to be difficult and painful, especially where they acquire their disability late in life. It is likely to involve redefining their lifestyles, learning to come to terms with their new dependency on others, facing up to difficulties they may have in fulfilling recognised female roles, and dealing with discriminatory or condescending attitudes on the part of others, all of which take their toll (see, for example, Campling, 1979). Their capacity to cope with the resulting pressures

– not just psychologically, but also financially and socially, is likely to vary according to employment status, educational level and level of familial income (Dangoor and Florian, 1994). Poorer women are less likely than women who are better off to be able to afford the extra costs associated with disability – the cost of adaptations to their living arrangements, of aids and equipment and of personal assistance services which make it possible or easier for them to continue to live independently. This is particularly true in countries like the Republic of Ireland, where no allowance is made for additional disability-related costs in the calculation of State benefits.

Women with a congenital disability may not have experienced a non-disabled life, but they are likely to be very clear about the ways in which they are excluded from their peer groups from childhood onwards. Girls with disabilities often find that they are treated differently than others of their age. Mary Duffy has spoken about the difficulty her parents had in ensuring that she attended school locally:

> My own schooling history involved a narrow escape from the segregated education system and my parents were determined that I would not be sent away from home. They enlisted the assistance of the local convent school in keeping me in my home school. This was done in opposition to the health and education authorities (Duffy, 1993).

Girls with disabilities may be prevented from joining in the activities of other girls of their age, sometimes because of their disability but often for other reasons – for example, because facilities are inaccessible or because the activities are arranged in ways which effectively exclude them or because of the attitudes of those who advise and decide. The result is that many girls with disabilities grow up in isolation from their peer group, with implications both for their self-image and social integration.

Some of the difficulties which disabled women face are linked directly to their disability, whether it is congenital or acquired – to the fact that there are certain things which they are unable to do because of the physical or mental constraints which this places on them. Many of the difficulties confronting them arise more from the social construction of disability, relating to the ways in which they are denied access to services and opportunities, and the ways in which they are excluded from the social, economic, cultural and political life of their communities and neighbourhoods. Problems arising from poor vision and mobility, for example, could be overcome in employment by the installation of appropriate technology and the making of necessary adaptations. And the presence of sign language interpreters at meetings and lectures would help overcome the difficulty faced by people with hearing impairment in taking part or following what is being said. Problems of access to buildings and within buildings, of streets which are difficult to negotiate, of access to information, of attitudinal barriers, of inadequate services and housing, of transport and of dependency could also be overcome if appropriate measures were introduced. In the absence of such measures, these problems accumulate to make it difficult, if not impossible, for the women to go about their everyday business independently, combining to exclude them from the options which are open to other women in the Republic of Ireland – education, employment, marriage, as well as everyday activities and services.

Because women with disabilities are so diverse in terms of the needs arising from their disabilities, the research implications are also very broad. There is a need to document the experience of women with different types of disabilities in different situations, a task which would ideally involve several different studies. Progress could be made quickly if researchers and research funders came to recognise this as an area worthy of attention, which does not generally appear to be the case at present.

Education

For women with congenital disabilities, in particular, and for those who acquired their disabilities at an early age, the education they receive – and whether they receive it in a mainstream school or in a special school – is central to their future life choices. Current Irish Government policy favours full integration of children with disabilities into mainstream schools as the first option, while keeping open other options such as that of complete segregation (White Paper on Educational Development, 1980, Department of Education, 1993). A flexible approach to the education of children with disabilities which would allow them to 'move from ordinary schools to special schools and back again' as their needs dictated (Department of Education, 1992) would require resources to fund the support services and adaptations essential to make this policy a reality, but such funding has not yet been allocated. In addition, because the Irish educational system has not to date been governed by legislation, disabled children and their parents have had no recourse to the law to assert their rights to education under the terms of the Constitution (Department of Education, 1993, Duffy 1993). The lack of a legal framework means that the right of disabled children to education, particularly in mainstream schools, is not guaranteed by law. In May 1993, the High Court found that the Ministers for Health and Education had deprived an eight-year old child of his constitutional rights under Article 42 of the Constitution, by failing to provide him with free primary education and by discriminating against him as compared with other children. This boy has significant physical and intellectual disabilities and the decision appeared to be a path-breaking one for all children with disabilities, female and male. The High Court decision has been appealed by the Minister for Education to the

Supreme Court and at the time of writing (November, 1995) the case has not been heard, so that the right of children with disabilities to education is not yet clearly established.

Special education was introduced in the Republic of Ireland in the mid-nineteenth century, with the establishment of schools for deaf and blind children. Schools for children with mental handicap or physical disabilities developed from small numbers in the 1950s to a total of 116 schools in 1994, of which 101 are specifically for children with disabilities. Substantial growth in the number of special schools took place in the 1960s, when they constituted the preferred form of educational provision for children with disabilities. Since the early 1970s, the policy shift to an emphasis on integration is evidenced by the significant growth in the number of special classes in mainstream schools.

Overall, approximately one per cent of children of school-going age receive their education in schools segregated from the normal school system in the Republic of Ireland. This figure is relatively low by international comparison – in the Netherlands, for example, the figure is approximately four per cent. The absence of statistical data on the number of disabled children in the country and their educational locations makes it difficult to assess whether the provision of segregated school places is adequate or how disabled children who are not being placed in segregated schools are progressing in their education (Duffy, 1993). Information is available, however, on the number of girls and boys attending special schools: in 1993/94, 2,896 girls attended schools for children with different disabilities, making up thirty-nine per cent of all pupils in these schools (see Table 1). The only special schools in which girls form the majority are schools for pupils with visual impairment: their predominance is explained by the fact that second level education for boys with visual impairment is provided in a mainstream setting.

Table 1: *Pupils Attending Special Schools, by Gender 1993/94.*

SCHOOL TYPE	GIRLS	BOYS	TOTAL
	%	%	%
Schools for pupils with mild mental handicap	38	62	100
Schools for pupils with moderate mental handicap	41	59	100
Schools for emotionally disturbed pupils	22	78	100
Hospital schools for pupils with physical disability	42	58	100
Schools for pupils with physical disability	43	57	100
Schools for pupils with hearing impairment	51	49	100
Schools for pupils with multiple handicap	22	78	100
Schools for blind/partially sighted pupils	60	40	100
Schools for pupils with reading disability	22	78	100
Total %	39	61	100
Number	2,896	4,507	7,403

Source: Department of Education, 1995.

In the absence of figures on the number of children with disabilities of school-going age, it is not possible to put the figures in Table 1 into proper context. There is evidence, though, that the incidence of learning disability in the Republic of Ireland is somewhat higher among males than among females, with females making up 46.3 per cent of the total population of people with learning disabilities in 1981 (Census of Mental Handicap, 1994). But females made up 43.6 per cent of the school-going age-group in this population, so unless the prevalence rates have changed dramatically in the past fifteen years, girls with disabilities are under-represented in the schools for children with mild or moderate learning disability, where they comprised 39.3 per cent of the pupils in 1993/94.

Further evidence of gender differences in the prevalence of disability is provided by the OPCS survey of children in Northern Ireland which reported that the prevalence of disability was greater among boys (four per cent) than among girls (2.9 per cent). This figure includes children with learning disabilities (mental handicap), physical and sensory disabilities, and behavioural problems (OPCS, 1992). While both this survey and the Census of Mental Handicap in Ireland indicate a higher incidence of disability among boys than among girls at an early age, it should be emphasised that the reported prevalence rates are based on diagnosed disability. In view of the fact that the gender differences in the reported prevalence rates were narrower in older age groups, it is worth asking the question whether disability is identified earlier in boys than in girls due to differing expectations about what constitutes 'normal' behaviour.

In relation to girls with learning disabilities in the Republic of Ireland and to girls with other disabilities, for whom there is no empirical evidence to suggest that the prevalence rate in the Republic is higher among boys than among girls, the question arises, where are the other girls with these disabilities receiving their education? Are they attending mainstream schools? If so, what special supports are in place to ensure that they benefit from the education provided? If they are not attending mainstream schools, are they being educated at all? In light of the High Court decision and the subsequent challenge to this by the Minister for Education, it is conceivable that they might not. In any case, what can be said with certainty is that girls with disabilities make up a minority of pupils in special schools. This pattern of under-representation has been noted elsewhere and it has been suggested that girls with disabilities are not seen as needing an education as much as boys with disabilities (Fine and Asch, 1989).

If girls with disabilities attend special schools, even if they are under-represented there, what is the consequence for them? The quality of special school teachers and their training has been widely recognised, as has the contribution of voluntary bodies in the operation of these schools (Department of Education, 1993). The weaknesses of the special system are considerable, though, and have practical implications for the kind of education which girls with disabilities receive. One of the disadvantages is a structural one: special schools are national schools, catering to pupils aged from six to eighteen. Girls with disabilities attending these schools generally do not follow a nationally recognised curriculum. While guidelines have been drawn up in certain curricular areas for pupils with moderate mental handicap, there are no curricular guidelines in relation to pupils with mild, severe or profound mental handicap in special schools. Girls in these schools are not required, at present, to do school or state tests, nor are they expected to do homework (Duffy, 1993). Thus, when girls with disabilities complete their time in these schools, they have not completed a nationally recognised course, not do they obtain a recognised certificate of education. There are some exceptions to this, as some of the special schools are now preparing pupils who are able to do so for the Junior Certificate examination but, for the majority, their education does not lead to any recognised qualification.

A further result of the classification of special schools as primary schools is that senior pupils with disabilities are attending school with young children, while their non-disabled peers are perhaps in the final year of second level school, about to transfer to further or third level education. This has implications in terms of the young girls' identity and self-confidence. The primary school ethos, which does not easily accommodate the changes associated with adolescence, reinforces their experience of being different or left out. Besides this, attendance at special schools limits their opportunities of mixing with their non-disabled peers.

> Segregated education... has separated young people from their peers – denied young disabled and non-disabled people the opportunity to learn from each other. Keeping young disabled people out of the mainstream has fuelled that fear that comes from unfamiliarity. It is damaging in terms of the quality of education delivered, but also in terms of relationships and access to experience and opportunity. Young disabled people are separated from their community and they grow up in extreme isolation, afraid of the non-disabled world which in turn rejects them because of their real and perceived institutionalisation (Wilson in *Making Connections*, 1992, p.24).

In mainstream education, considerable obstacles to gender equality have been removed in recent decades, but the debate about equality of opportunity for girls and boys has not impinged in any significant way on the educational opportunity for girls with intellectual disabilities. The recent Review Group on Special Education, for example, does not mention this aspect of educational provision at all. The lack of a national curriculum in special schools and the emphasis on training in living skills combine to maintain an emphasis on traditional gender role-related education for girls in these schools. A focus on the development of nationally recognised curricula in special education and on equality of opportunity for girls and boys within this system is well overdue. The introduction of a recognised programme of sex education, now in process in mainstream schools, needs to be extended to special schools. If anything, this programme is more urgently needed in special schools, given the greater risk of sexual abuse reportedly faced by girls with disabilities (Cole, 1991, Abilities, 1995, p.32).

Reference has been made above to the recent policy shift from special schools to an emphasis on special classes in ordinary schools. In 1993/94, there were 227 special classes in ordinary primary schools. In 1992, at post-primary level, there were forty-eight special classes for pupils with a mild mental handicap, catering to approximately 600 pupils. In addition to the special classes, an estimated 8,000 pupils with disabilities attend ordinary classes in mainstream schools (Department of on Special Education, 1993). No gender breakdown is available for these figures, however, and there is no information on how these pupils are faring in the mainstream schools. Curricular guidelines have been developed only for pupils with mild mental handicap in special classes in post-primary schools. In many cases, provision is made for some level of integration with mainstream classes, although this is made difficult by the fact that the pupils in special classes are enrolled on a separate roll, rather than being part of the general enrolment, with implications for the staff/pupil ratio should a teacher be willing to accept a pupil from a special class for part of the school day (Department of Education, 1993, p.65).

In a qualitative study of the experience of girls with disabilities in different types of schools (Duffy, 1993), half of the young women interviewed said that their teachers' expectations for them were lower than for non-disabled pupils, even where they attended mainstream schools. Most of the disabled girls did not take part in school sports, although half of them actively participated in sports after school hours. Most of them felt that they could have attended their neighbourhood school if their basic needs in terms of personal care, school equipment, access to the buildings and transport had been satisfied in those schools. Duffy concludes that the education system in Ireland fundamentally discriminates against disabled girls, mainly because of lack of access and disablist attitudes.

In a study of the experience of deaf students in higher education in Ireland (O'Reilly, 1993), students with hearing impairment – female and male – spoke about their primary and second level education. All of these students reported difficulties in participating in a speech-oriented education system. Sign language, while not officially permitted in all sections of schools for the deaf, was the preferred method of communicating between deaf people. They felt disadvantaged because of the continuous use of oral methods in the classroom, leading to lack of effective communication for them. As in the case of the girls with physical disabilities (Duffy, 1993), the deaf students reported that their teachers' expectations of them decreased as they moved on from primary to secondary school. Some felt that they were not encouraged to aspire to sit the Leaving Certificate examination, let alone go on to third level education. None of the female students had received help to prepare for third level.

The educational experience of girls with disabilities needs to be critically examined, both in terms of policy and curricular provision, in order to highlight the changes required to ensure equality of opportunity for these girls. These changes will not only affect the employment opportunities of girls and boys with disabilities when they complete their formal education, they will also affect their choices in terms of the adult roles they play and the opportunities open to them socially, politically and culturally.

Leaving School – Transition from Adolescence to Adulthood

Girls with disabilities experience particular difficulties when they enter adolescence, a time when they, like their non-disabled peers, are generally very sensitive to perceived social expectations. Duffy, in her study of the educational experience of girls with physical disabilities, comments on the difficulties which they face in moving to adulthood.

> As young women ... they are under pressure to conform to many sexual, physical and behavioural stereotypes. However, because of their physical impairments, they will also have to tackle the negative image of disability which pervades Western society – an image which is contrary to the ideal of femininity and womanhood (Duffy, 1993, p.2).

Like non-disabled girls of their age, the girls in Duffy's study aspired to work in a variety of occupations and, in some cases, to become parents. Underlying these aspirations, though, was a fear of being unloved in their adult lives, of never forming significant relationships, of being eternally dependent on their parents or being institutionalised. Almost all the girls in the study felt that it was more difficult to be a disabled girl than a disabled boy. They put this down in large part to the pressure on them to conform to accepted notions of feminine beauty and wholeness. If they were dependent on others for personal care assistance, they felt obliged to keep their cosmetic routines to the minimum. For two participants, this meant that they agreed to keep their hair 'cropped short like a boy's' – which they felt infringed on their desire to 'look feminine'. The high value which society places on physical beauty and 'wholeness' contributed to the difficulty and awkwardness which these girls felt (see also Campling, 1979). They also believed that the way in which women are perceived as carers mitigates against them as disabled young women (potentially dependent) being considered as partners.

This belief is in line with evidence from the United States and Canada that women who acquire a disability in the course of their lives are more likely to be abandoned by their spouses than are disabled men, while women with congenital disabilities often find it difficult to develop lasting intimate relationships (Fine and Asch, 1988). Frequently underlying these patterns is the expectation that these women will be unable to perform the expected female nurturing and reproductive roles, possibly combined with the view that they would be unfit as sexual partners. Another underlying factor making it difficult for a disabled woman to establish and maintain a relationship is the lack of social and employment opportunities, particularly if she is living in her parental home (Campling, 1981). As a result, women with disabilities are more likely than other women and disabled men to find themselves alone in life, whether or not they chose a single lifestyle. They are less likely to be involved in close sexual/ personal relationships and less likely to receive emotional or physical support than disabled men (Croxen-John, 1988).

Young women with learning disabilities also experience difficulties in the move from adolescence to adulthood. A study of parental expectations for their teenage daughters with learning disabilities in the Republic of Ireland found that the time of leaving school, which is generally associated with a move to independence, self-determination and autonomy, is a time of great anxiety and uncertainty about the future for many teenagers with learning disabilities and their parents (Redmond, in press). As a group, the parents in this study were fearful of the dangers which the adult world might hold for their daughters and many of them saw their daughters' emerging sexuality as an area of particular vulnerability. Rather than being a time of growing possibilities, the transition from adolescence to adulthood serves for many young women with learning disabilities to highlight how different they are from their intellectually able peers. Many of the girls in the study had few friends, quite restricted social lives and a limited degree of independence.

Although the women's movement has pushed for the recognition of women's sexual needs, women with disabilities are frequently regarded as being sexless and roleless, particularly if their disability is congenital. Linked to this is the implicit assumption that they will remain single, which has frequently led to practices which prevent them from meeting potential spouses in education, vocational training and other services for people with disabilities. A young woman with a learning disability, for example, is unlikely to be facilitated when it comes to mixing with men, forming relationships or deciding to form an intimate partnership.

Many women with learning disabilities in Ireland are not married. In (training) workshops in Ireland, some men and women go with each other and if they want to get married, they are stopped. Many people with learning difficulties don't know about the facts of life. They don't know about contraception. They don't know about AIDS. This is because many of us didn't get sex education (Lawlor, in *Making Connections*, 1992, p.4).

The limited information available on this critical phase of transition for girls with disabilities needs to be supplemented by more research on the subject and by greater public discussion of the issues which may arise, both for the girls themselves and for their parents, at this stage of their lives. Academics, professionals and the media all have a role to play in this. Only when more research becomes available and the problems faced by adolescent girls with disabilities are generally recognised, will they be enabled to move forward to adulthood with the kind of supports which are available to non-disabled girls.

Preparing for Working Life

Women with disabilities are virtually invisible when it comes to research on vocational training and participation in third level education in the Irish context. Given this gap, it is only possible here to highlight the main issues which require exploration.

Vocational Training

Young women leaving special schools are most likely to go on to attend a programme of vocational training in a rehabilitation training centre for people with disabilities. While their experience of training programmes in these settings has not been yet been the subject of study, evidence from a study of leavers from (European Social Fund) ESF-financed training programmes (NRB, 1994) indicates significant gender differences in the type of training programme pursued, with quite traditional patterns emerging. The findings of this study indicate that where women with disabilities attend vocational training programmes in special centres, they are likely to be prepared for occupations which are traditionally associated with women. Only recently has there been a move to introduce nationally recognised certification in these training programmes. Up to now, women leaving rehabilitation training courses have generally not had a skills certificate and have thus been at a disadvantage in seeking employment, as have men with disabilities completing these courses. This compounds the difficulty they face because of the stigma often attached by employers and the public at large to attendance at rehabilitation centres.

As in the case of special education, the debate on equality of opportunity for women has not taken place in relation to vocational training programmes in special centres, although it has in mainstream training. From a policy viewpoint, the priority currently lies in the introduction of recognised standards for vocational training provided in these centres, rather than on the gender dimension, concern with which was described as 'a relative luxury' in a recent official evaluation of training programmes for women (ESF Programme Evaluation Unit, 1994). The fact that this failure to prioritise equality of opportunity for women with disabilities has not given rise to public debate is a further reflection of the marginalised situation of women with disabilities in Irish society.

Apart from the question of access to and equality of opportunity within vocational training programmes, a range of supports are needed if women are to be able to avail of these training programmes. A report on the vocational rehabilitation of disabled women in the European Community (Croxen-John, 1988) highlighted the main shortfalls in this area – in the provision of the necessary financial and personal assistance supports which would enable women with disabilities to avail of training opportunities regardless of their disability and status; and in terms of the accessibility of vocational rehabilitation premises and of the medium of communication used. The extent to which these shortfalls impact on women with disabilities in the Irish setting needs to be researched.

Third Level

There is scant research on the experience of students with disabilities in third level education, not least because they have not attended third level institutions in great numbers until relatively recently. Anecdotal evidence suggests that factors external to the university itself often combine with the lack of support services within the colleges to cause students with disabilities to drop out – in particular, the lack of accessible public transport and the lack of personal assistance services. It could be the case that young people with disabilities just do not consider the option of following a third level course.

A study of the experience of deaf students in third level education in the Republic of Ireland found that, while many colleges had equal opportunities policies, this was seldom backed with the allocation of resources and support staff to ensure that this policy became a reality for students with hearing impairments (O'Reilly, 1993). Students in this study generally reported that, once accepted into college, they got no advice from college personnel on the general milieu of college life and only in a few cases was there a designated person in the college whom they could approach about areas of concern. They experienced great difficulty following lectures in mainstream lecture theatres and relied to a great extent on the goodwill of hearing students in trying to follow spoken lectures. Borrowing notes was very common, as few back-up facilities, human or technical, were available to enable deaf students to follow lectures. In all, only one sign-language interpreter was available for tutorials and the service did not extend to lectures. The students felt that if sign language interpreters were employed by the universities to interpret the lectures, it would be much easier for them to pursue their studies. They also felt that colleges should designate a person to deal with deaf students and their concerns. Socially, they felt that the greatest need is to educate hearing students and college and university staff about the problems of deafness.

While the participation of women with disabilities in third level education remains largely undocumented, several initiatives in recent years may have brought about an increase in their numbers. In the past few years, some colleges have undertaken to encourage the enrolment of students with disabilities and have taken initiatives to ensure that their premises are accessible and that students with disabilities have access to convenient parking facilities, as well as employing a resource person to provide support as required. The recently established Association for Higher Education Access and Disability (AHEAD), which promotes access to and full participation in third level education for students with disabilities, is currently planning to establish a National Advisory Centre for Disabled Students, providing information and advice to people with disabilities at third level, and support and encouragement to second level pupils with disabilities. The recent introduction of disability studies in a small number of third level courses and the development of disability awareness initiatives may set the scene for increased attention to this topic in the social science research agenda. The extent to which these initiatives promote gender equality as well as equality of opportunity for disabled students in general is a further area which would merit analysis.

Employment

No research has been carried out into the employment experience of women with disabilities in the Republic of Ireland, but evidence from the United Kingdom and the United States shows that women with disabilities participate significantly less in the labour market than disabled men (Martin et al., 1989, Danek, 1992). International research also shows that women with disabilities are more concentrated in semi-skilled or unskilled work than either non-disabled women or disabled men. Linked to this, women with disabilities earn significantly less, on average, than other women and men in the labour market (Danek, 1992).

In approaching this topic in the Irish context, a number of points need to be borne in mind. Firstly, since employment opportunities are shaped by the educational and vocational training programmes which people complete, they are therefore quite restricted for young women who attend special schools and special training centres in the Republic of Ireland. The fact that girls who attend segregated schools do not complete nationally recognised curricula or sit state examinations, combined with the fact that they have not received nationally recognised skills certificates on completion of their vocational training, means that they are at a distinct disadvantage when it comes to seeking employment. The perception by some women with disabilities that there is a stigma attached to attendance at specialist training centres needs to be explored. Women with acquired disabilities may have attended mainstream schools and further education or training centres, and have qualifications to offer, often combined with employment experience. But when it comes to securing employment, they face similar obstacles to women disabled from birth in terms of prevailing attitudes and medical procedures they are required to go through. In addition, if women with disabilities are to be enabled to work, more flexible work arrangements and personal assistance services would be required, to enable them to keep their jobs, sometimes in combination with their role of homemakers, as well as 'managing' their disability – getting up, toileting and getting dressed, which in itself may take several hours a day (Croxen-John, 1988).

At a policy level, as in the case of special education and vocational training, the equality of opportunity debates which have taken place regarding the employment of non-disabled women have not been addressed to the employment of women with disabilities. Research into their employment situation is needed, to stimulate this debate.

Conclusion

The lack of empirical data has been a major constraint in this chapter throughout. While a start has been made in some areas (such as education), the situation of women with disabilities is generally uncharted by social scientists in the Republic of Ireland. Their exclusion in research on vocational training, employment and adolescence has been discussed here, along with their invisibility in statistics and some questions which could form the basis for a research agenda have been raised. The picture is almost blank in a range of other areas central to the lived experience of women with disabilities which have not been discussed here, due to constraints of space. What is their experience in intimate relationships, or as mothers? Are disabled girls and women at greater risk of domestic violence and sexual abuse in this country as they are reported to be elsewhere? What is the experience of disabled women in using health and community care services? Are they at a greater risk of poverty than other groups in the population? Why has the debate on equality of opportunity for girls and women with disabilities – in education, training and employment – not taken place? These are some of the questions which need to be addressed by social scientists, so that issues facing women with disabilities can be identified and a policy debate initiated.

The challenge now facing researchers who set out to chart the lives and experience of women with disabilities in Ireland is to explore not only the negative aspects of their situation, but also the positive sides – their resilience, their ways of coping, the informal networks which they have developed to compensate for the inadequacies of formal services. And more generally, the challenge facing all researchers is to introduce a disability component into their research work as a matter of course, as has become widespread practice in relation to gender.

Discussion Topics

1. What analogies can be drawn between the situation of women with disabilities and the situation of marginalised women in general? In what way does their situation differ?

2. Consider and discuss you own attitude to disability. What positive and negative images do people have in relation to men and women with disabilities?

3. Adolesence receives considerable attention as a period of transition, often problematic, in the lives of young people. Yet the adolesence of girls with disabilities has virtually been ignored by researchers, counsellors and the media. Why is this?

4. Should women with disablties have children? Is the practice of sterilising women with diabilities without their consent ever justified?

References and Further Reading

Abilities, 1995. 'Confronting Violence Against Women' 22, Spring.

Callan, T, Nolan, B, Whelan, C and Whelan, B. 1989 *Poverty, Income and Welfare in Ireland* Dublin: ESRI Report No.146.

Campling, J. 1979 *Better Lives for Disabled Women* London: Virago.

Campling, J. 1981 *Images of Ourselves* London: Routledge and Kegan Paul.

Cole, S. 1991 Foreword to Sobsey, D, Gray, S, Wells, D, Pyper, D and Reimer-Hack, B. *Disability, Sexuality and Abuse – An Annotated Bibliography* Baltimore/London: Paul Stokes.

Conroy, P. 1992 'Facing the Issues' paper presented at the Making Connections Conference, Council for the Status of Women/NRB May.

Croxen-John, M. 1988 *The Vocational Rehabilitation of Disabled Women in the European Community. Programme of Research and Actions for the Social Integration of Disabled People.* V/600/89. Commission of the European Community.

Danek, M. 1992 'The Status of Women with Disabilities Revisited' *Journal of Applied Rehabilitation Counseling* Vol.23, No.4 Winter.

Dangoor, N and Florian, V. 1994. 'Women with Chronic Physical Disabilities: Correlates of their Long-Term Psycho-Social Adaptation' *International Journal of Rehabilitation Research,* Vol.17 No.2.

Department of Education, 1980 *White Paper on Educational Development* Dublin: Stationery Office.

Department of Education 1992 *Education for a Changing World.* Green Paper on Education Dublin: Stationery Office.

Department of Education 1993 *Report of the Special Education Review Committee* Dublin: Stationery Office.

Department of Education, 1995 *Special School Statistics.*

Duffy, M. 1993 *Integration or Segregation: Does it Make a Difference? A Study of Equality Issues Relating to the Education of Disabled Girls.* Unpublished thesis University College Dublin.

ESF Programme Evaluation Unit, 1994 *Women's Training Provision,* Dublin.

Fine, M and Asch, A. 1988 *Women with Disabilities. Essays in Psychology, Culture and Politics* Philadelphia: Temple University Press.

Finkelstein, V. 1980 *Attitudes to Disabled People: Issues for Discussion* New York: World Rehabilitation Fund.

Hanna, W J and Rogovsky H. 1991 'Women with Disabilities: Two Handicaps Plus' *Disability, Handicap and Society* 6, 1.

Lawlor, R. 1992 Speaking Personally Session, Making Connections Conference, Dublin.

Lonsdale, S. 1990 *Women and Disability. The Experience of Physical Disability Among Women* Basingstoke/London: MacMillan Education Ltd.

Making Connections. 1992 Papers presented at a conference organised by the Council for the Status of Women and NRB, May.

Martin, J, White, A and Meltzer, H. 1989 *Disabled Adults: Services, Transport and Employment* OPCS Surveys of Disability in Great Britain, Report 4, HMSO.

McCoy, D and Smith, M. 1992 *The Prevalence of Disability Among Adults in Northern Ireland.* PPRU Surveys of Disability – Report 1. Belfast.

Medico-Social Research Board. 1994 *Census of Mental Handicap in the Republic of Ireland,* Dublin.

Moran, B. 1992 *Women with Disabilities in Ireland: A Double Disadvantage* Unpublished thesis, University College Dublin.

Morris, J. (ed.) 1989 *Able Lives: Women's Experience of Paralysis* London: Women's Press.

NRB. 1991 *Righting the History of Wrongs. A Rights Approach to Issues Arising Out of Women's Experience of Disability* Submission to the Commission on the Status of Women. NRB, Dublin.

NRB. 1994 *Equal Status. A Blueprint for Action* Submission to the Commission on the Status of People with Disabilities. NRB, Dublin.

NRB. 1995 *Women's Health Issues* Submission to the North-Eastern Health Board.

Office of Population Censuses and Surveys, *Northern Ireland,* various years.

Oliver, M. 1990 *The Politics of Disablement* Basingstoke/London: MacMillan.

O'Reilly, J. 1993 *Students with Hearing Impairment. Equal Opportunity in Higher Education in Ireland? Institutional and Student Perspectives* Unpublished thesis, University College Dublin.

Redmond, B. 1996 *Listening to Parents. The Aspirations, Expectations and Anxieties of Parents about their Teenager with Learning Disabilities* Family Studies Centre, University College Dublin, Belfield, Dublin.

Rousso, H. 1978 'Daughters with Disabilities: Defective Women or Minority Women?' in Fine, M and Asch, A. 1989 *Women with Disabilities. Essays in Psychology, Culture and Politics* Philadelphia: Temple University Press.

Smith, M, Robinson, P and Duffy, B. 1992 *The Prevalence of Disability among Children in Northern Ireland.* PPRU Surveys of Disability – Report 2. Belfast.

Traustadottir, R. 1990 *Women with Disabilities. Issues, Resources, Connections* Center on Human Policy, Syracuse University.

Wilson, C. 1992 *Keynote Address*, Making Connection Conference, Dublin.

Section 9:
Women, Power and Politics

Women have been stereotyped in conventional accounts of political behaviour as being uninterested in politics, politically conservative and if married, influenced by their husbands. None of these stereotypes have been shown to be true (Lovenduski and Randall, 1993, Githens et al., 1994). Moreover, the stereotypes themselves emerge from a very narrow definition of politics which limits itself to looking at issues such as voting behaviour and the representation of women in formal political parties. Feminists would argue that what is conventionally defined as political depends on a male dominated view of politics. Male dominated political parties operate with a taken for granted notion of what is political. Such a definition excludes much of women's expertise and political concerns. Yet, as feminists have demonstrated, women do take part in political activities as conventionally defined. Women are active members of political parties, local councils and so on. However, feminists also argue that what is seen as political needs to be redefined. Working with the notion of the 'personal is political', feminists suggest that politics should be concerned with all power relationships in society and in particular with the power relationships between men and women both in the public and in the private sphere.

The three chapters in this section portray a feminist view of politics. They outline the numerous ways in which women have been politically active in challenging the laws and institutions that keep women in a subordinate role. All three chapters demonstrate the extent to which the state itself is a patriarchal political force. Eilish Rooney for example argues that the state in Northern Ireland has no coherent policy for funding women's groups. As a result, the state actively contributes to the marginal position of women in society. Breda Gray and Louise Ryan outline the role of the state in the Republic of Ireland in creating and maintaining the nuclear family and the role of women as wives and mothers. By depicting this family type as natural, normal and essentially Irish, the state plays an important role in constructing and maintaining the split

513

between the private and public sphere and thus contributing to the continued subordination and exploitation of women in both spheres.

Linda Connolly takes up this argument in her analysis of the women's movement in the Republic of Ireland. She demonstrates how the women's movement mobilised around issues of concern to women. The women's movement campaigned actively around contraceptive issues, abortion issues, divorce, assaults on wives and other problems that women experience in relation to men. She demonstrates how the state attempted to define such issues as private and moral rather than political issues. All three chapters demonstrate that women are not as politically passive as conventionally portrayed. Moreover, the section demonstrates that gender is an integral part of politics by highlighting the fact that the division between the public and the private sphere is in itself a political issue.

Gray and Ryan outline the ways in which the use of symbols and representations of Irishness are gendered and the material effects this has on Irish women. These issues are explored during two time periods; the decade after the Irish state was established in the 1920s and during the 1990s characterised by the presidency of Mary Robinson and the divorce referendum. In the first period, Gray and Ryan suggest that gendered symbols were manipulated by the media, the church, the government and the judiciary to create a distinct national culture. Simplistic sexist assumptions concerning the purity and integrity of women indicated the purity and integrity of the Irish state. The lived realities of women's daily lives were dismissed in favour of idealised representations of 'innocent, pure, unsexed, self-sacrificing motherhood'. These images were resurrected during the divorce referendum of 1995. The nuclear family was revered, cherished and epitomised as representing the Irish way of life and threats to the nuclear family were regarded as threats to Irish identity. The fact that the nuclear family was not the norm for an increasing number of women was underplayed or ignored. By locating women's roles in wider social, economic and political contexts, Gray and Ryan effectively challenge stereotypical images of women in Irish society.

Rooney explores the participation of women in local women's community groups and in electoral politics. She notes the male dominated composition of the formal political system in Northern Ireland. For example, no woman has ever been elected to the European Parliament and none of Northern Ireland's seventeen MPs at Westminster are women. Indeed, with the exception of Bernadette McAliskey (née Devlin) who refused to take her parliamentary seat, no woman has ever served as a Member of Parliament representing Northern Ireland. At the local community level however, the picture is less bleak. Focusing on three electoral areas representing unionist, nationalist and republican ideologies, Rooney examines the participation of women in local councils. She found that most of the major political parties in Northern Ireland have tried to make their organisations more women friendly by encouraging the participation of women and by setting up committees dealing with women's issues. However, such a strategy often serves to marginalise the needs and interests of women. Setting up separate committees to deal with 'women's issues' in many instances, results in women's issues becoming peripheral to mainstream party concerns.

Rooney examines the attitudes of male and female councillors to the gender dimension of local politics. Male councillors often viewed female councillors as women first and as councillors second. Moreover, many were unaware that they were making these distinctions. Women councillors saw their experiences as falling between being excluded and included in key party concerns. They suggested that their acceptance was conditional on not letting domestic responsibilities impinge on council business. Under the guise of treating women the same as men, such an approach serves to discriminate against women with specific gender commitments.

In a more positive vein, Rooney found that women actively participated at a local level in community based women's groups. However, several of the women in such groups rendered their fight against unemployment and poverty in their local communities as apolitical. To them, politics concerned the intra-fighting between Catholics and Protestants over the legitimacy and future of the Northern Ireland state. This is despite the fact that the main duties of local councillors tended to be concerned with 'apolitical' issues such as unemployment, housing and poverty. The way forward for Rooney is for a more coherent state policy regarding funding for women's groups and for women to work towards serving their collective as well as individual interests. The recently formed Women's Coalition, by simultaneously recognising the diversity and commonalties of women may provide an arena for the convergence of women's collective interests without sacrificing their individual concerns.

In the last paper in this section, Connolly develops the themes outlined above by presenting a theoretical appraisal of the women's movement in the Republic of Ireland. She charts the history of the women's movement as falling into three main stages: a period of radicalism, conflict and diversity during the 1970s; a period of re-appraisal during the 1980s and a period of new directions from the late 1980s onwards. By examining the aims and objectives of a number of core groups, Connolly demonstrates the concerns of feminists in Ireland. She also vividly captures the diversity within the women's movement and feminism through her analysis of the Irish Women's Liberation Movement and Irishwomen United.

Drawing on the literature relating to the dynamics of social movements, Connolly highlights the ways in which conflict and plurality continually plagued the efforts of women to establish a collective identity. Core mobilising issues such as access to contraception helped to unite different women's groups and encouraged co-ordination and coalition. On the other hand, the abortion issue was more contentious and divisive for women's groups in Ireland. Through an exploration of the debate surrounding the abortion issue, Connolly outlines how radical feminists moved from engaging in protest activities to operating within the mainstream system. While such action was motivated by the development of a counter social movement opposed to abortion in Ireland, the issue changed the direction of the women's movement in the 1980s as more and more feminists began to participate within the mainstream system either by involvement in formal politics or by actively campaigning for legislative changes on issues of concern to women. In the process, Connolly suggests the whole movement became more generically radicalised.

It is clear that as we approach the end of the millennium, organisations that empower women remain important and necessary. The ways in which the common and divergent interests of women can continue to be incorporated and promoted within the women's movement represents important challenges for the future.

References and Further Reading

Githens, M, Norris, P and Lovenduski, J. (eds.) 1994 *Different Roles, Different Voices: Women and Politics in the United States and Europe* New York: Harper Collins College.
Lovenduski, J and Randall, V. 1993 *Contemporary Feminist Politics: women and power in Britain* Oxford: Oxford University Press.

31.

(Dis)locating 'Woman' and Women in Representations of Irish National Identity

Breda Gray and Louise Ryan

Introduction

Jan Penrose (1995) points to the centrality of the nation-state and nationalism to the current world order and suggests that the idea of the nation involves three main elements: a 'distinctive group of people', a territory that this group occupies and a 'mystical bond between people and place' (1995, p.398). For a nation to be formed and maintained, it is necessary therefore, to establish that a distinct group of people exists and the idea of culture has always been central to proving this (Penrose, 1995). While language, religion and tradition are central to culture, these cultural resources are often drawn upon to develop symbols or representations of the nation which help to ensure the continued legitimation of the nation as an entity. Symbols and representations of nation are primarily related to Penrose's first condition of nationhood, that is the identification of a distinct group of people.

In this chapter we discuss two interconnecting themes. First, we examine the ways in which Ireland has been represented as female and secondly, we explore the subsequent links between national integrity and notions of 'appropriate' female behaviour. Anthias and Yuval-Davis (1993) point out that 'a female is often used as the actual symbolic figuration of the nation' (1993, p.28). They go on, however, to explore the complex relationship between women and nation. 'By dressing and behaving 'properly', and by giving birth to children within legitimate marriages, they both signify and reproduce the symbolic and legal boundaries of the collectivity' (1993, p.28). We explore these issues during the decade just after the twenty-six county state was established in the 1920s and the last decade of the twentieth century in the twenty-six county state. Our main aim is to explore how and why some symbols and representations might be used rather than carrying out a detailed semiotic analysis of the particular distinctions and connections that enable symbols and representations to have the meanings they do for particular groups.

Symbols are powerful in creating a collective imagination and collective identity but they go beyond that. The simplicity and naturalness with which they represent the collective identity of the nation often serves to disguise the daily work carried out particularly by women at family and community levels to maintain the national collective community and identity. Symbolic codes can also be galvanised into law and public policies which are often influenced by the view that women are the national guardians of morality and traditions (Mosse, 1985).

The eighteenth century classical Irish poetic genre of the 'aisling' used a range of female symbols of the nation, Ireland. These included the poor old woman grieving the loss of her sons (Sean Bhean Bhocht) and the beautiful young women making sacrifices for their beloved (Dark Rosaleen and Cathleen N° Houlihan). Tony O'Brien Johnson and David Cairns (1991) identify the potential problems with women representing Ireland's sovereignty or the land of Ireland.

> In so far as she stands for sovereignty, this is unrepresentable because it is an abstraction; and where she stands for the land, the earth/body analogy becomes the burden of woman, with an inevitably reductive effect which tends to undermine any notion of the woman being something more than her mere body (1991, p.4).

Rada Ivekovic sees gender as an organising principle within society upon which symbolic systems are built. The 'binary model of gender', she suggests, is the symbolic power system 'through which the symbolic works and onto which it projects itself' (Ivekovic, 1993, p.115). Ivekovic goes on to suggest that

> The feminine embodiment of such high ideals as 'Liberty', the 'Nation', 'Wisdom', 'Motherland', and 'Purity' are often used as a pretext to eliminate concrete women both in traditional mythologies and in contemporary politics The supposedly female figures for such great male ideas have nothing whatsoever to do with a concrete feminine experience (Ivekovic, 1993, p.123).

Ailbhe Smyth (1991) suggests that Irish nationalist discourse uses woman as a sign 'in a discourse from which women, imaginatively, economically, politically disempowered, are in effect and effectively excluded' (1991, p.11). In this way, women become the bearers of the symbols of nation but their everyday experiences and agency are denied. They are 'excluded from direct action as national citizens, [and] ... subsumed symbolically into the national body politic as its boundary and metaphoric limit' (McClintock, 1993, p.62).

Although symbols and representations can be resisted and challenged by re-interpretation or re-appropriation of the implicit or taken for granted meanings, it is impossible within the parameters of this chapter, to provide any analysis of processes of resistance or re-appropriation. In the next sections of the chapter, we present some case studies or exemplars which highlight the ways in which the use of symbols and representations of Irishness are gendered and have material effects for Irish women. Some of these exemplars relate to the decade after the twenty-six county state was established in the 1920s and others relate to the Republic of Ireland in the 1990s. Throughout our analysis we draw largely on newspapers of the period. We use newspapers, not as neutral and unbiascd sources of information, but as active agents in defining Irish national identity. Newspapers play a key role in 'selecting' what is news worthy and in highlighting certain issues over others. They do not merely report events they also interpret them. Newspapers are part and parcel of the society in which they operate. As Gaye Tuchman (1978) has argued, while the news media may claim to simply 'mirror' social events, they are involved in a complex reciprocal relationship with society: 'The news media are both a "cause" and an "effect"' (Tuchman, 1978, p.189). The section on the 1920s draws on two popular newspapers of the period, one national daily, the *Irish Independent* and one provincial daily, the *Cork Examiner*.

In the 1990s the profile of the Irish media is different from that of the 1920s with broadcasting via television playing a key role (Mullholland, 1995). British media is now widely available in television form and accounts for thirteen per cent of daily newspaper sales (Foley, 1993). In 1995 the Irish media lost three newspapers when the Irish Press newspaper group closed down and in 1996, the *Cork Examiner*, previously a provincial paper, entered the national newspaper market. Our discussion of the 1990s draws on the *Irish Times*, a national daily, and the national *Sunday Independent* and *Tribune* newspapers.[1] We draw on a mixture of direct quotes from politicians and clergy reported in newspapers as well as commentary and opinion columns.

Daughters of Eve or Sisters of Mary Immaculate: Irish National Identity, 'Woman' and Women in the 1920s.

In this section of the chapter we address the symbolic representations in the Irish Free State in the 1920s. The early 1920s represented a period of great political transformation stretching from the war of independence with Britain to the signing of the Anglo-Irish treaty and the outbreak of civil war. When the Free State was established in 1922, the Cumann na nGaedheal government attempted to restore law and order in the twenty-six counties which had been scarred by years of fighting and uncertainty. Meanwhile, the Boundary Commission, set up under the treaty to assess the border between North and South, meant that there was still a great sense of insecurity and expectation among those people living along each side of the border.

As a new nation, the Free State sought to assert its legitimacy by defining a unique culture and identity which marked Irish people apart and distinct to

British people. However, Irish culture in the 1920s was greatly influenced by the British print media and other forms of British entertainment and fashion, as well as by the growing enthusiasm for Hollywood films (Brown, 1987, Lyons, 1989). In addition to these external 'threats' to Irish culture, there were also internal barriers to a shared national identity. In the wake of partition and the civil war, the twenty-six counties were left with deep political rifts. Similarly, class, regional and religious divisions meant that forging a common sense of Irish identity was urgently required if the new state was to survive. The insecurity and uncertainty which characterised the new twenty-six county state could not be openly admitted by those in positions of authority. Instead, the state, church and media projected that vulnerability onto Irish womanhood by representing Ireland, albeit indirectly, as 'woman'. The purity of Irishness was symbolised by the purity of 'Irishwoman'. Threats to the integrity of Irish national identity were symbolised by foreign fashions corrupting the morality of Irish womanhood. In constructing symbols of Irishwomanhood, the Catholic Church, the State and the Press threatened to render real women invisible and exclude their lived realities from public discourse.

Before analysing particular examples of this process, it is necessary to clarify some of our terms. It may be tempting to speak of nationalism, nationalist discourse, nationalist policies in relation to the 1920s. But we would advise caution in using this language. During the 1920s, both the Cumann na nGaedheal government and the Catholic Church hierarchy distanced themselves from so-called 'nationalists' referring to the anti-treaty Republicans including Eamon de Valera, Mary MacSwiney and Constance Markievicz.[2] These 'nationalists' were strongly condemned for threatening the peace and stability of the Free State. They were represented as violent, dangerous and, in contrast to the law and order policies of Cumann na nGaedheal, they represented 'disorder'. Thus, while the state, church and media were certainly concerned with defining and moulding Irish national identity during the first decade of the Free State, they did not necessarily see this as a 'nationalist' project.

Catherine Nash (1993) has written about the contrasts between different schools of thought on national identity in Ireland at the beginning of the twentieth century. She refers to the 'celtic' symbols associated with the Literary Revival of Yeats and Lady Gregory. These drew on pagan mythology and represented a sexualised image of Irish womanhood perhaps best symbolised by Cathleen Ni Houlihan. On the other hand, there was a 'gaelic' notion of Irishness associated with the Irish Ireland movement of D P Moran and Daniel Corkery. This proposed a more sanitised, de-sexualised representation of Irish women symbolised by the Sean Bhan Bhocht. By the 1920s, Nash argues, the latter image had become most prevalent reflecting the rise to power of the Catholic middle classes. Nash's work is important because she indicates the existence of, and indeed opposition between, two contrasting symbolic representations of Ireland and Irish women. She also locates these discourses within wider religious, political and economic interests.

However, our research suggests that images of Irish womanhood were more complex and multi-dimensional in the 1920s. Far from being merely representations of innocent, pure, unsexed, self-sacrificing motherhood, public discourses included notions of women's vulnerability and need for protection. C L Innes (1994) argues women were frequently presented as culpable in their own and the nation's moral weakness. Similarly, Gerardine Meaney (1991) points out that women not only represent national honour and traditions but also susceptibility to foreign charms. This 'weakness' on the part of women legitimated the strong arm of the law in enforcing strict discipline and order on the society for its own good. Terence Brown in describing the group of middle class people who came to power in the Free State of the 1920s says:

> Their economic prudence, their necessarily puritanical, repressive sexual mores and nationalistic conservatism, encouraged by a priesthood and Hierarchy drawn considerably from their number, largely determined the kind of country which emerged in the first decades of independence. (Brown 1987, p.26).

In the newly independent Irish state, the family, as the locus of traditional Irish culture and morality, was deemed by the state, church and pressure groups to be in need of protection from foreign corrupting influences. Censorship laws were passed to ensure that these foreign influences were monitored and controlled. In 1923, the censorship of films act was passed, followed in 1929 by the censorship of publications act. By placing the family at the centre of Irish culture, the nation came to be increasingly symbolised by Irish motherhood.

Of course, such symbols as Cathleen Ni Houlihan, Sean Bhan Bhocht and others tell us little about women's real lives (Boland, 1989, Smyth, 1991). In fact, we would argue that such symbols tell us more about the interest groups who employed them than offering a realistic picture of Irish society. But these symbolic representations did contain messages about how women ought to behave. The kind of images generated by the church, media and state incorporated very strict dictates which sought to prescribe the appropriate lifestyles of women and young girls. The efforts to control the increasing 'immorality' of dance-halls provide a good example of how Irish identity was being actively constructed in the 1920s. It is apparent that notions of womanhood played a key role in these discourses of national purity but also national vulnerability. The victim/threat dichotomy underlay many of these representations of Irish women.

In analysing the role of the Catholic Church in the Irish Free State, Mark Ryan (1994) claims that 'Religion became central to the Irish state not only as a means of social control, but also as a symbol of independence from Protestant

England' (1994, p.89). He argues that far from being rooted in the Irish psyche, religion was constructed around the needs of powerful political elites.

> The church took to policing the most intimate details of people's lives, embarking on one of the most remarkable campaigns of moral engineering ever attempted .... The Irish people, and women in particular, paid a terrible price for the moral strait-jacket imposed by church and state (1994, p.91).

Liam O'Dowd suggests that both the Catholic and Protestant churches projected 'a predominantly private and familial role for women', however, the Catholic church, in the post partition period, idealised 'Irish motherhood' and attempted to 'police extra-familial sexual deviance' (1987, p.12/14).

On 12 May 1926 the *Irish Independent* newspaper carried a lengthy report of a sermon by Archbishop Gilmartin.[3] During the course of the sermon which concerned 'Foreign Dances and Indecent Dress' he explained that there were two types of women: 'The first was the daughter of Eve who ate the forbidden fruit', the second type was 'the sister of Mary Immaculate, who brought life and hope and comfort'. The first type of woman read bad books, exposed her physical charms and went to foreign dances. But she failed to realise that while men might be attracted to her 'they despised her in their hearts'. 'That type of woman was the occasion of ruin to men'. The Archbishop said that 'there was a time in Ireland when the prevailing type of woman was the sister of Mary Immaculate'. However, 'bad influences' were 'creeping in' through bad books, foreign dances and lack of parental control. He concluded by linking women's behaviour with the integrity and identity of the nation: 'The future of the country is bound up with the dignity and purity of the women of Ireland'.

It is not unusual for religion to draw on the dichotomy of good woman/bad woman – evil Eve versus pure Mary. The virgin/whore dichotomy was certainly not unique to Ireland. But what is especially significant here is the way in which such symbols of womanhood are linked to the future of the nation. The bad woman was not merely responsible for her own moral downfall and for the ruin of men but threatened the moral degeneration of the entire nation. Immoral literature, indecent dress and modern dances were all largely responsible for lowering the standards of Irish womanhood. All of these influences were represented as being foreign and hence alien to Ireland.

In addition to the two symbolic representations of women as virgin/whore and victim/threat, there was a third symbol – the 'furies'. These women were violent and dangerous but not because of their love of foreign fashions or dances. Furies were women who challenged the status quo, actively participating in the 'masculine' world of politics. In this way 'internal' divisions and 'threats' to national cohesiveness were also symbolised by 'woman'. Women in the Republican movement, in particular Cumann na mBan, were constructed as threats to the peace and security of the nation.[4] The Rev Dr Doorley speaking at a Confirmation service in Castlerea, advised children not to take up politics when they grew up. To the girls and women in the congregation the bishop proclaimed:

> If I had a little girl friend who took up politics I would give up praying for her. Women who go around taking despatches and arms from one place to another are furies. Who would respect them, or who would marry them? Never join a Cumann na mBan or a Cumann na Saoirse or anything else. Do your work as your grandmothers did before you (*Cork Examiner*, 18 May, 1925).

On the 23 February 1925 the editors of both the *Cork Examiner* and the *Irish Independent* commented at length on the lenten pastorals.[5] The editor of the *Examiner* agreed with the Bishops that Irish people were too fond of imported fashions and amusements. The editor warned that if this continued 'family life in Ireland would lose all its graces and its happiness'. A lengthy section of the editorial was devoted to the Archbishop's pastoral in which he singled out dance-halls for special criticism. He described dance-hall owners as 'slayers of souls'. The archbishop also condemned 'careless mothers' for allowing their daughters too much freedom. Again we see women, mothers and their daughters, being held responsible for falling standards of morality, and the linking of issues of moral rectitude to national stability.

Under the banner headline 'Warning to the People' the *Irish Independent* gave further coverage to the Hierarchy's condemnation of dancing. On this occasion the hierarchy, meeting in Maynooth, issued an appeal with a particular warning for young women. Frequenting dance-halls would bring them 'to shame' and necessitate their 'retiring to refuge institutions' (7 October, 1925). The risk of women becoming pregnant was never mentioned as such but, as in the piece cited above, it was widely hinted at.

Within this religious pre-occupation with the evils of dance-halls, so well publicised by the national media, symbols of Irish womanhood incorporated both negative and positive images. There was an unrelenting criticism of one image of women and a powerful prescription of another idealised image of how women ought to be. Between these two symbols the real experiences of women were grossly simplified. The tragic realities of Irish women who were sexually abused, became pregnant outside of marriage and were consigned to an institution for life, are reduced to a mere symbol of evil and immorality. Although the true extent of their suffering was never publicly acknowledged just enough of such misfortunes was made known to serve as a warning to others (O'Toole, 1994c, pp.79-83).

In the early years of the Free State, there was clearly a fear in many quarters that women were threatening to corrupt Irish culture by embracing new, modern and foreign fashions in music, clothes, reading material and dances. The threats which foreign corruption posed to Irish women symbolised the dangers of outside influences to the purity and integrity of an independent Irish state. Those powerful people who played a role in defining national identity, media, church, government and judiciary sought to preserve a particular image of Irishness which differed markedly from the culture which they saw emerging throughout the country. While they were certainly influenced by Catholic teaching, we argue that factors including conservative politics, Catholic morality and economic necessity influenced a strong desire amongst the dominant elites of the 1920s for a distinct national culture. Their widespread use of gendered symbols representing both good and evil cut across other divisions in the society. Class, regional, religious and political divisions were rife throughout the country. Simplified images of the good and bad woman and her relationship with Irish manhood as well as with the Irish nation could speak to all the classes and regions, bridging the yawning gulf between political viewpoints.

'Woman', Women, and Irish National Identity(ies) in the 1990s – Case Studies of the 'Irish Family' and President Mary Robinson

'Woman' and femininity are used in many ways by the state, pressure groups and the media in the 1990s to do different kinds of representational work. On the one hand, Irish women are firmly located within an idealised 'Irish family' by those who seek to define Irish national identity in terms of continuity and a particular way of life. On the other hand, Mary Robinson's election as President of Ireland is seen as symbolising a triumph for Irish women and a 'modernising, liberal agenda for Ireland, and as a defeat for those associated with nationalism and Catholic traditionalism' (Coulter, 1993, p.1).[6] Yet, the picture may not be as simple as these views suggest.

The Republic of Ireland in the 1990s is necessarily a more outward looking society in which national identity is being constructed in relation to its membership of the European Union (EU), the presence of a large number of multinationals within the state, an expanding tourist business, trends within the global music, electronics and other industries. The ongoing negotiations about the future of Northern Ireland is a further influence on the sense of national identity being projected by the state. Attempts to resolve the conflict in Northern Ireland have called many of the traditional symbols of Irish national identity into question.[7] National self-fashioning is, therefore, taking place within different spheres and not always along complementary lines. In this section of the chapter we focus on the interplay of two representations of Irishness in the 1990s, the idea of the marriage based 'Irish family' and the figure of President Mary Robinson.

Notions of an ideal 'Irish family' were most recently invoked during the 1995 Divorce Referendum which provides the context for our discussion of the family here.[8] The referendum campaign involved a struggle between pluralist and traditional Catholic versions of Irishness each of which focused on what Irishness means in the 1990s. Over a week before the Referendum, an *Irish Times* headline (November 15 1995, p.11) posed the questions 'Is nothing less than the kind of Ireland we want at the heart of the divorce debate? Is divorce un-Irish?' Dick Walsh in the *Irish Times* (November 18, p.14) noted that some of the anti-divorce campaigners linked the idea of the 'Irish family' to a traditional Irishness. He suggested that 'the cultural defenders' i.e. those who attempt to defend a 'traditional' Irish life from potential attack, 'would have us believe that marital breakdown is not in the Irish tradition'. In the event, 50.3 per cent voted for the introduction of divorce while 49.7 per cent voted against.[9] This close result may be testament to the continuing power of the view that marital breakdown is not part of a particularly Irish way of life.

Yet the typical 'Irish family' so powerfully invoked in the 1995 Divorce Referendum campaign and the Divorce and Abortion Referenda campaigns of the 1980s and 90s, is in fact only a recent phenomenon (O'Toole, 1994b). Fintan O'Toole suggests that the nuclear family only became the norm when Ireland underwent its own industrial revolution in the late 1950s and the 1960s. By the 1990s it is not possible to speak of the Irish family in terms of a nuclear family. Twenty per cent of all births in 1995 are outside of marriage (McGrath, 1995). 'The total fertility rate has fallen from 3.9 in 1971 to 3.1 in 1981 and 2.1 in 1991 (Walsh, 1993).[10] The figure for 1993 has reached the all time low of 1.93 (O'Rourke, 1995). In 1995 it is estimated that 80,000 marriages have broken down with the number of separations doubling since the divorce referendum in 1986. In addition, long-term unemployment and ongoing emigration continue to be significant factors in the break-up of families in Ireland in the 1990s. Indeed, John Waters in the *Irish Times*, (December 12 1995, p.14) suggested that those areas which voted most strongly against the introduction of divorce in 1995 were those most affected by high levels of emigration.[11]

Despite such evidence of changes in Irish families both the pro and anti-divorce campaigns for the 1995 Divorce Referendum emphasised the need to preserve 'the Irish family'. The Right to Remarry campaign focused on the message that people should be allowed a second chance and the right to remarry. Slogans used in this campaign included 'Give someone you know a second chance – vote Yes'. A Socialist Worker poster included the slogan 'Let the bishops look after their own families – vote Yes', alongside a photograph of the former Bishop of Kerry who was revealed to have a teenage son in the United States. The Right to Remarry Campaign did not overtly challenge the assumption that the 'Irish family' is based on a marriage contract and were forced to engage in a debate about the rights and entitlements of first, second and subsequent families.[12] One of the No divorce slogans read: 'Divorce destroys first family rights – Vote No'. Nuala O'Faolain in the *Irish Times* (15 November, 1995, p.11) suggested that 'compared to the anti-divorce language, which is confident and familiar, the pro-divorce language sounds frail'. Although the Divorce Action Group and the Right to Remarry activists had the support of the largest seven political parties who urged a Yes vote, the difficulties of arguing against the status quo and for the introduction of such potentially complicated family arrangements, proved considerable.

The anti-divorce[13] and No divorce[14] campaigns focused on a fear at all levels of society that Irish women might undermine the institution of the family by leaving it and 'walking away with it all'! The virgin/whore or victim/threat dichotomies so evident in the 1920s remain relevant in the 1990s. For example, the 1995 No Divorce campaign poster slogan 'Hello Divorce ... Bye Bye Daddy, vote No!' represented women and children as the innocent victims whose positions would be weakened by the threat to the institutions of marriage and the family. Judge Rory O'Hanlon (chair of the No Divorce campaign) also suggested that divorced women would be a drag on the marriage market as they would have children in tow. The 'No' lobby focused on fears that the nature of Irish society would be fundamentally changed by the undermining of Catholic marriage as a life-long contract in which women play the stabilising roles of wife and mother. Nuala O'Faolain, in her report on people's attitudes to divorce during the 1995 Referendum campaign (*Irish Times*, 14 November, 1995, p.7), suggested that,

> [t]he divorce debate is rich in ingenious woman-dislike. The fact that the overwhelming majority of separations and divorces are sought by women, for instance, is proof, to one man, 'that there's something in it for them [i.e. women]. They're the ones who walk away with it all'.[15]

Youth against Divorce, another campaign group in the anti-divorce lobby, clashed with Women's Aid when it used the group's slogan 'He gave her flowers, chocolates and multiple bruising' and added 'Don't give him the right to remarry' (quoted in the *Sunday Tribune*, 26 November, 1995, p.12).[16] Re-appropriation of language in this manner proved to be a significant strategy throughout the anti and No divorce campaigns.

Following a year of sex abuse scandals, the authority of the Catholic church had come into question and many commentators and activists were unsure about the potential effects of church interventions. For example, when Bishop Thomas Flynn said that people who divorced and remarried might not be entitled to the sacraments, the chair of the anti-divorce campaign rejected Bishop Flynn's comments and dissociated his campaign from the Catholic Church. There was open criticism of Bishop Flynn's intervention from a range of political circles. The Taoiseach, John Bruton's response was couched in terms of the separation of church and state and the establishment of a pluralist society.

> The State is not trying to stop any church preaching to all, or to stop it enforcing its own teaching amongst its own members. But each church should recognise that state laws must cater reasonably for all members of society, not just those who are fortunate enough to have a strong religious belief. Religious belief, like marriage, is something that requires ongoing personal commitment. It cannot be coerced by law (quoted in the *Irish Times*, 14 November, 1995, p.1).

Pope John Paul entered the Irish divorce debate just two days before the referendum when he addressed a group of Irish pilgrims at the Vatican. He called on Irish Catholics to 'reflect on the indissoluble character of the marriage bond ...' (quoted in the *Irish Times*, 23 November, 1995, p.8). The Pope's message came on the same day that pop stars appealed for a Yes vote, prompting the tabloid headline 'Bono versus the Pope' (quoted in the *Sunday Tribune*, 26 November 1995, p.12).[17] Mother Teresa also intervened in the debate via a letter to the Irish Catholic in which she wrote 'Dear People of Ireland, I pray that Ireland, by giving a No vote to divorce, will continue to be a sign of unity, love and peace where it must start, in the family' (quoted in the *Sunday Independent*, 26 November, 1995, p.6).

Yet the Catholic church was also a source of contradictory messages. While the archbishop of Dublin, Dr Connell, warned that the right to remarry would introduce 'a fundamental disorder into Irish society' (quoted in the *Irish Times*, 14 November, 1995, p.1), the Bishop of Cork, Dr Michael Murphy said that the divorce referendum was 'a civil matter and the State has to do what is feels is best for the people ... if a person feels divorce is the best solution, he can vote conscientiously Yes – no problem' (quoted in the *Irish Times*, 14 November, 1995, p.7). Sister Margaret MacCurtain, a historian, philosopher and Dominican nun publicly supported voting for the introduction of divorce in the 1995 referendum on divorce. She is quoted in the *Sunday Independent* (15 November, 1995, p.7) as saying ' We have to say goodbye to the cosy, unquestioned position that the family has held in our Constitution since 1937' ... we need to legislate as citizens of our state for the welfare of our children'. She represented the divorce referendum as offering Irish people

> an invitation to be [an] open, mature, generous-hearted society, that recognises the rights of different categories of people. It also gives us a chance to develop a code of ethics – we haven't had a chance to think outside the parameters of Catholic morality which has copper-fastened our thinking to a large extent .

Fintan O'Toole in the *Irish Times* on the day after the Referendum (25 November, 1995, p.6) suggested that religious devotion in Ireland since the

1960s had 'provided a layer of continuity' that enabled Irish society to cope with rapid change. He went on to assert that the lesson of the divorce referendum is that the opposite may also be true – 'in a time of crisis for the Catholic church it is harder, not easier, for Catholics to cope with change'. O'Toole concludes that in the face of a crisis in the church and political change the family becomes a source of 'refuge from uncertainty'. Such a view raises the question of where the Irish people in the 1990s seek stability and order. We are not sure that a return to 'family values' as recently heralded in Britain offers Irish women any more liberatory potential than the Catholic church has done in the past.

While tolerance, pluralism and openness to other ways of life were invoked during the Divorce campaign, not least in relation to Northern Ireland, the idea of an Irish marriage based family proved to have the greatest hold on the imaginations and hopes of Irish voters. Fintan O'Toole (*Irish Times*, 25 November, 1995, p.6) suggested that 'peace in Northern Ireland – had no discernible influence on the debate'

Seventy-five per cent of separations are initiated by women, yet, after all of this debate, women's disproportionate wish to leave marital relationships remains an under examined subject. Instead, the campaign, by the extreme tactics of the No Divorce campaign and the more tentative approach of the Right to Remarry activists, conspired to reinforce images of an idealised 'Irish family' which symbolises a particularly Irish way of life. Since the referendum, the Government has reinforced this idealised Irishness centring around the family by emphasising its commitment to pro-family policies. Denis Coughlan in the *Irish Times*, (20 January, 1996, p.10) suggests that the government move to establish a Commission on the Family is 'designed to deflect the complaints of those committed to traditional social and moral values'.

During President Clinton's visit to Ireland, Finola Bruton (wife of Taoiseach. John Bruton), reinforced the government's retreat to 'family values' when she stated that ' a loving married relationship between a man and a woman is a core value to be recognised, affirmed and supported' (quoted in the *Irish Times*, 20 January, 1996, p.10). The achievements of feminist activists and others during the divorce campaign were once again being redefined and re-appropriated. The apparent disagreement between women received an inordinate amount of attention in the media much of which served to trivialise the issues at stake and construct it as a fight amongst women. Headlines included 'Finola and the feminists: Backlash for a true radical' (*Sunday Independent*, 10 December, 1995, p.17); 'Mrs Bruton has split the women's movement – ICA', (*Irish Times*, 5 December, 1995, p.13); 'Why Finola Bruton rained on the feminist parade' (*Irish Times*, December 7 1995, p.9). These headlines highlight the unwillingness of the press to invest feminist debate with cultural authority. The tendency for the media to trivialise or demonise women by locating them either within the family or as a threat to the family and nation was evident throughout and after the campaign.[18]

On a symbolic level Mary Robinson's election as President of Ireland has been a significant event for Irish women partly because she acknowledges the gender significance of her achievements (Meaney, 1991, O'Reilly, 1991 and Smyth, 1992, see also Pilcher, 1995, p.495). However, when Mary Robinson commented, on NBC Superchannel, that the 1995 Divorce referendum was a simple matter of 'the right to remarry' and that a 'a very thoughtful infrastructure' of legislation had been put in place since the last divorce referendum, she received considerable criticism from No divorce campaigners. She was accused of overstepping the bounds of her office and misrepresenting the divorce referendum. Her comments evoked discourses of women not knowing their place and overstepping the boundaries of their roles. Her presence is tolerated and even admired when her influence is at the level of public relations and symbolic activities, however, any, even implicit challenge to the traditional perceptions of the 'Irish family', the bedrock of Irishness continues to trigger key tensions within Irish society.

Yet, a significant part of Mary Robinson's power as a symbol of a new Ireland and changing Irishness is her ability to touch on the tensions within Irish society. By her very presence, by speaking out and drawing attention to excluded groups, she holds up a mirror to Irish life. She is more than a symbol however, because she is effecting material changes in her role as President. Michael Mee, a senior law lecturer at Limerick University, points to the many changes she has made in the office of President and questions the constitutionality of these changes. He sees her as having changed the relationship between government and president – the 'old emphasis on presenting a united front in public at all costs seems to have been abandoned' (quoted in *Sunday Independent*, 28 January, 1996, p.2). Such criticism points to the material changes that Mary Robinson has made and the spaces within the state that she has been able to create which offer new political possibilities. While forces for the preservation of a patriarchal Irish nation underpinned by an idealised version of the 'Irish family' continue to hold sway in Irish society, Mary Robinson offers symbolic and material evidence of real and potential changes.

Conclusion

In this chapter, we have explored some of the complex and shifting relationships between 'woman', women and Irish national identity. While in the 1920s, symbols of women were used to signify threats to the purity and integrity of Irish culture, in the 1990s representations of women are often more diffuse. We have suggested that symbols and representations of women and Irishness need to be understood within changing economic, social and political contexts. From the 1920s to the 1990s, Ireland has witnessed massive socio-economic changes. Even so, there are some continuities in the ways that symbols and representations of women are employed to convey meaning. Although not used as overtly as in the 1920s, the virgin/whore, victim/threat dichotomies persist in present day Ireland.

During the 1920s, partition and the establishment of the Free State necessitated the construction of a collective identity which would bridge the gaps between class, regions and political divisions. Irishness was defined as a separate and distinctive identity. In attempting to free Irishness from foreign corrupting influences, the key architects of Irish national identity asserted its authenticity based on an 'ancient' and 'unique' culture. However, after centuries of British domination Irish culture was represented as fragile and in need of protection from the dangerous and immoral effects of imported fashions, amusements and entertainments. Preserving the purity and distinctiveness of Irish culture was a necessary part of maintaining the right of the Irish state to exist as a separate and cohesive entity. Within this context, gender was used as a key signifier as women represented both the purity and integrity of the nation as well as its vulnerability to foreign corruption.

While Ireland in the 1990s embraces foreign investment, economic markets and media, many of the tensions evident in the 1920s remain. The 1995 Divorce Referendum represents a watershed in the struggle between state, church, the media and the people of Ireland to define the kind of Irishness that is most relevant as we move towards the end of the twentieth century. Yet the campaign and the outcome forces us to acknowledge the tensions in modern Irish society between traditional and pluralist/secular versions of Irishness and how gender and family are employed to further both agendas. What is most significant is that despite the widespread use of advertising as a communication and persuasive device, images of women as victims or threats were relied on heavily by those against the introduction of divorce. While many commentators suggest that this was an unwise tactic given what they now call 'the Robinson factor' (i.e. the increased visibility and credibility given to women's issues influenced by Mary Robinson's presidency) it cannot be denied that such representations of women still strike a chord in Irish society.

Discussion Topics

1. Examine the changing relationships between Church, State and Media in twentieth century representations of Irish national identity and Irish women in the Republic of Ireland.

2. Discuss the impact of feminist activism and analysis on changing images of Irishness and Irish women.

3. How are representations of Irishness and Irish women affected by partition and ongoing negotiations about the future of Northern Ireland?

4. Explore the relationships between cultural images and the material lives of Irish women.

Notes

1. The extracts from the newspapers included here are necessarily selective. This does not mean that these extracts are unrepresentative of the newspapers of their day. In particular, those extracts from the 1920s newspapers are selected from a detailed survey of the press in the Free State currently being undertaken, see Louise Ryan (1996). The extracts from the 1990s newspapers provide the background to a wider empirical study on women, emigration and Irish national identity. The use of different newspapers for each of the periods under consideration reflects the different studies we are undertaking. We thought that some of our findings from these studies might be brought together productively to trace some changes in the relationships between representations of women and Irish national identity over time.

2. The Treaty with Britain which established the existence of the Free State and the partition of the island of Ireland into 26 counties in the South and 6 counties in the North was opposed by those groups who saw it as a 'sell out' of Republican aspirations. In the ensuing Civil War the pro-treaty government forces fought against the anti-treaty Republicans. This division on the treaty was to shape Irish politics for many years to come.

3. Archbishop Gilmartin of Tuam was quoted in detail by the *Irish Independent*. It was common practice for the newspapers of the period to give lengthy coverage to the sermons and pastoral letters of the Catholic hierarchy.

4. Cumann na mBan was the women's auxiliary to the Irish Volunteer Force. Set up in 1914 Cumann na mBan was initially limited to a supportive role in the nationalist movement but after the Rising of 1916 the women became more assertive and later played very active parts in both the War of Independence and on the Republican side of the Civil War (Ward, 1989). Women within the Republican movement were often strongly condemned by the Catholic church (Fallon, 1986).

5. It would not be entirely accurate to assume that only the Catholic hierarchy was concerned with the 'evils' of modern dancing. The Rev Nicolson, an Evangelist preacher addressing a congregation in Belfast declared 'I would sooner see my daughters dead than at a dance' (*Irish Independent*, 17 August, 1925).

6. Emily O'Reilly points out that 'all the political parties took her victory as a cue for updating, even altering, their own policies in a less narrowly nationalistic , more social-democratic and pluralist direction' (O'Reilly, 1991, p.153). Fianna Fail announced that it would produce a white paper on marital breakdown and repeal the laws on homosexuality (O'Reilly, 1991). John Bruton, the new leader of the Fine Gael party, announced new party politics on Articles 2 and 3 of the Constitution (articles 2 and 3 assert what is called a 'territorial claim' to Northern Ireland), and

put divorce back on the party agenda. The voices of Irish women whether it be Mary Robinson, the twenty women elected to the Dail in 1992 , Irish feminist activists and writers, women journalists etc. are now audible at most levels of public discourse.

7. A sub-committee of the Forum for Peace and Reconciliation has been set up to examine obstacles in the South to reconciliation. The Taoiseach, John Bruton, has recently asked officials to examine the procedures for commissioning a new national anthem because there have been complaints that Ambhran na bhFiann (A Soldier's Song) is offensive to unionists and a committee headed by T J Whitaker has been established by the Government to review the Constitution. The decision to introduce divorce in the 1995 (even if only marginally passed) is seen as making the Republic a more pluralist state in the eyes of Northern Unionists. John Hume, for example, called for a yes vote.

8. An Economic and Social Research Institute (ESRI) Report published in October, 1995 revealed that the Irish solution to martial breakdown involved the poor going for barring and maintenance orders and the better off for legal separation. It also showed that 75 per cent of separations were initiated by women.

9. Only 35.27 per cent of those who voted in the Divorce Referendum in 1986 voted for the introduction of divorce so there was an overall swing of 15 per cent towards a Yes vote between 1986 and 1995.

10. This rate represents the average number of children a woman bore during her reproductive years.

11. Waters also notes that these areas are unpopular with tourists and so are deprived of 'stimuli from without and within'. See Gray, 1996a and 1996b for a discussion of recent emigration, Irish women and national identity .

12. Eighteen pieces of legislation have been introduced since 1985 by successive governments to deal with issues arising from marriage breakdown. The Status of Children Act 1987 gives those born outside of marriage the same inheritance rights as those born inside marriage. The 1989 Judicial Separation Act was passed which addresses the division of assets, custody of children and maintenance of dependent spouses. The draft Family Law (Divorce) Bill 1995 set out the terms for divorce if the referendum was passed.

13. The anti-divorce campaign was chaired by Des Hanafin and included Professor William Binchy.

14. The No Divorce Campaign was chaired by Judge Rory O'Hanlon and had close links with the international fundamentalist organisation, Human Life International. The No Divorce group conducted an acrimonious campaign.

15. 75 per cent of separations in Ireland are initiated by women.

16. Women's Aid is an organisation that provides refuge and support to battered women.

17. The Vatican Newspaper, L'Osservatore Romano on the day after the Referendum dissociated the result from defeat for the Catholic church: 'The result of the Irish referendum ... on divorce is not a defeat for the church, as has been emphatically said. Logic and reason argue that it is a defeat for the family which loses one of its foundation stones, namely the unity and indissolubility of marriage' (quoted in the *Irish Times,* 28 November, 1995, p.4).

18. See McCafferty, 1985, Smyth, 1992 and 1994, Coulter, 1993.

References and Further Reading

Anthias, F and Yuval-Davis, N. 1993 *Racialised Boundaries: Race, Nation, Gender, Colour and Class* London: Routledge.

Barry, U. 1995 'A Changing Picture: Women in the Irish Labour Market' *Irish Reporter* 17: First Quarter pp.14-18.

Boland, E. 1989 *A Kind of Scar* Dublin: Attic Press.

Brown, T. 1987 *Ireland A Social and Cultural History 1922-1985* London: Fontana Press.

Coulter, C. 1993 *The Hidden Tradition Feminism, Women and Nationalism in Ireland*, Cork: Cork University Press.

Douds, S. 1995 'An Unlikely Prophet' *Fortnight* 344: 21 November.

Fallon, C. 1986 *Soul of Fire* Dublin: Mercier Press.

Foley, M. 1993 'The Political Lobby System' *Irish Communications Review* 3 pp.21-30.

Galligan, Y. 1993 'Gender and Party Politics in the Republic of Ireland' in Lovenduski, J and Norris, P. (eds.) *Gender and Political Parties* London and Newbury Park C A: Sage.

Gray, B. 1996a 'Ireland: The Home of Our Mothers or Our Birthright for Ages?' in Maynard, M and Purvis, J. (eds.) *New Frontiers in Women's Studies: Knowledge, Identity and Nationalism* London: Taylor and Francis.

Gray, B. 1996b 'Irish Women In London: National or Hybrid Diasporic Identities' *National Women's Studies Association Journal* 8:1, pp.85-109.

Innes, CL. 1994 'Virgin Territories and Motherlands: Colonial and Nationalist Representations of Africa and Ireland' *Feminist Review* 47, pp.1-14.

Ivekovic, R. 1993 'Women, Nationalism and War: 'Make Love Not War'' *Hypatia* 8:4, pp.113-125.

Lash, S and Urry, J. 1994 *Economies of Signs and Space* London: Sage.

Lyons, FSL. 1989 *Culture and Anarchy in Ireland: 1890-1939* Oxford: Oxford University Press.

McCafferty, Nell. 1985 *A Woman to Blame* Dublin: Attic Press.

McClintock, A. 1993 'Family Feuds: Gender, Nationalism and the Family' *Feminist Review* 44, pp.61-80.

McGrath, K. 1995 'Unwed Pregnancy Guilt Warning – But Not You' *Irish Independent* 19 October p.10.

Meaney, G. 1991 *Sex and Nation: Women in Irish Culture and Politics* Dublin: Attic Press.

Mosse, G L. 1985 *Nationalism and Sexuality* London: University of Wisconsin Press.

Mullholland, J. 1995 'After the Green Paper: What Next for Broadcasting in Ireland?' *Irish Communications Review* 5 pp.76-79.

Nash, C. 1993 'Remapping and Renaming: New Cartographies of Identity, Gender and Landscape in Ireland' *Feminist Review* 44, pp.39-57.

Nic Ghiolla Phadraig, M. 1995 'The Power of the Catholic Church in the Republic of Ireland' in Clancy, P, Drudy, S, Lynch, K and O'Dowd, L. (eds.) *Irish Society, Sociological Perspectives* Dublin: Institute of Public Administration.

O'Brien Johnson, T and Cairns, D. (eds.) 1991 *Gender in Irish Writing* Milton Keynes: Open University Press.

O'Dowd, L. 1987 'Church, State and Women: The Aftermath of Partition' in Curtin, C, Jackson, P and O'Connor, B. (eds.) *Gender in Irish Society* Galway: Galway University Press.

O'Reilly, E. 1991 *Candidate: The Truth Behind the Presidential Campaign* Dublin: Attic Press.

O'Rourke, T S. 1995 'Fall in Irish Birth Rates Welcomed' *The Big Issues* Issue 12: Feb 16-March 1, 11.

O'Toole, F. 1994a 'Rise and Follow Charlo' *Fortnight* No. 329: June, pp.32-33.

O'Toole, F. 1994b 'Mammy, Daddy and the Kids In One House' *Irish Reporter* 15: Third Quarter, pp.13-15.

O'Toole, F. 1994c *Black Hole, Green Card: The Disappearance of Ireland* Dublin: New Island Books.

Penrose, J. 1995 'Essential Constructions? The 'Cultural Bases' of Nationalist Movements' *Nations and Nationalisms* 1:3, pp.391-417.

Pilcher, J. 1995 'The Gender Significance of Women in Power: British Women Talking about Margaret Thatcher' *The European Journal of Women's Studies* 2:3, pp.493-508.

Quinn, R. 1995 'An Agenda for the Left' *Political Agenda* 1:3, pp.7-10.

Ryan, L. 1996 'The Massacre of Innocence: Infanticide and the Irish Free State' *Irish Studies Review* 14, pp.17-20.

Ryan, L. 1995 'Traditions and Double Moral Standards: The Irish Suffragists' Critique of Nationalism' *Women's History Review* 4, pp.487-503.

Ryan, M. 1994 *War and Peace in Ireland* London: Pluto Press.

Smyth, A. 1994 'Paying our Disrespects to the Bloody State We're In: Women, Violence, Culture and the State' in Griffin, G, Hester, M, Rai, S and Roseneil, S (eds.) *Stirring It: Challenges for Feminism* London: Taylor and Francis.

Smyth, A. 1992 ''A Great Day for the Women of Ireland ...' The Meaning of Mary Robinson's Presidency for Irish Women' *Canadian Journal of Irish Studies* 18:1, pp.61-75.

Smyth, A. 1991 'The Floozie in the Jacuzzi' *Feminist Studies* 17:1, pp.7-28.

Tuchman, G. 1978 'The Newspaper as the Social Movement's Resource' in Tuchman, Kaplan Daniels and Benet (eds.) *Hearth and Home: Images of Women in the Mass Media* New York: Oxford University Press.

Walsh, B. 1993 'Labour Force Participation in the Growth of Women's Employment: Ireland, 1971-1991' *Economic and Social Review* 22:4.

Ward, M. 1989 *Unmanageable Revolutionaries* London: Pluto Press.

Wills, C. 1994 'Review Essay: Rocking the Cradle? – Women's Studies and the Family in Twentieth Century Ireland' *Bullan* 1:2, pp.97-106.

Wilson, E. 1995 'The Rhetoric of Urban Space' *New Left Review* 209, Jan/Feb. pp.146-160.

32.

Women in Party Politics and Local Groups: Findings from Belfast

Eilish Rooney

Introduction

Women rarely receive a mention in the prodigious literature on Northern Ireland (NI). They are either assumed to be included or they are invisible. It amounts to the same thing. Women do not make a difference to the description or to the analyses of the political history or conflict in NI. They are generally viewed as not implicated in the 'man's war'. There is an emerging body of contemporary studies and publications on women in Ireland.[1] Some recent studies of women in NI take the view that the 'troubles' are an added burden to the lives of women struggling with poverty and 'armed patriarchy'. Others describe and celebrate women's activism in the achievements of the women's movement, of peace groups and of individual women. Most of this work has concentrated on women from nationalist or republican communities. The writer's political position on the ongoing conflict in NI, may be explicit, subtlety suggested or avoided. The writer's attitude towards women's agency in the conflict is an indicator of a political perspective. Those who see the state of NI as reformable see the 'troubles' as an avoidable, additional burden on women's lives. They generally applaud how women cope with and confront political violence. Those who see the state as not reformable see the troubles as a consequence of the setting up of the state. They generally support mainly working class women's political resistance to the state.

Setting out the range of political positions in this crude way simplifies the complexity of individual perspectives over time. The point is that the activity of researching and writing about women, of putting us in the picture, in NI is no more a 'politically innocent' activity than is any of the prodigious literature on NI. Ownership and definition of discourse is one other contest in the conflict of identities, sovereignty and policies that constitute debate about NI.

The ongoing political issue of sovereignty in NI, and the unresolved conflict of nationalisms, presents unique contexts for research into the historical and contested specificities of gender identity: of what it means to be fe/male at particular historical moments and within different political movements and ideologies. These meanings are part of the contested discourse in NI, and part of the background to the study from which this chapter is taken (Rooney and Woods, 1995).[2] The study was basically about building a picture of women's participation in political parties and their activities in local women's groups in three Electoral Areas (EAs) of Belfast City Council.

Starting Places

The study had a number of starting points relevant both to the research findings, to developments since the study was completed, and to debate on the future of women in NI. When looking at women and politics in NI the most obvious place to begin is with their absence. There are no women elected to the European Parliament and none of NI's seventeen MPs in the Westminster Parliament is a woman. The proportion of women elected to local councils in NI is twelve per cent with four of the twenty-six local councils having no women members (Equal Opportunities Commission NI, 1995). This compares with local councils in GB where 25.8 per cent of local councillors are women. When NI's female representation rates are further compared with other countries of the European Union (EU) the contrast can seem dramatic. Denmark has the highest percentage of female MEPs in the EU; 43.8 per cent of its MEPs are female (7 of 16). Germany with ninety-nine MEPs has the highest number of females in the European Parliament (thirty-four females or 34.4 per cent).

However, differences in populations, economy and geographic location, let alone political history, between European countries make conclusive comparisons difficult. Comparative figures may be useful for dramatic effect rather than for furthering analysis and understanding. Research on the interesting practical and theoretical question about whether or not an increase in women's participation rates *makes a difference* to decision making has led to the concept of 'critical mass' in women's political participation debates (Leijenaar, 1992, Lovenduski, 1986, Blom, 1988). Research indicates that when women are present in percentages greater than thirty per cent, their presence makes a difference to the topics for debate and to the priorities reached. For example, issues related to child care are prioritised.

When people are excluded or absent from electoral assemblies to the same extent on the basis of race, religion, or colour the inequity is more blatant and perhaps more easily recognised as discrimination. As it is, and as President Robinson has said from the vantage point of a privileged 'insider', the full participation of women in our society is perceived as an issue that is, *only* for women. And it is a short step from this to the position that such issues are, *merely* for women (Rooney, 1995, Robinson, 1992, my emphasis). Thus, women are ignored because they are assumed to be powerless and, being ignored, they may be affirmed in their sense of powerlessness.[3]

Dig Where You Stand: Local Groups

In contrast to the invisibility of women in electoral politics the upsurge of women's local groups and organisations in working-class neighbourhoods has been a noted development within NI in the last fifteen years (Taillon, 1992). This organising has an emerging and a hidden history. The emerging history is being recorded, largely by feminists who were active in the 1970s in setting up organisations that currently facilitate the proliferation of local groups (Abbot and Fraser, 1985, Devaney et al., 1989, Roulston, 1989, Evason, 1991, McWilliams, 1991, 1995, Workers' Educational Association, 1991, Rooney, 1992, 1995, Women and Citizenship Group, 1995). This activity has been formalised and influenced by funding from charitable trusts, churches and government initiatives targeted for areas of deprivation.

The hidden history of women's informal organising exists within living memory. In my childhood women 'organised' births, wakes, street parties, the rota borrowing of food and money, minding children, and mutual support (I also remember street fights between the same women!). Some of this still goes on. This local organising is barely visible beyond the local sphere. The point is that the local neighbourhood is a place that has traditionally been considered by women to be their territory.

So, what has been happening? In a research project based in the Centre for Research on Women, University of Ulster, we built a picture of women's activities in local groups and in electoral politics.[4] We wanted to know what women were doing in these fields and what impacts they thought their activities have. From the outset we took the view that women are under represented in decision making bodies in NI and that their participation in the electoral and local spheres should be supported and could be increased. This chapter will draw from the political dimension of the study to challenge the assumption that women are not interested in politics and are not involved; it will trace the historical, ideological and tactical continuum of debate about 'women' within the political parties; and it will show how women's and men's experiences of political participation are gender differentiated and how women are aware of this and men are not. It will report the responses of political parties to proposals for making party political participation more effective and 'woman friendly'.

The local activism dimension of this study challenges the view, held by women and men and supported in the literature, that women are under represented in electoral politics because of time consuming domestic responsibilities. In her work on citizenship Lister (1993) notes that poverty is a 'very time-consuming condition ... it is largely women's time that is consumed.' Coote and Pattullo (1990) also argue that, 'lack of time and lack of mobility, especially when combined with lack of money, as they frequently are, are key constraints on women's participation in formal politics'. Neither time nor poverty was a constraint on the women who participated in local groups and who took part in this study. The local group is a woman and child friendly place.[5] It is where women say they can make an impact on the local community which makes a difference to their own lives.

In this study women are seen by women and men to be 'different' in a number of respects arising from women's primary role in the home and family. These 'differences' are treated in a positive way in the local group. But in the council they are deviant differences and are treated in a negative manner. One male councillor made a delightfully concise contribution to the 'difference' debate when he said: 'Women are different but we treat them the same!' (Rooney and Woods, 1995). Being treated *the same* in the council and in party politics generally discriminates against women.

The Study: Plurality of Approaches

This is no more than a brief outline of the study approaches and methodology. One of the three Electoral Areas (EAs) returns all unionist councillors, another returns a combination of nationalist and republican councillors and the third, mainly unionist, returns a party mix. Each area stretches from the inner city, or its fringes, in the direction of east, west and north Belfast into suburban areas. Some of the highest levels of deprivation in NI are to be found in these areas (PPRU, 1988, NIHE, 1986). These EAs comprise some of the areas of highest deprivation in NI. Taken together they cannot be seen as representative of Belfast or of NI as a whole.

Four forms of data collection were used. Two were concerned with group activity and local community activism by women; and two were concerned with electoral politics in the EAs, and the presence or the absence of women in the formal political arena.

Women participate in a range of community based activities: youth and community projects, community employment schemes and community action groups to name a few. Women's roles in these groups would include those of members, workers, users and so on. We targeted local women's groups and defined such a group as any group of women who organise in their local community. In all, twenty-six of the twenty-eight groups contacted responded (ninety-eight per cent) and returned 213 questionnaires (forty-five per cent). Given the return rates to postal questionnaires this is a reasonably good response.

In order to supplement the survey and to deepen our understanding of community development and women's growing participation we conducted interviews and questionnaires with women and men (fifteen in all) who could be regarded as active in a professional and/or activist sense in these local communities. These people provided an historical dimension and overview context to the survey.

Sixteen councillors represented these EAs during this research; four of these were women. We invited them to participate in a structured, face to face taped interview. The response was very positive: fourteen of the sixteen agreed.

We were concerned to set the comments of councillors in the wider context of their political parties and of the parties' records as far as increasing women's participation was concerned. In all, seven parties agreed to provide a representative to be interviewed.

Action Outcome

Finally, we originally intended to disseminate findings of the research at a conference or seminar. When we were about half way through the study we decided that the priority of the dissemination process should be to inform the local women's groups who had participated in the questionnaire. This was the single set of respondents with whom we had no face to face contact and a number of queries had emerged in the early stages of data analysis which we wanted to discuss with them. We decided, therefore, to have community based dissemination and feedback workshops in each area. This proved a rich source of insight and has been important for the interpretation of the findings. Women enjoyed the experience and appreciated being told of the findings.

Issues Arising

It is a commonplace observation that research defines problems and shapes knowledge. It is worth repeating this observation each time we produce findings or aim for understandings. Why are we asking the questions? Why are we trying to answer them in this way? And who is paying? A simple instance of the way we 'shaped' our research lay in the way we selected the locality for the research. The study area was chosen to fit around how the city council and political parties organise. This bears little relation to how women in local areas organise.

The Parties: historical, ideological and tactical continuum

The political party representatives say that women are active and indeed crucial to the party machine particularly at election time. However, one women described their 'crucial' role thus: 'we are allowed to sell the ballots and make the tea but not the speech'. The larger parties claimed fifty per cent female membership whilst the smaller parties claimed around a third. There appears to be an historical, ideological and perhaps a tactical continuum in the history of debate and policy on women within the parties. In the 1970s-80s republican and left wing parties discussed and developed policy in relation to women (Communist Party of Ireland [CPI]; Sinn Fein [SF]; Workers' Party [WP]).[6] The Alliance Party (AP) and the Social Democratic and Labour Party (SDLP) have had women on their agenda since the mid 1980s. The association between civil rights, nationalism and feminism is one element in the history of emerging concerns with women in unionist parties (Morgan, 1992). The topic of women was discussed at the Democratic Unionist Party (DUP) and the Ulster Unionist Party (UUP) annual conferences in 1991. Several representatives of the parties involved in the various political 'talks' mentioned the initial absence and current presence of a woman amongst the delegations. If the latter is a form of tokenism it was nevertheless welcomed by the relevant party representatives.

A crucial factor in bringing about debate and policy decisions about women within parties seems to be the presence of key women who are prepared to push for a high profile for women's issues in the party. Awareness of these issues and campaigns outside the party is also a factor. Obviously it helps if these women can support their 'push' with reference to a constituency of women outside the party.

Women's membership of the parties is not reflected in decision making structures. In keeping with their history of awareness of 'women's issues' SF and WP operate quotas for women on their Ard Comhairle: SF twenty-five per cent; WP forty per cent. These parties also have a Women's Department or Committee and a policy of crèche provision for women standing for election. At election time SF publish a Women's Manifesto. CPI seems to have suffered from the feminist activism of its women members who have been active in promoting women's issues and organisations. The AP has a Women's Issues Group. It also has the highest percentage of female councillors and the highest estimated number of women local government candidates. The SDLP has a women's sub-group of the policy committee. The UUP has a long-standing Women's Council but this has not resulted in any major policy documents or debates on women. The DUP has recently begun to put women on the agenda.

These structures tell part of the story. At the annual party conferences of all these parties the meeting endorses policy and appoints the main executive committee. However, this committee, which may have an administrative role, is often not seen as the real source of power in the party. Another body the 'cabinet' type committee consisting of the party leader, elected representatives and others was said to be the real power base. The percentage of women in this body, in all of the larger parties, is lower than elsewhere in the structure. This clearly has implications for any party that would seek to redress opportunities for women within the party structure.

The Councillors — Inclusion and Exclusion

Questions to councillors about women as councillors generated a lot of comment and contradictory pictures emerged both among the men and women and between them. Women spoke from experience; men rationalised or explained how things are as they are. The male councillors expressed attitudes towards women in politics that may be tentatively categorised into three types: admiring-condescension; marginalisation and tactical acceptance.

Admiring-condescension

Some councillors saw women as special: women were admired as mothers, and treated as 'ladies' in the council. Several emphasised that women do not come in for the same barracking abuse as men. However, 'admiration' slipped into condescension when women were seen as good grass roots workers who, *know better than to get involved in council politics*. One male councillor said that women councillors, *hadn't broken any delph so far*. Another admired women's 'priorities' and said that political parties did not need crêches because women are not politically ambitious enough to sacrifice a child's interests for politics. The council is clearly seen as a place to be tough. The implicit passivity of women in these comments suggests that they are less successful in the job. Councillors with these views did not intend to seem condescending. At times during the interview they were keen to stress their support for women in politics.

Marginalisation

This outlook may be summarised in one councillor's comment that women coming forward had to be a 'special breed'; if she was of the, 'right calibre she would have no problems'. Implicit in this is that women had to be prepared to behave more like men. A number of comments from some councillors suggested that women do not behave as astutely as men and their party loyalty may be suspect. They are seen as more likely to collaborate, less likely to take committee business seriously and they, 'get diverted by petty issues'. One councillor said that, 'it's natural for women to get involved in women's issues but ... some councillors think there are more important things to be debated'. These comments may relate to past collaborations between nationalist and unionist women councillors in their opposition to Belfast City Council's decision to withdraw funding from Falls Women's Centre. This decision (later overturned) was seen by women as anti woman, as well as sectarian. These views on women's lack of political nous were mainly made by some unionist councillors. But across all parties there was the sense that being a councillor required a special kind of woman.

Tactical acceptance

These views tended to emphasise that women and men are not or should not be viewed as being different. These councillors emphasised party and policy as the distinguishing factors in council politics and in the contribution of women. Party not gender is the cleavage. These male councillors considered the presence of women in the council and the focus on women as representatives as a useful electoral strategy: women attract women and young voters. These councillors, all republican/nationalist, were aware of feminism. Some said that all issues were women's issues and that men should be encouraged to become involved with what is seen as women's issues. The virtual uniformity of some of these responses, and the alternative picture offered by women, suggest that there is a considered position, or 'party line', on women. Again, if this is a form of electoral tactics it is one which women welcome and which provides women with a place within the structures.

These attitudes are not necessarily male attitudes. They are the expression of dominant values and may also be held by women. They are not shared by the women in our sample.

It is when we turn to the responses of the women councillors to these questions that a rather different understanding of gendered perceptions and experiences emerges. Some things are affirmed, some are challenged. The women councillors in our sample have gone through the 'gate' of selection and election. They say this was not problematic for them, but once inside, they face other barriers. These are identified by women across parties. These barriers may be tentatively characterised as forms of inclusion and forms of exclusion. Women recognise the categories identified earlier. They see and say that they are excluded and they articulate the ways this exclusion works. And when they are included they see this as conditional. Women councillors see themselves perceived as women first and councillors second. This is something the men councillors did not say and seem unaware of.

Inclusion

Women's inclusion is provisional on their domestic responsibilities not impinging on council business and responsibilities. Being treated 'the same' as men is seen by some women as effectively discriminating against women, particularly women with children. Added to the activity of being a councillor some of these women spoke of having to get things ready at home before going to council meetings. They say they have less time to waste in useless dispute or debate. (This may be seen by some of the male councillors as not taking council business 'seriously enough'.) Definition of what is important is also a mechanism of inclusion. Thus, women's issues are an area that women councillors are expected to identify with but it is marginal; and female councillors become marginalised when they are closely identified with women's issues. One woman remarked that she saw women's issues as essentially working class community issues but she had failed to gain support for various initiatives from male colleagues who did not share her definition. These women note that no men identify with women's issues and for women to be taken seriously they have to show themselves able in all areas. From what a number of these councillors said it seems that subjects for debate are 'gendered': 'if they talk about parks ... they expect you to contribute whereas if they're talking about ... buildings they don't'.

Exclusion

The main form (perhaps forum) of women's exclusion is the 'boys' club' network that women say operates in Belfast City Council (BCC) and in the parties. One woman said that, unlike her male colleagues, she is never phoned with 'inside information'. She thinks that her male colleagues are a 'bit embarrassed' by having to deal with a woman. They don't know how to treat women. This may be linked to the mix of feelings of admiration and superiority outlined above.

The ways women can collaborate across party boundaries on issues of interest is seen as a strength by these women but they recognise that it renders them either invisible or suspect to some male councillors. They say they are more effective than men on some issues of which they have first hand experience. They do not gain inclusion on their own terms. One woman commented that when her party is attacked women councillors are never mentioned: 'we just seem to be irrelevant'. This woman interpreted being treated differently as tantamount to being ignored. Women councillors say that women listen more and talk less: 'they have to promise more and work harder'.

More equals better?

The political science literature on political participation of women in electoral assemblies in north European countries answers this question with a cautionary and disheartening: yes, eventually, when critical mass is secured (Leijenaar, 1992, Lovenduski, 1986, Blom, 1988). It is not surprising that when we asked the councillors if more women would make a difference to council business women say, yes business would be conducted more sensibly: meetings would be shorter, more efficient and women's issues would be on the agenda. However, one republican/nationalist woman said more women would not make a substantive difference; party lines would be the same.

The men said yes and no. One councillor felt that they would bring 'more dignity' to proceedings but then he qualified this: 'some of the women can fight as well as the men'. This response catches the contradiction differently expressed by other men: women 'could be a bit more sentimental and might give way on issues'; 'women can be just as bigoted and vicious as men'. Others decided that it depended on the type of woman or the party she came from. And others felt that more women would make no difference unless they were present in large numbers: 'Fifty women in BCC would make a difference'. Of the fifty-one councillors currently serving on Belfast City Council six are women.

Some Findings: Women in Community

We set about finding out which women become involved in local groups, why they become involved, what problems they confront and what they think they achieved by their involvement. We identified a total of thirty-one local women's groups in these areas as the basis for our study. These ranged from mother and toddler groups to community development groups. Three groups had disbanded by the time our work had begun. twenty-six of the remaining twenty-eight groups responded positively and distributed questionnaires to those who were actively involved in their group. A total of 213 questionnaires were returned, forty-five per cent of the total distributed. These are reasonable results as far as response rates are concerned.

These women were young; almost three-quarters were under forty years of age. Almost half were currently married with a further nineteen per cent being separated or divorced. Over three quarters of them (seventy-eight per cent) had children. While it appears that almost two thirds described themselves as economically active, that is, in work or looking for work, the unemployed formed the single largest category of these (thirty-six per cent). Group attendance was seen as an important part of the weekly routine of these women. Almost half attended their group for several days each week and ten per cent actually attended every day. They did so in order to meet other people, take their children out of the house and to get involved in the community. They were sustained in this activity primarily by friendship and support.

However, the groups are not seen as something for women alone. Over three-quarters of the women think that their group has an impact on their community. We asked the women at the feedback sessions what they meant by having an 'impact' in the local community and they gave a variety of answers. They said that they provide support services and education which helps people in the area. They said that as a result of working in the group they themselves had higher expectations for their children, especially for their daughters. Here they could see the importance of education and were more aware of sex stereotyping. The groups also were said to provide an escape both from isolation and from the 'troubles'.

Interestingly, and despite this conviction of having an impact, the women who attend the groups are definite that their groups' activities are not political in any way. Around two-thirds respond that their concerns are more to do with people than politics. When we pursued this in the feedback sessions women immediately identified 'politics' with intra-communal political division as a potential problem for the group. They distinguished between politics with a big 'P' and politics with a small 'p'. The former is divisive and could harm relationships and group work. The latter includes work around social security legislation, education and so on. We were reminded of the woman councillor who said that she could be, 'just as political as anyone else'. In the context, she obviously intended 'political' to be equated with the big 'P', with being divisive and aggressive.

Nevertheless, when asked about the role women could play in helping to resolve the problems in NI over half say that more women on Councils and as MPs is the way forward. But then the rub. This is not accompanied by the belief that women should become active in a political party. Only nine per cent of women selected this as important. When asked what would encourage women to become involved in electoral politics, over a third say that if political parties were more concerned about topics related to social issues women would be more encouraged to become involved. One of a number of ironies that emerged in this study is that councillors, men and women of all parties, say that most of their constituency work is devoted to dealing with just these issues; with problems related to unemployment, housing and poverty. Next in importance in encouraging women's political participation comes, valuing women and the contribution they have to make.

Inclusion and Exclusion

Like any organisation asked to assess its effectiveness women's groups link their effectiveness to their access to resources. In relation to this, some contrasts emerged between, for instance, church based groups, mother and toddler groups, and community development oriented groups in terms of their resources, control of resources and perspectives on the relationship to 'their community'. Groups appear to have 'constituencies', as it were, in communities just as councillors have in electoral areas. Groups do more than 'represent' themselves and their interests as a set of individuals. They see themselves as knowing the local needs and doing something to address them. One woman echoed the feelings of others in the feedback session when she said: 'groups like us help people in the community more than the politicians'.

Access to resources is a key means of being effective in the community. However, developments within local groups in the community sphere seem to occur in the wake of funders thinking of other things. For example, Ruth Taillon (1992) found that community relations funding tended to be available to groups engaged in 'cross community' work. A variety of groups responding to her study reported that they did not have much scope for cross community activity. Groups based in rural areas said that they had no access to a neutral venue for this work. Others said that their location, and their priorities of meeting the needs of local women did not leave much room for cross community work. Some groups in Taillon's study claimed to be cross community but were in fact predominantly of one community or the other.[7]

There is no sense of a coherent overall funding or support strategy to consolidate the activities of local women's groups or to aid women in their community participation. The involvement of the churches, of large voluntary sector organisations, and the development of centralised trust administration may, in some instances, have benefits for some of these groups and for their communities. The amorphous agencies and bodies in the voluntary sector in NI do not form an institutional structure. The problem of building a picture of women's participation in this context is that there is no apparent structure to 'deconstruct' in order to see how women's activities relate to decisive developments. In other words, it is difficult to see how women are included and excluded on the basis of strategy. There are three key funding areas: community economic development, community relations and community care. By definition, women's groups are excluded from the first. Their inclusion in community relations funding is conditional on satisfying criteria that may not reflect women's ways of working and of conceptualising dialogue.

The women and community dimension of this research began with an observation of growth and vitality. It is a precarious vitality. Some of the most influential and energetic women's networks have still, after ten years, been unable to secure resources. The absence of any coherent strategy for aiding women's participation at community level in NI may have adverse consequences for vital but vulnerable developments. Women in local groups are motivated to improve life in their communities. They contribute to the social fabric and they do so consciously and across communities through their group work. For as long as this contribution remains marginal within the voluntary sector and is unseen beyond and for as long as it goes unrecognised it cannot be developed to its full potential.

Anecdotal Theory?

What Rosemary Tong (1989) says of the importance of theory is useful. At its best (or perhaps in theory!) theory proceeds through description, explanation and prescription. It enables us to see where we have been and what the obstacles are to where we want to be. It also enables us to place our situation within a wider context; to inform that context and to learn from it. One of the frustrations of theory is that it has a symmetry that lived experience often seems to shatter. In this study some of the key concepts in feminist and political science literature were raised in passing by some of the participants. The 'difference' debate has already been mentioned. The contested but useful public-private dichotomy is problematized in NI where paramilitary, military and other forms of political activity have not been in the conventional public political domain. One woman in the local feedback session of this study responded to a question about whether or not the work of her local group could be seen as 'political'. She said, 'no ... we keep politics at home'. In a follow-up discussion it was obvious that this was an acknowledgement of political divisions within communities which, if admitted to the group, could wreck relationships and the work. It was also an acknowledgement of the subversive political activity which is not in the public domain in NI.[8] There are echoes here with research on women in conflict situations and in ethnic minorities (Molyneux, 1986, Horn, 1991, Mohanty, 1992, Waylen, 1992). In some instances the strategic political aim of a particular group may be set aside, perhaps temporarily, in favour of attaining practical objectives. In other situations the home, traditionally regarded as a site of women's oppression, becomes the site of women's resistance (Hassim, 1993). Politics are kept 'at home'. The implications are intriguing and beg for further understanding.

Conclusion

This research is spade work — unearthing what is going on, making connections with issues raised and concepts developed by others, whilst simultaneously erecting temporary frameworks for understanding what is uncovered. The local woman's group and the local council are very different sites for women's activities and agency. This research was carried out in the days of armed conflict. The temporary cease-fires and the debates that have flowed from them were unimaginable then. In the midst of hopes and fears for the future there is a widespread sense of a process of reconstruction and rethinking. This process threads through personal, communal, political and public encounters and debates. It fuels both uncertainty and aspiration. Women are in the debates but they remain outside the decision making and, largely, out of the picture.

Postscript

Since preparing this chapter, the NI Forum elections have been held and women, 'briefly' have been 'in the picture' in the form of the speedily mobilised NI Women's Coalition. The Coalition ran seventy candidates in the election and won 7,731 votes (one per cent of total cast) enabling them to have two representatives, Monica McWilliams and Pearl Sagar, at the all party talks. The emergence of the Coalition put 'women' on the party agendas. Virtually every representative of a political party interviewed in the media mentioned the presence of women in the party's electoral list. The Coalition generated a lot of support and critical debate amongst women's networks and local women's groups. Their manifesto called for women's voices at the talks table. They avoided some contentious issues by acknowledging the divided political perspectives within their ranks. But they took a progressive stance in opposing conditional admission to talks, on prisoners, the criminal justice system, and the Royal Ulster Constabulary.[9] Nevertheless, some groups and individual women (largely from republican communities) registered their misgivings seeing the Forum electoral process as essentially anti-democratic.[10] Fifteen of the 110 members elected to the Forum are women (fourteen per cent). The future impact of the Coalition is difficult to anticipate but the wonder is that the women behind the initiative saw the opportunity, seized it and used it to get to the 'table'. Women in local groups and women in other political parties will be listening and watching.

Discussion Topics

1. Why do you think there are such small numbers of women in electoral politics?

2. What might be the impacts on political decision making bodies if women were present in percentages that represent their population proportions?

3. Women active in local groups believe that their activism has an impact on their local community. When asked, they say that this is 'not political'. Do you think that this activism is 'political'? Consider why women in the study answer as they do.

4. A politically, and violently divided society presents particular problems for those women who want to unite and campaign on a women's agenda. Critically reflect on the difficulties, and the opportunities, facing such women within the context of divisions of class, colour, race, religion, nationality, sexuality, and/or dis/ability.

Notes:

1. The Centre for Research on Women, University of Ulster, Coleraine, and the Women's Studies Centre, Queen's University Belfast are two sources of information on research on women in NI. See R.L. Miller, R. Wilford and F. Donaghue (1996) *Women and Political Participation in Northern Ireland*, Aldershot: Avebury; also Celia Davies and Pamela Montgomery (1990) *Women's Lives in Northern Ireland Today*, University of Ulster.

2. The Central Community Relations Unit, Northern Ireland Office, funded this one year project: *Women, Community and Politics in Northern Ireland: A Research Project with an Action Outcome.* See the published report, Eilish Rooney and Margaret Woods (1995) *Women, Community and Politics: a Belfast Study*, Centre for Research on Women, University of Ulster.

3. For the purposes of this paper I take the view that women should be present in assemblies in numbers that reflect their percentage of the general population. I do not go into the philosophical or ethical issues of representation and gender in this chapter. For a discussion of these issues see Anne Phillips (1994) *Why should the Sex of the Representatives Matter?*, Paper presented at 'Women and Public Policy: the Shifting Boundaries between the Public and Private Domains', Erasmus University, Rotterdam.

4. Margaret Woods was appointed for one year as research assistant. See Rooney and Woods (1995 *ibid*).

5. In a contribution to the citizenship debates Carole Pateman (1988) argues that 'womanliness' (including emotions, sexuality, motherhood) should be incorporated on equal terms with the so called qualities of masculinity which have hitherto been the norm (i.e. disembodied presence). I am indebted to Carmel Roulston (1996) for this point. The local woman's group and citizenship are very different practices and concepts but the debates in citizenship and the practices in the local group have something to say to each other. See Women and Citizenship Research Group (1995) *Women and Citizenship: Power, Participation and Choice*, EOCNI: Belfast.

6. Since this research was carried out in 1992-3 a split has occurred within the Worker's Party which has resulted in the formation of the Democratic Left.

7. The Community Relations Council total grant aid to voluntary organisations in 1990-91 was almost ú97,000. Women's projects received just over ú7,000 of this (8%). Taillon's (1992) research and the Women's Support Network study of community relations thinking and funding has helped to sensitise various funding agencies to these issues, see Women's Support Network (n.d.) *W: Working for Women's Groups: S: Supporting and Informing: N: Networking to Change Policy: Women's Support Network Response to the Community Relations Programme*, Women's Support Network, Belfast. The words 'community' and 'relations' merit critical scrutiny, particularly in the context of political division and conflict in NI.

8. I have argued elsewhere that women have been and are politically vital in NI in this political private domain (Rooney, 1995). The postscript to this chapter supports this argument in ways that could not have been anticipated in 1995.

9. Sinn Féin, with over 15 per cent of the Forum vote, continued to be excluded from all party talks until the Irish Republican Army renewed its 1994 ceasefire.

10. The Northern Ireland Office (NIO) decided which political parties could and could not stand in the election. The Irish Republican Socialist Party was thereby excluded.

The party refused to participate in the process of making application to the NIO in order to participate. The form and function of the Forum was unclear at the time of the election with some unionists hailing it as a decision-making assembly and republicans saying they would not take their seats.

References and Further Reading

Abbott, M and Frazer H. 1985 *Women and Community Work in Northern Ireland* Belfast: Farset Co-operative Press.

Blom, I. 1988 'Women's Politics and Women in Politics in Norway since the End of the 19c' in *Retrieving Women's History: Changing Perceptions of the Role of Women in Politics and Society* Jay Kleinberg, S. (ed.) Oxford: Berg Pub. Ltd.

Centre for Research on Women 1995 *Democracy, Gender and the Politics of Women's Inclusion* Economic and Social Science Research Council funded study (in progress) University of Ulster.

Coote, A and Pattullo, P. 1990 *Power and Prejudice* London: Weindenfald and Nicolson; cited Lister 1993.

Davies, C and Montgomery, P. 1990 *Women's Lives in Northern Ireland* University of Ulster.

Devaney, F, Mulholland, M and Willoughby, J. (eds.) 1989 *Unfinished Revolution: Essays on the Irish Women's Movement* Belfast: Meadbh Publishing.

Equal Opportunities Commission of Northern Ireland 1995 *Women & Men in Northern Ireland* Belfast: EOCNI.

Evason, E. 1991 *Against the Grain: The Contemporary Women's Movement in Northern Ireland* Dublin: Atttic Press.

Hassim, S. 1993 'Family, Motherhood and Zulu Nationalism: the Politics of the Inkatha Women's Brigade' *Feminist Review* No.43 Spring.

Horn, P. 1991 'Post-Apartheid South Africa: What About Women's Emancipation?' *Transformations* 15.

Leijenaar, M. 1992 unpublished paper, Economic and Social Science Research Council Seminar: *Women's Political and Economic Participation in Northern Ireland* Belfast: Queen's University.

Lister, R. 1993 'Tracing the Contours of Women's Citizenship' in *Policy and Politics* Vol.21, No.1.

Lovenduski, J. 1986 *Women and European Politics: Contemporary Feminism and Public Policy* Amherst: University of Amherst Press.

McWilliams, M. 1995 'Struggling for Peace and Justice: Reflections on Women's Activism in Northern Ireland' *Journal of Women's History* Vol.6 No.4/ Vol.7 No.1 Winter/ Spring.

McWilliams, M. 1991 'Women in Northern Ireland: An Overview' in Hughes, E. (ed.) *Culture and Politics in Northern Ireland: 1960-1990* Milton Keynes: Open university Press.

Miller, R L, Wilford, R and Donaghue, F. 1996 *Women and Political Participation in Northern Ireland* Aldershot: Avebury.

Mohanty, C T. 1992 'Feminist Encounters: Locating the Politics of Experience' in Barrett, M and Phillips, A. (eds.) *Destablising Theory* Oxford: Polity Press.

Molyneux, M. 1986 'Mobilisation without Emancipation? Women's Interests, State and Revolution' in Fagen, R R, Deere, C D and Coraggio, J L. (eds.) *Transition and*

Development: Problems of Third World Socialism New York: Monthly Review Press.

Morgan, V. 1992 'Bridging the Divide: Women and Political and Community Issues' in Stinger, P and Robinson, G. (eds.) *Social Attitudes in Northern Ireland: The Second Report* Belfast: Blackstaff.

Northern Ireland Housing Executive 1986 *The Northern Ireland Household Survey 1985* Belfast: NIHE.

Pateman, C. 1988 *The Sexual Contract* Cambridge: Polity

Phillips, A. 1994 'Why should the Sex of the Representatives Matter?' paper presented at *Women and Public Policy: The Shifting Boundaries between the Public and Private Domains* Rotterdam: Erasmus University.

Policy Planning and Research Unit 1988 *Belfast Areas of Relative Social Need — 1981 Update* PPRU Belfast: Dept of Finance.

Robinson, M. President 1992 *Striking a Balance* The Allen Lane Foundation Lecture.

Rooney, E. 1992 *Women, Community and Politics in Northern Ireland: -Isms in Action* paper presented at the European Consortium for Political Research Conference Limerick.

Rooney, E and Woods, M. 1995 *Women, Community and Politics: A Belfast Study* Centre for Research on Women, University of Ulster.

Rooney, E. 1995 'Women in Political Conflict' *Race and Class* 37 1.

Roulston, C. 1989 'Women on the Margin: The Women's Movement in Northern Ireland, 1973-1988' in *Science and Society* Vol.53, No.2.

Roulston, C. 1996 'Feminist Theories of Democracy: An Overview of Recent Work' working paper in progress for Political Science Association Workshops, Glasgow University.

Taillon, R. 1992 *Grant-Aided ... or Taken for Granted?: A Study of Women's Voluntary Organisations in Northern Ireland* Belfast: Women's Support Network.

Tong, R. 1989 *Feminist Theory: A Comprehensive Introduction* London: Unwin.

Waylen, G. 1992 'Rethinking Women's Political Participation and Protest: Chile 1970-1990' *Political Studies* XL No.2.

Women and Citizenship Group 1995 *Women, Power, Participation and Choice* Belfast: Equal Opportunities Commission for Northern Ireland.

Women's Support Network (nd) *W: Working for Women's Groups: S: Supporting and Informing: N: Networking to Change Policy: Women's Support Network Response to the Community Relations Programme* Belfast: Women's Support Network.

Workers' Educational Association Women's Studies Branch 1991 *Women in Ireland in the 1990s: Report of a Conference* Belfast: WEA.

33.

From Revolution to Devolution: Mapping the Contemporary Women's Movement in Ireland
Linda Connolly

Introduction

T he changing course of the women's movement since the middle of the last century is invariably related to the opportunities for women to organise on their own behalf, the resources available to them, and their collective identity. The first wave of the women's movement (from about 1850 to 1921) was dominated by the question of suffrage and had extensive links with the nationalist movement. Post-independent Ireland was particularly hostile to women's rights and the women's movement receded (between 1922-1969). However, a small number of women participated in traditional women's organisations such as the IHA (Irish Housewives Association) and ICA (Irish Countrywomen's Association), and maintained a small indigenous network of social movement organisations until the end of the 1960s. The agenda of these organisations was limited by the social and political climate in the middle years of this century, manifested in a series of regressive laws excluding women from the public sphere in general.[1] These organisations focused primarily on achieving gradual reforms (such as, consumer rights) and strategically aimed to maintain their own organisation rather than developing extensive networks and forging a more radical women's movement.[2]

The contemporary, second wave of the women's movement in Ireland can be traced to the early 1970s when a number of groups increasingly mobilised, including the Irish Women's Liberation Movement (IWLM) and an *ad hoc* committee on women's rights set up in 1968, which was comprised mainly of those organisations that had maintained themselves as abeyance organisations post-independence (Staggenborg, 1991, p.8).[3] The first wave of the women's movement in Ireland has been significantly documented by feminist historians (Ward, 1983, 1995, Cullen-Owens, 1984, Cullen, 1985, Murphy, 1989) and recent publications have began to look at the second period denoted (Tweedy, 1992, Coulter, 1993, Connolly, 1996). This chapter focuses on the mobilisation of resources and collective action strategies from *within* which led to the resurgence of the women's movement in Ireland from 1970 onwards. Analysis of the role of the contemporary women's movement in Irish society has been based, for the most part, on speculative observation from the outside; elucidating the relationship between modernisation and the changing role of women; or discussing significant historical milestones.[4] These approaches provide a useful sociological context. However, overemphasising them as major explanations for the persistent transformation of the women's movement obscures empirical social processes within the movement and generates inaccurate interpretations (Ryan, 1992, pp.53-64).[5] Intricate qualitative research into the movement itself across time and space from a feminist epistemological stance, based on the *lived experiences* of activists, underpins this analysis. I aim to present a more inclusive, factual appraisal of the evolving women's movement.[6]

The evolution of the women's movement is analysed in this chapter by elucidating pivotal movement dynamics, over three stages of activism:[7] 1. radicalism, conflict and diversification (1970-79); 2. re-appraisal and the issue of abortion (1980-1988); and 3. emerging new movement sectors, particularly in education and working class communities (1989 until the present day).

Social Movements: A Review of the Field

The women's movement tends to evolve in an organic, decentralised pattern over time and place. This implies that a dynamic, inclusive definition of the women's movement as a social movement is applicable:

> Social movements involve the sustained activity of organised groups and often include a network of organisations that, although they may have different goals and members, have a shared sense of belonging to the movement. (Andersen, 1993, p.282)

New social movements in general are amorphous, complex and multifarious. Diani (1992) identifies three basic components of social movements: 1. networks of relations between a plurality of actors; 2. a shared collective identity; 3. engagement in conflictual issues.

The characteristics of social movement networks ranges from a very loose and dispersed pattern to tightly clustered networks. Networks link social movement organisations (SMOs) and underpin the distribution of resources for action (including information, expertise, material resources) which create the necessary preconditions for mobilisation.

Resource mobilisation theory emphasises political opportunities and an indigenous organisational base as major factors in the rise and decline of social movements (Taylor and Whittier, 1992). The availability of *resources* and a *pre-existing network* of SMOs play a central role in the generation of a social movement.[8] Grievances are present in the rise and decline of social movements, but resources and organisational structures are necessary for the emergence of a social movement. Resource mobilisation focuses on the specific conditions which acted as a catalyst for the resurgence of the women's movement from 1970 onwards. The respective success of SMOs in attracting media attention, executing campaigns, accessing resources and recruiting members, and how such factors influence the size and shape of the movement, are central to this framework.

In addition, however, the generation of a collective identity is an important catalyst in the mobilisation of a social movement and in defining its boundaries. Actors define themselves as part of a broader movement and, at the same time, are perceived as such by those within the same movement and by opponents or external observers (Diani, 1992, p.8). A plurality of ideas and orientations within social movement networks are integral to the generation of a collective identity. A collective identity is not static and is not based on a homogeneous set of ideas within and between SMOs. A wide spectrum of shared beliefs and orientations co-exist at any given stage of movement transformation and factional conflicts may occur at any given time. In particular, changing definitions and meanings of ideology over time influences intra movement relations. Resource mobilisation tends to relate the emergence of a social movement to public action and the political process (Tilly, 1978). It focuses on the conditions which facilitate or constrain the occurrence of conflicts. In contrast, the New Social Movements approach, which has dominated the field in Europe, places specific emphasis on conflict as a core element of a social movement.[9] Touraine (1981), for example, correlates the emergence of a social movement with the dominant conflict in a given society. Diani suggests that social movement actors are engaged in political and/or cultural conflicts, aimed at promoting or opposing social change either at the systemic or non-systemic level (Diani, 1992, p.11). It is clear that there is broad agreement in the field that in the process of social change, conflict is a distinctive feature of a social movement. However, there is a difference in emphasis.

The field of social movements has grown impressively in recent years and this appraisal merely provides a cursory account of the main developments.[10] The women's movement is analysed here as a social movement by conceptualising intramovement relations between SMOs and key movement dynamics which dominated the three pivotal stages of transformation identified. This approach reveals the complex web of social action within the women's movement, which by and large remains invisible in sociological analysis of Irish society.

1. Radicalism, Conflict and Diversification

The three core SMOs formed in the first stage of advancement and expansion were – the IWLM, which was formed in 1970 primarily by a small group of journalists, political (mainly women of the left and republican activists) and professional women, and had proliferated by 1972; the CSW (Council for the Status of Women/now the National Women's Council), which grew out of an *ad hoc* committee on women's rights established in 1968 by the IHA and the Association of Business and Professional Women; and the more radical IWU (Irishwomen United) which emerged in 1975 for a period of about 18 months and was the main catalyst for the formation of the CAP (Contraceptive Action Programme) in 1976, the first Rape Crisis Centre in 1977 and the first Women's Right to Choose group in late 1979. A number of SMOs (frequently in the form of small consciousness raising groups, single issue campaigns or with the function of providing services for women), were further offshoots from these core organisations throughout the 1970s or were formed by individual women conscientised by the activities of these SMOs.[11]

The increased receptivity to the political activities of long standing traditional women's organisations, including the ICA, the Association of Business and Professional Women and the IHA, in the late 1960s is intrinsically related to the resurgence of the women's movement. Tarrow (1988) elaborates on the notion of cycles of movement protest. He suggests that widespread protest is likely to occur when political conditions reduce the costs of collective action and increase the likelihood of success. In addition, the increasing interest of the mass media ensured the rapid spread of the movement. The IHA and the National Federation of Business and Professional Women in response to a UN Directive which encouraged all non-governmental women's organisations to lobby their respective governments to set up a National Commission on the Status of Women, formed an *ad hoc* committee on the status of women. The formation of this group facilitated mobilisation primarily because it precipitated a shared ideological foundation among women's rights proponents which was absent in the middle years (1922-1969).[12] The Commission on the Status of Women presented its findings to the Government in 1972. Subsequently, the Council for the Status of Women was set up to monitor the implementation of the recommendations of the Report.[13] The Council for the Status of Women increased its base of support throughout the 1970s, a major indicator of social movement advance. From the outset the Council worked closely with the State, employed a hierarchical structure, had several affiliate members and was a mass based, umbrella SMO.

Coinciding with the gradual consolidation and advancement of the traditional branch of the movement at this stage, a more radical group of women were mobilising and recruiting members in tandem in 1970. Their methods of protest were highly controversial and were extremely attractive to the media:

> A small group of women succeeded, in a remarkably short space of time, in attacking the sacred cows of social and political life in Ireland. They caught the attention of the media as no group of Irish women had ever done before shocking, controversial, galvanising substantial numbers of women to take action – or to publicly voice their support – on a whole range of new issues. (Smyth, 1993, p.251)

The direct action strategies and organising focus of this SMO shaped the course of this new wave of activism. There was only about twenty women involved initially. However, the staging of a series of media events propelled the IWLM into the public arena. In 1970, the IWLM's manifesto 'Chains or Change' was published. On 6 March 1971 the group were invited to appear on the Late Late Show which provided widespread exposure. A major turning point for the group was the staging of a public meeting in the Mansion House in April, 1971. Over 1,000 women attended, which was far in excess of the numbers expected. The demands of the movement were outlined and discussed. Following this meeting a number of groups were established. The dramatic presentation of confrontational demands in the media was a crucial tactic in gaining direct access to constituents and educating the public. In addition, this strategy 'by-passed' the limitations of established channels and the routines of news gathering. At the first delegate meeting a consensus was reached that contraception was a basic issue for women's liberation. The famous 'Contraceptive Train' in which members of the group travelled to Belfast and brought contraceptives illegally through customs in a dramatic manner at Dublin took place in May, 1971. The staging of this event created huge international media attention and publicity.[14]

The organising focus of the IWLM resembled those groups in the small group sector of the American women's movement. Consciousness raising, participatory democracy and autonomous direct action were common practice and distinctive ideas and self definitions of feminism were fused for many activists in this process. These ideas and methods were initiated by those members of the IWLM who had experienced the emergence of the radical sector of the American women's movement.[15]

There was clearly two distinct interacting movement strands in the early 1970s – a traditional, reformist, mainstream sector and a radical, autonomous sector. Initial tensions between these two movement strands were acknowledged by my interviewees. Organisations such as the IHA and ICA were viewed as 'conservative' in outlook by the first radical feminists in Ireland:

> There was quite a bit of tension between us. They thought we were 'old hat' and we were an establishment. In actual fact, we weren't an establishment.

> We were not funded (like the Council), we had nothing to do with the
> government, but we got that sort of thing. There was the feeling from our
> side that these young ones were coming up and we didn't object to what
> they wanted to do – but the methods they were using. People went so far as
> to say that they were putting back the women's movement. In the Council
> we didn't like their methods but we felt they were pinpointing the things
> that needed to be looked at and in fact we looked into their suggestions.
> Gradually now the strands have come together, there are so many facets to
> women's associations.[16]

The concept of ideology as a resource in the mobilisation process is
problematic. Previous accounts of the women's movement typically suggest
that SMOs correspond directly to a theoretical typology structurally embedded
in the women's movement, which has been static since its organising years
(Evans, 1980). In practice diverse ideologies co-exist and interact both within
and between SMOs.[17] At different stages these were a major source of internal
conflict (particularly in the 1970s). The importance of ideology in terms of the
maintenance and growth of SMOs and its utility in fomenting a collective
identity varies significantly across the movement over time and place. It is clear
that ideology was a perceived mechanism of group identity in the formative
years of the early 70s (particularly among radical, autonomous SMOs) and was
a source of great debate in organisations like the IWLM and IWU.

SMOs within the autonomous, radical sector experienced the greatest division
throughout the 1970s. After a period of intense activity, the IWLM began to
proliferate in 1971 and a large number of resignations and bitter exchanges
ensued. Sources of conflict included preferred tactics, disagreement over feminist
ideology, identification with the Left and diverging views on the political
situation in Northern Ireland. Consciousness raising, which initially had an
energising effect, became exhaustive. In essence, there was considerable
disagreement over what the focus of the women's movement and the most
efficient strategies in achieving its aims should be. There was a large turnover
of activists in this period.

Tensions were most acute in IWU, which emerged in 1975 to form a more
radical and politicised SMO than the IWLM. Its aims included the need for an
autonomous women's movement, self-determined sexuality, equal pay and the
establishment of women's centres. IWU was highly politicised and encompassed
a diverse group of left wing philosophies, including, the Movement for a
Socialist Republic, the Communist Party of Ireland, the Socialist Workers
Movement, the Irish Republican Socialist Party and the International Lesbian
Caucus (Fennell and Arnold, 1987, p.11). From the start open conflict was
inherent in the organisation. After a period of intense direct action, a significant
number of activists left these core autonomous groups and diffused into
alternative SMOs within the movement, concentrating their social movement

commitments on initiatives more congruent with their particular skills and ideological preferences.[18]

This diversification facilitated the continued advancement of the movement and cross fertilisation that occurred between SMOs in a number of sectors throughout the 1970s. Many activists became involved in practical action for women and the provision of services which complemented the more moderate, mainstream focus of the women's movement. A radical focus was maintained by political women who continued their involvement in specific campaigns. The widespread publicity and public reaction to the women's movement conscientised a broad constituency of feminists who became involved in the formation or progression of many of the campaigns and organisations which either emerged during the 1970s or were traditional organisations.[19] A number of co-ordinated campaigns emerged – including, the CAP and the campaign for a women's centre in Dublin. For example, members of IWU, which was the last *autonomous*, radical feminist group to attempt to foster a mass-based constituency, diffused into a number of SMOs, including the first Rape Crisis Centre in 1977 and the first Women's Right to Choose Campaign in 1979.[20] The radicalism of these women was to have an important influence on the movement as a whole during the 1980s.

Paradoxically, the process of movement growth and diversification throughout the 1970s was augmented by the ideological differences manifest among Irish women. In order for the movement as a whole to survive the conflicts which were apparent within and between SMOs throughout the 1970s diversification and proliferation ensured movement survival.

While there was a significant degree of conflict over ideologies within radical SMOs (and disagreement over a focus on mainstream or autonomous tactics between SMOs), it is clear that in practice many of the strategies and themes of radical, socialist and liberal feminism overlapped across the movement. In essence, while there were two movement sectors identifiable in the early 70s, they each drew upon an extensive repertoire of strategies (such as, the staging of media events, direct action, mass meetings, demonstrations, action through the courts, political lobbying, co-ordinated campaigns, establishing women-centred institutions and services) and were not uniform. The proliferation and advancement of the movement in the 1970s was not hierarchical or linear. It was diffuse, with several movement centres and mobilising issues emerging. This reiterates the complexity of the growth and diversification of social movements.

The growth of the movement in the wake of disputes over ideology and preferred strategies was further advanced by the cohesive effect of core mobilising issues. In particular, the multifaceted campaign for contraception produced unity and was characterised by co-ordination and coalition between

SMOs. Contraception was a core demand of the IWLM, IWU, individual politicians (Mary Robinson moved a bill in 1971 in the Senate), the CAP, legal cases (the McGee Case) and was provided practically by the newly formed SMOs of the proliferating women's movement (such as, the Well Woman Centres). The launch of the CAP in 1976 by members of IWU and direct action tactics employed had a considerable effect (which included opening an illegal contraception shop and market stall). These women went directly into housing estates and distributed contraceptives. Contraception was partially legalised in 1979. In essence, various SMOs mobilised around this question between 1970 and 1979, and there was a multi-levelled strategy which encompassed campaigning at the level of political and legal reform; direct action and dramatic movement events (such as, the Contraceptive Train and breaking into the Senate during Mary Robinson's Bill chanting 'we shall not conceive'), and the practical provision of services by SMOs (such as, the Well Woman Centres and the Irish Family Planning Association).

The experience throughout the 1970s was that there are real differences in ideological orientation among Irish activists.[21] However, it is clear that diversification did not threaten movement survival and in fact augmented it. The plurality of ideologies that exist within the women's movement did not undermine the capacity of the women's movement to organise in the interest of women after the 1970s. Ideological conflict and factionalism within SMOs was dealt with by proliferation and the formation of new SMOs. While this process facilitated the continued expansion and maintenance of the movement in a multiplicity of sectors (combined with the generation of a feminist constituency and synthesising mobilising issues), it also suspended the actual level of differences in movement identity clearly evident among activists.

2. Re-appraisal and the Abortion Issue

It is clear that by 1980 radical feminist SMOs retained a degree of autonomy, manifested in the increased activity of the Women's Right to Choose Campaign which centralised an issue strategically avoided by the majority of SMOs throughout the 1970s – abortion. Confining the campaign for reproductive rights to contraception reflected the divide on the abortion issue among the indigenous base of support for the women's movement and the conservative nature of Irish society in general, reinforced by the hegemony of the Catholic Church.

Since 1981, the mobilising issue of abortion was pivotal to the transformation of the women's movement. The emergence of a counter right wing movement; intensified mainstreaming and professionalisation across the movement; and constraints on radical activists, were key factors in the reappraisal and changing movement dynamics that occurred from within throughout the 1980s. There was a general trend of activists recognising the need to change from 'within' established institutions and to forge alliances with the State. This coincided with a significant decline in the formation of radical groups engaged in direct action outside the mainstream:

> Some people have gone into very radical left wing parties, some people have gone into social work, some people have gone into like maybe the Rape Crisis Centre, or Women's Aid or the Well Woman, so I'm not sure if it is quite mainstream in terms of say the commercial sector or something. But I think yes they have just moved into the positions where they have a bit more authority and a bit more power in the sense that they have the power to make some influence on things and can build some bridges...And I think that's positive.[22]

The change the women's movement took is intrinsically related to the role of the reproductive rights issue within various centres of the movement. The 1970s was a progressive period for women's rights in Irish society but, it was in 1980 that this progression met 'head on' the forces of conservatism and right wing Catholicism in Irish society, in the form of a highly resourced, politicised counter movement. While progress continued to be made by the women's movement on many fronts (for example, the increasing number of women in politics, expansion of services for women and self help organisations),[23] albeit at a less urgent pace, the campaign for abortion rights was pivotal to the transformation of the women's movement.

In general, radical feminists focused their social movement commitments on abortion in Ireland throughout the 1980s, an era described as demoralising by activists. As Ailbhe Smyth recalls:

> These were to be difficult and demoralising years, leading many feminist activists to a point of weary disenchantment. In retrospect, the encounters of the 1970s over contraception, rape, equal pay, appeared as mere skirmishes, a phoney war, prior to the battles of the 1980s against the serried ranks of church and state, staunch defenders of the faith of our fathers and the myth of motherhood. (Smyth, 1993, p.264)

The case of the social movement dynamics precipitated by the formation of the Women's Right to Choose Campaign and the networks forged with other SMOs in this period particularly exemplifies this point. This SMO was a catalyst for the changing course the movement took during the 1980s and re-defined the expression of radical feminism within the women's movement.

In late 1979, a small group of radical feminists established the first 'Women's Right to Choose Group.' The principal aims of the group were the decriminalisation of abortion and the establishment of a feminist pregnancy counselling service for women in crisis (Riddick, 1993). The first Irish Pregnancy Counselling Centre was set up in June 1980. In March 1981 a public meeting was held at Liberty Hall to publicise the demands of the group and recruit members. This meeting provided the first indication of organised opposition and hostility. There were counter pickets to the meeting and the audience was generally antagonistic to the pro-choice platform (Riddick, 1993). The counter right made itself visible and increasingly mobilised in 1981 by diverting the abortion debate into the legal/constitutional arena – an area which required extensive resources and expertise. Tactically, it aimed to block the women's movement from providing its services by actively campaigning for a constitutional referendum on the 'right to life of the unborn,' which the Irish electorate supported in 1983. Article 40.1.3 of the Constitution enshrined the absolute prohibition of abortion in the criminal law.[24]

Following the pro-amendment result in 1983, the increasingly marginalised pro-choice campaign responded strategically through the practice of abortion referral services. This was viewed as both a tactic and a practical means of helping women in crisis (Conroy Jackson, 1986, p.52).[25] A small number of autonomous, radical feminist SMOs mobilised resources with a view to flouting the law by providing information and counselling.[26]

However, the counter right responded strategically to this direct action through their attempt to block the women's movement from providing its reproductive rights. In June 1985 SPUC (Society for the Protection of Unborn children, the leading anti abortion organisation) issued civil proceedings against the Irish Pregnancy Counselling Service, and subsequently Open Door Counselling and the Dublin Well Woman Centre.[27] As a temporary measure, the Open Line telephone helpline was established in January 1987 to provide an alternative information and counselling service. Open Door Counselling subsequently appealed to the Supreme Court and the existing criminal law was extended to add further abortion offence – that of prohibiting professional service providers from giving practical information to women seeking legal abortion outside the jurisdiction.[28]

These cases drove this autonomous movement sector underground. However, in the long term such constraints acted as a catalyst for the emergence of new intra-movement alliances and tensions throughout the 1980s. This mobilising issue recruited a number of new radical activists who were not there in the 1970s – some who had illegal abortions themselves; discovered the extent of the problem as family planning practitioners or doctors; and others who were drawn into referral work by previous involvement in other related SMOs. The Women's Information Network (WIN) was established as an underground, voluntary emergency non-directive helpline service for women with crisis pregnancies in November 1987. The helpline was founded by a group of women appalled by the Hamilton ruling which banned the dissemination of abortion information. It was launched with the support and assistance of the then Defend the Clinics campaign. Contact with British abortion clinics was particularly important as a resource and the helpline volunteer group undertook continuous training in counselling skills and visited and monitored abortion clinics in Britain. WIN included twenty women working in a variety of professions (including psychologists, film makers, teachers, administrators, students) (WIN Information Pamphlet, 1993). These women did not reveal their identity in their information literature:

> We have produced this booklet in an attempt to break the silence around abortion in this country. Ironically many of us find we cannot follow the logic of this through fully by identifying ourselves publicly – the risks to individuals are still too high. Although the referendum last year was in favour of the right to information, at the time of going to press with this booklet the Government has still not clarified the circumstances in which information on abortion can be made legally available. (WIN Information Pamphlet, 1993, p.4)

Most women availed of their services clandestinely – a sympathetic doctor, a student's union, a public toilet door, a community worker, a piece of graffiti. This highlights the underground nature of the campaign for abortion services and the way in which support was garnered over time by employing such tactics.

There are three central movement dynamics discernible in this stage: 1. alliances between political campaigns and service organisations within the women's movement over this period ensured the survival of a radical movement sector which is integral to the survival of the movement as a whole (the Women's Coalition was a crucial SMO in the pro choice campaign); 2. the simultaneous use of and flouting of the law was tactically important; and 3. alliances with groups *around* the women's movement was a key strategy (particularly co-ordinated campaigning with students unions;[29] population activists; and legal and medical practitioners). As the issue gained more widespread awareness it mobilised a conscience constituency, which involved alliances with organisations within the social movement sector.[30]

These strategies evolved largely in response to the constraints placed on the continued advancement of radical demands and persistently aimed to push the boundaries of women's rights. The deployment of such strategies ensured success by 1992. In addition, the more moderate strands of the abortion debate (the provision of abortion information and the right to travel) were adopted by the Council for the Status of Women. This change of opinion in mainstream SMOs was influenced by rulings in favour of abortion information and the right to travel by the European Courts of Human Rights and Justice. Open Door Counselling appealed to the European Court of Human Rights in response to the Hamilton judgement and in October 1992 it found that the order of the Irish courts was in breach of the Conventions information rights clause, Article 10.[31] On 25 November 1992, the electorate voted for the freedom to obtain abortion information and the right to travel.[32] The ruling of the Supreme Court following the X case permitted abortion in some circumstances.[33]

This series of legal successes suggests that the long term outcome of the three main social movement dynamics in this stage ultimately produced partial movement success in 1992. In addition, the incorporation of this issue into the remit of mainstream SMOs was crucial to this success. The Council for the Status of Women directly encouraged the government to legislate on travel and information in 1992. However, the kernel of this mobilising issue – abortion on demand – remains unresolved and contentious within the Irish women's movement.

Whereas equal rights feminists intensified their strategy of mainstreaming and participation and alliances with the State in this stage, the emergence of a counter right movement forced radical feminists who mobilised around the issue of abortion throughout the 1980s to tactically engage in the mainstream – while simultaneously operating in an underground fashion. Abortion information and the right to travel were adopted as mobilising issues by interacting SMOs across the movement, including the Council for the Status of Women. Furthermore, mobilising issues such as, violence against women and rape (originally radical feminist issues) were increasingly incorporated into the remit of those organisations which were increasingly mainstreaming and professionalising. As a result, the original mobilising issues and ideas of autonomous radical feminism converged into the remit of those SMOs that aligned with the more traditional women's rights organisations since the 1970s. A number of movement centres were professionalising and mainstreaming generically. However, it is clear that the strategic challenges of radical activists, persistently pushing the boundaries of women's rights (albeit under severe constraints and with few resources), were as central to the process of continuity and change from within the movement as they have been at all stages of its development. As one activist says:

> Do we still need a radical women's movement? – I think so. I mean, I think that many people who work in the mainstream also have a radical edge to them that could equally be fertilised out there on the radical wing of the women's movement. I mean, people often 'wear those hats', it's not only a matter of say, there's this group of women who are working more in organisations, or in the Dáil or in the Civil Service, and there is this group 'out there' who are the radicals. I think it's also a matter of people knowing what they can do within the system that they are in – so in my case knowing that of course I need to negotiate with ministers, of course I need to negotiate with the Department of Health, that doesn't mean that I cannot actually have a more radical agenda of my own that may be practised

throughout the clinic – but they couldn't be subsidised by funds from the Department. So, you know, ... you sometimes have to maintain these things both within your person and the area you work in.[34]

3. Emergence of New Movement Sectors

By the late 1980s the abortion question was not resolved and a number of cases were still in progress. However, a number of new sectors were apparent including, the consolidation of women's studies networks, the flowering of feminist publishing and the 'mushrooming' of women's community groups. These trends were embryonic in the early 1980s, evident in the formation of the Women's Studies Forum at UCD, the formation of Irish Feminist Information (which preceded Attic Press) and the emergence of women's education groups in working class communities (such as, KLEAR). The recruitment of new members who were not active in the 1970s, ensured the continued growth of the movement:

> I'm thirty-seven now and the first time I got involved directly in the women's movement I would have been twenty and it would have been really two things I got involved in: one was the Women's Right to Choose group which Anne Connolly was a part of and the other was actually the Women's Studies Forum soon after that in UCD with Ailbhe Smyth.[35]

The extent of locally based women's groups and their impact on local communities is still not fully realised. A number of questions need to be addressed. A key issue is, is this sector organically part of the women's movement? Because it takes time for a movement sector to consolidate and form networks of SMOs, the outcome of this phenomenon is not yet clear. By drawing on a framework of social movements, I contend that these clusters of groups are organically *linked* to the women's movement as elements of the social movement sector in Ireland. However, are they part of the autonomous women's movement *per se*?

Recent accounts have relegated these groups as directly emerging from the women's movement (Coulter, 1993). However, they do not provide a theoretically informed analysis which demonstrates how this has occurred. There are different styles of community based groups emerging, including – working class, urban groups; suburban, middle class, spirituality groups, often based in community houses; rural, peripheralised groups with a focus on community development; and women's community writing groups. The lived experiences of women within this sector, with a common organising focus on *community*, have not been researched extensively by feminist researchers. However, research has been conducted on working class, urban groups and the various networks emerging (Mulvey, 1992).

The parallels of urban, working class women's community groups to the autonomous sector of women's movement in the 1970s in terms of the creation of a collective identity among these groups, a common goal of empowerment and liberation of women at the level of personal development and the distinctive lack of resources and constraints placed on women in this sector suggests that they are a distinctive movement sector evolving organically within the women's movement. A member of an urban, working class community group suggested that:

> The women's movement within the communities has evolved organically and is evolving all the time...There is no clear plan about where it is going to go except that it is happening, and within the communities women are identifying their own needs and are responding in as much as they can – depending on the resources that they have (e.g. childcare and a number of other things). These are key issues for local women in communities. There are a number of networks emerging – different to the traditional movement. There are different dynamics within the community movement than there is in the Council.[36]

Processes which indicate an evolving movement centre are often pervasive, decentralised and amorphous. The above analysis implies that it is not accurate to suggest that there is a uniform, hierarchical process of 'becoming part of' the women's movement. Typically SMOs emerge in a non-linear, organic manner. The main point here is that the current 'mushrooming' and focus of clusters of locally based women's groups is not a diverging course in the emergence of SMOs within the women's movement. The fact that the purpose of these networks of women's community groups is unclear, that there is no definite strategy of where these groups are going, that they are not tackling the 'structures' which uphold poverty and that there is no sophisticated ideological base articulated by these groups, is in fact a typical course for a social movement sector to take (particularly in the women's movement). In addition, the difference in style currently evidenced between what is now becoming the traditional movement in the 1990s (that which mobilised in the 1970s) and these newly emerging sectors reflects the diversity which in reality is inherent between cycles of the women's movement. The increasing professionalisation of SMOs throughout the 1980s and, in particular, the persistent expansion and institutionalisation of the Council for the Status of Women (National Women's Council), suggests that the women's movement has evolved more hierarchically in recent years. The grassroots women's community groups sector represents a striking alternative to the middle class image of the women's movement in the 1990s. However, on the other hand, it clearly represents the connection with the autonomous radical movement sector which dominated the praxis of the movement in the 1970s. Tilly (1978) contends that a repertoire of strategies is drawn upon by movements in later cycles. This repertoire includes the methods employed by women's community groups: consciousness raising/empowerment, decentralisation and participatory democracy.

In view of the widespread diffusion of the ideas and methods of radical feminism in the 1970s, it is apparent that consciousness raising is an equally radical strategy in women's liberation to that of 'tackling state structures' because it raises the consciousness of women who are not empowered to lead mainstream SMOs on a professional, hierarchical basis.[37] It is not unusual for radical women not to claim direct ownership of their collective social movement until a long period of time has lapsed. Since 1970, there has been considerable overlap and interaction between SMOs at various stages, which was not always explicit or apparent to the activists involved.

This analysis is tentative. However, it is clear that whether these groups are elements of the autonomous women's movement or not, they are influenced by *feminism*. By the 1980s, feminism had become more than just a 'list' of women's issues. Furthermore, feminism is not merely a constituency of women and in recent years women have organised against feminism, particularly in counter, new right organisations. Feminism has become a transformational politics and a comprehensive ideology that encompasses every level of Irish society.

This analysis has shown that societal constraints can ensure that visible structures are not the only indicator of feminist activism and the activities of SMOs at different stages were moving the hidden structures as well, particularly by concentrating their activities at the level of consciousness raising. It is essential that we ask questions about these newly emerging groups *within a feminist praxis* and to acknowledge that these groups are essentially working towards empowering women at many levels – which is a core element of feminism. In the 1990s there is a certain reluctance about asking such questions *as feminists*.

It is evident that in terms of the continued recruitment of activists and emergent SMOs; the persistent ability to organise organically when the need arises (for example, following the X case); and the emergence of new mobilising issues in the 1990s (such as, the recent Hepatitis C campaign and the emergence of groups in response to the Peace Process, such as, Clár na mBan),[38] the women's movement is still a vibrant force which is in a constant state of organic evolution over time and place. As one interviewee concluded:

> I still think it's a powerful force. It's capable of continuing that role. It's between those who want to deal with the immediacy of the here and now and those who take a broader view. When we have to, the different strands are capable of coming together on a common front and that will continue to be the case. The women's movement in all its different forms is still a powerful force. I have no doubt about that.[39]

Conclusion

This chapter focused on key social movement dynamics and mobilising issues in the growth, decline and maintenance of the women's movement since 1970. It is clear that key resources in the 1970s facilitated the rapid advancement of the women's movement. Diversification followed as a result of differences among Irish feminists primarily on the basis of ideological orientation and preferred tactics. The 1980s signalled a decrease in the direct action of the movement but the underground activities of radical feminists ensured the recruitment of new activists and the development of a conscience constituency around key mobilising issues. By the late 1980s, women concentrated their movement commitments by increasingly engaging with the institutions of the State, in education and in local communities. Arguably, the different SMOs submerged ideological conflict and fragmentation by working together for similar goals while ignoring their underlying differences in outlook (Ryan, 1992, p.37). Emerging working class women's community groups are now challenging this trend.

This analysis concentrated on elucidating key social movement dynamics and represents a starting point for much of the original research, theorising and making visible the lived experiences of feminist activists, that remains dormant. An agenda for research involves: 1. The need to *analyse further* the women's movement as a social movement in all its manifestations, including a more sophisticated analysis of the impact of ideology, grievances and symbolic meaning for feminist activism; 2. To *record* and incorporate the lived experiences of the women who have participated in social movement organisations at all stages; 3. To *theorise* differences among Irish women and develop a theoretical discourse within the women's movement;[40] 4. To *conceptualise* the 'mushrooming' of women's community groups within a social movements framework, from a *feminist epistemological stance*.

Discussion Topics

1. To what extent can the women's movement be regarded as a social movement in contemporary Irish society?

2. What have been the main achievements of the women's movement in the past twenty five years? What have been the deficits in its agenda?

3. What are the implications for the women's movement of the recent mobilisation of a counter right movement?

4. What strategies are required to ensure the continuity of a vibrant women's movement?

Notes

1. A ban was imposed on married women working in the Civil Service, local authorities and health boards until 1973; The Conditions of Employment Act (1935) granted government powers to obstruct women from working in certain industries. Women were effectively banned from sitting on juries; The 1937 Constitution relegated women's primary role to the domestic sphere. Article 41 states: 'The State recognises that by her life within the home, woman gives to the State a support without which the common good cannot be achieved.' 'The State shall therefore endeavour to ensure that mothers shall not be obliged by economic necessity to engage in labour to the neglect of their duties in the home.'
2. For a comprehensive review of this period see: Tweedy (1992), Coulter (1993) and Connolly (1996).
3. In a similar fashion to the Irish women's movement, the American women's movement in the years between the passage of suffrage and the 1960s was kept alive by its 'elite sustained' structure consisting of a small, exclusive and affluent core of women activists. For a more detailed treatment of the concept of abeyance in the Irish women's movement see, Connolly (1996), pp.43-77.
4. Major socio-historical texts such as, Lee (1989) and Breen et al. (1990) do not place any significant emphasis on the influence of the women's movement on the distinctive course of social change in Irish society. This genre relegates an unimportant, peripheral role to the women's movement in relation to the rapid modernisation of Irish society. It is the case empirically that an organised women's movement is at the kernel of the way in which Irish society has changed since the 70s . This is not acknowledged partly because the movement does not resemble established institutions, political parties etc. and established sociological models do not directly apply.
5. The women's movement tends to be conceptualised as some type of 'immaculate conception' with no previous legacy or roots in pre-existing networks; its emergence is connected primarily to the other movements of the 60s (such as, the Civil Rights, anti-Vietnam and New Left movements), which does not consider the existence of abeyance organisations and the recruitment and conscientisation of women with no links to these social movements. See Ryan (1992), pp.53-64 for a more detailed discussion.
6. Intensive interviews, from a feminist epistemological stance, were conducted with over 50 activists who have participated in a wide spectrum of social movement organisations as part of my Ph.D. research. Feminist research methods are generally reflexive and informal. See: Oakley (1993), Stanley and Wise (1993), and Lentin (1994).
7. I acknowledge that this is a general, broad praxis and there are no definitive watersheds between these stages. In practice, the movement is amorphous, decentralised and fluid across time and space. Different authors identify different stages in the current movement upsurge. For example, Evelyn Mahon (1995) identifies two activist peaks in the women's movement. The first occurred in the early 70s and focused on employment rights and contraception. The second occurred in the early 90s and addressed abortion (see also, Smyth, 1993).
8. For a broad treatise of the resource mobilisation perspective see: Zald and McCarthy (1977, 1987), Lyman (1995).

9. For a broad review of recent developments in this field, see Kriesi et al. (1995).
10. For example, Kriesi et al. (1995) is part of a collaborative project over seven years which is an ongoing comparative analysis of new social movements in Western Europe.
11. For a more detailed social history see: Connolly, 1996, pp.43-77, Smyth, 1993, Levine, 1982, Beale, 1986, Fennell and Arnold, 1987.
12. The *ad hoc* group comprised the IHA, Association of Business and Professional Women, Altrusa Club, ICA, Irish Nursing Organisation (INO), Dublin University Women Graduates Association, The National Association of Widows, The Soroptimists' Clubs of Ireland, Women's International Zionist Organisation, Irish Council of Women, Association of Women Citizens and the Association of Secondary Teachers of Ireland (ASTI))
13. These forty nine recommendations were related to equal pay, employment, training, sex discrimination, rural women, political and cultural life, the law, social welfare and maternity leave.
14. See Mahon, 1996 and Fennell and Arnold, 1987 for a more detailed outline of these events.
15. Interviewees recalled how two radical feminists from the US attended one of the first meetings of the IWLM at Mary Maher's flat, at the invitation of Máirín de Burca.
16. Interview with member IHA and Council for the Status of Women.
17. Leading activists were attracted to different ideologies within the IWLM (for instance, Nuala Fennell was clearly a liberal feminist and Máirín de Burca was a socialist feminist).
18. See Connolly, 1996 for a more detailed analysis of incentives to mobilisation.
19. New SMOs formed between 1970-1975 included, AIM (1972), Adapt (1973), Women's Aid (1974), the Women's Progressive Association (subsequently the Women's Political Association, (1970), Ally (1971), Family Planning Services (1972, now the Irish Family Planning Association), The Cork Federation of Women's Organisations (1972, representing seventeen local associations, was responsible for opening the first Citizens Advice Bureau) and Cherish (1972).
20. Including, Anne Speed, Anne O'Donnell and Evelyn Conlon.
21. Ideological disagreement was particularly manifest in the profound tensions within IWU, which evolved around the relationship between feminism and republicanism, feminism and socialism, state feminism, and radical separatist feminism.
22. Interview with member Women's Right to Choose Campaign, Women Studies Forum, Well Woman Centre.
23. See Mahon, 1995, especially for a summary of the political/legal gains accompanying the evolution of the women's movement.
24. The 1861 Offences Against the Person Act which was upheld in Ireland following independence in 1922, outlawed abortion as a criminal offence: *'Every woman being with child, who with intent to procure her own miscarriage shall unlawfully administer to herself any poison or other noxious thing...and whomsoever, with intent to procure the miscarriage of any woman whether she be or be not with child shall unlawfully administer to her or cause to be taken by her any poison or other noxious thing...with the like intent shall be guilty of felon, and being convicted thereof shall be liable...to be kept in penal servitude for life; and [W]homsoever shall unlawfully supply or procure any poison or other noxious think...knowing that the same is intended to be unlawfully used or employed with*

intent to procure the miscarriage of any woman whether she be or not be with child, shall be guilty of a misdemeanour, and being convicted thereof shall be liable to be kept in penal servitude for the term of three years.'

Article 40.3.3 of the Constitution of the Irish Republic adopted in 1983, copperfastened the 'right to life of the unborn':

'The State acknowledges the right to life of the unborn and, with due regard to the equal right to life of the mother, guarantees in its laws to respect, and as far as practicable, by its laws to defend and vindicate that right.'

25. Conroy Jackson (1987) examines the socio-historical background to the question of abortion in Ireland.

26. Including – Open Door Counselling, 3 Belvedere Place, Dublin 1 (24 hour answering service); Women's Right to Choose Group, c/o The Women's Centre, 53 Dame Street, Dublin 2; Women's Right to Choose Campaign, c/o 39 Reuben Avenue, Dublin 8; and the Irish Women's Abortion Support Group, 1 Elgin Avenue, London W1.

27. Referred to in High Court Record, No. 1985/5652P (quoted in Riddick, 1993).

28. 19 December 1986 the President of the High Court (the Hamilton judgement) declared:

'The right to life of the foetus, the unborn, is afforded statutory protection from the date of its conception...The qualified right to privacy, the rights of association and freedom of expression and the right to disseminate information cannot be invoked to interfere with such a fundamental right.'

The 1988 Order of the Irish Supreme Court (Open Door Counselling) confirms the ban on dissemination of abortion information but opened the way for a Human Rights appeal:

'The Court doth declare that the activities of the Defendants, their servants or agents in assisting pregnant women within the jurisdiction to travel abroad to obtain abortions by referral to a clinic; by the making of their travel arrangements, or by informing them of the identity of and location of and method of communication with a specified clinic or clinics are unlawful, having regard to the provisions of Article 40.3.3 of the Constitution.

And it is ordered that the Defendants and each of them and each of their servants or agents be perpetually restrained from assisting pregnant women within the jurisdiction to travel abroad to obtain abortions by referral to a clinic, by the making for them of travel arrangements, or by informing them of the identity and location of and the method of communication with a specified clinic or clinics or otherwise.' (Supreme Court Record No. 185/7 quoted in Riddick, 1993)

29. The 1991 European Court of Justice Ruling on Travel (Grogan) resulted from a case taken by SPUC against the students to prevent the provision of abortion information in their publications.

30. Movements typically mobilise conscience constituents who do not stand to gain directly from the achievement of the movement's goals (Staggenborg, 1991, p.6).

31. 'Everyone has the right to freedom of expression. This right shall include freedom to hold opinions and to receive and impart information and ideas without interference by public authority and without frontiers.'

32. 25th November 1992, the electorate voted to add to Article 40.3.3 the freedom to obtain information and the right to travel:

to allow for *'no limit to freedom to obtain and make available subject to conditions laid down by law, information on services lawfully available in another member (EC) state'* and that *'there shall be not limit to freedom to travel to another state.'* The electorate rejected a third amendment to the constitution:

'It shall be unlawful to terminate the life of the unborn unless such termination is necessary to save the life, as distinct from the health, of the mother where there is an illness or disorder of the mother giving rise to a real or substantive risk to her life, not being the risk of self destruction.'

33. In 1992 the ruling of the Supreme Court on the X case permits abortion to safeguard 'the equal right to life of the mother'. The European Court of Human Rights Ruling on Information (Open Door Counselling) asserts the right to abortion information, stating that: *'...the restraints imposed on the applicants from receiving or imparting information was disproportionate to the aims pursued by the Government of Ireland'* (in Riddick, 1993).
34. Interview with member Women's Right to Choose, Women's Studies Forum, Director Family Planning Clinic.
35. Interview with member Women's Right to Choose, Women's Studies Forum, Family Planning Clinic.
36. Interview with member of urban based, working class Women's Community Group.
37. See Mulvey's (1992) more extensive analysis of the focus of these groups.
38. The Hepatitis C campaign was mobilised in 1995 by a group of women only recently made aware that they were infected with contaminated blood during childbirth at different stages in the 1970s. Clár na mBan held a republican feminist conference in Belfast, in March, 1994. The conference was organised by a group of women with a history of activism at a political and community level who came together in 1992. A number of criticisms of the 'peace process' were proposed (Connolly, 1995, p. 119), and republican and nationalist assumptions about historical and contemporary Ireland were explored. The group have since held a second conference, published the proceedings and have made a submission to the Forum for Peace and Reconciliation.
39. Interview with member IWU, Women's Right to Choose.
40. The emergence of the first Irish Journal of Feminist Studies (I.J.F.S.) in March, 1996, which will be published twice yearly, provides an opportunity for this exchange.

References and Further Reading:

Andersen, M. 1993 *Thinking About Women: Sociological and Feminist Perspectives on Sex and Gender* New York: Macmillan Third Edition.

Beale, J. 1986 *Women in Ireland: Voices of Change* Dublin: Gill and Macmillan.

Breen, R, Hannan, D F, Rottman, D B and Whelan, C T. 1990 *Understanding Contemporary Ireland* Dublin: Gill and Macmillan.

Connolly, C. Summer 1995 'Ourselves Alone? Clár na mBan Conference Report' in Smyth A. et al. The Irish Issue: The British Question *Feminist Review* no.50 pp.118-126.

Connolly, L. March 1996 'The Women's Movement in Ireland 1970-1995: A Social Movements Analysis' *Irish Journal of Feminist Studies* Vol.1, Issue 1 pp.43-77.

Conroy Jackson, P. 1986 'Women's Movement and Abortion: The Criminalization of Irish Women' in Dahlerup, D. (ed.) *The New Women's Movement: Feminism and Political Power in Europe and the US* London: Sage.

Conroy Jackson, P. 1987 'Outside the Jurisdiction: Irish Women Seeking Abortion' in Curtain, C. et al. *Gender in Irish Society* Galway: Galway University Press, pp.203-223.

Coulter, C. 1993 *The Hidden Tradition: Feminism, Women and Nationalism* Cork: Cork University Press.

Cullen, M. 1985 'How radical was Irish feminism between 1860 and 1920?', in Corish P J. (ed.) *Radicals, Rebels and Establishment* Belfast: Appletree Press pp.185-201.

Cullen-Owens, R. 1984 *Smashing Times: A History of the Irish Women's Suffrage Movement 1889-1922* Dublin: Attic Press.

Diani, M. 1992 'The Concept of Social Movement' *Sociological Review*, 40, 1 pp.1-25.

Evans, S. 1980 *Personal Politics: The Roots of Women's Liberation in the Civil Rights Movement and the New Left* New York: Vintage Books.

Fennell, N and Arnold, M. 1987 *Irishwomen in Focus* Dublin: Office of Minister of State for Women's Affairs.

Kriesi, H, Koopmans, R, Duivendak, J W and Guigni, M J. 1995 *New Social Movements in Western Europe: A Comparative Analysis* London: UCL Press.

Lee, J J. 1989 *Ireland 1912-1985* Cambridge: Cambridge University Press.

Lentin, R. March 1994 'Feminist Research Methodologies: A Separate Paradigm? Notes for Debate' *Irish Journal of Sociology,* Vol.3.

Levine, J. 1982 *Sisters: The Personal Story of an Irish Feminist* Dublin: Ward River Press.

Lyman, Stanford M. (ed.) 1995 *Social Movements: Critiques, Concepts, Case-Studies* London: Macmillan.

Mahon, E. 1995 'From Democracy to Femocracy: The Women's Movement in the Republic of Ireland', in Clancy et al. *Irish Society: Sociological Perspectives* Dublin: Institute of Public Administration/Sociological Association of Ireland pp.675-708.

Mahon, E. 1996 'Women's Rights and Catholicism in Ireland', in Rowbotham (ed.) *Mapping the Women's Movement: Feminist Politics and Social Transformation in the North London*, Verso/New Left Review.

Mulvey, C. 1992 *Changing the View: Summary of the Evaluation Report on the Allen Lane Foundation's Funding Programme for Women's Groups in Ireland, 1989-1991* Dublin: Allen Lane Foundation.

Murphy, C. 1989 *The Women's Suffrage Movement and Irish Society in the Early Twentieth Century* London: Harvester.

Oakley, A. 1993 'Interviewing Women: A Contradiction in Terms' in Roberts, H. (ed.) *Doing Feminist Research* London: Routledge and Kegan Paul.

Riddick, R. 1993 *Abortion and the Law in the Republic of Ireland: An Overview 1861-1993* an Address to the New England School of Law, Boston, Massachusetts.

Ryan, B. 1992 'Feminism and the Women's Movement: Dynamics of Change' in *Social Movement Activism and Ideology* New York, London: Routledge.

Smyth, A (ed.) Jackson, P, McCamley, C and Speed, A. 1987 'Feminism in the South of Ireland: A Discussion' *The Honest Ulsterman*, No.83.

Smyth, A. (ed.) 1992 *The Abortion Papers Ireland* Dublin: Attic Press.

Smyth, A 1993 'The Women's Movement in the Republic of Ireland 1970-1990' in Smyth, A. (ed.) *Irish Women's Studies Reader* Dublin: Attic Press pp.245-269

Staggenborg, S. 1991 *The Pro-Choice Movement: Organisation and Activism in the Abortion Conflict* Oxford: Oxford University Press.

Stanley, L and Wise, S. 1993 *Breaking out Again: Feminist Epistemology* London: Routledge and Kegan Paul.

Tarrow, S. 1988 'National Politics and Collective Action: Recent Theory and Research in Western Europe and the United States' *Annual Review of Sociology,* 14 pp.421-40.

Taylor, V and Whittier, N. 1992 'The New Feminist Movement', in Richardson, L and Taylor, V. (eds.) *Feminist Frontiers III: Rethinking Sex, Gender and Society* US: MacGraw Hill pp.533-548.

Tilly, C. 1978 *From Mobilisation to Revolution* Reading, MA: Addison-Wesley.

Touraine, A. 1981 *The Voice and the Eye: An Analysis of Social Movements* Cambridge: Cambridge University Press.

Tweedy, H. 1992 *A Link in the Chain: The Story of the Irish Housewives Association 1942-1992* Dublin: Attic Press.

Ward, M. 1983 *Unmanageable Revolutionaries: Women and Irish Nationalism* London: Pluto Press.

Ward, M. 1995 *In Their Own Voice: Women and Irish Nationalism* Dublin: Attic Press.

Zald, M N and McCarthy, J D. 1977 'Resource Mobilization and Social Movements: A Partial Theory' *American Journal of Sociology,* 82: 6 pp.1212-1222.

Zald, M N. and McCarthy, J D. (eds.) 1987 *Social Movements in an Organisational Society* New Brunswick, NJ: Transaction Books.